THE CANADIANS 1867-1967

"Published on the occasion of the Centennial of Canadian Confederation and subsidized by the Centennial Commission".

"Ouvrage publié à l'occasion du Centenaire de la Confédération Canadienne, grâce à une subvention de la Commission du Centenaire".

Toronto   Macmillan of Canada

Edited by

J. M. S. CARELESS and R. CRAIG BROWN

With a fine-art section of monochrome and colour plates

THE
CANADIANS
1867-1967

Library of Congress Catalogue Card No. 67-14490

Reprinted 1967 (twice), 1968, 1969

Printed in Canada by the T. H. Best Printing Company Limited
for The Macmillan Company of Canada Limited,
70 Bond Street, Toronto, Ontario

Contents

List of plates   vii

List of illustrations in the text   xi

Introduction   xiii

PART ONE

1. The 1860s by Donald Creighton   3
2. The 1870s by George F. G. Stanley   37
3. The 1880s by W. S. MacNutt   70
4. The 1890s by John T. Saywell   108
5. The New Century by H. Blair Neatby   137
6. Through the First World War by Roger Graham   172
7. The 1920s by W. L. Morton   205
8. The 1930s by Kenneth McNaught   236

▼

9. Through the Second World War by Colonel C. P. Stacey 275
10. The 1950s by William Kilbourn 309
11. The 1960s by Laurier L. LaPierre 344

PART TWO

12. The Human Community by John Porter 385
13. The Land's Wealth by Roderick Haig-Brown 410
14. Industrial Development by O. J. Firestone 449
15. Unions and Co-operatives by Eugene A. Forsey 487
16. Transport by K. W. Studnicki-Gizbert 502

17. Communications by Wilfred Kesterton and John S. Moir 525
18. Science and Medicine by William Carleton Gibson 546
19. Education by George E. Flower 568
20. Religion by John S. Moir 586

21. Sport by Jack Batten 606
22. From Villages to Cities by Norman Pearson 621
23. Literature in English by Louis Dudek 639
24. Literature in French by Jean Basile 659
25. The Performing Arts by Thomas Hendry 675
26. Painting and Sculpture by Hugo McPherson 697

27. The Structure of Government by Norman Ward 713
28. Social Services by Albert Rose 734
29. The Fighting Forces by George F. G. Stanley 764
30. Foreign Affairs by Gérard Bergeron 785

Index 807

Plates

Between pages 700 and 701
(*denotes colour plates)

* 1. Cornelius Krieghoff: The Hunters, no date / oil on canvas
14½" x 17"
Owner unknown
Photo from the National Film Board, Ottawa

2. Aurèle de Foy Suzor-Coté: Indiennes de Caughnawaga, 1924 /
bronze 17¼" x 22"
The National Gallery of Canada, Ottawa

* 3. Homer Watson: In The Laurentides, 1882 / oil on canvas 26"
x 42"
The National Gallery of Canada, Ottawa

4. Maurice Cullen: The Old Ferry, Louise Basin, Quebec, c. 1907
/ oil on canvas 23¾" x 28¾"
The National Gallery of Canada, Ottawa

5. J. W. Morrice: Landscape, Trinidad, c. 1921 / oil on canvas
26" x 32"
The National Gallery of Canada, Ottawa

vii

* 6. Tom Thomson: Black Spruce and Maple, c. 1916 / oil on
panel 8¾" x 10½"
The Art Gallery of Ontario
Photo by Dennis Colwell

7. F. H. Varley: Self-portrait, 1919 / oil on canvas 24" x 20"
The National Gallery of Canada, Ottawa

8. Clarence A. Gagnon: Village in the Laurentian Mountains,
c. 1925 / oil on canvas 34½" x 51"
The National Gallery of Canada, Ottawa

* 9. J. E. H. MacDonald: The Solemn Land, 1921 / oil on canvas
48" x 60"
The National Gallery of Canada, Ottawa

10. Emily Carr: Forest Landscape (1), no date / oil on paper 36"
x 24"
The National Gallery of Canada, Ottawa

11. A. Y. Jackson: Early Spring, Quebec, c. 1926 / oil on canvas
21" x 26"
The Art Gallery of Ontario

12. Frances Loring: The Hound of Heaven, 1918 / bronze 39" high
The Pollock Gallery, Toronto
Photo by Dennis Colwell

*13. Arthur Lismer: Lily Pond, Georgian Bay, 1948 / oil on alu-
minum 12½" x 16"
The Art Gallery of Ontario
Photo by Dennis Colwell

*14. David Milne: Clouds, c. 1931 / oil on canvas
18" x 22"
The National Gallery of Canada, Ottawa

15. L. L. FitzGerald: Williamson's Garage, 1927 / oil on canvas
22" x 18"
The National Gallery of Canada, Ottawa

16. Jean-Paul Lemieux: Visiteur du soir, 1956 / oil on canvas
31½" x 43¼"
The National Gallery of Canada, Ottawa

*17. Paul-Emile Borduas: Sous le vent de l'île, c. 1948 / oil on can-
vas 45" x 58"
The National Gallery of Canada, Ottawa

*18. Jean-Paul Riopelle: Pavane, 1954 / oil on canvas, triptych
9'10" x 6'7", 9'10" x
4'11", 9'10" x 6'7"
The National Gallery of Canada, Ottawa

*19. Alfred Pellan: L'Affût, 1956 / oil on canvas 35" x 51"
The National Gallery of Canada, Ottawa

20. Alex Colville: Children in a Tree, 1957 / egg tempera on canvas 19¼" x 28"
The C.I.L. Art Collection

*21. J. W. G. (Jock) Macdonald: Nature Evolving, 1960 / oil on canvas 44½" x 55"
The Art Gallery of Ontario
Photo by Dennis Colwell

22. Albert Dumouchel: Premier labour, 1964 / relief print 20" x 27"
Hart House Collection, University of Toronto
Photo by Dennis Colwell

*23. Goodridge Roberts: Lake Orford, 1945 / oil on canvas 30" x 40"
The National Gallery of Canada, Ottawa

24. Jack Shadbolt: The Bush Pilot in the Northern Sky, 1963 / oil 18' x 37'
Edmonton International Airport
Photo from the Department of Transport, Ottawa

25. Gerald Gladstone: Female Galaxy in Recline, 1965 / welded steel 36" high x 60" long x 36" deep
Courtesy of the artist

26. Gordon Rayner: Homage to the French Revolution, 1963 / painted construction 70" x 46"
The Art Gallery of Ontario

27. Ted Bieler: Wall relief, 1965-6 / concrete, two entrance walls, each wall approximately 36' high x 24' long x 12' deep
Expo Administration and News Building, Montreal

28. Gordon Smith: Blue Painting, 1959 / oil on canvas 22" x 33"
Mr. and Mrs. C. R. B. Salter
Photo by Dennis Colwell

29. Robert Murray: Pointe au Baril I, 1963 / cedar and iron painted maroon 12½' high
Mr. and Mrs. Paul Arthur

30. Les Levine: Hanging Environ, 1964 / sprayed wood and canvas construction 61" high
The Isaacs Gallery, Toronto

*31. Jack Bush: Nice Pink, 1965 / a serigraph from the folio "Five Colour Prints" 26" x 20½"
The David Mirvish Gallery, Toronto
Photo by Dennis Colwell

32. Sorel Etrog: The Complexes of a Young Lady, 1961-2 / bronze 9' high
Mr. and Mrs. S. J. Zacks. On loan to Hart House, University of Toronto
Photo by Dennis Colwell

33. Jack Nichols: Clown and Prince, 1962 / lithograph 19½" x 15"
Courtesy of the artist
Photo from the Picture Loan Society, Toronto

*34. Harold Town: Sashay Set, 1962, from the series "Tyranny of the Corners" / lucite and oil on canvas 81" x 74½"
The National Gallery of Canada, Ottawa

*35. William Ronald: Mural, 1965-6 / acrylic and oil, 100' in circumference
St. Andrew's-by-the-Lake Rectory, Ward's Island
Photo by Dennis Colwell

36. John Meredith: Untitled II, 1963 / ink drawing 10½" x 14½"
The Isaacs Gallery, Toronto

*37. Graham Coughtry: Corner Figure, No. 13, 1961 / oil and lucite on canvas 78" x 54"
The Isaacs Gallery, Toronto

*38. Robert Hedrick: Landscape, 1959 / oil on canvas 36½" x 48½"
Mr. and Mrs. Percy Waxer
Photo by Dennis Colwell

*39. Jean McEwen: Entrelacs rouges, 1961-2 / oil on canvas 39" x 60"
The National Gallery of Canada, Ottawa

40. Greg Curnoe: Being Tickled, 1964 / oil on plywood 34" x 48"
The David Mirvish Gallery, Toronto
Photo by John Reeves

41. Michael Snow: Five Girl-Panels, 1964 / enamels, approximately 54" x 120"
The Isaacs Gallery, Toronto

*42. Yves Gaucher: Signals 3, 1966 / acrylic on canvas 48 x 60"
Gallery Moos, Toronto
Photo by Dennis Colwell

*43. Kazuo Nakamura: Blue Reflections, 4 Horizons, 1965 / oil on canvas 31¾" x 27¾"
From the Imperial Oil Collection

Illustrations

in the text

'The Political Giant-Killer, or "Canada First"'
From *A Caricature History of Canadian Politics*
by J. W. Bengough, Toronto, 1886, vol. I — 51

'Whither Are We Drifting?'
From *A Caricature History of Canadian Politics*
by J. W. Bengough, Toronto, 1886, vol. I — 58

From a print in the Public Archives of Canada — 76

'The Great Combination'
From a print in the Public Archives of Canada — 85

'Up Against the Solid Facts!'
From *Laurier Does Things . . .*, 1904 — 138

'An Irresistible Attraction'
From *Laurier Does Things . . .*, 1904 — 141

'Crumbling'
From *The Canadian Liberal Monthly*, October 1916 — 185

'If we do not have public control over finances . . . '
From *The Weekly News*, Winnipeg, October 16, 1925   217

'If We Don't Sell Our Wheat Abroad'
From the *Manitoba Free Press*, July 17, 1930   245

'The Shape of Things to Come'
From the paper *Cry Havoc* in the Woodsworth Papers Scrapbook,
1932-9, Public Archives of Canada   270

'Prophetic Harmony?'
From the *Winnipeg Free Press*, April 1, 1939   276

'Howdy Sheriff'
From *Toronto Daily Star Cartoons* by Duncan Macpherson   339

'Dig You Later, Pops'
From *Toronto Daily Star Cartoons* by Duncan Macpherson   342

From *Toronto Daily Star Cartoons* by Duncan Macpherson   348

'What Happened to my Strawberries?'
From *Toronto Daily Star Cartoons* by Duncan Macpherson   351

Introduction

Frugal and diligent, parochial and isolated, loyal to empires secular or holy, the people of British North America before 1867 seemed almost to live in a middle ages of their own. They were subjects of a distant imperial Queen-Protector. Their life in the main was rural; the church and family were powerful forces moulding it. Their settlements were small amid a vast wilderness, and they had known invasion and threat of attack from far more powerful American neighbours. Separate colonies had grown in diversity: in discord, above all, between French and English-speaking elements that could only be quietened, not resolved, by never-easy compromise.

Yet compromise became a means to unity for these colonials. Impelled by threat and dissension, they had come by the

1860s to look beyond a mere *modus vivendi* to wider, bolder opportunity, and to one transcontinental nation-state in a future which only they could make. They must reach for it across an empty expanse of prairie and mountain to an ocean so remote that men still journeyed there from eastern North America by rounding Cape Horn. Their new union must bear the birth-mark, lauded or deplored, of the conquest of French by British in 1760, and its citizens must always face the problems of living with the mighty continental power of the United States beside them. Their hope was bold; but the omens were by no means all propitious.

On July 1, 1867, these men of different regions, two languages and cultures, and sharp religious divisions, began their union, a broad confederation under the name of Canada. It was in the keeping of a score of leading colonial politicians, solid worthies in their black frock-coats, who yet had force and fervour in no way hampered by the guise of Victorian respectability. These politicians, in the soberly ordered language of the mid nineteenth century, had drafted terms for a new national entity, one that was already growing and changing as the words were proclaimed law. The federal Canadian authority that was to supply peace, order, and good government and express vital agreement between descendants of two nations, French and British, thrust out over the continent with almost incredible speed. It was like a fresh sail spread on a good wind, bearing the Canadians' Confederation from harbours on the St. Lawrence and Atlantic to Arctic and Pacific waters: to great northern barrens, the sweep of western grassland, and soaring coastal ranges.

The course for the Canadian union continued west and north for years to follow; but gradually long-established conditions seemed to dissolve. Old patterns changed and new emerged: the permanent protecting British Empire subsided and disappeared. The power of Washington and New York replaced it, to aid or involve Canada. Meanwhile railways pierced the western mountain barriers, and the prairies yielded classic riches of grain, then oil. Science and technology, immigration, industry, and dominating cities transformed the ways of an older, simpler, rural society, while the granite vastness of the Precambrian Shield, once the inhospitable core of the ancient Canadian wilderness, offered wealth from deep-cut mines, thick forests, and the reservoirs of countless lakes and streams. The canoes of an earlier Canada were gone; bush planes now anchored by the overgrown portage. And the complex modern country that had emerged faced problems and potentialities scarcely conceivable to the colonial Canadians of a hundred years before.

Thus the sweep of change in Canada since 1867, hardly to be contained in a few brief paragraphs such as these. They can only suggest the magnitude of the changes wrought in one hundred years, which require an entire volume to examine. That is the purpose of this book: to describe and assess the developments of a century in Canada, as its citizens stand at the hundredth birthday of their Confederation. It seeks to celebrate the changes of the hundred years, heralding achievements without forgetting failures – with a mixture of pride and doubt, hope and asperity, which is perhaps as distinctive of Canada as the centennial occasion being celebrated.

The contents of the work are as broad as its subject. They trace the activities and experiences of the Canadian people, in their many ramifications, through the century of rapid growth. To cover such a subject the book has been divided into two main sections. In the first, eleven historians record the life of Canada decade by decade since the 1860s. In each of these chapters much has been left to the individual perspective of the author, in the belief that no one view can necessarily embrace the variety of Canada, and that depths and dimensions may be more fully revealed by a multiplicity of viewpoints.

In the second section of the volume, nineteen authors describe special fields of interest in Canada's development since 1867. If the first section of the book is essentially narrative, this one is essentially topical. Once more a great deal has been left to the individuality of the authors in determining their approach and in shaping their essays. Uniformity was not the object, but – to adopt a Canadian truism – an appreciation of the Canadian entity through the recognition of its diversity. Nor was there any attempt to be encyclopedic in the treatment of topics. Authors were free to select, within their frame of reference, the aspects they wished to emphasize, in order to produce chapters or essays that had a viewpoint and offered an evaluation, and were not simply a comprehensive heaping-up of facts. It follows also that some contributors preferred to make their approach to their topic by surveying it in contemporary terms; others by tracing its course of growth across one hundred years.

The consequence is a volume that may have both gaps and overlapping. We accept both, as part of the nature of the enterprise. But any overlapping will provide the benefit of varied perspectives and comparisons, and any gaps would seem a minor price to pay for individually structured statements that form a major assessment of the Canadians over a hundred years – rich and broad enough in scope, in any case, that one pair of covers could scarcely fit in more.

THE AUTHORS

The authors of this volume themselves depict the diversity and sweep of Canada. No attempt, obviously, has been made to choose them in terms of ethnic, regional, or other quotas: the sole purpose was to gather thoroughly qualified writers with something to say on their subject. Yet – inevitably – the variety of Canada appears in them. They represent diverse Canadian regions and origins; they are academic scholars and professional writers, authorities in their chosen field.

In Part I, on the basis of his distinguished writings on the era of Confederation, Donald Creighton, Professor and former Chairman of the Department of History at the University of Toronto, opens the volume with an account of Canada in the 1860s, when Confederation was being shaped. George F. G. Stanley, Dean of Arts and Head of the History Department at Royal Military College, then continues with the 1870s; and W. S. MacNutt, Professor of History at the University of New Brunswick, takes up the 1880s. The 1890s are dealt with by John T. Saywell, Dean of Arts and Science and Professor of History at York University, while the first decade of the new century is treated by H. Blair Neatby, Professor of History at Carleton University.

The years surrounding the First World War are the concern of Roger Graham, Professor of History at the University of Saskatchewan. The 1920s fall to W. L. Morton, formerly Head of History at the University of Manitoba and now Master of Champlain College at Trent University. Kenneth McNaught, Professor of History at the University of Toronto, examines the 1930s. Colonel C. P. Stacey, former Director of the Historical Section of the Canadian General Staff and now Professor of History at the University of Toronto, describes the 1940s, the decade of the Second World War. William Kilbourn, Professor and Chairman of the Humanities Division at York University, deals with the 1950s. And finally, in this first section of the book, Laurier LaPierre, Director of the Institute of French Canadian Studies at McGill University, provides an estimate of the 1960s, with particular reference to French Canada, whose development has assumed such critical significance in this latest decade.

In Part II, John Porter, Professor of Sociology at Carleton University, begins with an examination of the human community in Canada. Roderick Haig-Brown of Campbell River, B.C., widely known for his writings on aspects of the Canadian natural environment, discusses the wealth of the land which the human population may utilize, consume, or waste. O. J. Firestone, Professor of Economics and Vice-Dean at the University of Ottawa, deals with the complex industrial development that has stemmed from the utilization of Canadian resources since the years of Confederation. And Eugene A. Forsey, Director of Research for the Canadian Labour Congress, treats the growth of unionism and the co-operative movement, major developments in themselves that have accompanied the rise of the modern Canadian economy. K. W. Studnicki-Gizbert, Associate Professor of Economics, York University, then continues the examination of vital aspects of a century of Canadian economic growth in the field of transport. And, jointly, Wilfred Kesterton, Associate Professor of Journalism at Carleton University and John S. Moir, Associate Professor of History at the University of Toronto, Scarborough College, take up the history of communications in Canada, a topic that moves naturally from socio-economic considerations into the realm of opinion, knowledge, and culture.

Thereafter, William C. Gibson, Professor of the History of Medicine and Science at the University of British Columbia, studies developments in these broad fields of knowledge and culture in Canada. George E. Flower, Head of the Graduate Department of Education Theory at the University of Toronto, deals with the imparting of knowledge through the system of Canadian education. John S. Moir, as an authority on Canadian church history, returns to deal with religion and a hundred years of religious organization in Canada.

Next, Jack Batten, Toronto journalist and staff writer on *The Canadian*, describes activities in a significant and considerably distinctive field of Canadian cultural endeavour – sport. Still further, Norman Pearson, Associate Professor of Planning in the Geography Department of the University of Waterloo, discusses emerging patterns in the transition from living and building in villages to the culture and architecture of cities.

Then varied other arts in the Canadian culture, literary, lively, or visual, are considered in turn. Louis Dudek, Professor of English at McGill University, treats the century's literature in English-speaking Canada: Jean Basile, literary critic for *Le Devoir*, the literature in French-speaking Canada. Thomas Hendry, Executive Secretary of the Canadian Theatre Centre, sharply assesses the performing arts in Canada, while Hugo McPherson, Professor of English at the University of Toronto, analyses Canadian painting and sculpture, assisted by vividly illustrative examples in a series of colour and monochrome plates.

Norman Ward, Professor of Political Science in the University of Saskatchewan, takes up Canadian political organization, examining the structure of government on its several levels. Albert Rose, Professor of Social Work in the University of Toronto, continues the analytical survey of major institutions in the Canadian state and society by treating the development of social services in the modern Canadian public system. And George F. G. Stanley, this time in his capacity as a military historian, considers those very specialized political and social institutions, the fighting forces of Canada. Finally, Gérard Bergeron, Professor of Political Science at Laval University, studies the Canadian state and society in its international aspect during the hundred years since Confederation, in the sphere of external policy and foreign affairs.

These are the contributors and their chapters which comprise the volume. But certain other names must be mentioned also. Gordon C. Trent of Toronto originally suggested a centennial work of this broad character and scope, and so inspired the present project. And James Bacque of Macmillans provided editorial services in connection with the book that constitute aid far above and beyond the normal call of duty. Another sort of highly valuable assistance came from the Canadian Centennial Commission, whose grant of $4,500 towards publication is herewith most gratefully acknowledged.

The end result of all this widely collaborative effort is a volume which does not seek to sum up Canadian activities and achievements since Confederation so much as to present their range, variety, and significance. It does so in the belief that whatever failures or shortcomings there may be, the experience of Canadians living and endeavouring together within their union for a century deserves to be remembered and appraised.

J. M. S. Careless
R. Craig Brown

PART ONE

PART
ONE

1. The 1860s

DONALD CREIGHTON

The 1860s was the decade of
the great decision – the decision to found a transcontinental
British American nation. It was a greater decision than any
that British North America had ever taken before, greater
than any it would ever take again: and it was reached only
after many hesitations and misgivings and a large amount of
anxious argument. The great decision was in fact preceded
by the great debate about the future of British America. The
debate had its climax in the prolonged and vehement controversy over the plan for a federal union drawn up at the
Quebec Conference; but its origins went back to the fears,
uncertainties, and questionings that had been inspired by
the opening of the American Civil War. The decade as a
whole saw the working out of a long process of self-realiza-

3

tion and self-determination. British North Americans were far more concerned than they had ever been before about their probable destiny in the New World; and this concern was prompted by an awareness both of their own internal development and of the vastly changed circumstances in which they lived. Two decades before, in the years immediately following the rebellions of 1837, the backwardness and frustration of British America had been obvious. Then the provinces had been small, relatively poor, widely scattered colonial communities, dependent both economically and politically upon Great Britain and limited by the narrow, parochial outlook of the colonial mind. They had come a long way since then. They were more aware than they had been of the promises and perils of the external world, and more curious about the place they might accept in it. They were conscious also of a new sense of maturity.

In 1861, some 3,230,000 British Americans faced what was to be the most critical decade in their history. Measured by the enormous extent of their territorial inheritance they seemed a very small people; and they were distributed unevenly at great intervals across the continent. The vast majority—approximately 2,500,000—lived in the Province of Canada, British America's empire province, the most populous, prosperous, dynamic, and aggressive of the lot. The Canadians outnumbered all other British Americans by three to one: they reduced the populations of the remaining provinces to very small proportions. The two largest— Nova Scotia with 325,000 people and New Brunswick with 250,000—seemed tiny communities in comparison; and the others were even smaller. Newfoundland, where persistent efforts had been made to limit the number of inhabitants for the benefit of visiting fishermen, had considerably fewer than 150,000 settlers; and Prince Edward Island, with a population of about 80,000, was smaller than the largest of the Canadian towns, Montreal. In the North-west and on the Pacific coast, where settlement had occupied only a tiny fraction of the vast and empty wilderness, the disparities were even more startling. The little company of whites and half-breeds at the junction of the Red and Assiniboine rivers numbered fewer than 10,000; and the population of the two small colonies on the Pacific coast, British Columbia and Vancouver Island, did not greatly exceed that total.

The two founding peoples of British America were the French who had remained in Canada after the Conquest and the English-speaking North Americans who had come up from the Thirteen Colonies before, during, and after the American Revolution. These first settlers had been outnumbered, though not submerged, by the huge, successive waves of immigrants which had kept flooding in from the British Isles ever since 1820. English and Scots had come in large and not unequal numbers; but the massive 'famine' migrations of the 1840s had left the Irish the largest of the three British groups. There were a few Germans and a good many Gaelic-speaking Scots; but British North America was, on the whole, a community of two languages, rather than a babel of many strange tongues. The French-speaking Canadians and the Acadians of the Maritime Provinces were remarkably homogeneous peoples; but the English-speaking communities, settled by Celts and Saxons, Protestants and Roman Catholics, Britishers and North Americans, were mixtures of incredible complexity and diversity.

It was a rural rather than an urban population. In 1861, Montreal was a city of 90,000 people, Toronto only half that size; and the Maritime towns, including the provincial capitals, were still smaller. Most British Americans lived in small villages or the open countryside, and farmed, fished, built ships, milled flour, or worked in lumber camps for a living. The provinces concentrated upon the production of a few basic staple products for export to more industrialized nations; and ever since the decline of the fur trade, early in the nineteenth century, the principal export staples had been wheat, flour, fish, timber, and lumber. In the past, ocean, lake, and river had been the chief avenues of transport; and wind- and water-power had driven the ships, moved the timber rafts, and worked the grist-mills and the sawmills. But now this old state of affairs was perceptibly changing.

The steam-engine, the railway, and the new machinery were diversifying the character, increasing the production, and hastening the transport of Canadian industry.

The industrial revolution first entered British America on the wheels of the new transport. Nova Scotia and New Brunswick each built short, provincially owned railways; Canada preferred to subsidize commercial companies, of which the most ambitious was the Grand Trunk Railway, an enormous system that ran all the way from Portland in the State of Maine to Sarnia on Lake Huron. Steamships were beginning to supplant sailing vessels on the Great Lakes, the St. Lawrence River, and in the passenger traffic between the Maritime Provinces, though neither Nova Scotians nor New Brunswickers ever succeeded in adapting their skills in wooden-ship building to the construction of the iron, steam-driven vessel of the future. Steam was also rapidly overtaking water-power as the main motive force in the saw-milling industry, and to a much lesser extent in flour-milling. Grist-mills and sawmills, which were linked so closely to the old staple trades, still accounted for over forty per cent of British American manufacturing in the 1860s; but the larger provinces, and particularly Canada, had already ventured into newer types of production – agricultural implements, tools, machines, and a variety of consumer goods – that would have been unheard of a generation earlier.

Yet, despite the advent of the new industrialism, British America still tended to think instinctively in terms of the old commercial age in which it had grown up. In the eyes of both Canadians and Maritimers, British America was a staple-producing economy whose prosperity depended upon the export of a few bulky, primary commodities, on highly preferential terms, to more mature industrialized nations. Great Britain's old Colonial system, with its tariff preferences and shipping monopolies, had given the northern provinces a very privileged place in imperial markets; and when, in 1846, the British adoption of free trade brought an end to these historic advantages, the first instinctive move of the British American merchants was to seek a comparable preferential treatment in the United States. The Reciprocity Treaty of 1854, which established free trade between the provinces and the United States in all major natural products, realized this aim successfully; and to many Canadians and Maritimers the Reciprocity Treaty came to seem the main basis of the prosperity which, with one great interruption, was to last for the next dozen years.

Yet the old commercial strategy did not dominate British American thinking and planning in quite the same way as it had done a generation before. The northern provinces were becoming far more conscious of themselves as a group of British colonies, far more interested in collective partnerships for a variety of purposes, and far more alive to the importance of their enormous territorial inheritance on the North American continent. In the past, British Americans had been inclined to consider that common membership in the British Empire was their most significant bond of union; but now, within the last few years, the idea of a British American nation and the ambitious hope of its westward expansion across the continent had awakened the interest of both Maritimers and Canadians. The discovery of gold on the Fraser River had dramatically revealed the great potential importance of the British inheritance on the Pacific slope; the westward drive of American settlement had brought up the portentous question of the future government of the chartered and licensed territories of the Hudson's Bay Company. More than a third of the North American continent lay waiting for occupation and development in the British American north-west; and for the first time the technology of modern industrialism had made its exploitation possible, even by the present generation of British Americans. Railways could make a united, transcontinental nation. The first stage in this giant enterprise – the Intercolonial Railway linking the Maritime Provinces with the St. Lawrence valley – was a practicable project which could be undertaken immediately. The next stage – the railway to the Pacific – was still for many people a dream for the future, though no longer for the far-distant future.

No province felt these importunate urges towards expansion more strongly than the Province of Canada; and no province was less fitted politically to carry them out. In form, Canada was a united province, with a single legislature; in fact, it was an unacknowledged federal system based on the unworkable principle of dualism. Canada East, which was largely French-speaking, and Canada West, which was overwhelmingly English-speaking, had been given equal representation in the provincial legislature; and the division of cabinet posts, the organization of government departments, and the appropriation of government expenditures were decided in general upon the same basis of sectional equality. Dualism ensured an almost chronic state of sectional rivalries and disputes: it also meant small, precarious majorities in parliament, short-lived governments, frequent elections, and a permanent condition of governmental instability. The Province of Canada could hardly govern itself within its existing limits; it was not capable, with its unreformed constitution, of any large expansion whatever.

The decade of the 1850s had been spent in vain attempts to escape from the maddening frustrations of dualism. Broadly speaking, the plans of reform fell into two main categories—the proposals, like George Brown's 'Representation by Population', which would have made the union a real legislative union, and those, on the other hand, which would deepen and formalize the division between the two sections of the Province. Soon it became clear that drastic solutions in either of these two directions were politically impossible. 'Rep. by Pop.', which would have placed French Canada in a hopeless minority in the united legislature, could never be voluntarily accepted by Canada East; and Canada West, which was convinced that it had suffered most from the injustices of dualism, could never quite bring itself to endorse such a desperate remedy as the dissolution of the union. Upper Canadians and Lower Canadians obviously did not enjoy living too closely together; but on the other hand they were not in the least attracted by the prospect of living completely apart. Federalism was the only system that seemed to combine the advantages of both union and separation; and by the end of the 1850s many Canadians were coming reluctantly to the conclusion that the 'federal principle' was probably the only effective remedy for provincial ills. In 1858, the Conservative government, with George E. Cartier and John A. Macdonald as joint leaders, proposed a federation of the whole of British America. In the following year, a convention of the 'Clear Grit' Reformers of Canada West, in which George Brown played a dominating role, adopted a plan for the federal union of the two Canadas. By the end of the decade, projects for two new unions, one national, one provincial, had been presented to the Canadian people.

II

Yet, when the decade of the 1860s opened, it seemed, strangely enough, as if both projects were dead and the great debate over the future of British America had temporarily fallen silent. The Conservative plan for a British American federation had been viewed mainly with indifference or hostility by the other provinces and with disfavour by the British government. The Reform scheme for a small federal union of the two Canadas had never won general acceptance among the party leaders and had foundered among the jealousies and quarrels of Grit politics. The ambitious plans for western settlement and railway building, with which the union schemes had always been associated, seemed also to dwindle into a temporary eclipse. The agitation for the annexation of the North-west, which had aroused such a furor in Canada West only a few years before, faded away into virtual silence; and the project of the Intercolonial Railway, for which plans had been made and re-made repeatedly during the 1850s, had apparently been completely abandoned.

It seemed as if the provinces had temporarily talked themselves out on the subject of political union. But they remained irrepressibly concerned about their future. They
could never quite rid themselves of the intimate conviction
that this future was to be a collective future; and in 1861,
when they least expected it, this belief was confirmed with
decisive force and passion. In 1861, the American Civil War
broke out; and during the four long years of its duration,
the war was to be a potent factor in all British American
calculations. It was, in the first place, a spectacle, a thrilling
and terrible spectacle for which Maritimers and Canadians
occupied front-row seats. It was exciting, but it was something else as well. It was dangerous. British America might
possibly become involved, either directly in the conflict itself, or indirectly through one of its unknown but fearful
consequences. The thought of involvement was an irrepressible apprehension. At times it almost disappeared in a
growing sense of security; at other times it grew suddenly
into an expectation of immediate crisis. But it was always
there, and it had been lodged in British American hearts
and minds, for the duration, at the very beginning of the
struggle.

On the 8th of November, not much more than six months
after the opening of the war, Captain Charles Wilkes, of the
U.S.S. *San Jacinto*, stopped by force the British mail packet
Trent and took from her two diplomatic agents who were
on their way to Europe in the hope of enlisting support
for the Southern Confederacy. Neither Great Britain nor
the United States wanted to make a war out of this incident.
Great Britain had ceased to play the role of a colonial power
in North America with any enthusiasm or conviction; and
the last thing she desired was a desperate struggle in the
new continent for colonies that most Englishmen now
regarded as liabilities rather than assets. For the United
States, a second war, which would have led almost certainly
to the independence of the South, would have been an
unrelieved disaster. But England was determined to obtain
reparation for Wilkes's affront to her prestige; and the

United States, where the excited populace seemed ready and eager to take on all comers in mortal combat, was unwilling to make too humiliating an apology. For nearly two months the outcome of the dangerous issue rested in suspense. Maritimers and Canadians, who realized that their provinces would inevitably be the first objects of American attack, braced themselves for a terrible encounter.

A remarkable demonstration of British and British American solidarity followed. The imperial government hurriedly dispatched transports bearing a force of nearly 14,000 men – the largest troop movement across the Atlantic since the War of 1812. The provincial governments called up their volunteers and tried to energize their militia units, long enfeebled by neglect and disuse. It was a moment of acute danger and anxiety; but it was also a moment of illumination in which the northern provinces suddenly comprehended their true character and their proper destiny. They realized that they wanted an independent existence in North America. They realized that they wanted to be linked with Great Britain and to remain separate from the United States.

Late in December 1861 the United States restored the captured envoys, though without an apology, and the *Trent* crisis was suddenly over. It had brought British America a moment of self-knowledge rare in its history; but it had by no means clarified or settled the ways and means by which its collective future might be realized. And once the crisis ended, the sense of urgency immediately slackened. The American Civil War was still big with menace; but in 1862-3, when the fortunes of the Confederacy were at their floodtide, its perils might well seem extremely remote. The South might win its independence – the outcome which most British Americans would have decidedly preferred. Even if it failed, it seemed certain that the conflict was going to be a very long one.

In these circumstances, the creative urge of 1858-9 did not return; the ambitious national planning of these years was not resumed. The provinces seemed to slump back into their accustomed state of provincialism and colonial dependence.

They did little to improve the militia forces whose inadequacy had been so clearly revealed in the crisis of 1861;
and to the intense exasperation of the British, the Canadian
Militia Bill of 1862, the one serious attempt at military reform that followed the *Trent* affair, was defeated in the
Canadian legislature. For years Great Britain had been attempting to transfer some of her North American obligations to the shoulders of colonies that were now so largely
self-governing; but British America was still in no hurry
to assume the responsibilities of maturity. The provinces
still shied away from the burden of their own defence;
they were not even doing very much to promote their own
internal development. Western expansion, intercolonial railways, and interprovincial trade could only be realized effectively through British American political union. But in 1862
and 1863, Maritimers and Canadians were thinking rather
of co-operative effort without political union, or, at any rate,
with no more political union than they already enjoyed
within the easy and flexible framework of the British Empire. In the Maritime Provinces only a handful of people
were giving any thought to political reorganization in British
America. In Canada, the principal authors of the plans of
1858-9 had been swept from the political scene. George
Brown, who had been defeated in the election of 1861, was
temporarily out of politics; and in May 1862, George E.
Cartier and John A. Macdonald resigned office after the
defeat of their Militia Bill.

The Canadian initiative had been abandoned, and the
men who assumed power after the defeat of the Cartier-
Macdonald government were not likely to take it up again.
These men—John Sandfield Macdonald, Luther Holton,
W. P. Howland, L. V. Sicotte, and A. A. Dorion—had no
definite policies and few clear political ideas. Apart from the
business of staying in power, they had no real purpose in
government. Their solutions for the major Canadian problems were essentially negative and temporizing. They proposed to make the unreformed Canadian union work ac-
ceptably to both sections of the Province by what was called

the 'double majority'–a principle which was supposed to require that government measures should have a legislative majority in the section or sections to which they were intended to apply. The three other principal Canadian projects–defence, western expansion, and the intercolonial railway–would, the ministers declared, be pushed forward cautiously, within the limits imposed by their professed desire for retrenchment and the monotonously repeated deficits of the past few years.

Even this modest program was singularly barren of results. In the actual circumstances of Canadian politics, the 'double majority' could hardly be more than a pious hope; and when the test came, Sandfield Macdonald permitted legislation applying to one section of the Province to be imposed by a majority of the members of the other section in exactly the same way as his predecessors had done. He made some progress with defence, though here he was probably moved less by his own wishes than by the constant urgings of the Governor General, Lord Monck. As for the twin projects of eastern communications and western expansion, they hardly advanced at all. The only way in which Canada could come to grips with the problem of the North-west was by buying out the territorial rights of the Hudson's Bay Company, or by challenging the validity of its charter in the courts; and both these courses were far too heroic for the impoverished Canadian government to take. It even failed in the end to honour an agreement with Nova Scotia and New Brunswick to divide the cost of the construction of the Intercolonial Railway. The British government, which had consented to guarantee the necessary loan, had imposed extremely onerous conditions for the sinking-fund that it required; and the Canadians, pushing their objections to these requirements to the limit, had in the end repudiated the agreement. Canada had not thrown over the whole idea of the Intercolonial; it had simply rejected a particular scheme for the construction. But at the moment the angry Nova Scotians and New Brunswickers were in no mood to notice this distinction.

By the autumn of 1863, two important facts had become

clearly evident: the first was that the attempt to promote western expansion and intercolonial communications without political union had failed; the second was that the hope of continuing the Canadian union without radical constitutional changes had been proved false. The realization of these two truths was the point at which the movement for political union had its beginning in both Canada and the Maritime Provinces. The two advances followed each other fairly rapidly; but it was New Brunswick and Nova Scotia that made the first move. The long-term sense of frustration and dissatisfaction was less acute in the Maritime Provinces than in Canada in the autumn of 1863; but the momentary feeling of injury and disillusionment was keener. In Nova Scotia and New Brunswick, the Canadian repudiation of the Intercolonial agreement of 1862 was regarded as a shocking, an outrageous, blow. 'Canadian perfidy' became the text of numerous angry sermons in which Maritime newspaper editors warned their readers that co-operation with Canada was impossible, that all thought of political union with Can·ada must be given up, and that henceforth the Maritime Provinces must draw close together and 'go it alone'.

III

It was out of this sense of angry and determined Maritime feeling of solidarity that the movement for a legislative union of the Atlantic provinces began to get under way. Its chief advocate was Arthur Hamilton Gordon, the Lieutenant-Governor of New Brunswick, a young man with very positive opinions on a wide variety of subjects and a strong desire to take a vigorous lead in the political reorganization of British North America. A general union of the northern provinces was, he believed, essential to their preservation independently of the United States; but he had come to the conclusion that such a union would not be feasible until the Intercolonial Railway was built, and the Canadian repudiation of the agreement of 1862 seemed to postpone that prerequisite indefinitely. In the meantime, he considered a smaller union, a legislative union of the Maritime Provinces, could be usefully undertaken, principally for its own sake, but also as a first step to a united British America. He was convinced that provinces as small and underpopulated as Nova Scotia, New Brunswick, and Prince Edward Island were simply overgrown municipalities, that their public affairs were parochial and petty, and that there were far too few men of ability and devotion to administer them. To govern such tiny provinces separately, with the elaborate organization of a provincial parliament in each, was simply to invite expense, inefficiency, corruption, and low buffoonery. The remedy was to unite the three provinces in a single province of some real consequence and genuine dignity.

Gordon's campaign for Maritime union had a certain limited success. He was able to persuade his own Premier, Samuel Leonard Tilley, as well as Charles Tupper, the Premier of Nova Scotia, that his scheme was desirable and might be practicable; but he had little real success with the politicians of Prince Edward Island, though for a time he fondly assumed that they were favourable too. This provincial separatism, the inward-looking parochialism that was such a dominant feature of colonial British America, confronted him everywhere; and nowhere were its manifestations more absurdly exaggerated than in the smallest of all the provinces, Prince Edward Island. During the winter and spring of 1864, all three provincial legislatures—Newfoundland was never included in the planning for Maritime union— passed resolutions empowering their executive governments to nominate delegates to a conference at which Maritime legislative union would be formally considered. But the highly unfriendly and critical reception which the little Island parliament gave to this resolution made the success of the projected Conference look very unlikely from the beginning. Even in Nova Scotia and New Brunswick, very few people seemed enthusiastic about Maritime union; a good many appeared indifferent or actively opposed to it. June 1864 came, and the very date and place of the conference had not been decided. It is quite possible that it would never have been held at all, if it had not been for a revolutionary change which in the meantime had taken place in Canada.

In the year that had elapsed since the general election of June 1863, affairs in the Province of Canada had gone from bad to worse. John Sandfield Macdonald had failed to improve his position in Parliament in the general election; and in March 1864, after vain attempts to secure further support from among the moderate Conservatives of Canada East, his cabinet resigned. A new Conservative government, led by Sir Etienne Taché and John A. Macdonald, took office. Its supporters in the Assembly were distributed in a fashion the opposite of that of the previous administration, for it was weaker in Canada West than in Canada East; but its following as a whole was no greater than that of its predecessor, if as great, and it remained in power by the narrowest and most precarious of margins. George Brown, who had returned to provincial politics in 1863, but in a much less partisan mood than he had ever shown before, had been pressing for the appointment of a parliamentary committee to examine the various possibilities of constitutional reform. The Assembly finally yielded to his persuasions, the committee was established, and on the 14th of June, Brown presented its report. On the very same day, the Taché-Macdonald government was defeated by two votes on a want-of-confidence motion.

The coincidence of the government's defeat and the presentation of the committee's report impressed George Brown deeply. He decided that he would try to take advantage of the first to realize the objects of the second. He let it be known through supporters of the defeated administration that he thought the crisis ought to be utilized to settle for ever the constitutional difficulties between the two sections of the Province, and that he was willing to give his support to this or any other government that would take up this question earnestly and vigorously with a view to its final settlement. The Conservative leaders responded at once to this invitation. A series of conferences between them and

Brown was held, and eight days later, on the 22nd of June, John A. Macdonald and George Cartier announced the formation of a Coalition ministry – a Coalition ministry that would have overwhelming support from both sections of the Province in the Assembly. Its program was constitutional reform through what was called 'the adoption of the federal principle', applied either to British America as a whole, or to the Province of Canada alone. The new government announced that it would first attempt, by sending special missions to the Maritime Provinces and England, to carry out the larger British North America federation. In other words, the two previous plans – the Conservative scheme of 1858 for a general British America federal union and the Reform scheme of 1859 for a federation of the two Canadas – had been combined in the Coalition's program; but the Conservative plan had been given priority.

The Maritime governments, which up to that moment had made literally no preparations for their own proposed meeting on constitutional changes, were electrified to receive dispatches from the Canadian Coalition, politely requesting permission to send delegates to the Conference on Maritime Union. The Maritimers replied that of course the Canadians would be welcome, though in an unofficial capacity, and they then quickly decided that the meeting would be held in Charlottetown, Prince Edward Island, beginning on the first of September, 1864. These three astounding circumstances – the formation of the Coalition government in Canada, the publication of its proposal of a general British American federation, and the announcement of definite arrangements for the approaching constitutional conference at Charlottetown – seemed in combination to constitute the greatest breakthrough in British American political history. Together they roused Maritimers and Canadians to a high state of speculation, planning, and argument. The government of Canada set out boldly and at once on an exhilarating career of constitution-making on a national scale. Speakers, newspaper editors, and pamphleteers began to argue the merits of federalism for British America. British Americans

everywhere were busily reflecting upon the potential implications of their federal union. They became more aware of
each other's existence, more interested in each other's activities, more excited than they had ever been before by the
prospect of a great transcontinental nation in which they
would all be united. The great debate on the future of British
North America had begun.

The year 1864 was the year of the 'coming together' of the
British Americans. They had never visited each other, entertained each other, talked, argued, feasted, and danced
with each other so often and for such long periods before.
Early in August, three weeks before the delegates were to
gather at Charlottetown for the conference on union, the first
of these interprovincial expeditions–an unofficial party of
Canadian politicians and journalists under the leadership of
that convinced Unionist, Thomas D'Arcy McGee–set out
for a tour of the Maritime Provinces. Travel between Montreal and Halifax and Saint John was far from an easy and
expeditious matter in those days. D'Arcy McGee's party went
by the Grand Trunk Railway from Montreal to Portland,
Maine; and then, in an overcrowded and extremely uncomfortable vessel, from Portland to Saint John, New Brunswick. They travelled by steamer up the St. John River to
Fredericton; they crossed the Bay of Fundy by steamer, and
at Windsor took the Nova Scotia government railway
train to Halifax. Everywhere the Maritimers turned out in
thousands to greet the Canadian visitors and everywhere
they were offered frequent and lavish entertainments.

Only a fortnight after D'Arcy McGee's touring Canadians
had said good-bye to Halifax, the official Canadian delegation to the Charlottetown Conference started down the St.
Lawrence to Prince Edward Island in the government steamer
Queen Victoria. The Charlottetown Conference, the first of
the conferences that built Canadian Confederation, was a
highly mobile, peripatetic gathering; the delegates spent
about half their time in travelling around the Maritime
Provinces, just as the unofficial Canadian visitors had done
only a few weeks before. But the real work of the Conference

was completed in Charlottetown in the first week of September. The only official item on the agenda was Maritime union; but the Maritimers courteously postponed consideration of their own project and the Canadians were given the opportunity of presenting their plan of a general federation first. For three days, the principal Canadian leaders – Cartier, Macdonald, Brown, and Galt – described and analysed in detail the scheme they had drawn up in cabinet meetings that summer. On the 7th of September, after another day of general discussion, the Maritime delegates reached a momentous decision. A British American federal union was desirable, they declared, and they were prepared to waive their own smaller project in order that this more ambitious plan could be fully examined and discussed. A few days later, at Halifax, the next stop in their travels, the delegates decided that a second conference would be held at Quebec on the 10th of October and that there a general federal union would be the official subject of discussion.

The *Queen Victoria*, bearing the jubilant Canadians back to Canada, did not reach Quebec until the 19th of September, and only a fortnight later it was steaming down the Gulf of St. Lawrence to pick up the Maritime delegates and transport them to the Canadian capital for the second and the most crucial of the conferences on union. There were twenty-one Maritime delegates to Quebec; and with them came five of their wives and nine young and marriageable daughters. By the evening of Sunday, the 9th of October, they had all reached Quebec and were comfortably established in the St. Louis Hotel, where the Canadian government, determined to equal or better Maritime hospitality, had put them up at its own expense.

IV

At eleven o'clock the next morning, Monday, the 10th of October, the Quebec Conference held its first session in that severely plain structure, the Canadian legislative building, which stood at the very edge of the rock of Quebec. The

Canadian federal plan, which Macdonald, Cartier, Galt, and Brown had sketched at Charlottetown, was the basis of the discussions; and it was laid before the Maritime delegates at Quebec in a series of resolutions, which were moved by various members of the Canadian cabinet, and which the Conference then debated and passed, sometimes with amendments. Each province, however large or small its delegation, had one vote, with two for Canada in view of the two sections into which it was divided. If they had so wished, the Maritime Provinces could have outvoted Canada two to one on any of the fundamentals of the Canadian plan; and the fact that they did not, and that the Canadian plan was accepted with only minor alterations, testifies to the basic similarity of political beliefs with which all British Americans approached the problem of a federal union.

They realized, in the first place, that the union would have to be federal. The absence of municipal institutions in the Maritime Provinces, and Lower Canada's insistence on a measure of autonomy in its own local affairs, made a single sovereign parliament for the whole of British America impossible. A federal union would have to be accepted, the delegates realized; but at the same time they regarded it with serious doubts and apprehensions. Federalism was alien to the political tradition and experience of Great Britain and British America. In the United States, where, alone among English-speaking nations, the federal principle had been tried, it had been deeply discredited by more than three years of bloody civil war. The 'federal principle' of government was a divisive principle which could be employed only in small quantities and within strict limits in British America. It must be purged of those centrifugal weaknesses that had brought on the Civil War in the United States; and it must be adapted to the British political traditions of monarchical institutions, parliamentary sovereignty, and responsible government.

In his opening speech to the Conference, John A. Macdonald told the delegates that the constitution they were framing for a united British America, must, in the words of

Governor Simcoe, be an 'image and transcript' of the British constitution. The fundamental principle of the Canadian plan was parliamentary government under the British Crown. The lower house of the new federal bicameral legislature was to be called the 'House of Commons' in conscious imitation of the Mother of Parliaments; and the upper house, though it was eventually named Senate, resembled the American Senate much less than it did a House of Lords composed of life peers. It was true that the essence of parliamentary institutions was the sovereignty of parliament, and that this could not be secured in British America if legislative power was to be divided between two levels of government and the resulting division set down in a written and binding constitution. The federal legislature of the future could not be an absolutely faithful 'image and transcript' of the Parliament at Westminster; but if it lacked sovereignty in theory, it could be given powers and controls which would approximate it in practice. The provinces of the future must under no circumstances be copies of the aggressive and powerful states that had broken up the American union. They must be subordinate, not co-ordinate, governments, simple, inexpensive, quasi-municipal in character, and concerned only with a relatively small number of local affairs.

It was easy for the delegates at the Quebec Conference to reach these conclusions, for these conclusions were the natural result of their entire political experience. Unlike the successfully revolting Thirteen Colonies, the northern provinces had never claimed or acquired sovereign powers. They wanted British protection and recognized British imperial sovereignty. There was thus no solid constitutional basis for the assertion of provincial rights at the Conference. There was no recognition of provincial sovereignty in the Canadian plan; instead the plan laid down strict limits to provincial legislative powers and provided the Dominion government with powerful controls over provincial legislation. In the United States, the equal sovereignty of the contracting states had been honoured in the provision that each, whether small

or large in population, was to have equal representation in
the federal Senate. In British America, this alien precedent
was consciously and deliberately rejected. The Canadian
plan provided for an upper house based on the quite different principle of regional representation, with Canada East
and Canada West as the first two regions, and the Maritime
Provinces together forming the third.

In the crucial matter of the division of legislative power,
the Quebec Conference also deliberately refused to follow
the American example. In the constitution of the United
States, all powers not specifically granted to the federal government were reserved to the states and the people. The
Canadians regarded this as a mistaken and dangerous principle which they must completely reverse. In the Canadian
plan, residuary powers were granted, not to the provinces,
but to the federal government; and this distribution, though
opposed by a small number of individual delegates, was
accepted by a unanimous vote of all provincial delegations.

On the 27th of October, the delegates left Quebec for a
tour of the Province of Canada – a tour in which the Maritimers received the same kind of hearty welcome that they
had given the travelling Canadians during the summer.
Early in November they were all scattering to their homes;
and at about the same time the Quebec Resolutions, the
fruit of their labours, were published in most newspapers
throughout the provinces. By the time the delegates were back
among their constituents, the British American electorate
knew exactly what had been done at Quebec; and from that
moment Confederation and the future of British North
America became a subject that everybody could debate with
knowledge as well as interest. The murmur of discussion
and argument could be heard everywhere; but its pitch and
volume varied considerably from province to province and
region to region. The debate was perhaps least animated,
though for very different reasons, in Canada West, and in
Newfoundland and Prince Edward Island, than it was elsewhere.

In Canada West, which might have looked on the Quebec

scheme as virtually its own, there was little significant opposition. In Newfoundland and Prince Edward Island there was so much that, despite the efforts of a handful of devoted Unionists and the support of a few influential newspapers, the chances of a favourable reception, or even of a serious discussion, were very slight from the beginning. Opinion in Canada East was rather more evenly divided. There the influence of Cartier's *Bleus*, the dominant political party in the section, ensured widespread and general support for the scheme; but at the same time a British American union seemed to many to mean an uncertain future for French Canada, and the Seventy-two Resolutions obviously provided for a highly centralized federation. The *Rouges*, though politically a small minority, did their best to promote and exploit this vague, general apprehension over the prospect of the survival of the French-Canadian individuality in a British American nation. They had some success in their novel role as the conservative defenders of the historic identity of French Canada; but on the whole the discussion of the Quebec scheme in Canada East continued on a reasoning and unexcited level. It never approached the vehemence of the argument that rapidly developed in Nova Scotia and New Brunswick.

There the Quebec Resolutions were attacked from two different, and, indeed, completely contradictory, points of view. The plan was criticized in the first place precisely because it provided for a federal rather than a unitary system of government—because it was based on the 'federal principle' whose fatally divisive character had obviously wrecked the United States. In the second place, it was criticized, and with equal trenchancy, as a too strongly centralized federal union—a federal union that concentrated power in the federal parliament, where the larger provinces would be dominant, and left the local legislatures only insignificant duties and very little revenue with which to carry them out. The first criticism was, of course, an expression of British America's characteristic preference for legislative unity and parliamentary sovereignty—of the belief in strength as the essence of the great transcontinental nation of the future. The second and contradictory criticism was prompted by two other characteristic British American habits of mind – the widespread and deep-rooted sense of provincial exclusiveness and the inherited colonial feeling that membership within the unconfining framework of the British Empire already supplied all the unity that the northern colonies needed or desired. It was Joseph Howe, an early imperial federationist out of tune with his own age, who gave most eloquent expression to this older idea of British and American union. In his view, the Atlantic provinces were more naturally members of a great maritime British Empire, based on sea power and ocean commerce and linked with metropolitan London, than of a North American continental union governed from backwoods Ottawa.

It was in New Brunswick, however, that the two contradictory criticisms of the Quebec scheme united to achieve their greatest political success. Soon after his return from Quebec, the premier of the province, Samuel Leonard Tilley, had been persuaded, or forced, to announce publicly that the Seventy-two Resolutions would not be presented to the provincial legislature until after the next general election. The next general election did not need to be held for another six months; but Tilley, who was under considerable pressure from his Lieutenant-Governor, Arthur Hamilton Gordon, decided, against his better judgement, to risk his doubtful chances in an immediate winter contest. His government, old and tired, with a somewhat unsavoury reputation, was vulnerable politically; but even Tilley himself may not have anticipated the extent of the disaster that now overtook it. The elections, beginning on the 28th of February, were spread over a period of about a fortnight. But as early as the 4th of March it was known that Tilley and all his principal Unionist friends had been defeated and that the next government in New Brunswick would be opposed to Confederation.

That week-end early in March 1865 was the blackest hour in the long struggle for Confederation. A British American union would certainly be able to get along for a while – and perhaps for a long while – without either Newfoundland or Prince Edward Island; but New Brunswick, which supplied the necessary link between Canada and Nova Scotia, was absolutely essential to any union that was worthy of the name. Without New Brunswick, Confederation simply could not be. Without New Brunswick, the movement towards union could make no further progress. Tilley's defeat fortified the strong resistance in Prince Edward Island and Newfoundland; and in Nova Scotia, where the division of opinion was more keen, it gave the Anti-Confederates new hope and confidence. The passage of the Quebec Resolutions, which was to have been completed in all the provinces during the session of 1865, must now be held up indefinitely. Within another year, the Coalition government in Canada would probably have to abandon the longer project of Confederation and take up its second alternative of a federal union of the Canadas. If that ever happened, the hope of British American union was gone for a generation. And how could the second-best alternative be avoided, unless the Anti-Confederate government in New Brunswick was overthrown, and quickly?

V

Up to this point the movement for British American federation had been prompted largely by domestic interests rather than by external pressures. Maritimers and Canadians were, of course, always aware of the wider imperial context of their public affairs and of the serious effects which the American Civil War might have upon their relations with the United States; but so far any influences from outside upon the movement for union had been general and indirect, rather than particular and immediate. Then, in the autumn of 1864, this relative immunity from external pressure ended. As the Civil War went on, and as the fortunes of the Confederacy grew more desperate, there was an increasing likelihood that the South might attempt to distract the

North, to throw it off balance, by raids or surprises from
British North America. The affair of the *Chesapeake*, which
had alarmed Halifax in December 1863, was a foretaste of
what might happen; and now nearly a year later, after the
campaigns of the summer of 1864, the Confederacy was close
to the end of its tether. On the 19th of October a score of
commissioned Confederate soldiers, operating secretly from
a base in Canada East, made a small, ineffectual raid on the
town of St. Albans, in Vermont.

The St. Albans raid was of no military benefit whatever
to the cause of the Southern Confederacy; but it roused the
Northern Americans to a state of fury against the Province
of Canada. The Americans were aware that by this time
public opinion in British America had become largely pro-
Southern in sympathy; and they were convinced that in failing to stop the raid on St. Albans the Canadians had been
guilty of a glaring violation of their neutrality. Relations
between the republic and the northern provinces, which had
never recovered completely from the effects of the *Trent*
crisis, now deteriorated with frightening rapidity. Northern
politicians, generals, and newspapers threatened savage re-
prisals against Canada. The United States served notice to
Great Britain that it no longer considered itself bound by
the Rush-Bagot agreement, which limited naval armaments
on the Great Lakes. The American Congress angrily began
to discuss the early termination of the Reciprocity Treaty
with British North America.

Canada was badly alarmed. So also was Great Britain. The
British were already aware that in the United States they
too were angrily accused of pro-Southern sympathies and
unneutral actions; and the St. Albans raid and its consequences simply brought home to them more vividly the
enormity of the potential danger they faced in North
America. Everybody knew in the winter of 1864-5 that the
American Civil War, after nearly four long years of carnage,
was coming inevitably to an end. What if the triumphant
Union were now to seek revenge for the injuries it claimed
to have suffered at the hands of an unneutral British Em-

pire? What if the Americans should attempt to exact a re-
compense on the St. Lawrence for their losses on the Potomac? To Lord Palmerston, the British Prime Minister, it
was inconceivable that in such an event British America
should be left to its fate; but, though most of the British
governing class grudgingly accepted this obligation, they did
their best to reduce its scope and weight. As W. E. Gladstone,
Chancellor of the Exchequer, argued, it was quite possible
to 'shift the centre of responsibility' in defence and to compel
the colonies to accept a much larger part of the burden of
their own protection. Lieut.-Colonel Jervois was sent over
to plan a new defence system for Canada; and the British
government earnestly pressed the Canadian government to
consider the matter seriously and to assume the major responsibility in a new arrangement.

But the settlement of the defence question by itself was
not enough. As Gladstone and Edward Cardwell, the Colonial Secretary, began to realize very quickly, the problem
of the future of British America was political as well as military. If Canada was to become a principal in its own defence,
if it was to take over the control of the Hudson's Bay Company's territories and thus assume the guardianship of a
third of the North American continent, it must cease to be
an ordinary colonial dependency of the Crown. If British
North America as a whole was to become the residuary
legatee for British properties and commitments in the northern part of the new world, then obviously it must, in Gladstone's words, be brought closer to 'a national sentiment and
position' than it had ever been before. For its own imperial
reasons, the British government welcomed Confederation.
In Confederation lay the best chance of its own orderly and
dignified withdrawal from its North American responsibilities. And as early as December 1864 the Colonial Office had
given its cordial approval to the Quebec scheme.

But now Canada desperately needed stronger support.
The combination of defeat in New Brunswick and danger
from the United States seriously alarmed the Canadian government; and England was the only power to which the Prov-

ince could appeal in its extremity. The news of the Anti-
Confederate victory in New Brunswick was a shattering
blow; but the Coalition cabinet put on a bold front against
adversity. On Monday, the 6th of March, Macdonald announced in the Canadian Assembly that the Ministers did
not regard the reverse in New Brunswick as a reason for any
change in their program, but simply as a spur to 'prompt
and vigorous action' in carrying it out. The 'prompt and
vigorous action' that the government proposed was a special
mission of senior ministers to London – a mission that would
try to obtain stronger British support for Confederation and
for defence against the United States. In the spring, Macdonald, Cartier, Brown, and Galt – the 'big four' of the
Canadian Coalition – crossed the Atlantic for talks with the
British ministers.

They had a fair measure of success. Galt's elaborate and
extremely expensive defence plans were, of course, rejected
by Whig-Liberal politicians who were determined to do no
more for Canada than they absolutely had to. But England
and Canada exchanged pledges to defend British America
with all their forces in the event of a war with the United
States; and the British commitment, though the London
newspapers did their best to belittle its significance, re-
assured the worried and apprehensive Canadians. They
were also encouraged by the British government's promise
to use all its influence with the Maritime Provinces in favour
of Confederation. There were obvious limits to what Great
Britain could do. She could rely only on moral authority
to give weight to her earnest exhortations. But the Colonial
Secretary's reasoned dispatches, reprinted through the Atlantic provinces, might win over Maritime voters; and Maritime lieutenant-governors, instructed to do all in their power
to forward the Quebec scheme, might be able to influence
the course of provincial politics.

The pressure of danger from the United States and of
persuasion from England made together a heavy impact
upon British America; but it was not this combined external
force which, in the main, overcame the resistance of the

Anti-Confederate government in New Brunswick and thus cleared the road for the advance of the Union movement. Influences from outside were strong; but they were not so serious as the inward weaknesses and differences of opinion that divided and enfeebled the Anti-Confederate forces throughout the Atlantic provinces and from the start brought dissension and trouble to the new government at Fredericton. The fact was that the majority of the Anti-Confederates were not opposed in principle to the idea of British American union: they simply disliked the Quebec scheme; and it was this completely negative feeling that alone held the heterogeneous elements of the Anti-Unionist party together. Of the two leaders of the new New Brunswick government, one, R. D. Wilmot, opposed the Quebec scheme because it was not a legislative union, and the other, Albert J. Smith, attacked it because it was a too highly centralized federation. If the Anti-Confederates could not discover a viable alternative to Confederation, they were very likely to split apart over the very issue that had united them.

Yet where were viable alternatives to be found? The only obvious substitutes for union with Canada were a continued and possibly closer association with Great Britain or a closer commercial and railway connection with the United States. Joseph Howe's plan for colonial representation in the imperial House of Commons was an expression of the first idea; Wilmot and Smith, with their scheme for the 'western extension' of the provincial railway to the American border, were in effect basing their hopes upon the second alternative. But, in the circumstances of the time, both policies were hopelessly unrealistic. The prevailing anti-colonial sentiment in the United Kingdom made Howe's vain hopes impossible of achievement; and the animosity with which wartime United States regarded British America sealed the fate of New Brunswick's designs for closer economic relations with the republic. Smith could not induce any group of capitalists to build 'western extension' as a commercial enterprise, and the province was too poor and debt-ridden to undertake it as a public work. The American abrogation of the

Reciprocity Treaty was an even more crushing reverse; and
when it became clear that the United States would not listen
to any proposals for the prolongation of the Treaty in any
form, the only New Brunswick alternative to Confederation
had obviously reached a dead end.

By the autumn of 1865, the divisions inside the Smith-
Wilmot government and its growing unpopularity with the
New Brunswick electorate were both becoming manifest.
Early in November the New Brunswick Confederates won
an important by-election in the County of York; and the
York by-election encouraged and strengthened the Unionist
cause over all British America. It reunited the Canadian
Coalition cabinet, which had been on the verge of a split
over the course it would pursue if a general union proved to
be unrealizable; and, more important still, it proved to be
the first sign of the rapid decline and fall of the Anti-Confederate government in Fredericton. By this time, R. D.
Wilmot had accepted the Quebec scheme as the only practicable form of British American union; and this was a
conflict, at the very heart of the Fredericton government,
that Lieutenant-Governor Arthur Hamilton Gordon was
able to exploit with telling force. He persuaded the wavering
and undecided Smith, as a price of his remaining in office,
to make a half-hearted public avowal of belief in some form
of union; and when Smith, who seemed ready to betray both
sides in his determination to remain in power, repeatedly
postponed doing anything to carry out his pledge, Lieutenant-Governor Gordon brusquely forced a decision upon
him. In April 1866 Albert Smith and his Anti-Unionist colleagues angrily resigned; a new Confederate government,
with Wilmot as one of its leaders, took office; and in another
six weeks a second New Brunswick general election ended in
a Unionist victory even more decisive than the defeat of the
previous year.

The resignation of the Smith cabinet and its subsequent
defeat at the polls ensured the success of Confederation in
both New Brunswick and Nova Scotia. The crisis in Fredericton could hardly have come at a more fortunate time for

the Confederates. A year before, the American Civil War had come to an end, and the Union Army, long dreaded in British America, had been quietly disbanded. But the Fenian organizations, now greatly enlarged with veterans of the Civil War, had concocted their crazy scheme of striking a blow for Irish freedom by invading British America; and the first of the abortive Fenian raids miscarried on the borders of New Brunswick only a few days after the Smith government had resigned. The Fenians publicly announced that they had come to prevent Confederation and to sever the connection between the provinces and Great Britain; and for many people this declaration placed an indelible stigma of disloyalty on the Anti-Confederate cause. The vain Fenian raid of April clinched Tilley's victory at the polls in May and June. It also noticeably strengthened Charles Tupper's position at Halifax; and in April, at the height of the Fenian excitement, the Nova Scotian legislature passed a resolution authorizing its delegates to continue the negotiations for British American union in London.

By June of 1866, Confederation had become a virtual certainty. Nothing—neither American threats, British persuasions, nor Canadian argument—could overcome the obstinate resistance of Newfoundland and Prince Edward Island; but if the islands had rejected union, the continental colonies had accepted it as the only way in which the survival of a separate British North America could be ensured. By this time the Anti-Confederate cause had been proved bankrupt: its leaders had failed to provide viable alternatives to Confederation or develop successful policies for a future of provincial isolation. Their failure had left them irresolute and purposeless; and this inward deterioration was the main cause of their movement's defeat. Many Anti-Confederates, however much they disliked the Quebec scheme, had always assumed, at bottom, that union was the ultimate destiny of British North America. Now, in the troubled and dangerous times of 1865-6, it began to look as if union was not merely desirable for the future, but necessary in the present.

It was too late for the British Parliament to unite the

three provinces by imperial legislation during the session of
1866; but delegates from Canada, Nova Scotia, and New
Brunswick met in London in the late autumn in good time
before the re-opening of Parliament in February of 1867.
The London Conference, which made some significant but
no fundamental changes in the Quebec scheme, completed
its final review of the new constitution before the end of
December. The British North America Act, based on the
London Resolutions, passed the imperial Parliament in
February and March with only trifling amendments; and on
the 1st of July, the three provinces were united to 'form and
be one Dominion under the name of Canada'.

VI

The members of the first Dominion cabinet took office on
the 1st of July; and on the 6th of November 1867 the first
Parliament of Canada listened to the Governor General read
the first speech from the throne. The machinery of government had begun to turn; but the task of integrating the new
union and of promoting its welfare had barely begun, and
the business of nation-building on a continental scale had
got only as far as its first preliminary stage. The three provinces that united on the 1st of July formed only a part—
though a very important part—of what the Fathers of Confederation hoped and believed the Dominion of Canada
would one day become. In the east, the two islands, Newfoundland and Prince Edward Island, remained obstinately
aloof; and in Nova Scotia Joseph Howe was leading a popular and determined agitation for the repeal of the Union.
In the west, the Hudson's Bay Company still retained its
feeble hold on the vast domain of its chartered territory; and
on the Pacific slope, the future of Vancouver Island and
British Columbia, those two remote outposts of British
power in North America, remained uncertain. In both west
and east there was much to be done; and if a rough balance
was to be maintained in national expansion the work in both
directions must be carried forward simultaneously.

In the east there were provinces still to be won over; there was also serious resistance to be met in one province already a part of the Dominion. In Nova Scotia the Anti-Confederates, taking advantage of their first chance to show the strength of their popular support, made virtually a clean sweep of both the provincial and federal general elections; and in 1868 another Nova Scotian delegation, headed by Howe, left to beg the imperial Parliament to release their province from Confederation. Outwardly the Anti-Confederate cause seemed powerful, as it had done in New Brunswick three years before; but once again there was no real alternative to Confederation for which the Anti-Unionists could work with resolution and, if necessary, by radical methods; and all about them was the resistance of existing commitments and established authorities, new and old. In the words of Sir John Macdonald, the Dominion refused even to admit that repeal of the Union was 'a matter for discussion'. In Great Britain, Disraeli's government, which had sponsored the British North America Act, declined to undo its own handiwork at the request of one discontented province; and in the late autumn of the year when the Liberals, led by Gladstone, formed a new administration, this decision was confirmed, even though John Bright, who had shown some sympathy for the Nova Scotians, was a member of the new cabinet. Obviously constitutional methods had completely failed: and the defeated Anti-Confederates could not agree on the course they must now pursue. Howe, old, tired, and disillusioned, was ready for any honourable capitulation; and, on its part, the Dominion government was prepared to offer Nova Scotia substantially better financial terms in Confederation.

In the autumn of 1868, when Macdonald was making his first conciliatory approaches to Howe, the Dominion government also took its first definite step towards the acquisition of the North-west. The Canadians were now prepared to recognize, what they had always previously declined to admit, that the Hudson's Bay Company held proprietary rights which would only be surrendered for adequate compensation; and Sir George Cartier and William McDougall,

an early Reform advocate of Western expansion, were sent
over to London to negotiate realistically for the cession of
the territory. The terms of transfer—a cash payment by Canada of £300,000 and the retention by the Hudson's Bay Company of one-twentieth of the fertile belt—was ratified by the
Canadian Parliament, which also passed a statute setting up
a temporary provisional government for the Northwest Territories. Parties of engineers and workmen were already busy
cutting roads that would link Lake Superior with Red River;
and in the summer of 1869 a group of surveyors went west
to begin the enormous enterprise of the survey which would
open up the Canadian North-west for settlement. Late in
September, William McDougall, the first Lieutenant-Governor, set out with a small staff for his new domain. The
transfer of the territory was to take place on the 1st of December.

   The resistance that Confederation met in the Red River
settlement and the gravity with which the Dominion government regarded it can be fully understood only in the
broad context of North American power politics. The tension with which the decade had opened, between the United
States on the one hand and Great Britain and British America on the other, had never been really relaxed; and until
the destined continental limits of the new nation had been
reached, there was always the dangerous possibility that
one or other of the still detached parts of British America
might fall into the control of the republic. The United States
had never recognized and accepted the new Dominion; she
and Great Britain had never reached a settlement of the
issues outstanding from the American Civil War. The crim-
inally unneutral conduct during the struggle with which
Great Britain was charged had now become the basis of fantastic claims for reparations, and the new American President, General U. S. Grant, and his Secretary of State, Hamilton Fish, were hoping and urging that a penitent England
would 'withdraw' from the North American continent and
that all or most of her possessions would fall into the hands
of the United States. Behind them a small army of interested

Americans – governors, senators, congressmen, members of
state legislatures, railway promoters, newspapermen, State
Department special agents, and American consuls – were
steadily working towards the same end.

The United States would not, of course, adopt an official
policy of intervention; but American citizens might exploit
the gaps and weaknesses in the partly built structure of Confederation so successfully that in the end official intervention would become inevitable. The strange, remote settlement at Red River was a potential centre of resistance to
Canadian nationalism. The unrest in Nova Scotia and the
detachment of Newfoundland and Prince Edward Island
could be used to weaken the Canadian union and prevent
its expansion. In the summer of 1868 Senator Benjamin
F. Butler led a congressional party on a visit to Nova Scotia
and Prince Edward Island. A year later, Senator Alexander
Ramsay of Minnesota, a state that took an eager interest in
the fate of the British American North-west, succeeded in
having an American consul, Oscar Malmros, appointed to
the little outpost at Red River. Obviously Malmros's only
important duty was to watch over and encourage tactfully the
anti-Canadian feelings of Fort Garry. Butler's purpose was to
emphasize and reward Prince Edward Island's separatist tendencies by offering to it alone the generous reciprocal trade
agreement for which all Canada had been vainly hoping ever
since the abrogation of the Reciprocity Treaty in 1866. The
Butler mission and the new consul were two fingers of investigation hopefully probing for a weakness in the per-
functory defences of the new Dominion.

It was not Malmros who inspired and directed the resistance at Red River in 1869-70. This was the work of the
Métis, the French half-breeds, led by Louis Riel and supported and advised by the French-speaking priests Lestanc,
Ritchot, and Dugas. The Métis, a semi-nomadic people, with
a rough military organization derived from buffalo hunts,
were the strongest political force at Red River. They saw in
Confederation and the coming of mass immigration the inevitable extinction of their own free, wild way of life. With

Louis Riel as their political theorist and revolutionary
leader, they prepared to resist; and they were aided by the
French-speaking priests, who, through a combination of
religious bigotry and devotion to their half-savage charges,
were prepared to use any means to delay the advent of the
hated English-speaking Protestants from Ontario. It was
Louis Riel's Métis who stopped Lieutenant-Governor Mc-
Dougall and his party at the international border, occupied
Fort Garry, and imposed a so-called 'provisional government' on the little community. Such a protest by force was
bound to perturb the government of a state that was little
more than two years old; but for Macdonald's cabinet more
than half of the importance of the Red River rising derived
from its place in the complex of North American power
politics. The publication in 1869 of Butler's report of his
mission to Prince Edward Island had prompted the Canadian government to make another serious effort to persuade
the Island to enter Confederation. Now the prominence of
Americans in the inner counsels of the new 'provisional government' and the excited interest of the press and people of
Minnesota and the American north-west were more than
enough to make Macdonald suspect that Riel might be
only too ready to appeal for support to the United States. As
the last year of the decade closed, the Canadian government
was selecting and briefing the emissaries who were to go to
Red River in the hope of satisfying the settlement's grievances and ending its resistance. The vast transcontinental
design lay incomplete. If British Americans had made the
great decision, it had yet to be fulfilled.

2. The 1870s

GEORGE F. G. STANLEY

As 1870 opened, Canadian eyes were on the troubles at the Red River settlement, which had delayed the transfer of the great North-west from the Hudson's Bay Company to the new Dominion. Forces of resistance ruled at Red River, where Louis Riel, youthful, idealistic, and vigorous, had organized the Métis National Committee to prevent William McDougall, Canada's governor designate, from entering the colony, had arrested a party of Canadian settlers who sought to back up the installation of Canadian authority by armed force, and had proclaimed a provisional government with headquarters at Fort Garry. In response the Macdonald government in Ottawa, having refused to accept title to the troubled Northwest on December 1, 1869, as originally planned, took

belated steps to explain Canada's intention to the inhabitants of Red River. Bishop Taché of St. Boniface was summoned back from Rome, where he had been attending the
Vatican Council. Two distinguished French Canadians were
dispatched to the colony to allay the suspicions of the Métis,
and Donald A. Smith, an official of the Hudson's Bay Company, was also sent out as a special commissioner to investigate the situation at Fort Garry. There Smith attended two
large public meetings at which he put forward the Canadian
case. He was sufficiently impressive that the Red River
settlers resolved to draw up a list of rights and send delegates
to Ottawa to confer with Sir John Macdonald and the members of the Canadian government.

All would undoubtedly have gone well had not the Canadians in Red River resolved to try another show of force.
They had resented the imprisonment of sixty-five of their
number in December and, goaded by several escapees, they
organized a small armed force at Portage la Prairie. The
Portage party planned to join another group from the lower
parishes. The ostensible purpose of their demonstration was
to compel Riel to release his prisoners. Again the whole
movement fell flat for lack of adequate support, and when it
became generally known that Riel had, in fact, already given
the prisoners their release, the Portage Canadians turned
around and set off for home. The Métis, however, had been
alarmed by the threat of attack, and as the Canadians were
passing Fort Garry – their action in returning so close to the
fort was an unnecessary provocation – the Métis horsemen
rounded them up and herded them into the cells recently
vacated by the previous prisoners. Determined to make an
example of one of the troublemakers, Riel picked upon
Thomas Scott, a belligerent Irish Canadian from Ontario,
whose conduct in prison was both violent and insulting. Scott
was tried by a Métis court-martial and executed by a firing-
squad on March 4.

Scott's execution aroused the racial and religious animosities of the Orangemen of Ontario, who demanded the immediate despatch of a punitive expedition to the west and

the arrest of the delegates of the provisional government, then on their way to Ottawa. Despite the Orange agitation and the efforts of Ontario Liberals to make political capital out of it, the Macdonald government received Riel's emissaries and concluded a mutually satisfactory agreement with them. This was embodied in an act passed by the Canadian Parliament in May. Known as the Manitoba Act, it provided for the entry of the Red River settlement into the Canadian Confederation as a province. The transfer of the territories of the Hudson's Bay Company to Canada then took place, and on July 15 the Red River settlement became the fifth province of Canada, under the name of Manitoba.

These political developments had removed all urgency for the dispatch of a military force. However, Macdonald went ahead with the proposed military expedition, if only to satisfy the demands of his Ontario constituents and to afford protection to the new lieutenant-governor, A. G. Archibald, when he should reach Fort Garry. The troops arrived in Red River before Archibald, and Louis Riel fled to the United States. At the last moment he had been warned by a friendly Hudson's Bay Company man that the Ontario militia was determined to avenge Scott. All along Riel had protested his loyalty to the Crown: subsequently he was able to give proof of that loyalty when the Métis rallied under his leadership to resist a threatened Fenian invasion of Manitoba in October 1871. But for the present it was thought better that he remain out of sight. In later years Riel himself ran for Parliament and was elected several times, but, always fearing for his life, he never took his seat. Finally, in 1875 he was exiled for five years.

At the same time that Canada acquired Manitoba as a province it also acquired the remainder of the Hudson's Bay Company territories. This vast, unorganized region was administered, during the eighteen-seventies, by a governor and council appointed by Ottawa. Territorial administration continued, with the later introduction of elected members, until the formation of the provinces of Saskatchewan and Alberta in 1905.

Once the North-west became firmly part of Canada, the next step in Macdonald's great design for a transcontinental union was to open negotiations with the British colony on the Pacific coast. As long as the prairies remained under Company rule, there could be no effective union between the eastern and western parts of British North America. However, by 1866 the question of the future of British Columbia was becoming urgent. The economic situation of the colony was precarious and men were talking of either union with Canada or annexation to the United States. The latter was by no means impossible. After all, who were the Canadians? A people living far to the east, over the Rocky Mountains. Only a small number of them had reached the west coast and they had not made any great impact on the political life of the colony. As far as the colonial governor and his officials were concerned, they wanted union neither with Canada nor with the United States. Confederation or annexation was bound to mean the introduction of responsible government and the end of their specially privileged position. They hoped that things would remain as they were.

In spite of the opposition of the pro-American element and of the little group who controlled the government there were forces at work in favour of union with Canada. Led by James Trimble and Amor de Cosmos, the latter a Nova Scotian whose original name was William Smith, a Confederation League was formed in 1868 to publicize the advantages of Confederation. This body organized a series of public meetings throughout the colony of British Columbia, the most important of which was held at Yale on September 14. This 'Yale Convention' adopted various resolutions prepared by de Cosmos, a leading proponent of responsible government for British Columbia and incorporation of the colony in Canada. Governor Seymour sent these resolutions to the Colonial Secretary, but attached a letter to them belittling their importance. However, in 1869 Seymour died, and the way was clear for the appointment of a man sympathetic to the union idea. Macdonald himself favoured Anthony Musgrave, the Lieutenant-Governor of Newfoundland, who had already proved his devotion to the Confederate cause by his efforts to bring about the union of Newfoundland with Canada. Musgrave accepted the appointment when it was offered by the Colonial Office, and persuaded his Legislative Council to suggest the kind of union terms that might be acceptable to them. The next step was to appoint delegates to go to Ottawa. It was all done very quickly; and when Canada accepted the British Columbian proposals, the Legislative Council of the colony passed an address to the Crown asking for admittance to Canada as a province. The Canadian Parliament adopted a similar resolution and the union was given legal status by an imperial Order-in-Council dated May 16, 1871. A little over a month later, on July 20, 1871, the Canadian union was augmented by the addition of its sixth province, British Columbia.

The terms under which the west-coast province became part of Canada included not only the assumption by the federal government of the debt of the pre-Confederate colony, a favourable subsidy, and fully responsible government, but also the promise of a transcontinental railway to be started within two years and completed within ten. The railway stipulation was, in fact, the most important clause in the agreement between Canada and British Columbia. The ten-year limit was to be the guarantee of Canada's intentions to honour its agreement with its new Pacific province.

Newfoundland's delegates had also returned from the Quebec Conference of 1864 enthusiastic about the idea of British North American union. But they had found their colleagues considerably less so. The government leader, Frederick Carter, felt it advisable to postpone public discussion of the issue, particularly when he saw Tilley thrown out of office in New Brunswick on the same issue and Tupper reluctant to broach the matter in his Nova Scotian legislature. There was no use talking about Confederation in Newfoundland when the other Maritime colonies showed no desire to have any part of it. When the reverse experienced by the Confederates in the Maritimes proved to be only temporary, however, Lieutenant-Governor

Musgrave prompted Carter to re-open the question in 1869. Possible terms of union with Canada were discussed in the legislature and a delegation headed by Carter was appointed to go to Ottawa.

Before going to the Canadian capital, Carter gave a positive undertaking to submit any agreement reached in Ottawa to the people of the colony. Accordingly, in November 1869, a general election was fought in Newfoundland almost exclusively on the federation issue. Despite the support of the Lieutenant-Governor in St. John's and the Colonial Secretary in London, the people of the island voted against the Confederates. Carter was thrown out of office and the Anti-Confederate Charles Bennett left no doubt in anyone's mind that union with Canada was dead as far as Newfoundland was concerned. The Lieutenant-Governor wondered if perhaps the imperial government might not coerce the colony into union with the mainland; but the Canadian Prime Minister, Sir John Macdonald, would have nothing to do with coercion. In any event, he was, at the time, much more concerned about the future of Prince Edward Island than about that of Newfoundland. Britain's 'oldest colony', with its appendage, Labrador, therefore remained outside the Canadian Confederation until 1949.

The Prince Edward Islanders had shown far less partiality for union at the Quebec Conference than had the New-foundlanders. Almost invariably they had been the men who presented the most embarrassing problems and who raised the most controversial issues. Nevertheless, the Island delegates had accepted the Quebec scheme and when they returned to Charlottetown felt obliged to stand by it. But there was no such obligation on the part of the members of the provincial legislature. And with hostility to the Quebec Resolutions apparent throughout the whole of the Island there was little doubt that Confederation would have a rough time of it. In the legislature the supporters of union were outnumbered and out-argued, and an address to the Queen was adopted praying Her Majesty 'not to give her Royal Assent or sanction to any Act or Measure . . . that would have the effect of uniting Prince Edward Island in a Federal Union with Canada . . .' Subsequently the Colonial Office endeavoured to convince the Island government that it should modify its attitude, but without success. The Islanders were adamant in their opposition to the wishes of Great Britain and Canada alike.

Then in 1869 came the news that General Benjamin Butler of Massachusetts, an advocate of the annexation of British North America to the United States, was on his way to Charlottetown to discuss the possibility of American trade concessions in return for special privileges for American fishermen in Island waters. The Canadians were so alarmed at the implications of Butler's mission (particularly after they read his report) that Macdonald felt it advisable to forget about Newfoundland and bend his efforts towards winning the Prince Edward Islanders away from the wily Americans. The astonishing thing is that the Islanders were able, in 1869, to resist the combined efforts of London and Ottawa to induce them to renew negotiations for the union of the Island and Canada. Some of the members of the legislature might be disposed to take a second look at union; but the people themselves remained coldly aloof. Clearly, unless some crisis arose, Prince Edward Island would not voluntarily unite its future with that of Canada.

Then the crisis came. The Islanders, who in 1866 had not wanted to pay for the building of an intercolonial railway for the benefit of Nova Scotia and New Brunswick, decided in 1871 to embark upon an ambitious program of railway construction on their own. Rather too ambitious. Some of the members wondered if they might not find themselves saddled with a debt higher than anything that union with Canada would involve. However, the supporters of the line talked optimistically and convincingly about the prosperity it would bring, the new industries, the additional population, the American tourists. But the opponents of the line were right. The line did cost more than expected and the Islanders did find the provincial debt mounting by leaps and bounds. So strained were the finances of the colony and so embarrassed the banks that had underwritten the railway that both feared a financial collapse. The way out of the difficulty seemed to be Confederation. The bankers urged it as well as some of the politicians. With great reluctance the premier, Robert Haythorne, appointed a delegation to go to Ottawa in February 1873. The Canadians, led by Macdonald, did not take advantage of the Islanders' journey to Canossa. They offered fair and generous terms and these were accepted. In the general election that followed, Haythorne was defeated; but Confederation was not an issue. The new government of J. C. Pope was pro-Confederate, and after further negotiations on matters of detail, Prince Edward Island agreed to enter the Canadian union.

The terms included the assumption of the Island debt by Canada and the advance of $800,000 to buy out the absentee landowners. The federal authorities also agreed to take over the railway guarantee and to establish and maintain 'efficient steam service for the conveyance of mails and passengers . . . between the Island and the mainland of the Dominion, winter and summer, thus placing the Island in continuous communication with the Intercolonial Railway and the railway system of Canada.' In May 1873, the Island legislature unanimously adopted a resolution in favour of Confederation with Canada on the terms outlined above. In Ottawa, at the same time, a similar address was adopted. On June 26, an imperial Order-in-Council authorized the formal union of Prince Edward Island and Canada effective 'from and after the first of July, 1873'.

'I greatly desire to complete the work of Confederation before I make my final bow to the Canadian audience,' Macdonald had once written. Now, within the short space of six years after the four original provinces had come together in 1867, that work was virtually completed. Only Newfoundland still remained outside. Canada was a country extending 'from sea to sea and from the river to the uttermost ends of the earth', a country of seven provinces and a vast region known as the North-West Territories. Before the decade of the eighteen-seventies had even reached a half-way mark,

Canadians had become proprietors of half a continent. It was a great and mighty achievement. Just how great only a few of them as yet appreciated. Perhaps time would help them to understand.

II

The union of 1867 had, in large measure, been the response of British North America to the threat of absorption by the United States. This threat had not taken the form of open warfare since 1812, but war still remained a possibility. The Fenians had come near it, with their unsuccessful raids upon Canadian territory in 1866 and their equally unsuccessful raids upon Quebec and Manitoba in 1870 and 1871. If these raids had not had official backing of Washington, there were still many Americans who believed in the doctrine of 'Manifest Destiny'. William Seward, President Lincoln's Secretary of State, and Charles Sumner, the Republican leader of the Senate, both adhered to Benjamin Franklin's view that the division of North America was 'unnatural'. In July 1866, before Confederation had been achieved, General N. P. Banks of Massachusetts introduced into the American Congress a bill providing for 'the admission of the States of Nova Scotia, New Brunswick, Canada East and Canada West and for the organization of the Territories of Selkirk, Saskatchewan and Columbia'. It was the answer of American continentalists to the national union movement north of the United States' frontier. The continentalists did not want to see a British-sponsored union; and Congress was persuaded to pass a joint resolution to the effect that the United States should view the Canadian Confederation 'with extreme solicitude', on the grounds that it contravened the Monroe Doctrine.

If Canadian-American relations had been bad prior to Confederation, after 1867 they grew steadily worse. Seward's purchase of Alaska was frankly designed to strengthen American influence in British Columbia and to assist the annexationists in that colony. It was, said Seward, 'a visible step in the occupation of the whole North American continent'. Minnesotan interest in the Hudson's Bay Company territories was well known to and encouraged by official circles in the United States' capital. In June 1869, two years after Confederation, Secretary of State Hamilton Fish approached the British ambassador with the suggestion that Great Britain should cede Canada to the United States in payment of the damages inflicted by the *Alabama* and her sister ships, built in British shipyards during the Civil War. Several times Fish returned to the same proposal, urging in 1870 that the time was ripe to remove all sources of friction between Washington and London by turning over Canada to the American republic. Edward Thorton, the ambassador, might have returned a strong reply to this preposterous proposal; instead he merely remarked that Great Britain would not initiate such a cession without Canadian consent, although the British government might be 'willing and even desirous' of doing so. That a British official should speak so mildly, and so cautiously refrain from pressing the Canadian demands upon the United States for compensation for the Fenian damages, seemed to suggest that Great Britain was no longer a pillar on which Canadians might lean. The proposed withdrawal of the British troops from their Canadian stations gave credibility to this idea, unpalatable as it might appear to Sir John A. Macdonald and to most Canadians at that time.

Most of the heat between Canada and the United States arose from the friction generated by the abrogation of the Reciprocity Treaty of 1854. On January 15, 1865, three months before Lincoln's assassination, the American Secretary of State gave formal notice that the treaty would terminate in one year's time. There is no doubt that Canada had profited more from the treaty than the United States, particularly while the Americans were busy fighting a civil war; but the treaty was not a one-sided affair. It had given the Americans a privilege of which they were very jealous, that of fishing in the waters of the British North American colonies. After 1866 this privilege was denied them. At first the

British colonials were disposed to exercise the right to exclude their rivals in a conciliatory manner, asking only the payment of a licence fee; but when the Americans abused this privilege and neglected to take out the required licences, the Canadian authorities resolved to enforce the letter of the law. The energetic federal Minister of Marine and Fisheries from New Brunswick, Peter Mitchell, fitted out several cruisers to protect the rights of Canada, and arrests of American interlopers became frequent—so frequent that even Macdonald became alarmed at the possible consequences.

The situation rapidly developed into a crisis. In December 1870, President Grant denounced the 'harsh treatment' meted out to American fishermen by the Canadians and threatened retaliation. Great Britain, deeply concerned over the implications of the German victories in the Franco-Prussian War in Europe, became alarmed at a prospective breach with the United States over a few colonial codfish. After all, did they not have their own problems with the Americans over those *Alabama* claims? Accordingly the suggestion was advanced that a joint high commission be established by Great Britain and the United States to discuss and settle all outstanding controversies between the two countries. Sumner wanted to make it contingent upon the United States' obtaining in advance an undertaking that the British flag would be withdrawn from all North America; but Hamilton Fish did not wish to kill the commission before it was born and Sumner's proposed ultimatum was ignored.

When the names of the British commissioners were announced both Canadians and Americans were surprised to see included among them that of the Canadian Prime Minister, Sir John Macdonald. It was the first time a colonial politician had received such a distinction. But the British recognition of Macdonald did not involve the recognition of any special Canadian right to be represented. Macdonald was not a Canadian commissioner; he was a British commissioner on the same terms as his colleagues. And the other members of the commission did not let him forget it.

The joint high commission held its sittings between Feb-

ruary 27 and May 8, 1870. During these ten weeks Macdonald frequently found himself at odds with the other members of the British team. Canadian claims against the United
States or Canadian demands for substantial trade concessions in return for the granting of fishing privileges to the
Americans were ignored, not only by the Americans, but,
what was more irritating to Macdonald, by the British. The
latter were anxious, dreadfully anxious, for an accommodation with the Americans and were prepared to give them
almost everything they wanted if only war could be avoided;
why wouldn't the Canadians be willing to accept a money
payment for their miserable fish? What could Macdonald
do? He knew that Canadian claims were going to be sacrificed in the interest of appeasement. Should he agree with
his British colleagues and be a party to an agreement of
which he could not, at heart, approve; or should he withdraw from the commission and imperil any chances of an
Anglo-American accord? He protested; he threatened the
rejection of the draft treaty by the Canadian Parliament; but
in the end he signed.

By the Treaty of Washington the Americans obtained
from Canada the fishing privileges they wanted in return for
a cash payment, the amount of which was to be subsequently
agreed upon. They also obtained the free navigation of the
St. Lawrence River. From Great Britain they obtained satisfaction for the *Alabama* claims. The British in return obtained a relaxation of tension between Great Britain and
the United States. Canada seemed to get nothing, except the
privilege to navigate freely on several obscure Alaskan rivers
and a tentative promise from the British that they would pay
the Fenian claims which the Americans ignored. But, in
reality, the provision for Canadian ratification of the fishery
articles of the treaty signified American acceptance of an
emerging Canadian nation on her northern border.

In Ottawa it was Macdonald's task to see the unpopular
treaty through the Canadian Parliament. The British government's offer to pay the Fenian claims would be of some
help; but Macdonald felt the Canadian sacrifices were worth

more than that and insisted upon a British loan to help finance the new railway to British Columbia. Finally the British agreed to guarantee a loan of £2,500,000. Macdonald fulfilled his share of the bargain by cajoling and arguing the members of his own party into supporting the Washington Treaty and voting for its ratification by the Canadian Parliament. In May 1872, one year after the treaty was signed, the ratification was complete. The Canadians had not succeeded in making the fisheries a lever to restore reciprocal free trade with the United States, but they could console themselves with the thought that the British loan would strengthen the bonds of Canadian unity and make the Pacific railway something more than a scheme on the drafting board.

Even though Macdonald had failed signally to obtain any trade concessions, much less a renewal of the Reciprocity Treaty, while in Washington, there were those Canadians who felt that the effort should not be abandoned. Alexander Mackenzie's Liberals felt that a truly free-trade party might stand a better chance of success if they could deal with the Americans. In 1873 they won power, following charges of glaring scandal in negotiations for the Pacific railway which effectively discredited the Macdonald Conservative government. The Liberals had the opportunity now to approach the Americans, particularly with reports reaching George Brown, former Liberal leader and still a power in the party, that Washington might consider a trade agreement in return for the fisheries, rather than the cash payment that had orginally been proposed. Filled with self-confidence— had he not always been an advocate of reciprocity and an ardent supporter of the North during the Civil War?— George Brown left his Toronto *Globe* office and hurried to Washington. But Hamilton Fish was no more interested in reciprocity in 1874 than he had been in 1871. Brown was annoyed to discover that he was looked upon as a kind of political beggar coming to pick the crumbs from the great man's table. But he choked down his resentment and continued his negotiations. A draft treaty was finally drawn up. But Fish would not sign it until he had the opinion of the

Senate. That opinion came–one year later. It was unfavourable. Not that the Americans were hostile to Brown; rather
they were completely apathetic. Reciprocity, as the Canadians defined it, was not for them.

Brown's failure was a disappointment both to him and to
Mackenzie. The Liberals had counted heavily upon a trade
agreement with the United States as the answer to the severe
economic depression into which the country had sunk in
1873. Without reciprocity, the Liberals had virtually no
economic policy to offer the people of Canada other than
retrenchment and careful administration. The impact of
depression weakened the bonds of a scarcely formed new
nation-state, causing a resurgence of provincial or sectional feelings and disillusionment with the nation-building
dreams of Confederation. The Atlantic provinces chafed
restlessly in a union that many Maritimers felt had benefited
central Canada at their expense. British Columbia grew
increasingly impatient over the Mackenzie government's
failure to proceed fast enough with a Pacific railway–especially when Edward Blake, a brilliant orator and Mackenzie's strongest rival within the Liberal party–denounced
the extravagance of a railway to the west at such a time.

Blake was loosely associated with a little group of eager
young national idealists known as the 'Canada First' movement. They, like him, looked for measures to advance Canada's development as a nation, and applauded his ringing
speech at Aurora, Ontario, in 1874, when he spoke elo-
quently of 'four million Britons who are not free'. But,
again like Blake, they were not sure if the answer lay in an
imperial federation giving the leading self-governing colonies
a voice in the British Parliament or in enlarging Canada's
own national status in the world. Blake and the 'Canada
Firsters' assuredly did not seek to break with Britain. But
more conservative Liberals like Mackenzie and Brown feared
the trend of their ideas–and particularly their association
with Goldwin Smith, the free-trade British liberal and former Oxford professor, who had settled in Toronto and first
advocated outright independence for Canada and subse-

THE POLITICAL GIANT-KILLER; OR, "CANADA FIRST."

From *A Caricature History of Canadian Politics* by J. W. Bengough,
Toronto, 1886, vol. 1.

quently annexation of Canada to the United States.

But the young nationalists did not take over the Liberal
party. When Blake returned from dissent to membership in
Mackenzie's government, 'Canada First' lost its zealous drive,
and Goldwin Smith was left a powerful but isolated figure

denouncing the emptiness and partisan vehemence of Canadian politics. The Mackenzie régime had other difficulties with its supporters. It was weak in Quebec, where the French-Canadian *Rouge* Liberals who had opposed Confederation were still rather lukewarm towards it. And *Rouge*-ism, which had long sought to curtail church influence in secular affairs, if not outright separation of church and state, was under heavy attack for its anti-clerical or 'irreligious' views from the growing spirit of Catholic ultramontanism in French Canada.

For the present, ultramontanism was in the ascendant. It had crushed the Institut Canadien, intellectual centre of *Rouge*-ism. The Guibord case of 1875, when ultramontane forces succeeded in preventing the burial of an Institut member in consecrated Catholic ground, marked the final collapse of the old *Rouge* organization. Fortunately for the Liberal party a young French-Canadian politician, Wilfrid Laurier (a lesser minister in Mackenzie's cabinet in 1877-8), began laying a new basis for liberalism in Quebec by asserting that it was not associated with the anti-Catholic, anti-religious European form so much opposed by the Church, but really derived from British roots that had long been linked with religious and Christian causes.

But whatever Laurier might do for the Canadian Liberal party in the future, he could do little now. The Mackenzie regime's problems continued in Quebec and all across Canada – as did the unremitting depression. Meanwhile Sir John Macdonald watched and waited. Although he did not like the attempt by George Brown to regain American reciprocity as an answer to Canada's problems, he kept his silence during 1874. But in 1875 there was no need for him to reserve judgment any longer. He knew what the answer was to the depression and the ills it had brought to Canada: the 'National Policy', a modified protectionism that would remedy the trade depression, foster a national economy, prevent Canada from becoming the dumping-ground for American goods, and encourage home industry. Macdonald correctly gauged the strength of the growing opinion in favour of protection and the resentment with which Canadians had viewed the uninterested, uncooperative attitude of the government at Washington. Thus, when Mackenzie appealed to the electorate in 1878, he found Canadians ready to vote for the National Policy and for the man who had proposed it. The fact is that the people of Canada were weary of the uncertainties and the hesitations of the Liberal regime. They wanted positive, dynamic political leadership. And from Macdonald they believed they would get it.

The return of Macdonald to power in 1878 and the Tilley tariff of 1879 were followed by good times. The economic revival was to be of short duration, but Canadians did not know that as they welcomed the New Year in 1880. They believed that they had discovered the touchstone of prosperity. There would be no more starving of Canadians into an annexation they did not want; no more running, cap in hand, to Washington for trade concessions they would not get. A good dose of nationalism was the answer to Canada's economic ills. Henceforth Canada would chart her own course, political and economic, in the years that lay ahead.

III

Bonds of steel as well as of sentiment were needed to hold the new Confederation together. Without railways there would be and could be no Canada. For years prior to the union of 1867, men had talked about uniting the Maritime colonies with those on the St. Lawrence. The first proposal, in 1836, was to build a railway line between the New Brunswick port of St. Andrews and the city of Quebec. It came to nothing when the United States queried the location of the boundary line. The railway builders would have to wait until Webster and Ashburton had decided where the frontier actually lay. Even so, St. Andrews was much too close to the United States, and subsequent proposals were based upon the idea of Halifax rather than St. Andrews being the eastern terminus of any railway line. During the eighteen-fifties and -sixties the Grand Trunk had built a series of railway lines in Canada, linking the major cities of the upper provinces with Chicago in the west and with Rivière du Loup and Portland in the east. And in the Maritimes two new lines were built, including a line from Halifax to Truro and another from Saint John to Shediac.

Meanwhile routes for the proposed intercolonial railway between the Maritimes and Canada were surveyed. Three possibilities offered themselves: the Frontier route by way of the St. John River, the Central route, and the Bay of Chaleur route. The Canadian engineer Sandford Fleming was asked to select the most suitable route, and in 1865 he recommended the last–the north shore or Bay of Chaleur route. Fleming believed that this would provide the greatest financial return for the money expended, if only because it would pass through rich lumber country and would touch at the various fishing villages along the coast. Even more significant was the fact that it was a long way from the American frontier and could be reached by ships from Great Britain carrying troops in the event of war. At the Quebec Conference in 1864 and at London in 1866 the construction of a railway between Truro and Rivière du Loup had been stated by the Maritime delegates to be a *sine qua non* of any union. And so it was asserted in the British North America Act of 1807, section 145, 'it shall be the duty of the Government and Parliament of Canada to provide for the commencement within six months after the Union, of a railway, connecting the River St. Lawrence with the City of Halifax in Nova Scotia, and for the construction thereof without intermission, and the completion thereof with all practicable speed.'

It took nine years thereafter to build the Intercolonial. It was not an achievement of private enterprise but a government work, built with money raised by the Canadian taxpayers and by British loans backed by an imperial guarantee of four per cent on three-quarters of the total amount. The road was intended to be a political as well as an economic bond pulling the interior and coastal regions together; it was never intended to be a purely commercial venture. Responsibility for the administration of the line was given to four commissioners appointed by Ottawa, and the engineer who superintended the work was the Canadian who had chosen the route, Sandford Fleming. The line was opened in 1876. Other lines already built in the Maritimes were taken over and in 1879 the section between Rivière du Loup and Quebec, built by the Grand Trunk, was turned over to the Intercolonial. Arrangements were made for running privileges on the Grand Trunk line between Quebec and Montreal. Thus the Intercolonial was able, eventually, to operate its trains from the two great seaports of Canada, Montreal and Halifax.

Equally essential was a railway to the west. Sandford Fleming had talked about the advantages of a line to the Pacific in 1858, when Allan Macdonnell of Toronto obtained a charter for his North West Transportation, Navigation and Railway Company. But neither Macdonnell's company nor Fleming's dream was realized at that time. In 1863, Edward Watkin of the Grand Trunk, who had his eyes on the acquisition of the Hudson's Bay Company territories, made tentative plans for the building of a telegraph line across the prairies from Fort Langley in British Columbia to Fort William; but when the Canadian government refused its financial backing unless a road was built also, the telegraph project too was set aside for the time being. There were vague references in the list of 'rights' that Riel's delegates took to Ottawa in 1870 about 'uninterrupted railroad communication between Winnipeg and Saint Paul, and also steam communication between Winnipeg and Lake Superior', but no formal demand was put forward during the negotiations and nothing appeared in the Manitoba Act. The British Columbians, however, left no doubt in anyone's mind that, like the Maritimers, they too wanted their railway and were prepared to make it the price of their entry into Confederation.

When Macdonald came to consider the problem of the Pacific railway he resolved upon a policy quite different from that followed in building the Intercolonial. The Maritime line was bearing heavily upon the financial resources of the federal government, and Macdonald wanted the new railway built by a private company. Two possibilities offered themselves: the Canada Pacific, headed by Sir Hugh Allan of Montreal, the founder of the Allan Steamship Line, and the Interoceanic, headed by David Macpherson, a Toronto financier. Macdonald would have liked both syndicates to come together and pool their resources. But Macpherson did not trust Allan, whom he believed to be backed by a number of leading American railroad financiers such as G. W. McMullen and Jay Cooke, who were also interested in the Northern Pacific, a rival American transcontinental line; Allan would never consent to Macpherson's demand that he, Macpherson, should appoint the majority of the board of directors. Allan glibly denied his American associations and eventually received the promise of the charter for the Pacific railway from Macdonald. The Prime Minister, owing to his long political and personal friendship with Macpherson, was unwilling to expose himself to the charge of favouritism that a grant of the charter to the Toronto financier would bring.

At this point Allan's American friends took over. They had put up the money that Allan needed and were determined that they were not going to be excluded from the control they intended to exercise over the Canada Pacific. One of them, G. W. McMullen, went to Macdonald and threatened to reveal to the public the fact that Allan had contributed substantially to the Conservative campaign fund during the election of 1872 and especially that he had assisted Sir George Cartier, albeit unsuccessfully. McMullen's threat was political blackmail. But he and his associates were unscrupulous men and ruthless. And McMullen carried out his threat. The files of Allan's solicitor in Montreal were rifled and the necessary incriminating documents were stolen. These were then turned over to the Liberal party. On April 2, 1872, Seth Huntington, the Liberal member for Shefford, rose in his place in the House of Commons and charged the government with having accepted a bribe from

Sir Hugh Allan in return for the railway charter. Macdonald was sustained by a majority vote in the House; but the charges were too serious to be pushed aside in this fashion, and he himself proposed the appointment of a royal commission to take evidence on oath and report to Parliament.

The debate over what became known in our history as the 'Pacific Scandal' made a tremendous impact upon the people of Canada. Macdonald defended himself well in Parliament. Some authorities say that he gave the best speech of his career with its dramatic gesture, 'These hands are clean!' But the Liberal disclosures shocked the none-too-tender consciences of the people and shook the loyalty of some of Macdonald's supporters. Finally, on November 5, 1873, Macdonald resigned, and Mackenzie took office. McMullen had paid back Allan; but in doing so he had discredited Macdonald, whom Lord Dufferin, the Governor General, regarded as 'by far the ablest man in Canada'.

The defeat of Macdonald meant the end of Allan's contract and the end of the Canada Pacific. It almost meant the end of the railway scheme itself. The Liberals, when in opposition, had made it clear that while they welcomed British Columbia into Confederation they were strongly opposed to the railway concessions promised by Macdonald. Now they were in power, they were anxious to modify the terms to which Macdonald had agreed. British Columbians protested. In fact they had already protested to Macdonald during the summer of 1873, prior to his resignation, that he was not living up to the terms of his agreement, by failing to start the railway within the two-year limit. When they heard that Mackenzie in his nomination speech at Sarnia in November of the same year had declared that there would be an entirely new railway policy instead of the 'insane' thing Macdonald had devised, they stormed the legislative buildings of Victoria, denouncing the Liberal Prime Minister's words as a breach of solemn contract.

Mackenzie was a stubborn Scot. He had made up his mind and he was not going to allow it to be changed by a few noisy British Columbians. He sent James Edgar, the young, per-

WHITHER ARE WE DRIFTING?

From *A Caricature History of Canadian Politics* by J. W. Bengough,
Toronto, 1886, vol. 1.

sonable Liberal whip, to Victoria to talk with the provincial
premier, George Walkem, to suggest to him that the ten-
year time limit was wholly absurd. After all, the Pacific line
was at least five times as long as the Intercolonial, and the
Intercolonial was not yet finished after seven years. How
could the longer line be built in ten? Mackenzie's may have

been a thoroughly rational approach but it was not a politic one. The British Columbians wanted 'the bond and nothing but the bond'. They would tolerate no compromise. Throwing politics to the winds, Mackenzie refused to listen to the British Columbian demands. He would go ahead with his own plans and build the Pacific railway as a public work, building sections of the line as the country's means warranted and settlement demanded, and using existing waterways and American lines to fill the intervals.

So incensed were the people of British Columbia at Mackenzie's attitude that they appealed to the Colonial Secretary. Walkem hurried to London to convince Lord Carnarvon that the Canadians had dishonoured their agreement and that something should be done about it. Carnarvon felt that Walkem's views were not without some justification and urged Mackenzie to speed up the surveys and make larger financial appropriations for the railway. At the same time he recognized that the ten-year time limit was probably too short and recommended that it be extended to 1890. Armed with Carnarvon's proposals – they were in his eyes an ultimatum – Walkem returned to Victoria where 'Carnarvon or Separation' became the battle cry of the west-coast province. Either Mackenzie would live up to the Carnarvon terms or British Columbia would leave Confederation.

The Conservatives rather enjoyed Mackenzie's discomfiture. They prodded the government and encouraged their friends and supporters in British Columbia to do likewise. Tupper denounced Mackenzie's effort to build the line as a public work and demanded that it be turned over to a private company. Mackenzie would probably have agreed. But where was the company? These were the dark days of depression and no one had come forward to take the place of the Canada Pacific. Tempers grew shorter and words sharper as the weeks passed and Mackenzie sought some way out of the horrible mess in which he was caught. But there was no easy way out and Lord Dufferin wrote to the premier of British Columbia suggesting that if the Canadian government did not make a bona fide start on that portion of the railway to be built in British Columbia by 1878, then there should be a general conference in London with the representatives of Canada and British Columbia and the Colonial Secretary.

But the proposed conference was never held. In 1878 Mackenzie went to the people and they rejected him. They wanted Macdonald back again. They wanted the man who had said 'Until this great work is completed our Dominion is little more than a "Geographical Expression". We have as much interest in British Columbia as in Australia, and no more. The railway once finished, we become one great united country with a large interprovincial trade and a common interest.' And with the return of Macdonald came the return of brighter days.

For two years Macdonald carried on much as Mackenzie had done as far as the railway was concerned. He had made a bad choice once when he had given the railway charter to Sir Hugh Allan. He could not afford to make another such blunder. Which of the prospective syndicates should he choose? There was the Grand Trunk, the Canada Company, the Canada Central Railway, and firms in England and France, all of which were said to be interested. But Macdonald wanted a Canadian firm, and in the end the charter went to a body called the Canadian Pacific Railway Company headed by George Stephen, the president of the Bank of Montreal. Stephen was backed largely by Canadian capital, although there was a small amount of foreign capital from Great Britain, France, and the United States. On October 21, 1880, Charles Tupper, Macdonald's Minister of Railways and Canals, and George Stephen penned their signatures to the contract that was to build the first Canadian transcontinental railway.

Mackenzie's administration had occupied five years of the eighteen-seventies, from 1873 to 1878. They were dull years; years of frugality, of depression, and of restlessness in the provinces, in New Brunswick over the separate-school issue, in Manitoba over the natural resources issue, in British Columbia over the railway issue. With all his integrity Mackenzie was never a popular figure; perhaps because he lacked imagination; perhaps because he lacked the qualities of leadership. When Canada needed boldness he gave it caution; when it demanded large constructive measures he gave it small practical necessities. Canada did receive during his regime the Royal Military College of Canada, the North West Mounted Police, the western Indian treaties, the Supreme Court of Canada, and the secret ballot – all of them good and necessary measures, but none of the stature that would inspire the admiration of foreign observers or the pride of Canadians. Goldwin Smith's jibe, 'Mr. Mackenzie was a stonemason; he is a stonemason still,' was unkind; but it had an element of truth in it.

IV

The Canada that had been formed in 1867 was not the outcome of a grass-roots movement. It was not the product of a strong sense of nationalistic idealism. It was, instead, the practical answer of practical politicians to the problems of the eighteen-sixties. It was the achievement of the few, rather than of the many; the work of governments, rather than of peoples.

There were not really very many people in the new federation – not, at least, by European or American standards. The first federal census, published in 1871, gave the population of Canada as 3,492,878, to which could be added 102,358 Indians to bring it up to three and a half million people. Canadians were distributed among the several provinces in much the same proportion as they are today, with about eighty per cent concentrated in Ontario and Quebec. There were very few people of racial origins other than British or French, with the latter numbering about thirty per cent, much as they do at the present time.

During the next ten years the population of Canada increased by 831,932 to a total of 4,324,810. Part of this increase was due to the incorporation of Prince Edward Island in the federal union; but if we subtract the 108,891 people this

province added to the Canadian population, the increase
was 723,041, or about twenty per cent. This was a net increase only; for the number of births during the decade was
estimated at 799,000, and the number of immigrants at
342,000, making a total of 1,141,000. Obviously there was,
during the same period, a drain of about 400,000 people to
the United States. This exodus may be attributed largely to the
demand for labour in the mill towns of New England, and
partly to the opening for settlement of the American west,
where there were no trees and no large stumps to remove,
and where lands were readily accessible to the railways.

From time to time during the eighteen-seventies efforts
were made to persuade expatriates to return to Canada.
Other efforts were made to divert Canadian emigrants towards Manitoba. But neither of these attempts was really
successful in stemming the human flow to the United States.
Only a strong national patriotism could have achieved this;
and in the first decade after Confederation, national patriotism had not taken firm root in the minds of Canadians in the
various parts of Canada. Everywhere there was the same cry,
both in French and in English: the young people were not
content to remain on the farm but were seeking the more
exciting life of the cities and the better-paying jobs in the
American factories.

The typical Canadian of the period was a countryman,
living on a farm, in the bush, or in some fishing village along
the Atlantic coast. In the whole of Canada there were not
more than nine cities with populations over 10,000. Montreal, Quebec, and Toronto were the largest with 115,000,
59,699, and 59,000 respectively. Then followed Saint John
with 41,325, and Halifax and Hamilton in the twenty thousands. Ottawa had 24,141 people; London 18,000, and
Kingston 12,407. Others ranged from Charlottetown with
8,807 to Winnipeg with 241. As the population grew between 1871 and 1881, so too did the proportions of countrymen and city-dwellers change. Whereas in 1871 eighty per
cent of all Canadians were classified as rural, by 1881 this
figure had declined to seventy-four per cent. There was

already a strong trend towards urbanization, which has gone on unchecked to the present.

The very earliest farms in Canada had been self-sufficient subsistence units. During the nineteenth century, under the impact of the prosperity which Canadians enjoyed under the Reciprocity Treaty, there was a change from self-sufficiency to emphasis upon a single cash crop, wheat in particular. However, after Confederation wheat growing tended to give way to greater diversification in farm production. The invention in Sweden of the de Laval centrifugal cream separator, replacing the old method of skimming cream by hand, gave an impetus to dairying. Regional specialties began to appear – fruit in Niagara, cheese in the Ingersoll and Belleville districts of Ontario, and garden truck in the vicinity of the large cities. Changes of this nature necessitated greater knowledge on the part of the farmer, and agricultural schools were started. The first of these had been opened in 1859 at Ste. Anne de la Pocatière. Others were founded at L'Assomption in Quebec in 1867 and at Guelph in 1874.

Improved mechanical aids to farming also became a familiar sight on Canadian farms. The average farmer of the eighteen-seventies required a wheel cultivator with long shovel-shaped teeth to tear up the soil, a set of harrows, a horse-drawn seeder, a 'buckeye' mower, and a hay rake. The reaper was the common harvesting implement until the twine binder came into use in the eighteen-eighties. Threshing was done largely on a contract basis, if only because of the expense involved in buying a threshing machine. Some farmers still used horse-power for threshing but by the end of the seventies the steam thresher was the common machine on all farms in Canada.

Because Canada was still in 1870 a land of countrymen, barter was a familiar method of exchanging goods in the rural areas. In every village the general store was always the main feature, after the church. Usually located in the centre of a village or town, the general store often had a porch or verandah to which a man might descend from his horse or his buggy without getting directly to the ground. In the back was the warehouse, where the bulky barrels and heavy goods were stored. Along the side walls were the rows of shelves displaying their stock of hardware, dry goods, harness, and foodstuffs. At one end, near the door, would be the post office, for the proprietor often doubled as postmaster and storekeeper. In the main body of the store would be the stove around which men would gather to talk about the wild feuds of the Black Donnellys in Biddulph Township, Macdonald's role in the 'Pacific Scandal', Louis Riel's appearance in the House of Commons in Ottawa, or the great fire in Saint John. The general store was the centre for gossip, political argument, or a quiet game of checkers.

In spite of the hardships of the great depression of 1873, there were many improvements in living conditions during the years that followed. In the Maritimes and in the upper provinces, the expansion of the railways made personal travel and the transportation of goods easier and cheaper. The completion of the Intercolonial in 1876 ended the isolation in which both Canada and the Maritimes had previously existed during the long winter months when the St. Lawrence was closed by ice. The adoption of trawl-line fishing brought improved catches for the Lunenburg fishermen, and during the eighteen-seventies Halifax grew as the entrepôt for the large fish-export firms that drew their supplies from as far away as Gaspé. In Cape Breton the demand for coal for the railways and steamships acted as a stimulus to mining on the island, and Sydney became an important coaling-station for vessels en route to Montreal. There were active sugar refineries in both Nova Scotia and New Brunswick at this time; but generally speaking, manufacturing in the Maritimes was held back by too little capital and too severe competition from both the United States and the Upper Canadian provinces. Perhaps the outstanding general feature of the economic life of the Maritimes during the years of the seventies was the gradual shift of business from the schooners to the railways.

In the St. Lawrence valley there was the same emphasis upon railway and steamship transportation, both of which combined to make Montreal into a great metropolis. Other factors contributed to this development; such as the insistence from 1871 upon proper qualifications for ships' officers, and the expansion of the system of lighthouses and buoys by the federal marine department. The discovery of petroleum in Ontario during the late fifties had provided lighthouse-keepers with a mineral oil that was a vast improvement over the animal oil previously used for signal lights; and although the Ontario oil industry went into a decline during the eighteen-seventies, increased oil production in the United States provided a cheap and easily acquired substitute for the Canadian product.

The lumber industry remained an important economic activity during the seventies, particularly in Ontario, where great timber rafts still floated from the upper reaches of the Ottawa, and down the St. Lawrence from Kingston to Quebec, where they were loaded on ships bound for Europe. But there were also new industries that were attracting attention: for instance, the silver mine at Silver Islet in Lake Superior, which produced over three millions of dollars' worth of the precious metal between 1868 and 1884; and the asbestos mine opened at Quebec in 1878. The demand for iron and steel grew, especially with increased railway construction, and this demand led to a revival of iron-mining in Canada. In the field of farm machinery, Canadian companies like the Massey company, which had been originally established near Newcastle, and the Harris company, at Beamsville, both expanded their production in spite of American competition. The Massey works had won the highest award at the Paris Exposition in 1867 for their mower and reaper. They took out the first Canadian patent for a self-binder and in 1878 introduced a new harvester. In the same year they moved to Toronto to take over the Toronto Reaper and Mower Company. Meanwhile, the Harris company moved to Brantford in 1872, whence it found its way to Manitoba, even prior to the building of the transcontinental railway, to open a distributing agency in Winnipeg in 1879.

By the eighteen-seventies Canada was well beyond its
pioneer days, except, perhaps, in Manitoba and the North-
West Territories. The brick house had increasingly replaced
the frame house and in some places the stone house, particularly in Ontario. Picturesque eclecticism dominated the
architecture of all public buildings. Every city had its 'villas'
and its 'mansions' on well-treed lots behind ironwork fences.
Most of them were not much different in size and shape from
the farmhouses to be seen in the country, but they were more
pretentious and more elaborately trimmed with gingerbread.
Inside a visitor would recognize the fringed sofas, the em-
broidered stools, the fire-screens, the whatnots, and the easel
with the portrait or landscape on it. There would be the
marble fireplaces with the gold-framed mirrors over the
mantelpiece, the heavy draperies, and the mahogany furniture with the machine-carved ornaments. The lighting might
be by gas; more frequently it was by kerosene-oil lamps. On
the tables would be found stereographs by Louis Vallé, W. J.
Topley, or James Esson; or, if the houses were in the Maritimes, by J. S. Climo or James Notman, a younger brother of
the more famous William of Toronto and Montreal. Outside,
the streets were still seas of mud after heavy rainstorms; but
there were improvements there too. Scarcely any town worth
the name did not possess gas lighting by the seventies. In 1876
Alexander Graham Bell succeeded for the first time in transmitting speech over a telephone wire. On August 3, in Wallis
Ellis's general store in Mount Pleasant, Ontario, he received
a telephone call from his uncle a few miles away in Brantford. A new era was on the way. During the seventies the
well-off Canadian took the waters at the Grand Hotel, Cale-
donia Springs, married within his own circle, paid an occasional visit to 'the old country', invested his money in gilt-
edged bonds. But as often as not he would haggle over ten
cents with the local grocer, for he was usually not more than
one generation removed from the farm.

Life in the eighteen-seventies was not all a matter of pushing the plough or driving in a carriage or cab to the office.
There may not have been as much time for play as there is

today; but there was still plenty of play. Some people found their relaxation in the bottle, for many Canadians were hard drinkers, if we can believe the reports of contemporary visitors or judge from the number of temperance societies and the passing of the Canada Temperance Act in 1878. Dancing, too, was popular, whether it was carried on in the ball room, in the barn, or in the local community hall. Regattas and canoe races on the lakes and rivers were popular in the summer as well as political picnics and excursions of all kinds; and in the winter there was tobogganing, skating, carrioling, and curling. This last sport was introduced into Quebec during the last years of the eighteenth century by Scottish officers of the British garrisons. It is probably the game that has retained its popularity in Canada longer than any other. And this in spite of the fact that a large segment of the population, the French Canadians, always had difficulty in understanding what amusement there could be in hurling large pieces of granite over the ice to the cries of 'Soop! Soop!'

Curling enjoyed considerable popularity during the years we are discussing. At the last great open-air bonspiel at Burlington in 1875 there were no fewer than 360 curlers present; and, according to the *Annual Report* of the Ontario Curling Association, 'The Bay presented a most lively and festive appearance. Crowds of spectators, including many of the fair sex, on foot and in sleighs, covered the Bay during the contest.' In the following year, 1876, the first bonspiel was held in Winnipeg, with the prize, a barrel of oatmeal, being presented by the winning team to the Winnipeg General Hospital. During this period the Toronto Red Jackets, who played together between 1868 and 1878, dominated the Canadian curling world.

There were, of course, other sports. Cricket was played in many centres and was stimulated by tours of Canada by visiting British teams. One such tour took place in 1872. Lacrosse was popular, as was also soccer football, which seems to have become an almost universal game. Christenings, weddings, and funerals were then, as now, occasions for

social gatherings; charivaris were still the noisy and sometimes riotous affairs of earlier years; meetings of the 'national' societies, such as the St. Andrew's Society, the St.
George's Society, and the St. Patrick's Society, were well
attended; so too were the parades of the militia, the firemen,
the St. Jean Baptiste Society and the Orangemen. Both in
the towns and in the country there were horse races to be
seen and bets to be placed, although the more sophisticated
and well-to-do in Toronto went to see the steeplechase at the
Toronto Hunt Club, where they could display the latest
fashions in bustles and top hats. For the countrymen in particular, there were the provincial ploughing-matches. These
began in the early years of the nineteenth century and have
maintained public interest ever since, although it is probably a declining interest with the increase in urbanization.

Declining, too, is the excitement that once attended Canadian elections. In the nineteenth century they were always
occasions of jollity, often of fisticuffs, and sometimes of
fatalities. The prohibition of alcohol on election days and
the introduction of the ballot have done much to rob elections of the violence and glamour of our grandfathers' day.
It was the early seventies that witnessed the first use of the
secret ballot in Canada. It was introduced into Nova Scotia
in 1870, British Columbia in 1873, Ontario in 1874, Quebec in 1875, and New Brunswick in 1876. The Parliament
of Canada adopted the ballot for federal purposes in 1874,
although it was not put to use until the election which returned Sir John Macdonald to power in 1878.

Canadian society in the eighteen-seventies was not only
predominantly rural in character, it was also basically conservative. Unlike the United States, Canada was not the
product of a revolution, of a defiance of established authority;
it was, on the contrary, the achievement of the Establishment—of government, church, army, and traditional loyalties. Even in the west, where the frontier influence might be
expected to be strong, law and order were maintained by a
para-military body, the North West Mounted Police. There
were no vigilantes on the Canadian prairies. And in British

Columbia the presence of the Royal Engineers had checked any early lawlessness in the gold-mining camps.

Because they were conservative, because they had not willed the new federal union, the people who lived in the provinces that became Canada were not, in the eighteen-seventies, really Canadians at heart. They were Nova Scotians, New Brunswickers, Islanders, French Canadians, Westerners, British Columbians, and Ontarians. Confederation was still, as Macdonald put it, 'in the gristle'; it had not hardened into bone. It was still too early to expect a Maritimer to feel a deep bond of kinship with an Upper Canadian whom he knew only by distant report. How could a French Canadian feel a sense of identity with the Anglo-Saxon Protestant Ontarian, from whom he was separated by language, law, and culture? When French Canadians became nationalists—as they did to defeat Sir George Cartier in Montreal in the election of 1873—it was nationalist in the narrower French-Canadian sense, not in the broader supraracial sense. And the Ontarian, when he thought himself wildly nationalist – as he did when he listened to 'Canada First' voices like William Foster or the *Nation* – was really demonstrating only his Upper Canadian nationalism. 'Canada First' was too prone to identify Canada with Ontario and the British supremacy. In British Columbia there were comparatively few ties, economic or family, with the remote region called 'eastern' Canada.

The grey stone Victorian Gothic structure in Ottawa, which had been opened in 1867 and housed the Parliament of Canada, was the symbol of the new nation that some of the Fathers of Confederation had talked about in 1864. But in the critical years of the seventies, it was still only a symbol of the future. Canada was as yet only a federation of provinces. Nevertheless, as the eighteen-seventies ended, times were improving. Macdonald the nation-builder was back in Ottawa, and many Canadian people looked hopefully ahead, trusting that the next decade might achieve for them the strong transcontinental union the politicians had talked of building when Confederation had first set forth its outlines.

3. The 1880s

W. S. MACNUTT

No decade in Canadian history has opened more hopefully. Providence seemed to be smiling upon the great national enterprise that Canada had become, and the idea of nationality, daring by reason of its novelty a dozen years before, was being trumpeted throughout the land. Blandly and self-confidently Macdonald and his Conservative ministers enjoyed the tide of good fortune that was allegedly the consequence of their policies. The C.P.R. was building, and Canada was becoming all of one piece. Only the dourest Grit in opposition or the gloomiest of pessimists could deny that the experiment of 1867 seemed to be successful. Pessimism, such as that of Goldwin Smith, was possible only on the philosophical plane. The national prosperity and the rapidly increasing rate of immigration that prevailed at the opening of 1881 were ample proof of the righteousness of nationality and of the measures of economic nationalism that Macdonald had introduced. The tone of life was buoyant.

Canadianism had become a living force, though it was encompassed in a more universal loyalty. Disraeli's period of power in Britain had ended in 1880, but the imperialist sentiments he had fostered were affecting the habits of thought of the British at home and overseas. Being British was tantamount to being successful, and the world had been forced to admit the paramount position of the island race and its numerous offshoots on all the continents. To the Canadians being British especially meant the ability to look the Americans in the face on something better than equal terms. America was still adolescent but the British Empire was established and supreme. All its citizens could acquire an increased sense of self-importance by reason of its triumphs in peace and war.

The new sense of imperial unity that became so noticeable in the eighties was the more novel because of the old and well-founded Canadian conviction that Britain had little enthusiasm and regard for her overseas possessions. But the disruption of the historic balance of power in Europe caused by Bismarck's triumphs, culminating in the defeat of France in 1870 and the establishment of the German Empire, had made the British people more aware of their world heritage. Canadians were being flattered by a new and respectful regard for their country expressed in British newspapers. The strengthening of the historic ties with the Mother Country, that often had visibly been weakened, was more than superficially reflected by the presence at Rideau Hall in Ottawa of Lord Lorne, the son-in-law of the Queen. Sensing the imponderable and highly symbolic possibilities in the appointment of a new governor general, Disraeli in 1878 had won the consent of Queen Victoria to the dispatch of her fourth daughter, the Princess Louise, to Ottawa. 'Her Canadian Majesty', the consort of Lorne, who was the chief scion of the great Campbell clan and the heir to the duke-

dom of Argyll, might presume to represent an aspiration to
imperial unity as dazzling as the Crown of India, so recently
presented to Her Royal Mother.

Initially the appointment of Lorne appeared to achieve
the results hoped for. The public felt complimented and the
Scots of Canada, never an element to allow pride of place to
others, were exuberant. To the empire-minded men of the
time Canada appeared a field for statecraft, and the office of
governor general, though nominally a sinecure, was a post
from which real influence could be exercised. To Disraeli
Canada had been 'one of our great vice-royalties', and the
panoply of imperial power throughout the world presented
no sharp contradiction to Canadians whose great ambition
was a nation extending from sea to sea. The mother-image
of the Queen, the embodiment of all the virtues cherished
by Victorian moralists, was a real factor in sustaining this
view of Canada's place in the world that was challenged only
by the querulous and the academic. On the Ottawa scene the
vice-regal court, which became more notable by reason of
the presence of royalty, seemed to represent a North American version of British world power.

Yet, though Canadians were impressed by visitations of
royalty and vice-royalty, the consequences were impermanent. The outpourings of imperial sentiment on occasions
of state, the genuine affection for the person of the Queen,
the triumphal arches bearing the inscription of 'Lorne and
Louise' that appeared on the streets of every community of
consequence during the season of summer travel, could
make but a transient impression on the North American
quality of the people that was emerging. A Canadian vice-
royalty, it was pointed out very firmly, could never be the
equivalent of that at Delhi. Public functionaries solemnly
performed their duties on occasions of state in the best British tradition. The most bucolic of politicians rivalled one
another in professions of loyalty to the Crown and to British
institutions. Yet, so far as civil affairs were concerned, this
was almost the only heritage of the Old World that really

counted. Though accepting 'the court' and the whole superstructure of vice-regal state, Canadians were almost unanimous in declaring that theirs was a country in which social
distinction did not count. Only in Quebec City was the
acceptance of an aristocracy openly defended in the press.
Everywhere else opinion was tempered by a considerable
degree of levelling egalitarianism. A little of this drew inspiration from radical opinion in Britain, much more from
the hostile and sneering tone of a portion of the American
press that liked to remind its readers of the dangers of
monarchic institutions in the Western Hemisphere. Canadian journalists, ambitious for notoriety and eager to shock
their readers, liked to reproduce racy items of gossip from
British and American sources that had the effect of mildly
discrediting monarchy. The bolder condemned 'court tom-
foolery'. The Toronto *Telegram*, then allegedly a paper of
annexationist sympathies, could declare that Canadians had
become a nation of toadies.

British institutions were in favour but the British pattern
of society was alien to the Canadian soil. Politicians could
accept knighthood, but unknightly deportment was more in
favour with the public. Prejudices against pretensions to
social superiority were easy to evoke so that the idea of an
aristocracy beyond the portals of Rideau Hall was really
unacceptable. The Governor General had to learn to be un-
shaken when expatriate Scots failed to remove their caps in
his presence. Independence of demeanour was a popular
Canadian affectation. Independence could be asserted not
only against the class system of Britain but against un-
warranted intrusions from south of the border. Americans
who too roundly applauded the Canadians for similarity to
themselves were frequently reminded that there was a great
deal about the United States, too, that Canadians did not
like. American ignorance of Canada could be just as irritating as that of the British, and was less excusable. In March
1881, when the Chicago *Tribune* reported that 'Lady Tilley,
one of the Court ladies at Rideau Hall, gave a grand ball
last week, and no wine was served, an unusual innovation at

the table of an English nobleman,' the nation laughed in contempt as well as in amusement.

The ideas of the Canada Firsters constituted a kind of vanguard of opinion that all were obliged to follow to one degree or another. Macdonald could not gainsay the feeling that prevailed throughout the country on the necessity of keeping Canada's particular interests before the attention of the imperial authorities. At London Sir Alexander T. Galt, just appointed as Canadian High Commissioner, harassed the Foreign Office by aggressive demands for a virtually independent role in commercial negotiations with foreign states. Political independence was a goal kept before the public by those who clamoured for complete freedom from Britain. Enraged opponents retorted that independence was wanted only as a prelude to annexation. The more moderate would not deny that political independence was a reasonable objective, insisting that it did not imply separation from the Mother Country. The only objection to independence, said the *Illustrated News* of Montreal on March 7, 1881, was that the people were satisfied with things as they were, a statement that, in the light of events for years to come, might be considered a fair one.

Great satisfaction was derived from the Proclamation of the Imperial Privy Council of 1880 which annexed Britain's Arctic territories to the Dominion and added the Eskimos to the Canadian population. There were ill-humoured reflections in the newspapers on how the United States in 1867 had, in spite of geography and the doctrine of natural frontiers, filched Alaska. American schemes for establishing a protectorate over Panama, voiced by Secretary of State Blaine, aroused protests from the people of the Maritime Provinces who, with a ton of shipping afloat for every individual in the population, boasted of the third, or perhaps fourth, greatest merchant navy in the world. This high level of self-estimation that was in the wind acquired a note of shrillness with the remark of Nicholas Flood Davin, a newly arrived Irish journalist, who wrote for the *Canadian Monthly* that 'three or four of our statesmen' could have become

Prime Minister of Britain. Almost every newspaper in the country carried the quotation, but comment was guarded.

Much of this confidence represented only the beginning of adolescence, but the years of the early eighties were producing evidence of the commencement of a real national life. On the material side the Conservative policy of knitting the country together by tariffs and railways seemed to be working wondrously. A frequent remark of foreign visitors at the time was that Canadians seemed totally absorbed in the business of becoming rich. Especially on the English-speaking side there had been general lamentation on the absence of cultural advancement. But the work of the Royal Canadian Academy of Art, established in 1880, was being supplemented by that of many local art societies. The Royal Society of Canada came into existence in 1881. In spite of the parochial jealousies of artists, savants, and journalists, both of these organizations were spurred into activity by the Governor General. The Royal Society was compelled to face a curtain of hostility and indifference drawn by the press of the country that professed fears for the egalitarian character of Canadian society. It would be, said the Toronto *Globe*, 'a mutual admiration society of nincompoops'. Yet both performed in a fair way the task of making Canadians more conscious of one another. The literary *élan* of French Canada had been sparked by the award of the Prix Montajou to its leading poet, Louis Fréchette, by the French Academy in 1880. In this realm French Canada's leaders had no doubt about their own superiority. How could a people such as the English Canadians, with their roots barely fixed in the soil, acquire a respectable degree of literary and philosophical achievement? The French Canadians successfully demanded ten of the forty seats in the Royal Society. Their poets, moralists, and philosophers continued to be preoccupied with the pathos of their past. Young English Canadians of literary enthusiasms were fired by the fame that accrued to the young New Brunswicker, Charles G. D. Roberts, who published *Orion* in the same year. The first distinctive school of English-Canadian poetry was in the making.

From a print in the Public Archives of Canada.

II

The prosperity of the early eighties softened the discontent
that had, in some parts of the country, accompanied the
early years of Confederation. In the Maritime Provinces the
union was now being accepted with some grace. The oceanic
economy of the great days of wood, wind, and water was
enjoying its last decade of real importance. But the little
secondary industries that depended almost exclusively on
local markets were succumbing to the competition of the
new manufacturing giants of Montreal and Toronto. The
Intercolonial Railway, completed in 1876, served as a unifying force primarily for the manufacturing industries of central Canada. The traffic was largely one-way, for Maritime
goods of appreciable value and quality were not wanted
in Montreal. The merchants of Saint John and Halifax,
schooled in the lore of an international traffic, were discovering that, owing to the high levels to which Macdonald had
raised the tariff in 1879, goods from abroad could not be
imported at salable prices. More and more their activities
were becoming tributary to those of Montreal. Along the
route of the Intercolonial the National Policy had conjured
up some small manufacturing industries. Many Nova Scotians, rejoicing in the notion that the coal of Pictou and
Cape Breton would make their province the Black Country
of the Dominion, were certain that great prosperity would
come. But the buoyancy of the country at large was not generally reflected in the demeanour of the people of the three
provinces. At Confederation Maritimers had been told that
they would exercise an influence of approximately one-third
in the life of the new nation, that they could derive a prepon-
derant advantage from an endemic hostility between Quebec and Ontario. Notions of this kind had been thoroughly
dissipated and the general humour was one of regretful
resignation. On Dominion Day flags still flew at half-mast in
the Annapolis Valley and the idea of secession, though dor-
mant, was not far removed from practical politics. The
Chronicle of Halifax sustained memories of the great coer-

cion of 1867. On the fourteenth anniversary of union with
Canada it declared that not one honest heart in the province
would rejoice upon the event.

Within the structure of Confederation Quebec rested
easily. The safeguards guaranteed to her in the B.N.A. Act
seemed to serve their purpose. French Canadians were so
busy with their own political quarrels that they seldom
bothered to complain of domination by 'les Anglais'. At
Ottawa nothing of great consequence could be done contrary to the wishes of the Quebec bloc of ministers, and one
of Macdonald's great concerns, in the course of the infight-
ing during the parliamentary session, was to keep his large
number of Quebec supporters in line. A common complaint
among English-speaking Canadians was that Quebec's dominating place in Confederation was well-nigh intolerable.
This was modified by the expectation that it could not last
for long, and that as the English-speaking provinces were
filled by new immigrants Quebec would lose what was virtually a right of veto in the conduct of Canadian affairs.

The factories of Montreal were annually increasing their
production. Port activities enjoyed similar expansion as the
export trade gained the benefits of the aggressive work of
Canada's Grand Trunk Railway, which by this time was
moving into Chicago and tapping much of the traffic of the
northern mid-west of the United States. New textile mills
were opening in Sherbrooke and other centres of the Eastern
Townships. In the great river valleys of the province, where
the primeval forests had long been hewn down for square
timber, the pulp-and-paper industry was commencing to
thrive on the new growth. Making every effort to keep its
people at home, rather than allow them to emigrate to the
United States, the French Catholic church was organizing
colonies wherever fertile land could be had, sometimes making bad choices of areas that were barely marginal. Owing
to its systematic formation of new communities of French
Canadians, the Eastern Townships were rapidly losing their
character as an English-speaking land. The fastening of the
parish-school system of education on this Protestant country-

side resulted in the withdrawal of the original Anglo-American stock in large numbers.

Amid Gallic fury Quebec continued to endure its Holy War. There were many nuances of opinion, but fundamentally the question was whether or not those who called themselves liberal in the European sense of the expression, who were willing to separate the religious and the profane, who would allow the State a large share in the direction of human affairs, could be regarded as trustworthy Catholics. The conservative, ultra-Catholic, ultramontane *castors* held hard to the Syllabus of Errors of Pius IX, turning their backs on the science and progress of the nineteenth century. The integral Catholic state was their grand aspiration. Liberal Catholics and Catholic Liberals (there was a difference) believed that Church and State could march side by side, but that each could be largely free of the other. 'Muzzling the clergy' was the avowed aim of Liberal *Rouge* extremists. Montreal opposed Quebec, and Laval University endeavoured to prevent the establishment of infant colleges that were to be the seedlings of a new university in the larger city. Even the hierarchy of the Church was divided as the aged Bishop Bourget of Montreal, the grand protagonist of the *castors*, with his fervent disciple, Bishop Laflèche of Three Rivers, endeavoured to restore French Canada to 'its true principles'. The question could not, of course, be confined to theological circles. Young Wilfrid Laurier, who prided himself on being a Liberal after the English fashion, found the going difficult in his great effort to free his party from the innuendo of being Freemason and un-Catholic. The clergy persisted in regarding the *bleu* of Conservatism as their favourite colour. 'Le ciel est bleu, l'enfer est rouge' was still enunciated from Quebec pulpits at election time, and the Liberals, beneath the weight of this great prejudice, continued to labour at a disadvantage.

Ontario was asserting its role as the strong backbone of Confederation. In the making of national policy and in the winning of national elections her influence was becoming more and more pronounced. Proud of her prosperity and

favoured by the new tariff, Ontario was developing a sense
of community, a consciousness of being the great heartland
of Canada to which all other elements must be ancillary.
Oliver Mowat, the Liberal premier, was the foremost champion of what were beginning to be called provincial rights
and he thought of his province as 'our country', a glaring
contradiction to the concept of Confederation that was in
the ascendancy under the Macdonald Conservatives at Ottawa. Ontario was the province in which peaches were given
to the pigs. Local pride became more notable as the industry of the cities became more productive. Toronto was becoming famous for its indulgence in congratulating itself
upon its brand-new industries, its eighty churches, and its
educational institutions. Its rivals ringing it about accused it
of greedy monopoly. At Hamilton, already known as the
'Ambitious City', it was frequently boasted that the opulent
county of Wentworth could always challenge Toronto either
in industry or in the arts.

Assimilation of the elements making up the population
was proceeding more rapidly in Ontario than in the other
provinces. At Berlin German-speaking crowds still sang 'The
Watch on the Rhine', but boasts of loyalty to the British
Crown were as frequent here as elsewhere. Newly arrived
English and Scottish immigrants, taking to the manufacturing towns between Toronto and Sarnia, quietly became
absorbed in the mixture of Loyalist gentility and brash
Yankeeism that had made up the old frontier. In Toronto
there was a large Irish community with an archbishop who
was sometimes called a Fenian and who was endowed, it was
said, with a marvellous capacity to organize the Irish vote at
election time. Occasionally he challenged the dicta of the
Minister of Education on the content of the school curriculum. The summer of 1882 saw a great controversy on the
issue of whether or not Scott's *Marmion* was a subject of
study fit for the children of the province.

The exuberance that prevailed on the purely provincial
scene in Ontario was given increased emphasis by the success
of the contest over Dominion and provincial powers that

Mowat waged with Macdonald. The great Conservative chieftain, largely by the judicious exercise of Ottawa's powers of patronage, had been able to keep the smaller provinces in accord with the policies of the federal government. But Ontario proved her bigness by an ability to fight Ottawa. Mowat and his Grits never flagged in their legal battle against Macdonald's wide interpretation of Ottawa's powers as defined by the British North America Act. A sustained action at law, with a comic-opera setting, over the powers of licensing taverns and tavern-keepers, was finally won by Mowat in 1884. In the same year there came Mowat's victory on the Rivers and Streams Act that gave to the provinces the right to control navigation on provincial rivers. The law-lords at Westminster, cogitating upon problems of Canadian jurisdictions, were leaning more and more heavily on the Property and Civil Rights clause of Section 93, and the Dominion government was emerging in a thoroughly weakened condition. Sensing the tide of provincial self-righteousness that developed in the wake of these decisions, Macdonald, thinking above all things of keeping his majority in Parliament, would no longer employ the power of disallowance which, ever since Confederation, he had used to chasten provincial governments. Mowat was the first of a long line of Canadian provincial premiers to acquire great repute by boldly and successfully challenging the government at Ottawa.

It was an old conviction of the Grits of Ontario that their province should extend to the Rockies. By the establishment of Manitoba Macdonald's government had commenced a process of division of the west by which, it was supposed, a large number of small provinces, puny in their powers, would eventually emerge. But the bigness of Ontario could not be denied. Between the two there was a great area in dispute: part of the land of Keewatin – the land of the bleak north wind, as it was known to the Indians. Rat Portage, later renamed Kenora, was the only place of consequence in the territory which contained considerable reserves of valuable timberland. In the time of Alexander Mackenzie an Ottawa tribunal had awarded it to Ontario, the argument

hinging on the limits of Canada as ceded to Britain in 1763,
but Macdonald, upon his coming to power in 1878, had
refused to honour the decision. During the following years
Ontario and Manitoba clashed in more than legal array. In
the summer of 1883 Mowat sent magistrates and constables
to contest Manitoba's jurisdiction at Rat Portage. Police-
men of each province found themselves in the other's gaol.
Ontario's constables were kidnapped and packed off on the
long journey to Winnipeg, and the Manitoba gaol was set
on fire. One incident of violence was reported as the work of
both 'Mowat's carpet-baggers' and 'a Tory band of thirty-
four ruffians'. Very unconstitutionally the Manitoba government ordered the Winnipeg Field Battery to the scene.
But again Mowat won, this time his greatest triumph. When
he returned to Toronto from London in September 1884,
with the favourable opinion of the Privy Council in his
portmanteau, he was received as a conquering hero who had
humbled Ottawa in the dust.

The great era for the opening of the west seemed finally
to have arrived with the eighties. The year 1881 saw the
greatest immigration in Canadian history, and the traffic
through the United States, from St. Paul down the Red
River Valley, tripled in volume. Thousands of Ontario
farmers, it was said, were preparing to join the colonization
trains for Manitoba. There was no doubt concerning the
future of Winnipeg. It stood at the front door of a vast new
empire that would reveal new riches with the years. Its situation as a distribution centre for the entire North-west could
not be excelled. Already there was talk of the short haul by
rail from it to the open water of Hudson Bay. With its
population of ten thousand, Winnipeg was ugly and unfinished, its main streets long, crooked, and flat as a billiard
table. But land of questionable title on imaginary streets was
selling at seven hundred and fifty dollars the running foot.
High wages made the industrious independent, and the high
cost of living eliminated the laggards who hoped to escape
work. But all was not raw and materialistic. The city
abounded with churches and schools, and to the north there

would arise a university to which all religious denominations had pledged their support. From the time of the establishment of the province law enforcement had been secure. No gangs of vultures and land-sharks, whose activities made the American west so spectacular, were found here.

A railway ran from Winnipeg to Portage la Prairie. Westward the traveller was dependent on the jolting Red River carts and buckboards that smashed so readily on the prairie sandholes. The Saskatchewan was served by two remarkable steamers, the *Northcote* and the *Lily*, stern-wheelers about 130 feet long and drawing twenty-two inches of water. Occasionally they employed the huge spars and tackle that were carried on their decks for 'walking' and 'pushing' from shoals and sand-bars, looking like great grasshoppers or spiders floating on the river. The lovely valley of Qu'Appelle, which in the summer season bloomed with roses, was forlorn and neglected: only the occasional pocket of white men had taken possession for Canada of the country to the west of Manitoba. Battleford had recently been made the capital of the Northwest Territories, yet nobody was proud of the designation, for the Dominion government had not yet opened a land office. The white squatters were in the humour to encourage the more vocal malcontents among the Métis, who ever since 1870 had been migrating to the Saskatchewan, and at Ottawa Macdonald, fearful of the greed of land speculators, was in no hurry to legitimize the huge claims of those who hoped for easy riches.

The prairie between Battleford and Fort Calgary was still red man's country. Domestication, the consequence of the policies of the Dominion government, had made considerable progress among the Cree, though not to their great improvement. But the Blackfoot were still untamed, still capable of mobilizing two thousand braves, well-equipped and presenting a formidable, warlike array as they did for Lord Lorne at his crossing of the Bow River in September 1881. Calgary itself was an outpost of the cattle industry from over the border. Cattle-breeders were emphatic in their point of view that the land was worthless for agriculture.

Macleod could produce Canada's best version of a wild west. The famous Camoose House, kept by an ex-trader, ex-preacher, and squawman, was the resort of all the whisky vendors, bull-whackers, and mule-skinners of the region who called themselves ranchers.

Guarded by the few hundred constables of the North West Mounted Police, the west was fairly in Canada's grip, despite the possibility of new Fenian raids and of the overflowing of American immigrants who might establish American claims by actual possession. Until Sitting Bull led his tattered lodges back over the border in July 1881, there was always a danger that American forces would cross the line in order to apprehend him. But the Police had managed the expatriate Sioux as well as they had kept their own Canadian Indians in order and had persuaded them peacefully to return to American territory.

Convinced that the west needed only publicity to fill its unpeopled plains, Lord Lorne proceeded on a tour in 1881 as far as the foothills of the Rockies, taking with him a large number of British and Canadian newspapermen. His efforts were singularly successful. Even *The Times* of London, always convinced that there was little above the commonplace in Canadian life, came around. A country, it said, that had been declared to be hopelessly sterile by the only authorities supposed to know had been shown to be exactly the opposite of what had previously been believed. The best lands in Canada had been left for the last immigrants.

III

The grip on the west could be made permanent and sure only by the modern method of economic exploitation – the construction of a railway. Through the years of the early eighties Macdonald anxiously contemplated the fitful construction of the American Northern Pacific on its slow progress from St. Paul to Seattle. Railway-builders had by this time learned that a railway could grow and make money for its shareholders only by establishing a monopoly of control

THE GREAT COMBINATION.
Let Monopoly tremble in its boots!

From a print in the Public Archives of Canada.

over the traffic of a territory. New and unexploited areas of virgin soil such as the Canadian west, obviously the resort of tens of thousands of immigrants in the approaching years, challenged the ambitions of monopolizers, and the men of the Northern Pacific had their eyes on the territory to the north of the forty-ninth parallel. If they could drain off its traffic the west would come within the American commercial orbit and Canadian sovereignty would become increasingly dubious.

Commercially, British Columbia had always been a part of the American hinterland. San Francisco was its metropolis and a whole generation of merchants and traders of Victoria were oriented to it. Canada had failed to hold to the union bargain of 1871. The government of Alexander Mackenzie had honoured it only by piecemeal and unsubstantial tokens, having no conviction that a railway line to the Pacific through British territory could be justified either by engineering or by commercial realities. At Victoria the government of George Anthony Walkem, calling for 'the terms, the whole terms, and nothing but the terms' of union, was resorting to expediencies that Macdonald called blackmail. The Vancouver Island party in provincial politics wanted more than anything else a railway from Nanaimo to Esquimalt which they declared Canada should build as a penalty for its failure. Secession was a powerful cry and behind secession there was a disposition, not overt but nevertheless real, to seek annexation to the United States. In the spring of 1881 a provincial delegation, headed by the blustering Amor de Cosmos, left Victoria for London to seek repeal of the union. Until a railway could be constructed to the Pacific, British Columbia would gravitate to the United States. The 'very British' upper crust of society would find it difficult to keep things in hand until the steel link with Canada should pierce the Rockies.

But Macdonald had swung into action. The Canadian Pacific Syndicate, organized in 1880, headed by George Stephen, was moving swiftly. In Parliament the Grits were vehement, certain that the C.P.R. contract represented the surrender of the natural resources of the west to a corporation whose influence would be much greater than that of the Hudson's Bay Company had ever been. Yet Edward Blake, so verbose and self-righteous, had declined an open debate on the great contract with the Minister of Railways and Canals, Sir Charles Tupper, and there was little doubt that the temper of the country favoured Macdonald's sanguine point of view. Stephen made a number of epoch-making decisions completely at variance with the gloomy economic and engineering calculations in which the Grits had been so prone to indulge. He would run his line along the swamp and muskeg of the Lake Superior shore, always considered the most hazardous and expensive route. Instead of building north through the Rockies by the Yellowhead Pass he would go farther south in order to intercept the anticipated invasion of Canadian territory by the Northern Pacific. In August of 1882 this gamble was justified by the exciting telegram from Major Rogers which announced a convenient pass through the Selkirks where no tunnel would be required. These short cuts would reduce both the costs and the time taken to fulfil the contract.

When William Van Horne joined the Canadian Pacific Company in the spring of 1882 the work of exploration, survey, and construction moved at what seemed like lightning speed. New techniques for track-laying quickened the completion of the easy prairie section from Portage to the Rockies. From Port Arthur hundreds of men worked to the eastward, and the frightening complications of the lake shore, so feared by the experts, did not materialize. Over the rough obstacle of the Canadian Shield, through the difficult country by which La Vérendrye and the first French voyageurs had made their way to the prairies, the railway moved, by-passing the myriad lakes and swamps, spanning the many portages. Communities of workshops and shanties dotted the route, and almost everywhere the bagpipes skirled to give inspiration. Up the valley of the Fraser, from Emery's Bar to Savona Ferry, Andrew Onderdonk and his imported army of Chinese labourers blasted their way. Stephen had announced 1886 to be the year of completion of the entire line and when the last spike was driven in a remote pass of the Rockies, named Craigellachie in respect to the Scottish antecedents of Stephen and his cousin, Donald Smith, the mood was one of self-congratulation but not of surprise. In the view of those who thought of Canada as a real entity – there were few scoffers now – the work of Confederation had been consummated.

Yet the triumph was achieved painfully. The construction

proceeded so rapidly that the facilities for financing it were
outpaced. The tens of thousands of immigrants expected did
not move into the west to provide the C.P.R. with revenue
by purchase of the twenty-five millions of acres of land the
company had been awarded by its contract. Stephen, self-
confessedly, was like a man walking along the edge of a pre-
cipice. In March 1884, the government came to the aid of
the company to save it from its creditors. But Macdonald
had to combat in Parliament not only the Grits to whom the
whole story of the C.P.R. was one of reckless misappropria-
tion of the national heritage. His own majority was dubious
as the credit of the Canadian government became plighted
to that of the C.P.R., as the whole destiny of Canada became
more and more synonymous with the company's success or
failure. Quebec Conservatives blackmailed the government
for local concessions in return for their support for the
required financial measures in Parliament.

Much of the trouble was caused by the malignant rivalry
of the Grand Trunk. It had first been indifferent to the idea
of opening up the west by a railway, but when Stephen
secured lines through eastern Ontario to Montreal, when
he moved on to Quebec City by acquiring the line along the
north bank of the St. Lawrence, when he entered Toronto
and tapped the Grand Trunk monopoly in parts of southern
Ontario, the Grand Trunk opened its talons. Because the
government was committed to the success of the C.P.R.,
Ottawa was Stephen's citadel. London was the battleground
on which Sir Henry Tyler and the board of Grand Trunk
directors could fight the C.P.R. with assuredly greater prospects of success. It was intolerable to the Grand Trunk that
this new upstart, the spoilt darling of the Canadian government, should compete with it for funds for Canadian development, and its hostile propaganda helped to destroy
Stephen's prospects for getting money on the London
market. The great news media of the world – Reuters, the
Associated Press, *The Times* of London – all played the game
of the scribblers who seemed determined to destroy the
credit of the C.P.R. and with it the credit of Canada.

Early in 1885 the government again had to come to the aid of the company. The pay car was ready to leave for the west but there was no money. This crisis was averted by the news that rebellion on the Saskatchewan had been ended by the rapid transportation of Canadian soldiers to the scene of conflict over the railway which Parliament and the nation had seemed on the point of repudiating.

IV

The results of the election of 1882 reflected the prosperous and contented state of Canada. But the C.P.R. crisis of 1884 reflected a turning for the worse. In the summer of 1883 the land market in Manitoba had suddenly broken, and panic replaced the buoyant optimism that had reigned at Winnipeg for five years. Embattled farmers of Manitoba, where the population had risen to over seventy-five thousand, organized themselves for protest, blaming Ottawa for all their troubles–the high tariff on American agricultural implements, the high freight rates they paid to the C.P.R., which enjoyed a monopoly over the grain traffic, the alleged exactions by the Ogilvie monopoly of grain elevators, the laborious intricacies of Ottawa's policy for the sale of land. The real remedy for the trouble lay not in anything Canada could do. The rich, black soil required no cultivators so long as the price of wheat on the great exchanges of the world remained miserably depressed. The great days of the west had not yet come. Almost simultaneously an industrial slowdown struck the east. Bear markets ruled at New York and London. By the summer of 1884 bad times had come to the Treasury, and Tilley, the Finance Minister, reported to Macdonald that revenues were diminishing.

The months of late 1883 and early 1884 marked a minor turning-point in Canadian history. For five years prevailing tendencies had moved in the direction of greater unification and towards consolidating the work of Confederation. Now the winds had shifted. New forces were arising that could lead to disintegration. Ruling Canada became a business of holding hard to what had been accomplished rather than creating new industries and forming new provinces. Population failed to grow at a satisfactory rate. Immigration dwindled and, in London, Galt failed to interest the British government in the proposal to move the surplus and unwanted population of Ireland to Canada for the purpose of forming new Manitobas in the west. Again natural increase seemed to be totally absorbed in the movement to the United States.

As success faded, politics lost the veneer of good humour and joviality that had been so notable in Macdonald's halcyon days. The aging Prime Minister, fondly contemplating retirement amid more plenteous times, could not find a willing successor who could carry the party's confidence. He was rapidly becoming a lone survivor of the old guard who had made Confederation. Sir Charles Tupper, preferring to be on the fringes of politics and succumbing to the importunities of his wife, who enjoyed the refinements of titled English society, took the office of High Commissioner in London in 1883. His violent, sometimes coarse, counter-attacks upon the Opposition during the great moments of debate in the House of Commons were sorely missed by the Conservatives. Tilley, in poor health, was becoming a spent force. Sir Alexander Campbell, Macdonald's old law partner, wanted to retire. Nobody of Cartier's stature had appeared to manage the large bloc of Quebec Conservatives in the House. Macdonald had accomplished all he could for Confederation. He now had no choice but to hold on to office, in poor times, until a strong and acceptable candidate for the leadership should appear. D'Alton McCarthy, the highly qualified young barrister of Orillia, had to remain in his large practice to pay his debts. John S. D. Thompson of Halifax was induced to enter the Cabinet as Minister of Justice in 1885. He had all but one of the necessary qualifications for leadership. It was not so bad that he was a Roman Catholic. But a Protestant turned Roman Catholic, however able and moderate, could not instantly overpower the prejudices of the great Orange contingent of the party. For the leadership and the Prime Ministership he would have to wait.

Macdonald was on the look-out for talent of all kinds and did not care where he found it. There is an account of how, one summer day in the 1880s, he drove into Kingston and tied his horse to a hitching-post half a block away from Municipal Hall, the stage for the old parliament of the Province of Canada, from which he could hear a clear, mellifluous voice, pitched in good, strong cadences. He enquired about the speaker and was told that it was George Foster from New Brunswick lecturing on temperance. 'Get him into politics,' said the Prime Minister. A few months later the young university teacher was in politics and but a few months more had passed before he was Macdonald's Minister of Marine and Fisheries.*

The first great testing time for Confederation was at hand, and Macdonald was fortunate in the quality of the opposition that faced him. The Liberal party had no real discipline and no grand conviction. Ousted from the leadership in 1880, Alexander Mackenzie, not really aged, though broken, held to his rigid principles and could not compromise as the march of events impelled elasticity of belief and action. Through the entire decade he faithfully cherished the great principle that Toryism was the personification of evil, but became increasingly helpless as the muscles in his throat refused to voice his contempt for his infuriatingly successful rivals. Edward Blake, the leader, was eloquent, high-minded, and negative. He professed to believe during the Canadian Pacific debate that the west was merely 'a sea of mountains'. By his determination to be in the forefront of opinion on the development of Canadian nationhood, particularly on Canada's right to make trade treaties of her own, he failed to help the cause of his party and sometimes created in the public mind the impression that he was disloyal to the Empire. The Liberals offered wisdom without hope and failed

* Told to the writer by the Rev. Dr. G. M. Young of Fredericton. Dr. Young was a brother-in-law of Sir George Foster and died in 1963 at the age of 96.

to find the flair that was necessary to win the electorate's confidence. Sir Richard Cartwright's fatalism of economic thought was a dead weight to the party in its disjointed and uninspired struggles. There may have been many reasons for the Conservatives to lose elections, but the Liberals presented no alternative that seemed attractive.

The dictum that Canada is a difficult country to govern was already proverbial in the eighteen-eighties. Regional cross-currents often threatened to upset the constitutional and party structure that held Confederation together. The farmers of Manitoba showed no gratitude to the government and to the C.P.R. that had linked their country with the outside world. They wanted other links as well, principally to the south. Their resentment was concentrated against the monopoly clause in the C.P.R. contract that guaranteed the company freedom from competition for a period of ten years. Macdonald was compelled to accede to their demands in 1888. Then, in return for their support of financial measures of assistance to the C.P.R., Maritime members of Parliament successfully demanded their 'short line' from Montreal to Saint John through Maine, while Quebec, largely by reckless and improvident subventions to railways, had gotten into such financial difficulties that the Dominion government was constantly called to her relief. Her politicians, according to an unfavourable comment of the time, could be bought and sold like steers by the railway contractors who lurked about the committee rooms of government. And as for the most powerful region of all, it was already customary in Toronto blandly to identify Ontario's interests with those of 'the nation'.

Intrusions from the outside sometimes made the management of Parliament more difficult. Racial as well as religious causes contributed to the diversity of the scene. The Irish Home Rule movement of the early eighties converted the Canadian Irish into a homogeneous element in politics. Right across the country they were acutely aware of the tensions in their native land, and they organized themselves to demand of the Canadian government some kind of action that might persuade Britain to moderate her Irish policy. In countless constituencies their votes could be mobilized to win or lose seats for the government.

To keep power Macdonald was compelled to yield to their demands, consenting to the passage in Parliament of resolutions favouring Home Rule for Ireland. Canadians, it was argued, had suffered from Fenian outrages and, out of their federal experience, had the right to advise the British government on how to solve the Irish constitutional problem. But masterfully he took the sting from the resolutions that were prepared in their original form by one of the most violent sympathizers of the Irish extremists, Timothy Warren Anglin of New Brunswick. Taking advantage of the rules of procedure, he steered them through in drastically amended and much more moderate form. Even so, they reached Britain at the time of the horrible Phoenix Park murders and drew angry replies from all British circles, official and non-official. The British government virtually told Canada to mind her own business. The Canadian Parliament, suggested *The Times*, was guilty of levity of thought and had passed the resolutions merely for electioneering purposes. Goldwin Smith, rejoicing in what he thought was a clear illustration of the sham of British loyalties in Canada, told *The Times* that the whole affair had been an electioneering dodge to win the Irish vote. 'You see the real value of the loyalty of colonial politicians.'

The affair created embarrassments and demanded explanations, but Macdonald, having taken a gentle tilt at the British, had the Irish vote delivered to him in the elections of 1882. A few extremists continued to cause mild alarms. The new Governor General, Lord Lansdowne, who arrived in 1883, was threatened with assassination for the prominent part he had played in arousing the resistance of the Irish landlords to the Home Rule movement. Many Canadians became partisans of either 'the tyrannical landlords' or 'the cowardly Fenian assassins who hocked horses and maimed cattle', but as the Irish agitation at home became more subdued, the Irish in Canada became more quiescent.

V

All these problems were minor, compared to the first great crisis of Confederation, which originated on the prairies in the eighties. Ottawa was slow in coming to grips with fundamental problems of the organization of the west, particularly the disposal of land. While the Canadian Pacific was being constructed over the southern prairie, discontents to northward attained the dimensions of a rebellion. Around Battleford, the Métis of the Saskatchewan, who had migrated there following the Red River episode of 1870, again became exposed to the exercise of governmental authority. Again Canadian surveyors divided the country into square sections, ignoring the historical predilection of the Métis to strip farms fronting on the river. Still the government persisted in refusing land-scrip to the Métis, preferring to believe that their claims were fraudulent, as, indeed, in many cases they were. At Battleford white settlers themselves encouraged the Métis to adopt their truculent attitude. Macdonald considered the whole fraternity of the north Saskatchewan a band of blackmailers, and would take no action. His agents in the west warned of impending troubles, but the Prime Minister held to his great conviction that time was the healer of difficulties of this kind.

Early in 1884 a delegation of the people of the Saskatchewan, headed by Gabriel Dumont, rode off to Montana for the purpose of inviting Louis Riel to take the leadership of this mixed community that contained Scots and other racial ingredients as well as French Métis. The leader of the provisional government of the Red River had lost no prestige among his people with the passing years. He was articulate, even eloquent, gifted with a capacity for putting bold and resolute plans into action. What was to become more novel was his capacity to see visions and to dream dreams. The great question as to whether he was patriot or scoundrel, sane or insane, can be dismissed with the observation that there is a little of each of these in all men.

Riel believed in the possibility of establishing a half-breed nation in the west. But following his return to Canada his demeanour was at first orderly, for his activity consisted chiefly of urging upon the government civil measures that would assure his people of their rights. Having established his ascendancy, he employed it for private purposes. At the very moment the government was about to honour the demands of the half-breeds for land-scrip, which, Macdonald believed, they would spend on whisky, Riel intimated that he was willing to leave Canada if his own personal claims to land in Manitoba, valued at one hundred thousand dollars, were bought out for thirty-five thousand. Ignoring this blackmail, the government reinforced the North West Mounted Police and took measures to appease lesser lights among the Métis.

Coupled with this cupidity, never revealed to his followers, Riel exhibited a fanaticism suggestive of a Moslem Mahdi in the desert. He described himself as a prophet destined to lead 'the New Nation' to freedom. He would divide the west among the Catholic nationalities of Europe. As excitement mounted on the Saskatchewan his faith became more unorthodox and schismatic, reflecting to some extent the competing tendencies in the Catholic world. The records of his errant imaginings may be dubious, but according to one authority he would destroy not only England and Canada but Rome and the Pope. Apparently rejecting the new orientations of Leo XIII, he would make Bishop Bourget, leader of Quebec's ultramontanes, Pope of 'the New World'. Alarmed by these eccentricities, his clerical mentors of the Saskatchewan, especially Father André, deserted him.

On March 17, 1885, Riel established a provisional government with himself as president and Gabriel Dumont as adjutant-general. A few days later a detachment of Mounted Police under Superintendent Crozier, attempting to establish control over the country about Duck Lake, proved to be unequal in marksmanship to the Métis. Twelve police were killed. This battle, so trifling in dimensions, began the Saskatchewan rebellion and reopened the whole question of

the future of the Canadian North-west. Though the white
settlers turned against him, behind Riel were the Cree and
the Blackfoot, who could sense the last opportunity to contest the complete domination of the plains by the white
man. With considerable reason Riel could boast of American assistance, for the frontier was lined with Fenians and
irresponsible expansionists who would make what they could
of trouble in Canada.

Sensing real crisis, the kind of crisis that could undo so
much of what had been done for Confederation, Macdonald
acted swiftly. By March 27 Major-General Frederick Middleton, the British commander of the Canadian militia, reached
Winnipeg. On the night of the same day he left for Qu'Appelle with the Winnipeg Rifles. Within the next few weeks
he had under command a force of over 3,200 men, drawn
chiefly from the militia battalions of Quebec and Ontario.
Colonel Thomas Strange, a retired British officer who was
cattle-ranching near Calgary, led a force of westerners down
the Saskatchewan from Edmonton to Fort Pitt, where he
joined the eastern formations. These rapid movements were
made possible only by the near-completion of the C.P.R. The
Métis were unready and unable to deal with the overwhelming forces that so suddenly converged upon them.

After four days of fighting, Batoche, the rebel stronghold, was stormed and taken by Middleton on May 12. The
rebels fought well but they were overpowered by numbers.
On May 15 Riel sullenly emerged from hiding and surrendered to a small scouting formation. This was the first
purely Canadian military enterprise in history and the
triumph heartened the nation at a time when little else, not
even the certain completion of the C.P.R., could give it
heart. In Quebec, where the hierarchy of the Church gave
its blessing to the expedition, the jubilation was as great as
elsewhere. British and American newspapers had written
forebodingly and disparagingly of a long-extended war in
the west, but the rebellion had been quickly crushed by
what appeared to be the remarkable effort of a united Canada. Yet, when the year 1885 was out, it was disunion that

emblazoned the Canadian scene. Riel was tried for treason at Regina and convicted. The defence rested its case on insanity, but Riel himself, in his highly emotional address to the jury, repudiated this contention. The Crown invoked the famous McNaghten judgment to show that the accused, at the time of the crime, had been able to distinguish right from wrong.

The great question was not that of Riel's guilt but one of whether or not the government should act on the jury's recommendation for mercy and commute the sentence of execution. During the trial excitement had risen in Quebec. For all his failings, Riel was a Frenchman. In a strange, mystic kind of way his career was symbolic of the rapidly receding hopes for a French Canada in the west, of the idea, dominant at Confederation, that the west could be bilingual. The fact of Riel's insanity was accepted as an excuse for his violent eccentricities. It was noted with bitterness that his English-speaking secretary, Jackson, had been found insane and allowed to escape across the border. Mercy had been extended generally to other rebels, even to Gabriel Dumont. Within the Cabinet, in Parliament, and throughout Quebec, French-Canadian opinion welled up in the conviction that the government should act mercifully and commute the death sentence.

Yet opinion favouring the execution was the stronger. In Ontario the feeling was that Riel should hang, not so much for his recent treason as for the alleged judicial murder of Thomas Scott, the brash young Orangeman who had been shot at Fort Garry in 1870. Revenge for Scott was the great impulse that moved opinion not only in Ontario but all through English-speaking Canada. Was it reasonable, men argued, to spare the life of a blackmailing scoundrel who was responsible for the deaths of thirty-eight Canadians in a rebellion that cost the country five million dollars? The recommendation for mercy became primarily a matter of politics, though the judicial apparatus was kept in motion until the end. Twice Macdonald suspended the execution. From July until November the great decision hung in the

balance while convulsive fits of feeling became more notable
on each side of the Ottawa River. On November 11 opposition among Quebec members of the Cabinet was overcome.
Interpreting the decision brutally, it was a question of political analysis. Quebec's opinion was less certain than Ontario's.
By commutation of the sentence Macdonald would lose more
seats in Ontario than he would gain in Quebec should he
decide on mercy.

All this time Riel had waited in prison, daily visited by
medical practitioners and spiritual advisers, retracting his
heresies but announcing new fantasies of nocturnal interviews with an angel. His priest, declaring he was not responsible, readmitted him to the communion of the Church. On
November 16 the sentence was executed and the trap sprung.
Macdonald could not bring himself to believe that the gibbet
at Regina could become the symbol for the great tragedy he
had always sought to avert—the division of opinion in Canada on the basis of racial antipathy. His career had been a
succession of triumphs for the idea of the confederation of
races. Yet the execution of Riel was to unloose new forces
which he, in his remaining lifetime, would be unable to
master.

VI

At Ottawa the affair of Riel apparently blew over easily and
much as Macdonald had anticipated. Blake, making a seven-
hour speech in the Commons, was tactically outmanoeuvred.
Seventeen Quebec *Bleus* deserted the government, but
twenty-three English-speaking Liberals refused to vote for
the motion deploring the passing of the death sentence.
Many Quebec Conservatives, Sir Hector Langevin told Macdonald, felt it necessary to deliver one vote against the government. The bishops and archbishops of the province sor-
rowfully held to the point of view that Riel's execution was
justifiable.

But Ottawa and its allies in the hierarchy lost the leadership of French-Canadian opinion. On November 22 the

greatest mass meeting in the history of Canada was held at
the Champ de Mars in Montreal. There the eloquent Wilfrid
Laurier burst the bonds of Liberal refinement and consti-
tutionalism by declaring that he, too, had he lived on the
banks of the broad Saskatchewan, would have shouldered a
musket and fought with Riel. Ultramontane *Bleus* and radical *Rouges* united to proclaim the monumental injustice that
had been inflicted on the French race and to mourn the death
of Riel, who, on this great occasion, became a deathless
symbol of the martyred French groups of the west now passing under English domination. The hero of the afternoon
was not Laurier but Honoré Mercier, a Liberal newspaperman and politician, who professed to see great urgencies in
the hour and could present greater necessities. 'Riel, our
brother' had died because of the fanaticism of Sir John A.
Macdonald and the treason of the Quebec cabinet ministers,
who, privately opposing the execution, had nevertheless collaborated in the act in order to keep their portfolios. The
French race, said Mercier, could redeem itself only by uniting in the formation of a national party. The cheering on
the Champ de Mars was so loud that the artist Robert Harris,
who had just completed his picture of the Fathers of Confederation, could hear it as he leaned from his window a
mile and a half away. He was not the only English-speaking
Canadian who would condemn 'this murder for policy'.*

The formation of a purely French-Canadian party was a
solution of vengeance, a program of practical action that ran
counter to the whole Canadian tradition. It affronted the
memories of Lafontaine, Cartier, and all other French-
Canadian leaders who had believed that the two races could
work together within a single constitutional system. It
offended the sensibilities and faith of Laurier who said that
Riel at his worst was a subject fit for an asylum, at his best a
religious and political monomaniac. But Le Parti National
came into existence. Its philosophical basis was a mystic faith
in the virtues of the French race, of memories of how Charle-
magne had championed the papacy in the Middle Ages, of

* From a letter in possession of the writer.

the great tradition of St. Louis and Joan of Arc and of
Champlain and Brébeuf. Mercier had been something of a
Rouge, tinged with anti-clericalism, but it was easy for him
to identify his violent racism with a militant Catholicism.
In the provincial elections of October 1886 the Conserva-
tives lost their majority, and out of the confusion that ensued
in the legislature Mercier emerged as the leader of a new
Quebec government early in 1887.

Le Parti National spared no pains to convince its following that it was anti-British and anti-Protestant, determined
to avenge the insults and injuries of the past. The English-
speaking reaction was no less violent. The Toronto press
led the van of the counter-attack, professing to believe that
Mercier's ascendancy in Quebec was the prelude to the
break-up of Canada, reminding its readers that they were
the successors to the conquerors of 1763, warning that they
might be compelled to fight in order to retain the fruits of
the conquest. These strenuous threats and retorts inspired
Mercier to still greater excesses in his own utterances. To
an alert and prejudiced Protestant public his legislation
suggested the coming of a life-and-death struggle between
the two races. Anticipating a great cry of the future, he
warned French Canadians that the propaganda of the Imperial Federation League might result in the sending of
their sons to die for the British Empire 'from the icefields
of the North Pole to the burning sands of the Sudan'. For
friendship he looked to Rome, Paris, New York, and Brus-
sels, never to London and Ottawa. He behaved like a head
of state and, as his policies gained popularity in Quebec,
the hierarchy regarded him more warmly. Far in the depths
of the minds of Mercier and some of his supporters was the
dream of a French state, not merely French-Canadian but
Franco-American as well, that would include the 350,000
French Canadians of New England as well as those of the
St. Lawrence. It was candidly believed by many Franco-
Americans at the time that Confederation was like a house
of cards and would soon collapse. Out of the debris an independent French state might arise.

The Jesuit Estates Act, passed in the Quebec legislature in 1888, sustained the racial strife that the execution of Riel had engendered. Within its own context it was a reasonable measure. Ever since the eighteenth century, when the Jesuit Order had been suppressed by papal decree, its vast properties in Canada had been administered by the government, largely in the interests of education. Returning to Canada in 1831, the Order had steadily regained influence in French Canada, powerfully contributing to the ultramontanism of Bishop Bourget and becoming embroiled in Quebec's tangle of Church-State politics. An agitation arose for the return to the Order of its property. This, Mercier was prepared to stop by buying out its claims for a monetary compensation. Other religious orders pressed for shares in the financial returns which were to be devoted to education. So scrupulous was Mercier in apportioning the funds that he reserved sixty thousand dollars for the Protestant Committee of Public Instruction.

Fierce Protestant reaction throughout Canada was aroused by the stipulation in the Act that the Pope should decide upon the distribution of four hundred thousand dollars to Catholic foundations. Papal authority was invoked in the Act's preamble and it became evident that the Bishop of Rome was about to dispose of property rights in a British country. Through the nineteenth century, Protestant Canada had developed with the doctrine of separation of Church and State as one of the cardinal articles of its belief. The Church establishment and system of tithes in Quebec were regarded as alien and outmoded. In extreme Protestant circles the Jesuit Estates Act was described as insulting to the character of Canada and to the intelligence of its people, and threatening to Protestant populations in other parts of the country. Eastern Ontario, said an editorial in the Toronto *Mail*, would become the victim of French and priestly aggression and be detached from Protestant civilization.

The immediate outcry in Ontario was for disallowance of the Jesuit Estates Act by the federal government. Weighing carefully the political odds as well as the legal considera-

tions, Macdonald decided against it. Disallowance would
merely strengthen Mercier in Quebec and deepen the increasing gulf between the two races. At this stage the initiative in maintaining the cultural and racial conflict passed
to Ontario. There came into existence the Equal Rights
Association, an organization whose objectives, if realized,
would force French Canada to the will of the English-
speaking majority, would deny to Catholics the 'privilege'
of separate schools financed by public money, would refuse
to French-Canadian clergy any influence in civil affairs—
would make of Canada a melting-pot in which English-
speaking, Protestant, secular culture would be supreme.
The Jesuit Estates Act passed to the theatre of the House
of Commons, where the motion of the Orange Colonel
W. E. O'Brien, demanding disallowance, gained but thirteen supporters. But throughout rural Ontario, the west,
and the Maritime Provinces they were widely acclaimed as
'the noble thirteen'. English-speaking Canada, too, acquired
a well organized bloc of embittered extremists.

Racial conflict spread to other quarters. In 1889 D'Alton
McCarthy proceeded west and toured Manitoba, advocating
anti-French measures in a province where the French language stood on a legal footing equal to that of English. In
1890 Thomas Greenway, the leader of Manitoba's government, an aggressive politician who was seeking a new basis
of popularity amongst the overwhelming English majority,
brought to the legislature a bill that denied the official character of French as a language and abolished the system of
separate schools, contrary to the guarantees of the Manitoba
Act of 1870. In the same year McCarthy successfully introduced to the House of Commons a bill which could have
effectively destroyed the equal status of the French language
in the Northwest Territories and precipitated a division in
which party lines were broken down and race voted against
race for the first time in Canada's history. Simultaneously
attacks were made in the House of Commons on the use of
the French language in the schools of eastern Ontario.

VII

The cultural conflict between the two great races of the country was not the only reason why men were saying, in the last five years of the decade, that Confederation could not last. The concept of Canada as a unified state received a whole succession of damaging blows from a cluster of provincial premiers of whom Mercier was merely an outstanding example. The Judicial Committee of the Privy Council at Westminster had placed such heavy emphasis on the Property and Civil Rights clause of the British North America Act that it was becoming possible to think of Canada as a loose league of provinces. Mowat's legal victories were considered by his supporters to be the commencement of the process by which the authority of Ottawa could be subordinated to provincial pride. The authority of Ottawa, in the minds of the Grits of Ontario, could be identified with the sinister methods, the unscrupulous tactics, the loose moral character of Sir John A. Macdonald.

From the east there emerged another threat. In 1884 William Stevens Fielding, the editor of the *Nova Scotian*, a product of the old anti-Confederate school of Howe and Annand, became head of the government at Halifax. Disappointed hopes and bad times rejuvenated the old conviction that Nova Scotia was entitled to a destiny of her own, that her prosperity could be found in an oceanic and international economy, freed from the tariffs and railways of a continental state. Temperamentally Fielding was cautious. But in 1886, after an unsuccessful attempt to extract larger subsidies from Ottawa, he introduced to the legislature resolutions favouring Nova Scotia's secession from the union, coupling them with the other old plan of a union of the Maritime Provinces and the secession of all three. Not only did he succeed in this, but he went to the people on this drastic program and routed the Conservative opposition. The first open challenge to the union of British North America, sanctioned by the people of a province in an electoral contest, had been made.

Honoré Mercier enjoyed the support of a goodly number
of provincial premiers when he called a constitutional conference at Quebec in October 1887. His objective was to
bring about a general surrender of powers from the Dominion to the provincial governments. The provinces, it was
reasoned, should appoint half of the members of the Senate
for life. The federal power of disallowance of provincial
legislation should be abandoned. Larger financial subsidies
should be paid by the Dominion to the provincial governments that would enlarge their spheres of influence. Mowat,
the pre-eminent champion of provincial rights, was present.
Fielding, though refusing to compromise on his grand objective of secession, agreed to take part. John Norquay, though
he had always been Macdonald's man, had his back to the
wall in Manitoba and felt compelled to participate for the
purpose of securing the removal of the C.P.R.'s monopoly
over the traffic of the west. From New Brunswick there came
Andrew G. Blair, the leader of a hard school of legislative
trimmers who declined party labels. He had risen to emi-
nence as a non-party man, but by 1884 he had deemed it
politic to wear a Liberal tag. Six members of his cabinet
called themselves Liberal-Conservatives.

Macdonald's answer to the passage of the resolutions at
Quebec, which would, if carried out, change the whole character of the Dominion, was a highly conscious profession of
masterful inactivity. The Parliament of Great Britain would
amend the British North America Act only following the
joint address of the Senate and the House of Commons of
Canada. The two provinces of British Columbia and Prince
Edward Island had been unrepresented at Quebec. The Dominion government had abstained from taking part. The
conference, therefore, could be said to have absolutely no
legal basis or any basis of consent on the part of the people
of Canada. As the provincial premiers returned to their
strongholds to proclaim the new dispensation and to introduce to their legislatures the Quebec resolutions, some appreciably modified and weakened, Ottawa's attitude was one

of aloofness and gentle disdain. Acting on their own, the provincial premiers could accomplish nothing.

Initiative in the affairs of Canada had fallen into the hands of a new school of provincial politicians whose stages, originally intended to be miniature, had become marvellously expanded. Yet Macdonald could not be dislodged from his central and commanding position. In February 1887, realizing that time was working against him, he went to the country and emerged the undoubted victor in a short, sharp campaign. The Liberals seemed constitutionally incapable of taking advantage of the enormous underlying factors working in their favour. Canada was in a humour for new departures. But Blake stultified the Liberal effort by violently breaking with a free-trade wing of the party, led by Cartwright, on the issue of commercial union with the United States. In spite of the logical appeal of free trade he could not bring himself to betray the interests of the manufacturing belt, extending from Montreal to Sarnia, that the National Policy had so notably developed. In this he was supported by the aging titan Alexander Mackenzie. The idea of Canada not merely as a nation but as a national economy, bound together against its great neighbours by a tariff fence, survived a great peril in this election of 1887. In moments of despair, or something akin to it, when all commercial activity seemed incapable of rousing itself from a cloying depression, closer relations with the United States could exercise a general appeal. In 1887 the idea of nationality appeared to come at a high price. The only good explanation for the Conservative victory was the ineptness and indiscipline of the rival party, a factor on which Macdonald could count heavily. Out of the Liberal discomfiture there came a new leader, Wilfrid Laurier.

The electoral victory brought no new enthusiasm and freshness of ideas to the Conservatives. As the decade drew to a close the strength of the government seemed more and more to rest upon the aging Macdonald. Confident Tories had acquired the habit of saying that he would never die, but in 1887 he was seventy-two and new strains had come to the problem of holding Canada together. Corruption in the Department of Public Works struck down Sir Hector Langevin and intensified the prejudice of many Canadians that the vocation of politician was sinister and dishonest. While heads hung in shame at Ottawa no Canadian could take an ebullient pride in the character of his country. The Imperial Federation League, by stimulating within a thin band of the population a violent desire for the closer integration of the British Empire, antagonized the French Canadians and gave to Mercier and his separatists new reason for the cry that Canada as a nation could not function. To this highly emotional appeal Macdonald never acceded. Galt, McCarthy, and George Foster succumbed to the blandishments of Imperial Federation, but the Prime Minister could see in these real obstacles to the integration of Canada as a state.

Old tensions from across the border acquired new form as the Americans, less outwardly hostile than in former years but apparently no less cunning and underhanded, seemed to snatch at every opportunity to weaken the slender foundations on which Canada was constructed. The government at Washington began to seize Canadian sealing vessels in the Bering Sea, putting forward the pious pretext of conservation but at the same time permitting its own sealers to operate from the Pribilof Islands. James G. Blaine, the American Secretary of State, who had risen to political affluence as a baiter of Britain and as a hero to the Irish vote, deepened the insult by professing to regard Canada as a colony, by attempting to deny Canadian participation in the negotiations that followed with Britain. For years almost all Canadians had nourished hopes for freer trade with the United States. Macdonald and the Conservatives, though committed to the policy of high tariff on manufactured goods, had watched for openings that would enable them to bargain with Washington for lower rates on Canadian farm produce. These aspirations were dealt a cruel blow by the McKinley tariff of 1890, which especially penalized the importation of Canadian cereals. The old cry that Yankee politicians were attempting to starve Canada out, the deep suspicion that they were using commercial policy to force Canada to sue for annexation, acquired fresh poignancy.

Canada was a North American country with but two abiding marks of distinction – its British institutions and its bilingual culture. In 1890 there was no certainty that the constitution of 1867 could restrain the tensions that divided the two great races. Confederation, it could soberly be argued, had reached its limits. Perhaps the solitary mark of grandeur on the bleak and unpromising scene was the withering but unflagging figure of the Prime Minister. For twenty years he had been a favourite target for moralistic propagandists as well as professional politicians. But behind the veneer of cynicism and worldly wisdom, beneath the deep knowledge of men's frailties gained from a long career of public administration, there were faith and constancy. To his life's mission, the building of a nation from sea to sea, he was holding hard.

4. The 1890s

JOHN T. SAYWELL

We have come to a period in the history of this young country when premature dissolution seems to be at hand.... How long can the present fabric last? Can it last at all? All these are questions which surge in the mind, and to which dismal answers only suggest themselves.' As the decade opened, there were many Canadians who agreed with Wilfrid Laurier, leader of the Liberal Opposition. The high hopes of the founding Fathers had not been fulfilled. The statecraft of veteran Sir John A. Macdonald, the charcoal sketch of the Canadian Pacific across a still-unsettled west, and a slim volume containing the ever-increasing tariff schedules seemed to be the only tangible instruments of Canadian unity. Yet the old Conservative's fingers were weakening and losing their grasp, and the instruments of the National Policy were blunted and suspect.

Provincialism, unequivocally supported by the Judicial Committee of the Privy Council in the nineties, threatened the delicate fabric of unity, with a cancerous decentralization, dissolution, or annexation as the price of its triumph. However gradual its pace, the economic growth of the country was creating a sharply divided society; the overture promised a fully orchestrated symphony of class consciousness and conflict. Between English and French Canada lay a gulf of incomprehension bridged only by the necessities of politics. Bigotry was widespread, finding outlets in the traditional French-English and Catholic-Protestant conflicts, in hostility to any strangers in the land, and in sharp rivalries among Protestant sects. The tone of the nineties was rough and discordant.

While bigots fanned the embers of racial and religious controversy in readiness for a new conflagration and even a cynical population was increasingly disturbed by mounting evidence of gross political corruption, the central issue as the decade opened was the question of Canada's commercial policy. A growing disenchantment with the National Policy of tariff protection had been reinforced by the slump of the late eighties. Low yields and low prices led to meagre returns for the farmers. Manufacturers attempted to relieve the pressure on profits by increasing that on the workers. While bank presidents informed shareholders that debt and mortgage payments were being met, post-office savings banks reported a marked decline in the number of depositors and the size of the balances. The Liberals looked to Sir Richard Cartwright's utopia of Unrestricted Reciprocity, which was to open up American markets by removing tariff barriers between Canada and the United States. D'Alton McCarthy tempted Tories with the virtues of Imperial Preference, to enlarge trade within the Empire through a structure of preferential duties. Macdonald and the National Policy Conservatives prepared once again to defend their beleaguered fortress.

By late 1890 Sir John had concluded that his maxim 'time

and I against any two men' would have to be set aside. Only
a modern economist could have seen in increased government revenues, increased imports, and an upswing in export
prices the early signs of a turn in the business cycle. Far more
obvious was the threat of another bad harvest and, worse
still, the fear of the McKinley tariff that was to close the
United States to Canadian exports. Ahead too were the well-
documented revelations of party scandals and the threat
posed by the Manitoba Schools Question to the unbelievable
Basilica-Lodge alliance on which the party rested. For the
moment, however, the Liberals were more divided than the
Conservatives. Mercier's nationalistic, extravagant, and corrupt policies in Quebec had alienated many English Canadians, and important elements in the party, led by Blake and
Mowat, were dragging their heels over Unrestricted Reciprocity, dubious themselves of its consequences for Canada.

As early as 1889 Macdonald had realized that economic
statistics would be impotent weapons with which to defend
the National Policy, and that his opponents could only be
felled by psychological warfare. Patriotism and loyalty to a
Canada within the Empire—a war cry, not a weapon—would
have to be the issue. Canadians would be forced to choose
between collective survival as a Britannic community or
possible individual betterment as Americans. Macdonald's
polarization of the trade issue in terms of loyalty ('A British
subject I was born') .and treason ('a deliberate conspiracy,
by force, by fraud, or by both, to force Canada into the
American union') had already been attempted by Colonel
George Denison and the Imperial Federation League and
had been used to good effect in a by-election in South Victoria.

In the short campaign that followed the snap dissolution on February 2, 1891, the Conservatives were ordered
to hammer home loyalty versus treason. So boldly stated it
seemed believable, even to dyed-in-the-wool Grits. Moreover, Catholic ecclesiastical declarations against annexation
seemed only to have one meaning. The silence of Blake and
Mowat added to the uncertainty and suspicion. Far more

was at issue than political allegiance. There was, said J. C.
Patterson of the Toronto *Mail*, in asking Canadians to place
patriotism above partisanship, nothing less at stake than the
survival of a superior culture. What Canadian could be so
diabolical, he asked, as 'to throw Canada, with her lofty
ideals of religious, political and civil liberty, her noble educational institutions, her unstained judiciary, her pure social
and domestic life, her high standards of commercial integrity, into the arms of the United States which to put it
mildly, in all these particulars, stands on a much lower level?'

Of course loyalty could not be expected to carry the entire
election. Traditional methods of patronage and promises–
even promises of a tunnel to Prince Edward Island–were
called into service. The financial and industrial community
was alerted to the dangers of reciprocity, although, feasting
as it did on duties and bounties, it was unlikely to need the
reminder. The C.P.R.'s Van Horne wrote publicly to Drummond of the sugar trust–as if he needed to be told–that the
interests of manufacturers, financiers, transportation officials, and the working men lay with the National Policy, and
later could boast that not one C.P.R. employee in a hundred
was doubtful.

The combination of conventional weapons and psychological warfare was irresistible. Loyalty–not boodle or Sir
Charles Tupper, confessed the Liberals–swept the Maritimes. The Conservative popular vote rose in Quebec, although the Liberals capitalized on Tory dissension to gain
seven seats. Reciprocity had too firm a hold among the
farmers of south-western Ontario to be broken, but elsewhere the Conservatives triumphed easily. Significantly
enough, many of the victorious Conservatives were members of the Imperial Federation League, and in eastern Ontario the central issue of the election was often overshadowed
by the Protestant Equal Rights campaign and anti-Jesuit
agitation. Conservatives swept the cities, despite the disaffec-
tion of the working class, and were eminently successful
along the main line of the C.P.R. For the last time Macdonald had given his party a comfortable victory. In June

even time deserted him. The Old Man and his era passed away, although his party remained in office five more years, under the last election he had won for them.

II

Whatever else it accomplished, the election did not solve the problems of the Canadian economy. Publication of the census of 1891 confirmed the most gloomy suspicions and dismayed its readers for, despite the boom years of the early 1880s and immigration levels not exceeded until after the turn of the century, population growth had not even kept up with the natural increase. Prospects for the 1890s seemed bleaker. The birth-rate was falling. Immigration declined and remained well below emigration as Canadians flocked to the farms and factories of the United States. Increasing urbanization—about 6 per cent a decade between 1880 and 1900—was accepted as a beneficial effect of the National Policy in central Canada. Until late in the decade, however, there were few optimistic signs in the Maritimes and the prairies. In Manitoba and the North-west low prices, unusually dry years, and the difficulty of finding methods of cultivation suitable to semi-arid lands served as a process of natural selection. But while some deserted farmhouses and almost empty settlements were the marks of failure, the increasing use of machinery and experiments with windbreaks, seeding, and summer fallowing were gradually bringing the land under man's control. Beyond the mountains British Columbia, not yet integrated into the Canadian economy, enjoyed its first boom since the Cariboo gold rush. American enterprise and capital, encouraged by the generous policies of a government of entrepreneurs, opened up the rich mineral lands of the southern interior and began the war of devastation on virgin timberlands. And American railways threatened to confirm the dictate of geography and turn much of the province into the hinterland of a commercial empire based on Spokane or, if J. J. Hill had his way, Tacoma.

There was generally a modest improvement in Canada's economic conditions between 1891 and 1893. Reasonably good harvests, an increase in the value of agricultural products, and diversification which enabled many farmers to take advantage of urbanization and an expanding British market aided agriculture. While the United States was the chief beneficiary of this expanding British market, following the end of the slump of the 1880s and the inability of the Russians to maintain food exports, increased Canadian sales to Britain helped to offset the American barriers of the Mc-Kinley tariff. The volume of business grew and, while some business suffered from over-expansion and severe competition, good profits were reported in banking, manufacturing, and transportation. Improved economic conditions were undoubtedly one reason why the Conservatives won back eighteen Ontario seats (and lost only three) in the carefully staggered and well-managed by-elections between 1891 and 1893.

But a downturn began late in 1893, and the middle years of the decade were bleak. The crash of 1893 had an unsettling effect on the financial world. Agricultural production and prices fell. A British embargo on live cattle and the competition to horses posed by increasing use of electricity dealt the farmer further blows. Contraction was marked in banking, manufacturing, transportation, and construction. Banks reported that farmers were borrowing, not buying, and falling behind in mortgage payments. Business failures increased; there was a general pressure on profits. Wages fell and unemployment increased. In June 1896 the general manager of the Bank of Commerce gloomily reported that for the first time in years 'we have not been able to take a forward step' and that the year had 'been one of constant anxiety and almost unexampled difficulty in making profits and avoiding losses'. For another sector of society there was perhaps some consolation when beer fell to an all-time low of 32 cents a gallon in 1896 – indicative of the level of commodity prices. The trough was reached in 1896 and early 1897. It was little wonder that Laurier was convinced that

the Liberals could win the 1896 election, if only the distort-
ing race and religion issue could be removed from national
politics.

The pace of industrial growth fell sharply in the nineties,
but the role of the large firm became more important as the
depression stimulated efficiency and consolidation. Mount-
ting popular criticism of monopolies, combinations, and
price-fixing was based on more than suspicion. Avoiding
such areas as textiles (where it was well known that a cotton
combination flourished behind a constantly higher tariff and
paid dividends of 32 per cent) a select committee in 1888
found: a grocers guild in league with an association of sugar
refiners; an association of coal dealers that fixed prices, made
identical bids on public tenders, and awarded the contract to
the company that paid the highest premium to the association,
and drove out competition; an association of oatmeal millers
to fix prices, establish quotas, and buy out competitors; and
organizations to control the production and price of binder-
twine and barbed wire. An anti-combines bill introduced by
a Conservative back-bencher was taken over by the government, watered down, and sent to a committee whose members readily yielded to the lobby that descended on Ottawa
before it was passed; it was then sent to the Senate, where it
was further emasculated. The act was not only half-hearted,
it was fraudulent; so frequently did the words unlawfully,
unduly, and unreasonably appear that the measure actually
weakened the old common-law restrictions on combinations,
and was an inducement rather than a deterrent to them—
unless one accepted the official government view that the
common-law restrictions were so severe that no judge would
convict. (At some point a clause was inserted that removed
the protection given to trade unions in 1872.) Such an act
did nothing to alter the trends in business organization established in the eighties and intensified in the nineties.

III

As the plutocracy grew, so too did the class consciousness of its employees. Until late in the decade the times were not auspicious for rapid trade-union growth, and, given high unemployment, the Yellow Dog, the Ironclad, or the Agreement must have been powerful instruments in the hands of management. Wage rates were depressed and working conditions for men, women, and children were often inhumane; withheld wages or payment in kind or in truck were commonplace. As a royal commissioner commented in 1889 'there seems to be no idea of any obligation existing between the employer and his operatives, any more than the mere payment of wages. To obtain a very large percentage of work with the smallest possible outlay of wages appears to be the one fixed and dominant idea.'

The large mass of the working class, crowded into city slums, was unorganized, and the trade unions – Knights of Labor, local unions, or the Trades and Labour Congress – were largely ineffectual as a political pressure group. Repeated demands for a wide range of protective or remedial economic, social, and political legislation went unheeded in Ottawa. Mowat proved more responsive in Ontario, and there by the mid nineties legislation concerning hours and conditions of work, workmen's compensation, and some of the social consequences of urbanization had been placed on the statute books. Increasingly, however, working men looked to some form of political action. Gradually a left-wing program began to emerge. Except in British Columbia, however, the movement for independent political action was fitful and ineffectual.

The new urban proletariat found few sympathizers or champions. While in literary realms Archibald Lampman and D. C. Scott lashed out at the squalor and injustice of the new industrial society, there was nothing comparable in Canada to the American muck-rakers. Some religious leaders realized that they were losing contact with what one of them called 'the unconverted masses', but churches and chapels seemed too established to make the structural and ideological adaptations necessary to meet the challenge. Classes, wrote the editor of the *Christian Guardian* in 1884, 'must exist as long as there are different degrees of thrift, intellect and religious education in a community', and the antagonism to the church among the lower classes, he felt, was 'to some extent the outcome of the feeling of the unsuccessful and the needy against those who are successful and comfortable'. Their energies absorbed by denominational conflict and their funds by the construction of magnificent buildings housing high-rent pews, the organized churches left the work in the streets and slums to the revivalist movement of the 1890s and the Salvation Army, which mushroomed in the industrial cities. By the middle nineties more thought was being given to social questions. Some Methodists, for example, grudgingly accepted the legitimacy of trade unions, although not the right to strike, and even allowed that a reduction in hours worked might not be matched by an increase in sin. And in 1894 the Methodist Conference even declared its sympathy with 'the struggling masses everywhere' and affirmed hopefully that 'when society had become impregnated with the teaching of Jesus of Nazareth, trusts, monopolies, heartless combinations and oppressive economic conditions shall have been superseded by universal brotherhood'.

The 1890s also witnessed the first stage of the agrarian revolt in Canada. Rural Canada was slowly losing its paramountcy. In 1880 over 75% of the population was rural; by 1900 37.5% was urban. In some rural counties in Ontario there was an absolute decline in population. Parents watched the family unit being broken up as sons and daughters headed for the godless fleshpots of the cities. Economic hardship made more acute the bitterness felt towards the producers of farm goods and implements, sheltered by a high tariff and combining to fix prices. Since the 1870s the Grange had stimulated the development of a rural class-consciousness and had undertaken a wide range of social and economic activities to demonstrate the advantages of collective action.

The movement had declined in the eighties, largely because of its unwillingness to accept political action.

When an American organizer for the Patrons of Industry, an American farmers' association with social, economic, and political objectives, appeared in Ontario in 1889 he found the field ripe for expansion. By 1892 there were 1,400 lodges with 30,000 members and by 1894-5 over 50,000 members, including 5,000 in Manitoba and the North-west. By 1891 the Patrons had severed their American connection and had started to work on a national political program. Their major concern was the tariff, and in 1893 they presented a petition with over 40,000 signatures calling for tariff reform. By this time the Patrons had successfully entered the political field in Ontario and Manitoba. In the Ontario election of 1894 the success of seventeen Patrons indicated the extent of agrarian discontent. But like the Progressives a generation later, the Patrons found their reluctance or inability to be a party and their preference for the Liberals over the Conservatives a barrier to effective action. Moreover, although united on major economic issues, the Patrons were divided over the racial and religious issues that emerged in the mid nineties, as well as over prohibition. The high hopes for the federal election of 1896 were not realized, as only three Patrons were elected. By 1900 the Patrons were a spent force and were unable to field a single candidate. Their revolt against the economic and social biases of the National Policy, however, was to remain a permanent force in Canadian politics.

Competing with the Patrons for farm support was the Continental Union movement, which got under way late in 1891. Inspired by Goldwin Smith and supported financially by wealthy American annexationists, the advocates of continental union found a ready audience among the farmers of south-western Ontario. Support given the movement by Liberals enraged Oliver Mowat, who even charged that the Toronto *Globe* had become an annexationist organ, and he warned Laurier that if continental union was 'to be the policy of the Dominion Liberal party, I cease to be a mem-

ber of it'. The reaction against continentalism, the effect of
Blake's West Durham letter with its doubts that unrestricted
reciprocity could be combined with independence, and repeated defeats in the by-elections convinced the Liberals
that a change in policy was essential before the next federal
election.

IV

The occasion was the national Liberal convention in Ottawa
in June 1893. Elected chairman, Mowat used his address to
emphasize the British connection and warn that any notion
that the convention disagreed with him on such a matter
'would cause a sufficient stampede from the reform ranks to
make our success at the next general election out of the
question'. Laurier too emphasized his loyalty, but added
that 'the commercial interests of England are not the interests of Canada'. After a battle over the critical tariff resolution moderate Liberals were victorious. The Liberal tariff
was to be based not upon the protective principle, but upon
the requirements of the public service, and would be 'ad-
justed as to make free, or bear as lightly as possible upon the
necessaries of life, and should be so arranged as to promote
freer trade with the whole world, more particularly with
Great Britain and the United States'. A second resolution
underlined the importance of broad and liberal trade relations between Canada and the United States.

The new platform was the first stage in the ultimate
Liberal acceptance of the main principles of the National
Policy. Almost at once it had its effects. As William Mulock
wrote from Toronto, 'it is conceded that our platform is
proof against the disloyalty cry while the moderate character of our trade policy fails, apparently, to create alarm in
monetary circles'. Old friends lost in '91, he added, 'are all
coming back'. And by late 1894, while Cartwright was woo-
ing the Patrons, Laurier was cultivating what financier
George Cox called 'the leading financial men in this Province'.

Criticized from all sides, the Conservatives were aware that every effort would have to be made to increase Canadian prosperity within the framework of the National Policy. In 1892 the five-year-old act creating the Department of Trade and Commerce was proclaimed, and the elderly Mackenzie Bowell was appointed Minister. The Department gathered statistics, appointed trade commissioners, and encouraged Canadian exporters, and Bowell followed a trip to Australia by hosting the 1894 Colonial Economic Conference. While Bowell could describe attacks on the trusts 'as a species of socialism' he and the Minister of Finance, George Foster, undertook a survey of the tariff in the summer of 1894 in response to universal criticism. As Foster reported to the Prime Minister: 'Bowell and I have done Montreal, Toronto and Hamilton in Tariff and shall polish off St. John and Halifax and Quebec week after next. . . . It is hard work, but it is doing good. The interests like to talk out the various subjects and we get many good pointers and some information. . . . What fools the Opposition have been. If they had struck tariff reform and gone into . . . details they would have made it hot for us.' To cool down criticism the government introduced a new schedule in 1894 which lowered the duties on such items as farm implements, binder-twine, nails, wire, and fencing. The reductions had little effect on the public, but gravely disturbed the manufacturing community. The editor of the *Canadian Manufacturer* asked in disbelief why Foster should have felt it necessary 'to deal such a fearful blow to his political friends and supporters', but trusted that the rates would soon be revised 'to conform to the requirements of the country and the expectations of the manufacturers', which clearly were synonymous. That trust kept most of the business community loyal to the Conservatives in the election of 1896.

V

Far more menacing than the clash of socio-economic interests was the failure to respond to the challenges of a
pluralistic society. Within a decade of Confederation Pierre
Chauveau had written, 'English and French, we climb by a
double flight of stairs towards the destinies reserved for us
on this continent, without knowing each other, without
meeting each other, and without even seeing each other, except on the landing of politics.' In the 1880s the landing of
politics had become increasingly turbulent and in the 1890s
was a battleground of bigotry where race battled race, and
creed fought creed.

Although it stopped short of the rack and the stake, the
Protestant hatred of Catholicism was intense. 'Jesuit! Jesuit!
Jesuit! Dislike of the Jesuit is part of the blood and bone of
these people,' wrote the editor of the *Globe* in 1889. Orange
Lodges, the Equal Rights Association, and the Protestant
Protective Association (later called the Canadian Protective
Association), an offshoot of the American Protective Association, were openly determined to rid the country of the
menace of Catholicism. The churches were officially less
outspoken, but religious bigotry was a major obstacle faced
by every non-denominational institution. Bitter rivalries and
hostilities even divided the Protestant sects.

The religious conflict was overwhelmed and to a large
extent absorbed by the more serious ethnic conflict. While
many English Canadians doubtless shared Goldwin Smith's
view of the habitant as 'a French peasant of the Bourbon
day . . . simple, ignorant, submissive, credulous, unprogressive', what was fundamentally at issue was not individual
incomprehension, but two widely different conceptions of
the nature of the Canadian nation. Many English Canadians
in their search for a meaningful nationality adopted the pan-
Anglo-Saxonism that afflicted late-Victorian England. In a
nation so defined and among a majority firm in the belief
in racial superiority there was little room for French Canadians. The great question facing Canada, trumpeted D'Alton

McCarthy, is 'whether this country is to be English or French
– and it is this problem and the apparently insoluble character of the difficulties that it presents that are driving people
openly to look on annexation as the only means of escape.'
Imperial Federationists, many of them members of the Equal
Rights Association, were of the same mind. John Charlton
confided to his diary that 4,000 Montrealers gave him the
greatest applause when he 'asserted that a successful French
nationality on the North American continent was a hopeless
dream, for that question had been settled on the plains of
Abraham'. 'I would suggest that if the other provinces are
maintained out and out English,' wrote another Ontario
Liberal to Premier Greenway of Manitoba, 'French must
disappear from Quebec. There would be no overflow places
for the French to go and knowing this, the French would
learn English'. 'I am satisfied that sooner or later this crisis
had to come,' wrote John Willison. 'It may be that Confederation will be the main sufferer.'

Impotent when national politics centred on race, facing
the politics of the 'reserve' doctrine, and with its survival
openly threatened, French Canada resorted to every defensive mechanism at its disposal. And many French Canadians,
like the young Jules-Paul Tardivel, must have dreamed
'd'un Canada français autonome, d'une vraie Nouvelle-
France. . . . A l'heure marquée par le Dieu des nations
. . . formeront un vrai peuple . . . et dans cinquante ans
peut-être, il [Quebec] prendra place parmi les nations de la
terre.'

The celebrated Manitoba Schools Question sprang from
and helped to crystallize sentiments about the duality of
Canada. The issue arose in 1890 when an English-Protestant
majority in Manitoba deliberately removed the legal linguistic and religious privileges or rights of a French-Catholic
minority there. As confirmed in the Northwest Territories
two years later, the action made it clear that wherever possible the majority was determined to make the public
schools the vehicle for creating a Canadian nationality
which, without definition, would be English. In French

Canada the issue became 'une question nationale, une question de notre avenir comme race, de la position que nous
devons occuper dans la Confédération'. In English Canada
it was much the same. Tragically, the objectives were diame-
trically opposed. Here lay the dilemma facing the federal
government, empowered by the constitution to protect
minority rights.

The Conservative party was ill-equipped to face such a
crisis. Macdonald had been losing his touch in his last few
years, and had not only failed to contain the McCarthyites,
but had also refused a necessary reconstruction in Quebec.
After his death, his successor as Prime Minister, Sir John
Abbott, persuaded Langevin, Macdonald's chief French-
Canadian lieutenant, to offer his resignation in return for a
lenient report from the committee investigating the Mc-
Greevy political scandal in which Langevin was implicated,
but refused to promote the strongest Quebec Conservative,
J. A. Chapleau, to the position of Quebec federal leader.
Abbott, however, soon tired of the game – 'if it were not for
the deputations wanting money and lands, and the people
wanting situations and plunder, I should get on pretty well'
– and gave way to Sir John Thompson in November 1892.
Under pressure from the Ontario wing, where he was already suspect because of his conversion to Catholicism,
Thompson refused to yield to Chapleau's demands and unwisely sent him to Spencer Wood, the luxurious residence
of the lieutenant-governors of Quebec, from which pinnacle
Chapleau continued to exert an enormous influence on Quebec politics. His replacement was the ultramontane A. R.
Angers, whose brilliance and integrity were matched only
by his impotence in the constituencies. Thompson's appointment of Clarke Wallace, Grand Master of the Orange Order,
might have balanced the government, but it was unlikely
to facilitate a settlement of the schools question.

Thompson was dead and the lacklustre Mackenzie Bowell
was Prime Minister when, in January 1895, the Judicial Committee of the Privy Council ruled that the federal government had the right to take remedial action on behalf of the

Manitoba minority. For the next year the Cabinet was rocked by resignations and revolts as Bowell and his colleagues proved unable to take a firm and united stand. In March Sir Charles Hibbert Tupper resigned when Bowell reversed a decision to go to the country and secure a mandate for remedial action, but was persuaded to return by Sir Donald Smith and Senator Drummond. In July the three French-Canadian ministers threatened to resign when the Cabinet refused to answer Manitoba's refusal to restore separate schools by introducing remedial legislation. Angers fulfilled his threat, but Caron and Ouimet came to heel after a visit from Drummond 'in his role as peace-maker and purse-bearer'. In December Clarke Wallace left office, after months of publicly advocating national schools while the government was committed to remedial action. In January seven English-Canadian ministers resigned in a calculated attempt to force the Prime Minister to resign in favour of old Sir Charles Tupper, who had journeyed from England to be on hand at such a time. But the Governor General, falsely assuming that the resignations were designed to prevent remedial legislation, refused to accept Bowell's resignation. The Prime Minister's belated success in securing a replacement for Angers, the fear that Lord Aberdeen would call on Laurier, and Bowell's agreement to resign after the session brought an end to the Cabinet crisis. But a prolonged filibuster prevented the Conservatives' remedial bill from passing before Parliament was dissolved.

The Liberals were as divided as the Conservatives but enjoyed the immense advantage of being in opposition. For six years Laurier remained silent, confessing that 'it was impossible to take a bold and well-defined attitude without breaking the unity of the party. Indeed such a rupture may be unavoidable in the end. But to exhibit the spectacle of a divided opposition would have been simply playing the game of the government.' By the fall of 1895 he had gone no further than to recall the fable of the man who shed his coat for the sun, not the wind: 'if it were in my power, I would try the sunny way.' And in moving rejection of the coercive remedial bill on March 3, 1896, he assured the House that his policy would be based 'not upon grounds of Roman Catholicism, not upon grounds of Protestantism, but upon grounds which can appeal to the consciences of all men, irrespective of their particular faith . . . .' Meanwhile in Quebec Israel Tarte could promise that Laurier's sunny ways would provide the best deal for the Manitoba minority and that his victory would 'relever le prestige de notre race'. And in Ontario Liberals could pledge that provincial rights would be inviolate under a Liberal Prime Minister.

The Quebec Liberals were afraid that old Sir Charles Tupper, who took over from Bowell in April, could entice Chapleau back into the Cabinet with the offer of the Quebec leadership. But Chapleau rejected the offers and Angers, selected in his stead, recruited the entire French-Canadian wing from the ultramontanes, thus insuring that many moderate Conservatives would swing to Laurier. However, it was not the ultramontanes the party relied on to win the election in Quebec, but their ecclesiastical allies; lacking political leadership the Conservatives turned to spiritual. The Quebec bishops had long demanded the restoration of separate schools, and the influential Father Lacombe had publicly stated early in 1896 that 'the episcopacy, like one man, united with clergy, will rise up to support those who may have fallen in defending us'. After endless correspondence, the reconciliation of serious internal divisions, and anxious soul-searching the bishops issued a *mandement* to be read without comment in the churches commanding the faithful to support only those candidates solemnly pledged to support remedial legislation. 'Ce grave devoir s'impose à tout bon catholique,' intoned every parish priest on May 17, 'et vous ne seriez justifiables, ni devant vos guides spirituels, ni devant Dieu lui-même, de forfaire à cette obligation.'

Conservatives were disappointed and Liberals relieved, for the *mandement* was weak. Although its intent was clear, and some priests made sure their parishioners understood 'la pensée intime' of the bishops, it did not prohibit Liberal support, and all but eight Liberal candidates signed a declaration supporting remedial action. Far more to the taste of the Quebec Conservatives was the action of Bishop La-flèche, who denounced Laurier's March 3 speech as 'l'affir-mation du Libéralisme condamné par l'Eglise la plus caté-gorique qui ait jamais encore été faite à ma connaissance dans une assemblée législative de notre pays. . . . L'homme qui parle ainsi est un Libéral rationaliste,' support of whom would be a mortal sin. But Laflèche stood alone and the power of the *mandement* was not sufficient to overcome the absence of political leadership. Laurier and the Liberals swept to a decisive victory in Quebec.

The bishops were not alone in taking a stand. Protestant conferences had declared unequivocally against Catholic schools, and the pulpit was a vehicle for political education. A Methodist minister in Western Ontario informed his flock that a Liberal vote 'would stare the voter in the face at Judgement Day, and condemn him to eternal perdition', while a Presbyterian divine assured Clarke Wallace that 'the country is with you in its truer conscience and God is, and the Pope and the Devil are not.' In Ontario suspicion of Laurier was probably stronger than doubts about the Con-servatives, and many Conservative candidates openly and with Tupper's permission refused to support remedial ac-tion. The total Ontario Liberal vote and the percentage of the Conservative popular vote fell, as 30,000 voters followed McCarthy or the Independents and another 30,000 voted for the Patrons of Industry. The net result was a draw as both Liberals and Conservatives won forty-three seats in the big English-speaking province. Elsewhere the Liberals made substantial gains, an indication perhaps that the racial and religious controversy was less intense. Over-all the Liberals emerged with a comfortable 118-88 margin over the Con-servatives.

The Manitoba Schools Question was not the only, and in some areas it was not even the main, issue in the election of 1896. Bad times, trade and tariff policies, agrarian and work-ing-class discontent, Liberal indications of sympathy for prohibition, Conservative disintegration, and, with falling

revenues and strict orders from the Minister of Finance in
1895 to cut out all unnecessary expenditures, a decline in
the extent of patronage and boodle, all played their role.
The schools question cut across these issues and, probably
for all time, made a firm analysis of the election impossible.
However enigmatic, the election did bring one period of
Canadian political history to an end. The next four years
were to see whether the Liberal revolution could be consolidated.

<h1 style="text-align:center">VI</h1>

The Laurier Cabinet reflected the basis on which the party
had been re-organized and the victory won. The appointment of W. S. Fielding rather than Cartwright as Minister
of Finance and the selection of William Mulock, William
Patterson, and R. R. Dobell (all sympathetic to the major
principles of the National Policy) confirmed the pledges concerning commercial and fiscal policy. The entry of Mowat
guaranteed loyalty and religious moderation. The presence of
Tarte and the virtual exclusion of the old *Rouges* strengthened the still-tentative alliance with moderate conservatism
in Quebec. The presence of strong provincial figures–
Mowat of Ontario, Fielding of Nova Scotia, Blair of New
Brunswick, and Sifton of Manitoba–suggested that an era
of centralization had passed. The only serious criticism of
the Cabinet came from Quebec, where *Le Temps* described
it as 'la plus profonde humiliation nationale qui eût pu
être infligée à la race française', and *Le Monde*, recalling
Laurier's promise to base his policy neither on race nor on
creed, commented bitterly, 'M. Laurier a tenu sa promesse;
il a oublié qu'il est Canadien français et catholique.'

Laurier's first challenge came from Quebec, where the
shocked bishops were determined to mount a counter-attack.
Conciliation depended upon a favourable settlement of the
schools question and Laurier sent an ex-Conservative and
respected Catholic, Judge Routhier, to Manitoba to soften
up the Catholic community. Clifford Sifton's deferred Cabi-

net appointment and Greenway's desire for better terms, in addition to the greater willingness of Manitoba Liberals to negotiate with their federal counterparts, facilitated a compromise. And by mid November a settlement had been reached whereby instruction in faith and French were allowed under certain conditions. But the hierarchy was in no mood to accept a compromise which Archbishop Bégin described as an 'abandon unjustifiable des droits les mieux établis et les plus sacrés de la minorité catholique'. At the same time L. O. David saw his tract on the clergy placed on the index because he described Laflèche's action during the election as a subversion of political liberty and constitutional government, while Ernest Pacaud's *L'Electeur* was forbidden to Catholic readers because he reprinted extracts from David's pamphlet.

Laurier had already realized that no solution to the problem would be found in Canada. As in 1877, an appeal would have to be made to Rome. Armed with a lengthy statement from Liberal members of Parliament, which outlined the issues involved and emphasized the Catholic dilemma in a democratic pluralistic society, Abbé Proulx left for Rome. The bishops entrusted their case to four of their members. As Proulx wrote from the Vatican, 'presque tout le Canada va se transporter à Rome; ce serait bien plus simple qu'un seul, au nom de Rome, se transportât au Canada.' Charles Fitzpatrick, Laurier's Solicitor-General (a leading Quebec Liberal, and once counsel for Louis Riel), also hastened to Rome. So earnest were his devotions and so successful his diplomacy that Mgr. Merry del Val was sent to Canada. Like Mgr. Conroy two decades earlier, del Val soon saw the realities facing the Catholic minority in Canada. Thus, while the encyclical *Affari Vos* refused to criticize the hierarchy and described the settlement as inadequate, it urged Catholics to accept it as partially satisfactory and to work to secure additional improvements. The bishops could hardly continue their relentless struggle with the Liberals, and in time Laurier's friendship with Archbishop Bruchési and other prelates not only lessened the hostility but made Liberalism almost respectable.

Meanwhile, the government had turned to the equally pressing problem of economic policy. The Liberal victory had had a further unsettling effect and the winter of 1896-7 was a low point in the recession of the mid nineties. Soon after taking office the government reduced the interest rate in its own savings banks to three per cent and lowered it again the following year. After discussions with the Americans, Fielding, Cartwright, and Patterson held tariff hearings in the major industrial centres. When the new tariff was presented in 1897 the Cabinet had obviously not only agreed with Sifton that 'the free trade theory, which has already been shattered' should 'not be permitted to stand in the way when it is clearly not in our business interests', but had found the manufacturers' case almost as impressive as had the Conservatives. While many duties were lowered in the interests of the farmer and the consumer, the general level remained high and the protection of such basic industries as textiles and iron and steel remained undisturbed. To offset free-trade criticism the Liberals included a broad preferential system with reduced rates for countries offering reciprocal privileges. The double schedule had little effect, however, for despite British preference the United States continued to improve its position in the Canadian market.

The 1897 tariff both placed export duties on nickel, copper, and lead and held out the offer of reciprocity with the United States. This ambivalence ended after the failure of talks at the Joint High Commission and the enactment of the highly protective Dingley tariff. The offer was deleted in 1898 and the Canadian government threatened to place a duty on the export of logs and pulpwood if the Americans placed a tariff on newsprint. At the same time the Ontario government prohibited the export of logs cut on Crown lands in a further attempt to strengthen Canadian manufacturing and force Michigan lumbermen to mill in Canada. A federal subsidy to the Canadian Pacific to build the Crow's Nest Pass line into the Kootenays was not only a lever to secure reduced freight rates to the prairies, but was also designed to contest American commercial control of the southern interior of British Columbia.

These measures coincided with the rapid growth of American capital investment in Canadian natural resources and the establishment of branch plants in significant numbers. By 1897 American direct investments totalled about $160 million: $55 million in each of mining and manufacturing, $18 million in agricultural enterprises, $13 million in railways, $10 million in marketing, and $6 million in oil. The pace of investment quickened during the prosperous years at the end of the decade when the *Economist* estimated that another $100 million was poured into mines, forests, and manufacturing.

Increased American investment was only one manifestation of the new prosperity of the late 1890s. Recovery was slow through the later months of 1897, but by 1898 virtually all indices – prices, government revenue, exports and imports, immigration, construction – moved forward. The boom has usually been attributed to the 'conjuncture of favourable circumstances' – technological changes, freight rates, gold supply, end of the American frontier, increased urbanization, rising prices, and increased rainfall – which made possible the full development of the wheat economy of the prairies. The western boom was by far the most significant aspect of a general economic advance, and in attracting millions of immigrants and billions of dollars in capital investment in the next decades it provided an immense stimulus to manufacturing, lumbering, transportation, banking and insurance, and service industries, including even the coal, iron, and steel industries on the eastern seaboard.

Such rapid expansion intensified the socio-economic consequences of industrialization and urbanization. Concentration of economic power increased, as men such as George Cox could consolidate an interlocking empire of banks, trust and insurance companies, brokerages, and railways. Combinations and monopolies flourished, undeterred by the 1889 legislation or the provision in the 1897 tariff that protection

could be removed if it encouraged monopolies. Although
warned in advance of the consequences, the Liberal government made minor changes in the regulations concerning the
transportation and sale of crude oil and kerosene which, with
preferential treatment from the Grand Trunk and the Canadian Pacific, enabled Standard Oil to present its subsidiary,
Imperial, with a virtual monopoly of the central Canadian
market. (Ironically, seventeen manufacturers, including
Massey-Harris and Dominion Bridge, cried to Laurier that
'since the Standard Oil Company secured the control of the
product there has been a tendency to curtail the supply and
reduce the quality as well as to advance the price materially.')
Trade unions grew in number, size, and power. Labour-
management relations became increasingly tense and bitter.
Evidence published by the young Mackenzie King revealed
that nothing had changed for the better since the 1889 Royal
Commission report. In the west farmers mounted an offensive against inadequate grain inspection, elevator monopolies, lack of branch lines, and price syndicates.

The government had more pressing problems than industrial or agrarian unrest. In July 1897 ships docked at Seattle
and San Francisco with the news – and the gold to back it
up – that in the previous summer Lying George Carmack,
Skookum Jim, and Tagish Charley had found a mother lode
on the Klondike. In the spring of '98 thousands of prospectors and camp followers tempted fate on the Skagway Trail,
the Chilkoot Pass, and the treacherous waterways leading to
the Klondike. By the summer Dawson, with 18,000 inhabitants, was the largest Canadian city west of Winnipeg. With
surprising ease the Mounted Police established their authority, but the civil administration was less successful in
minimizing inefficiency and corruption.

Conflicts over territorial jurisdiction, customs fees, and
bonding privileges in the north strained Canadian-American
relations to the breaking-point, and there were frequent
rumours of an American military expedition to the Alaskan
panhandle. Attempts to find or manufacture an all-Canadian
route, such as the ill-fated Yukon railway, failed. But the

Canadian government hoped that because of the ill-defined panhandle boundary they could manufacture a case for control of the heads of inlets and access to the overland passes. Diplomatic negotiations failed and discussions at the Joint High Commission in 1898-9, which merged with talks concerning sealing, the fisheries, and reciprocity, were fruitless. By 1903, when a quasi-judicial tribunal rejected the Canadian case, the rush was over. But the anti-American feeling caused by the boundary controversy stimulated Canadian nationalism and imperialism in the last years of the century.

VII

Even prosperity could not blunt the edge of racial tension and conflict that re-emerged in the late nineties, largely as a by-product of Canada's relations with Britain. Until the late 1880s discussion of Anglo-Canadian relations had turned largely on constitutional and economic questions. A few Canadians were quickly caught up in the early phases of the imperial federation movement in England, and in 1885 formed the first branch of the I.F.L. in Canada. The League languished for several years until it became the instrument through which loyalists cultivated imperial sentiment as an antidote to continentalism or annexation. As the British League declined the Canadian flourished. Most of the members were Tories, but by 1896 many of the leaders, such as Colonel George Denison, Principal Grant, and D'Alton McCarthy, had become supporters of the Liberal party. As Denison wrote to Lord Salisbury, the imperialists were delighted with the 1897 tariff. 'They [the Liberals] have come out straight in favour of the Imperial idea, have wrapped themselves in the old flag to the intense satisfaction of all parties except the extreme partisans in the Conservative ranks. . . .'

Laurier's conduct at the 1897 imperial pageant of Queen Victoria's Diamond Jubileee delighted the Canadian imperialists. His vision of a French Canadian at Westminster and his heady references to imperial representation were far more eye-catching than his careful motion at the conference that relations were for the moment satisfactory and would remain so as long as Canada remained a colony.

Yet this newly awakened imperial enthusiasm was a serious threat to Laurier's object 'to consolidate Confederation, and to bring our people long estranged from each other gradually to become a nation'. Imperialism seemed to be strongest in circles inhabited by the Noble Thirteen, the Equal Rights Association, the Protestant Protective Association, and the advocates of national schools. Imperialism was in many ways the reverse side of English-Canadian nationalism, and another instrument in the forging of a Canadian nationality–'We are Canadians, and in order to be Canadians we must be British' declared the annual meeting of the British Empire League in 1898. Racism and social Darwinism were explicit or implied in the literature of these nationalist-imperialists. George Parkin, for example, could subtitle his book *Imperial Federation* 'The Problem of National Unity'. Like countless other English Canadians, Parkin echoed Chamberlain's boast of 'that proud, persistent, self-asserting and resolute stock that no chance of climate or condition can alter and which is infallibly destined to be the predominating force in the future history and civilization of the world'. It was unlikely that many French Canadians could share this view of Anglo-Saxon superiority and supremacy.

Just as many Canadians shared the doctrines of racial supremacy and conflict–even business reports reflected it– that underpinned much of the late-Victorian western imperialism, so too did they exhibit many other symptoms of the disease. Military writers were prominent and military ardour increased. There was a greater interest in athleticism and combative sports, the ultimate sport of course being war. The press of Canada showed many of the signs of the so-called yellow press in Britain and the United States, leaving some bewildered greybeards to marvel at the new vicarious interest in gossip, sports, crime, and war. Nor was it surprising that in Canada, as in Britain, the new evangelism was carried forth under the militant banners of the Salvation Army, with its journal *The War Cry*, and to the rousing strains of Sir Arthur Sullivan's 'Onward Christian Soldiers'.

VIII

Many of these tendencies in western civilization could be shared by English and French Canadians alike. In Rhode Island the young Canadian Olivar Asselin could encourage recruiting and he raced to join the colours when the Spanish-American war broke out, just as thousands of English Canadians living in Canada flocked to the American consulates to participate in the adventure against Spain. While some Canadians were uneasy about the Anglo-Saxon bond that drew England and the United States together, most were pro-American and endorsed racial solidarity. The *Mail and Empire*, however, warned that further absorption of Latin territory would, because of intermarriage, ultimately weaken the race and 'the dominating influence of Anglo-Saxondom will become less powerful'. The same paper also commented on a banquet in Montreal under the headline 'They Cheered for Spain — French Canadians show their sympathies in the crisis'. If this was true, French Canadians were reacting as did continental Europeans to Anglo-Saxondom's determination to conquer and cleanse the world.

Back in Quebec a year later, however, Asselin wielded his pen to denounce Canadian participation in Britain's war to conquer and cleanse the Boer Republics in South Africa. For the Boer War moved the question of Anglo-Canadian relations from the levels of visions or logic to those of reality and emotion. Once again it revealed the conflicting ideas about the nature and future of Canada, demonstrated the divergence of French and English views, and confirmed the weakness, if not the impotence, in times of crisis of a cultural minority in a democratic majoritarian state.

In Britain, the Colonial Secretary, Chamberlain, and the imperialists saw the war as an admirable opportunity to

demonstrate imperial unity and establish a precedent for
the collective imperial defence that had been rejected at the
1897 conference. In Canada, English Canadians were overwhelmed by imperial fervour and regarded resolutions of
sympathy and frenzied flag-waving as inadequate expressions
of loyalty or solidarity. They wished to identify and participate, however vicariously for most of them, in a triumphant
war. French Canadians could not identify. As the Governor
General, Lord Minto, wrote of Laurier, who felt the war
was just, 'the Frenchman in him precluded the possibility
of any British enthusiasm – there was not a spark of it.' And
as *La Presse* observed, 'Canada is for us the whole world;
but the English-Canadians have two countries, one here and
one across the sea.' Moreover, many French Canadians
either did not believe in the justice of the war or tended to
identify with the Boers, whose collective survival, like theirs,
was threatened. To English-Canadian demands for a contingent, Israel Tarte replied 'not a man, not a cent for South
Africa'.

Laurier's policy of 'parliament will decide' was much less
successful in his hands than in those of his Liberal successor,
William Lyon Mackenzie King. 'It is not constitutional
authority that the Government lacks to send Canadian troops
to the Transvaal,' thundered Hugh Graham's Tory-im-
perialist Montreal *Star*, 'it is moral courage to do its duty at
the risk of offending a disloyal element, which objects to
any action that tends to strengthen the bonds which unite
England and Canada.' 'The French rulers of Canada are
holding back the loyal Canadians,' trumpeted its Toronto
counterpart, the *News*. 'This Dominion is in the grip of
foreigners who have no taste for British advancement. Their
ideas are not those of the Anglo-Saxon. They would cast off
their allegiance to Britain's Queen tomorrow if they dared.
Only a wholesome fear of what would happen to them at
the hands of the more virile people of Ontario and the West
restrains them.' As usual Laurier sought a compromise that
would divide Canadians least. After a stormy two-day session
of the Cabinet, with Tarte's resignation in the balance and

Mulock once stalking angrily from the room, the government authorized a contingent, later followed by another, to be organized and equipped by Canada but paid for by Britain. The action was not to be regarded as a precedent, but the nationalistic-minded Henri Bourassa knew a precedent when he saw one, and resigned his seat in protest. The seed of future tragedy was sown.

Laurier had planned an election for December 1899, but the furor over the war forced him to postpone it. Since 1896 the Liberals had won virtually every by-election, yet the party was not in a good position for an election. The sessions of 1899 and 1900 had been unsatisfactory. Irish Roman Catholics were disaffected. Prohibitionists felt betrayed, and were not convinced by Laurier's arguments that the slight majority for prohibition—slight because Quebec had voted overwhelmingly against it— was insufficient, or that the government could not afford to lose seven million in revenue from taxes on liquor. The neutrality of the C.P.R., a power in seventy-five constituencies, it was said, had been lost. Some businessmen felt that the government was too sympathetic to labour. The party organization in Ontario was hopeless. The Conservatives, on the other hand, had benefited from the fierce energy of Tupper and, thanks to generous donations from the Grahams, the Drummonds, the Danbys, and the Gooderhams, had an efficient paid organization and ample funds. Liberal pundits believed their party would win in the Maritimes, Quebec (where the Conservative cry 'Laurier is more imperialistic than Tupper' sounded absurd), and in the west, but would be lucky to hold their own in Ontario.

The pre-election speculations were close to the mark. Liberal strength increased substantially everywhere but in Ontario. With excessive simplicity Liberals and Conservatives alike attributed the results in Ontario to the race and creed cry. Conservative campaigners, while seldom attacking Laurier openly, had fastened on the allegedly disloyal Tarte, describing him as the real master of the administration. 'The writing of the leading opposition papers in Ontario has been

positively wicked,' wrote Lord Minto, 'simply aiming at
stirring up hatred of French Canada.' The Sons of England,
Orange Lodges, and the P.P.A., converted into the 'purity
association' and assisted by the A.P.A., became branches of
the Tory party. Emotion-charged demonstrations for returning veterans a week before the election set a tone that lasted
through election day.

After the election the Toronto *World* gloated that 'it was
the voice of the lion saying "thus far and no further".' And
Charles Eaton of Bloor Street Baptist Church wrote to
Laurier that 'I am sadly convinced that the chief menace to
the future of Canada is the unreasoning blind bigotry of
English-speaking Toryism, and pardon me if I venture to
say that you cannot overestimate this danger – I cannot suggest a remedy because the evil is not amenable to reason,
but I hope the good sense of the rest of Canada will avert a
calamity.'

Laurier was despondent, and again wondered if a French-
Canadian Catholic could successfully lead a national party.
But he tried to look hopefully on it all, as he asked Bourassa
in the House, 'Can we not hope – I ask my honourable friend
himself – that in the grave shall be buried the last vestiges
of our former antagonism?' Unfortunately, neither good
sense nor countless graves were to overcome antagonisms or
avert future calamities.

5. The New Century

H. BLAIR NEATBY

$\mathbf{I}$n 1891 Goldwin Smith had
seen no future for the Dominion of Canada, composed as it
was of four separate regions cut off from each other, and
doomed to remain the backward and impoverished northern
fringes of the continent. But now, at the turn of the century,
pessimism was outmoded and Canadians had become brag-
garts. When the Chambers of Commerce of the British
Empire held their congress in Montreal in 1902, the delegates must have been surprised to learn that they now found
themselves 'in the largest and chief commercial city of the
Dominion of Canada – a city which is at once the London,
the Liverpool, the Manchester, the Birmingham, the Leeds,
the Bradford, the Sheffield, the Northampton, the Oxford,
the Cambridge of North America'. So exaggerated were

UP AGAINST THE SOLID FACTS !

From *Laurier Does Things*, 1904.

many of the claims made by citizens of the Dominion that
another British visitor at this time commented that it was
difficult to talk to Canadians about their country; 'They
have been told so often what a fine country they have, they
tell themselves so often what a fine people they are, that any
touch of criticism, even amid general admiration, is resented
as though it were a studied slight.' Canadians had become
vociferous optimists and the Canadian question was no
longer whether Canada would survive but rather how populous and how prosperous it would become.

There was much to justify the optimism. Prosperity was
the central fact of the first decade of the century. The *Canadian Annual Review* was founded at the beginning of the
decade to provide each year 'a summary of current progress
in a country now steadily growing in importance', and each
succeeding volume did present an impressive record of economic progress. The economic foundations of the Dominion
seemed so secure that Sir Wilfrid Laurier's boast of the

twentieth century belonging to Canada seemed more an appraisal than a prophecy. At the end of the decade the spiral of material progress was still ascending.

But if prosperity was the central fact, it does not fully explain the changes in Canada during the decade. Some Canadians did not share in the sense of national achievement because they had no share in the benefits of prosperity or because they were dissatisfied with their share. Farmers and labourers resented the profits of businessmen and manufacturers; the Maritimes and the prairies were jealous of the greater prosperity of central Canada; French Canadians were disturbed by the increasing influence of English Canada. Authors who described Canada at the end of the decade still saw prosperity as the major theme but they now wondered whether material progress alone could nurture a nation-state. The multi-volume history *Canada and its Provinces* was in preparation by this time. The decision to write such a history was proof of national pride, and the editor, in his preface, was still enthusiastic about the visible signs of economic growth. But pride was now tempered by the warning that 'the national character is not moulded exclusively by economic causes' and that 'the danger of sectionalism, in spite of material success, is greatly to be feared, unless this destructive tendency is met by the positive and constructive idea of the Nation'.

The harsh truth was that the nation was not yet built. The leaders of the scattered British colonies in North America had created a political union in 1867 and by the first decade of the new century an integrated transcontinental economy – an economic union – had been shaped. But some of the fundamental divisions within the union still remained and prosperity had brought new divisions into focus. National pride was there, and a new-found assurance that Canada would survive and prosper, but there was as yet no way of knowing what Canadian society would be like or what kind of nation-state Canada would become. Canadians were still searching for a sense of national identity.

I

And high above the sea and lands,
On peaks just tipped with morning light,
My dauntless spirit mutely stands,
With eagle wings outstretched for flight.

Frederick George Scott

The Canadian spirit took flight with the flocking of immigrants to the Canadian prairies. For years, even before Confederation, this 'great lone land' had created hopes and fostered national ambitions. Canadian politicians had forestalled the northward expansion of the United States by taking over the Hudson's Bay territories and by luring British Columbia into the union, and had then linked these regions to the St. Lawrence with the steel ribbons of the Canadian Pacific Railway, but the National Policy, the grand design of a transcontinental economy, depended on making the western lands productive. The tariffs had been imposed, the railway built; all that remained was prairie settlement. For a generation the high hopes had been frustrated; now in the first decade of the new century the settlers came and the grand design became a reality.

There were fewer than half a million people living on the Canadian prairies at the beginning of the decade, most of them in what was then the tiny province of Manitoba. Ten years later the prairie population had trebled and homesteaders could be found in all the arable regions of the prairie. The density of settlement would increase in the following decades and settlers would push northward into the Peace River country, but 'the last best west' of North America was no longer a frontier by 1910. The railway lines that criss-crossed the prairies were knotted every few miles by villages, with grain elevators in each village to receive the harvest. Some communities, favoured by nature or by railways, became distributing centres. Saskatoon, for example, was little more than a general store on the South Saskatchewan at the beginning of the century, linked with the outside

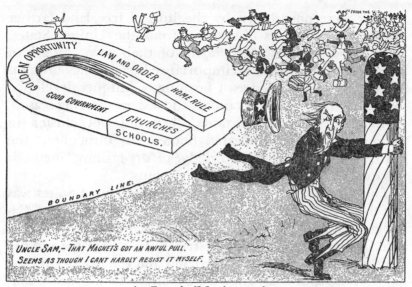

An Irresistible Attraction

From *Laurier Does Things*, 1904.

world by a branch line running south to the main line of
the C.P.R. at Regina. In 1902 Saskatoon was organized as a
village, although the storekeeper later recalled that 'it was a
hard struggle to effect this, the ordinance calling for twenty
houses within a mile square. By counting all the shacks we
managed it.' Then the settlers established themselves on the
prairie lands to the south, and soon two new railways, the
Grand Trunk Pacific and the Canadian Northern, crossed
the river at Saskatoon and opened up new territory to the
west. Saskatoon was incorporated as a town in 1903 – although they had difficulty in finding the necessary nine councillors who had the qualification of a year in residence. By
1905 it had received a city charter and by the end of the
decade it had a population of almost twelve thousand, a university was being built, and Saskatoon was no longer a
frontier community.

It was not difficult to attract settlers in these years. Nearly
all of the free homestead lands in the United States had
been occupied by 1890, and land-seeking immigrants from

Europe were now drawn by the lure of free land farther
north. Many settlers also came from the United States,
farmers' sons who wanted farms of their own. American
immigrants were of special importance because they brought
with them the knowledge of farming techniques developed
for a region with limited rainfall and a short growing season.
Unlike European immigrants, they did not cluster in
national colonies but located homesteads throughout the
prairie region, and their knowledge of 'dry-farming' methods
was quickly acquired by their neighbours.

The disappearance of free land in the United States was
not the only factor that stimulated settlements on the Canadian prairies. Wheat-farming was becoming more profitable. The growth of large industrial cities in Europe and the
United States increased the demand and the prices paid for
food. At the same time, large-scale manufacturing meant that
the cost of the lumber and farm machinery required by the
homesteaders did not rise as quickly. Technological advances
also provided other advantages. Ocean freight-rates fell, and
so wheat could be shipped to Europe more cheaply. A farm
in the Canadian west was now a far more attractive venture
than it had been before.

The Canadian government had long been ready to welcome immigrants to the prairies. As early as 1870, when the
province of Manitoba was created, the federal government
had retained control over its natural resources; it would
retain the same control over the lands in the provinces of
Saskatchewan and Alberta when they were formed in 1905.
In this way the federal government could grant any bona fide
settler a free homestead of 160 acres without any interference
from the governments of the three prairie provinces. Other
prerequisites for orderly settlement had also been provided
before the turn of the century. The Indians had been located
on reserves, the North West Mounted Police were enforcing
the law, the Canadian Pacific Railway had been built, the
land had been surveyed, and municipal and territorial
government had been established. Immigrants would not be
coming to a turbulent and lawless frontier.

This did not mean that the Canadian government calmly waited for immigrants to come. Sir Clifford Sifton, Minister of the Interior from 1896 to 1905, was a dynamic salesman. Sifton gave priority to advertising Canadian homesteads in the United States, and exhibitions of Canadian farm products at American state and county fairs, combined with free railway excursions to the Canadian west for American newspaper editors, helped to destroy the myth of a 'frozen north'. In Europe, the British Isles had provided most of the emigrants that had peopled the New World in the nineteenth century, but by this time British emigrants came from industrial cities rather than rural areas and these newcomers needed a long period of apprenticeship before they could become successful farmers. Sifton shifted Canadian publicity to rural areas in central Europe. There were growing criticisms during the decade of a policy which established colonies of central Europeans in western Canada, colonies which brought prairie land into production but which preserved languages, customs, and a way of life that were different and alien. Sifton ignored the criticism. 'I think', he said, 'that a stalwart peasant in a sheep-skin coat, born on the soil, whose forefathers have been farmers for generations, with a stout wife and a half-dozen children, is good quality.' It was enough for Sifton that these immigrants would grow wheat on what had been unproductive prairie sod.

Under Sifton, the Department of the Interior did more than advertise the opportunities in the west to attract immigrants. Departmental regulations were simplified and even ignored in order to make it easier for the immigrant to become a settler. Clifford Sifton, himself the son of an early immigrant to Manitoba from Ontario, had no sympathy for red tape. 'One of the principal ideas western men have is that it is right to take anything in sight provided nobody else is ahead of them,' he once wrote. 'As a rule it is sound policy for the government to fall in with this idea and encourage the people to go ahead.' Newcomers to the prairies had enough problems to face, building barns and houses, 'sod-busting', surviving cold winters and arduous summers before they had a crop to sell. Under Sifton's administration they were at least spared many of the frustrations of red tape and officious bureaucrats when filing homestead claims and earning title to their land.

The life of these new settlers in western Canada differed greatly from the pioneer life of an earlier era. The settlers were not pioneers in homespun, growing their own food, cobbling their own shoes, making their own furniture, and living a self-sufficient life. From the beginning they expected to share in the advantages of an industrial age. The first homes might be log cabins or sod huts on the treeless plains, but such accommodation was always considered temporary. Most farmers either began with or soon moved into frame houses built of lumber sawed in Ontario or British Columbian mills and roofed with cedar shingles. Clothes, kitchen utensils, and farm machinery were usually imported from eastern Canada. Settlers usually had vegetable gardens and pigs and chickens for their own use, but they were far from self-sufficient. They were businessmen who produced a product that might be sold to consumers on another continent, and who lived on the profits of their enterprise.

II

This kind of farming meant that settlers were completely dependent on efficient transportation services. Railways made prairie settlement possible. When a fierce blizzard cut off the train service to many prairie communities in the spring of 1907, the pioneering families faced the possibility of starvation or of freezing to death until the tracks were cleared of snow. Only railways could bring in the food, fuel, and equipment on which the settlers depended; only railways could move out the millions of bushels of wheat that they grew. Canoes and Red River carts had served in an earlier era, but the iron horse created this wheat kingdom.

Railways extended beyond the settled areas at the beginning of the decade, but in the next few years railway construction failed to keep pace with settlement. In 1900 rail-

way lines fanned out west of Winnipeg in the province of
Manitoba; in the Northwest Territories there was the Canadian Pacific with the 'Soo Line' south to the United States
and branch lines running north from Regina and Calgary.
The flood of immigrants in the next few years, however,
meant that the only available homesteads were soon thirty
or forty miles from the nearest railway. And as early as 1901
the combination of an increased acreage under cultivation
and a good crop showed that the Canadian Pacific's single-
track line from Winnipeg to Fort William and its limited
supply of box-cars could not handle the harvest. Some of the
grain had to be stored on farms over the winter in what
became known as the 'wheat blockade'. The need for more
railways was glaringly apparent.

The farmers' demands for better railway facilities fell on
receptive ears. Many Canadian businessmen were now convinced that long lines of box-cars would soon be needed to
carry the wheat from the prairies and wanted to share in the
profits; a visit to the west in 1902 convinced Edmund Walker
of the Canadian Bank of Commerce that 'the extent of land
for agriculture exceeds even my fondest hopes . . . within
four or five years every railroad in the country will have to
double-track its lines to handle the traffic.' But private investors would still be inclined to wait until the existing
traffic ensured an adequate return on their investment. Canadian politicians were not prepared to wait for private
enterprise to take the initiative because any delay would
retard settlement. As Sir Clifford Sifton wrote to a friend,
'I think for the government to shut down on railway policies
would be a suicidal policy. . . . Twenty years ought to see at
least twelve million people in Canada. But if this result is to
be accomplished, small ideas of cutting off expenditures on
railways and public works will have to be dropped. For my-
self I am altogether in favour of going ahead.' With politicians ready to subsidize railway construction and with
entrepreneurs willing to build, it is not surprising that railway mileage increased dramatically during the decade.

This eagerness for railways did not answer the question of

how many lines should be built, who would build them, and where they would be located. Each western farmer wanted a branch line as close to his own homestead as possible, but the farmers had developed a deep-rooted suspicion of the Canadian Pacific, which they blamed for the wheat blockade and which they believed had taken advantage of its monopoly to provide inadequate service at extortionate rates. Political pressure from the west ensured that governments would favour rivals of the Canadian Pacific. These rivals, however, had ambitions that went beyond providing railway services for new prairie communities. They wanted to create trans-continental railways, carrying the lucrative long-haul traffic to and from the west.* Added to this was the fact that Canadians in other parts of the country also wanted railways. The federal government could largely determine what railways would be built because railway construction depended on federal subsidies, but the many pressures and the optimism of the period meant that more than prairie railways would be built.

Donald Mann and William Mackenzie were the first to take advantage of the situation. Mann was a tough, barrel-chested construction boss, while Mackenzie was a small and neat business promoter; the two combined to form one of the most amazing partnerships in Canadian affairs. At the turn of the century they already owned a few short lines in Manitoba which went by the name of the Canadian Northern Railway. The Canadian Northern was a frontier railroad, cheaply constructed, using old steam-engines and boxcars bought second-hand from other railway companies, and depending for revenue on such local traffic as the hauling of firewood into Winnipeg. But these two men were ambitious and daring. They applied to the Manitoba government for a subsidy to build a line from Winnipeg to the Great Lakes and so create an alternative outlet to the Canadian Pacific

* Few people realized at the time that wheat would continue to be shipped through the Great Lakes, because even after paying storage costs over the winter it was cheaper than shipping grain all the way by rail.

from the prairies. The Manitoba government was more than willing and even subsidized the construction of the section located in the neighbouring province of Ontario. By 1902 the Canadian Northern extended to Port Arthur on Lake Superior. An English traveller gave a description of Fort William and Port Arthur soon after – 'the shanties, the miry roads, the railway tracks in chaos, the humped elevators, the snorting and evil-odoured engines' – but he also commented that here was the wheat funnel of the world.

But for Mackenzie and Mann this was only the beginning. They had visions of a transcontinental railway. Money was no obstacle because federal and provincial governments were generous and private investors had confidence in Canada and in these two men. By 1910 Mackenzie and Mann had borrowed more than two hundred million dollars and their railway consisted of some three thousand miles of track, mainly in western Canada, with construction under way across the Rockies to Vancouver and across the Canadian Shield to eastern Canada. Even in this era of optimism, this was a fantastic achievement. The partnership of Mackenzie and Mann had shown that there was scope for the talents of daring entrepreneurs in the Canada of the twentieth century.

The Canadian Northern was not the only railway to expand in this decade. The Grand Trunk Railway had benefited from the prosperity in central Canada after years of near-bankruptcy – but Charles Hays, the aggressive general manager, was not satisfied; he wanted the Grand Trunk to get a share of the traffic of western Canada. As early as 1902 he proposed that the Grand Trunk build a line north of the Great Lakes to Winnipeg and beyond Winnipeg across the northern prairies and the Rockies to the Pacific. It would have been more logical for the Grand Trunk with its eastern network to combine with the Canadian Northern and its western lines, but Hays was not interested in 'that little bunch of lines up around Winnipeg', and in any case Mackenzie and Mann were too ambitious to merge with the Grand Trunk. The directors, shareholders, and bond-holders of both railways were so optimistic about the future of western Canada that they were ready to take the financial risk of building two new transcontinental systems.

Charles Hays's plans for the Grand Trunk depended on government aid; without federal subsidies there could be no western extension. Hays did not need to worry about a receptive hearing at Ottawa. Sir Wilfrid Laurier was even more eager than the Grand Trunk to have railways built. He justified his sense of urgency in a speech in the House of Commons:

> We cannot wait because the prairies of the North-west, which for countless ages have been roamed over by the wild herds of the bison or by the scarcely less wild herds of red men, are now invaded from all sides by the white race. They came last year one hundred thousand strong and still they come in still greater numbers. Already they are at work opening the long-dormant soil; already they are at work sowing, harvesting and reaping. . . . We consider that it is the duty of all who sit within these walls by the will of the people to provide immediate means whereby the products of these new settlers may find an exit to the ocean at the least possible cost and whereby likewise a market may be found in this new region for those who toil in the forests, in the fields, in the mines, in the shops of the older provinces. Such is our duty; it is immediate and imperative.

With such a vision of the future, it is not surprising that Laurier welcomed discussions with Charles Hays. But Laurier's vision created a serious complication. He wanted a railway that would be a national railway carrying Canadian goods through Canadian territory, and so strengthening the National Policy. In the speech already quoted he gave vivid expression to the nationalist view that the United States must be excluded from the western traffic:

> Heaven grant that it is not already too late; Heaven grant that while we tarry and dispute, the trade of Canada is not deviated to other channels and that an ever vigilant competitor does not take to himself the trade that properly belongs to those who acknowledge Canada as their native or adopted land.

Unfortunately for the Grand Trunk, its Atlantic terminus was Portland in the state of Maine. There would be no federal aid until there was some assurance that the Grand Trunk would not deflect Canadian traffic to an American seaport.

Laurier therefore made a counter-proposal to the Grand Trunk. The federal government would give subsidies if the Grand Trunk would build a railway sweeping north in an arc from Winnipeg to Quebec city, bridging the St. Lawrence and extending to Moncton. This would ensure an all-Canadian route and also have the advantages of opening up new areas for French-Canadian settlement in northern Ontario and Quebec and of winning popular support in the Maritimes. If this proposal was accepted, the government would then be ready to subsidize Grand Trunk construction west from Winnipeg to the Pacific.

Charles Hays did not like this proposal because western goods would not travel on the old Grand Trunk lines in southern Ontario. But Hays could not be stubborn; he was intent on westward extension and he needed federal aid. It was finally agreed that the federal government would build the line from Winnipeg to Moncton, which was named the National Transcontinental, and would lease it to the Grand Trunk when it was completed. The government then agreed to guarantee the interest on a large part of the money borrowed by the Grand Trunk for the construction of the line west from Winnipeg to Prince Rupert.

These arrangements involved the construction of some 3,500 miles of railway. Still to come were the branch lines that would funnel the prairie wheat to the main Grand Trunk line. Construction was well advanced on most sections of the main line by the end of the decade, although the railway would not be completed until 1914, and the bridge across the St. Lawrence at Quebec, after collapsing twice during construction, would not be opened until 1917. The total cost of construction would be more than $250 million, with the federal government spending $60 million of this total on the National Transcontinental and guaranteeing bonds to a total of $75 million on the western line. Canadian

nationalism could be expensive. At the time, however, few
politicians or observers worried about the cost; the economic
boom, partly induced by the huge expenditures on railways,
seemed to justify any extravagance.

John A. Macdonald's National Policy had encompassed
more than prairie settlement and railways. It also involved
a protective tariff to exclude foreign manufactures and so
ensure a monopoly of the growing prairie market for goods
manufactured in Canada. The Liberal party had argued for
lower tariffs in the days of Macdonald, but accepting the
National Policy meant accepting the principle of protective
tariffs as well. The imperial preference had lowered the
tariff on imports from other parts of the British Empire, but
even this lower tariff still provided adequate protection to
Canadian manufacturers. In 1907 an intermediate tariff was
introduced, falling between the general tariff and the imperial preference, which was useful for negotiating trade
agreements with other countries, but again the protective
principle was preserved. Growing demands for freer trade
from western Canada worried the government later in the
decade and led to reciprocity negotiations with the United
States, but even these talks involved free trade in natural
products rather than in manufactured goods. Economic
nationalism effectively smothered the free-trade sentiments
that Liberals had espoused in a less prosperous era.

The three-fold National Policy was truly national in this
decade because it linked all of the hitherto isolated economic
regions of Canada by creating an interdependent economy.
While the production of wheat spiralled, the value of manufactured goods produced in Canada more than doubled; iron
and steel, lumber and coal, and minerals were produced in
greater quantities than ever before. In spite of the flood of
immigrants to the prairies, the urban population increased
more rapidly than the rural population, and Ontario and
Quebec grew in numbers almost as quickly as the three
prairie provinces. It was true that the benefits of the National
Policy were not evenly distributed—manufacturing in the
Maritimes actually declined, with the exception of the iron

and steel industry there, which was stimulated by railway construction – but although regional differences attracted some attention, regional jealousies were tempered by the increased prosperity in all areas.

Industrial expansion meant more than increased production. The structure of Canadian industry was also being modified. The typical manufacturing enterprise in Canada had been owned by a family or a small group of business associates. By 1910 many of these companies had become or had been absorbed into large and impersonal corporations. The Canada Cement Company, for example, was formed by a horizontal merger of the major cement firms in the country; the Steel Company of Canada was a vertical merger which combined blast furnaces, rolling mills, and finished iron and steel products. All such mergers were made possible by the expanding Canadian market; large-scale production and greater specialization now seemed both possible and profitable.

This consolidation of industry required talents much different from the technical ability or salesmanship of successful businessmen of an earlier era. The new 'captains of industry' were financiers and promoters, often with little knowledge of the manufacturing process but with the daring and skill to negotiate large mergers and with the confidence of the bankers and investors who supplied the capital. The outstanding example of such a promoter is Max Aitken, later Lord Beaverbrook. Aitken was twenty-six years old when he moved from Halifax to Montreal in 1907. He was already director of Royal Securities Corporation and the trusted adviser on investments of many wealthy businessmen. Within the next three years Aitken had promoted the merger of three huge corporations – the Canada Cement Company, the Steel Company of Canada, and Canadian Car and Foundry, with an authorized capital of almost one hundred million dollars – and had found investors to provide the necessary funds. Aitken himself showed little interest in these corporations after they were formed. 'I am a builder,' he explained. 'When the building is finished I do not stay in it but move on to build another.' The financial success of the firms he built

testifies to his talents as a promoter as well as to the opportunities for large-scale enterprises in this decade of expansion.

III

The 'wheat boom' was not an unmixed blessing. J. S. Woodsworth, a young Methodist minister in Winnipeg, was outraged by the abject poverty and degradation of immigrant
labourers in the city, and the slum conditions he saw at the
All People's Mission in North Winnipeg were duplicated in
most Canadian cities. Woodsworth, however, was an exception; most Canadians turned a blind eye to the tenements or
blamed the plight of this urban proletariat on their lack of
initiative or their taste for alcohol. Even the slum-dwellers
themselves were virtually untainted by the heresy that
poverty might not be their fault.

There were, however, more privileged groups who became
increasingly dissatisfied during the decade, and who were
able to organize and take collective action to improve their
lot. Wheat farmers, who were producing the staple commodity on which the prosperity was founded, were convinced
that others were growing wealthy at their expense. The
more skilled industrial labourers begrudged the difference
between their wages and the owners' profits. The collective
action of each of these two groups reflects the growing
complexity of an interdependent society and the emerging
tensions of class conflicts.

Prairie farmers in this decade showed a remarkable talent
for collective action. In spite of their varied racial backgrounds, their linguistic and religious differences, and the
immediate problems of transforming a homestead into a
farm, these settlers quickly found that they shared common
interests. They all faced the challenge of a rigorous climate
and the dangers of drought, frost, and grasshoppers. They
grew the same crops for the same remote market, which
meant they shared the same suspicion that they were being
exploited by railways and elevator companies, or by manu-

facturers, bankers, and politicians, who seemed to control market conditions. By the end of the decade the sense of being an economic group had largely transcended the divisions of race and creed.

Farmers first organized to protect themselves against the most obvious form of exploitation. Grain elevators were an essential link in shipping wheat to the distant market. Farmers could sell their grain to the elevator company, or, if they had a thousand bushels or more, they could pay the elevator company to load their grain in a box-car for shipment to Winnipeg, where it would be sold through the Grain Exchange. Farmers were soon convinced that elevator companies were taking advantage of the situation by giving dishonest weights, offering low grades for the grain, and levying excessive charges for storage. Farmers who might have travelled ten miles with a wagon-load of wheat and who needed the money were in no position to refuse the offered price and take their wheat home again.

The most obvious grievances were eliminated by the federal Grain Act of 1900 which prohibited excessive handling and storage charges and appointed an inspector to prevent improper weighing and grading of the grain. Farmers, however, still believed that they were being exploited by the elevator companies. These companies were theoretically competitors for the farmers' wheat, and in most villages there were two or more elevators beside the railroad track. In practice there was no competition, for the companies had formed an association and offered identical prices and terms for the grain. Farmers were convinced that this association was a conspiracy against them but soon discovered that the law offered no redress because the courts ruled that it was not an 'undue' restraint of trade. Disillusioned by this decision, the farmers decided to take direct action.

E. A. Partridge provided the initiative. Partridge had come to the prairies from Great Britain in the 1880s, and had built a sod hut as his first home. He was a socialist who believed that the farmers were involved in an inevitable class struggle against the vested interests of capitalists and politicians, and although few farmers shared his philosophy their immediate sense of injustice was so intense that many responded to Partridge's agitation for collective action. It was agreed that a co-operative association should be formed to buy a seat on the Grain Exchange. Farmers could then sell their own wheat on the Exchange and end their dependence on the elevator companies.

This simple solution encountered a series of obstacles. The federal government first refused to incorporate the Grain Growers' Grain Company on a technicality, and the farmers' organization had to be satisfied with a more limited provincial charter. Then, after a seat on the Grain Exchange had been purchased, the officials of the Exchange disbarred the company on another technicality. The company was reinstated but only after a public outcry had persuaded the Manitoba government to exert some pressure on the Exchange. Farmers were more convinced than ever that the protection of their interests depended on their own collective action.

Collective action naturally meant political action in the prairie provinces, where most of the voters were farmers and where provincial governments reflected this fact. The seat on the Grain Exchange did nothing for farmers who did not grow enough wheat to ship a carload to Winnipeg; they still had to sell to the elevator companies. By the end of the decade some farmers were agitating for provincially owned elevators. The Manitoba government agreed to purchase and operate some elevators, and the Saskatchewan government appointed a royal commission to investigate the idea. On the prairies at least, collective action meant that provincial governments, whether Conservative or Liberal, quickly became farmers' governments.

The farmers' organizations were less effective in federal politics. Farmers had long argued that the protective tariff benefited Canadian manufacturers at their expense. Wheat producers had to sell their product abroad but they had to buy such things as farm machinery from Canadian manufacturers because the tariff excluded foreign competition. They saw little justification for a policy that prevented them from buying similar machinery in the United States at lower prices; it was easy to believe that manufacturers in eastern Canada were taking advantage of the monopoly that the tariff created. Local Grain Growers' associations and their organ, *The Grain Growers' Guide*, led a sustained attack against the policy of protection. The federal tariff policy, it was argued, was a form of economic imperialism designed by the vested interests of central Canada to hold the west in tutelage.

This version of the National Policy was not readily accepted at Ottawa. The national Conservative party had long been committed to the protective tariff and its position was not significantly modified during the decade. Westerners had more confidence in the federal Liberal party, which had free-trade traditions and was in office, but as years passed without major tariff reductions there was growing disillusionment with both national parties. The reins of political power, it seemed, were securely held by 'big business', and western protests were being ignored. 'The only hope of the farmers in Canada,' *The Grain Growers' Guide* asserted in 1910, 'is to realize that they have no more to expect from one political party than another. They must step aside and secure men to represent them who will stand out boldly in the interests of farmers at all times.' If the federal Conservatives and Liberals continued to represent eastern interests it might be necessary to organize another political party to represent the west.

By 1910, however, the Liberal government at Ottawa was at least aware of the danger of independent political action by the farmers. Sir Wilfrid Laurier made a western tour that year and was impressed by the petitions for tariff reduction that were presented at every stop. Later in the year a mass delegation of some eight hundred farmers came east with the same request; such a formidable demonstration by an organized pressure group was so unprecedented that the event became known as the 'Siege of Ottawa'. The readiness of the government to discuss a reciprocity agreement with the United States was clearly a response to this agitation.

IV

The farmers were not the only economic group to turn to collective action. The decade saw trade-union membership grow from some twenty thousand to more than one hundred and twenty thousand. Union activity was piecemeal and the benefits gained in one craft or one industry had little effect on the majority of unorganized workers, but some workers at least were responding to the tensions of an industrial society. More significant than the improvements in working conditions was the pattern of union affiliations that emerged, and the shaping of a government policy in industrial disputes.

The Canadian labour movement at the turn of the century was largely the northern expansion of the American labour movement. Although there were Canadian trade unions, most locals in Canada belonged to international unions with their headquarters in the United States. These 'international unions' can be explained by the earlier development of trade unions south of the border and by the fact that whether they lived north or south of the border, workers in the same crafts had the same problems and wanted the same working conditions. The political boundary, however, created serious complications. The Trades and Labour Congress of Canada had been formed to act as a spokesman for all trade unions in the country and to bring pressure on Canadian legislators for the benefit of all workers. Union rivalries in the United States, however, disrupted union activity in Canada. In 1902, in a test of strength within the Canadian Congress, the unions affiliated with the American Federation of Labor expelled Canadian unions if international unions of the same craft existed, and also expelled any international unions not affiliated with the Federation. The result was that from 1902 the Trades and Labour Congress was little more than a regional division of the American Federation of Labor.

American influence was not accepted without opposition. The national pride and the national ambitions of Canadians in the decade were shared by some Canadian workers. The Canadian Federation of Labour was founded by the Cana-

dian trade unions as a reaction against the subservience of
international unions to American leadership. Yet another
development was the organization of Catholic trade unions
among French-Canadian workers in Quebec. These locals
were usually organized and directed by a parish priest, and
the religious rather than secular concept of the rights of
workers was an illustration of the cultural difference between
English and French Canada. Like the Canadian Federation
of Labour, however, the Catholic unions had only a small
membership by the end of the decade. To the extent that
labour was organized in Canada, it was still an extension of
an American movement.

The federal government took an active interest in labour
problems in these years in spite of the weakness of trade
unions. This concern was not with organized labour directly.
An employer was not required by law to negotiate with a
union; he could dismiss union organizers and replace them
by more submissive workers at any time. But the government
did want to prevent strikes that might interfere with the
National Policy. A labour dispute involving railway workers,
for example, could disrupt the national economy; it is no
coincidence that the labour policy of the federal government
was first formulated to avert railway strikes.

W. L. Mackenzie King was the architect of this policy.
Mackenzie King was young, energetic, and ambitious, with
an active interest in industrial relations. As Deputy-Minister
of Labour in 1900, at the age of twenty-six, and later as the
first Minister of Labour, he had his ideas put on the statute-
books. King believed that strikes could be avoided if employers and workers behaved like reasonable men, for it
seemed obvious to him that both parties to a dispute would
suffer if work stopped. At the same time, King did not believe
in coercion; he saw that there could be no industrial stability
if either employers or workers were forced to make concessions against their will.

King's solution to this dilemma was government intervention to delay strikes until employers and workers had tried to
negotiate a settlement. The Railway Labour Disputes Act

of 1903 allowed the Minister of Labour to forbid a strike
until the dispute had been investigated by a board that he
appointed. The railway company and the workers then presented their arguments before the board. Neither party had
to accept the recommendations of the board – there would be
no direct coercion – but King believed that the public hearings would force each side to present a reasonable case and
that reasonable arguments on both sides would make a peaceful settlement possible. The publicity given to the investigation and to the recommendations of the board would also
help to persuade each party to reach an agreement.

A few years later this policy was extended. A coal-miners'
strike in Alberta in 1906 threatened to bank the fires in railway steam-engines and prairie homes. The Industrial Disputes Investigation Act of 1907 broadened the policy of compulsory investigation to include mines and public utilities.

This form of government intervention in labour disputes
continued to be the policy of the federal government for
many years to come. It did not prevent strikes, because the
company or the workers could refuse to accept the recommendations of the board. But by permitting the workers to
present their case effectively it did give some recognition to
the rights of labour and helped to eliminate the worst forms
of exploitation by employers. In later years, organized labour
would object to a policy that might prevent strikes from
being called at the most effective moment, but in this decade
government mediation in any form was a radical innovation.

V

Derrière deux grands boeufs ou deux lourds percherons,
L'homme marche courbé, dans le pré solitaire,
Ses poignets musculeux rivés aux mancherons
De la charrue ouvrant le ventre de la terre.

Il s'imagine voir le blé gonfler sa grange;
Il songe que ses pas sont comptés par un ange,
Et que la laboureur collabore avec Dieu.

William Chapman

This scene of rural bliss has little in common with the English-Canadian poet's metaphor of a dauntless spirit outstretched for flight, and during this decade the contrast in the attitudes of French and English Canadians was to become even more marked. French Canadians did not share the nation-building enthusiasm of their compatriots because to them prairie settlement and industrialization seemed remote and almost irrelevant. Instead of sharing the optimistic vision of spiralling national prosperity, many of them believed that nothing in the French-Canadian way of life had changed, and, what was more, they believed that nothing would or should change. The few who sensed that their society was being affected deplored the changes. Life on the remote prairies or in industrial cities seemed morally inferior to the idealized family life in the rural Quebec parish. French Canadians, always conscious of their distinctive identity, were becoming more defensive and more than ever determined to preserve their traditional way of life.

The great migration to the prairies in this decade did not include many French Canadians. There had been a time when some of their leaders had hoped to create a second Quebec in the Canadian west. French-speaking Roman Catholics had been an important group in Manitoba when it became a province in 1870, and the provincial constitution had included guarantees for their language and for Roman Catholic schools. In the years that followed, however, few French Canadians had migrated west and the English-speaking majority in the province had revoked these guarantees. Manitoba had become a second Ontario rather than a second Quebec, and the bitter controversy over the Manitoba Schools Question had shown that Manitobans were determined to live in an English-speaking province with non-sectarian schools. It was clear to French Canadians that their form of Canadian society was not welcome in the western province.

Nor was there any warmer welcome in the newly created provinces of Saskatchewan and Alberta in 1905. Provincial status involved little change for the people of the Northwest

Territories. The Territorial Assembly already controlled local administration, having won a form of responsible government, and had already established English as the language of the Assembly and the courts. French Canada had little interest in the discussions as to whether there should be one province or two, whether the federal government would retain control of Crown lands, and how large the provincial subsidies would be, and the final decisions on these issues roused no serious opposition. The federal government created two provinces and retained Crown lands – federal control of land policy would ensure that free homesteads would still be given to new settlers – but in exchange the new provinces received generous subsidies. Only the schools question provoked heated debate.

From the point of view of the people in the Territories there was no problem. A series of Territorial Ordinances had transformed the original dual system of Protestant and Catholic schools into one in which a single department of education administered both 'public' and 'separate' schools, with little difference between the two except in the teaching of religion. Roman Catholic students could be taught by Roman Catholic teachers in the separate schools but these teachers were expected to qualify for a teaching certificate by attending the same normal school as the public school teachers, and for the teaching of most subjects they used the same textbooks as the public schools. The people in the Territories had accepted this modified system of separate schools without any serious criticism and it was taken for granted that the same system would continue after provincial status was conceded.

Sir Wilfrid Laurier, however, was not satisfied with this arrangement. He feared that the Protestant majority in the new provinces might introduce administrative changes in the future that would further reduce the Roman Catholic character of the separate schools; the events in Manitoba ten years before convinced him that the minority needed a constitutional guarantee of their rights. Laurier did not raise the question of the language of instruction – he seems to have taken it for granted that the west would be an English-speaking region—but he did insist on a constitutional guarantee that there would be no interference with the religious character of the separate schools. Roman Catholics in this part of Canada were to be assured of schools of their own faith. Thus the first draft of the legislation creating the new provinces was designed to protect the separate schools from secular pressures by the provincial departments of education.

This guarantee almost defeated Laurier's government. Sir Clifford Sifton argued that this legislation would really restore the completely separate and dual system of schools that the people in the Territories had already rejected. Sifton himself resigned from the government in protest. W. S. Fielding, the Minister of Finance, threatened to resign. Robert Borden and the English-speaking Conservatives denounced this interference with the right of the provinces to choose the educational system they preferred, and strong protests came from the Territories. On the other hand, many French Canadians insisted on this guarantee for the Roman Catholic minority in the west; English-Canadian opposition to the legislation only confirmed their fears that without such a guarantee separate schools would be suppressed.

The government survived because Sir Wilfrid Laurier yielded to English-Canadian pressure. He did not believe that any constitutional guarantee would be effective if the majority in a province was not prepared to accept separate schools. In the long run he was sure that minority rights depended on the tolerance of the majority and he was sure that there would be even less tolerance if he tried to coerce the majority. He therefore introduced an amendment to the legislation which declared that the existing separate school system would be preserved but which left the administration of the schools under the control of the new provincial governments. Most of the Liberals, whether English- or French-Canadian, accepted this compromise and the amended legislation was approved.

The compromise was accepted but it was not applauded in French Canada. French Canadians could not share in the

national enthusiasm for prairie settlement if English was to
be the dominant language of the region and if separate
schools were to be almost indistinguishable from non-
confessional public schools. Henri Bourassa, the grandson
of Louis Joseph Papineau and a brilliant young French-
Canadian orator, had little confidence in the tolerance of the
majority. He had tried to persuade Laurier to force the
original legislation through the House of Commons even if
it meant the resignation of many English-Canadian Liberals
from the party, and the amendment which Laurier called
a compromise Bourassa called a surrender to Protestant
fanatics. Bourassa was joined by French-Canadian Conservatives in the House, who denounced Laurier's policy and who
also denounced the official policy of their own party for the
same reason.

The bitterness at being treated like aliens and foreigners in
the western provinces of their own country survived long
after the political crisis had ended. The French-Canadian
Conservatives under F. D. Monk seriously considered separating from the English Conservatives in protest, and the
break came a few years later with the next crisis. And
Bourassa reported that many French Canadians had come to
believe that only in Quebec could they be themselves:

> I regret every time I go back to my province to find develop-
> ing that feeling that Canada is not Canada for all Canadians.
> We are bound to come to the conclusion that Quebec is our
> only country because we have no liberty elsewhere.

VI

Even in Quebec, however, prosperity had brought many
changes. Montreal was both an industrial and a transportation centre, and the growing importance of transatlantic
commerce, which was one aspect of the 'wheat boom', meant
that Montreal, as Canada's major Atlantic port, was directly
affected by prairie settlement. One visitor has left this impression of his first sight of Montreal after a voyage from
Europe:

Montreal! There is the city, swathed in smoke, like Sheffield itself. Through the dust-pall pierce factory chimneys and church spires and mammoth grain elevators. The docks are full of shipping, the winches are busy, and the cranes swing. Bales and machinery are being hauled from that ship. Grain is rushing in a yellow stream into that. Cattle are hoisted into another. Lumber rafts surround a fourth. There is the uproar of a busy town. Before you land you hear the shrill buzz of the racing electric cars, and on the great bridge spanning the river, nearly two miles wide, rumbles an express of the Grand Trunk Railroad.

But Montreal was not French Canada. Some fifty years earlier half the population of this city had been English-Canadian; it was now predominantly French-Canadian in numbers, but the French Canadians, mainly labourers who had migrated from rural areas, had little influence in the city. The railways, the banks, the commercial houses, the industrial firms – all were English-speaking institutions, owned and directed by English Canadians or by Englishmen or Americans. The workers might be French Canadians but they had no voice in the management or the policies of these firms. A prominent Frenchman noted that

Visitors may pass whole weeks there, frequenting hotels, banks, shops, railway stations, without ever imagining for a moment that the town is French by a great majority of its inhabitants. English Society affects unconsciousness of the fact, and bears itself exactly as though it had no French neighbours. They seem to regard Montreal as their property.

Montreal was still an English enclave in French Canada.

French Canadians showed little resentment at this alien domination of Montreal. French-Canadian leaders, then as always, were intent on *la survivance*, the preservation of French-Canadian society. They feared that the distinctive qualities of this society could not survive in an urban and industrial world. Montreal meant more than the dangerous association with English Protestants; it also meant a materialistic way of life which was a threat to the ties of family and faith. As an influential churchman said in 1902:

Our mission is not so much to manipulate money as to
wrestle with ideas; it consists less in lighting factory fires
than in keeping alight the luminous hearth of religion and
making it shine from afar. . . . While our rivals claim . . .
supremacy over industry and finance, we are eager above all
for the honor of the faith and the victory of apostleship.

With this view of the destiny of French Canada, Montreal
was alien territory and the French Canadians there seemed
already lost to French-Canadian society. The Quebec in
which they could be themselves lay outside of Montreal.

The champions of *la survivance*–churchmen, politicians,
and journalists, many of whom lived in Montreal–reacted to
the dangers to French-Canadian traditions by extolling the
virtues of rural life. They appealed to their compatriots to
remain untainted by contact with the English language, the
Protestant religion, and the materialistic way of life, and they
painted an idyllic picture of French Canadians tilling the
soil and going to mass, with all the moral values of a close-knit
family life. To the leaders of French Canada, *la survivance*
meant the preservation of this rural society.

This ideal had one serious flaw. The children of large
families grew up and had families of their own and the family
farm could not support them all. For generations there had
been a steady exodus from rural Quebec to the textile towns
of New England. As Franco-Americans, these emigrants lived
in an English-speaking and urban world; it seemed only a
matter of time before they lost their language and their faith.
In this decade Montreal probably absorbed a higher proportion of the rural emigrants, but Montreal was little better
than New England to the defenders of *la survivance*.

To most French Canadians the answer seemed obvious.
The sons who left their fathers' farms must clear more land
and establish new rural communities in which the traditions
of French-Canadian society would be preserved. This had
been the solution advocated by French-Canadian leaders for
generations. It had been the policy of George Cartier, of
Bishop Bourget, of Curé Labelle, and of Honoré Mercier,

and it became the policy of Sir Wilfrid Laurier and Henri Bourassa. The National Transcontinental railway was seen by Laurier as a colonization railway opening up new areas south of the St. Lawrence between Moncton and Quebec City, as well as in northern Quebec and in northern Ontario. European immigrants, he argued, would go to the prairies. Only the French Canadians were prepared to carve farms out of forests, and hence 'all the forest lands in Quebec and even in Ontario are the patrimony of French Canadians'.

It would be many years before the limitations of this colonization policy were understood. The soil that produced the northern forests did not yield bountiful cereal crops, and August droughts and September frosts made every spring-time seeding a gamble. The settlers who moved north had to supplement their income in the early years with pick and shovel on railroad construction gangs or with axe and saw in logging camps, and even after their farms were cleared they still depended on winter work to survive. Louis Hémon, writing just after the end of the decade, described the life of the Chapdelaines in the Lake St. John area, the three sons spending the winters in logging camps to earn the only cash the family received, and returning in the spring to 'make land':

> The forest still pressed hard upon the buildings they had put up a few years earlier: the little square house, the barn of planks that gaped apart, the stable built of blackened logs and chinked with rags and earth. Between the scanty fields of their clearing and the darkly encircling woods lay a broad stretch which the axe had but half-heartedly attacked. A few living trees had been cut for timber, and the dead ones, sawn and split, fed the great stove for a whole winter; but the place was a rough tangle of stumps and interlacing roots, of fallen trees too far rotted to burn, of others dead but still erect amid the older scrub.

And yet after a few more years of toil, when the farm was cleared, the Chapdelaines would still be off to the *chantiers* in the winter in order to survive. Small wonder that the

Maria Chapdelaines of the province were sometimes tempted by the distant glamour of a crowded city.

Nonetheless, the colonization of northern Quebec and adjacent territories remained the accepted solution to the problems of French Canada. Henri Bourassa was one of the advocates of northern settlement. Bourassa was not a narrow French-Canadian nationalist, for he believed that Canada should be a bicultural country – a country in which French and English communities should have equal rights from the Atlantic to the Pacific. But he was sadly disillusioned by the debate over separate schools in Saskatchewan and Alberta. In 1907 he withdrew from federal politics to concentrate on the problems of colonization in the province of Quebec. Here at least was a part of Canada where French Canadians could be themselves.

Bourassa knew that these northern pioneers had grievances, but instead of blaming poor soil he blamed the provincial government at Quebec. He believed that this government was impeding colonization by leasing large areas to lumber or pulp-and-paper companies and thus excluding settlers. Bourassa won popular support by championing the rights of the colonists. His campaign drew support from those who wanted to strengthen a rural French-Canadian society, as well as from the French-Canadian nationalists who resented the activities of English-Canadian and American corporations in northern Quebec. If the other provinces were to be English-Canadian, rural Quebec at least should remain French.

Bourassa did not overthrow the provincial Liberal government by his attacks but he did alter the political balance within French Canada. He and a few young Liberal followers found ready allies within the provincial Conservative party. The collaboration of Bourassa and Monk on the schools question was soon duplicated by the collaboration of Bourassa and the French-Canadian Conservatives in Quebec on the colonization issue. This alliance was a protest against both of the national parties, which always seemed to heed English-Canadian demands and to ignore the interests of French

Canada. It was, in fact, the beginning of a sectional French-Canadian party and its emergence was a response to the growing isolation and estrangement of French Canadians from their English-speaking compatriots.

This isolation might have reduced friction between the two societies except that the isolation could never be complete. French Canadians, like the farmers in western Canada, found that they were affected by the policies at the federal as well as the provincial level. In the past the divisions between English Canadians and French Canadians at Ottawa had been blurred by the structure of the national political parties, in which cultural differences were tempered by party loyalties. The alliance between Bourassa and Monk and the Quebec Conservatives, however, meant that the party loyalties for this group coincided with French-Canadian loyalties, and within the federal Conservative party the withdrawal of the French-Canadian wing meant that this party was more and more an English-Canadian party. A clash between the two societies on a federal issue would be less easy to cushion because of this changing political alignment.

VII

It was not long before the clash occurred. Early in 1909 the British government announced that the tremendous expansion of the German navy constituted a critical threat to British security. The development of the torpedo had transformed naval tactics, and the emphasis was now on large capital ships with big guns that could engage the enemy at long range. The development of the Dreadnought, with its strength, speed, and twelve-inch guns, made older battleships obsolete. By 1909 German construction of this new type of capital ship threatened to outdistance British construction. Public opinion forced the British government to undertake a major naval construction program, with eight new Dreadnoughts to be laid down in 1909 and a total of eighteen within three years. The 'naval scare' of 1909 quickly became an issue in the British Dominions. The Royal Navy had always been the first line of imperial defence and the tremendous cost of this construction program convinced many people, both in Great Britain and in the Dominions, that the cost should be shared. In Canada, the question was whether the federal government would respond to this pressure.

Sir Wilfrid Laurier had successfully avoided any naval expenditures until 1909. The British Admiralty had pressed for contributions to the Royal Navy at the Colonial Conference of 1902, arguing that 'the sea is all one and the British Navy therefore must be all one'. Laurier however had argued that such contributions would be incompatible with Dominion self-government. How could the Canadian government control its defence expenditures and its defence policy if it had to pay levies to the Royal Navy? He admitted that Canada should take more responsibility for naval defence but announced that his government was contemplating a local naval force. Nothing was done in the years that followed because there had been no popular support in Canada for any form of defence expenditures. Since the choice between a contribution to the Royal Navy or building a separate Canadian navy was certain to be controversial, Laurier preferred to procrastinate. The 'naval scare' of 1909 forced the government to act.

The Naval Service Act of 1910 was Laurier's response; there would be a Canadian navy which at the same time might become part of the Royal Navy. This compromise was designed to satisfy most Canadians but at the same time it accurately reflected Laurier's view of the proper relations between Canada and Great Britain. Laurier was a staunch defender of Canadian autonomy but to him autonomy did not mean separation from the Empire. He believed that the Royal Navy contributed to Canadian security, and if British naval supremacy was in danger that it would be in the interests of Canada 'to support England with all our might'. To him, Canadian autonomy meant that Canadians would decide whether to participate in a British war – there would be no automatic commitment – but it also meant, in case of a major war, that Canadians would decide to be at Britain's side.

The Naval Service Act therefore declared that the Canadian government had the authority to place the Canadian naval force at the disposal of the British Admiralty in time of war, and the naval force itself was designed so that it could be easily integrated with the British army. The Act thus asserted a Canadian autonomy that was neither colonial subordination nor national independence.

This compromise was unacceptable to the Conservative Opposition. English Canadians were becoming more conscious of their ties with Great Britain; this was the era of Kipling and jingoism, and it was also a time when the major role played by the British market and British capital in the 'wheat boom' strengthened the emotional ties. Many expressed horror at the implication that Canada might refuse to participate in some British war. R. L. Borden argued that 'such inaction or declaration will amount virtually to a declaration of independence'. Other Conservatives argued that the new naval force would be inadequate – they called it 'Laurier's tin-pot navy' – and demanded a direct donation of the cost of two Dreadnoughts to Great Britain. In effect, the Conservative Opposition was advocating a closer commitment to participation in British wars than Laurier was willing to accept.

Laurier's compromise, however, was equally unacceptable to many in French Canada. French Canadians had few ties with Europe; as Bourassa said, they were French in the same way that the Americans were English. To them, the attachment of English Canadians to Great Britain was a form of colonial subservience and a proof of their failure to develop a true loyalty to Canada. In 1899 Bourassa had denounced Canadian participation in the South African war because he felt Canada's interests were not involved, although at the time most of his compatriots had been able to tolerate the

idea of a Canadian contingent of volunteers. French Canadians were less tolerant a decade later. Not only was their
isolation more complete but they had become more suspi-
cious of English-Canadian motives. F. D. Monk argued in
the House of Commons that Canada was in no danger of
attack and so the only possible reason for spending money
on a Canadian Navy was to strengthen the Royal Navy. The
Canadian navy might be Canadian in time of peace but
English Canadians would make sure that it was British in
time of war. In Quebec Bourassa joined Monk in denouncing the Act as a betrayal of Canadian autonomy. In contrast
to Borden's position, these French-Canadian leaders were
advocating a greater separation from Great Britain than
Laurier was willing to accept.

The Drummond-Arthabaska by-election in the fall of 1910
showed that many French Canadians shared the suspicions
of Bourassa and Monk. Laurier opened the constituency to
challenge the opposition in Quebec to the Naval Service Act,
but the opposition proved to be unexpectedly strong. The
constituency, long a Liberal stronghold, elected an independent candidate who had campaigned against Laurier's
naval policy. The federal election of 1911 would prove that
this was not an isolated incident. French Canadians, like the
western farmers, were ready to support a third party because
neither of the two national parties seemed sensitive to their
special outlook.

VIII

In retrospect it must have seemed to most Canadians that
the decade had justified the boast that the twentieth century
would belong to them. The 'Dominion from sea to sea' was
no longer a mere geographical or political expression; physical regions with distinctive natural features and provinces
with separate histories were now bound together by interdependent economic activity. New railways were crossing the
continent and nurturing new towns and cities, and the 'wheat

boom' dispelled the fears of earlier decades that Canada was an artificial creation that could never become a nation.

But although Canadians in 1910 no longer doubted that the federal union would survive, they were still uncertain about the future. Prosperity had linked regions but it had not erased the divisions. The context of regional rivalries had changed but the divergence of regional aims and aspirations had not been resolved. Material progress had not created a sense of common purpose or common identity. National unity continued to be the slogan of every Canadian politician because unity of purpose was still no more than an elusive goal.

6. Through the First World War

ROGER GRAHAM

At the outset of the second decade of the twentieth century, in the late autumn of an age, violent winds of trouble were beginning to blow in distant quarters of the globe. But, accustomed to relative order and tranquillity, conditioned by good fortune and their prevailing outlook on life to anticipate continued progress, the Canadians had no more reason to guess than most people, and perhaps much less than many, that mankind was about to pass over one of the great watersheds of history into a time of war and revolution, of profound moral and intellectual unsettlement, and of almost unremitting anxiety.

Of course they were not oblivious to all that was happening in the world. There was much newspaper talk, for example, of the ambitions of Kaiser Wilhelm II, self-styled

'Admiral of the Atlantic', whose imperial German navy challenged British mastery of the seas. Disquieting reports came from places far away and only vaguely apprehended: St. Petersburg and Belgrade; Bosnia and Bulgaria; Salonika, Constantinople, and Fez. But in the view of most Canadians, these clouds appeared small, on a remote horizon. The naval challenge struck closest to home, and they argued about it heatedly, but it seemed inconceivable that Germany, for all her military might, her industrial capacity, and her imperial swagger, could successfully dispute the sea supremacy of the vast maritime empire of Great Britain. As for the mad ambitions and absurd rivalries of the Balkan kingdoms and principalities, the chronic violence and obscure intrigues of North Africa, the dim, mysterious rumblings in the Russian Empire, these could hardly be of real danger to a country as securely situated as Canada. Minor wars might be fought but major crises would be averted or, if not averted, solved by diplomatic accommodations. With power balanced between two rival alliances of great European states a large, all-consuming conflict was hardly imaginable. So it doubtless seemed to most Canadians in that year of grace 1911; so it seemed in the years thereafter until the news from Sarajevo destroyed the illusion in 1914 and brought an epoch to an end.

For Canada, these were years of hope abounding, of spacious visions and happy expectations. The population was growing at an unparalleled rate, thanks chiefly to the swelling wave of immigration that had begun to roll about the turn of the century and was now approaching the crest it would reach in 1913, when over 400,000 people, the biggest number ever, settled in Canada. A large proportion of these newcomers found their way into the great, sparsely settled stretches of the prairie provinces, that 'last, best west' of which Sir Wilfrid Laurier had spoken, thus adding flesh and sinew to the thin frame of the country. Harvests, production, and construction were all increasing prodigiously. The most striking accomplishment was the building—with generous public financial assistance—of two new transcontinental railways to serve what, with more enthusiasm than good judgement (they fell on evil days a little later and had to be nationalized), were thought to be the needs of a rapidly developing, increasingly prosperous nation. One could not guess that the boom would shortly end, to be revived only by the grim demands of war; one could not anticipate the fact that easy optimism and confident faith would soon give way to doubts and sullen disillusionment, and the near-fracture of a country that in 1911 looked so fit and so secure.

Nor was it to be imagined when that year began that a startling political upset was in the offing. The decade, in fact, was bounded at either end by a political milestone, the defeat of Laurier at its start and the retirement of his successor, Sir Robert Borden, as it drew to a finish. The Laurier government looked as strong when 1911 opened as any government had a right to be after fourteen consecutive years in power. The Liberal party had won four general elections in a row, won them handily, and Laurier himself had come to be almost as much a national institution as a mere leader of men. With the country progressing splendidly there appeared to be no compelling reason for a change of government, and yet, before 1911 was over, Laurier was defeated. He lost because of fears created by two of his major decisions. Both decisions had a bearing on Canada's relations with Great Britain and one bore on the equally explosive subject of her relations with the United States; both therefore touched the emotions and aroused passionate debate.

The first was Laurier's naval policy. As an alternative to direct contributions of men and money to strengthen the imperial fleet, of the sort advocated for some years past by the British Admiralty, he proposed that Canada assume responsibility for her naval security with a navy of her own, which, however, might be placed at the disposal of Great Britain in time of emergency. It was a compromise and it caused widespread dissatisfaction. Criticisms came from two opposite directions. There were many in English-speaking

Canada who, while not necessarily against a separate Canadian navy in principle, believed that only by outright cash contributions to build up British naval power could Canada effectively aid in meeting the immediate and actual danger, the menacing growth of German strength on the seas. To them Laurier's policy was ineffectual and unrealistic, a weak-kneed surrender to anti-British elements in the nation. The policy was attacked with equal bitterness but for quite contrary reasons by the French-Canadian Nationalists, led by Henri Bourassa. In their view the establishment of a navy under the terms of Laurier's Naval Service Act of 1910 was hardly less obnoxious than the gifts of money so much desired by the Admiralty and so zealously advocated by many Canadians. In the absence of any conceivable threat to the naval security of the country, they argued, the expense of acquiring and maintaining a naval force would be unjustified. Worse than that, possession of such a force would needlessly involve Canada in imperial adventures that were no concern of hers, especially since it was stipulated that Canadian ships and their crews might be handed over to Britain in the event of war. This last feature of the policy convinced them that Laurier was, as they had long suspected, *un vendu*, that he had sold out to the imperialists and betrayed his own people. These, by and large, were also the opinions on the matter expressed by F. D. Monk, the leading French-speaking Conservative in federal politics.

The second of Laurier's fateful decisions at that juncture was to discuss with the Americans the possibility of reciprocity in trade between Canada and the United States. Thus was revived a project that for nearly half a century, ever since the abrogation of the Reciprocity Treaty of 1854, Canadians had talked about a great deal and from time to time attempted unsuccessfully to promote. Discussions were succeeded by actual negotiations and the result was a formal agreement which was to be implemented by concurrent legislation in the two countries. It provided for free trade between them in natural products, as well as in a selected list of semi-finished and fully manufactured articles, and for

reciprocal tariff reductions on a number of other goods as
well. These arrangements were approved by the American
Congress, which more than once in the past had balked at
reciprocity with Canada, but in the Parliament at Ottawa
and in various parts of the Dominion a formidable antagonism to the scheme began to take shape. The parliamentary
Conservative party seemed at first to be somewhat discon-
certed by the agreement – as much so as the government was
pleased with it, for its terms looked very favourable to Canada. However, as evidence of opposition mounted and as
signs appeared of a serious split in the Liberal party over the
issue, with a group of prominent Toronto Liberal businessmen issuing a manifesto denouncing the agreement, the
Opposition in Parliament began a filibuster against the
scheme that was carried on in the midst of an increasingly
acrimonious and emotional debate across English-speaking
Canada.

Faced with resourceful obstruction of his measure in the
House of Commons and without a closure rule enabling him
to bring it to a vote, Laurier at length decided to appeal to
the country, and Parliament was dissolved. In the ensuing
election campaign critics of the agreement attacked it not so
much on purely economic grounds as because it would bring
Canada too much into the orbit of the United States, would
in fact place her political independence in jeopardy. It was
a disloyal policy, they contended, likely to lead to the severance of Canada's ties with the mother country and her
annexation to the United States, a charge given some truth
by the numerous annexationist statements made by men of
some prominence in American public life and by certain
American newspapers. Meanwhile Quebec was ringing with
denunciations of Laurier's naval policy. There the Nationalists made common cause with the Conservatives against the
Liberal party, with the result that Laurier's hold on his own
province, the foundation of his long power, was seriously
weakened. Thanks to this, to their gains in some other provinces, and to their near sweep of Ontario, the Conservatives
came into office with a commanding majority.

The new Prime Minister, Robert Laird Borden, was a Nova Scotian who had become leader of the Conservative party in 1901. Less elegant and less brilliant than Laurier, he had little of the urbane charm and eloquence of his great adversary. However, Borden brought distinguished gifts of his own to the office: patience and persistence, courage and common sense, strong convictions about duty and honour, and solid integrity. He was to need all these personal resources in the years of storm and stress during which he led his country.

Borden's troubles began to appear even before the outbreak of war in the summer of 1914. Most important in the immediate political sense was the loss of much of the support in Quebec that he had enjoyed in the election. The Conservative-Nationalist alliance in that province was an unnatural union that began to dissolve shortly after the purpose for which it had been formed – the defeat of the Laurier administration – was achieved. Its dissolution was hastened, though not entirely caused, by the decision of the new government to replace the Laurier naval plan with an outright cash contribution to the enlargement of the British navy. Parliament was to be asked to appropriate $35,000,000 for the construction of three large battleships which would be units in a single imperial fleet. This was strenuously objected to by Monk, who held the Public Works portfolio. Failing to persuade the Prime Minister to submit the question to the voters in a referendum, Monk resigned from the Cabinet. The alienation of Quebec from the Borden government had begun. As it turned out, though, the contribution of the three ships was not made. Borden's Naval Air Bill ran into stormy weather in the House of Commons, the Liberals obstructing its passage just as the Conservatives had that of reciprocity in 1911. With the aid of a new closure rule, the handiwork of a young, ambitious, and able back-bencher from the west by the name of Arthur Meighen, the Bill was finally approved by the Commons, only to be rejected in the Senate, where the Liberals were in control.

II

Although the naval issue revealed a deep cleavage in Canada over the general subject of imperial relations, when war finally broke out in Europe in 1914, Canadians were united in believing that they must join forces with Britain and her allies. With the British declaration of war on Germany on August 4, Canada was then automatically at war as well, and most Canadians heartily approved of this arrangement. It was thought that the war would be over and won in short order, would in fact be something of a glorious adventure. Few yet understood the extent to which the resources and the unity of the country would be tested. There was much display of patriotic fervour as young men, a large proportion of them recent immigrants from Great Britain, flocked to join up.

Everywhere in the Dominion people greeted the war with enthusiasm; crowds sang patriotic songs in the streets, and the Minister of Militia and Defence, Sir Sam Hughes, was deluged with offers of volunteers. Hughes, who always knew better than his professional advisers, discarded the carefully prepared mobilization plan for the Canadian Militia and substituted a scheme of his own whereby a Canadian contingent would be mobilized at Valcartier Camp near Quebec City. All during August and September volunteers poured into Valcartier, where, in spite of the bungling and bombast of the Minister, they were formed into the battalions of the Canadian Expeditionary Force. On the 3rd of October 32,665 men embarked for England.

At home the economy, which had lagged somewhat in a short pre-war recession, was mobilized to supply small arms and ammunition, boots and uniforms, food, metals and timber, medicines and bandages, horses and wagons. All across the land photographers' shutters clicked so that soldiers and their families might have something to remember each other by.

In England through that autumn and winter, the First Canadian Contingent trained in the wet misery of Salisbury

Plain, and, although the soldiers did not know it, the rain, mud, and cold of that desolate camp was to be a fitting introduction to the campaigns that lay ahead. Early in February the First Canadian Division, under Lieutenant-General E. A. H. Alderson, a British officer, arrived in France and was gradually introduced into the fighting line in the Armentières sector.

April 1915 brought the Canadians their first major battle. On the 22nd the Germans suddenly attacked in the Ypres Salient, advancing behind yellow clouds of chlorine gas which rolled over the French colonial divisions on the Canadian left. A gaping hole was torn in the Allied front, but the green troops from the Dominion stood firm. The Canadian line extended to provide a thin screen across the gap, and the German drive was halted. The fighting at this second battle of Ypres was a bitter foretaste of the heroism and sacrifice that was to come, for in four days Canadian casualties totalled 6,037.

Less than a month later the Canadian Division was back in the thick of the battle. In the middle of May at Festubert and in June at Givenchy, the Canadians were launched in suicidal frontal attacks against impregnable positions. Such attacks were to be the hallmark of Allied strategy for the next three years. In September 1915 a second division arrived in France, and in December a third division was formed.

The First Division had had its baptism of fire at Second Ypres. In April 1916 the Second Division was thrown into an equally confused and desperate battle for possession of the St. Eloi craters. The troops fought with their usual courage and tenacity, but bad staff work and inadequate commanders prevented them from gaining firm possession of the worthless holes in the ground that were their objective. The following month Lieutenant-General Sir Julian Byng replaced Alderson as Canadian Corps Commander.

The year 1916 was to be marked by a tremendous Allied effort on the Western Front. The Germans had been pressing the French hard at Verdun, and the British Commander-

in-Chief, Sir Douglas Haig, intended to relieve this pressure
by breaking through the German lines on the Somme. Before
Haig was ready to mount his great offensive, the Germans
launched a number of limited spoiling attacks, one of which
overran some Canadian positions near Sanctuary Wood and
Mount Sorrel. The Canadians were in no mood to accept
such reverses, and on June 13 the First Division, attacking
through a black night filled with driving rain, recaptured
the lost ground.

For the British and Dominion troops, the history of the
remainder of 1916 can be summed up in two ominous words
– 'the Somme'. Fortunately, the Canadians had no part in
the débâcle of the 1st of July, when Haig's soldiers advanced
under a bright blue sky to meet the bloodiest repulse ever to
befall British arms. The Newfoundland Regiment was there
on the fatal first day of the Somme, being practically wiped
out at Beaumont Hamel before the soldiers so much as
reached the German wire, but the Canadian Corps was not
committed to the holocaust until September. By then Haig
was no longer aiming at a breakthrough and the offensive
had degenerated into bitter, bloody, step-by-step slogging
of a type never before witnessed on any battlefield. The
Canadians attacked again and again – at Pozières Ridge,
Flers-Courcelette, the Sugar Factory, Fabeck Graben, and
Regina Trench. They gained their objectives, or most of
them, but when the winter rains at last forced Haig to call
a halt, the Canadians had lost 24,029 men.

By the end of 1916 it looked as though the war might go
on forever and in all the belligerent nations the mood of the
people had hardened into a sort of angry despair. The peace
proposals that Pope Benedict XV made in December were
rejected out of hand by both sides, for both the Allies and
the Central Powers were determined to settle for nothing
less than victory. In Canada too this feeling was apparent,
although by no means all Canadians were deeply committed
to winning the war. Profiteering scandals rocked the government; farmers and industrial workers were making unprecedented earnings; and angry voices in Quebec were begin-

ning to repeat the Pope's condemnation of the conflict as 'this senseless carnage'. The men in France had little in common with the aspirations and emotions of the people at home. The daily tasks of the battle-zone demanded all the soldiers' energy, but by now the Canadian Corps had already been welded into a magnificent fighting machine with a corporate pride and confidence that later events were fully to justify.

Easter Monday, April 9, 1917, brought the first Allied-offensive success of the war on the Western Front. On that day the entire Canadian Corps of four divisions stormed forward in the early dawn against the imposing heights of Vimy Ridge. With driving sleet and snow at their backs, the Canadian soldiers crashed through three successive lines of German defences and reached the crest of the ridge by mid-morning. Before nightfall the name of Canada was ringing around the world, for the Allies, after so long being starved of success, were inclined to exaggerate the importance of this splendid, but minor, victory. Vimy Ridge became a symbol of Canadian achievement, and the pride engendered on the bloody slopes of that commanding hill did much to bring Canada to full nationhood.

That summer Sir Douglas Haig was resolved to strike again in the west. With irrational confidence he still hoped to achieve the final breakthrough that had so long eluded him. The British offensive was to be launched across the most difficult terrain on the Continent, the undulating low-lands beyond Ypres around Passchendaele. As a diversion, the Canadian Corps, now commanded by a Canadian, Sir Arthur Currie, was ordered to capture Hill 70 near Arras. On August 15 the Canadians took the hill in a dashing assault and held it firmly against all counter-attacks. Indeed, from the capture of Vimy Ridge on, the Canadian Corps invariably gained its objective every time it was committed to battle. Never-theless, the fighting at Hill 70 had been costly. In ten days Canadian casualties totalled 9,198.

Worse was to come. Although Haig's Passchendaele offen-sive had met with no appreciable success, he persisted in his

attacks long after all hope of victory had disappeared. The
British had begun attacking on July 31 but there had
been long pauses—coinciding, ironically, with the brightest,
dustiest weather—in August and September. The autumn
rains set in by the evening of October 7 and quickly turned
the shell-drenched landscape into a muddy morass where
movement was all but impossible. This did not prevent Haig
from sending the Canadians to the Ypres Salient or from
committing them to action on October 26. The nature of
the fighting that autumn about Passchendaele defies adequate description. Men struggled forward to attack through
waist-deep mud and icy water; the wounded often slipped
off the greasy boardwalks to drown or smother in the mud;
and all the while the Germans, who held the higher ground,
saturated the entire area with shell-fire. Yet the Canadians
struggled agonizingly forward to capture each successive
objective. The last Canadian troops were not relieved in the
Salient until November 20, by which time they had taken
the ruins of Passchendaele village and were the possessors of
an insignificant area of flooded swamp. The cost to the Corps
had been 15,654 casualties.

By now, however, the war was drawing towards its
climax. Russia, torn by revolution, made a separate peace
with Germany in December, and large numbers of German
troops were freed from the Eastern Front for deployment in
the west. The United States had entered the conflict on the
Allied side in April, but it would be midsummer of 1918
before significant numbers of American troops could take
their place in the fighting line. Therefore, the spring of 1918
was a crucial time for the Central Powers. The German High
Command decided to launch a last desperate offensive in the
hope of winning the war before the weight of American manpower and industrial production could make itself felt. The
German attacks began in March; great holes were immediately torn in the British front and the Allied line bent alarmingly back towards Paris. For the first time since the bright,
adventurous summer of 1914 it appeared as though Germany
might win the war within a matter of days.

During all this desperate fighting, the Canadian Corps was held in reserve, but when the German offensive was at last halted and the time for counter-attack came, the Canadians again formed the spearhead. The great counter-blow was launched on the morning of August 8 near Amiens. Canadian, British, Australian, and French divisions, utilizing surprise for the first time in an unimaginative four years, broke cleanly through the attenuated German lines and advanced joyously into open country. The battle of Amiens convinced the German High Command that the war was lost and that peace would have to be made. The end was now in sight, and all ranks of the Canadian Corps could sense that victory was almost in their grasp. Yet bloody, bitter battles still remained to be fought. The Canadian Corps was continuously used as the hard-hitting hammerhead of the relentless Allied assaults. The Canadians broke through the Drocourt-Quèant Line and the Hindenburg Line and then, in one of the most brilliant and daring conceptions of the war, advanced through the narrow funnel of the dry bed of the Canal du Nord to fan out on the far side in another victorious attack. By the end of October the harried German forces were everywhere falling back, with the pursuing Allies hard on their heels. When the Armistice brought an end to hostilities on the morning of November 11, the Canadians were on the outskirts of the Belgian city of Mons, almost exactly where, four years and three months previously, the British had first brushed against the enemy.

III

In every way the First World War had been the most tragic episode in Canadian history. Gone for ever was the old, pleasant, half-somnolent world, in which most Canadian communities had borne a striking likeness to Stephen Leacock's sunshiny little town of Mariposa. A terrible total of 61,326 Canadians had been killed, and 172,950 had been wounded. On top of that, national unity had been dealt a grievous blow by a prolonged and passionate controversy

over how to maintain the supply of men for Canada's forces
overseas.

The Canadian Corps was both a highly effective fighting
force and the proudly regarded symbol of Canada's identity
as a partner in the Allied cause, which made the question of
maintaining its strength all the more vital. This problem,
which became crucial in 1917, arose fundamentally from the
unexpectedly long duration of the war, the shockingly high
wastage of men at the front, and the fact that the Canadians
were present in force and more or less continuously in action
from early in 1915 to the very end of the struggle. Even
under the best conditions at home these brute, inescapable
realities might well have caused trouble in recruiting the
needed reinforcements.

But conditions at home were not of the best, and the most
serious feature of the worsening situation here was an ever-
widening breach between Quebec and the rest of the nation.
At the outset of the war the French Canadians were, by and
large, at one with the mass of their fellow countrymen in the
belief that Canada must participate to the fullest extent, a
belief to which Laurier gave characteristically eloquent
tongue. Other spokesmen of French Canada, in both Church
and State, also expressed this conviction, as did the French-
language newspapers, and urged the young men of Quebec
to enlist, which many did. However, as time went by angry
voices began to accuse the French Canadians of not contributing their fair share of men to the forces, and asserting
that Quebec was lagging behind, with smaller numbers enlisting in proportion to her population than were coming
from the other provinces. Not only that, it was pointed out,
a substantial proportion of the volunteers from Quebec belonged to her English-speaking minority.

That there was such a discrepancy was true but there were
reasons for it. If one left out of the reckoning the British-
born recruits, most of whom lived outside Quebec and who
supplied so large a part of the volunteers in the first two
years of the war, and compared the response of native Canadians from the various provinces, the discrepancy was not

Crumbling

From *The Canadian Liberal Monthly*, October, 1916.

nearly so great. But in any case the people of French Canada
could not be expected to answer the call to arms with quite
the readiness and enthusiasm shown by their compatriots of
British descent. Appeals to a sense of kinship and duty to
Britain and the Empire did not touch their emotions in the
same way. Nor had they their own comparable feeling of
loyalty and affection for France, from which they had long
been separated both politically and sentimentally; the argument that she deserved their aid in her hour of peril left
them relatively unmoved. Indeed, to most of them Europe

seemed quite remote, even irrelevant. The war as it dragged
on came to look less and less like a noble crusade and more
and more like another in the long series of struggles between
the big European powers for wealth and territory. The
French Canadian would willingly die for the defence of
Canada, and especially of his homeland in the St. Lawrence
valley, but he found it increasingly difficult to believe that
Canada was in danger or that her defence might best be
mounted in the muddy trenches of Flanders.

In addition to feeling isolated from Europe and unin-
volved emotionally in its problems the people of French
Canada felt antagonized and their tempers were frayed by
certain errors of judgement made in recruiting and organizing the overseas force, errors for which the flamboyant, ego-
centric, and bull-headed Sam Hughes was largely responsible. As Borden's Minister of Militia until 1916, his failure
in the beginning to establish distinctive French-speaking
units and his policy of dispersing French-speaking recruits
among predominantly English-speaking battalions annoyed
the people of Quebec, as did his tendency to overlook qualified French-Canadian officers when promotions were decided.
If his ingrained Orange prejudice and his suspicion of Quebec annoyed French Canadians, he had as remarkable a gift
for annoying almost everyone with whom he came in contact. But, unfortunate as his influence was in many ways, the
importance and seriousness of his errors were exaggerated by
his critics. He was not the author of the manpower problem,
only an exasperating aggravation of it.

A more serious grievance of the French Canadians, one
entirely extraneous to the war but powerfully destructive of
Canadian unity while it was being fought, was the Ontario
government's policy of restricting the use of French as a
language of instruction in the schools of the province. In
the eastern and northern regions of Ontario, and to a lesser
extent in the south-western corner, there was a marked concentration of French-speaking people. Acting on the finding
of a commission of inquiry that children were graduating
from some of the schools in these districts without an ade-

quate knowledge of English, the provincial Department of Education in 1912 issued an administrative order—the notorious Regulation 17—placing severe limits on the use of French in teaching. The strenuous protests of those directly affected by this policy found a noisy echo in Quebec, where the rights of the French-speaking minority of Ontario were widely regarded as more important and better worth fighting for than the cause of the Allies in Europe. Canadians were dying overseas, allegedly in defence of freedom, justice, and democracy, at the hands of the Prussian enemy. But should not justice, like charity, begin at home and the fight be waged against Anglo-Saxon 'Prussianism' in Ontario? Such was the cry raised by some leaders of opinion in Quebec, most insistently by Bourassa and his newspaper, *Le Devoir*. Here was a distraction for which the Dominion government was in no way responsible and which it was constitutionally powerless to remove. Borden's private representations to the authorities in Ontario urging a modification of the policy were rebuffed and the language issue remained alive to bedevil the country throughout the war.

Although the most alarming feature of the situation that developed during the war was the growing estrangement of Quebec and the evidence of hostility towards her elsewhere, a reluctance to enlist for overseas service was, needless to say, not confined to the young men of that province. War weariness and disillusionment became more prevalent everywhere. Furthermore, the war, by placing heavy demands on Canada's productive capacity, created a pressing need for labour on the farm, in the mines and mills, and in the factories and the forests. These all competed with the armed forces for men and it was not surprising that many men, despite the social pressures on them to enlist, preferred to remain employed at home rather than embark upon the hazardous and ill-paid life of soldiering.

The shortage of reinforcements for the army began to be serious in 1916, especially during the second half of the year, and in the early months of 1917 it became worse, with only about half as many men enlisting as were being lost in action.

Faced with this fact, knowing that its various efforts to stimulate recruitment had failed and finding itself under
mounting bi-partisan pressure from English-speaking Canada to adopt conscription, the government was forced to
reappraise its manpower policy. Borden himself had more
than once stated that he had no intention of resorting to compulsory service and had tried to put the best possible face on
the situation. By the spring of 1917, however, it was no longer
possible to pretend that without conscription the additional
soldiers could be found. In May of that year the Prime Minister came home from a visit to England and France convinced by discussions there and by first-hand observation
that conscription would have to come.

Borden's announcement on his return of the fateful decision to abandon voluntary enlistment was followed shortly
by efforts, at length successful, to construct a coalition cabinet of Liberals and Conservatives who favoured conscription. He first invited Laurier to join such a ministry, but Sir
Wilfrid, unable to endorse the new manpower policy, declined. Discussions were then opened with a number of
English-speaking Liberals and at last, in October, Borden
completed the formation of the Union Government, a government in which the French-speaking people of Quebec
were not effectively represented. In the meantime there had
been stirring scenes and much eloquent oratory in Parliament. A bill embodying the principle of selective compulsory
service was drafted and enacted after long debate between
opposing forces which to a disturbing degree reflected the
division between Quebec and the rest of the country. One of
the most poignant features of those dramatic days was the
desertion of the venerable Laurier by many of his leading
lieutenants and followers outside of Quebec and the disruption of a party which under his leadership had become a great
power in the land. But the unity and *esprit de corps* of the
Conservative party were hardly less seriously injured by these
developments. Its French-Canadian wing was almost totally
alienated by conscription, and many dyed-in-the-wool Conservatives, both in Quebec and elsewhere, were bitterly

opposed from the party standpoint to even a temporary coalition with their traditional enemies.

With party lines thus drastically altered, and with passions at a high pitch over the conscription issue and the increasing antagonism between Quebec and the rest of the country, the Union Government went to the polls in the autumn of 1917. It did so under a franchise that had been cleverly modified by another bitterly disputed enactment of the recent parliamentary session. This extraordinary measure, the Wartime Elections Act, was clearly designed to weight the electoral scales against the anti-conscriptionist opposition. By enfranchising the female near-relatives of men who had served or were serving overseas it added a significant number of voters who could be expected to support conscription. By disfranchising people who were of enemy alien birth or habitually spoke an enemy alien tongue, and who had not become British subjects until after March 1902, it removed from the rolls a class who on the whole had supported the Liberal party in the past and might be counted on to continue following Laurier now. This change in the suffrage presumably accounted in part for the great victory scored by the Union Government, whose candidates won a majority of seventy-one seats in the new House of Commons. But there was a most disquieting feature in the outcome of the voting. All but twenty of the eighty-two seats captured by the Laurier Liberals were in Quebec and that province therefore appeared to be pitted against the rest of Canada. Many of the utterances on both sides during the election campaign, indeed, not only indicated belief in the existence of such a confrontation but did much to separate the two peoples.

Enforcement of the conscription law, the Military Service Act, was most difficult in Quebec, where there was widespread evasion of the law. In Quebec City, there was rioting against it. However, the measure was also widely unpopular elsewhere, especially among those liable to service, as the very high number of claims for exemption in all provinces testified. The government's cancellation early in 1918 of certain exemptions hitherto granted, in particular those to farmers'

sons, brought stormy protests. Seldom if ever had a policy
given such apparently resounding electoral support encountered so much obstruction and aroused so much resentment
among the populace. Partly because of this and partly because
the Act was in force for only about ten months before the war
ended, relatively few men – upwards of 80,000 – were raised
by conscription. Not much more than half of these actually
went overseas and but a small number of those who did
saw active service. It therefore made no significant military
contribution, though it might have done so had the war
continued longer, which seemed quite possible at the time
conscription was adopted.

Although dislike of conscription was not confined to
Quebec, in the main the issue did divide Canadians on 'racial'
lines. At the height of the crisis of 1917-18 it appeared that
the very survival of Confederation might be in doubt as the
verbal violence of recrimination mounted on both sides. In
the closing months of the war, however, a more moderate
spirit made its influence felt. While the crisis left a lasting
legacy of misunderstanding and distrust, with conscription
remaining a potent political issue in Quebec for many years
to come and affecting profoundly the course of Canadian
politics, passions were in some measure subdued as with the
end of the war new political developments and controversies
took precedence.

IV

The post-war political situation was indeed new, and different from anything known before in Canada. Any expectations there may have been of a speedy return to 'normalcy'
(equated by many people with pre-war conditions) were
doomed to disappointment. For one thing those years witnessed an exuberant radicalism, especially in the western
provinces, which in some of its manifestations was new in
kind as well as in magnitude. For another, and this was partly
an effect of the radical temper, the familiar party system,
still suffering from the conscription issue, was being further

weakened by a rebellion of the farmers against the two old parties, and even against the party system as such. New farmers' parties, or 'movements' as many of their supporters preferred to call them, were in the process of being formed, both in the provinces and on the national scene.

If there was an element of genuine radicalism in this resort to direct political action by the farmers, they were also in a sense driven by an impulse that was conservative, not to say reactionary. Though some of them exhibited a fondness for up-to-date reform ideas about direct democracy and group government, ideas largely borrowed from similar agrarian movements in the western United States, they were unconsciously reacting against the increasing domination of government and society by modern industrial capitalism. Making a desperate last-ditch stand in defence of the agricultural community, they were in a way political romantics attempting to preserve a fast-vanishing Arcadia. Of course they could also be hard-headed realists when it came to gauging their own immediate interests and determining how best to advance them. They had long since organized for collective action through various agencies to protect themselves from the ruthless exploitation practised by banks, railways, and grain companies. However, they had stopped short of creating their own political parties, relying instead on their united strength to put sufficient pressure on existing parties to secure the legislation they desired.

Before the war a lot of dissatisfaction with this method had appeared among the farmers, a growing conviction – strengthened by the defeat of the reciprocity agreement that most of them favoured – that both the Liberal and Conservative parties were dominated by groups hostile to the agricultural class and to the interests of western Canada in particular. Justice for the farmers, many of them came to believe, an influence in determining national policies commensurate with their numbers and importance, could only be achieved by electing their own candidates to Parliament, by presenting a united political front. Since agrarian influence in Liberal and Conservative councils was so slight, being invariably subordinated to the power of the great business aggregations of Ontario and Quebec, a new farmers' party there must be.

The process of its formation was interrupted by the war, the winning of which took precedence and which, in any event, by temporarily restoring agricultural prosperity, softened somewhat the anger and dissatisfaction of the farmers. At the same time, though, the creation of the Union Government facilitated the process by freeing many of its farm supporters from their allegiance to the Liberal party, which the majority in the west had followed before that time. This made it easier for them to find their way into the fold of the new agrarian political movement, instead of rejoining the Liberal ranks, when the day came to desert the Union Government. That regime they regarded as only a transitory war-time necessity. They not only disliked some of its measures, especially the conscription of farmers' sons and hired hands, but had little hope that in peace-time its policies with respect to the tariff and other domestic issues would be satisfactory from their point of view. In 1918 the Canadian Council of Agriculture, claiming to represent all the farmers in the country, adopted a platform known as the New National Policy. Two years later the National Progressive party came formally into being, made that platform its own, and, led by Thomas A. Crerar, an erstwhile Liberal from Manitoba who had resigned the previous year as Minister of Agriculture in the Union Government, prepared to appeal to the nation in the next general election. Meanwhile provincial farmers' parties were also being organized. In 1919 one of them, in Ontario, scored a sensational victory and, with the co-operation of a number of labour members also elected to the legislature, formed a government. The revolt of the agrarians was assuming large proportions, to some people alarmingly so. It was a new fact of political life which would have to be taken seriously.

The farmers were not the only ones who were more than usually restive at the end of the war. Their entrance into politics as a new force, though worrisome to the leaders of the old parties and to conservatively-minded people in general, was less frightening than the increasingly radical opinions popular in a section of the trade-union movement and the revolutionary talk indulged in by some of its leaders. In the past Canadian unions on the whole had been moderate in outlook and peaceful in methods. Of course there had been strikes and some violence in labour disputes but by and large little evidence of basic dissatisfaction with the capitalist system. When the war came to a close, however, such dissatisfaction was a good deal in evidence and, as with the discontent of the farmers, was most intense and most vehemently stated in the west.

There were varied and rather complex reasons for the disgruntlement of the western working men. For one thing they felt aggrieved by certain war-time policies, as well as by some economic consequences of the war and of the return of peace. Many of them, at least of those who did not enlist in the army, had opposed conscription, and many of the 'New Canadians' among them had been disfranchised for the time being by the Wartime Elections Act. A large proportion, whether unionized tradesmen or unorganized labourers, had been employed in the construction industry, which had been badly hit by the diversion of capital and materials to the war effort. In the absence of substantial, efficient, and well equipped industrial plants in the west to attract large war orders that would generate a demand for labour, many workmen sought refuge from adversity either in the army or on the land. Those who continued to be employed in the cities worked at wage rates rather lower than were paid in the east. Consequently they were especially hard hit by the war-time rise in prices, a rise made harder to bear by high freight rates, to which western Canadians had long since become accustomed but never reconciled. Thus much of the urban working class in the west did not benefit greatly, if at all, from the prosperity created by the war.

The situation was aggravated by the economic dislocations that occurred following the armistice in Europe. The abnormal war-time demand for many Canadian products ceased.

Large-scale unemployment was one of the results of this, and the rapid demobilization of the troops did nothing to improve matters, only adding to the surplus of labour. The federal government, in its plans for re-establishing the soldiers in civilian life – plans more generous and advanced than those of any other country, relied mainly on a scheme of assisted land settlement. But the results of this were disappointing. The vast majority of the returning veterans showed no interest in availing themselves of the help offered in acquiring land, preferring to take their chances in the cities and towns, where for the time being there were not enough jobs to go around. Hence at a time when the cost of living remained high a potentially explosive state of affairs was coming into being.

Its explosiveness was increased by disillusionment with the 'system' – with an economic mode, a structure of society, and a form of government which to many of the disenchanted hardly exemplified that democracy whose final victory in the world the war had been fought to ensure. Was it worth dying for a country, was such a country democratic, in which the personal sacrifices and material rewards of the war seemed to be so unequally distributed? One had only to contrast the lot of the privileged few, who made great fortunes, were granted titles of nobility, and controlled governments in their own interest, with that of the many who were expected to do the fighting and the dying for a soldier's pittance or to produce the materials of war for a subsistence wage. Nor did there seem, to those who saw things in this light, to be any prospect of a change for the better when peace returned. The propertied classes were firmly in command of the state. They had used and would continue to use their power to suppress the propagation of political, social, and economic doctrines with which they disagreed. They would continue to exploit those upon whose toil their wealth and security depended, resisting all efforts by the working class to improve its condition and to gain an influence in keeping with its size and value to the community.

From this unhappiness with the framework of government and society there flowed a more specific discontent: a rising impatience with the timid, cautious leadership of the national trade-union organizations in the east. These bodies, influenced by the views of Samuel Gompers in the United States and by the practice of American labour organizations, shunned direct political action through a distinctive labour party, depending instead on pressing leaders of existing parties for desired legislation and reform. But among the working men, as among the farmers, the conviction took root that because the old parties were controlled by the 'interests' this way of proceeding was bound to be ineffectual. The moral some of them drew was that a labour party ought to be formed, as in Great Britain. Others, though, more radical and less patient in spirit, turned away from that path in the belief that ballot-box democracy was an illusion that would trap the working class, instead of providing the sure means to power and reform.

They favoured, rather, the more dramatic and, as they believed, more effective weapon of the general strike. Sharing the outlook of the Industrial Workers of the World, a body strong in the western United States and much imbued with Marxist ideology, they looked forward to the creation of One Big Union which, speaking and acting for the whole of the labouring class, would use the paralysing power of the general strike to compel a surrender of power by the 'bosses' and bring about a socialist reconstruction. Some of them were given to heady revolutionary talk and to predictions that the Russian Revolution, which they greatly admired, would shortly be imitated in Canada. This did nothing to diminish the 'great Red scare' weighing heavily at that time on all those, mainly in the United States but also in Canada, who were haunted by the spectre of communism.

The strength of this radical movement seemed to make itself felt – to the consternation of many people – in a rash of strikes, some of them of large proportions, in various Canadian cities during 1918 and 1919. But the climax of it came

in the Winnipeg General Strike in the spring of the latter
year, a stormy episode precipitated by a dispute about collective bargaining in the metal and building trades. In a vote
conducted by the Winnipeg Trades and Labour Council the
workers in the whole city chose by an overwhelming majority
to stage a general sympathy strike.

It lasted for several weeks, removed about 30,000 people
from their jobs, and divided the residents of Winnipeg into
two sharply opposed camps. It was finally ended, after some
violence and loss of life had occurred, by the decisive intervention of the Dominion government, which became convinced that the municipal and provincial authorities could
not control an essentially revolutionary situation. Several of
the strike leaders were tried on a number of charges, including seditious conspiracy, and with one exception were convicted on all or part of the indictment. In retrospect it can be
seen that all the bellicose talk about the strike being the start
of a national Bolshevik revolution should not have been
taken at its face value, that the strike was intended, not to
touch off a revolutionary upheaval, but to gain acceptance of
the principle of collective bargaining. Nevertheless, a case
can be made for the view that a general strike, regardless of
its leaders' intentions, must in order to succeed result in a
usurpation of public authority—as happened to some extent
in Winnipeg—and in that sense inevitably becomes a revolutionary act. In any case, considering the widespread fears
excited by the Russian Revolution and the violent language
used by some of the radical figures in western Canada, it was
not surprising that many people in Winnipeg felt that they
had been confronted by an overt revolutionary effort.

V

If most farmers and some industrial workers were restive and
impatient with their lot, so too were members of still another
large and underprivileged class – the women of Canada.
Their organizations were as numerous and active as waves
on the ocean, busy with all manner of worthy causes, mostly

devoted in one way or another to moral uplift and reform. In fact women then appeared to have more of a self-conscious, collective will, more sense of power and mission, more verve and energy to accomplish their purposes than were to be seen half a century later when for the most part they had long enjoyed political and legal equality with men. Such equality, however, was denied them before the First World War and the prime objective of many of their organizations was to break the male monopoly of the franchise.

The cause did not receive anything like unanimous support from women – some were outspokenly opposed and many, perhaps most, were indifferent – but it was given devoted and effective leadership by a group of reformers, both male and female, whose efforts were crowned during the decade with remarkable, if as yet incomplete, success. These people regarded the vote as a fundamental right, of course, but not so much an end in itself as a means for the removal of the legal inferiority from which the sex suffered at the time, and for abolition of such other evils as liquor and the white-slave traffic. Not only that, the enfranchisement of women, it was argued, would have a salutary effect on Canadian public life, helping to cleanse it of corruption and baseness. The ruffianly behaviour natural to an exclusively male occupation would give way to something nobler if politicians had to justify their actions directly to the gentler sex and admit women to their hitherto closed society. Canadian advocates of electoral reform watched with interest the movements for female suffrage in the United States and Great Britain, and were much influenced by them. But the Canadian campaign was less marked by violence and disorder: there was no equivalent of Mrs. Pankhurst to incite rebellion, although that redoubtable feminist visited Canada to lend encouragement. However, the Canadians did not lack for zeal on the part of those women who took an interest in the subject.

Bodies specifically devoted to furthering the cause were established, such as the Canadian Suffrage Association, the Equal Suffrage Society, the Equal Franchise League, and the

Political Equality League, and were backed by other organizations such as the Women's Christian Temperance Union. Women prominent in the fight—Nellie McClung in Manitoba, Dorothy Davis in British Columbia, Flora Denison and Margaret Gordon in Ontario, to name a few—were indefatigable in addressing meetings and badgering public men. Resolutions were drawn up, approved by assemblies of women across the land, and presented to the politicians, demanding the removal of an unjust anomaly that was pithily described by one speaker as follows: 'The ballot to-day includes bad men and good men, men of all colours and even dead men, excluding only paupers, idiots, criminals, minors, and women.'

The response of most men to the pleas of the reformers was not very positive or encouraging at first. Perhaps many of them agreed with a British M.P., Lord George Hamilton, that to 'put women on an equality with men is contrary to Heaven's Act of Parliament, and to the everlasting law of Nature and of fact'. But Premier Sir Rodmond Roblin of Manitoba had a more flattering and guileful justification of his opposition. 'I think too much of woman,' he said, 'to have her entangled in the mesh of politics. She would be stooping from the pedestal on which she has sat for centuries.' Advocates of the suffrage, however, were willing to stoop in order to conquer. That famous pedestal was about to be vacated.

Considerations of reason and justice, it may be, are seldom wholly absent from politics in a well ordered democratic state —nor can politicians remain blind for too long to the party advantage that may accrue from extending the franchise to a large class thus far excluded. Whatever the causes, during the war the opposition to votes for women suddenly crumbled away in much of Canada. During 1916 and 1917 the five provinces west of Quebec all extended the suffrage and in the latter year came the partial enfranchisement afforded by the Wartime Elections Act. Before the 1917 election Sir Robert Borden promised that if he was returned to power he would introduce a measure granting the vote in national elections to all adult females, and in 1918 a bill to this effect was approved by Parliament. Women, for electoral purposes in the Dominion and in five provinces, were now officially distinguished from idiots, paupers, and criminals. It was a triumph of democracy.

One of the motivating impulses behind the women's suffrage movement, in fact one of the pronounced characteristics of Canadian sentiment in the century's second decade, was a fervour for moral reform. While it was much in evidence before 1914, it seemed to be intensified by the wartime atmosphere of sacrifice, self-denial, and righteous indignation against the foe. The 'Prussian tyrant' was the chief one, of course, but while the soldiers were waging that battle there was also a battle to be fought by those on the home front against other forms of evil, against crime and vice, drunkenness and indolence, and even, according to a few advanced reformers, against poverty and human hardship.

But of all the forms and causes of human degradation attacked by the moral reformers none was fought with greater enthusiasm, with more stirring eloquence and effectively concerted action, than the 'drink evil'. None was fought with as much apparent success.

Many social evils were considered to be produced or at least much aggravated by 'the curse of alcohol'. If it were conquered they would be much diminished. At the beginning of the decade the prohibitionist elements, among whom were numbered many so-called 'temperance' people, had made substantial progress. Prince Edward Island had a Prohibition Act in force, and elsewhere, under a variety of local option laws, the number of districts voting to become dry was increasing year by year. This partial success, though, did not satisfy such crusaders as Nellie McClung, the Reverend Ben Spence of Toronto, and J. H. Roberts of Montreal. They not only worked to increase the number of dry areas under the local option system but agitated for laws to 'ban the bar' in those that remained wet. Churches, with their clergy and their well organized women in the van, were joined by a number of prohibitionist groups such as the Dominion Alliance and the W.C.T.U. and by an assortment of moral and social reform leagues to marshal their forces for a mighty onslaught on demon rum. The war, far from diverting their attention, only intensified their efforts by affording them a number of additional arguments. The vast sums of money spent each year on beverage alcohol should be diverted to war purposes. The war demanded an end to self-indulgence. Canadians must be mentally alert and physically fit; was it not true that alcohol dulled the mind and wracked the frame? High productivity was required on farm and in factory; who could deny that strong drink caused absenteeism and inefficiency?

While the brewers and distillers fought a losing rear-guard action, backed by champions of individual liberty, disgruntled critics of the 'sin-hounds', and some trade-union leaders defending the right of the workman to his pint, the campaign for total prohibition was pressed through the war and through the victory. One after another the provinces, except for Quebec, enacted prohibitory laws, which were strengthened by federal Orders in Council forbidding the importation and interprovincial shipment of beer, wine, and spirits. The government of Quebec, where through local-option votes prohibition of sale had made substantial strides forward, was on the verge of following the lead of the other provinces, but held back when signs of a public reaction against the policy were seen. Indeed, after the war ended, evidence of dissatisfaction mounted in the rest of the country as well, and the anti-prohibitionists began to find new heart for the struggle. Certainly it proved to be one thing to enact 'temperance' legislation and quite another to enforce it. Spirits for medicinal, scientific, or mechanical purposes were permitted, along with sacramental wines, and soon stories multiplied about how the laws were being flouted by people with well disposed physicians. It was alleged, for example, that one doctor in British Columbia wrote more than four hundred liquor prescriptions a month. This kind of mal-practice, according to some reports, was much encouraged by the great, terrifying influenza epidemic in the fall of 1918, which took the lives of thousands of people. Many in the

medical profession, it was claimed, displayed a quite un-
scientific faith during that emergency in the preventive and
curative powers of alcohol. However, despite the difficulties
of enforcement, and they were many, the spread of prohibition impressively demonstrated one fact: that a large, well
organized, and vigorously led pressure group can wield enormous power, especially when it is able to take advantage of a
prevailing mood like the determination and moral righteousness of war-time, and the desire to make some sacrifice, however small and unheroic, that would give one the sense of
sharing in a noble cause and a grievous ordeal.

VI

When the ordeal of the war ended, Canadians, like the other
victorious peoples, gave vent to their feelings of relief and
thankfulness in exuberant celebration. Now, many thought-
lessly took for granted, life in its essentials would resume the
old pre-war pattern. In some ways, no doubt, this expectation
was fulfilled, but in other important respects the old order
had vanished beyond recovery. The luxury of isolation
from the controversies and conflicts of world politics, which
Canada had enjoyed in the pre-1914 era, was gone for ever.
Thanks partly to Borden's complaints during the war that he
was not being properly consulted by the British on matters
of policy affecting the whole Empire, Canada and the other
dominions were given places in the small Imperial War
Cabinet that was set up by Lloyd George shortly after he
became Prime Minister of Great Britain late in 1916. Again
owing in part to Borden's insistence the dominions were
represented on their own account at the Paris Peace Conference of 1919 and were accorded seats of their own in the
League of Nations established under the Treaty of Versailles.
Such advances in status, such marks of recognition, were
pleasing to Canadians, whose war effort did much to foster
national pride. But as well as affording Canada recognition as
something above a mere colony and conferring on her the
right to be heard in the councils of the Empire and the world,

these changes imposed upon her international obligations and responsibilities. For Canada the age of innocence was over.

In politics, the new awareness that the old order had disappeared was heightened by the departure of the two men who had dominated the scene in the war and pre-war years. Early in 1919 Sir Wilfrid Laurier died. He had sat in the House of Commons for nearly half a century, had led the Liberal party for over thirty years, and had been Prime Minister for fifteen. All Canadians, regardless of partisan feeling, sensed that his going marked the end of an age. His death was followed in the summer of 1920 by the retirement of Borden. The two, for all their disagreements, all the spirit with which they had done battle against each other, had a great mutual respect and liking. Under their direction Canadian politics had shown a certain civility, a quality of grace and gentlemanliness that was to be destroyed under their successors, whose intense personal animosities would loom large during the following decade.

The new Liberal leader was William Lyon Mackenzie King, who had been Minister of Labour in the last years of the Laurier administration. Aloof from politics for the most part during the war, he had been employed for much of that period by the Rockefeller Foundation to investigate labour-management relations. The work he did enhanced his considerable reputation as an expert in that field. Convinced that Laurier regarded him as his rightful political heir, and that he was ordained by Divine Providence to govern Canada, King managed to win the leadership at a national party convention in August 1919. Borden's successor was Arthur Meighen, who had come to Parliament in 1909 as a small-town lawyer from Manitoba. After first achieving prominence by his important role in the introduction of closure in 1913, he had gone on to become one of the three or four most active and powerful figures in the war-time government. Because of his acidulous manner in the House of Commons, where he was a highly skilled debater, and his close connection with so many controversial policies – including conscription and the related manipulation of the franchise in 1917, railway nationalization, and the suppression of the Winnipeg strike – Meighen had made many enemies during his rise to the top: too many, in the opinion of some Conservatives, for him to be a successful leader of the party. King and Meighen were as dissimilar as two men could be, in appearance, temperament, outlook, and style; and this lent a special fascination to the exceptionally bitter contest between them.

There was a marked contrast between the spirit and outlook of Canadians in 1920 and the confident optimism they had shown ten years before. At the opening of the decade they had looked forward with assurance to continued progress and prosperity, but when it closed the future seemed far less certain. It was not only that the changes in the structure, issues, and leading personalities of politics had unsettling effects. Nor did Canada's new status in the world, so gratifying to the national pride of her people, fully explain the air of misgiving and unease; for most Canadians failed to realize as yet that there was no longer any safe retreat from a world that remained more deeply troubled than they knew. In many ways, however, their collective experience during that time of stress and suffering had a sobering effect, bringing them face to face with harsh realities. They found satisfaction in Canada's contribution to victory in what the majority still regarded as a just cause, but some of them, at least, knew that victory had been purchased at a high price: at great cost of human life and disablement, and a strident renewal of the old antipathies of language and culture. They knew that during the war, perhaps in some obscure way as a result of it, there had begun to appear new, troublesome signs of social unrest, with accompanying class antagonisms that added a further dimension to the besetting problem of Canada – her fragmentation and lack of cohesion. They knew that their country faced difficulties in adjusting from a wartime to a peace-time economy, in finding markets for her goods and jobs for her people. All in all, in some undefined and perhaps indefinable way, life seemed to have become infinitely more complicated on the after side of the great divide of the world war. On New Year's Day, 1911, the Canadians had contemplated under sunny skies what looked to be a happy, satisfying future, with more people enjoying more of the good things of life than ever before. On New Year's Eve, 1920, they could only peer anxiously through mists of confusion and uncertainty into a doubtful future.

7. The 1920s

W. L. MORTON

Canada in 1920 entered the
decade that stood between the Great War with its aftermath
of revolution and the Great Depression with its sequel of
disintegration. The Great War of 1914 had blown off the roof
of nineteenth-century civilization. The walls and foundations
still stood, cracked but erect, and the inhabitants of the
western world lived on bravely in them until they too tumbled down in 1931, and men moved numbly into the spiritual
tents and mental huts in which they have lived ever since,
involuntary bedouins in a desert of the soul. The great myths
of the nineteenth century, the century of modern Canada's
creation, still glowed with life: order in freedom; stability in
progress; truth despite contradiction; hope against despair.
In the Canada of 1920, a colonial, imitative, and derivative

society in which no idea had first been declared and only one or two discoveries had ever been made, these myths still flourished and the actual wreckage of war was far distant. The thunder of the guns was fading into a crackle of rifles in the forests of Russia and among the hills of Turkey. The growing hush was thought to be the return of day, a day that would restore the yesterday that had ended in 1914.

The decade, then, is defined in event by war and depression. The definition in character is a subtler matter. On a surface still troubled by war and revolution, waves of nostalgia ran back to the pre-war past. To resume the growth anticipated in 1914, to bring in immigrants, to break new fields, to turn out the new machines, to fill the long trains rumbling day and night to the seaports, to fill the wilderness with the prosperous and comfortable homes of a simple, democratic people, to realize at last the fantastic visions of the first decade of the century–these were the hopes renewed in 1920.

Yet the currents that were to flow from the decade of the twenties into that of the thirties were already running deep and strong. The dream of a Canadian nation like the American, the British, or the French had been dissolved. To the old happy acceptance of nationhood as the crown of civilized existence had been added the strange, disturbing doctrine of internationalism, the doctrine that nationalism was not enough, that nations must modify their newly asserted sovereignty and independence. And as emotional nationalism chafed against internationalism, economic nationalism abraded the imperial tie that for many Canadians was a sufficient internationalism. The former tension the Liberal party embodied, the latter the Conservative. The romanticism that had gilded Canadian art and letters was eaten into by a realism that made more astringent the bleakness of Canadian life and the harshness of the Canadian landscape. And Canadian churches, committed to a missionary and social role, found their foothold in the actual world narrowing rapidly between the erosion of a blind fundamentalism on the one hand and a popular scientism on the other.

In outcome this decade, therefore, was by definition an interim one. It stood between a century of uneventful intellectual and material progress, and one in which that progress had already begun to crumble, or to writhe perversely into forms and to flow in directions never intended. It was a decade of transition from a century in which chaos was steadily reduced to order to one in which order was to be increasingly disintegrated. The Canada that had been in 1914 did not return after 1920. After 1930 it was to be a very different country in aspiration, thought, and deed.

Very few Canadians sensed how deep the currents were running. Most were occupied in navigating the troubled surface waters. The first thing that stood out for all to see in 1920 was the post-war boom, a boom that had become an inflation. An abundance of money could not, after the expenditures of war and demobilization, purchase a sufficiency of goods. Agricultural and industrial prices were unprecedentedly high. Wages also were high, although salaries had not kept pace with rising prices. All seemed to prosper; few were really prosperous. The inevitable stresses of inflation therefore caused economic, social, and political discontent. The upward movement of the trade cycle set running by the demands of the war had reached its peak and was about to crest and break.

Deflation would then follow inflation. In the economic thought of the day this was regarded as being natural, therefore inevitable and right. The economy was thought to be self-regulating. Government controls on economic life had long been thought to be mistaken and even immoral, because controls would interrupt and distort the distribution of the resources of productive effort by the automatically adjusting free market in goods and services. The prevailing economic thought of the times therefore required that the government's control of parts of the economy devised since 1917 should be ended as quickly as possible, and that the process of deflation should be initiated. (That the latter was itself a matter of control escaped observation.) Thus it was possible for the editor of *The Canadian Annual Review* to write on the first page of the volume for 1920: '. . . the banks would have much to say in hastening a period of deflation and compelling the lowering of prices upon which the existing situation so largely turned'. Mr. Castell Hopkins, the editor of the *Review*, was neither an uninformed nor a reactionary man; he was rather a mirror of all that conventional men of affairs thought.

No one, of course, questioned then or would question now the need for deflation. The boom had become genuinely inflationary and the general interest required that it should be checked. But the particular mistakes of economic thought at the time were two. The first was the assumption that the existing economic system was a 'natural', that is, a non-political, one, and that no control should be exercised over it. Yet Hopkins's statement reveals that the banks did possess power to control the economy, that they deliberately exercised it, and that they were expected by men of business to do so. The second was that the means the banks used—the raising of interest rates on loans or the refusing of loans—did not have the effect of easing the throttle and slowly reducing the speed of the economy. Instead they had the effect of a sudden jamming on of brakes, and they brought the whole hurtling trade cycle to a grinding, shuddering halt.

The tightening of credit was, of course, the chief as well as the customary mode of producing deflation in 1920. But its depressing and indeed needlessly harsh effect was aggravated by the abolition of the last war-time government control: the Wheat Board, created to ensure a flow of grain to Britain in 1917 and used thereafter to stabilize the price paid to the wheat farmer and the wheat consumer. By 1920, when the price of the top grade of Board wheat was $3.15 a bushel at Fort William, it had come to be a guarantee that the western farmer would not only continue to enjoy the high prices of the immediate post-war period, but that he would be able to pay interest and principal on the debts incurred in increasing production and his standard of living. He desperately hoped that the Board might be continued to handle the crop of 1920, to moderate the inevitable decline in prices, and to win time to ease the load of indebtedness. But established opinion prevailed. The Board ended operations on August 31, 1920, and no amount of agitation by the grain growers' organization or the governments of the three prairie provinces was to get it restored. The price of wheat fell, and deflation swept over the western grain lands like a dust storm.

The special case of the Wheat Board, itself at once an expedient of the war and a prophecy of the future, illustrated the great weakness of the classical mode of deflating the economy. Not only did deflation bring the prosperity train to a shuddering stop; it fell with grievous and indefensible inequality on different segments of the economy. The working man, the farmer, and the small businessman were struck with the special force of a crushing blow. Major business was slowed but did not suffer severely, and the banks who had imposed the deflationary measures for the general good did not suffer perceptibly at all. No doubt that was why they administered so drastic a medicine with such philosophic calm and such unflinching courage.

II

Deflation, then, although an economic necessity, was applied in 1920 in a way that was socially intolerable and politically unacceptable. An old remedy was to produce both its expected consequences and a new resistance. Unemployment, a necessary aspect of deflation, was ceasing to be a price that people would willingly pay; farm foreclosures were a grim result not to be accepted without protest by a generation schooled in organization and enlightened with the gospel of economic co-operation. Labour would organize, farmers enter politics, as a result of the classical use of deflation like a surgeon's knife, without ether or antiseptic. This reciprocating stroke of old and new was a perfect example of the decade's essential character.

The year of deflation was therefore followed by a year of revolt. In the development of Canada, 1921 is indeed a watershed. It displayed, recorded in the decennial census, the results of the decade of the Laurier boom and the decade of depression, war, and inflation that had succeeded. The west had now been settled, the country's railway system completed, the east industrialized. Agricultural and rural Canada had reached its limits; industrial and urban Canada had become its equal, and was moving with a momentum that would carry it into first place. This momentous change, economic, social, and, as it was to prove, moral, was exhibited simply in the percentages for the totals of rural and urban population. These were: rural, 50.48%; urban, 49.52%. In this regard the decade was Janus-like, facing back to a predominantly rural past and forward to a predominantly urban future.

The balance of rural and urban populations of the agricultural and industrial economies was not, however, to be a peaceful equilibrium. The momentary equipoise indicated by the census meant that the fundamental struggle that had begun at least as early as the 1850s between the agricultural and the industrial interests of Canada, each seeking to ensure that national policy was in its favour, would only be intensified as the agricultural interest realized how formidable was the challenge to its place in the national life. For if Canada had always been mainly a rural and an agricultural country in population and in the nature of its economy, above all it was so still in sentiment and in morals. The twenties would witness a long battle between the two great interest groups of the country, the agricultural and the industrial.

Deflation had been urban and industrial in its inspiration, and, its incidence dramatized by the ending of the Wheat Board, it fell with particular weight on the countryside. Thus the great revolt of 1920 set the organized farmers against the old parties, parties led and largely manned in Parliament and the provincial legislatures by lawyers. The roots of the revolt ran far back into the farmers' organizations that had risen and fallen since Confederation. But the agrarian movement had gained strength and a body of doctrine with the rise of the Grain Growers' and United Farmers' organizations. Their original aims had been co-operation among their members and pressure on governments. But disappointments and necessities – the defeat of reciprocity in 1911, and the failure of the Union Government to take heed of the Farmers' platform of 1915 and lower the tariff – had strengthened the argument of those who urged that political action should be added to economic. Such political action, to avoid disruptions of the primary organizations, had to be on a non-partisan, non-political party basis. It had to be, as the word was, occupational. Already, the United Farmers of Ontario had captured the provincial government, and those of Alberta the government of that province. In Manitoba they had reduced the government party to a plurality. And already a separate 'Progressive' group had been formed in the House of Commons and a full and far-reaching political program framed, a program called defiantly 'the new National Policy'.

The fires were thus crackling in the bush and running on the prairies when the ending of the Wheat Board, and the refusal of the national government to restore it, prepared the dry and torrid weather that made possible a fire across the land. It was ignited when in June 1921, in a by-election in Medicine Hat, the government candidate was overwhelmingly defeated by a farmers' representative. Prime Minister Arthur Meighen, who had in 1920 succeeded Sir Robert Borden as Conservative leader, took note and called a general election in December 1921. The result was the return of sixty-five 'Progressive' members from British Columbia to Ontario, a sixty-five that might easily have been as much as seventy-five. The Liberal party had the larger number of members of the two parties, but with one hundred and seventeen were one short of half the House. Only fifty Conservatives were returned. The Progressives had not quite gained a balance of power, but they had upset the working of the old two-party system. They were in a position to bargain for the particular interest they represented, that of agricultural and rural Canada.

III

The farmers' revolt, however, was only part of the disruption of 1921. Even more important was the sectional character of the parties in the House of Commons. Thirty-seven of the Progressives themselves were from the prairies and they were always regarded, not wholly unfairly, as a sectional group. Of the Conservative party's fifty members, thirty-six were from Ontario, nine of those from Toronto. The Liberal party drew sixty-five of its members from Quebec, much of the remainder from the Maritimes, and only a sprinkling from across the rest of the country, some of them from constituencies in which the French vote was important. In short, the traditional parties had been disrupted as 'national' parties, and Parliament had become a congeries of sectional and occupational interests. Canada had reverted to its inherent parochialism.

Nowhere was this truer than in Quebec. There also, revolt was beginning. It was, however, a revolt masked by the provincial and federal Liberal parties. The revolt of Quebec spoke, if in muffled accents, through its unqualified support of the Liberal party, the party that had opposed conscription. Every French member, as every English member, from the province of Quebec was a supporter of the Liberal party. The revolt failed to speak through the provincial party because of the intellectual training and practical experience of the people who led it. By economic and political conviction they thought it necessary and even desirable to co-operate fully with the Anglo-Canadian economic ascendancy in Montreal. They could have no overt ties with a nationalism that was emotional and clerical, and that in its one clear purpose sought to end the unity of Canada, on which the fortunes of Montreal's business rested.

French-Canadian nationalism had grown steadily since the Red River resistance of 1870. It was, however, partly secular nationalism and partly ultramontane clericalism. Even when greatly inflamed by the Boer War, the revival of the schools

question in Ontario and Manitoba after 1913, and the conscription crises of 1917, it remained clerical as well as secular
in nature. Given the role of the Church in the maintenance
of the French language and culture, there could be no other
result. Yet the struggle to preserve French nationalism in
Canada could not, ultimately, be only resistance to Protestant
and English culture. It would have to become a revolt against
the clerical, educational, and political regime in French
Quebec itself. While, however, the leadership of the Quebec
revolt still lay in the hands of clerics such as the Abbé Lionel
Groulx, gifted and devoted scholar though he was, it would
not fully realize its own nature or gain its goals.

One might argue that for French Canada to live fully and
freely in Canada, it had to become a North American community in all respects – in the relation of Church and State,
in the substance of education, in the character of its politics,
in its attitude to the Vatican – and that until it did, its young
people would remain handicapped in their choice of careers;
its politics would remain corrupt and detached from popular
life; the Church would carry a burden of responsibility for
which it was not designed. During the 1920s, at any rate, the
idea of a 'Laurentian' republic remained a romantic wish
among a limited group of French nationalist idealists, the
Liberal government of Prime Minister A. L. Taschereau
remained the puppet of Anglo-American capital, and French
aspirations were misunderstood and opposed in some parts
of English Canada as aggression by the Roman Catholic
Church. The practical political result was the return of a
body of some fifty French members to Ottawa (including
some men of notable talent such as Ernest Lapointe) who
largely enabled the Liberal party to form the government of
Canada and yet stood sufficiently apart from the views of their
English-speaking colleagues that the government's conduct
became essentially that of finding the least division between
its French and English supporters. This brought a negative
attitude in domestic affairs and a positive pursuit of broader
'national' rights in the external field.

IV

The sectional disruption of 1921 thus at bottom meant that English and French Canada cancelled one another out in politics, and the west was too inexperienced, too limited in its own aspirations, too deferential to the established leadership of the east, to resolve the deadlock. This situation was faced by the new Liberal leader, William Lyon Mackenzie King. King had to preserve the façade of national unity, to preserve it at all costs, and, if possible, to give it some substance. A highly trained sociologist, a creative civil servant, a politician who, in spite of misfortune, had reached the top – King was extraordinarily well equipped to lead a community moving from an agricultural to an industrial order. But because of the revolt in Quebec – not because of that of the Progressives – King had to set aside his special training and experience and devote himself to the negative politics of national preservation. In turning away from his training, he in fact reverted to himself, the grandson of the rebel of 1837, the son of an inadequate father and of a possessive mother who had spent her childhood in exile. He was a shy, lonely, highly respectable son of the Canadian middle class, trained to that class's devotion to hard work, self-discipline, and plain common sense.

Because of the political ancestry he cherished, King, moreover, was in one aspect a doctrinaire, wedded to the Grit ideas of popular democracy, responsible government, and the popular 'mandate'. These ideas he was sure he must realize in their final fullness in an independent Canadian nation and so justify the rebel grandfather whom his mother had adored. He had no idea that, logically developed, those ideas could lead to an irresponsible dictatorship of the Prime Minister. He did not comprehend that they could work to damage both Cabinet and Parliament, and even the Canadian federal structure – that they might bring government in Canada down to closed meetings of political chiefs. If emotions had not swayed his intellect, he might well have realized these things. As it was, by the fate of circumstance and his own personality, King was largely reduced to preserving national unity by the pursuit of expedience. Canada, with all its anomalies of nationality, class, and economic interest, was to be governed by the politics of opportunism.

V

The basic line of opportunistic politics was very simple. It consisted of keeping things as they were in Quebec and of attempting to win back the former Liberal voters in Ontario and on the prairies. No one then had any idea of how things might be really changing in Quebec—not even the nationalists. What Canadian politics required was, first, the negative condition that Quebec should continue to take a formal part in national politics. The second was a positive matter, the winning back of the prairie vote, for the things the western Progressives wanted were few and simple—the restoration of the Crow's Nest Pass Railway rates on grain, the re-establishment of the Wheat Board, the building of the Hudson Bay Railway, and the lowering of the tariff. These were not too remote from what the Liberal party could do without alienating any considerable Liberal or business support elsewhere. King had failed to bring the Progressive leaders into his Cabinet in an attempt in December 1921, but he was able to govern in the knowledge that, except on a few matters such as the above, the majority would support him in preference to Meighen and the Conservatives, or to a general election. Meighen and the Conservatives, for their part, were ostentatiously not opportunists – more so than their conduct warranted. Yet they made no overt advances to Quebec and few concessions in defending the National Policy of tariff protection as needed.

In these circumstances the King government met Parliament in four sessions. Its policy of expediency at home was made to seem positive by a nationalist policy abroad. In the Chanak affair of 1922 it refused to support the British government against insurgent Turkey. In 1923 it refused to allow the Commonwealth to become more than a meeting of governments at the Imperial Conference of that year. The signature of the Halibut Treaty with the United States earlier in the same year had shown a similar resolution, and ended the formal diplomatic unity of the Empire. For the same purposes of national assertion, lip service was given to the League of Nations.

The country in general approved this relatively insignificant nationalism. Quebec merely smouldered. The Progressive movement was beginning to disintegrate. The Crow's Nest Pass rates had been temporarily and partly restored. The Wheat Board had been refused, but the grain-growers had turned to the new idea of 'pooling' their wheat sales. Some slight gains had been made by political action, but the new form of economic action was drawing the farmer's attention, and his hope, away from politics. Politics would go back to the politicians. Above all, the distress of deflation was over. The crops of 1923 and 1924 were good, agricultural prices were once more rising, and business was reviving. The class and sectional distresses of the post-war deflation were subsiding, although some industrial unemployment remained, and Canadian life and Canadian politics might return to their usual pattern.

They indeed proceeded to do so, but the political beneficiary in the general election of 1925 was the Conservative party. It returned to Parliament with one hundred and seventeen members in a House of two hundred and forty-five. The Progressives elected only twenty-four representatives. And the Liberals were sent back with only one hundred and one members, one half of them from Quebec. The Prime Minister and a number of his English-speaking colleagues in the Cabinet were defeated at the polls.

The result might well have been a change of government, but King now revealed that octopus-like tenacity in keeping office that marks the true politician to whom the possession of power is everything because it alone makes anything possible. By means of loose agreement with the Progressives he continued in office, was then elected member for Prince

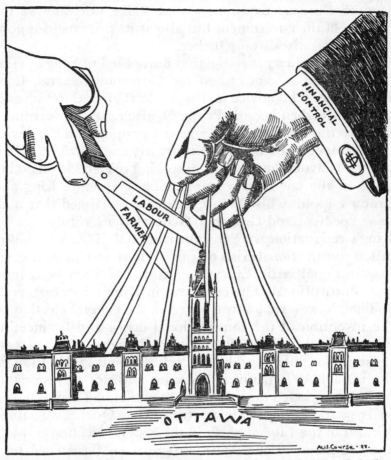

If we do not have public control over finances, we are going to have control of the public by financiers. We can take our choice.—Mr. Good, (Brant), Hansard, March 4, 1925.

From the *Weekly News*, Winnipeg, October 16, 1925.

Albert, and faced once more the triumphant and expectant Meighen. The master of expedients faced the master of words. King ought to have been destroyed by his experienced and brilliant opponent, because on the heels of electoral defeat came the revelation of government scandal. Investigation by a parliamentary committee revealed corruption in the Department of Customs, corruption that almost certainly involved the responsible minister, the Honourable

Jacques Bureau. Exposure would strike not only at the honesty of the government but also at its principal support, its representatives from Quebec.

The preliminary investigation indeed led to King's defeat in the Commons and, when the Governor General, Lord Byng, refused his advice to dissolve Parliament, to his resignation. Meighen became Prime Minister, and endeavoured to finish the session with Progressive support and the device of a Cabinet made up of ministers without portfolio. (This last was to avoid the necessity of seeking re-election on taking office, as the law then required.) The desperate King and Ernest Lapointe, his Quebec lieutenant, claimed that both this expedient and Governor General Byng's insistence on King's resignation were unconstitutional. This was the so-called constitutional crisis of 1926. There was, of course, no constitutional crisis. Everything done had been both legal and constitutional. The crisis was in King's own career.

That, however, he surmounted in the general election by the invention of the constitutional crisis, and by meeting demands of the western Progressives. Meighen made no concession. He could not take the 'crisis' seriously. He thought the tariff both a national necessity and not unreasonably high. He expected the wave of success that had begun to run in 1925 to continue. He was mistaken. Quebec remained faithful to the Liberal party in the general election of 1926, and the majority of western Progressives, threatened by a revival of the protectionist party, either supported the Liberal party openly or at least voted for its candidates.

One hundred and twenty-nine Liberals and liberal Progressives faced ninety-one Conservatives, nine Progressives, eleven U.F.A. members from Alberta, and three Labour members. King, with the ferocity of a cornered animal and a prodigious effort of imagination, had saved his career. And the class and the sectional antagonisms of 1920 were now to be both soothed by prosperity and blanketed by a national Liberal party, indeed by a return to the two-party system in Parliament. Only the U.F.A. and Labour members in the

Commons, the farmers administrations in Manitoba and Alberta, and the clerical and intellectual nationalists in Quebec, remained of all the tumult and revolt of 1920. Canada had survived the shock of the war and the strain caused by the transition from the old rural order to the new industrial one. The remainder of the decade would perhaps give Canada time to study and to find itself. One may venture to peer into the national mirror, note the lineaments of the face, and endeavour to see the mind and spirit behind the puzzled eyes.

VI

To look at the physical face of Canada as a whole in 1926, from the blue and sombre cliffs of Cape Breton and the sweeping shorelines and mountain horizons of the St. Lawrence cleaving Quebec, the woods and waters of Ontario, the rock and waters of the Shield, the long roll of the prairies, and the forest-clad slopes of the Rockies plunging to the Pacific, is to be struck by the way these vast horizons, these great reaches of land and rock and water were held together by a net of railways. Ships plied the great waterways, but distance made them seem few. Roads bound farm to farm, town to town, but were straight and narrow and mean. Few were yet sweeping, challenging highways. But the railways were everywhere, criss-crossing around the great cities, winding through the granite ridges and muskegs of the Shield, crossing the north with an imperious directness from Quebec to Prince Rupert. Four were even probing the farther north towards Hudson Bay, the Peace River, and the Mackenzie. Among the fields and villages of the Maritimes and central Canada the traveller crossed and re-crossed them. The camper in the northern woods came upon their steel spans silent over the rushing waters, their rails running with insistent purpose through the cleft forest. The farmer in the western wheat-fields worked within sight of the tracks that cut across the square survey from landmark to landmark of elevators. The great river valleys of British Columbia were scarred by their rights of way winding by cliffside and through timber stands.

The railway was the symbol of the Canada it had made possible and indeed created. The rolling plume of smoke by day, the echoing whistle by night, were the marks of the progress of civilization in Canada, whether by the riverside at Trois Pistoles, or in the sweeping grasslands of Battle River. And a potent symbol it was. Nothing had ever meant more to Canada. Nothing concerned more Canadians more. Nothing material in Canada more struck the eye with its might, majesty, and power than a great steam locomotive sliding with leashed strength into the station, or thundering with its long train through the countryside, the great strokes of its piston rods slashing the miles down like a scythe in the roadside weeds.

Nor was the symbolism merely picturesque. Canada had almost one mile of railway for every 200 persons. It had indeed built beyond its resources, and the collapse of the Canadian Northern and the Grand Trunk Pacific during the war had not been caused wholly by the conditions of wartime. One great task of the Union Government of 1917-20, and of its successor under Meighen, had been to prevent a collapse of national credit brought about by the collapse of the credit of the railways. Its efforts to preserve the credit and good name of the government left the government with the two railways on its hands, to which the Grand Trunk Railway was later added. The three were combined under one management as the Canadian National Railways in 1921. Whatever the financial cost, whatever the devotion to economic principle, the railway services of Canada had to be preserved, by private enterprise if possible, as in the case of the Canadian Pacific Railway, by government ownership if not. Now a great railway man, Henry Thornton, was endeavouring to make the Canadian National Railways a railroad system despite the diverse origins of its constituent railways, and to make it earn a profit despite the over-capitalization that was greatly excessive even after the sharp reduc-

tions effected by the reorganization of 1917-21. Canada, it
was hoped, would yet grow up to the railways it had built.

In the old settled areas, however, the automobile lurching
along dusty roads was a foretaste of a means of transport that
would end the supremacy of the railway in Canadian life,
and make impossible the slow reduction of deficits of the
government railways by national growth. Growth in general
had been going on in spite of deflation and the uncertainties
of politics. In the long-settled areas some rural counties were
losing population, but to the growing cities, or to the expanding wheatlands of the farmer, or to the new towns of
the north. The pattern here of a small farm behind its fences
of rail, stone, or stump, the farmsteads with their tree-shaded
lanes down to the public roads–or in Quebec and the Maritimes with unpainted porches peering onto the roadways–
was much the same; it was already old, sometimes gracious
with trees and ivied houses, sometimes bare and dilapidated.
The towns were lapping into the neighbouring fields. Sometimes a raw new factory took over an orchard or a barley-
field, but most of them, in spite of their crude red-brick and
smoking chimneys, fitted into the countryside. Only in the
greater cities–Montreal, Toronto, Hamilton–did one hear
the real clangour of industry, or in Vancouver encounter a
pre-1914 rush of speculative building and suburban growth.
Winnipeg, its tap-root of traffic cut by the Panama Canal,
fretted in stagnation. Older Canada was fattening, rather
than extending, the structure that the settlement of the west
had built.

Growth as Canada knew it, in terms of prairie sod broken,
or mine shaft opened, or mill site cleared, was taking place
on the northern prairies and in the aspen-growth country of
the Manitoba Interlake, in Saskatchewan north of its great
river, or in the Peace River country of Alberta and British
Columbia.

There the shifting farmer and the immigrant, following
the grain belt as it was advanced north by new strains of
wheat bred in the experimental stations, cleared the scrub
and drove the breaking-plough. New fields were turned

black, and the next year grew green and golden under the long sunshine of the north. And at the dam sites of the rivers coming down from the plateau of the Shield, new dams rose grey and rigid, to send waters down the whirling turbines summer and winter, to stroke from the dynamos the electric current for the mines and the pulp-mills. In Kirkland Lake and Abitibi the hard-rock miners were cutting ever deeper into the mineral rocks of the Precambrian Shield after gold, silver, and the base metals that American industry increasingly sought in Canada. And along the southern edges of the black-green spruce forests that lay across Canada like a hunting tartan, and on the tree-covered Pacific slopes, pulp-mills and paper-mills rose and gathered towns around them to print the daily records of the crimes, follies, and sports of men in a thousand American cities. To lumber and wheat, national growth was adding the metals, noble and base, and the paper that held together an urban and industrial civilization. The rocks the immigrant had passed by, the spruce woods the lumbermen had scorned, the water that had run untrammelled to the lakes, were adding new wealth to Canada, and a new population neither agrarian nor urban.

The northern wilderness immediate to settlement, hitherto the haunt of the miner and the summer camper, was yielding to exploitation. This much of untouched Canada had been opened by the new demands of industry and urban life and the great railways built to haul wheat. But the immense Canadian northland, flung out towards the Pole, remained beyond the reach of exploitation except in the old way of the trapper. The missionary, the fur-trader, and the Mounted Police lived or travelled in these vast wastes, in tent, igloo, or cabin, by canoe, snowshoe, or dog-sled, to serve Indian and Eskimo and to maintain the Canadian claim to areas yet unoccupied. The north was in effect a barren empire that Canada ruled and Canadians ignored. Their interests, like their railways, ran east and west, but rarely north.

Yet in the north also change was occurring, like the first summer thaw along the face of southward-facing Arctic cliffs. Oil had been found in 1920 at Fort Norman on the Mackenzie River, a first portent of the mineral riches of the Arctic. And now the Hudson Bay Railway, its roadbed abandoned since 1915, was reaching towards the Bay to begin a line of northern sea traffic and become a jumping-off place into the islands of the eastern Arctic. And most important of all, 'bush-flying' by means of planes equipped with pontoons for summer's open water and skis for the level ice of winter was opening the north to the surveyor, the prospector, and traffic as never before. Edmonton, Winnipeg, Quebec City—all suddenly saw the deep north as a new hinterland. The airplane was to bring the north into Canadian life with an immediacy and an intensity never known before.

VII

The face of Canada, so far as it had been altered by human action, reflected the material purposes of Canada. It did not, and fortunately, reflect the mind of Canada, except in so far as that was scientific. Science, particularly science applied to some material end, was solidly established and widely flourishing in Canada. The National Research Council, founded during the war, was now turning its efforts to building up the scientific establishment of Canada, and to distributing the government grants in aid of scientific research. The one dazzling scientific achievement in Canada during the decade was the discovery in 1922 by Doctors F. G. Banting and C. H. Best of the nature and function of insulin. It was perhaps in the national character that the discovery should have been in medicine, for in Canada the doctor enjoyed much of the reverence only the clergy had had, and many of the best men, mentally and morally, of earnest middle-class homes went into the practice of medicine as a vocation. But science went much beyond research. It had become the basis, with mathematics, of popular education in Canada, and as religion and the humanities declined in popular influence, science succeeded them, not only as a material utility but also as a world view.

Learning in the humanities did little to affect this change. In Canadian schools and universities, instruction in literature and philosophy was, in general, inhibited and dull, and well behind the movement of ideas and events in the world at large. In professional philosophy, the speculative idealism of the great John Watson of Queen's University still remained the chief philosophic influence in Canada, and particularly on theology and the life of the Church. But idealism, although it continued to be taught by R. C. Lodge in the University of Manitoba, was no longer to lead philosophy in Canada. Philosophy now took many forms, the chief being that of the historical understanding of philosophy of G. S. Brett of the University of Toronto. For the decade, however, philosophy became academic, its achievement that of laying foundations for later edifices. And the same was true of the study of literature and history. Historians were active in producing good and learned books, such as R. G. Trotter's *Canadian Federation* (1924) and Chester Martin's *Empire and Commonwealth* (1929). Others, such as O. D. Skelton, turned to political service in the Department of External Affairs. But the most publicly influential scholar, in part because of the nature of his science, was Adam Shortt, economist, editor, and adviser of government. Still lacking was a Canadian idiom for the discussion of ideas and affairs, the golden bridge between the detached world of learning and the committed world of action.

The public schools, on the other hand, were becoming steadily less concerned with academic training and more and more involved as agents of social policy. It was becoming their prime function, undeclared but imperative, to diminish the distinctions caused by home and class among their pupils, and to produce from diversity of background and national origin the social conformity a democratic society required. In the process academic excellence suffered before the demands of social mediocrity. The power to discriminate, to differ, to divine new relations, had to share the teachers' concern with the power to conform, to co-operate, to conciliate. The school of learning had become the school of manners, and, all unwittingly, the new generation was being prepared for the demagogue and the advertiser.

Literature in Canada was no prophylactic against change so fundamental and subtle. It was popular, optimistic, pragmatic, and romantic. Perhaps the most widely read novelist in English, Ralph Connor (Rev. Charles W. Gordon), was a clerical Jack London, combining violence with virtue in a recipe that sold thousands of volumes. His books contain not a single memorable character, or one noteworthy statement, but they had the great virtue that one could read them without ever being disturbed. Connor wrote for the less demanding members of the middle class; a similarly typical novelist, Sir Gilbert Parker, wrote for the more worldly of the middle class, for the established businessman and his family – novels of remote and aseptic action with the fruity accent and cigar-smoke atmosphere of the clubroom and the den. Such writers appealed to the romanticism, the desiccated nostalgia of a people raised on the romantic writings of Scott and Tennyson, of Longfellow, Lowell, and Whittier, and quite unused to an imaginative and searching discussion of their own society, and in their idiom. Literature was in Canadian experience unreal, and an amusement, never a criticism of life.

When an immigrant writer, Frederick Philip Grove, gravely and successfully attempted this task, his books were received in silence, or with self-conscious and damning praise. When a Canadian writer, Sara Jeanette Duncan, in *The Imperialist* (1904), for example, described Canadian life in realistic but by no means brutal terms, her book was not recognized for what it was, the beginning of a native criticism of life. In short, all sense of realism, and above all of tragedy, was lacking from Canadian writing, even from the excellent academic verse of genuine poets like Duncan Campbell Scott and Bliss Carman. In French and in English, Canadian writers and the Canadian literary idiom were derivative, sifted, and genteel. Only the poetry of E. J. Pratt in his *Newfoundland Verse* (1923) promised the emancipation of poetry from the polished and the soignée. Emancipation had yet to be won from rural conservatism and a Victorian prudery.

In art little was worthy of note except the painting of the Group of Seven. The art of these men was considerable in both execution and vision. It did open Canadian eyes to the northland and the character of the country. But it too was essentially derivative and romantic, and it caught the public eye, not because of its vigour and skill, but because, strong as it was, it too could be fitted into the prevailing local romanticism.

Art and letters, then, had done little, if anything, to resolve the fierce transition in Canada from a Victorian world of rural conservatism to the astringent, realistic, and abstract world of sophisticated, scientific, urban volatilism. Canada had not felt the psychological impact of the Great War, and it had escaped in consequence the smothering disillusionment that descended on Europe and the United States in the twenties. Thus the mind of Canada was floundering in a world it had not experienced; it could not prepare for the future because it had not caught up with the present. Hope there was in the work of Grove and the first novel of a new writer, Morley Callaghan—his *Strange Fugitive* (1928). It was a grim, overdone story, but a story, flatly reported, of bootlegging taken up as merely another line of business, and of urbanized people in Toronto who had neither tradition nor values, who were amoral creatures of appetite. Canada had indeed been strangely fugitive from reality all the decade.

VIII

If so backward in mind, what was Canada in spirit? The Christian churches in Canada had been and still were essentially missionary and 'pioneer' churches. They had not only to care for souls, but also to create a Christian milieu. They had created and were incorporated in the rural conservatism that still constituted the Canadian mind. The churches were therefore little prepared to deal with the new scientific, urban, and industrial culture that was changing the mentality and morals of Canadians in ways Canadians themselves could neither understand nor control.

The traditionalist as well as the fundamentalist churches were caught in this self-created prison. The Roman Catholic Church was concerned either with the cultural survival of French Canada or with the advancement of immigrant and depressed groups – Irish, Scots Highlanders, Ukrainians. It was a vast, arduous, and necessary task, called for by the basic ethics of Canadian life, never openly avowed, and continually pursued. The Anglican Church, the church of the northern missions and of the recent British immigrant to the west, was in the east, along with the Presbyterian, the garrison church of the Anglo-Scottish and Protestant Irish ascendancy.

The Protestant churches were also, sociologically speaking, bringing their congregations up to the middle-class status, again a necessary work of civilization and improvement. How true this was is shown by two things. One was the steady revolt of fundamentalist sects from the 'old line' churches; the other was the gnawing concern, best exemplified in the careers of Salem Bland and J. S. Woodsworth, of the Methodist Church with the 'Social Gospel', once proclaimed by Wesley himself and now re-awakened amid the great social changes of the century.

In all this social effort the churches became confused and lost control of events through their own self-induced contradictions. The traditionalist churches ignored the challenge of science and failed to adapt their world view to the new material culture that science and industry were forcing on society. The Protestant churches, with their fundamentalist roots, accepted the challenge of science and were shattered by it, and veered uncharacteristically to what was essentially a gospel of good works: social reform and prohibition. The Canadian churches, as fragmented as the country they served, were bankrupted intellectually and spiritually, not in the decade as such, but more definitely during the decade than before or after.

This was revealed by two events. One was Church Union.
The succession of unions between the Methodist and Presbyterian churches was a Canadian phenomenon based on
practical considerations, and it prepared the way for the
union of the Methodist Church with the Congregational
Church, and with the majority of Presbyterian churches.
This great ecclesiastical event was nevertheless much more
a matter of pooling resources and aiding the weaker rural
churches than an exercise in Christian brotherhood or the
ecumenical spirit. In many ways it was a Protestant rally
against the steady growth of the Roman Catholic Church.
Because it was these things it left the new church increased
in numbers and in wealth, but uncertain in doctrine and
weaker in spirit and influence than before.

The other event was prohibition, an enterprise of the
churches, mainly the Protestant, and of the rural voters, and
particularly the newly enfranchised women. In nothing did
rural conservatism speak in more authentic accents. A contemporary journalist accurately observed: 'it is clear . . .
that it has always been the countryside – its prejudices as
well as its interests – that has been the prime factor in shaping Canadian legislation.' The abuses attacked by legislation
were real and indefensible. The difficulties prohibition had
to encounter were great because in Canada only the consumption of alcoholic drinks could be prohibited, not its
manufacture and sale for export. Moreover, and this was
the fundamental error, it was an attempt to enforce a moral
code by legal means. The result was both the failure of the
enterprise – not complete, because drinking habits were to be
improved – and serious damage to the law itself, as in the
shifting of the onus from the Crown to the accused, and to
respect for the law and for law-officers. Bootlegging flourished in direct proportion to the degree of prohibition. The
law was flouted and the police were corrupted. Fortunes
were made, one at least still among the greatest in Canada.
The unsophisticated morality which among many Canadians
passed for religion had overreached itself and was discred-

ited. The churches that had supported prohibition suffered too in loss of influence. And the way was widened for the advance of the secular spirit.

IX

What, then, was the central vortex of Canadian life in the decade of 1920-30? It was the opposing drives of what may be termed the nostalgic and the propulsive elements in Canadian society. Canadians, looking backward with sentiment, were being driven forward by desire.

The elements of the Canadian nostalgia were, first, a Christianity essentially missionary in impulse and rural in assumption. And then a rural conservatism that was materialistic, even primitive, and committed to simple living and moral endurance. What had been a necessity was defended as a thing good in itself. And beneath both of the religions of primitivism and rural conservatism was an unthinking individualism, essentially optimistic in spirit. A university president might question progress, but the popular mind in Canada accepted without thought the doctrine of continual, automatic progress, moral as well as material. One had only to persevere in the plain, hard way, and all would be well.

Such was the outlook, with varying degrees of sophistication and clarity, of the bulk of Canadian society, French as well as English, of the urban middle class as well as of the farmers, lumberers, and townsmen of the countryside and the frontier. Yet nothing could have been more illusory. Not only the great obvious changes wrought by the growth of cities and industry made that outlook unrealistic. The very acts of the farmer leaders, of the exponents of rural thought, of the behaviour of any prospering Canadian, denied the outlook. Every advance of science and industry was welcomed; none was questioned. The fundamental grievance of those who followed the rural life was that it lacked the amenities and advantages of urban life. The very changes sought would change rural life itself, would industrialize and urbanize it.

The spinning vortex, however, was working more than a change from rural to urban mores and values. The social structure was being altered to incorporate a permanent and organized labour force with its own values and its own outlook. The grim misery of the urban slums was forcing a new concept of social obligation and of the role of the state. The virtue of charity became a matter of scorn because of its inadequacy in the new conditions, and its social assumptions were intolerable in the new society. It was being replaced by the concept of social welfare, the beginning of the rise of the social worker, the advent of the service state. In the municipalities and the provinces human needs were to be met by public means and scientific training.

Such changes were happening, but were still anathema to the general conscience. Yet the slow extinction of social laissez-faire was being pressed also on economic laissez-faire. Free enterprise, still in the ascendant, was challenged by the spectacular rise of the Wheat Pools in the prairie provinces between 1923 and 1928, and by the persistence of labour representation in the Commons after 1921, the fruit of the Winnipeg General Strike of 1919. Few as they were yet in number, the shoots of a social democratic movement were struggling to the surface. If not socialistic in doctrine, they were socialistic in spirit. In 1927 the leader of the movement, J. S. Woodsworth, won his first victory in the passage of the Old Age Pensions Act, the act by which the government and people of Canada admitted that personal effort and private charity could not be left alone to provide for the care of every member of the community. It was the affirmation in personal affairs of the same principle the provinces had been asserting in industry, that human life could not, in all cases, be regulated by private contract and have all its needs met by personal effort alone.

Not less significant, perhaps more so, was a change of thought on monetary matters that had begun to trickle through the fissures of public discussion. The harsh defla-

tion after 1920 had renewed interest in the monetary doctrines of American populism and in a new monetary theory
propagated in England under the name of Social Credit.
Both were forms of under-consumption thought. When the
Canada Banking Act was reviewed in 1923 the Alberta Progressives had arranged to have the leader of the Social Credit
movement, Major C. H. Douglas, called as a witness. Thus
the principles of Social Credit were spread on a public document, to defy with its inflationary spirit the orthodox dogma
of enforced deflation applied in 1920. This, and the writings
of W. C. Good, Progressive member for Brant, on the cyclical
theory of budgeting, ensured that as economic individualism was challenged by social welfare, financial orthodoxy was
also queried, queried by principles which in more sophisticated terms Maynard Keynes was to make respectable and
effective in the next decade.

X

The same wrestling of the nostalgic and the progressive
occurred in literature and in thought, more faintly and less
decisively. By the end of the decade romanticism had re-
treated to the pages of the ladies' magazines, or, heavily
spiced with sin and realism, had entered into its euthanasia
in Mazo de la Roche's *Jalna* (1927) and *Whiteoaks of Jalna*
(1929). Grove and Callaghan among novelists, E. J. Pratt
among poets, were recognized as the emerging artists because
they spoke in tones of convincing realism and dealt with
tragic as well as comic themes. And in thought there was
some beginning of realization that the firm world of optimism was cracking, that progress was probably not automatic, perhaps not necessarily desirable. This failure of
Canadian contemporary thought in general to grasp how the
assumptions and values of the previous century had collapsed at least left the nation free to rejoice in the prosperity
of the second half of the decade and in the victories of the
political opportunism that had triumphed in the election of
1926. That was a victory of nationalism, but a superficial

victory, for the troubles of Canada were more fundamental than nationalism could be. They were the difficulties of secular change – economic, social, and moral – and could be changed only by experience and suffering, not by the expedience of politicians. Nationalism was a mist that hung over the vortex of Canadian life; it was, in its drift and changes, lit by sunlight, eye-catching and seemingly solid, but it was in large part mist.

So far as it was not, what it was appeared through the rare insight of a writer, John Mitchell, to be known later under the pseudonym of 'Patrick Slater' for his tale *The Yellow Briar* (1933). Canada had become, so the title of Mitchell's book proclaimed, *The Kingdom of America*. It had, but did its people accept the fact, and would they give their allegiance to a king of Canada? This too was mist for two more decades at least.

Because, however, nationalism triumphed in 1926, that year and its successors saw the consequences of nationalism. These were the Imperial Conference of 1926 and the Dominion-Provincial Conference of 1927. The former declared, in the famous Balfour formula, the equality in status of the Dominions with the United Kingdom and set in train the achievement of equality of function enacted in the Statute of Westminster of 1931. In the acid of nationalism, Emppire had dissolved into Commonwealth. Because, however, equality of function would mean national control of the constitution, a matter of great importance to the provinces of Canada, a Dominion-Provincial conference met in Ottawa in 1927 to consider, among other things, the amendment of the constitution by a process wholly Canadian that would end the still necessary reference to the Parliament of the United Kingdom. The conference marked the beginning of the endeavour, not yet completed, to find such a process. It may also be taken as marking the establishment of the national-provincial conference as part of the working, if not of the formal, constitution of Canada. Both the failure to agree on a method of amendment and the continued use of the conference were to reveal how superficial was the nationalism of the decade, and how much Canada was a country *sui generis*. The basic truth was that the changing nature of the British Empire brought Canada face to face with the task of finding its own internal cohesion, whether in nationalism or in its own peculiar federalism. A percipient writer in *The Canadian Forum* saw as much, and wrote: 'If the [British] Empire were to fall apart, no cohesive force in the Canadian Confederation could hold it together.'

The logic of the nationalistic course was furthered in international affairs also. Not only was a British High Commissioner sent to Ottawa, to mark the new relations between Canada and the United Kingdom, but a Canadian minister, the Honourable Vincent Massey, was also sent to Washington in order that relations with the United States might be handled directly. And in the League of Nations, Canada, who had used the League in the assertion of its own nationality, itself declared by the 'Canadian resolution' that it would not have to go to the defence of other nations. This effectively ended Article X of the Covenant, by which all members of the League were committed to the defence of any member of the League. No Canadian supporter of the League, apparently, foresaw that the right of national self-determination might be used to destroy a state member of the League, such as Czechoslovakia, or indeed Canada itself. And few noted that as Canada became more independent of the United Kingdom it became more dependent on the United States.

No such thoughts disturbed the celebration in 1927 of the Diamond Jubilee, the sixtieth anniversary of Confederation. It was the avatar of a Confederation vindicated, of a nation restored to a unity, disturbed but not broken by the events of the preceding decade – the Great War and the conscription crisis.

Canada, therefore, rode the crest of opportunist politics, romantic nostalgia, and economic prosperity into the great and unintended deflation that closed the decade. The Liberal regime of Mackenzie King, having survived the hazards that might well have destroyed it, was content to survive.

The regime did nothing after 1927, and stayed busy doing it. Political expediency had paid off. The threatening forces of agrarian revolt and Quebec nationalism had been lulled. Abbé Groulx, although less aggressive than before or after, continued his essentially nationalistic studies, and the little group of U.F.A. and Labour members in the Commons were quieted if not silenced. Why do anything to arouse them, or to give the representatives of labour and agrarian discontent material for bitter speeches to the complacent benches in the Commons?

Not only the character of the political regime was responsible for this euphoria. Canada, with its practical instinct for material success, was sharing the great American boom. Even the farmers were relatively well off, and the record crop of 1928 seemed to put them beyond any need for complaint. More and more roads were built for more and more motor cars. The cities grew, particularly Vancouver, which surged ahead of Winnipeg in size. The country home became steadily more like the city home. What was needed but more and more effort in order to enjoy more and more of life in a country dotted with the well lit, well warmed homes of a simple and democratic people? Nationhood had been achieved, except for a few details. Germany was in the League, and the war forgotten. The United States was revealing with its usual exuberance what science and productive drive could do. War had been abolished by the Kellogg-Briand Pact of 1928, an amiable gesture inspired by Mr. Kellogg, whose name every Canadian knew, and by M. Briand whose pictures in the press were so friendly and reassuring. And in 1928 the Washington Senators had won the World Series, which proved that any good luck was possible in a peaceful and prosperous world. An unfortunate interruption – an accident, appalling, but an accident – the Great War and its aftermath, had been surmounted and left behind. Canada was once more on the high road it had been following in 1914.

Such was the mood of 1929. Then in October came the crash of the Wall Street stock market; shares tumbled in

Montreal and Toronto. Prosperity continued but only as a
hope–the old car was not turned in, and the old suit was
made to do. What had been forgotten since 1920 now re-
appeared in the news and grew steadily–the black disease of
industrial and urban society, continuous mass unemployment. The financial and administrative structures of municipalities and provinces, not prepared for this dead weight
of the new society, took the impact and shuddered. The
spectres of the next decade, the unemployed, began to walk
the city streets and ride the freight cars. And the great crop
of 1928 had been sold to the Pools at levels too high to allow
them to carry the loss on falling markets. The western grain
crop, for a generation the great nourisher of the national
economy, now became a national problem, and the carry-
over a burden lightened only by the beginning of the driest
decade the west was ever to know.

The decade thus ended as it had begun, with deflation.
This deflation, however, was the result not merely of the
ending of a post-war boom, it was the result of the ending of
an epoch, that which had begun in 1815 when England had
saved the world for industrial capitalism and the United
States had opened the Mississippi Valley for the settler. The
decade of 1920-30 was devoted to an attempt to continue
that epoch. In it Canada had accomplished little that was
positive and had learned little of the new realities. Some
novelties had begun to stir: a political labour movement,
strange ideas of Social Credit and cyclical budgeting, a saving realism in a few writers. Some social experience had been
acquired, and prohibition had failed and been replaced by
government control of the sale of liquor. City ways were not
quite so alien and so menacing to rural conservatism. So
much, it would seem, and perhaps no more.

But Canada had still to learn from the next decade that the
world of 1914 was beyond all recall.

8. The 1930s

KENNETH MCNAUGHT

The grim world-wide financial collapse of 1929 dictated to Canada a basic condition of life in the 'hungry thirties' for which the country was unprepared. Both the politics and the economic growth of the twenties bequeathed basic political preconceptions which acted like a constitutional strait-jacket. The economic growth and collapse were constitutionally the concern of the provinces, and the provinces were still strong to defend their rights, or extend them, at the expense of the federal government. Lassitude seemed to hang over the weakened Government of Canada.

Prime Minister King, after weathering the political storms of the twenties, was reluctant to challenge the provinces by advocating any broad federal program to meet the depression. Moreover, he and his Liberal colleagues were by no means convinced that federal spending, subsidies to the provinces, and deficit financing were good policies *per se*. Quite apart from King's 'obsession with the sense of our constitutional difficulties', as J. S. Woodsworth put it, the Prime Minister was no further along the Keynesian path than was the ex-Progressive President of the United States, Herbert Hoover. Surrounded in his cabinet by men of basically conservative temperament, such as Charles Dunning (Finance), Ernest Lapointe (Justice), Peter Heenan (Labour), and Thomas Crerar (Railways), Mackenzie King doggedly defended the barren ground of rugged individualism. The government's response to demands for positive leadership was well illustrated by Heenan's remark that 'unemployment insurance will be adopted in Canada only after public opinion has been educated to the necessity for such legislation.'

Rattled by the mounting spirit of political discontent King compounded his sins of inactivity by dropping the injudicious remark that he would never give 'a five-cent piece' to any province with a Tory government. While he was irritated by the evidence of rising unemployment, falling wheat sales, and regional inequities, he vastly underestimated their political impact. Continuing to think in terms of tariff tinkering he called an election in the autumn of 1930. Long since laid to rest is the legend that he foxily anticipated defeat in order to saddle the Conservatives with responsibility for the worst of the depression. In fact he was confident of victory. His decision to go to the country was reinforced by contact with the occult and he recorded in his diary on the eve of the election: 'I believe we will win with a good majority.' He also noted his conviction that R. B. Bennett was 'not so good a leader as Meighen', and this personal misconception was to be a major cause of Liberal defeat. When the votes were counted the Conservatives took 49 per cent of the total, the Liberals (with Liberal-Progressives) 45.6 per cent. Minor parties and independents accounted for the remaining 5.4 per cent. This gave the

Conservatives 137 seats to the Liberals' 88. R. B. Bennett, the rich and bombastic bachelor lawyer from Calgary, was Prime Minister for the next five years.

The 1930 election spelled out the principal Canadian themes of the decade. Liberal defeat revealed that the country was not content to endure depression nourished only on memories of ephemeral prosperity. Bland promises of sound administration and retrenchment – 'the record' – were met with loud cries for farmers' protection against New Zealand butter, retaliation against rising American tariffs, and, on the left, the demand for a more collectivist legislative philosophy. Although the Dunning election budget had increased imperial preference and provided for a response to American tariffs it had been mild in both directions. Bennett saw this and castigated the Liberals for 'timidity and vacillation'. Representing a party tradition that was not philosophically averse to positive government action he declared that he would use Canadian tariffs to 'blast a way into the markets that have been closed', put on foot large-scale public works, and assume the provinces' share of the cost of old-age pensions. Anticipating F. D. Roosevelt's 1932 assault on Hoover, Bennett thundered: 'Mackenzie King promises you conferences; I promise you action. He promises consideration of the problem of unemployment, I promise to end unemployment. Which plan do you like best?' Although the Conservative program was even less specific than Roosevelt's and in practice was to accomplish even less towards ending the depression, it did acknowledge the circumstances of the day. Together with the programs and activities of new federal and provincial political parties and of voluntary organizations, Bennett's blustering was an appropriate harbinger of a decade in which Canadians sought a new definition of national purpose. Despite, and partly because of, economic frustration, it was an energetic, speculative decade – one that created a new national sentiment and many of Canada's most important modern institutions.

The crucible of depression was certainly well heated. The ten million Canadians of 1930 were hit as hard as any comparable group in the world by economic chaos. In some respects, because of the boom of the late 1920s, the impact was much greater than in many other countries. The depression was also, because of the extent of the Dominion and the variety of occupations, very uneven in its incidence. Urban centres that had grown rapidly in the 1920s remained nearly static in the 1930s. Thus, many middle-class families suffered relatively little, while a swollen urban working class bore the brunt of lowered wages and unemployment created by business policies designed to protect prices rather than jobs. Yet, even so, the Atlantic provinces and the prairies undoubtedly reached the lowest depths in Canada.

For the country as a whole, both income and gross national product actually declined slightly over the ten years following 1929. But in the Maritimes and on the prairies the decline was catastrophic. The national net farm income plunged from $417 million in 1929 to $109 million in 1933 and by 1939 had only recovered to pre-depression levels. Hit by disastrous drought in the early thirties, as well as by shrinking external markets for wheat, the prairies suffered total economic collapse. Saskatchewan, the greatest of the wheat producers, had to apply for loans from the federal government, to meet even the provincial share of federal-provincial relief payments. The shock-waves from the western dust-bowls spread quickly through the national economy, affecting transportation, banking, commerce, and industry – and were not tempered by any substantial recovery of world markets.

For a country that was still overwhelmingly dependent upon exports of farm produce and raw materials the figures of foreign trade tell the story briefly. The total value of domestic exports was $1,152,416,000 in 1929, sank to $489,883,000 in 1932, and by 1939 had climbed back only to $924,926,000. For central Canada and British Columbia a fairly steady market for mine products (especially gold) and pulp and paper helped to ease the shock, but also aggravated the regional differences. The Maritimes, which had benefited little from the prosperity of the twenties, reached a near-subsistence level as fisheries, lumbering, and steel production withered. Fish exports, for example, fell from a 1929 value of $38 million to $19 million in 1932 and had reached less than $30 million by 1939. By 1933, in addition to the social devastation on the Atlantic seaboard and the prairies, approximately 23 per cent of the labour force was unemployed (compared to 3 per cent in 1929). This meant that, besides farmers, there were well over one and a half million Canadians without any source of earned income.

While the statistics are revealing, they fail to conjure up the reality of wasted lives, of long lines of forlorn men stretching away from the city soup-kitchens or shivering against the wind on the tops of freight cars as they rode hopelessly about the country in search of non-existent jobs. Nor do the abstract figures tell the real story of farms lost to mortgage companies, of the accumulated savings of a generation vanished with the sale of a fishing schooner, the closing of a corner store, the shutting down of a small plant. Least of all can the statistics portray the bitterness of newly pauperized classes forced to forgo amenities and even adequate food while the salaried and *rentier* groups suffered little. Highly protected industry and monopolistic control of prices served to emphasize the inequities of a chaotic capitalism. The social nadir was sketched briefly in the Commons by J. S. Woodsworth, who emerged in these years as the rallying-point for the country's conscience:

> In the old days we could send people from the cities to the country. If they went out today they would meet another army of unemployed coming back from the country to the city; that outlet is closed. What can these people do? They have been driven from our parks; they have been driven from our streets; they have been driven from our buildings and in this city [Ottawa] they actually took refuge on the garbage heaps.

The rumbling of political discontent that had reverberated through the election of 1930 grew louder as the depression deepened. In the west the old feeling of betrayal and exploitation brought forth new political groupings which grew naturally out of the background of Progressivism. In Ontario and British Columbia, provincial Liberalism threw up demagogic leaders and these provinces also sustained active branches of the new socialist party, the Co-operative Commonwealth Federation (C.C.F.). In Quebec, spreading unemployment led to a combination of social radicalism and French-Canadian nationalism. There, the urbanization and industrialization that had been stimulated in the twenties by English-Canadian, British, and American investment was exploited politically as evidence of growing foreign domination. In fact, urbanization was a factor in the decline of French-Canadian influence in the power élite of Quebec. Owing to lower rural educational levels, farmers' sons who went to the cities ended up in unskilled, lower-level occupations and thus emphasized the non-French control of Quebec's economic life. In the Maritimes, while new political movements failed to emerge, the sentiments that gave rise to the 'Maritimes rights movement' in the twenties continued to find vigorous expression in both the old parties.

Plainly, the breakdown of the Canadian system, both economic and political, required the definition and implementation of new policies at all levels of government. The municipalities and the provinces had discovered that their sources of finance were utterly inadequate to the roles imposed upon them by unemployment relief and general welfare as well as by the industrial and urban growth of the preceding decade. Many Canadians also felt that since the economic problems were nationwide in their impact the federal government should assume, or be given, power to establish more uniform levels of welfare and opportunity— in short, to establish a new 'national policy' with a strong tinge of collectivism. In this mood many French Canadians shared with English-speaking Canadians despite the extreme *nationaliste* politicking that emerged in Quebec under Maurice Duplessis.

II

The initial response of the new Bennett government to the national calamity was to convene a special session of Parliament early in September of 1930. Twenty million dollars was voted for emergency relief work to be administered by provincial and municipal governments, without any national plan being worked out, and the tariff was raised more sharply than at any time since the institution of the 'national policy'. While King was horrified by this 'fiscal irresponsibility', it did represent action, and there was no substantial opposition to it in the House. On the other hand it was action along archaic lines. While Bennett, as the offspring of an old New Brunswick Loyalist family, was prepared to use his power positively, he had had little preparation, as a corporation lawyer, for the socio-economic needs of a semi-industrialized country faced by the collapse of world markets. His argument rested on the assumption that he could provide 25,000 jobs by protecting Canadian industry and also use the tariff to bargain for the entry of agricultural and primary products to foreign markets. In practice this over-simple response had the same effect as did the autarchy adopted by other western nations at the same time. The Canadian trade balance was transformed from a deficit of $125,332,000 in 1930 to a surplus of $187,621,000 in 1935. Financiers on Bay Street and St. James Street found this gratifying, especially since the government also refused to devalue the dollar. Undoubtedly, too, the Tory fiscal policy saved some Canadian firms from bankruptcy (particularly by rigorous application of new anti-dumping features of the tariff) and thus protected some Canadian jobs. But while the policy lessened the depression in profits, dividends, and prices this very virtue militated against recovery in the vast areas of the economy that depended upon exports. And by keeping the price structure artificially rigid it added appreciably to the misery of millions of people living on relief or on drastically reduced incomes.

Allied to the initial tariff-monetary policies was Bennett's use of the Imperial Economic Conference, held in Ottawa in 1932, to wring concessions from the United Kingdom. 'From that Conference', declared the Governor General in his 1932 prorogation speech, 'may arise a power which will bring enduring harmony out of economic chaos.' Bennett had prepared his ground by almost acrimonious insistence during the 1930 Imperial Conference that while he firmly believed in an extension of the system of imperial preferences he also believed in 'Canada first, then the Empire'. Disavowing the Laurier-King principle that imperial preference in the Canadian tariff should be voluntary and unrelated to specific reciprocity in the British tariff, Bennett had irritated the Labour government by his suggestion that it was time for Britain to abandon free trade and construct a genuine imperial commercial system. But between 1930 and 1932 Bennett's position was markedly strengthened. Not only had negotiations with the United States, Germany, and France failed to produce any significant concessions, but in Britain Ramsay MacDonald had survived the collapse of his Labour government and emerged at the head of a National (or thinly-disguised Conservative) government that was very interested in regrouping the Empire-Commonwealth in the face of both economic and possibly military difficulties.

Thus, when the Conference assembled amidst much fanfare in Ottawa, the ebullient Canadian leader drove a hard bargain. With the Canadian tariff already raised by about 50 per cent Bennett agreed to raise the general level still further while exempting Britain from the second-round increases. He also agreed to lower the Canadian tariff on some significant items as a second way of increasing the imperial preference. But in return he got the British agreement to ban dumping of foreign goods in the British market, and to provide free entry for a considerable range of Canadian farm and primary products, as well as preferential treatment for others, ranging up to 33 per cent. In addition to the British agreement, bilateral trade pacts were worked out with other members of the Commonwealth.

In the years following the Ottawa agreements a consider-

able shift in Canada's trading pattern occurred. Britain and
the Commonwealth took about 12 per cent more of Canada's
total exports, but the continued failure to expand exports to
the United States and Europe more than balanced this shift.
One thing the agreements did prove: with determination the
Commonwealth system could be fleshed out by trading benefits. In a world in which tariff warfare was painfully ubiquitous the Ottawa initiative showed some positive advantages.
Had the tariff policies been accompanied by a mild inflation
these advantages might have been enhanced by lowering
the price of Canadian exports (as well as the cost of living)
and thus improving Canada's competitive position in other
foreign markets. The other Bennett depression policies,
however, were framed within a hard-currency context.

In the most critical centre of economic collapse, the prairie
west, a series of stopgap measures was applied. When the
Wheat Pool, with its system of initial payments, was forced to
wind up its operation in 1931, small subsidies were paid by
the government for wheat brought to market in that year.
This was followed by government purchasing on the open
market – which failed to sustain prices to any appreciable
degree – and in 1935, with over 200,000,000 bushels of
government-owned wheat in storage, the Wheat Board was
re-established to bring permanent order into the western
grain economy. Aid to the provinces, to provide for relief of
farmers and the unemployed, was continued, but its administration through provincial and municipal bodies was largely
ad hoc and no system of co-ordinated public construction was
worked out. In many of the relief camps for single unemployed men the conditions of life provoked rioting, while
extreme distress in the cities created grave class tension. To
these continuing problems Bennett's further responses were
a curious mixture of government planning and outright
reaction.

In 1934 Conservative legislation established the Bank of
Canada in an attempt to give greater stability and order to
the country's finances as well as to have a useful financial
adviser to the government. However, the Bank legislation

If We Don't Sell Our Wheat Abroad

From the *Manitoba Free Press*, July 17, 1930.

was criticized by many because it provided for a much greater private than public equity in its stock ownership. It was not until 1938 that the Bank was fully 'nationalized', and in the meantime it served to bolster the restrictive credit policies of the private chartered banks. In the case of the railways, which were in sore straits because of reduced traffic, the government reorganized the C.N.R. and permitted a limited degree of pooling in passenger services with the C.P.R. But the full recommendations of the Duff Commission which had been appointed to examine the railway problem were not implemented, and it was not until 1937 that the C.N.R. was relieved of some of the huge debt burden with which it had been saddled for the relief of bondholders between 1917 and 1922.

The government also undertook one unsuccessful and two successful programs of national enterprise. Negotiation with the United States for the joint building of a St. Lawrence deep waterway was completed and signed in 1932, but failed to obtain ratification by the American Senate. A far more significant action was taken in 1932 when Parliament passed an act establishing the Canadian Radio Broadcasting Commission (renamed the Canadian Broadcasting Corporation in 1936). Although scarcely an anti-depression move, the development of public control over the airwaves was symptomatic of the new sense of national purpose that had grown with widespread discussion of the problems thrown up by the economic crisis. Across the country, groups of professional and business people either had been established or had rapidly increased in membership during the 1920s. Expressing a revived concern about the maintenance of political independence and the nourishment of cultural growth, such groups extended their activities in the thirties.

An outstanding example of such activities was the Canadian Radio League, which turned into one of the most successful pressure groups in Canadian history. With members in all the provinces and the support of key men in the political parties it was the work of this organization, more than any other single factor, that induced the government to frustrate the ambition of private interests, such as the C.P.R., which were preparing to commercialize radio on the basis of cheaply imported American programs. Enjoying support in both French- and English-speaking Canada the new publicly owned network provided services in areas considered of no value from a profit point of view. It also provided employment for musicians and actors, as well as developing an objective national news service and stimulating the exchange both of people and of ideas amongst the regions.

Implementation of public control and enterprise on the

airwaves rested upon a 1932 decision by the Judicial Committee of the Privy Council confirming federal jurisdiction in broadcasting. Another ruling of the Privy Council in the same year validated the 1927 Aeronautics Act, which asserted federal control of the airways. Both decisions seemed to express the general feeling that provincial powers had been overblown by previous legal decisions and economic trends. The mysterious ratiocination of the Judicial Committee had somehow reflected the new national feeling in Canada, and encouraged by the airways decision the government laid the basis of a national air-transport system, partly as a relief construction project. In 1937, under the Liberals, Trans-Canada Air Lines was chartered as a public corporation to operate intercity, transcontinental, and international flights. As with the C.B.C., where private radio stations were not eliminated but put under public control with the public corporation dominant in the field, so private air lines continued to operate, but with T.C.A. the dominant national line. In both cases the private sector was permitted to expand in later years and the debate about the virtues of mixing the two economic methods continues.

Despite a willingness to assert the directing authority of the federal government Bennett could do so only within a rigidly orthodox framework of 'sound money' and protection of investments – at least until the 1935 election. He could increase federal grants to technical education and raise the federal share of the cost of old-age pensions from 50 to 75 per cent (neither of which measures appealed to Mackenzie King), but when it came to proposals of inflation and 'unbalancing' the budget he was as the rock of Gibraltar. In 1932, when credit had all but disappeared in most sections of the economy, Bennett's Finance Minister, Edgar Rhodes, proclaimed increases in all forms of taxation, declaring: 'The preservation of our national credit is an indispensable prerequisite to the return of prosperity.' The proposal of the agonized western farmers, seconded by J. S. Woodsworth, that the dollar should be devalued and both currency and credit completely nationalized was rejected out of hand. The

King Liberals were equally horrified by this financial heresy, and as King told his nervous caucus, 'I pointed out how extreme it was, that I doubted if those who were for supporting it understood it, that it wd. make conditions worse if such a policy were adopted.'

Faced with radical proposals and deeply conscious of the inefficacy of his own policies Bennett was persuaded that Canada was on the verge of revolution. Moreover this fear was very personal. The Prime Minister was sensitive to the charges that filled the opposition air about his dictatorial methods of handling Parliament and caucus. He was furious at the widespread use of such terms as 'Bennett buggies' to describe horse-drawn farmers' automobiles for which owners could not afford gasoline, and 'Bennettboroughs' to designate the shanty-towns of tin and tar-paper where many relief families lived in the urban areas. When camps were established in 1932 for transient unemployed men their 20,000 inhabitants were placed under military discipline enforced by the Department of National Defence. When large delegations of farmers, or of unemployed, sought interviews with the Prime Minister they were either refused (on the ground that the government was already aware of their problems and proposals) or they were met with an exaggerated show of force. During the 1932 session when one such delegation declared its intention of meeting with the Prime Minister armoured cars were called out, the city police were reinforced, armed groups of R.C.M.P. were deployed on Parliament Hill, and a mounted detachment was posted in reserve behind the buildings. The delegation dispersed peaceably after a few hortatory words delivered by the Prime Minister from the Tower steps. Inside the House tempers flared as Woodsworth asked how much longer the people of Canada would stand the spectacle of a millionaire Prime Minister, surrounded by the military, lecturing 'poor people' because they did not speak to him in the most polite language.

Across the country many municipal and provincial governments and much of the press shared Bennett's view that protest groups and mass meetings of unemployed were, by definition, revolutionary in intent. The Minister of Justice, Hugh Guthrie, gave quick support to such local authorities in their war against the largely imaginary 'reds'. When financial incapacity forced the prairie and Maritimes governments to eliminate their police budgets, the R.C.M.P. was assigned the responsibility of police duty in those provinces, and in the bill that reorganized and expanded the R.C.M.P. provision was made for the swearing in of special unpaid constables whose recruitment was largely from the ranks of private industrial groups. In addition to stepping up its invigilation of the trade unions by 'labour spies' (despite the fact that union membership declined sharply between 1929 and 1936) the Justice Department ordered the Mounties to put a tight clamp on any large-scale movement of 'transients'. When a strike of British Columbia relief-camp workers led to a 'march on Ottawa' in 1935, the workers' delegates were stopped by the R.C.M.P. at Regina and turned back amidst scenes of bloody riot. Censorship of 'seditious' books was intensified through anonymous officers of the Department of National Revenue, and aliens (some of whom had lived in Canada for twenty years) were arrested without warrant for deportation without court trial or right of *habeas corpus*. Communists and radicals were jailed under the terms of Section 98 of the Criminal Code, which, like the authoritarian amendment to the Immigration Act, had been passed as a 1919 emergency measure and which gave an open-ended definition of sedition.

The development of such a semi-police state was opposed step by step by Henri Bourassa, the Quebec nationalist and social reformer, J. S. Woodsworth, and even Liberals like Ernest Lapointe, who seemed to forget Liberal acquiescence in the repression of Cape Breton coal-miners in the twenties. Woodsworth's motion to repeal Section 98 was met first by Bennett's attempt to refuse debate and then, simply by Guthrie's derogatory innuendo: 'If there was a reason to pass such a section in 1918 [sic], there is certainly a reason to keep such a section in force in the year 1933. . . . Section 98 is not in any sense a hindrance to any right-thinking person.' Those who spoke out against the drift toward totalitarianism were labelled red. In large measure this was because the proponents of liberty were also the chief castigators of the *status quo*. It was they who charged that the old national policies of high tariffs, balanced budgets, subsidies to transportation, coal production, and immigration, had ceased to work – or, rather, were working excessively well for the protected parts of the economy. Moreover, they pointed out, those policies had nourished the growth of monopoly and had led to a concentration of economic control in Montreal and Toronto that made virtually impossible an equitable distribution of the country's wealth – let alone the adequate realization of that wealth. As the Stevens Report on the spread of prices between the producer and the consumer put it in 1934:

> It [the Commission's evidence] has shown that a few great corporations are predominant in the industries that have been investigated; also that this power, all the more dangerous because it is impersonal, can be wielded in such a way that competition within the industry is blocked, the welfare of the producer disregarded, and the interests of the investor ignored.

Not only were there sharp contrasts between social classes within each of the regions and between the regions themselves, but there was an inability (stemming from constitutional as well as political inhibitions) to enact anything like adequate social reforms. Trade unions remained unprotected against limitations of their organizing and bargaining rights, unemployment insurance and other welfare legislation languished as abortive proposals while the government, like its predecessor, pleaded the limiting effect of the B.N.A. Act. Substantial transfer payments from Ottawa to the provinces remained unpredictable and thus an infirm basis on which to plan provincial welfare measures. The depression had made it plain that the federal division of legislative fields and financial resources – a division that had come under critical provincial review in the preceding decade – was totally unrealistic. Either the federal government would have to assume large new responsibilities or the provinces would have to be granted new jurisdictions and assured sources of revenue. To meet these complex problems of the constitution, the economy, and social welfare, new political parties sprang into being at both levels of government, and even the Bennett Conservatives (or, at least, Bennett himself) agreed by 1935 that reform would have to come. It was a part of the subtlety of this dynamic decade that a deepening reform sentiment led both to intensified nationalism and to strong expressions of provincialism in regions as different as Quebec and Alberta.

III

On the national stage the first and most significant of the new parties was the Co-operative Commonwealth Federation (C.C.F.). At its founding convention held at Regina in 1933 the C.C.F. adopted a platform announced as the Regina Manifesto, which condemned the capitalism system in its entirety and advocated a far-reaching program of social democracy. The Manifesto closed with the sentence: 'No C.C.F. government will rest content until it has eradicated capitalism and put into operation the full programme of socialized planning which will lead to the establishment in Canada of the co-operative commonwealth.' Horrified editorials in most of the country's press analysed the new party as a mixture of bolshevism and impractical idealism. In fact the C.C.F. was a natural outgrowth of previous Canadian experience and politics as well as a relatively moderate response to the savage impact of the crisis of capitalism.

In a political sense the new party was a grouping of farmers' protest organizations whose experience went back through the Progressive movement to the years preceding the First World War, of small urban socialist parties with an equally lengthy if less influential history, and of urban intellectuals. Trade unions as such were not founding partners in the C.C.F. although A. R. Mosher was a delegate to the Regina convention as president of the largest national railway union. With the spread of the C.I.O. in Canada after 1936, unionists became more active politically and in 1938 the first union affiliated directly with the C.C.F. This trend culminated in the establishment of the New Democratic Party in 1961, jointly sponsored by the Canadian Labour Congress and the C.C.F.

Ideologically the C.C.F. reflected many influences, all of which added up to a distinctive brand of Canadian socialism. Its first leader, J. S. Woodsworth, brought to the party a combination of British Christian socialism and Fabianism, the American Social Gospel, and political unionism of the British Independent Labour party brand. An ex-Methodist minister, he had sided with the Winnipeg strikers in 1919 and been charged with sedition for quoting from Isaiah. Elected to the federal Parliament in 1921 as the candidate of the Manitoba Independent Labour party, he had co-operated with U.F.A. and other Progressives in the 'Ginger Group' throughout the 1920s, seizing every opportunity to expound the rights of labour unions, the need for unemployment insurance and other welfare measures, as well as the virtues of socialism. From his experience in the House of Commons Woodsworth became convinced that the political left would have to accept the Parliamentary-party system as it existed. Other Progressives, such as Robert Gardiner of Alberta, came to agree with him. Thus the C.C.F. was from the beginning both a movement and a political party, although it was controlled by democratically elected conventions and ruled out election contributions from business sources. Elaborating Canada's history of railway, customs, and other kinds of party corruption, and with the contemporary Beauharnois scandal fresh in the public mind – a scandal in which both old parties were implicated in accepting money from the beneficiaries of the alienation of public power-rights in the St. Lawrence River – the C.C.F. appeal to party democracy and political purity cut deeply.

The party also benefited from the moral indignation and the nationalist sentiment of the thirties. With the General Conference of the United Church condemning the profit motive of capitalism, and many ministers of that and other denominations active in the new party, many of its club meetings and conventions took on the tone of evangelistic enthusiasm that had also characterized the early phases of Progressivism. Moreover it had the effective support of one of the period's many national-interest groups, the League for Social Reconstruction. Formed in 1932, the L.S.R. was a Canadian version of the Fabian Society with members drawn largely from the universities and the professions. Conceived in the midst of depression and doubts about the validity of the Canadian experiment, the L.S.R. emphasized the necessity of completing Canadian independence, retaining British legal and parliamentary institutions, and defining social purposes. The pamphlets, broadcasts, and meetings of the L.S.R., together with contributions to the small but influential *Canadian Forum*, did much to create interest in democratic socialism as an answer to planless capitalism, and it was a committee of the League that wrote the first draft of the C.C.F.'s Regina Manifesto.

Electorally the C.C.F. made rapid headway. By 1934 there were hundreds of C.C.F. clubs and locals across the country and a federated section of the party in each province. In British Columbia and Saskatchewan the C.C.F. had become the official opposition. In Manitoba, Alberta, and Ontario, C.C.F. candidates had won seats in the legislatures and in many municipal bodies. In the Maritimes the new party made some headway in the mining districts, but in Quebec the firm anti-socialism pronouncements of the Roman Catholic hierarchy blocked the party, and social protest in that province took a different form. In the federal election of 1935 the C.C.F. polled nearly 400,000 votes and elected seven M.P.s, including M. J. Coldwell and T. C. Douglas, both of whom were to become successors of J. S. Woodsworth as leader of Canada's social democratic party.

The influence of the C.C.F. was pronounced, not only upon the leftward trend of other party platforms in the 1935 election, but also upon the Liberal government after 1935. As with the earlier Progressive movement, Mackenzie King

was conscious of the need to express a sufficient amount of
nationalism and social-reform sentiment to prevent the socialists from achieving further gains. By 1940 the Liberals
had secured an amendment to the B.N.A. Act that enabled
them to provide a national system of unemployment insurance, the Criminal Code had been amended so as to guarantee the right to join a trade union, and the Bank of Canada
had been nationalized. C.C.F. pressure in the provinces had
also produced a considerable advance in welfare legislation
and the movement for family allowances was well under way.
In 1935 the C.C.F. vote would undoubtedly have been substantially larger had it not been for the splintering of the
protest vote in that election. The ephemeral Reconstruction
Party and the Social Credit Party between them took some
600,000 potential C.C.F. votes, and the division in the Conservative party over a sudden 'radical' turn taken by Bennett
served further to distort the vote. All of this reflected the
social-economic turmoil of the period.

One startling aspect of the 1935 election was the capture of
seventeen seats by the new Social Credit party, with less than
half the vote garnered by the C.C.F. This was possible because Social Credit took all fifteen of the Alberta seats (plus
two in Saskatchewan). Behind this success in the foot-hills lay
the political magic of a fundamentalist lay preacher, William
(Bible Bill) Aberhart. Founder of the Prophetic Bible Institute of Calgary, Aberhart was an ex-Ontarian schoolteacher
who had read the curious monetary theory of the English
engineer, Major Douglas. To the simplistic idea that poverty
in the midst of plenty could be ended by printing and distributing 'social dividends', which would keep purchasing
power and productive capacity in balance, Aberhart added
the evangelistic fervour of frontier revivalism. The new inflationary gospel of Social Credit was preached every Sunday
over a province-wide radio network rented by the Prophetic
Bible Institute in 1934. By election time in 1935 Social Credit
organization was complete and huge audiences could be
assembled to hear Aberhart announce: 'You remain in the
depression because of a shortage of purchasing power im-

posed by the banking system. If you have not suffered enough, it is your God-given right to suffer more.' The gospel was close enough to that preached previously by the U.F.A. movement to strike a familiar note and new enough to give a sense of excitement to the brilliant hortatory powers of Aberhart. The older spokesmen for the farmers went down to defeat first in the August provincial election of 1935 and again in the October federal election. In provincial elections down to the present, Alberta has remained solidly Social Credit.

The astonishing political unity exhibited by Albertans can best be explained by the homogeneity of their social-economic structure. A society of more-or-less-independent primary producers, the majority of people in the province constituted a sort of rural *petite bourgeoisie* with an identical interest in loosening credit facilities and defending themselves against national protective policies that favoured the industrialized region of central Canada. Fundamentally the province's Social Credit governments have been conservative in their 'radicalism' – in the sense of claiming to protect private enterprise, whether on the farm, the ranch, or, more recently, the oil and natural-gas fields. But in the 1930s an attempt was made to give effect to some of the Social Credit election promises. Legislation was passed to license and tax federally-chartered banks, to issue 'social dividends', and (revealing the basically illiberal, one-party-state assumptions of Social Credit) to gag the press. All of these bills were eventually disallowed by the federal government or declared unconstitutional by the judiciary. Indeed, the fate of Alberta Social Credit legislation was one more sign of the growing emphasis in the 1930s on the need to assert federal powers. That it was also evidence of the influence of entrenched 'eastern' financial interests did no harm to Social Credit's political appeal in Alberta. At the federal level of government Social Credit's impact was not comparable to that of the C.C.F., and its Ottawa representatives remained narrowly interested in provincial rights and an impossible monetary policy. Like some other forms of North American agrarian radicalism, the movement exhibited a disturbing trend toward anti-Semitism and restrictions of civil liberty.

Worried political response to the depression was also evident in policy divergences made by the provincial wings of the Liberal party in British Columbia and Ontario. On the Pacific coast the Liberal T. D. Pattullo won office in 1933 with a Rooseveltian pledge of positive government. Having promised 'work and wages' in the campaign, Pattullo put on foot extensive public works, increased the scale of relief payments, subsidized mining and fishing, and secured legislation governing hours of work and minimum wages. It was the most energetic program of its kind in Canada during the depression, and, when the necessary deficit budgeting led to fiscal difficulties requiring either financial aid from Ottawa or a redistribution of revenue sources between the two governments, the resulting controversy caused a serious review of Dominion-provincial relations.

In Ontario the Liberals came to power in 1934 under Mitchell F. Hepburn, who thus broke the nearly thirty-year sentence of Liberal opposition. More 'populist' in some respects than the Social Crediters themselves, Hepburn was in a long Ontario tradition of liberal radicalism dating back at least as far as George Brown. It was the tradition of the businessman farmer of the south-western Ontario peninsula, able to attract the support of the province's rural interests, yet identified in actual policy terms with the merchant-manufacturing class of Toronto. At the outset of his administration Hepburn secured marketing legislation to protect the price of some farm products and even made a bid for labour votes with legislation to safeguard trade-union rights. But he moved steadily closer to the power élite of the Toronto Mining Exchange and the American branch plants. Much less willing than Pattullo to budget for a deficit in the interest of welfare and economic recovery, Hepburn with his rather uncouth and bumptious political hyperbole soon identified the growing trade-union movement, with its potential support in the semi-organized unemployed, as the major threat to Ontario's well-being. This threat he met by adding substantially to the ranks of the provincial police and thundering against the irresponsibility of radicals – amongst whom he drew no distinction between C.C.F.ers, the U.F.O. (which affiliated with the C.C.F. in 1934), Communists, trade-union leaders, and the unemployed.

The climax of Hepburn's anti-labour policy came with a strike against General Motors in Oshawa in 1937. Leaders of the United Automobile Workers, who were backed by the newly formed C.I.O. in the United States, were denounced by the Premier as 'foreign agitators', and the full force of the Ontario government was brought to bear in support of the American-owned company. Although the U.A.W. was eventually successful in its organizing drive, the managers of other American branch-plants, the northern mine-owners, and most of the mercantile community were not ungrateful to the little 'onion farmer'. While Hepburn lost from the Cabinet his two most liberal ministers (David Croll and Arthur Roebuck), he remained politically entrenched. In a bitter personal feud that broke in the late thirties between Hepburn and the re-established Mackenzie King, Hepburn retained the support of much Toronto business (including the ex-Liberal *Globe*, which was purchased by a mining millionaire in 1937 and amalgamated with the Tory *Mail*). It was only the overriding necessity of war-time federal leadership that finally enabled King to undercut his Ontario rival. In the process the provincial Liberal party was left in ruins and until at least 1948 the C.C.F. was the most serious opposition challenge to Ontario toryism – a challenge based in large measure on the growing strength of the unions, especially the C.I.O. unions.

The pattern of provincial political unrest was similar in Quebec, but there it was still further complicated by the growing industrialization which transformed many farmers into urban wage-earners. Moreover, racial nationalism was exploited by a clever political opportunist. In the 1935 provincial election the corrupt Liberal administration of L. A. Taschereau came within an ace of defeat and during the succeeding months a new party was formed. The *Union*

Nationale combined French-nationalist Conservatives and, incongruously, social-reform Liberals who were disillusioned by the utter indifference of the Taschereau government to the sordid social condition of the province. Under a master ex-Conservative politician, Maurice Duplessis, the *Union Nationale* won power in 1936.

Ignoring his electoral promises of reform and improved social welfare for the workers, Duplessis proceeded to consolidate his power. Making a system of corruption, he gave favours to the farmers and winked at the extension of control over economic resources by outside capital – the precise object of his most virulent pre-election attacks. Like Hepburn, Duplessis focused attention on 'radicals' and trade-unionists as the source of Quebec's troubles; and for good measure he rode forth against Ottawa in defence of the special Quebec rights. Like Aberhart, Duplessis aligned himself closely with his province's dominant religious orthodoxy and from it drew grateful support in his war against radical reformers. Symbolic of his method was the outrageous Padlock Law which permitted the seizure and closing of any premises suspected of being used to propagate communism. Communism was not defined in the law and it thus crippled attempts to establish the C.C.F. and to extend the limited range of the province's trade-union organization.

The Padlock Law was simply the most extreme expression of a quasi-police state. Duplessis found himself supported not only by the Church but also by a growing body of conservative opinion amongst the propertied classes. Clerical corporatism, stimulated by the success of General Franco in Spain, allied itself in Quebec to American capital and ran happily in harness under Duplessis. When Woodsworth in the House of Commons sought either federal disallowance of the Padlock Law or its reference to the Supreme Court, he declared that 'Twice every three days for six months the provincial police have carried out execution without judgement, dispossession without due process of law; twenty times a month they have trampled on liberties as old as Magna Carta.' The Canadian Bar Association petitioned against the Act, and a

Canadian Civil Liberties Union was founded with the first
purpose of opposing such legislation; yet to Woodsworth's
protests in the House, the Minister of Justice, Lapointe,
would reply only 'In spite of the fact that the words are so
unpleasant to the honourable member for Winnipeg North
Centre, I do desire to say that the reign of law must continue
in this country, that peace and order must prevail.' Lapointe
prepared to order the R.C.M.P. to support Hepburn's anti-
labour campaign in Ontario, and he was quick to act against
the Alberta legislation affecting the federal powers in finance.
Why, then, did he not protect the federal interest in criminal
law and civil liberty?

The answer is complicated but important. While Canadian
nationalism was at high tide and deeply anxious to define new
national purposes and policies, Duplessis's power was based
upon exploitation of the most powerful prejudices against
such purposes and policies. Unwilling to change social policy
in Quebec to meet new conditions he posed as the defender
of French-Canadian rights against the threat of Ottawa's
intervention and the tentacles of American ownership. Fear
of Duplessis was a major part of the explanation for the
failure to launch vigorous federal domestic policies in the
late thirties as well as for the dangerous refusal of Mackenzie
King to permit the debating or definition of Canadian
foreign policy. The alliance of Duplessis and the Church,
furthermore, effectively blocked the establishment of partnership between the C.C.F. and the social democrats in
Quebec, thus further emphasizing the introverted separateness of the province and the political dangers which that
involved.

IV

Ottawa's response to the political undulations in the provinces was governed by the outcome of the 1935 federal election. Major party programs in the election, in turn, were
largely determined by analysis of the provincial trends. Mackenzie King decided that the Liberals would be most likely

to regain power if they posed as the moderates in a sea of radicalism and racialism. With the slogan 'It's King or Chaos' the Liberals were to win a handy majority of seats with a minority vote almost the same as that with which they had lost in 1930. The events of the preceding twelve months made King's decision a clever, if not a very daring, one.

In the Conservative party Bennett found himself confronted by forces demanding an extension of positive federal action and the leader himself was gradually converted to this point of view. The Minister of Trade and Commerce, H. H. Stevens, argued that economic recovery was being blocked, and equitable distribution of purchasing power prevented, by monopolistic rigidities. When Bennett gave him a royal commission to investigate the methods by which retail prices were kept alarmingly higher than was justified by the wages of employees or the prices paid to producers and small manufacturers, Stevens made public comment upon the evidence as it was being assembled. Since some of the chief offenders were also supporters of the Conservative party an inner crisis resulted in the resignation of Stevens from the government. In 1935 the ex-minister led an *ad hoc* 'Reconstruction Party'. With a platform calling for regulation of business along early New Deal lines, Reconstruction candidates polled votes scattered across every province. Their total was about equal to that polled by the C.C.F., but only in Stevens's own constituency was it sufficiently concentrated to elect a member.

Despite the Stevens crisis the Prime Minister's brother-in-law, W. D. Herridge, continued the campaign to shift Conservative policy towards intervention in economic life. As ambassador to the United States Herridge was deeply impressed by the vigour and social purpose of Roosevelt's New Deal. Heeding Herridge's urgent call for government action to save the nation from the collapse of capitalism, and recognizing the political necessity of counterbalancing the favours that Conservative policy had granted to industry, Bennett acted with characteristic impetuosity. In a series of dramatic radio broadcasts early in 1935 he announced his intention of legislating a New Deal for the Canadian people. Conservative

Members of Parliament (who had not been previously consulted) and the country at large listened in astonishment as the Prime Minister declared that the capitalist system was responsible for the depression and for the continuing insecurity of millions of people, and that the system now lay in ruins. Only a total revamping of the system could enable it once again to serve the national interest. In the speech from the throne the reform program was again spelled out with the preface: 'In the anxious years through which you have passed, you have been the witnesses of grave defects and abuses in the capitalist system. Unemployment and want are the proof of these. Great changes are taking place about us. New conditions prevail. These require modifications in the capitalist system to enable that system more effectively to serve the people.'

Although Bennett declared that his inspiration came from reading the lives of Conservative reformers such as Lord Shaftesbury, in fact the program that he presented was derived from the whole reform tradition of the English-speaking people in the twentieth century and every part of it had been demanded by either Progressives or Liberals or C.C.F.ers in the Canadian Parliament. It stopped short of advocating the co-operative commonwealth of the socialists but was even more comprehensive than F.D.R.'s experiments – although, like the American New Deal, it was consciously designed to save capitalism. Its shock value lay in the fact that it sought to make use of the rising demand for a new national policy by deliberately asserting federal powers that by any objective reading of past judicial interpretation were bound to be contested and in most cases declared *ultra vires* of Ottawa's jurisdiction. As passed by the pre-election session the Bennett New Deal consisted of five principal acts – the Unemployment and Social Insurance Act, the Weekly Rest in Industrial Undertakings Act, the Natural Products Marketing Act, the Minimum Wages Act, and the Limitation of Hours of Work Act – together with several lesser bills concerned with farm and other credit, some of which were extensions of existing legislation.

The whole program horrified many supporters of the Conservative party in the business community, especially because it was accompanied by the threat of serious measures against price-fixing and the establishment of an economic council with potential regulatory influence. In the House the C.C.F. applauded and derided the new policy, claiming that it was inherently good in its reformism but that it stopped far short of adequacy and that it was worthless until there was assurance that the constitution would permit its implementation. Mackenzie King established Liberal election attitudes by castigating Bennett for the dictatorial manner in which he had 'insulted' Parliament by giving the speech from the throne in pre-session radio talks and imposing 'his' policy on a party whose caucus had not even discussed it.

The centre of the Liberal critique, however, was the charge that the whole program was a deliberate deception perpetrated in the knowledge that it would be disallowed by the courts. King declared that the government should have sought a judicial opinion and, if necessary, obtained an amendment to the B.N.A. Act before introducing such legislation. He challenged Bennett to 'tell this house whether as leader of the government, knowing that a question will come up immediately as to the jurisdiction of this parliament and of the provincial legislatures in matters of social legislation, he has secured an opinion from the law officers of the crown or from the Supreme Court of Canada which will be a sufficient guarantee to this house to proceed with these measures as being without question within its jurisdiction.' On the question of Liberal opinion about the inherent propriety of the Bennett social reform program King was cagey. On the one hand he argued that such legislation could come only after careful discussion with the provinces and determination of the division of powers. On the other he declared that the whole approach was wrong: 'I tell the Prime Minister that, if he wants to reform the capitalist system, the way to begin is by sharing between labour and the community as well as capital, the control of industrial policy. Let labour and the community, which are as essential to industry as capital, be represented around a common board to determine the policy that is to govern, and very soon these questions of maximum hours, minimum wages, sweat shops and other evils . . . will be remedied in the one effective way, namely, by the parties themselves who are directly concerned having an effective voice in the determination of the conditions under which they shall work.' While some historians have been quick to charge Bennett with insincerity in his sudden conversion, they have perhaps been less ready than the case warrants to charge King with insincerity manifested in his careful hedging of the Liberal position on reform.

The election was fought along the general lines of the throne-speech debate and the Conservatives lost sufficient votes as a divided party to carry the Liberals back to office. With the worst of the depression past, and bearing in mind the increasing business support for the Liberal party, King made it clear at once that he would act on social reform only after the constitutional position had been clarified. The Bennett legislation was referred to the Supreme Court in 1936. The Court's opinion that the main items affected fields of provincial jurisdiction and were thus unconstitutional was confirmed by the Judicial Committee of the Privy Council in the following year. The judicial decisions reversed the apparent trend of the aeronautics and radio cases of 1931 and ran directly counter to the sense of national emergency. Indeed, the Judicial Committee specifically refused the Dominion's argument that the residual powers of Section 91 of the B.N.A. Act – the federal responsibility for 'peace, order and good government' – and the enumerated powers to regulate trade and commerce were being used to meet a national emergency. Revealing an equally impenetrable logic the Privy Councillors struck a crippling blow at the authority of Ottawa in external relations by announcing that Section 132 of the B.N.A. Act was insufficient basis for the labour laws of the Bennett program. Enacted as fulfilment of obligations undertaken as a member of the International Labour Organization the hours and wages legislation was declared to infringe the powers of the provinces. The granting of power to Ottawa in Section 132 to carry out the duties of 'Canada or of any province thereof, as part of the British Empire, toward foreign countries, arising under treaties between the Empire and such foreign countries' was announced to have died with respect to any matter touched with a provincial interest – on the ground that Canada possessed the right to make her own treaties and that the I.L.O. agreement fell into this non-imperial category. Not only did this aspect of the decisions create mischief at the time, it was to be used, ironically, in the 1960s by anti-British Quebec nationalists as partial justification for claiming a large degree of provincial control over Quebec's external relations.

Rather than launch an immediate campaign for amendments to the B.N.A. Act to undo the erratic pronouncements from London, King welcomed the decisions as proof of his warnings about Bennett's high-handed and 'unconstitutional' policy. The return of the Liberals was also the occasion for intensification of the demands of provincial rightists. The provincialist case put forward at the 1927 Dominion-provincial conference seemed to be revived as strident claims to jurisdiction came from Quebec, Ontario, Alberta, and British Columbia. Even amendments that would have given power of indirect taxation to the provinces were dropped when they met opposition in the Senate. No agreement on a method of transferring to Canada the actual mechanics of amendment had been reached at a conference late in 1935, and when the Privy Council decisions of 1937 gave added strength to the provincialists' assertions, King appointed a royal commission to examine 'the economic and financial basis of confederation and the distribution of legislative powers in the light of the economic and social developments of the last seventy years'. While the problem of an agreed procedure on amendments was important the question of what amendments might be desirable was even more so, and King left this question in the lap of the commission, which was headed by N. W. Rowell and Joseph Sirois. Although the commission did not report until the spring of 1940 at a time when one might have expected an emphasis on war-inspired federal initiative, its research and the main lines of its recommendations had been well advanced prior to the outbreak of war.

The Rowell-Sirois Report was one of the principal expressions of the nationalism of the 1930s. Its brilliant analysis of Dominion history since 1867, with its special studies of economic, social, and constitutional trends, revealed a fresh understanding of the need for identifying and enabling new 'purposes of the Dominion'. Moreover the Report left no doubt that neither the French- nor the English-speaking founders of Confederation had anticipated the halting and ineffectual role assigned to Ottawa by the Privy Council jurists, some ambitious provincial premiers, and the investors of foreign capital. Reviewing the fiscal chaos, economic stagnation, and national frustration of the depression years, the Report made sweeping recommendations for redistribution of responsibilities and revenue sources – a redistribution which the commissioners believed would restore the balance of powers as originally conceived. Key controls over the economy were to be definitively in federal hands, as was the responsibility for essential services of national welfare such as unemployment insurance and relief. As further expression of national goals the existing system of provincial subsidies was to be replaced by national adjustment grants that would enable the provinces to maintain educational and social services at an average Canadian standard. In order to launch this ambitious and realistic plan without mortgages, provincial debts were to be assumed by the Dominion. To enable Ottawa to shoulder a revived federal planning role it was to enjoy exclusive rights to income and corporation taxes and succession duties.

Implementation of the Rowell-Sirois plan would have required a combination of amendments to the B.N.A. Act and policy agreements between Ottawa and at least a majority of the provinces. Such agreement was not reached. Throughout the Commission's period of research it was virtually boycotted by the governments of Ontario, Quebec, and Alberta, and when the Report was issued in 1940 these governments,

supported by British Columbia, expressed marked hostility
to the recommendations. At a Dominion-provincial conference called in 1941 to consider the recommendations in detail
Premier Hepburn led a provincialist opposition that resulted
in collapse of the conference. In 1940 the King government
obtained an amendment to the B.N.A. Act empowering
Ottawa to establish a nation-wide system of unemployment
insurance, at least in part because it was worried by signs of
growing C.C.F. support, but the war and post-war periods
were to see only *ad hoc* adjustments to the federal balance of
responsibilities and revenues. This outcome was of crucial
importance to the future of Canada, for it meant that the
nation was to emerge from the potentially unifying experience of war without a clear conception of the nature of its
own constitution. It was an outcome that was the result of a
too hesitant federal political leadership in the 1920s and
1930s – a leadership that feared the political risks of open confrontation of particularist provincial prejudices and feared
equally the task of consolidating a public opinion that was
ready for an extension of social democracy at the federal level
of government. Bennett's conversion came too late to be
credible, and King took only those steps that were essential
to avoid immediate defeat. The technique of issue-dodging
permitted the firm establishment of provincial governments
allied in an essentially anti-national program of exploiting
local sources of power – foreign investment that found provincial governments more pliable than Ottawa, narrow self-
interest that denied the justice of equalization policies, and
prejudices both of race and of religion. The same method of
issue-dodging was highly developed in the field of external
policy, and here the long-term results were to prove equally
dangerous.

V

The problem of Canadian foreign policy in these years was
intimately related to the problems of the constitution and
the Liberal political tradition. In fact the speed with which

the implications of the imperial conferences of 1923, 1926, 1929, and 1930 were worked out in the 1930s was very embarrassing to Canadian leaders, many of whom had not really thought out what they wanted to do with independence either in domestic or in external affairs. The Statute of Westminster, passed by the imperial Parliament in 1931, left Canada with only those restrictions on her sovereignty that she herself desired. Power to amend or repeal the B.N.A. Act was left in Westminster only because Canadians had not decided on an amending procedure acceptable in Canada, and appeals to the Privy Council were retained principally because some economic and some minority groups felt them to be a needed safeguard. To some extent the lack of confidence in purely Canadian control of the constitution stemmed from Mackenzie King's ambivalence towards Parliament – a policy that insisted on the one hand that in all matters Parliament must be the final arbiter, yet on the other hand endeavoured either to remove contentious issues from debate in the Commons or to present the House with virtual *faits accomplis*. The success that had attended King's 1926 appeal to the electorate in avoidance of a decision in the House seemed to encourage the Prime Minister's reliance on a kind of plebiscitary democracy through which the power of the Cabinet was enhanced while policy assumptions were left ill-defined.

The abdication crisis at the end of 1936 illustrated this trend in a precise constitutional context. One of the aspects of Dominion 'independence' asserted by the Statute of Westminster was the right of Dominion Parliaments to assent to 'any alteration in the law touching the Succession to the Throne or Royal Style and Titles'. Section 4 of the Statute declared that no British Act should apply to a Dominion 'unless it is expressly declared in that Act that the Dominion has requested, and consented to, the enactment thereof'. In accordance with these provisions, when Edward VIII decided to abdicate, the governments of the Dominions were all advised on December 9, 1936. The Instrument of Abdication was signed by the King on December 10, and the British

Parliament met to pass the legislation necessary to give effect
to the abdication. In Canada, Parliament was not specially
summoned to deal with this constitutional problem. Instead,
the Cabinet requested the application to Canada of the
British Act of Succession because there was not, in Mackenzie
King's opinion, enough time to summon Parliament.

When the Canadian Parliament did assemble in January
1937, the government sought passage of an address of loyalty
to George VI. C. H. Cahan for the Conservatives and J. S.
Woodsworth for the C.C.F. protested the procedure as being
government by Order in Council and a denigration of Parliament. Woodsworth argued that the address should not be
passed until after the Succession Bill was debated and passed,
and that the oath of allegiance to George VI should not have
been administered to the members. Between the prorogation
and reassembling of Parliament the King of Canada had been
changed by order of the Liberal party. While there was no
serious possibility of parliamentary rejection of the British
Act the constitutional propriety of the Cabinet's action was
dubious since the Order in Council, as Cahan pointed out,
rested upon no statutory authority. Pursuing the logic of the
situation, Woodsworth suggested that if the Prime Minister
could decide such important matters unilaterally he could
also declare war by the same method: 'Surely if the King of
the United Kingdom can be distinguished for legal purposes
from the King of Canada, then the recognition of the King of
the United Kingdom as King of Canada can wait until there
is time to call Parliament. If the selection of the King of
Canada is of such minor importance, the question arises:
why a King at all?'

Defending his course of action the Prime Minister reiter-
ated his conviction that time had been of the essence and
announced that 'If there ever was a time in British history
when it was of importance that the unity of the British Empire should be demonstrated to all the world, it was when
a question affecting the Crown itself was under consideration.' Like many of Mackenzie King's statements this one
was heavily laden with ambiguity. A pronounced advocate

of absolutely responsible government, he was particularly emphatic on Canada's freedom from imperial obligations. The course marked out during the Chanak crisis in 1922, and in the succeeding imperial conferences, as well as in the gradual growth of separate Canadian diplomatic representation abroad and disinterest in the League of Nations, continued after 1935. While the Bennett government had made it very clear that Canada would expend neither men nor money in support of any League endeavour to roll back Japan's invasion of Manchuria, and in other ways rejected the League in favour of a passive acceptance of British policy in international affairs, under King there was an even greater insistence on non-commitment.

In 1935 Canada's representative in Geneva, W. A. Riddell, proposed that the League add oil to the list of economic sanctions against Italy. Since the Mussolini war machine was absolutely dependent upon oil imports in its barbaric assault on Ethiopia, the 'Canadian' proposal would have brought that war to a halt and in so doing would have redeemed the League from the impotence to which Anglo-French policy was consigning it. Riddell, however, had misinterpreted the views of the new King government before making his proposal, and when news of his startling initiative arrived in Ottawa his action was quickly repudiated. When King explained his position in the House it was with the rhetorical question: 'Do honourable members think it is Canada's role at Geneva to attempt to regulate a European war?' Similarly, when in 1936 Germany violated the Versailles treaty by formally repossessing the Rhineland, King argued that Canada should keep out of the ensuing negotiations and defined Canadian 'policy' thus: 'the attitude of the government is to do nothing itself and if possible to prevent anything occurring which will precipitate one additional factor into the all-important discussions which are now taking place in Europe.'

King's evasions and his reluctance to have foreign policy even debated in the House sprang from his strong desire to keep Canada united. Fearful of arousing the deep resentment that swept French Canada during the conscription

THE SHAPE OF THINGS TO COME

From the paper *Cry Havoc*, in the Woodsworth Papers Scrapbook (1932-9), Public Archives of Canada.

crisis of the First World War and conscious of the readiness of Duplessis and other Quebec 'nationalist' politicians to use the lingering suspicion of English-Canadian 'imperialism' as a certain source of votes, King sought to avoid definition of his real policy. That policy was to commit a 'united' Canada to the support of British military action should the European peace be shattered in a war of aggression. Like other western leaders he continued to indulge in the wishful thought that Hitler could be contained by judicious appeasement without serious revitalization of the League and without a Russian alliance. In 1937 he talked with the German dictator, whom he completely misunderstood, and then went on to London, where he left Prime Minister Chamberlain in no doubt about Canada's support of Britain in the event of a European war. In 1938 he informed Chamberlain, upon the British leader's return from Munich, that 'the heart of Canada is rejoicing tonight at the success which has crowned your unremitting efforts for peace'.

In the country few people questioned King's policy. Lamenting the emasculation of the League, John Dafoe of the *Winnipeg Free Press* asked after Munich, 'What's the cheering for?', and in the Commons Woodsworth spoke for a Canadian initiative to reinvigorate the League. But even stronger than the voices that began to call for rearmament and recognition of the real threat posed by Hitler's Germany were those that spoke from the crest of North American isolationism. Taking their cue partly from the neutrality campaign in the United States and partly from the decade's surge of Canadian nationalism a probable majority of Canadians believed that their country could in fact remain neutral in the event of a European war. King did little to disabuse the public mind in this respect, while at the same time he himself never had any doubt about the decision that would quickly be taken in the event of war. While he parried the first British suggestion that Canada become the base of a Commonwealth air-training program he did not discourage further discussion of the subject and as early as 1937 began cautious increases in the military budget. The government also made no objection to the placing of large British munitions orders in Canada in 1938 while it declared in the House that 'we have no more information than is in the possession of the honourable members.'

With this policy of preparing to support a British war effort while continuing to deny such intention, King's chief Quebec lieutenant, Ernest Lapointe, was in complete agreement. Lapointe believed that although a British declaration of war was still legally binding upon Canada, according to the old Laurier formula the nature and extent of Canadian involvement remained a matter for Ottawa's decision. He also believed that Quebec would go along with a Canadian entry into war once the crisis arrived, but that it would be too risky to test Quebec opinion without the assistance of crisis pressures. Thus, like King, he was very short with parliamentary questions that sought to elicit the government's real policy. In 1938 when the Minister of National Defence, Ian Mackenzie, incautiously declared in public that Canada must stand by Britain, Lapointe was asked to say whether this was government policy. He refused to support Mackenzie and asked the questioner, 'Does my honourable friend want to split the country right away?' Conversely, when J. T. Thorson of Selkirk moved a resolution in 1939 declaring a Canadian right of neutrality, King refused to entertain it, with the now standard rhetorical question and brief comment: 'Why divide Canada to provide against a contingency that may not arise, or if it does, may not come until the situation has materially changed? The same consideration of the overwhelming importance of national unity which has led this government to decline to make premature and inappropriate statements of possible belligerency prevent it from recommending actions to declare possible neutrality.' Requests that the government should embargo shipments of strategic materials to the fascist nations and Japan met with the same response.

The King-Lapointe policy beyond doubt brought Canada into the Second World War without substantial overt division. Without a formal declaration of the right of neutrality Canada was, by the judgement of her own Minister of Justice, at war from the time of the British declaration on September 3, 1939. Yet the government acted as if this were not the case. In a special session of Parliament authorization for a separate Canadian war declaration was obtained with only J. S. Woodsworth rising to oppose the move in an unrecorded vote. Between September 3 and the Canadian declaration on September 10 the United States regarded Canada as neutral, but the legal right to that fictitious neutrality was established only with the declaration of war itself. While a number of French-Canadian members of Parliament voiced opposition to the war none rose to oppose the vote in the House. Clearly the majority accepted the leadership of Lapointe and the government's assurance that there would be no conscription. In English-speaking Canada in the years preceding the outbreak of the war many who had been supporters of neutrality began to shift their opinions as Hitler's implacable purpose became harder to deny, and by the summer of 1939 even the C.C.F., which was committed to neutrality by its preceding national convention, was deeply divided on the issue. The very successful visit of King George VI and Queen Elizabeth in the summer of 1939 also did much to undermine neutralist feeling amongst English-speaking Canadians and thus make possible a wider 'automatic' support of British policy.

Yet the extent of the 'unity' can be exaggerated. With a population slightly over eleven million there were still some 529,000 Canadians unemployed. Despite the signing of a trade agreement with the United States in 1937, which ended the sequence of tariff retaliation, and an extension of that agreement in 1938, which further reduced tariffs between the two countries, the Canadian economy was recovering but slowly from the long depression. As a result, many of the enlistments for the first Canadian Division were the products of relief camps and work projects for the unemployed who brought with them a feeling of resignation rather than patriotic enthusiasm. Again, the C.C.F. gave support to the war declaration on the assumption that Canada's contribution would be basically economic, and this was certainly true also of most of French Canada. For Quebec, 'unity' was represented by J. A. Blanchette who, for the government, seconded the Address in Reply to the Speech from the Throne: 'It cannot be reasonably contended, after due reflection, that it would not be wise to co-operate to a reasonable extent with France and England in the present conflict, taking into account, however, our resources, and our capacity, and without sacrificing our vital interests . . . .'

Unity had been bought by the methods of evasion. 'Our vital interests' was a phrase that meant different things to different classes and different regions and was given no precision by federal leadership. In Quebec there had been strong sympathy voiced for General Franco and for the cororatist form of government during the Spanish Civil War, while the war with Germany, when it came, was still widely regarded as another British imperial conflict. Failure to clarify a specifically Canadian relation to the events that led to the conflict, let alone to exercise any influence upon those events, meant that the nation drifted into the greatest crisis of the twentieth century by default. While the war appeared to 'solve' such problems as the right of neutrality, the slackness in the economy, and even the federal distribution of powers, and while it called forth extraordinary courage and organizing abilities from the Canadian people, in fact it merely swept under the table the unresolved questions of the thirties.

9. Through the Second World War

COLONEL C. P. STACEY

In the autumn of 1939 it was just ten years since the onset of the Great Depression; and Canada, not yet fully recovered from the long and debilitating struggle against economic misfortune, found herself plunged, for the second time in a generation, into a world war. It was the beginning of six years of conflict. Those years would bring the Dominion triumphs and frustrations, achievements and embarrassments, glory and sacrifice on foreign battlefields, and crisis and recrimination on Parliament Hill.

I

In September 1939 approximately 11,300,000 people lived in Canada, whereas the population when the First World

War broke out in 1914 had been less than 8,000,000. The worst of the depression was long over; yet in 1939 estimates of the number of the unemployed still ran as high as 600,000, the federal government was still spending great sums on relief, and many of the young men who would have to fill the ranks of the services in the new war had seldom or never had a steady job. Factory-owners, hungry for orders, were disappointed that the Canadian and British rearmament programs had produced so few. The national government's revenues, which in 1933 had fallen to the lowest point since 1918, had climbed by 1938 well above the then record-breaking total of 1929; but export trade was still depressed.

Canada's approach to war had paralleled Britain's. Economic disorganization had been accompanied by political uncertainty. Isolationism, nourished by the memory of the

Prophetic Harmony?

From the *Winnipeg Free Press*, April 1, 1939.

blood-bath of 1914-18, and with no politician daring to challenge it, had yielded very gradually to the realization that Hitler would be checked only by force. Political leadership was largely hamstrung by recollections of how the country had been split by the conscription controversy of 1917-18 and fear of a repetition of it. Only in the last week of March 1939, when Hitler, by tearing up the Munich agreement of the previous autumn, had made war virtually certain, was a temporary answer to this dilemma found. It was enunciated by Dr. R. J. Manion, the leader of the Conservative Opposition: 'full cooperation with Britain in wartime', but 'no conscription of Canadians to fight outside our borders in any war'. Three days later the Prime Minister, Mr. King, associated himself with this fateful formula.

In those days few Canadians drew much comfort from the new national status that had been won for their country by the soldiers of the old war. Under those lowering skies the fact that in 1931 the Statute of Westminster had established the formal independence of the Dominions within the Commonwealth did not seem a matter of dominating significance, any more than the fact that there were Canadian diplomatic missions now in Washington, Paris, and Tokyo. Canada's action – in contrast with 1914 – in issuing her own declaration of war against Germany, and issuing it only on September 10, 1939, after one week of purely formal neutrality, was to appear perhaps rather more important in retrospect than it did at the time. What men asked themselves at the moment was what unknown horrors the war would let loose, and whether the always shaky unity of English and French Canada, so sadly buffeted two decades before, could stand the strain of this new conflict. No one sang 'Rule Britannia', as people had in 1914. Grimly, but of their own free will and in a spirit of reluctant resolution, the Canadians went into their second war against the formidable folk of Germany.

It fell to the third administration of Mr. Mackenzie King, formed in 1935, to lead the country through the whole six years of conflict. It was not a government of warriors, though it did include a number of men who had fought in the 1914

war, and one – J. L. Ralston – who had been a legendary
battalion commander in the Canadian Corps and, it was
said, would have got the Victoria Cross had exception not
been taken to his having exposed himself in a manner
unsuitable to his rank. King himself was the most civilian
of men, and has been credited by one of his numerous official biographers with possessing a 'deep-seated and life-long'
distrust of the army – not perhaps the best of qualifications
for a minister conducting a great war. Until nearly the end
of the struggle, the controlling factor in his military policy
was the determination to avoid overseas conscription at
almost any cost. But his was certainly an able government:
possibly the ablest that has ever ruled in Canada. Such people as C. D. Howe, who as Minister of Munitions and Supply
showed himself something of a genius in matters of war
production, and J. L. Ilsley, the rugged Maritimer whose
transparent honesty helped him as Minister of Finance to
retain the liking and confidence of Canadians even while
taxing them as they had never been taxed before, were not
untypical of it. Angus L. Macdonald, the popular Premier
of Nova Scotia, joined the Cabinet in 1940 as Naval Minister. Ernest Lapointe, the senior representative of French
Canada, deserves a high place on the roll of Canadian
patriots; and when he died in 1941 King, by what turned
out to be one of his most fortunate strokes, was able to replace him with Louis S. St. Laurent, distinguished alike for
ability and integrity.

Whatever else the government was, however, it was not
glamorous; and glamour is a useful thing in time of war.
King's own flabby person and personality carried little suggestion of forceful leadership. There was no one on the
government front bench who could strike sparks from the
House of Commons or the country. The ministers were,
some of them at least, genuinely great public servants,
but they lacked the capacity to inspire their countrymen.
The most compelling Canadian personality of the war
period was not a politician but a soldier – General A. G. L.
McNaughton; and when, in an evil hour for himself, Mc-

Naughton went into politics, it was under conditions that made him ineffective. King was childishly incensed when Canadians spoke of 'our leaders, Churchill and Roosevelt'; but Canada possessed no personality to challenge those two, and it is possible that the strongly marked hostility of the Canadian forces to their own government (and to King particularly) was influenced by a certain embarrassment born of comparing the Canadian Prime Minister with the dynamic and dominating British and American chiefs.

II

The Canadian war effort had an unimpressive beginning. The military policy of limited liability, which London had finally thrown over in the spring of 1939, before the actual outbreak, ruled in Ottawa until the collapse of France over a year later. Peace-time ideas of economy and treasury control were still dominant; the program was tailored to the domestic political situation rather than to the menace posed by the enormously dangerous enemy whom Canada had chosen to challenge. Such policies can be safely indulged in only by countries with powerful friends and great geographical obstacles standing between them and their foes.

On September 1, 1939, orders were issued to mobilize the 'Mobile Force' of two divisions provided for in the Militia's existing Defence Scheme. Four days later, when great numbers of men had already been enlisted, the Chiefs of Staff were instructed that there was to be 'no stimulation to recruiting at the present time', and almost at once recruiting was suspended in a good many units. In spite of this official cold water, the men of the country came forward in their thousands. Patriots, idealists, adventurers, perhaps some who were merely hungry, they volunteered in numbers greater than the examining doctors could cope with. Over 58,000 were taken into the army in the first month. Many others were rejected, among them numerous old soldiers of 1914-18 who were anxious to serve once more but who could no

longer meet the medical standards. Much smaller numbers
were enlisted by the navy and the air force.

There were two provinces where recruiting was slow:
Saskatchewan, basically agricultural and with a population
containing large numbers of recent European immigrants,
and predominantly French-speaking Quebec, still nursing
the memory of the hated conscription measure of 1917. Yet
French Canadians did enlist in very considerable numbers,
and some French-speaking units were among the first to
reach full strength.

Indeed, the dominant fact in these early days was the
unity of the country. After the pre-war controversies and
apprehensions it seemed hard to believe, and people who
had had little sympathy with King's policy of avoiding commitments and postponing decisions were heard expressing
surprised satisfaction with its results. Nevertheless it is evident in retrospect that the unity of 1939, vital as it was at
that moment, was largely artificial. It owed its existence in
great part to the government's policy of a 'moderate' war
effort, and above all to its adoption of the Conservative
leader's formula, the rejection of overseas conscription. But
unfortunately moderate war is a contradiction in terms, and,
as the struggle continued and the strain increased, the policy
of limited liability was certain to break down, and the unity
of Canada would break with it. Only a short war could have
fully vindicated the King policies; and this war was to be a
long one. For the moment, however, unity was remarkably
complete, and in Quebec André Laurendeau, then a youthful extremist agitating actively against taking part in the
struggle with Hitler, had the feeling of not being followed
by the mass of his French-Canadian compatriots.

That the country in general was prepared for the moment
to accept the King war policies was demonstrated by two
political crises that arose within the first six months. Maurice
Duplessis, the nationalist premier of Quebec, chose to call
a provincial election on the issue of war measures infringing
provincial autonomy; it came close to being a threat of a
declaration of neutrality. The Quebec members of King's

Cabinet, led by Lapointe, met this really appalling menace squarely. Against the Prime Minister's advice, they proclaimed that if Duplessis were returned they would resign, leaving Quebec without representation in the Cabinet at Ottawa; at the same time they reaffirmed the government's pledge against overseas conscription. In the election of October 26, 1939, Duplessis was heavily defeated, and did not return to power until 1944.

The second crisis came on King's other flank, in Ontario. The premier of Ontario, Mitchell Hepburn (a Liberal, but bitterly hostile to King), put through the legislature in January 1940 a resolution condemning the federal government's war policies as weak and inadequate – precisely the reverse of the criticisms that had come from Quebec. King's response was to dissolve Parliament (which was nearing the end of its legal span of life) and appeal to the people. In the election of March 26 the government swept the country; it won every seat but one in Quebec and a majority of those in Ontario. King had made an acute calculation in going to the country before the war had entered a critical phase, before violent passions had been aroused, and at a time when his 'moderate' war effort still commanded general support. He was now firmly in power for the duration of the war. The Conservative parliamentary opposition was and remained extraordinarily inefficient and ineffective, and the most formidable threats to King's position, as time passed, came from within his own Cabinet, the results of the developing strain of the war.

The mainspring of Mackenzie King's conception of the national effort was his fear of conscription for overseas service and its adverse effects upon the country's unity and, doubtless, his party's chances of continuing in power. It followed that he was consistently hostile to a large army. He saw the Canadian contribution to the war as centring in the development of war industry (which in addition to enabling many Canadians to make money would keep them safely at home), with the military effort concentrated in the air force and to a lesser extent on the navy. Those services, he thought, were unlikely to make demands on manpower that might result in conscription. Nevertheless, these conceptions were in great part defeated: by the logic of the situation and the way the war developed; by the pressure of some of King's colleagues; and by the fact that the Canadian people, conditioned by memories of 1914-18, perversely persisted in thinking of a war effort primarily in terms of a fighting army.

By about the middle of September 1939 the government had decided upon the main lines of its military program, including the dispatch of one army division overseas; and on September 19 it announced it. The program also included a large air-training scheme, for which the British government had asked. But on September 26 that government broached a much bigger project – which became the British Commonwealth Air Training Plan. Had it been proposed earlier it is possible that no army expeditionary force would have gone to England that year; for the Canadian government, and King in particular, embraced the idea with enthusiasm and sought to make it the country's chief military contribution. An important contribution to victory it was, for in the end the Plan produced over 131,000 air-crew personnel (Britons, Australians, New Zealanders, and – the majority – Canadians). But it brought troubles in its train. Indeed, it broke the back of the Royal Canadian Air Force. The strength and energy of the R.C.A.F. were diverted into training in Canada, and when Canadian graduates of the Plan began to become available in numbers most of them were dispersed through the Royal Air Force remote from Canadian contact or control. Basically this was because in 1939 the Canadian government felt unable to spend the money to maintain them. The so-called R.C.A.F. squadrons formed overseas had, for a long period, partly Canadian air crew but British ground crew and British-financed equipment; and even the Canadian air crew were paid by the British taxpayer except for the difference between British and Canadian rates! As long as this situation lasted the 'Canadianization' program pursued from 1941 onwards by the energetic and compassionate Air Minister, C. G. Power, with a view to producing as far as possible a genuinely Canadian overseas air force, was largely illusory. After Canada, in 1943, assumed the whole cost of the R.C.A.F. overseas the program began to show more results.

The catastrophic Allied reverse in France in the early summer of 1940, the Dunkirk evacuation, and the French collapse marked a tremendous divide in the Canadian effort. Canada and the Commonwealth looked into the pit of defeat. The dollar suddenly ceased to seem important. Limited liability was abandoned – except in the important item of manpower, for the government continued to stand by the pledge against overseas conscription. The National Resources Mobilization Act of June 1940 authorized the use of compulsion for home defence. With the great army of France suddenly swept from the board, more divisions were desperately needed, and for a time, it seems, even Mackenzie King did not oppose the expansion of the Canadian Army or the dispatch of more troops overseas. Four Canadian destroyers – the whole available effective force – sailed across the Atlantic to join the fight in the waters around the British Isles. Similarly, an R.C.A.F. fighter squadron was hurriedly dispatched and fought in the Battle of Britain later in the summer. And with British orders for equipment pouring in, and the expanding Canadian forces themselves in great need of weapons, the Canadian economic front suddenly began to develop in a manner unknown in the early months of the war.

Starting late, and from a very narrow base – for the country had almost no peace-time munitions industry – the production effort did not reach its peak until 1943; but it achieved proportions far beyond anything hitherto seen in Canada. Whereas in 1914-18 no weapons had been made except Ross rifles, now a wide variety of small arms and guns, ships, and aircraft were manufactured. The outstanding achievement was in the automotive field; nearly 800,000 motor vehicles were produced for the Allied forces. At the summit of the effort in 1943, some 1,100,000 persons were employed in war industry, as compared with a total of

1,086,000 who ever served in the armed forces. The estimated gross national product at market prices rose from
$5,598,000,000 in 1939 to $11,897,000,000 in 1944. The
Dominion government's total expenditure was $553,063,098
in 1939, and was up to $5,322,253,505 in 1944. These sta-
tistics make the financial calculations of the government and
its advisers in the first year of the war look timid indeed.

Canadians on the home front were lucky by comparison
with the people of Britain, infinitely lucky by comparison
with those in countries overrun by the enemy. Yet they did
suffer privations, and some of them were more serious than
the sad fate of being unable to buy a new car in the peace-
time manner whenever they chose. Rationing did not appear
on any considerable scale until after the further intensification of the war following the attack by Japan at the end
of 1941, but during 1942 coupon rationing of gasoline and
various foods began; for the rest of the war Canadians made
do with half a pound of sugar each per week. Alcoholic
drinks were in short supply. Clothing was not rationed, but
production of civilian garments was controlled. The disappearance of silk and nylon stockings was a blow to women.
The public, however, had reason to be grateful to the War-
time Prices and Trade Board, which operated the country's
price controls. The Board, with proper pride, calculated that
the cost of living in Canada rose only 19 per cent during the
six years of the Second World War, as compared with 54 per
cent in 1914-18.

Economic discomforts on the whole were cheerfully borne.
They were minor compared to the sorrow and deprivation
resulting from the prolonged absence overseas of hundreds
of thousands of sons and husbands, the constant fear for
their safety, the all-too-frequent telegrams bringing news of
death or wounds suffered in action against the enemy by
land or sea or air. And many a home was broken by the long
separation, leaving tragic social consequences which are felt
to this day.

III

'Senior Service' by virtue of British inheritance if not of Canadian history, the Royal Canadian Navy remained throughout the war the smallest and the least publicized of the three services, happy in that its operations seldom became matters of political controversy. Yet it grew enormously in the course of the conflict, and there were few seas where its guns were not heard before the war was over.

The navy of 1939 – its fighting element comprised six destroyers – was far too small to fight an independent naval war. The Canadian government kept the ultimate control of the force, and Canadian naval units were not sent out of Canadian waters or transferred from one theatre to another without the consent of the Cabinet War Committee in Ottawa. In most situations throughout the war, however, Canadian ships served and fought under the operational control of the Royal Navy. There was one considerable exception. In the summer of 1941 the R.C.N. organized a Newfoundland Escort Force with headquarters at St. John's. Later in the year, as a result of arrangements made between Churchill and Roosevelt at their Argentia meeting, this force was transferred to U.S. naval command, even though the United States was still neutral. This arrangement lasted until 1943, by which time few United States ships were operating in the area. Then the Canadian North-West Atlantic command was set up and a Canadian naval officer took charge of operations in the ocean areas off Canada's east coast, subject only to the qualification that the United States retained strategic responsibility for the whole Western Atlantic.

The Royal Canadian Navy was mainly a small-ship navy; its main battleground was the North Atlantic and its chief antagonist the German submarines that sought to sever the vital line of communications joining the fighting forces and the factories of North America to the United Kingdom. The battle was fought with destroyers, corvettes, frigates, and minesweepers, supported by naval and still more by land-based aircraft. It was conducted under the grimmest conditions of peril and discomfort, on one of the nastiest seas in the world. The seamen who manned the ships sought relaxation in Halifax, a place they apparently did not find particularly agreeable. Perhaps their feelings found expression on VE day – the day of victory in Europe – when mobs in which sailors were prominent wrecked a good part of the city.

Before that day came the R.C.N. had destroyed, or shared in destroying, 27 German submarines. It had also been active in the naval war in European waters, taking part in the landings at Dieppe and in the Mediterranean, and making a very considerable contribution to the Normandy D Day and the operations that preceded and followed it. The tiny service of 1939 had expanded to a strength of about 100,000 men and women, and it was a commonplace that some of the best seamen were lads from the prairies who had never seen the sea until they went down to it in the ships of the R.C.N.

The Royal Canadian Air Force was much larger – roughly 250,000 men and women served in it – and its tasks were even more varied. Nearly 100,000 of its personnel were absorbed in conducting the great British Commonwealth Air Training Plan in Canada. A large Home War Establishment guarded Canadian coastal waters, fought submarines – at home and abroad the R.C.A.F. was credited with destroying, or sharing in the destruction of, 23 U-boats – and took part in the air operations against the Japanese in the Aleutian Islands in 1942-3. And overseas a total – ultimately – of 48 R.C.A.F. squadrons, becoming more and more truly Canadian as Mr. Power's 'Canadianization' policy made its slow and painful progress, fought the enemy around the globe. At the same time a great number of individual Canadians, graduates of the Air Training Plan, served in units of the Royal Air Force. The controversy goes on still as to whether a national squadron was more effective than one of these mixed R.A.F. squadrons in which air crew from half a dozen different Commonwealth countries served cheerfully together. Canadians did a great deal of air fighting but got only a limited share of air command. Only one operational air vice-marshal's appointment was available to them over-seas – the command of No. 6 (R.C.A.F.) Group in the R.A.F. Bomber Command, which was formed at the beginning of 1943. The final strength of the Group was 14 squadrons.

Mackenzie King and his colleagues, when they authorized the heavy commitment of the R.C.A.F. to Bomber Command, certainly did not realize what this meant in terms of loss of life. No military task of the war took a more appalling toll than the strategic air offensive against Germany; none called for greater or more sustained fortitude than that demanded of the young airmen who made the long flights against Berlin or the Ruhr, carried out grimly night after night in the face of searchlights, radar, flak, night fighters, and all the concentrated resources of German defence science. This was a battle in which few of the casualties lived to be recorded as wounded or prisoners of war; the vast majority of those shot down died. No one knows how many Canadians served in Bomber Command; but just under 10,000 lost their lives in it. This (nearly double the Canadian Army's loss in the 20-month campaign in Italy) accounted for far more than half of the R.C.A.F.'s total of 17,000 fatal casualties – and for the fact that the air force had far more such casualties in proportion to its strength than either of the other services.

The air force and the navy were both fighting the enemy on many fronts and on an increasing scale before the army really got into action. Yet as we have already said the Canadian people certainly in some degree equated the war effort with the army. This may have been partly because the army was the largest service – all told, some 730,000 Canadians served in it – and therefore closest to the community as a whole. It was certainly due in part to national memories of 1914-18 and the Canadian Corps. But there was probably also a consciousness, if only a dim one, that the army, inheriting the old Corps' traditions, was the most national of the three forces. The Royal Canadian Navy was overshadowed by the Royal Navy and fought dispersed across the seas, often under British or American local command. The Royal Canadian Air Force overseas had a long struggle before it achieved something like national status. But the overseas Army–until the great aberration of 1943 – served as a national body, under a leader of vivid personality whose Canadianism was very evident. In action it fought under British higher head-quarters–the Eighth Army in Italy, the 21st Army Group in North-West Europe; but it fought in united national formations.

National spirit had moved strongly in the old Corps, espe-cially in 1917-18 under Sir Arthur Currie; but this new Army was in one sense more genuinely Canadian. Of the men of the Canadian Expeditionary Force of 1914-18 only 51.3 per cent were Canadian-born. In 1939-45, no less than 84.6 per cent of the Army's personnel reported Canada as their native country.

Its experience was also quite different. The C.E.F. was in-volved in heavy fighting from the spring of 1915 onwards. The overseas force in the second war, which had expected to join the British Expeditionary Force in France in 1940, found itself condemned by events to years of garrison duty and training in England. During those years it was built up, under General McNaughton's direction, from a single half-trained division of infantry to an efficient small Army of two corps, comprising five divisions (two of them armoured) and two independent armoured brigades.

Not the least interesting phenomenon of these garrison years was the development of the Canadians' relationship with the British people. It began badly in the cold winter of 1939-40, the days of the 'phony war', when 'boredom, home-sickness and a feeling of not being really needed' led the sol-diers to write letters about England that shocked the censors who read them. Then came the Battle of Britain and the 'blitz', and the British people and their country suddenly began to look much more admirable to the troops. As the months passed, individual Canadians found their way into British homes and in many cases became almost members of the family. By the spring of 1944 the censors were reporting that in a batch of nearly 12,000 Canadian letters 'not one adverse comment' on British civilians had been seen. And when the war was over Canadian servicemen brought some 43,000 wives home from the British Isles. It was an extraordinary episode in social history and Commonwealth relations.

Only in December 1941 did the Canadian Army fight its first battle, when two battalions took part in the hopeless defence of Hong Kong against the Japanese. These troops were sent from Canada and had nothing to do with the force in England. That force had its baptism of fire in the bloody and unsuccessful raid on Dieppe (August 19, 1942). Both these tragic operations, followed as they were by further periods of inaction for Canadian troops, produced bitter, violent, and ill-informed discussion in Parliament and outside it. As time went on and the Army was still not fighting, demands that it should fight were heard in the press, on the platform, and at the council table. Ralston, the Defence Minister, and Lieut.-General Kenneth Stuart, the Chief of the General Staff, took this line. General McNaughton, commanding the First Canadian Army in Britain, was opposed to fighting for the sake of fighting, and had no doubt that the morale of his men would withstand even more prolonged inaction. He acquiesced when the Canadian government prevailed upon Mr. Churchill to insert the 1st Canadian Division into the order of battle for the Sicilian invasion in the summer of 1943. That autumn, when Ralston and Stuart, with the rather reluctant assent of Mackenzie King, got the British government to force upon the Allied Mediterranean command a Canadian corps headquarters and an armoured division that they did not need and did not want, there was almost an open break. At that moment the British War Office raised the question of McNaughton's fitness to command an army in the field. They were no doubt sincere in feeling that the heavy military and quasi-political responsibilities of the past four years had told upon him. At any rate, this, coming simultaneously with his difficulties with his own government, made McNaughton's position impossible, and he was forced out. The command passed after an interval to Lieut.-General H. D. G. Crerar, a competent and experienced Canadian professional soldier who had been commanding the Corps in Italy and who was now to command the First Canadian Army through the 1944-5 campaign in North-West Europe.

After its long period of inaction, the Canadian Army had its fill of bloody fighting in the final phases of the war. There is no need to relate in detail the story of its part in the great campaigns that began in Sicily in the south and in Normandy in the north. The battle honours on its regiments' colours will tell the tale for ever: Sicily, the Hitler Line, the Gothic Line; Normandy Landing, Caen, Falaise, The Scheldt, The Rhineland. Although the Canadian government at a remarkably early date began to ask for the return of the Corps that it had insisted on sending to Italy, the war with Germany was nearly over when the two segments of the Army were reunited under General Crerar's command in North-West Europe. British and other troops filled the gap in the First Canadian Army while the 1st Canadian Corps was fighting in the British Eighth Army far to the south. If one counts English, Scots, Irish, and Welsh, nearly a dozen nationalities fought under Crerar; and though the Canadian divisions were always the Army's solid core, the smooth and loyal co-operation of these varied national elements against the common enemy was a particularly inspiring element in its campaign.

Though the Germans were on the defensive by the time the Canadian Army got into major action, and the two campaigns in which it played its part were in general an unbroken series of victories, victory seldom came easily. The fierce house-to-house struggle at Ortona in December 1943, the desperate little fight beside the frostbound Maas at Kapelsche Veer in January 1945, may stand as types of bloody local operations; the figures published by Field-Marshal Montgomery, showing that the two Canadian infantry divisions had heavier casualties than any other divisions under his command in Normandy, testify to the burden Canadians bore in the major battles. Yet the total loss was

far below that exacted by the carnage of the Western Front
in 1915-18; the Army's fatal casualties in the Second World
War, including deaths from natural causes, amounted to
about 23,000.

<h1 style="text-align:center">IV</h1>

Canada was in 1939 a formally independent country, as she
had not been in 1914. It remained to be seen how much this
independence meant in practical international terms in the
midst of a great war, when a nation's status is measured less
in constitutional formulas than in the numbers of divisions
it places in the field.

The war in its first stage (1939-40) was conducted on
behalf of the Allies by an Anglo-French Supreme War Council. It appears that Canada never either sought or was offered
a seat on this body or any direct relationship to it. For a
country bent on a 'moderate' war effort and having no desire
to be pressed to do more, this modest policy may have had a
practical appeal. At any rate, except that the established
diplomatic relations with France continued, Canada's relation to the direction of the war was through the Commonwealth channel; and that channel itself was not very active.
A minister (T. A. Crerar) visited London in the autumn of
1939; there was day-to-day liaison through the High Commissioner in Ottawa and London; but when in the spring
of 1940 the Chamberlain government in England proposed
a conference of Commonwealth prime ministers, Mackenzie
King successfully discouraged the idea. He argued that it
would be politically difficult for him to leave Canada and
that he should be available there 'in the event of a situation
arising in which he might be called upon to assist in maintaining the most friendly relations between Great Britain
and the United States'.

After the French collapse which shortly followed, Canada
continued to take a similar line. The war was conducted by
the British War Cabinet (but increasingly, in practice, by the
new Prime Minister, Churchill, and the three Chiefs of Staff),

with limited consultation with the Dominions. Australia wanted an Imperial War Cabinet as in 1917-18; Churchill and King unitedly – though clearly from different motives – opposed it. The importance of the United States to British victory was obvious; and King continued to see himself as playing a vital part in relations with that country. He was a whole-hearted adherent of the theory that saw Canada as the 'linchpin' of Anglo-American relations. For a time in 1940 it seemed that that theory held the field, and King scored an independent point with his meeting with Roosevelt in August and the issuance of the 'Ogdensburg Declaration'. This certainly initiated a new era in Canadian-American relations, and few dogs on either side of the border barked against it. But the linchpin theory suffered a serious setback, and King himself a severe shock, in August 1941, when Churchill and Roosevelt held their meeting in the waters of Newfoundland without previous consultation with or notice to him. For a short period of the war Canada had been Britain's strongest ally; that period drew to a close when Hitler attacked Russia in June 1941, and its western twilight ended abruptly on December 7, 1941, when the bombs that fell on Pearl Harbor blew the United States into the war. Thereafter Canada was a very junior partner and sometimes treated with scant ceremony.

The Combined Chiefs of Staff, set up early in 1942 to co-ordinate the military effort of the alliance, was a purely Anglo-American committee. Canada, as a considerable munitions producer, sought membership on the Munitions Assignment Board, which allotted completed stores among the Allies; her application was rejected, though she might have achieved limited membership. She did become a member of two of the four Combined Boards that supposedly co-ordinated other aspects of Anglo-American war affairs (the Combined Food Board and the Combined Production and Resources Board), but these were not really very powerful or important bodies. Canada, in common with other 'middle powers' of the alliance, was excluded from the great strategic conferences where war policy was decided. This applied even

to the two conferences held at Quebec in 1943 and 1944, but
the point did not greatly trouble Mackenzie King. 'I said to
Ralston,' he wrote in his diary, 'the important thing was to
have the meeting held at Quebec. That, of itself, would cause
all else to work out satisfactorily.' Having the conference held
on Canadian soil seemed to him a great political advantage to
himself and to his party. That Canada had no voice in the
higher direction of the war he regretted, but he never made
a very serious protest.

V

We have referred to the adoption by both major political
parties in 1939 of the formula 'no conscription for overseas
service'. Neither departed from this formula in the general
election of the early spring of 1940. But from the time when
the war was intensified following the collapse of France
demands were increasingly heard from English-speaking
Canada for not merely the home-defence conscription authorized by the new National Resources Mobilization Act
(above, page 283), but unlimited conscription. At the Cabinet
table Colonel Ralston was mentioning such conscription as a
possible if remote future requirement as early as April 1941.
The attack by Japan eight months later produced an immediate agitation for repeal of the section of the N.R.M.A.
forbidding the use of compulsion in connection with military
service abroad. And after much soul-searching Mackenzie
King decided that the best course was to appeal to the people
in a plebiscite to release the government from its pledges
against overseas conscription. This was announced when
Parliament met in January 1942.

The result was a serious rift between English and French
Canada, shattering the precarious unity of 1939. French-
speaking Quebec considered (with good reason) that the 1939
pledges had been mainly addressed to itself, and took the view
that the government was now trying to wriggle out of them
by the device of a plebiscite in which the vast majority of
voters would be English-speaking. For the first time the

element in Quebec actively opposing the war found itself possessed of a popular and powerful issue. The *Ligue pour la défense du Canada* was formed to encourage French Canadians to vote 'No'. André Laurendeau, once discouraged by the public reaction in 1939, now found the movement growing 'like an avalanche'. And in the vote taken on April 27, Quebec isolated itself. In the country as a whole 2,945,514 people voted 'Yes' (for release) against 1,643,006 voting 'No'. In Quebec the proportion was reversed: 376,188 voted 'Yes'; 993,663 voted 'No'.

King had no intention whatever of actually introducing compulsory overseas service unless and until he was forced to; but the government proceeded to amend the National Resources Mobilization Act by removing the prohibition on such service. The result was the resignation of one French-Canadian minister, P. J. A. Cardin. At the other extremity of the Cabinet, J. L. Ralston resigned in a dispute over the procedure to be followed if circumstances demanded the actual application of compulsion. He was prevailed upon to stay; but his resignation remained in King's hands. Under the amended act, conscripts were sent to serve in various areas of the North American zone, but none were dispatched to Europe until late in 1944.

It was the heavy infantry casualties in Normandy in 1944 that precipitated the final conscription crisis. 'General service' enlistments (as distinct from compulsory call-ups for service in Canada) had fallen off seriously since early in 1943; and when the Normandy battles took a heavier toll in infantry, and a lighter one in other arms, than the Allies' calculations had anticipated, the supply of trained infantry reinforcements overseas was not equal to the demand. In Canada, however, there were thousands of trained conscript infantrymen who refused to 'go active'. The immediate overseas expedient was to 'remuster' men of other corps as infantry and give them emergency training. The result was that inadequately trained men were sent into battle. Colonel Ralston made a quick visit to the fighting fronts and returned to Ottawa on October 18 to recommend that the trained 'zombies' – the opprobrious term some too-clever person had coined for the conscripts – be sent overseas. King was not yet ready to consent. After prolonged wrangling, the Prime Minister, remarking that he still held Ralston's 1942 resignation, dismissed the Defence Minister on November 1. Ralston was succeeded by General McNaughton, who had been his bitter enemy since his own dismissal a year before, and was now prepared to make a final attempt to make the voluntary system work.

The attempt failed. After three weeks during which the great majority of the 'zombies' continued to resist appeals to them to accept general service voluntarily, the Chief of the General Staff (Lieut.-General J. C. Murchie) and the other military members of the Army Council reported on November 22 expressing the considered opinion that the voluntary system could not meet the immediate reinforcement problem. Mackenzie King seems to have told some of his confidants later that this action by the generals represented a grave threat to constitutional government and that, faced with something like a military revolt, he was 'struck dumb'. This is poppycock, though King almost immediately convinced himself that it was true. Actually, he had come by November 22 to feel that overseas conscription, which he had opposed so long and so bitterly, had become a necessity if his government was to survive. Public opinion in English Canada had taken a long time to harden on the conscription issue – the defeat of the conscriptionist Conservative leader Arthur Meighen by a C.C.F. candidate in a Toronto constituency in February 1942 was evidence of this – but now it was virtually unanimous. The Army was at last in full action, and it must be supported. This feeling was powerfully reflected in the Cabinet. When King heard from McNaughton the news of the generals' advice, the superstitious Prime Minister wrote in his diary,

> This really lifts an enormous burden from my mind as after yesterday's Council it was apparent to me that it was only a matter of days before there would be no Government in

> Canada. . . . As I look at the clock from where I am standing
> as I dictate this sentence, the hands are both together at 5
> to 11.

The following day the government tabled in Parliament an
Order in Council providing for the dispatch overseas of
16,000 conscripts – approximately the number required to
fill the reinforcement pools overseas.

King and his government and party were saved. One minister – C. G. Power – resigned. Ralston, who probably could
have brought the Prime Minister down and, in the light of
the treatment he had received, could scarcely have been
criticized for doing so, supported the new policy. The House
of Commons gave King a vote of confidence – though 34
French-Canadian members of his party voted against him.
There was a wave of desertion among the conscripts – 7,800
were missing at one point – and there were what amounted
to mutinies (a word avoided at the time) in some of the camps
in British Columbia, where great numbers of home-defence
troops had been concentrated in 1942 to provide against a
Japanese menace that existed only in the excited imagination
of the people of the province. But nearly 13,000 conscripts
were actually sent overseas, where those who got into action
performed much like any other reinforcements. Thanks to
their arrival, and to the fact that casualties in the final phase
were fewer than had been feared, the Canadian divisions
were fully up to strength in their last battles.

King had overcome the most serious challenge he had ever
faced. For the rest of his time in office his power in his party
and in Parliament was more absolute than ever. He suffered
only one humiliation – not a serious one, though it had about
it a flavour of poetic justice: his defeat, by the service vote, in
his own constituency of Prince Albert in the general election
of 1945. It was McNaughton, whom King had used to save
himself, who paid the price. The general failed of election to
the House of Commons in a by-election and subsequently in
the general election, being defeated by nonentities. He had
deserved better of the Canadian people. He resigned the

National Defence portfolio in August 1945, after the defeat
of Japan. It was the measure of that extraordinary man that
this reverse was not the end of him. He was to go on to a
further distinguished career of many years in the public
service.

Although the servicemen apparently could not bring
themselves to vote for Mackenzie King personally, they –
and other Canadians – did vote pretty heavily for his government in that general election of June 1945, held after the
defeat of Germany. (The armed services have voted Liberal
ever since.) The country was evidently satisfied, on the whole,
with King's conduct of affairs. At any rate, it was not prepared
to turn him out in favour of the 'Progressive Conservatives'
led by John Bracken, a former Manitoba premier who,
though chosen leader in 1942, had followed the curious tactic
of not seeking a seat in the House of Commons until the general election. The Liberal majority was materially reduced,
but not to the point of danger. The Co-operative Commonwealth Federation, which King had once thought more dangerous to him than the Conservatives, got only 28 seats,
almost all in the West.

VI

There was no post-war 'slump' in any extreme sense after
1945, though in 1945-6 there was a material decline in employment from the 1944 peak. By 1947 there was again 'full'
employment. The gross national product at market prices
rose from $11,759 million in 1945 to $15,450 million in
1948. The post-war years were essentially an extension of the
period of economic growth initiated by the war, and as usual
prosperity brought contentment and political stability.

On the whole, it was remarkable how smoothly and easily
the country's one million service men and women were
absorbed back into the civilian economy. The generous
veterans' benefits accorded them contributed to this while
at the same time giving the economy a fillip. Educational
benefits brought many thousands of ex-service students into

the universities, whose resources were strained as they were
not to be again until the sixties. Although Canada remained
a country whose prosperity depended on staple exports, the
economy in which the new graduates found places was more
industrialized than before the war; and industrial expansion
continued. With it, inevitably, came increased urbanization.
The census of 1951, which indicated an increase of population from 11,507,000 to 14,009,000 in the past decade, also
showed that 62.9 per cent of Canadians were now town-
dwellers as compared with only 54.4 per cent in 1941. A
change in the definition of the terms 'urban' and 'rural' between the two censuses had the effect of somewhat exagger-
ating the change, but it is clear that the pace of urbanization
had greatly quickened.

A new element on the Canadian peace-time industrial
scene was the continuance of some of the defence industries
created during the war. The fact that Canada was now maintaining much larger defence forces than before 1939 contributed to this. Some of these production facilities were
directly owned by the national government, others (the
aircraft and shipbuilding industries in particular) owed
their continued existence mainly to government orders and
encouragement.

Among the industries rapidly 'reconverted' from war production to peaceful purposes, none was more notable or more
representative than the automotive industry, whose war-time
achievements had been so striking. At the end of hostilities
the demand for civilian cars was enormous, and the industry's
resources were strained to cope with it. And the statistics of
production rose year by year: from 104,819 cars and trucks
'made for sale in Canada' in 1946, to 262,775 three years
later. The number of motor vehicles registered in Canada
rose similarly – from 1,497,081 in 1945 to 2,290,628 in 1949;
and the increase continued rapidly thereafter. The motor
car was no new thing in 1945; but it was the generation after
the Second World War that was to feel the full impact of the
revolution wrought upon society by the internal-combustion
engine. In 1939-45 it had added a new dimension to warfare,

enabling campaigns to move across the map at a speed hitherto unknown; but at the same time it produced a new set of
tactical problems, threatening to destroy the mobility it
created simply by strangling the armies in their own traffic
jams. It was now to do the same for civilian communities.
Millions of dollars' worth of super-highways were required
for cross-country movement; great cities found themselves
throttled by increasing motor traffic, and were forced to
spend more millions to provide new high-speed routes to
carry it in and out; the death-toll in accidents rose steadily
with the number of cars on the roads; and Canada's expensive
railways, so grossly overbuilt early in the century, found
themselves faced with ruinous competition from highway
transport just when increasing population seemed to hold
out the hope of genuinely economic operation.

In another respect too the motor industry was representative of the trends of the time. A British official history of the
Second World War remarks, truly enough, 'The industry of
the Dominion was dominated to an undue extent by automobile production. . . . Moreover, the whole of this industry
and a large part of the others had been created by American
firms. . . . The dependent character of Canada's industrial
development was betrayed at many points.' These tendencies
were reinforced after the war; indeed, the Canadian economy
as a whole acquired an increasing dependence on the United
States. Between the two world wars the United States had
displaced Britain as the chief non-resident investor in Canada; and between 1945 and 1949 the total U.S. investment
in Canada rose from $4,990 million to $5,906 million. By
1948, 39 per cent of Canadian manufacturing industry was
controlled by residents of the United States. The figure
increased sharply in subsequent years, and it was in the fifties
that Canadians became painfully aware of the situation and
began to be vocal about it; but the trend was well established
long before 1950.

Another trend was a modest movement in the direction of
the welfare state. Mackenzie King liked to think of himself
as a social reformer and the friend of the working man; and

within rather narrow limits he can be so regarded. His third administration passed at least two fairly notable pieces of social-security legislation. An amendment to the British North America Act passed in 1940 to establish the right of the Dominion Parliament to establish unemployment insurance – which had been successfully challenged in the courts – was followed immediately by the enactment of the Unemployment Insurance Act. In 1944 came the Family Allowances Act, providing what was popularly called the 'baby bonus' – a monthly payment to parents of up to eight dollars for each child under the age of sixteen. There was long discussion of a non-contributory system of old-age pensions; but the Old Age Security Act did not become law until 1951 (following yet another amendment to the B.N.A. Act) – twenty-four years after the Dominion's first ineffective old-age pension act, and forty-three years after Lloyd George's act in Britain.

VII

The conscription question, which did so much harm in 1917-18, had a less damaging effect in 1942-5 on relations between French and English Canada. The conscription policy of the First World War was introduced and administered with little regard for the feelings of the French-Canadian minority. In the Second World War the country was ruled by a prime minister whose power was largely rooted in Quebec, and who made it the cornerstone of his war policy to avoid overseas conscription, or at the very least to postpone it to the last moment. Although the French-Canadian extremists hated King as much as the English-speaking conscriptionist extremists did (it is interesting that the former were largely quite young men, while the latter frequently belonged to the 1914-18 generation), it is evident that the French-Canadian community as a whole recognized King's government as far more satisfactory from their point of view than any that could conceivably replace it were it defeated. When King was finally forced to accept overseas conscription to keep his Cabinet together, many Quebec members, we have seen, voted against him. Nevertheless his party continued to control the federal representation from Quebec; and it was largely thanks to him that the country came out of the war somewhat less divided than it had been in 1918.

Within the armed forces themselves 'French' and 'English' got on rather better than their civilian compatriots did. It was in the services that many a Canadian actually met for the first time members of the other section of the community. It would be idle to claim that the result was always to the advantage of national unity; but most people who were there would probably say that it was oftener good than bad, and sometimes it was very good indeed. The comradeship of the battlefield was an admirable solvent of traditional prejudices. Even among servicemen in Canada who never saw a battlefield, there were good effects. The men from Quebec who served in British Columbia came home with a heightened sense of Canadian realities (and it may not be out of place to remark, on the evidence of those in the best positions to know, that it was not French-Canadian soldiers who organized the disorders in the west-coast camps in 1944).

The Province of Quebec in the post-war era remained under the *Union Nationale* government of Maurice Duplessis. In the election of 1944, which brought him back to power, the electors rejected not only the Liberal ministry of Adélard Godbout, but also the ultra-nationalist, anti-war *Bloc Populaire*. Duplessis's strength lay mainly in the rural areas. His policy within Quebec may be described as authoritarian and anti-intellectual. Towards Ottawa he took an intransigent attitude, refusing, for instance, to co-operate in the construction of the Trans-Canada Highway (authorized by a federal act of 1949). Nevertheless it seemed evident that the events of 1939-45 had done little if any permanent damage to the relations of French and English Canadians. So far as English Canada was concerned, there had probably never been a time when there was so much disposition to understand Quebec and co-operate with her. And in 1949 a French-Canadian, Roman Catholic prime minister won the greatest electoral victory in the Dominion's history.

VIII

In the sphere of Commonwealth relations the independence of Canada was already almost complete; but in certain matters of detail it was widened. In 1947 the Canadian Parliament passed a statute of this tendency: the Canadian Citizenship Act established for the first time a status as Canadian citizen additional to that of British subject. The year 1949 (after King's actual retirement) saw two other measures. The Judicial Committee of the Privy Council in London ceased to be the highest court of appeal for Canadian cases; these would now stop at the Supreme Court of Canada. Had this been done earlier it would have been well for the powers of the central government. The other measure was the amendment of the British North America Act to permit further amendments to be made without reference to the British Parliament in matters not affecting the powers of the provinces.

Relations with the other point of the North Atlantic Triangle contained many more uncertainties than those with Britain and the Commonwealth. Intimate contact with the United States dated only from 1940 and the Ogdensburg Declaration, which announced the establishment of the Permanent Joint Board on Defence, Canada–United States. King undoubtedly was proud of the part he had played in bringing about this *rapprochement*, and considerable evidence is now available to document his tendency to overvalue the American connection and undervalue the British one. This tendency was probably natural to him, but it was encouraged by O. D. Skelton, the isolationist and anti-British Under-Secretary of State for External Affairs, who, until his death in 1941, was King's closest adviser. Nevertheless King's experience as the war proceeded seems to have somewhat moderated his enthusiasm in this direction; he became aware, for instance, of the assurance with which American officers operated in the Canadian North, acting as if they were on their own soil and sometimes omitting even lip-service to Canadian sovereignty. And the President with whom King had been on terms of a degree of personal friendship vanished from the scene in the spring of 1945. In these circumstances the war-time co-operation between the two countries continued into peace-time, but it was hedged about with safeguards. The statement issued jointly by the two countries in February 1947 announcing that military co-operation through the Permanent Joint Board would go on emphasized that the collaboration would be 'limited' and that pains would be taken to protect each country's sovereignty. The only new joint activity undertaken in the North in King's time was a modest program of weather stations.

Perhaps more important for the future was the government's changing attitude towards international organization and collective security. Canada played an active if modest part in the organization of the United Nations in 1945. Her representatives were not pleased with the attempts of the great powers to ensure a dominant voice for themselves in the new body – only great powers were invited to the Dumbarton Oaks conference where the plan was drafted, and the constitution of the Security Council gave each great power not only a permanent seat there but a right of veto – but they did not lead a crusade on the subject. In marked contrast to her attitude towards the League of Nations between the wars, she did not object to the U.N.'s being allowed to have 'teeth' to help it keep the peace. And Canada was glad to be elected a temporary member of the Security Council for the years 1948 and 1949.

More striking events were coming. As the Cold War between East and West took shape, the Canadian government made no attempt to isolate itself from it. As early as the autumn of 1945, the revelations of Soviet espionage activity in Ottawa as well as other Allied capitals had shocked the Canadian government and people. The year 1948 produced alarming developments: the *coup* that brought the Communists to power in Czechoslovakia, the Soviet blockade of Berlin. Canada had no share in the improvised Anglo-American airlift that maintained the life of West Berlin; but as discussion developed in and between western capitals on the desirability of forming some sort of western alliance to check the further advance of communism, the Canadian government took an active lead in the movement. It was apparent now that new men and new ideas were stirring in that government; whether they met any resistance from the Prime Minister it is impossible to say. Until 1946 the portfolio of External Affairs was held by the Prime Minister himself; but in September of that year Mackenzie King resigned it and Louis St. Laurent succeeded him. Just two years later an able and popular professional diplomatist, Lester B. Pearson, was prevailed upon to join the King Cabinet; he took the External Affairs portfolio, St. Laurent returning temporarily to the Department of Justice, of which he had formerly been Minister. As early as April 1948 (shortly after the *coup* in Czechoslovakia) St. Laurent declared that the best guarantee for peace was 'the organization of collective defence' under British, American, and French leadership; and no party in the House of Commons seriously challenged the proposition. In June the Vandenberg Resolution, incorporating the same principles, passed the U.S. Senate. In August St. Laurent became leader of the Liberal party; in November he succeeded King as Prime Minister. In April 1949 the North Atlantic Treaty was signed by twelve nations, including Britain, the United States, France, and Canada. The Dominion thus committed itself to an alliance whose members agreed to 'maintain and develop their individual and collective capacity to resist armed attack'. In pursuance of this obligation, Canada in 1951 and later years was to contribute an infantry brigade and an air division to the European forces of the North Atlantic Treaty Organization. Co-operation with the United States outside of NATO was also advancing. By 1949 'an early warning system to cover certain vital approaches and areas' was being developed in the North.

It is evident that the five years after the war – and especially, whether by coincidence or not, the period immediately preceding and following the retirement of Mackenzie King – witnessed a revolution in Canadian external policy. The policy of 'no commitments', which had ruled until the outbreak of war in 1939, had been entirely abandoned in favour of defensive alliances. The commitments that pre-war governments had refused to make to Britain had now been made to an alliance in which Britain was a partner; and it was fairly evident that there were other commitments, unpublished and perhaps undefined, to the United States under arrangements stemming from those of 1940. At the same time, as we have seen, Canada was maintaining armed forces very much larger than it had kept up before 1939. Neither aspect of the new policy was meeting any real criticism from Parliament or the public. The Second World War and the advent of the atomic age had clearly had a powerful effect upon the outlook of the Canadian people and their government.

External relations were a constant source of anxiety; internal relations – in the sense of relations between the Dominion government and the governments of the nine provinces – also presented unsolved problems, chiefly financial. The Royal Commission on Dominion-Provincial Relations (the 'Rowell-Sirois Commission') had reported in 1940, recommending a new basis for the division of revenues and responsibilities, but several provinces, notably Ontario, would have nothing to do with it. After the war the Dominion succeeded in negotiating individual financial agreements with seven provinces (all but Ontario and Quebec), but these were stopgap arrangements and no final and general solution was achieved.

In 1949 the nine provinces became ten. Newfoundland had stood aside at the time of the original Confederation in 1867, and thereafter when opportunities for union arose they were rejected by one party or the other. Union between Canada and Newfoundland was one of the good results of the Second World War.

It was perfectly obvious that the island of Newfoundland was an area of first-class importance to the security of Canada, and indeed of North America at large. Its significance for transatlantic aviation was clear long before the Second World War. Yet before 1939 Newfoundland had no defences whatever; and the island had lost its dominion status in 1934,

when economic disaster forced it to call upon the United
Kingdom for help, and government by an appointed commission was instituted. From the outbreak of war there was
close co-operation between the Newfoundland and Canadian
governments; and at the time of the French collapse in 1940
Canadian troops and aircraft were sent to the island, and an
agreement was made placing Newfoundland's forces under
Canadian command. Almost simultaneously the 'destroyers-
for-bases deal' between Churchill and Roosevelt gave the
United States military bases in the island, and U.S. forces
began to arrive there early in 1941. For the rest of the war
there were essentially two separate defence organizations –
Canadian and American – in Newfoundland. The Canadian
Army garrison rose to a total of nearly 6,000 men. Mackenzie
King was very conscious of the importance of protecting
Canada's permanent interests in the island.

War-time contacts no doubt somewhat diminished the
Newfoundlanders' old anti-Canadian prejudices. After long
debate the island's people went to the polls in 1948 to decide
their future. Three choices were before them: continuance
of commission government, revival of responsible government, and confederation with Canada on terms that had
been discussed with Ottawa. Commission government was
eliminated, but a second referendum was required to decide
between the other two possibilities. It resulted in a small
majority for union with Canada. Essentially it was a victory
of the 'outports' over the commercial community of St.
John's. Final terms of agreement were signed on December
11, and the union became effective at midnight of March 31–
April 1, 1949. There were seven Newfoundland members in
the new Canadian House of Commons that assembled later
in the year; and the first premier of Newfoundland under
the new regime was the formidable and irrepressible 'Joey'
Smallwood, who had led and won the battle for union with
the Dominion. The union brought Canada the completion
of her 'natural boundaries', a piece of territory of great strategic importance, and some 325,000 excellent citizens. It
brought Newfoundland more security than she could create

for herself, and the benefit of the Canadian social services, the payments under which were a useful stimulus to the island economy.

Confederation with Newfoundland provided a final triumph for Mackenzie King, for, though he had retired before it was completed, the vital arrangements had been made under his administration and he had actively encouraged the project. At the same time it was a very auspicious beginning for the government of the new prime minister, Louis S. St. Laurent.

> He to the Commons' feet presents
> A Kingdom for his first year's rents.

The advent in 1948 of the Dominion's second French-Canadian prime minister seemed to encourage the hope that an era of good feeling might lie ahead. He was a very different person from King: a married man with a large family, of whom several had been in the services during the war. Unlike King, he enjoyed not only the respect but also the warm affection of many of his colleagues and subordinates. But he seemed to have many of his predecessor's political gifts, and in the general election of June 1949, as we have already said, he and his party won a victory unparalleled in Canadian history. The new Progressive Conservative leader, George Drew, a former premier of Ontario, was no more fortunate than John Bracken had been; his party got only 41 seats to the Liberals' 193, and 25 of the 41 were in Ontario. The Liberals remained what King had made them – the only party with a solid base in every region of Canada.

Mackenzie King died on July 22, 1950. Very few people, it would seem, had loved him; not many had even liked him; some had entertained an almost psychopathic hatred of him; but vast numbers had voted for him. He had some unpleasant characteristics; we know more about them now than we did when he was living. As a political strategist and tactician, however, he has perhaps no equal in Canadian annals. His greatest political achievement was doubtless the creation and maintenance of a genuinely national party. There were

Canadians – probably a good many of them – who were not partial to King but who nevertheless voted for him and his party simply because it *was* a national party and the only one in the field.

As a statesman, King left his mark on his country and his times, and for better or for worse the mark was deep. His zeal for national unity – a thing good in itself, but in the circumstances of the day particularly good for the Liberals and for King – may not have rendered the country more genuinely united than it had been before, but at least it helped to prevent an explosion that would have made things much worse. Above all, he had left Canada a more independent community than he had found her. How genuine national independence can be in a world cowering under the threat of the Bomb, or how far independence even deserves to be considered a good thing in a world that has suffered so much from the destructive power of nationalism, are questions for the philosopher rather than the historian. Perhaps the measure of King's achievement will be found in the use his country makes of the status which – with the powerful assistance of thousands of more ordinary Canadians wearing various colours of battledress – he did much to win for her.

10. The 1950s

WILLIAM KILBOURN

It was a time of prosperity and civil peace. On the surface at least, the structure of society and politics appeared to change little. The values and influence of a small self-perpetuating upper middle class held sway over French and English Canada. Labour dug in to consolidate its gains or cut its losses, after the militancy and violence of the forties in the auto and steel and asbestos industries. The power and leadership of big business was not seriously challenged. The universities were hotbeds of quietism. The Protestant churches, if one looks no deeper than the newspaper, appeared to spend a good deal of energy fighting their old enemy, drink, and some of their money at least on full-page ads against proposed new violations of the Protestant Sabbath. Perhaps most people were simply content to live in decent and comfortable obscurity, aspiring to an affluence almost within reach, and to think as little as possible about the searing experience of depression and global war they had lived through for twenty years and might momentarily be plunged into again.

In the realm of applied ideas, a thoroughgoing pragmatism held sway. One economist complained that the Gordon Report, for which most of Canada's best economic brains had been mobilized, contained no new philosophy of growth, not even a basic new approach to economic policy. In most spheres of government the predominance of the federal power and the secondary role of the provinces was widely taken for granted. The expanding federal civil service, now administering the welfare state introduced in the 1940s, continued to exhibit its customary professional skill and competence. Its life style remained that of the archetypal Ottawa man who 'did nothing by halves which could be done by quarters'. Politics was dominated by the spirit of Mac- kenzie King, who was indeed still alive in 1950. His two chosen successors followed him into the Liberal party leader- ship, and his self-appointed disciple from Prince Albert suc- ceeded to the leadership of the Conservatives. The dominant political style of the age was either that of iron-bound dedica- tion to adopted positions and principles, in the manner of C. D. Howe or George Drew (it was, after all, the age of Churchill and Dulles, Stalin and Pius XII), or else, more successfully, the style of firm avuncular blandness practised by St. Laurent, Eisenhower, and Macmillan. The most suc- cessful Canadian politician of the decade managed to com- bine something of both styles. If hyperbole may be permitted, it can be said that John Diefenbaker stood in general for morality and strong principles, like George Drew, and in particular for nothing, like Louis St. Laurent. Even his astonishing victory in 1958 may be partly attributed to a nostalgic popular yearning for a past that was already gone, or regarded as another manifestation of the Canadian custom of having only one national, governmental party at a time.

Yet if one looks closely there were already signs in the fifties of the political activism and new directions of the years that followed. The pace and scope of economic growth were so great that they were bound to create far-reaching changes in the structure of society and business. The economic élite of the 1960s were perceptibly different in background and outlook from their counterparts in the 1940s. The heads of the major industrial companies and of the banks and the railways were no longer so predominantly recruited from the topmost echelon of Canadian society. The new men of influence in the churches and the professions, the universities, and the senior civil service also appeared to come from a broader spectrum of society.

If such changes in the structure of social power and prestige came slowly, there were other kinds of change during the 1950s – in culture and technology and the man-made environment – that amounted to nothing less than a revolution. In 1950 Canadians lived in a world without tranquillizers and polio vaccine, jet travel and computers, super highways and shopping plazas, metro government and pedestrian malls. Several of Canada's vast new suburban municipalities still consisted in 1950 mostly of farms and bush, gravel roads and village stores. Cities like Kitimat and Schefferville in the northern wilderness had not even been conceived, let alone built. Television, stereo, transistors, beatniks, Sunday sports, Stratford, the Canada Council, and abstract art were not yet part of Canadian culture.

Names that were to become household words in Canada during the next decade or so – René Lévesque, 'Wacky' Bennett, K. C. Irving and Robert Stanfield, Pierre Berton, Harold Town, Nathan Cohen, and Marshall McLuhan – were in 1950 scarcely heard of or unknown. Jean Lesage was a young back-bencher in the House of Commons. Paul-Émile Léger was teaching theology in Rome. Such nineteenth-century giants as John Dewey and William Randolph Hearst, men who had profoundly influenced the lives of all English-speaking North Americans, were still alive. George Bernard Shaw was still being heard from; so was B. K. Sandwell. A dozen of the Privy Councillors appointed by Laurier and

Borden were living. T. T. Shields still thundered against
French Canadian popery from his Jarvis Street pulpit, as if
the fires of the Inquisition had but recently been lit; and
for Jehovah's Witnesses and Roman Catholic liberals in
Duplessis's Quebec, Dr. Shields was not entirely wide of the
mark.

During 1950 the voices of Rawhide and his troupe of
friends were becoming familiar to Canadians, much to the
alarm of a prominent ecclesiastic and historian, who called
their radio program 'a public avowal of irreligion that Godless Soviet Russia could hardly improve upon', and an M.P.
who denounced the CBC for cluttering its airwaves with
these 'ravings'. Other leading Canadians were more concerned that the CBC had begun to squander its money at the
horrifying rate of $3,000 a week (about two per cent of what
an opera on television cost in the sixties) on a new forced diet
of culture for Canadians called CBC Wednesday Night.

At the turn of the half-century, in January 1950, a
Maclean's Magazine article predicted that in the coming year
the British Labour government would be re-elected with Sir
Stafford Cripps telling people to eat less, that the French
cabinet would reshuffle itself seven times, that the St. Lawrence Seaway project would be re-opened for discussion for a
short time, only to be deferred once more, and that the
Toronto subway would be two feet closer to completion.
Canada's population, it went on, 'now about thirteen millions, would, owing to immigration, emigration, births, deaths
and sheer exhaustion, increase to about thirteen millions'.
The same article looked ahead over the next half-century to
Monday, January 1, A.D. 2000, when, 'with the Toronto subway completed and the housing shortage finally solved, some
politician, speaking by ultra-radio to the entire population
of Canada (thanks to immigration, emigration, etc., now
about thirteen millions) would affirm that "the twenty-first
century belongs to Canada".'

The head of the Canadian state in 1950 was King
George VI, represented in Ottawa by a British Governor
General. Canada was a member of a United Nations with

only about half the members it had admitted a decade and a half later, and of a Commonwealth dominated by Britain and the four white Dominions. Canada was taking the unprecedented step of sending troops to Europe in peace-time as part of its obligations under the new NATO alliance. But the idea of a Canadian presence in Korea or Viet Nam or the Gaza strip would have seemed at the very least improbable – as improbable as a Russian victory over the American space program, over Canadian hockey teams, or over the spirit of Joseph Stalin.

Obviously from the vantage-point of the 1960s, the physical and spiritual world that Canadians lived in a decade earlier could seem very remote indeed. Perhaps one final example will suffice to sum up the difference and suggest the pace and scope of change. Imagine a typical Canadian university as it was just after the Second World War veterans graduated and the temporary disruption and excitement they brought had passed. In the early fifties it was still a quiet liberal-arts college, perhaps run by the church, but in any case essentially the same place its founders had built at the turn of the century. The students all knew each other, and the subjects and courses they took were pretty much the same ones their parents had taken there before them.

By the mid sixties, however, the original Gothic halls were almost lost in a vast university city of glass and concrete. Several professional schools, a new art gallery, and the elegant polygon of a nuclear reactor now graced the campus. Honours courses were offered in subjects unheard of in 1950 or only mentioned in science fiction. The church had relinquished its control and handed over its university as a gift to the people of Canada, yet there were more courses in religion than ever before, now taught as an arts subject by professors of several faiths and of none. There were more Ph.D. candidates than there had once been freshmen, and it was quite possible for the average staff member not to know everybody in his own department. A young lecturer's starting salary had moved up from about $2,000 to $7,000, more than the president earned back in 1950.

The federal government began giving support to Canadian universities for the first time during the fifties, and the rising cost of universities (many of them newly founded), along with the even larger cost of expanding school systems, made education much the largest item in provincial budgets. By 1960 the universities were the very centre of an opulent urban society whose attitudes were being studied and programmed by social scientists and computers, and whose way of life was being altered beyond recognition by automation and electronics and a new industrial alchemy which seemed capable of turning any substance into anything else.

II

The raw statistics of that new society's growth in Canada are formidable. The gross national product doubled between 1950 and 1960 from eighteen to thirty-six billion dollars, and appeared certain to double again well before the 1960s were over. The difference is all the more impressive when one remembers that 1950 was regarded as a year of unparalleled prosperity, while Canadians were glad to see the last of 1960, the worst year of unemployment since the days of the great depression. The value of manufactures produced nearly doubled during the decade, and the value of services rose two and a half times over.

Among the primary industries, Canada maintained her position as producer of half of the world's newsprint, which was still her largest export, and by 1960 she was producing a billion and a half dollars' worth of pulp-and-paper products annually. The most important growing edge of the economy, however, was unquestionably in mining and oil. With the opening of new fields in Alberta, crude-petroleum production increased five times in volume during the decade. So did iron-ore production thanks to the development of vast deposits in Labrador and northern Quebec, with the remarkable result that Canada moved from the position of being a net importer in 1950 to that of one of the world's great iron exporters in 1960. Planning for Canada's first atomic-power station began in 1955, and a year later Canada had become a leading uranium producer, though in the total picture this development was perhaps relatively less important than the continued growth of such giant operations as those of the Aluminum Company of Canada and the International Nickel Company.

The sixty billion dollars' worth of new housing and other buildings constructed during the decade was more than double the total value of buildings put up during the quarter-century before 1950 and probably greater than the value of all the buildings put up since Confederation. The demand for building materials, as well as for such consumer goods as new kitchens and cars and television sets, led to vast new investment in the Canadian steel industry. Far from cutting back capacity and production, as it had been forced to do in the twenty years that followed the First World War, the steel industry achieved an amazing fivefold increase in the same period after the Second World War.

The one great exception to the unprecedented growth during the 1950s was in agriculture, which could still at the beginning of the decade be described as Canada's most important industry. The dollar value of agricultural production remained the same in 1960 as it had been in 1950 – 1.7 billion – and the number of Canadians employed on the farm actually declined. An increasing number of people during the decade were, relatively speaking, reduced to rural poverty, and there were Canadians outside the cities, many of them Indians, who survived on the edge of bare subsistence. Their problems were left to a later period to identify and solve. The fifties ended forever in Canada the predominance of the small mixed farm and the hired man who lived in, the plough horse, and the hand-stooked wheat in the fields, which were a familiar sight during the Second World War. Even so, the aggregate of farm production increased during the fifties. The bumper wheat crops of the earlier part of the decade ran over four times larger than those of the first great western wheat boom before the First War. Agriculture, like other industries, moved rapidly along the path of mechanization

and automation. It was the great demand for farm implements, in fact, that provided one of the initial sparks of the
post-war boom.

Such prosperity was not expected. The Great Depression
of the thirties had never really ended but had rather been
absorbed into the war effort. Few Canadians could escape the
nagging fear that in peace-time it would inevitably return.
There were many reasons why it did not. Keynesian fiscal and
monetary policies, ignored or disdained during the early
thirties, were now understood and accepted, however difficult
they might be to put into effective practice. Such new sources
of consumer purchasing-power as the old-age pension and
the baby bonus were now available. The Central Mortgage
and Housing Corporation made it possible for thousands of
Canadians to become home owners for the first time. Consumer demand was sustained throughout the decade by a
dramatic rise in the birth rate, which by 1955 was up to 27
per thousand, one of the highest rates in the world; and
nearly a million and a half immigrants arrived in Canada
during the 1950s. There was a better distribution of wealth:
wages in manufacturing, for example, rose by about 75 per
cent during the decade. Because the Second World War had
been financed by taxation and people's war savings and
because inflation had been kept rigidly in check by price
control, there was far less dislocation in the post-war period
than there had been after the First War. In spite of the great
pressure caused by the rapid expansion of the fifties, the
consumer price index was only 28 per cent higher in 1960
than it had been in 1949.

In spite of all this, there were times during the decade
when it seemed that the prophets of doom might be right
after all. The two brief recessions of 1948-9 and 1953-4 were
each followed by periods of rapid expansion, but the economy
experienced three sharper and longer setbacks between 1957
and early 1961. The growth of real per-capita income slowed
down to less than two per cent. The numbers of unemployed
during 1960 approached the level of 1939. The daily average
number of shares traded on the Toronto Stock Exchange in

1960 was down to two million, compared to six million in the boom year of 1956. The flow of immigrants slackened off, but not the exodus of emigrants to the United States. By 1960 the total population of this second-largest country in the world was still only eighteen millions.

The improvised and unplanned character of much of the expansion that took place between 1949 and 1957, besides the very speed of it all, goes far towards explaining the period of painful readjustment that followed. Canadian investors tended to concentrate on the two extremes of investment in blue-chip stocks and bonds on the one hand, and gambling on volatile penny mining stocks on the other. Partly because of an unsuitable tax structure, they paid all too little attention to the intelligent use of risk capital in investment opportunities between the two extremes. So, too, many Canadian manufacturers and labour leaders moved easily from a depression psychology to its opposite. Some assumed that almost anything they could make could be sold no matter what its price. They were encouraged further in this by shortages caused by the Korean war. By 1957 such easy proliferation of high-cost operation and inefficiency met its nemesis. European and Japanese industries were now fully recovered after the dislocation and destruction of the Second World War. They had the extra advantage, in competing with Canadians, of the high value of the Canadian dollar, now riding about 5 per cent above the American. This was all the more serious because the greatest Canadian expansion of the early fifties had taken place in the primary and export industries, which were the most vulnerable to change in the economic climate. However, once some of the inefficiencies had been shaken out of the economy by 1961, once demand had caught up with the vast investment in industrial capacity made during the middle fifties, and above all once the American economy recovered from its own less serious recession, Canadian economic growth resumed. From the perspective of 1966, looking back over what was already the longest single period of sustained and balanced growth in the whole of Canadian history, the economic troubles of the later fifties can be seen as those of readjustment rather than depression.

More than ever before, however, Canada's economic destiny since 1950 has become tied to that of the United States. In the decade before the Second World War, Britain had been Canada's best customer, but by 1956 the United States bought more than three times the amount of goods purchased by Britain in Canada and accounted for 60 per cent of all Canadian exports. From the United States came some 70 per cent of Canada's imports, reaching a high point of 4.1 billion dollars in 1956, which made Canada a better customer of the United States than the whole of Europe or Latin America. While there was a rise in the percentage of Canadian trade with Britain during the later part of the decade, the economic ties with Britain were by 1960 far more tenuous than they had been a decade before. The percentage of direct British investment in Canadian branch plants and subsidiaries declined from 20 per cent to 15 per cent of the total of all external direct investment. The five-per-cent difference was accounted for almost entirely by new European investors. The American percentage of direct investment remained steady at about 75 per cent throughout the decade, but its absolute increase in crucial areas was striking. Direct American investment in Canadian manufacturing plants, for example, went up from less than two to more than four and a half billion dollars, and half of Canada's manufacturing industry was American-controlled by 1960. In fact the sheer number of American subsidiary firms had reached such a point by 1965 that the giant privately owned Canadian company, Eaton's of Canada, was advised to drop the last part of its name, because the words 'of Canada' had now become interchangeable in the public mind with 'American branch plant'.

Many people regarded the growing integration of the Canadian and American economies in the post-war period as a big step towards the inevitable disappearance of Canadian independence. After all, it had been the east-west pattern of communication and transport which, ever since the fur trade shaped the political boundaries of the country, had fostered and maintained a separate national identity. The two most dramatic changes in transportation were the building of the St. Lawrence Seaway and the Trans-Canada gas and oil pipelines. The Seaway helped fulfil that age-old dream at the heart of Canadian history, the Empire of the St. Lawrence, by bringing major ocean shipping two thousand miles into the interior of the continent. The pipelines were heralded as a new version of the Canadian Pacific Railway, bridging the difficult passage between east and west across northern Ontario with government help, and so tying western resources to the markets of central Canada. Certainly the flow of oil and gas across the country pointed ahead to a day when pipelines would become perhaps the most important of all bulk carriers, moving not only gas and liquids but solids as well across the country. But both developments also linked Canada more closely than ever to the United States. The Seaway's most important single new cargo was Canadian iron ore brought from Labrador and northern Quebec to the heartland of the American steel industry south of Lakes Erie and Michigan. The Trans-Canada pipelines also opened up the possibility of the export of oil and natural gas to the United States and pointed ahead to another energy export, hydroelectric power, from two of the largest sources in the world, Labrador's Churchill Falls and the giant Columbia River.

Nevertheless the fifties did see certain developments which unequivocally strengthened Canada's traditional east-west pattern. The most important of these was the construction of a 4,000-mile microwave network by the Canadian Broadcasting Corporation, the longest in the world, and the establishment of national television service from coast to coast. The fifties saw a revolution in the technology of passenger travel. By 1960 the airlines were carrying five and a half million passengers annually, a number equal to almost a third of the country's population. And on April 1 of that year, the first jet aircraft went into service on the Toronto-Vancouver run, cutting to five hours what was still a three days' journey by train, and preparing the way for still larger volumes of passenger air travel during the sixties. If a community is made more viable by the face-to-face meeting of its leaders from hundreds of different scattered political, commercial, professional, and religious groups, then this giant, sprawling, divided nation received at last, in the second half of the twentieth century, the form of passenger travel suited to its size and nature.

Since airplanes cannot tow steel beams, however, and since giant trucks are inefficient long-distance carriers, the railway age, which had given birth to Canadian confederation, was far from over as the nation's second century began. Before the end of the decade the railways showed the first signs of emerging from the ailing and archaic condition in which they had languished for nearly two generations. They moved into a successful battle against an aging union's blind protest against automation – the firemen's strike of 1958. They purchased Canada's first industrial computer and put plans on the drawing-board for automatic freight yards to sort trains by electronic control panels. And they bought up transport companies in order to integrate trucks and piggyback into a unified system of transportation. By the end of the decade, the age of the steam locomotive was over and the last of the great 6000-class engines had gone to the scrap-yard or the museum. The Canadian National had redesigned its public image and was painting its new symbol on everything from box cars to dinnerware. There were even signs that it might soon begin to lure back passengers that had been lost to the automobile.

The automobile, of course, was one of the prime symbols and facts in the vast economic and social change of the mid century. It stood for the aspiration of everyone to a life of affluence and leisure, for private rights over public, for the dissolution of old communities and traditional values. It had also killed more Canadians by 1960 than had the Second World War, and its demand for space and pavement was a voracious consumer of provincial budgets and urban land.

Of all the decade's social change, however, the urban revolution and the new values and styles that came with it

was probably the most significant. Canadians had slowly
been turning into an urban people ever since 1867. But
even as late as 1939 one Canadian worker in three was employed in agriculture, and the figure was still as high as one
in four at the end of the Second World War. By 1960 it had
dropped to one in eight. Over half the labour force was
employed in the urban-oriented service industries, and the
chief place of work for those who lived in the countryside
was in the towns and cities. According to the 1961 census,
two out of every three Canadians lived in urban areas. Most
of the decade's new immigrants went not to the farms but to
the cities. Canada's dozen largest metropolitan areas grew
by half their former size in the short space of ten years. As
dormitory suburbs grew round old cities many times larger
than the original core, the down-town areas suffered from
abuse and neglect, and local governments designed for a
horse-and-buggy age were totally inadequate to the needs of
the vast new conurbations. Canadians were made aware for
the first time that their precious resources of land and air
and water did not exist in unlimited abundance, that they
were using their skies as vast garbage dumps, drinking steri-
lized sewage from their streams, and facing the day when
their peach orchards and vineyards would go the way of the
passenger pigeon to extinction. By the decade's end, thanks
to the very gravity of the problems, a few promising signs
of solution had already appeared: conservation authorities
and the first forms of regional planning, down-town redevelopment, and better public transit, some of it underground, and the separation of pedestrian and cars. Some
solutions, of course, such as the tearing down of old houses
in favour of prisonlike new apartment blocks, were worse
than the disease. Not only did much new building cost far
more than rehabilitation of the old, but its bleak sameness
produced a kind of soul-destroying mass accidie. Other
solutions such as metropolitan government and large-scale
amalgamation came just in time to prevent the total breakdown of municipal services.

Nowhere did the decade effect greater changes than in the

character of metropolitan Toronto. For the first time it
became a cosmopolitan centre for the whole of English-
speaking Canada. Toronto acquired the somewhat dubious
distinction of being the fastest-growing big city in North
America, in population, tax assessment, construction, and
retail trade – almost anything you could name. Plans were
laid for the construction of the world's widest multi-lane
expressway, through what was recently the farming country
of North York and what would be by the end of the sixties
the geographical centre line of the metropolitan area. Specialists in business and professions that had scarcely existed
before in Canada set up offices in Toronto. The city became
one of the world's largest centres of television and radio
production. Canadian trade publishing became a big business for the first time as publishers added dozens of new
Canadian titles, including paperbacks, to their lists, where
previously they had survived almost entirely on a diet of
school texts and books imported from abroad. Canadian
advertising agencies increased the dollar volume of their
business three times over during the decade, and the quality
and quantity of their design staffs many times more than that.

Toronto had once been a stronghold of the religion of
Empire and the Orange Lodge and the W.C.T.U., but by
1961 less than half of the people of the central city were
British in racial origin, and Roman Catholics outnumbered
Protestants. Toronto became one of the world's large Italian
communities. The post-war immigrants played an important
part in transforming the parks and shops and supermarkets,
the restaurants and coffee houses, and the downtown bohemian villages. One successful place displayed a sign that
read, 'If you like home cooking, stay home.' Toronto became
known as one of the best places on the continent for jazz
groups and folk singers to make a living. That time in the
1940s when Torontonians who wanted a weekend of excitement and night life took off for Buffalo was a distant memory.
'Returning to Toronto', wrote a British visitor in 1959, 'was
like finding a Jaguar parked in front of the Vicarage and the
padre inside with a pitcher of vodka martinis reading *Lolita*.'

III

Canada experienced a revolution in the arts during the 1950s. The old indifference and neglect of the depression and the war years gave way to an atmosphere of excitement amid the wealth and leisure of the new decade. Metropolitan newspapers from coast to coast for the first time devoted extensive news coverage to the arts, and a few of them even began to employ a roster of serious critics. Richer patrons and more powerful pressure groups appeared to promote the cause of the arts and the condition of artists.

Perhaps the most important new generator of interest and creative friction was CBC television, which began in 1952. Not only the newest of the lively arts itself, and to some degree a creator of artistic sophistication in the mind of a large public, it provided employment for a great variety of people whose chief vocation still lay in one of the traditional arts. The apotheosis of cultural promotion came in the 1961 rally of the Canadian Conference of the Arts at which large numbers of artists, critics, patrons, academics, officials, and arts councillors, representing every type of art, craft, and locality in Canada, were stirred up together for three days at the O'Keefe Centre in Toronto.

Taking up a recommendation of the Massey Report of 1951, the Canada Council was created in 1957, and many municipal and provincial governments have followed this federal move with new and increased support for the arts. Although the Department of Transport's enlightened policy in the design and furnishing of its new airports was the exception rather than the rule, it did point ahead to various forms of discriminating governmental and business patronage during the 1960s. Even the universities began to take the role of patron more seriously during the fifties, as the separation between the academic world and creative artists began to disappear.

The new awareness of a crisis in North American education was graphically demonstrated when Sputnik and the Edsel, the rival symbols of East and West, were launched in the same month of 1957. But the need to train the senses and the imagination as well as the mind was one to which most educators were still blind. Even the Canada Council's funds were directed primarily to universities and scholars rather than to artists. Although it spent its budget of one million dollars a year for the arts with superb discrimination and noticeable effect, this amount was only a third of what one single European company, the Vienna State Opera, was receiving annually from its government, and one-fifth the amount that Canada's Department of National Defence was spending annually on military bands. (The latter, curiously enough, did help to subsidize art in a roundabout Canadian way, by supplying several local orchestras with good brass players they could not otherwise have afforded.) Few serious Canadian performers acquired an income-tax problem during the 1950s. No good creative writer made even a bare living out of his writing alone, and the best composers were lucky if royalties paid for the paper they used for their scores.

In 1950, Samuel Marchbanks (alias Robertson Davies) pointed up the plight of the Canadian theatre in a letter to an aspiring playwright, Apollo Fishhorn, Esq.,

> What is the Canadian playhouse? Nine times out of ten, Fishhorn, it is a school hall, smelling of chalk and kids, and decorated in the Early Concrete style. The stage is a small raised room at one end. And I mean room. If you step into the wings suddenly you will fracture your nose against the wall. . . . The lighting is designed to warm the stage but not to illuminate it. . . . Write your plays for such stages. Do not demand any procession of elephants, or dances by the maidens of the Caliph's harem. Keep away from sunsets and storms at sea. Place as many scenes as you can in cellars and kindred spots. And don't have more than three characters on the stage at one time, or the weakest of them is sure to be nudged into the audience.

Yet in 1960, just ten years later, one critic could complain that halls of exaggerated vastness were being built, while intimate productions – reviews, readings, repertory theatre, and chamber music – were what directors wanted to put on

The new friends of the arts were accused of having an edifice complex, and certainly many enterprises seemed to benefit civic pride and the construction industry more than the artists themselves. Nevertheless, artists did reach new audiences during the fifties, in new theatres like those in Vancouver, Edmonton, Calgary, and Stratford, and some of the more complex art centres of the sixties such as those in Montreal and Charlottetown were already in the early planning stage. The climate for the performing arts had changed drastically during the decade, as had the quality of what was being produced.

Native professional theatre appeared in strength for the first time, replacing the American road companies and the amateurs who competed in the Dominion Drama Festival, which was no longer now the most significant training-ground for actors and audiences. The companies of Stratford, the Théâtre du Nouveau Monde, and the Manitoba Theatre Centre, to be followed later by repertory companies in Halifax and Vancouver, along with the tours of the Canadian Players and the National and Royal Winnipeg Ballets, and the various summer festivals, all generated new interest and high standards.

The opera school of the Royal Conservatory was training literally dozens of fine singers who were to find employment later in the opera houses of Europe, or in the short but excellent seasons put on by the Canadian Opera Company, although the appearance during the fifties of such superb musicians as Glenn Gould, Maureen Forrester, Lois Marshall, and Jon Vickers did underline the fact that Canadians were as yet better as interpreters than as creators of great work in the performing arts. In some fields, particularly film and television drama, Canadians usually had to go to London and New York if they were to reach the top of their profession. In film production, apart from the stimulus of television, there were no major new departures such as the forties saw in the flowering of the National Film Board and the genius of Norman McLaren, and the sixties in the long-overdue beginning of feature-film production in Canada.

The late 1940s may have marked an all-time low for the visual arts in Canada, particularly in design, from typography right through to the architecture of whole new environments. Painting, with the exception of the work of a few isolated veterans and newcomers, was in the doldrums. Canadians were still largely living off the spiritual capital of the Group of Seven, whose best work had been done by 1920. There was little encouragement for new directions from either private or public patrons. As the Massey Report pointed out, there was a staff of exactly four full-time professionals at the National Gallery, while by contrast the art museums of Toledo, Ohio, had twenty-six, and Worcester, Massachusetts, forty-three. Yet before the fifties were over, several dozen good new painters had appeared and were selling their work at new commercial galleries like the Isaacs in Toronto; the best of them were being exhibited at the world's major exhibitions and had indeed twice won the national group award at the Guggenheim International. The National Gallery had experienced a transformation at the hands of Alan Jarvis.

By the end of the fifties the design profession too had achieved new standards of excellence. The worst of the postwar insurance companies and housing subdivisions had been built, and the impact of a number of new architects of the calibre of Arthur Erickson, Robert Fairfield, and John C. Parkin was being felt upon the environment.

IV

Though she still lacked certain attributes of sovereign nationhood, both legally and psychologically, and though she possessed less than half of one per cent of the world's population, Canada nevertheless emerged from the war years and their immediate aftermath as the fourth most powerful nation on the earth. The nations of continental Europe, which had now suffered defeat and enemy occupation on both sides, still lay ravaged and exhausted from their ordeal. Japan and China had been fighting for a decade, and the long Chinese civil war only reached its real conclusion in the first week of 1950. Indonesia had just emerged from its war of independence against the Dutch, and India and Pakistan from the terrible blood-letting of their partition. The independence of the new nations of Africa lay in the future.

Beside the might of the two superpowers, the U.S. and the U.S.S.R., and that of Britain, whose war-time courage and sacrifice had given her status for the time being nearly equal to theirs, Canada's power seemed almost insignificant. But because she was not one of the great powers, and because she possessed the unique if unearned advantage of being a wealthy western nation without an imperial past, Canada had an important role to play as a presence in international disputes.

By 1950 Canada was in spirit, word, and deed thoroughly committed for the first time to an internationalist position in peace-time and to new and unfamiliar responsibilities in the world community. Mackenzie King himself had never quite been able to grow out of that slightly smug, slightly fearful attitude of North American isolationism with which he so well mirrored Canadian opinion for two decades between the great wars. King had delivered the *coup de grâce* both to the older, imperial form of Canadian internationalism, and to effective action by the potential new form, the League of Nations. But in the post-war era, King's French-Canadian external affairs minister and successor, Louis St. Laurent, allayed his fears, and spoke for a new Canada. Perhaps his first and most important act as Prime Minister was to answer the threat of the Cold War by committing Canada to the NATO alliance and to a new role in a strong Atlantic community. St. Laurent, in turn, gave complete support and great scope to his foreign minister, L. B. Pearson, who personally represented the new spirit of Canada's small but highly respected diplomatic corps. Pearson during the 1950s became the first Canadian politician well known abroad and the first to play a major role in world affairs. As the decade opened, Canada had just finished her first term on the United

Nations Security Council, to which she would be re-elected
again in 1958, and in 1953 Pearson was elected president of
the General Assembly.

It is fair to say that at the end of the forties the climate of
Canadian opinion in respect to the great questions of war
and peace was one of anxiety in a world of immobile positions and rigid attitudes. The Cold War had come early to
Canada when Igor Gouzenko walked out of the Russian
Embassy in Ottawa with enough documents to prove the
existence of an elaborate Soviet spy ring against her allies.

The Stalinist *coup d'état* in Czechoslovakia in 1948 finally
hardened North American opinion in the belief that a new
military alliance with Europe was needed. In that year, 51
per cent of all Canadians, according to a Gallup Poll, believed
that a third world war was coming and that it was coming
soon. Mackenzie King in his last year in office acted as if he
were one of them. Specifically, he was afraid that it was coming in Korea (a thing that seemed at that time most unlikely),
and he threatened to resign if Canada's involvement in the
U.N. commission on Korean elections was not withdrawn.
It took a counter-threat of resignation by St. Laurent himself and a highly unorthodox appeal by Pearson through the
Canadian ambassador in Washington to President Truman
to persuade King to allow Canada to fulfil this U.N. responsibility.

King's fearful prophecy – the result, it turned out, of a
conversation he had had with his late friend Franklin Roosevelt through a spiritualist medium in London – was not
entirely wide of the mark. The Korean war broke out on
June 25, 1950. Of the sixteen United Nations members
whose forces went to South Korea to resist aggression, Canada's contribution was exceeded only by those of Britain and
the United States. Canadian soldiers were not finally withdrawn from Korea until 1955. Canadian diplomats in
Geneva and New Delhi contributed to the negotiations that
led to Communist China's release of U.N. war prisoners.
The outbreak of the Korean war in 1950 thus marks the
beginning of a fundamental shift of interest and focus in

Canadian extra-continental foreign policy from an almost exclusive concern with Europe to one that included other parts of the world, particularly Asia. Canada's membership, with Poland and India, in the Indo-China Control Commission which emerged from the Geneva conference of 1954 was indicative of this new role in Asia. In spite of her refusal to recognize the new Peking regime because of the feelings of her principal ally, Canada maintained tenuous but significant contact with China. A Canadian cabinet minister, James Sinclair, had meetings in 1955 with Chinese leaders in Peking, and Canadian business and university leaders have been there regularly since. The *Globe and Mail* correspondent in the Chinese capital was the only North American newspaperman in Peking during the whole decade; he was followed by CBC reporters and film-makers in the sixties. The most important single Western hero and saint of the Chinese revolution, other than Karl Marx himself, was the Canadian doctor Norman Bethune. Trade negotiations led to the huge wheat contracts of the 1960s. It was clear enough that Canadian relations with China were one area of sharp if subdued difference between Ottawa and Washington, particularly from the time of Canada's plea for restraint during the dangerous confrontation between the two great powers over the offshore islands of Quemoy and Matsu in 1955.

Canada's new role in world affairs is particularly illustrated by her function in what was increasingly 'an Afro-Asian commonwealth of nations'. Canada went far towards making such a Commonwealth possible when at the end of the forties she persuaded Britain and Australia to accept the idea of a new kind of association that could include republics that owed no allegiance to the Queen, and this of course was to be the pattern for new members in the future. In 1950 Commonwealth members met at Colombo and a new foreign-aid scheme was born, by which Canada was to provide India with an atomic reactor among other things, Pakistan with the Warsak dam, and other Asian members with supplies and technical personnel. Although the per-capita Canadian contribution to all foreign aid lagged disturbingly behind that of Britain and the U.S., it did gradually increase during the fifties and sixties to one half of one per cent of the gross national product.

Canadian participation in Afro-Asian affairs was more that of a disinterested observer than it was in Europe. She did not, for example join the South-East Asia Treaty Organization, preferring to maintain a position like that of Nehru's India. This position proved to be valuable during the Suez crisis of 1956. It enabled Canada to initiate and mount support for the idea of a United Nations Emergency Force, and to supply both the commander and the largest military contribution once the force was formed.

Although Pearson was denounced by some Conservative anglophiles at home for siding with Nehru's India rather than with Britain in her hour of need, it was obvious that Canada emerged from the crisis, as did the United Nations, with the grudging or approving acceptance of all parties concerned.

Five years later when another crisis in Commonwealth relations arose, the Conservative Prime Minister was to go further than the Liberals earlier thought feasible or proper. John Diefenbaker sided with Indian and Afro-Asian members against Britain and Australia, and so determined South Africa's departure from the Commonwealth, and the potential rebirth of the Commonwealth as a true multiracial partnership. Even the declared intention of the new Conservative government to achieve closer relations with Britain by means of a shift of Canada's foreign trade away from the United States and back towards Britain failed to materialize during the later part of the decade. The Conservative foreign minister, Howard Green, however, did his best to pursue an increasingly independent foreign policy for Canada, and one that was more disliked in Washington than anything the Liberals had done. Although his and Canada's efforts may not have contributed directly to the atomic-test-ban treaty that was finally achieved in 1963, they did represent, in concert with the policies of many other nations, the real if intangible pressure of world opinion encouraging the two great powers to arrive at their agreement.

The years of Conservative power after 1957 saw a certain decline in Canada's relative influence in world affairs, for which the Conservative government cannot be held responsible. The change in her world position was, in fact, inevitable once the recovery of Europe was accomplished and the rise of the Asian nations had begun. Even Canada's ranking in 1962 (estimated by R. A. Sutherland of the Defence Research Board) as eighth or ninth among the world's military powers could lead Canadians to an exaggerated sense of their own importance. Canada's position as a middle power, however, pursuing an independent foreign policy within the limits of the Western alliance, remained significant and valuable. Without it her role in the Congo and Cyprus and her military and educational contribution in East Africa, particularly Tanzania, would have been impossible. It was not so much a matter of her physical strength *vis-à-vis* the great powers – a relatively small quantity can hardly be compared to something like the absolute – but rather a matter of function. There was a series of jobs to be done that no great power, especially one with an imperial past or present, could possibly perform.

The central problem and concern of Canada's foreign policy during the 1950s, however, remained that of her relationship with the United States. More than ever before Canada seemed in danger of losing her identity in the American cultural sphere of influence and becoming completely dependent on the United States for her economic well-being and military defence. Ever since the Japanese attack on Pearl Harbor in 1941 brought the United States into the war against the Axis powers, the defence of North America, from the Alaska Highway to the American base in Newfoundland, had been treated as a single problem. After the war, Canada became the chief frontier and buffer state, another potential Belgium, on the bomber and missile path between the United States and the Soviet Union. Early co-operation in schemes of northern air defence culminated in the signing

of the agreement to build a series of radar stations across the
Canadian Arctic, the Distant Early Warning Line, which
was to be entirely paid for by the United States. With the
DEW Line's completion in 1959, there were more American
military personnel in the Canadian north than there were
Canadian. The NORAD agreement for North American air
defence was signed in 1958, after a joint command with an
American in charge and a Canadian deputy had been set up
in Colorado Springs the year before. The magnificent Avro
Arrow, whose production was cancelled in 1958 before it
could cost the nation half a billion dollars it could not afford,
was the last Canadian attempt to develop a major weapon
for the western alliance. After that the Canadian armed
forces were almost completely dependent for the development of complex new weapons systems upon American industry and upon military research done by such bodies as
the RAND Corporation. In return, Canadian factories were
given a share as sub-contractors in joint Canadian-American
defence production projects and, in effect, became an integral part of the American military establishment. None of
this precluded an independent Canadian initiative at the
United Nations or in any other situation of crucial concern
to Canada, but did require the exercise of a mature blend
of forbearance and firmness in relations with the United
States of a kind rarely demanded or forthcoming from the
Canadian public in the past.

There were, moreover, a number of areas in which the
direct conflict of economic interest was inevitable. Canada
was replaced as the world's leading wheat exporter by the
United States, thanks to the American department of agriculture's support prices, while Canadian farmers saw their
unsold surpluses growing larger and larger. American lobbies
saw to it that imports of Canadian oil or any other commodity that seriously threatened American producers were
severely restricted by means of tariffs and quotas. The problem of flood control on the Columbia River and the use of
its vast hydro-electric potential was also an occasional source
of friction, until some questionable Canadian compromises

began to move negotiations towards final settlement in the treaty of 1964.

Potentially, American ownership of Canadian branch plants could lead to their use as an instrument of American foreign policy, although such actual cases as that in which the Ford Motor Company of Canada was prevented from participating in Canadian-Chinese trade may have been the exception rather than the rule. Growing Canadian trade with China and Cuba, at a time when American trade embargoes existed and American diplomatic recognition was withheld, were inevitably causes of friction. They were undertaken for the economic advantage of Canada and of two powers unfriendly to the United States, and they were the reflection of a pragmatic Canadian approach to politics and world affairs that differed sharply from that of the United States.

American attitudes and policies towards communism during the decade contributed further to difficulties already inherent in the situation. Canada's foreign minister (in company of course with several American leaders) was consistently described by the Chicago *Tribune* as a pinko and by North America's largest newspaper, the New York *Daily News*, as being soft on communism. At the height of Joseph McCarthy's reign of terror, in January 1954, two of his colleagues, Senators Jenner and McCarran, arrived in Canada for the purpose of questioning the former Russian Embassy clerk, Igor Gouzenko. Although the incident resulted from Gouzenko's own initiative, and the senators were required to operate not in their usual free-wheeling public manner but in closed session under Canadian rules, there was criticism in Canada that they should have been admitted at all. McCarthy soon passed from the scene, but American attitudes and practices which had made him possible did not. The staff of the Senate's permanent subcommittee on investigations indulged in repeated acts of public vilification which led in 1957 to the suicide of one of Canada's most respected public servants, Herbert Norman.

The appearance of the radical right in all its virulence

served to underline the fact that Canada, in spite of being
a thoroughly North American society, was also a society
with qualities quite different from that of the United States.
These qualities, produced by a fundamentally different
history, were rightly cherished by Canadians. But in addition to feeling a justifiable pride, Canadians also covered
their own envy and sense of inadequacy, in the face of the
real achievements of American democracy and economic
progress and culture, by identifying things American with
the worst of American television, with the infiltration of
Mafia mobsters into Canada, and with the tactics of Teamster
Union officials.

Towards the end of the decade and on into the sixties
there was a growing public debate in Canada about ways
and means of preventing Canada from being totally absorbed
into the American sphere of influence. Pressure groups
mounted campaigns to prevent Canada from acquiring
nuclear arms, particularly the American Bomarc missile with
nuclear warheads, or to have her opt out of the Western
alliance in favour of a neutralist position. One influential
journalist, Charles Lynch, proposed the donation of the
Canadian armed forces to the United Nations. Another,
James Minifie, wrote a best-seller which invited Canada to
decide whether she wanted to be 'Peacemaker or Powder-
monkey'. The Conservative government expressed an intention to reduce Canadian dependence on American imports,
and the Liberals on their return to power in 1963 managed
to outreach the Conservatives in experimenting to reduce
American economic influence in Canada. Ways of taxing
Canadian editions of American magazines were tried, withdrawn, explored by royal commission, and tried again. The
overlords of Canadian radio and television, the Board of
Broadcast Governors, required television stations to put on
a schedule that was at least fifty-five per cent Canadian in
content.

V

Canadian–American relations were inextricably bound up, as they so often had been in the past, with the central political issues of the 1950s and after. The period's greatest turnover in political power, the Diefenbaker victory of 1957, could hardly have taken place without strong feeling among some sections of the public that the Liberal government had been too willing to let American business shape the Canadian economy, to tolerate the excesses of McCarthyism where they affected Canada, to accept the foreign policy of John Foster Dulles, and to join the United States against Britain during the Suez crisis.

Except for a few months following the Diefenbaker victory of 1957, Parliament in the 1950s was dominated by a powerful government with a huge majority at its back. The landslide victories of the Liberals in 1949 and 1953, after which they outnumbered the official Opposition by 190 to 41 and 170 to 51 seats respectively, and the even more astonishing Conservative triumph of 1958 in which the tables were turned on the Liberals, by 208 seats to 49, led to further erosion of a parliamentary system that was already ill suited both to the structure of Canadian federalism and to the needs of the Canadian situation in the middle of the twentieth century. The role of the back-bench M.P. receded in importance, and there was little compensating committee work for him to do of the sort that helped the American congressman play such a powerful and effective part in the process of government.

The official Opposition, not only because of its numbers but because of the experience and calibre of its members, was hard put to look like an alternate government. The Opposition was further handicapped by the fact that it rarely represented more than one major section of the nation. In the Parliaments elected in 1949 and 1953, the Conservatives were largely an Ontario party, led by the old-fashioned Tory, George Drew of Toronto. In turn the Liberals in 1958 suffered the staggering loss of all their members from the four

western provinces, and the majority of their former cabinet
ministers and parliamentary assistants. They were in numbers predominantly a French-Canadian party, with no
members from English-speaking constituencies outside Ontario and Newfoundland.

Elections had turned into something very close to plebiscites on the performance of the Cabinet and on the personality of the party leader. Canada, it seemed, only wanted
one national party at a time, expressed in a powerful cabinet
that represented a consensus of the different parts of the
country. For purposes of government the Cabinet seemed
more like the extension and superstructure of the federal
civil service than of its party in Parliament. In fact, Mackenzie King and the Liberals had established a tradition
whereby the public service was one of the main routes to
position in the Cabinet. Another route was a distinguished
career outside politics entirely, which was the way taken by
the two dominant figures in the Liberal Cabinet of the
fifties, Louis St. Laurent and C. D. Howe.

Louis St. Laurent seemed by 1957 almost more of a national
president or reigning monarch than the head of a political
party. His courtly presence and firm but subtle grip on
power lent the office of prime minister a dignity and respect
and nationwide acceptance of a sort it had never had before.
His corporation lawyer's penetrating mind and pragmatic
approach to the problems of government enabled English
Canadians, particularly businessmen, to regard him as their
country's leader and as one of themselves. For his own people
his presence in office helped him heal wounds as old as the
hanging of Louis Riel and the English rejection of Laurier
in 1917, and to move French Canada out of its spiritual
isolation. Though he was never a French-Canadian political
leader, let alone a *chef*, in the manner of either Lapointe or
Duplessis, his prime-ministership formed a useful period of
transition between the old servility of the past and the
mature, proud, but self-preoccupied nationalism of the
future. St. Laurent helped English Canada too to grow out

of the attitude of colonial dependence in which it had prolonged its adolescence. The decision to appoint the first
Canadian Governor General was St. Laurent's, and it was fitting that the first amendment to the British North America
Act made without reference to Westminster should have
been introduced in Parliament by his government.

As the Liberal regime entered its third decade of continuous power in 1956, its failure to read the mood and
temper of the times, its poverty in new ideas and men, and
its assumption of a kind of administrative divine right grew
too great even for a prosperous and complacent Canadian
public. Ironically, the downfall of the St. Laurent government was prepared by the most powerful and effective minister who has ever served in a Canadian cabinet. After a successful career as university professor, engineer, and head of
his own construction business, C. D. Howe had played the
central role in managing Canada's economy during war-
time and the difficult period of readjustment that followed.
In the fifties he was general manager of the post-war boom.
He still held some of the war-time powers he had been
granted under the Defence Production Act, though their
extension was limited as a result of Opposition protest in
1955. In 1956 he had set his heart on the construction of the
world's longest natural-gas pipeline – his version of the
C.P.R. – to unite the industry of the east with this vital new
source of energy in Alberta. In order to build it to a tight
schedule, he persuaded the Liberal Cabinet to put the necessary legislation through Parliament by means of a misuse of
the rule of closure. The wild and bitter debate that followed
brought Parliament to life again and firmly registered an
impression of Liberal arrogance in the public mind that was
to last for many years to come. (It was also, less happily, the
precursor of obstructive abuse of their privileges by some
members of the parliamentary opposition in the following
decade.) The overthrow of such a competent and experienced government during boom times, however, seemed so
little likely that Canada's national magazine could put its

post-election issue to bed over a week before the election with
a lead editorial on the tasks facing the new Liberal administration. Yet on June 10, 1957, the Conservative party gained
a narrow plurality at the polls over the Liberals and in 1958
went on to the greatest triumph in Canadian parliamentary
history. More than anything else this astonishing turn of
events was due to the impact of one man whose style and
temperament were suited to the occasion, and who knew how
to make the most of them.

In replacing George Drew, who was forced to retire because of ill health in 1956 after years of devoted service in
the wilderness, John Diefenbaker remade the Conservative
party in his own image. It became a party of protest—against
big business, big government, the intellectual establishment,
and the status quo. Of neither British nor French stock, he
was the first unhyphenated Canadian to be prime minister.
He brought into politics the sort of people who had not been
there before—a Chinese M.P., an Indian senator, a Ukrainian minister of labour, and from the biggest group of
second-class citizens, the first woman to hold cabinet rank.
The city of Hamilton was plastered with 'Martini for
Diefenbaker' signs in 1958 for the election of the first Italian
parliamentary secretary in Canadian history. Diefenbaker
was also the first English-speaking leader to whom French
Canada was to give its trust since Macdonald—an astounding
61 per cent of Quebec's vote in the 1958 election.

Diefenbaker was a genuine folk hero, a battler like Harry
Truman, David assaulting Goliath, a vindicator of Parliament and people, the poor newsboy who talked to Sir Wilfrid
Laurier early one morning in 1909 and knew then he would
be prime minister some day. He was for the little man; he
was the outsider, who had to survive nine defeats before he
gained the success he always knew would be his. He failed
to get elected mayor of Prince Albert; he was defeated four
times in federal and provincial elections before he finally
entered the House of Commons in 1940; and he was twice
rejected by his party for the House leadership before they
turned to him in 1956. 'The weird manic grandeur' of his

"Howdy Sheriff"

From *Toronto Daily Star Cartoons*, by Duncan Macpherson.

public manner, larger than life, was balanced by the warmth and humour, by the feeling for local tradition and the fundamental verities, by the earnest intimacy streaked with a talent for mockery, of his private conversation. As he said himself, his greatest sins were those of the heart; they were not cold or mortal ones and most people for a time were as willing for him to indulge them as he was.

The difficulty was that heartfelt feelings if they were to last had to be translated into thought and action. Strong slogans and nostalgia for the simpler days of Canada's rural childhood were no substitute for hard decisions, particularly during the difficulties of recession and unemployment which arrived at the beginning of Diefenbaker's term of office. He kept putting off decisions himself, yet he would not trust his colleagues, especially the stronger ones, to make decisions of their own. He kept testing the winds of public opinion for every breeze blowing in his favour. That egocentricity and mystic relation with the common man that had made him a leader blossomed into a consuming jealousy of rivals. 'Dear John' became 'Ivan the Terrible'. With an overwhelming majority behind him, he still acted as though he were Leader of the Opposition.

Though Diefenbaker ended the decade still in an apparently unbeatable position, his own shortcomings as a prime minister, underlined as they were by Canada's economic troubles, were taking their toll. In 1960, for the first time, public-opinion polls showed the Liberals ahead of the Conservatives in the projected percentage of the popular vote. The new Liberal leader, L. B. Pearson, who had never been completely identified with the old ways of King and Howe, succeeded after a shattering start in rebuilding his party and attracting a wide variety of uncommitted opinion to him. As a means of finding policies, his Kingston Conference in 1960 may possibly have been the idle, ivory-tower occupation for which it was mocked by the *Globe and Mail*. But as a political symbol to attract a variety of thoughtful Canadians and as the unintended instrument for finding workers and candidates for the next two elections, it was an unqualified success. The Nobel-Prize-winning diplomat began to look like the head of an alternative government; and the very thing for which he was most criticized, the failure to act like a professional politician, worked partially in his favour.

Canada's Fabian socialists, the C.C.F. party, had also been shattered by Diefenbaker's victory in 1958. The party lost its western agrarian base, and was reduced to a corporal's guard of members from the heavily unionized sections of British Columbia and Northern Ontario. This suggested the obvious move towards a closer link with the labour movement which was itself entering a new period in its history.

In 1956, following a similar move in the United States, the old conservative Trades and Labour Congress and the industrial-based Canadian Congress of Labour were merged in the Canadian Labour Congress under the presidency of Claude Jodoin. After the C.C.F.'s most effective parliamentarian, Stanley Knowles, was defeated in 1958, he was made C.L.C. vice-president and from this position he played a prominent role in preparing the way for the founding convention of what was to become the New Democratic Party. Although that party was only able to attract between ten and twenty per cent of the popular vote in the early sixties, at least it ensured the survival of the old C.C.F. in a new and more urban form. It also served as a reminder that the 1957-8 Parliament of minorities, which was the exception in the fifties, would prove to be the rule of the following decade, and it provided a new and vital role for what was often the most effective and valuable group of M.P.s in the House.

However, the most important of all secular trends in the political history of the 1950s was the increasing strength of the provinces and their governments, after the war-time and post-war period of centralization and increased federal power. New economic and social conditions required greater government activity in areas that had been defined by the courts and the B.N.A. Act as matters of provincial concern, in everything from education to highways to the social services. By the end of the decade the provincial civil services began to change from small second-rate organizations, often ridden with patronage, to the large and sophisticated operations that were needed. The increased provincial power of the sixties was forecast in Quebec's nationalism under Duplessis, even though it was disguised in an outmoded and semi-Fascist form, and in the new prosperity of Alberta and British Columbia, as they developed their mineral and forest resources.

The provinces also continued to play one of their traditional roles in Canadian history, that of providing an effective political opposition to the federal government. The first sign of revolt against the national Liberal monarchy came

"Dig You Later, Pops"

From *Toronto Daily Star Cartoons*, by Duncan Macpherson.

with the Conservative victory under Hugh John Flemming
in the New Brunswick provincial elections of 1952, and this
was followed by the victory of Robert Stanfield in Nova
Scotia in 1956. The new pattern in British Columbia was
established in 1952. Both the traditional parties there practically disappeared from the scene, and the contest from then
on was between a right-wing, free-enterprise Social Credit
party under Premier W. A. C. Bennett and a socialist party,
the C.C.F., which had come within one seat in 1952 of being
the new government. Again in 1960 it was within striking
distance of victory in the first trial run for the forces that
formed the New Democratic Party in 1961. By 1960 no fewer

than five provincial Liberal governments had been thrown out and the only one left was that of Premier Joseph Smallwood of Newfoundland. In 1960 this same trend began to move against the federal Conservative party, with the Liberal victory of the young Acadian Louis Robichaud in New Brunswick. Thanks in part to the enterprise of the man whom Robichaud eventually had to oppose, K. C. Irving, New Brunswick had already begun to recover from the economic stagnation in which it had lain almost since the time of Confederation. Nova Scotia, too, under Premier Stanfield, developed a policy of attracting new industry. Foreign firms such as Volvo and Canadian companies such as Clairtone moved in to take advantage of planned industrial estates, tax concessions, and relatively low labour costs. In Newfoundland, Premier Smallwood had also used the instrument of the state to undertake various experiments in the development of provincial resources. But outstripping all these in its national significance, both for economic and for political change, came the triumph of the provincial Liberals over the old Duplessis machine in Quebec in 1960. The decade thus ended with the appearance of the most dynamic and revolutionary government ever to take power in Canada, and the beginning of a new chapter in the history of relations between the country's two founding peoples and cultures.

11. The 1960s

LAURIER L. LAPIERRE

Canada – to borrow Arthur Lower's words – is the 'substance of things hoped for'. And the things most hoped for in Canada often involve the reconciliation of irreconcilables: the ideals of the nation and *la nation*, of east and west, of federal and provincial claims; all within a framework complicated by size and lack of unity of purpose, economic disparity and social inequality. The 1960s were no exception to this general rule.

Indeed the attempt to make one whole out of the varied pieces of the Canadian mosaic seems to have been particularly taxing during this decade. This was no doubt due in part to the absence of dynamic national leadership and to the dislocation of power that necessarily followed. But above all, it was due to the re-emergence of a militant French-Canadian nationalism which has managed to turn the entire edifice of Confederation inside out. In fact, the shape of the sixties has been dictated by Quebec's *révolution tranquille*, the reactions it has generated, and the adjustments it has imposed on the rest of the country. For the first time in their history, perhaps, Canadians are being seriously asked to define themselves as a people and to evaluate Canada as their *patrie*. The sixties have proved their *crise de conscience*.

From January 1, 1960, to November 8, 1965, three federal elections and fifteen provincial elections took place.* Of these eighteen elections, nine were held before the expiration of the usual four-year term. In each of the elections held before the end of the traditional term of office, the need for a 'workable majority' was given as the primary reason. The provincial governments were more successful in this search than their federal counterpart. In fact, one of the dominant characteristics of Canadian political life in the sixties was the apparent bankruptcy of federal leadership. More and more, Canadians tended to view the federal government with suspicion and appeared to be unable to make up their minds about its role within Canadian society.

In many ways this feeling was understandable. By 1957, the gigantic task of transforming a war economy into one for peace-time had been accomplished. Canadians began to concentrate on the immediate necessities of their daily lives: education, social services, and security. Because the constitution and the courts have given the provinces prior responsibility in education and social security, and because provincial governments are closer to individual citizens than Ottawa, they were considered better instruments to fulfil these immediate needs than a distant federal government. This development coincided with the appearance on the provincial scene of a new breed of politician, more alert, dynamic, and

* This article has taken January 1966 as a terminal date. Since the end of 1965, Quebec (where Mr. Lesage was defeated by the Union Nationale), Prince Edward Island (where the government also changed hands), Manitoba, Newfoundland, and British Columbia also held elections.

in touch with popular feeling than those on the federal scene. In contrast, Ottawa was increasingly dominated by old men, a trend that has continued in spite of the promises of 1958 and the Diefenbaker era, and the discovery of the American New Frontier at the beginning of Mr. Pearson's regime.

In 1958, John G. Diefenbaker was re-elected with the largest majority ever recorded in the annals of Canadian political history (208 seats out of a House of 265). After the many decades of Liberal rule, which had ended in the pipe-line debate and Black Friday, the Canadian people whole-heartedly placed their trust in Diefenbaker. They looked forward to the realization of a policy which he had enunci-ated on February 12, 1958: 'Sir John A. Macdonald ... opened the west. He saw Canada from East to West. I see a new Canada – *A Canada of the North!*'

Four years later, on June 18, 1962, a federal election left Diefenbaker with 118 seats, and a year later, April 8, 1963, another election further reduced his following in the House of Commons to 95 seats. Although the man himself was still to be a powerful presence on the political scene (to the sur-prise of almost everyone, except himself), the Diefenbaker era had ended.

Many reasons have been offered for Diefenbaker's demise. Many Canadians believe that his chronic indecision and his determination to make the Conservative party a personal instrument of power alienated the bulk of his followers. His handling of Canada's acquisition of nuclear war-heads serves as a good example.

By the commitments made by the Diefenbaker administra-tion in 1957 (the establishment of the North American Defence Command and the new NATO role of 'strike and reconnaissance') Canada, it was generally admitted, had ac-cepted a defence policy based on nuclear arms. By the begin-ning of 1963, $685 million had been spent on new planes, rocket installations such as the BOMARC sites in North Bay, Ontario, and La Macaza, Quebec, and other equipment designed to receive nuclear war-heads. However, the Diefen-baker government appeared incapable of making up its mind to purchase the war-heads. Cabinet ministers such as George Hees, Douglas Harkness, and Pierre Sévigny insisted on fulfilling Canada's nuclear commitment. However, Mr. Diefenbaker temporized. Finally on Monday, February 4, 1963, an exasperated Harkness resigned as Minister of Defence. George Hees and Pierre Sévigny followed, and soon the Conservative caucus was in open revolt.

In the House of Commons, Mr. Harkness explained the difference between himself and Mr. Diefenbaker:

> I differ from the Prime Minister in this way, that I believe we should have obtained nuclear warheads for our weapon carriers as soon as the latter were ready. I thought throughout that by remaining in the Cabinet I could better achieve this purpose than by taking the easier course of resigning. I resigned on a matter of principle. The point was finally reached when I considered that my honour and integrity required that I take this step. . . .

Diefenbaker had enunciated his own point of view a few weeks before. This was based on his assessment of the Kennedy-Macmillan talks in Nassau in December 1962. Diefenbaker insisted that it had become quite apparent that 'more and more the nuclear deterrent is becoming of such a nature that more nuclear arms will add nothing material to our defence'. For his part, Mr. Harkness believed that Canada's defence policy and her international agreements since 1957 made imperative the Canadian acquisition of nuclear war-heads as quickly as possible. This interpretation was essentially supported by General Norstad, the retired NATO Supreme Commander, in a press conference on January 2, 1963, and by the American government, which did not hesitate to issue press releases attacking the Diefenbaker position.

The government was not able to withstand the onslaught of Harkness's resignation and the palace revolution that followed. On February 6, 1963, Mr. Diefenbaker was defeated in the House. He asked for a dissolution and called for a general election on April 8, 1963.

The issue in this election essentially revolved around the

From *Toronto Daily Star Cartoons*, by Duncan Macpherson.

question of leadership and decision-making. Mr. Pearson, who had changed the nuclear policy of the Liberal party by insisting that Canada's international commitments demanded nuclear weapons, promised 'Sixty Days of Decision', and went on to attack the vaccillations and delays of the Diefenbaker administration. On polling-day, Canadians appeared unable to make up their own minds. Mr. Pearson's party obtained 129 seats, while the Conservatives elected 95, Social Credit 24, and the N.D.P. 17.

Most pundits agreed that John Diefenbaker had really defeated himself. His indecision over defence, the disappearance of the 'Vision of the North', his anti-American pronouncements, his inability – or unwillingness – to speak to

and to understand French Canada: all of these contributed
to *la déroute*. Peter Newman in his book *Renegade in Power*,
published in 1963, explained:

> By the time he had been forced into the 1963 election,
> Diefenbaker's indecision and mismanagement had been
> publicly revealed by his inability to reach a sensible defence
> policy and by the disintegration of his cabinet. He had com-
> promised so many convictions during six years of power
> that he no longer seemed to have any clear idea himself of
> the kind of future he was offering his followers. Sensing this,
> even some of his most loyal disciples began to regard him as
> a man to be cherished for his symbolic value, rather than
> for his capabilities as prime minister.

Very few were prepared to question this assessment.

If Diefenbaker contributed to the decline of federal prestige, Lester B. Pearson and his Liberal party have not emerged
as the means to refloat federal fortunes. By June 1963, the
famous 'Sixty Days of Decision' had become days of indecision and fumbling. The budget presented by the Minister of
Finance, Walter Gordon, on June 13 proved to be the beginning of the Liberals' difficulties. Mr. Gordon, who in the
1950s had presided over an important royal commission on
the economic prospects of Canada, was determined to revive
Joseph Israel Tarte's conception of 'Le Canada pour les
Canadiens'. His first budget withdrew many sales-tax exemptions and laid down measures to prevent the persistent
American take-over of Canadian industries. Many viewed
these policies as a curtailment of the expansion of the economy, and the business community cried for vengeance. The
fact that Mr. Gordon had had the assistance of 'three special
consultants who joined the Department of Finance on a
temporary basis shortly after the government took office', all
of whom had contributed to the drafting of the Liberal platform, added to the furor. In the face of the tumult, the Prime
Minister, refusing to accept Mr. Gordon's resignation, decided to fight. The result was that on July 8 Mr. Gordon
presented a new budget which seemed to pacify almost
everybody but retained few of his original propositions.

During the following two years of his prime-ministership, Mr. Pearson's government went from one catastrophe to another. Two of his ministers were accused of having bought furniture on extremely generous credit terms. One of his ministers without portfolio had to resign after it was alleged that he had accepted a bribe of $10,000 to facilitate the obtaining of a racetrack permit for his constituency. And in the fall of 1964 it was divulged in the House of Commons that the Executive Assistant to the Minister of Citizenship and Immigration had offered a bribe of $20,000 to a Montreal lawyer to allow bail in the case of Lucien Rivard, a narcotic smuggler. A considerable sum of money was also to be deposited in the coffers of the Liberal party, and the Minister of Justice was accused of being delinquent in the pursuit of his duties since he failed to inform the Prime Minister and to refer the matter to his law officers. The Opposition saw the Rivard affair as an immense conspiracy, since most of the people involved were supporters of the Liberal party.

With characteristic indecision, the government did nothing until it was finally forced to name a royal commission of inquiry. In the summer of 1965, the Royal Commissioner, Chief Justice Frédéric Dorion of the Superior Court for the Province of Quebec, presented his report, in which he severely censured the Minister of Justice and insisted 'that there is certainly "prima facie" evidence of an offence under the Criminal Code'. Faced with such a rebuke, the Minister of Justice, Guy Favreau, resigned to become President of the Privy Council.

These scandals merely intensified the feeling of frustration that had been a part of federal politics for quite some time. They also seemed to have sapped the vitality of the Liberal party, with the result that many Liberals feared the outcome of a possible election. And to add to its problems, the Liberal government seemed unable to recover from the demise of its first budget, and the bitterness of the long and protracted debate on the new Canadian flag.

The early sixties saw the resurgence of two smaller political parties which added to the confusion in federal politics. The

"What Happened to My Strawberries?"

From *Toronto Daily Star Cartoons*, by Duncan Macpherson.

first was the New Party Movement, which ended in the creation of the New Democratic Party. Growing out of proposals made in the Winnipeg Declaration of 1958 which had attempted to re-direct labour politics, the party was officially founded between July 31 and August 4, 1961, after three years of active discussion. Its program, which rejected thoroughgoing socialism and nationalization, was dedicated to full employment, effective economic planning, a national investment board, job retraining and relocation, public and co-operative ownership of utilities and national resources, more effective control of the Canadian economy through the

curtailment and supervision of foreign ownership, free education, and a national labour code. Its defence and foreign
policies tended to support the United Nations and its various
activities, and to reject NATO and NORAD since these
military alliances depended on nuclear weapons, which the
New Democratic Party rejected. On matters of national
unity, the New Democratic Party went further than any
other federal party, aside from the Créditistes, to adapt itself
to Quebec's quiet revolution. It had no hesitation in accepting the theme of the two 'nations' and in adjusting its federal
policies to meet Quebec's demands for greater autonomy.
Although unsuccessful in Quebec, the New Democratic
Party made impressive gains elsewhere in the various federal
elections in the early years of the sixties. By the middle of the
sixties, it had become a political force that could – in time –
lead a movement to the left.

Social Credit was the phenomenon of the 1962 federal
election. In that year the party, under the co-leadership of
Robert Thompson and Réal Caouette, managed to win 30
seats, 26 of them in Quebec. Pundits have been at a loss to
explain this development. In simplest terms, it may be stated
that many French Canadians, disappointed in the failure of
'old' parties to cope with the plight of those living in areas
where unemployment was rife and economic conditions
poor, seized upon Réal Caouette's claim that they had nothing to lose and voted accordingly. In the 1963 election, although its strength was decreased by six seats in Quebec, it
still remained a considerable force. Caouette, a fiery leader
with an unusual knack of being able to communicate, managed to retain his popularity in spite of the attempts by the
Liberals to ridicule him through the rhetoric of Yvon Dupuis
and the economic lectures of Eric Kierans, then President of
the Montreal Stock Exchange.

After the election, however, Mr. Caouette terminated his
entente with Robert Thompson. He had accepted the Associate State theory for Quebec and had even courted separatist
support during the elections. His views on foreign and defence policy resembled more those of the N.D.P. than those

of Mr. Thompson, and it is an open secret that Mr. Thompson believes more in the spirit than in the letter of Social Credit economic policies, a heresy that Mr. Caouette cannot easily forgive. The party therefore split between the Social Credit party headed by Mr. Thompson, and the Créditistes, led by Mr. Caouette. In addition to the four parties represented in Parliament after the election of 1962, federal politics were now further confused by the vociferous presence of a fifth.

In the face of all these developments and weaknesses, it was relatively easy for the provincial leaders to assert their will and effect what has been called the 'processes of decentralization', or, to use a more colloquial phrase, 'the ganging up' of the provinces against Ottawa. Increasingly, the provinces – much more than the federal government – appeared the best vehicles for Canada's economic and social development.

In a way, the federal government itself assisted in this process of decentralization. The sixties confirmed a trend in this direction that had become apparent in the 1950s. Mr. Diefenbaker had done much to begin it, not only by the better financial terms he granted to the provinces, but also by his solution of the vexatious problem of grants to universities.

Although there had been much discussion over the years of federal assistance to education, the federal government had never embarked on what was essentially a by-passing of the provincial authorities through a system of direct subsidies to provincial institutions, scholars, and students. It was not until the beginning of the 1950s that the federal government created a system of federal grants to be paid directly to Canadian universities and colleges in order to assist them to meet their operating costs and capital investment. Propelled by the Report of the Royal Commission on National Development in the Arts, Letters and Sciences (the Massey Commission of 1951), the federal government provided for a per-capita subsidy of 50 cents in aid of university education. In 1957, this was raised to one dollar, and every province except Quebec availed itself of federal moneys. By 1960, the Canadian University Foundation, which had replaced the National Conference of Canadian Universities, held in trust some $25 million for Quebec.

To remedy this situation, the federal Minister of Finance proposed an amendment to the federal-provincial tax-sharing agreements to give an additional abatement of 1% in the rate of corporation tax in the province to any province that did not wish to accept federal grants to universities. Thus was the opting-out formula with full fiscal compensation introduced into Canada's already complex constitutional framework.

As the sixties progressed, the crisis within Canadian Confederation demanded some reassessment of the relations of Ottawa with the provincial governments. All the provinces asked for such a reassessment and every province participated in the process of decentralization. Provincial dissatisfaction with Ottawa was general over the questions of the Canada Pension Plan, Medicare, the development of health facilities, and the division of revenues.

However, the attention of Canadian public opinion was focused on the Province of Quebec, for only that province availed itself of the negative formula called 'opting out'. By this method any Canadian province may withdraw from a joint program (that is, a program conducted jointly by the federal and provincial governments) and receive its cash equivalent, to be spent within the province, without federal supervision. Since only Quebec has used the opting-out formula, and since Quebec has also declared its intention to withdraw from all the joint programs, the result has been that many mistakenly believe that the federal government is making important concessions to that province and that the French Canadians are dictating to the rest of the country. But because these joint programs arise out of concurrent jurisdiction, in truth no concessions are being made to Quebec. The impression created by the opting-out formula has certainly injured Canadian unity.

The Pearson government liked to use the phrase 'co-operative federalism' to describe federal-provincial relations. By co-operative federalism was understood a gentlemen's agreement that both levels of government would facilitate the other's task, would not attempt to force one level to accept the views of the other, and would undertake to have their legislative bodies pass the necessary legislation embodying the agreements reached at federal-provincial conferences. Over the years, this agreement has been severely tested. For example, at the March-April federal-provincial conference of 1964, two different communiqués were issued, one by Prime Minister Pearson in the name of the federal government and the nine English-speaking provinces, and one by Mr. Lesage in the name of the Province of Quebec. Although a solution was found, it met only the need of the moment. Co-operative federalism was not established on a sound and permanent basis. In January 1966 it was further placed in jeopardy by the provincial government of Quebec. Like the other Premiers of Canada, Mr. Lesage had originally agreed to the Fulton-Favreau Formula for amending the Canadian constitution and had accepted the responsibility of presenting the necessary resolutions in the legislature of his province. While the Premiers of the other provinces presented such resolutions and gained their endorsement (with difficulty in some cases), a re-evaluation of the Fulton-Favreau Formula was going on in Quebec. Many felt that the acceptance of the Fulton-Favreau Formula would mean in the long run placing the constitutional evolution of Quebec in a strait jacket. After months of indecision and vacillation, the Prime Minister of Quebec wrote to Mr. Pearson to withdraw his endorsement of the formula. The gentlemen's agreement which demanded that the provinces should adhere to collective agreements was broken. This was a heavy blow to 'co-operative federalism'.

In operation, that principle led to a considerable increase in the number of federal-provincial conferences held. So frequent were these conferences, so far-reaching their conclusions, and so disturbing the secrecy of the negotiations, that many wondered if the legislative responsibilities of this country had not passed from Parliament and the provincial legislatures to the conference. In fact, the conferences began to develop a quasi-constitutional status. Members of the elected bodies began to feel that they were required to pass almost automatically the decisions that had already been agreed on. The speed and secrecy that surrounded some of these meetings, the hurried plane trips at night, the last-minute summoning of assistants, fascinated some editorial writers, who predicted the eventual impotence of the legislatures and of Parliament. However, in spite of this, as the sixties continued, the elected legislative bodies not only survived but managed to initiate new social welfare measures.

II

The federal government – sometimes helped and at other times hindered by the provinces – laid down the foundation of significant social legislation. For instance, through the Agricultural Rehabilitation and Development Act (ARDA), the most important achievement of the Diefenbaker regime, the war on rural poverty, was begun in June 1961. Its basis was a general recognition that one of Canada's top priorities was to improve the economic opportunities and living standards of the country's rural areas. Through better land use, regrouping of farms, and the introduction of a more diversified economy, it was hoped that this goal would be attained. By 1970, the federal government will have spent close to $125,000,000 in co-operation with the provinces on this project.

Furthermore, the Conservative government passed the Technical and Vocational Assistance Act in 1960. This Act provides federal assistance for the building and equipping of vocational training facilities, the training of technicians, vocational teachers, and students in technological training programs, and the training or re-training of many categories of Canadian citizens. By the end of the fiscal year of 1964, the federal and provincial governments had accepted projects valued at more than $583,400,000 to provide 292 new schools and 159,417 new places for students.

For their part, the Liberals contributed the Canada Assistance Plan to help the provinces in the constant fight against misery and destitution, and following in the footsteps of the Conservatives they have encouraged the expansion of technical education and the mobility of the labour force. However, at the time this article was written, no legislation had as yet been presented on manpower development and allied services, though the federal government had begun to attack the problem through the moving and re-training of the unemployed and unskilled. Finally, with the official announcement in 1965 of a Canadian 'war on poverty' and the establishment of a Company of Young Canadians, Ottawa showed that it intended to launch a major offensive against the worst problems in Canadian society.

It was also in the sixties that Canadians acquired the beginning of a universal and portable pension plan to ensure dignity and security after retirement. On July 18, 1963, the then Minister of Health and Welfare, Miss Judy LaMarsh, introduced the pension measure in the House of Commons. The plan was to be entirely self-financing with the exception of the flat-rate pension of $65 a month ($75 by 1964) at the age of seventy. Employers and employees were to share the payment of the 2 per cent contribution to the first $4,000 of annual earnings. A procedure was established to calculate the eventual increases in wage standards.

Unfortunately, the plan was unacceptable to the two largest provinces, Ontario and Quebec. The provinces were well served in their arguments, since it was generally conceded that they had prior constitutional rights in matters of social welfare. The controversy became more acute and bitter as the months progressed, and it was not until April 1964 that a solution was finally found. By then, relations between Quebec and Ottawa had become so bad as to endanger the course of Confederation. Yet, by the end of 1964, almost every Canadian was assured of a more secure old age and of a fund of $4 billion which would become available within the space of ten years for various provincial developments. In order to meet Quebec's insistence that social welfare was a provincial responsibility, the Canada Pension Plan provided for the establishment of provincial pension plans with 'comparable benefits' to its own. Quebec is the only province so far to have made use of this formula, although there are some indications that Ontario may wish to do the same in some not too distant future.

During the early years of the sixties, medicare was also uppermost in everyone's mind, and it was hoped that by the time Canada celebrated its first centenary, a universal medical care plan would be in existence, although this now appears an unrealizable goal. However, the same problem over constitutional jurisdiction has already arisen, since many provinces have already established medical care programs of their own, while others have signified their intention of doing so.

Such legislative action suggests that at long last the era when social welfare meant government handouts to indigents and misfits has ended, and that a new era of social justice has begun. This new awareness is essentially due to the intensive growth of urbanization and industrialization since the end of the Second World War. The census of 1961 showed that almost 70 per cent of Canada's population lived in urban centres, while only 12 per cent of her population lived on farms or in rural areas of less than 1,000 population. In fact, 53 per cent of Canadians lived in or on the fringes of urban centres that had a population of 30,000 or more.

These developments increased the individual's feeling of insecurity. More and more the state became the only instrument capable of providing him with services that could minimize this vulnerability. There thus emerged a consensus that a democratic society must take the necessary steps to alleviate poverty, eradicate disease, and guarantee the equality of all its citizens by providing them with equal opportunities. There is no doubt that during the early sixties Canada made a considerable advance in the realization of that noble ideal.

III

After the débâcle in international relations of Diefenbaker's regime, a new feeling of international responsibility emerged when Lester B. Pearson took office. In fact, if in the fifties Canadians had taken a new interest in world affairs, in the sixties their views became more sophisticated and more independent of American pressures as they became more and more involved in international politics. The 'fireproof house' theory had indeed become obsolete. Much of the credit for this belongs to Mr. Pearson himself, for as Peyton V. Lyon remarked: 'The Prime Minister himself had more success dealing with world affairs than with Canadians.'

During the years after 1963, Canada continued its support of American involvement in Viet Nam, although the Canadian government and particularly Mr. Pearson advocated a quick and peaceful settlement. The Prime Minister even risked his good relations with Lyndon B. Johnson by suggesting, on American soil, important changes in the United States' policy towards Viet Nam and China. Mr. Pearson was no doubt encouraged by the fact that more and more Canadians were becoming disenchanted with the American position and Canada's tacit support of it. Protest marches, sit-ins, and demonstrations outside American consulates in Canada often expressed this Canadian dissent.

In other areas of international involvement Canada attempted to regain its former status as the disinterested middleman. Canadians kept up their peace-keeping missions in Kashmir, Indo-China, the Gaza strip, Cyprus, and the Congo, and also in the corridors of the U.N. and in NATO. At the U.N. the Canadian delegates continued their attempts to solve the financial impasse and to press for disarmament; while in Geneva they tried, with little success, to break the deadlock between the great powers. Disarmament also became a fashionable conference topic at private meetings of industrialists and professional groups, perhaps a further sign that Canadians in the sixties were more interested in the international scene.

In Commonwealth meetings Canadians were more successful in fulfilling their almost traditional role of middleman.
Both Mr. Diefenbaker and Mr. Pearson tried to prevent the
Commonwealth from dividing along racial lines over the
issue of South African and Rhodesian racial policies, first in
London in 1961, and then in Lagos in 1965. At Lagos, where
the attempt to reconcile the cautious Britons and the militant
Africans over Rhodesia seemed almost impossible, it was
finally agreed to wait and see what effect the British policy of
economic sanctions would have on the Smith regime. Later
when Rhodesia cut off Zambia's oil supplies Canadian aircraft helped to fly in oil. Although Britain welcomed Canadian support, and even Canadian initiative, at these times,
she was embarrassed by Canada's insistence on Commonwealth trade protection during the difficult talks preceding
her attempts to enter the European Common Market in
1961-2. The growing and increasingly complex problems of
the Commonwealth caused the Afro-Asian nations to propose
the creation of a permanent secretariat. Canada's traditional
opposition to such proposals was abandoned – perhaps yet
another sign of a new approach to international affairs – and
a senior Canadian diplomat, Arnold Smith, became the first
Commonwealth Secretary-General.

As always Canada's relations with the United States were
the most controversial and demanding area of international
relations. Canadian-American relations, already strained by
differences between President Johnson and the Prime Minister, were not improved by diverging attitudes towards France
and General de Gaulle. Mr. Pearson and the Secretary for
External Affairs, Paul Martin, were determined to resist any
measures that might give the French grounds for pulling out
of either NATO or the U.N. Canada remained sympathetic
as de Gaulle attempted to return to France's traditional
European policy of the balance of power even if it meant
closer ties with Russia. For this reason the U.S. proposal that
NATO acquire its own nuclear force received little support
in Ottawa. Canadian policy towards South Viet Nam, France,
Cuba, Russia, and the Congo was certainly influenced by her

military agreements with the United States as well as by an instinctive sympathy for her most vital North American neighbour.

The extension of U.S. control over Canadian industry alarmed many Canadians, who complained that no other nation allowed another power so much influence and profit within its borders. Their concern was accentuated by the constant shifts in government policy as both Conservatives and Liberals at times favoured a large and growing U.S. investment in Canada and at other times criticized our economic dependence. This erratic behaviour was particularly apparent in the dismissal of James Coyne as Governor of the Bank of Canada during a quarrel with the government over his support of a nationalistic economic policy.

The sections of Walter Gordon's 1963 budget designed to limit U.S. control disappeared in an unprecedented barrage of criticism and dissension in the government, the House, and the press. Yet the government still enacted legislation to protect Canadian banks against foreign ownership and pointedly issued guide-lines to shape the behaviour of U.S. companies as good Canadian citizens. Wheat sales to Communist-bloc countries, particularly to Red China, ran counter to both the Canadian policy of not recognizing Peking and the wishes of the U.S. State Department. George Hees, as Minister of Trade and Commerce, exuberantly welcomed the possibility of an increase in Canadian sales to Cuba, leaving other members of the government to reassure an aroused Washington that the trade would not involve military equipment. Canada's exports to Cuba then declined in dollar value until 1964, when they rose again and at $60 million were almost as high as those to Venezuela. Far from appreciating the benefits of U.S. investments, it seemed that Canadians could not even make up their minds what they wanted from their own trade or from U.S. investment in Canada. To some it was a disaster, the sale of our birth-right. To others, equally qualified to judge, it was an unquestionable good.

The same ambivalence appeared in Canada's attitude to-

wards the management of resources. The long negotiations
with the United States on the use of the Columbia River
resulted in the signing of a treaty that was quickly rejected by
Premier Bennett of British Columbia. Ottawa and Victoria
proved no easier to reconcile than Ottawa and Washington,
and further negotiations were necessary before a solution
agreeable to all parties could be found. The public's sudden
awareness of their fundamental resources, highlighted by a
growing knowledge of the effects of water and air pollution,
produced instant disagreement over how to use these resources. Certain Americans referred to 'continental water
resources', and Canadians replied that they had never before
heard the Mesabi iron range or the Butte copper deposits
described as 'continental'. Further advanced than Canada,
and pressed for resources, especially water, Americans were
impatient with Canadian ignorance of their problem and the
benefits of a mutual solution. The emotionalism of the water
resources discussion was a compound of ignorance, old quarrels over continentalism, and strongly nationalistic press reports. Here again, the Canadian ambivalence appeared. The
possibility of a sale of Canadian water, highly hypothetical,
provoked lively comment, while the existing ownership and
exploitation of Canadian forest, iron, and oil resources by
Americans was not seriously disputed by anyone. Even the
critical negotiations over the auto parts agreement raised
relatively little discussion. Yet this agreement, signed in
1965, provided, for the first time in North American history,
virtually free trade in a single manufacturing industry. It was
designed by the government as a major step in reducing
Canada's balance-of-payments problem with the United
States, and by 1966 it had already begun to function as expected, although it caused severe hardship to many Canadian
auto workers. As Canadian wheat sales continued to increase,
and as wheat prices began to rise, Canada's old imbalance-of-
payments problem was lessened, if not actually solved.

By the end of their first century, Canadians expected more
skilful and effective diplomacy than they had had in the past.
While they had tolerated the wavering, often ineffectual

idealism of the Diefenbaker era, they approved of Lester Pearson's more productive, if less high-minded, policies. By the mid sixties, although Canadians were still often troubled, if not divided, by the conflicting loyalties that had been so apparent during Suez and even the Cuban crisis, some identifiable 'policy' towards international relations was emerging. The trade and resources agreements, the peace-keeping missions, and the positions taken at NATO and at the U.N. – none of them really new approaches – were all part of this 'policy'. Gradually some Canadians came to think of their country as having a foreign policy, not merely isolated reactions to the problems of others. Essentially, although some Canadians tended to sound pretty pious about the benevolent role of their country in international forums, this policy was based on intelligent self-interest, as a realistic foreign policy inevitably must be.

IV

In the search for greater equality among the citizens of Canada, the provincial governments have had to provide strong leadership, since on their shoulders rests most of the responsibility. Yet, for the most part, provincial action has been limited to the expansion of already available services, in spite of a booming economy and a wave of popular enthusiasm for reform on which the provinces could have capitalized to reassess and adapt their welfare and educational services.

There were, of course, notable exceptions. In Newfoundland, the Premier established free university education with a living allowance for all university students. Newfoundland was thus a pioneer in recognizing an essential element in the battle for social equality. In New Brunswick the government of Louis Robichaud has undertaken long-overdue reforms. Fighting their own war on poverty, the people of New Brunswick have launched a threefold attack against the poverty and backwardness that have plagued their province for so long. Through a Youth Assistance Act and various educational reforms, through economic planning, and through a complete overhaul of municipal power and responsibility, the province can look to better days ahead.

And there was, of course, the Medical Care Act of the Province of Saskatchewan, making it the first province to provide complete medical insurance. Unfortunately, its beginnings were marred by a conflict between the government and the doctors, who objected in principle to a universal, state-operated medical care program on the grounds that such a scheme would disturb the sacred doctor-patient relationship and would transform them into civil servants. Having staffed emergency hospital services in 31 hospitals (out of 147) with some 240 doctors, between 400 and 500 physicians went on strike on July 1, 1962. After three anxious weeks during which the government saw to it that the irresponsibility of the doctors did not endanger human life, an agreement was reached with the medical profession which appears relatively satisfactory, at least sufficiently so for the Liberal Opposition, who opposed the legislation violently when it was passed, to leave it intact when they gained power a few years later.

Medicare appeared to be only one of the symptoms of the provinces' growing pains. In fact, provincial governments reflected more closely the needs and desires of the Canadian people. The growth of urbanization affects the provinces more than Ottawa, since they are primarily responsible for urban renewal, municipal affairs, and social security. Provincial expenses for most services surpassed federal expenditures, and many observers felt it not too far-fetched to suggest in the early sixties that unharnessed provincial economic power could well destroy the federal government's ability to direct the Canadian economy and to maintain a proper balance between the have and have-not provinces.

The danger of provincial exclusiveness – or a tendency to consider the part more important than the whole – is best demonstrated by the startling and disturbing 'renewal' that took place in the Province of Quebec. As was suggested above, the sixties have above all focused on the emergence of a new Quebec, and on Canada's adjustment to that fact. Quebec's 'renewal' was startling because it appeared to be so sudden. And it was disturbing because Quebec in the process of her reassessment put an end to many Canadian myths.

Yet, many conditions made Quebec's renewal in the sixties almost imperative. Since the Second World War, Quebec's population has increased by over 8 per cent and by the middle of the sixties more than four million of its citizens live in urban centres. One can easily imagine what this has meant in terms of industrialization and urbanization, expanded facilities and opportunities, and the conflict with older values. As Michael Oliver has remarked, Quebec's social revolution, greatly aided by the development of mass communications, especially television, has 'led to a transformation in the image of the good life and the good society which most French Canadians hold'. The old concept of a Quebec of large families grouped and protected by their parish has become untenable. The urban concept, with its mobility, more sophisticated services and opportunities, its broader vision, and the constant and needed intervention of the state, has replaced it, and French Canadians are now entering into the mainstream of North American society.

The seeds of this social revolution were planted in the 1950s. That they did not come to fruition until the sixties was essentially due to the presence of Quebec's benevolent despot, Maurice Duplessis, who governed the province with a firm hand from 1944 until his death in 1959. Duplessis's conservatism would not allow the transformation of structures and traditional institutions to meet the demands of the new era, and so the social revolution grew in the catacombs. No sooner had Duplessis died than his successor, Paul Sauvé, acknowledged its presence. When Jean Lesage came to power in 1960 on a platform of social reconstruction, Quebec was already prepared to receive his message.

If one looks for a simple way to explain what has been taking place in Quebec in the sixties, one can say that 'the days of Maria Chapdelaine are over'. Even in the sixties,

Canadians have been accustomed to consider the following
passage from Louis Hémon's novel as the basic philosophy of
Quebec:

> C'est pourquoi il faut rester dans la province où nos pères
> sont restés, et vivre comme ils ont vécu, pour obéir au com-
> mandement inexprimé qui s'est formé dans leurs coeurs, qui
> a passé dans les nôtres et que nous devrons transmettre à
> notre tour à de nombreux enfants: Au pays du Québec rien
> ne doit mourir et rien ne doit changer.

From this philosophy, the image of an agricultural, clerically
controlled, monolithic, and politically unconcerned Quebec
society emerged. Yet Quebec has changed, and is changing.
A refusal to grasp this fact is an essential reason for what has
become the 'crisis of Canadian national unity'.

Many people suggest that French Canadians are merely
attempting to catch up with the rest of Canada. But what is
going on in Quebec in the sixties is not 'catching up'. It is the
collective effort of hundreds of thousands of individuals to
reassess completely their individual and collective values,
their institutions, their ways of thinking, their way of life,
and even the relationship that binds them to their Creator.
Such profound soul-searching means a massive program of
adaptation, a careful assessment of priorities, and a constant
effort to maintain the momentum of reform.

Since the government of Jean Lesage came to power in
Quebec in June 1960, the province has been experiencing an
upheaval, *la révolution tranquille*. The fundamental goals
of this revolution are a radical reconstruction in education;
the improvement of living standards, especially in rural
areas; the creation of a viable economy in which public and
private ownership can both flourish; a sharp break with the
patronage-plagued political morality of the past; the development of a managerial class which is French-speaking and
which takes its place in the business community of Canada
and of the world; a complete re-appraisal of the relations between Church and State; the elaboration of a coherent social
welfare program; increased assistance to those French-speak-

ing Canadians who live beyond the borders of Quebec; the emergence of a new type of French-speaking politician in Ottawa (on whom rests most of the responsibility for creating a truly bilingual and bicultural Canada); the nourishing of French culture by closer association with the French-speaking community of the world; and ultimately the realization of the dream that French-speaking Canadians can play an equal role within Confederation.

Since 1960, much has been done to implement this program. Because education is at the root of Quebec's *révolution tranquille*, the first reforms were to begin to equip Quebec with an educational system based on the realities of the present. To change the obsolete system which had been conceived almost a century before and which was dedicated to the maintenance of a clerical and professional élite, the Lesage government appointed a royal commission to suggest extensive reforms. The task of the Parent Commission was to devise a way to move Quebec's educational system out of the nineteenth century and into the twenty-first, ignoring the fact that in education Quebec has really missed the twentieth century.

In 1963 the Commission presented its first report, which dealt with the administrative structure of the educational system in Quebec. The Commission recommended the creation of a Ministry of Education to govern and co-ordinate every aspect of education in the province. At the same time it advised the establishment of a Superior Council of Education, a non-confessional and bilingual body, to serve as the watchdog of the Ministry. The Council was to be aided in this task by a Catholic Committee, a Protestant Committee, and several commissions which would look into primary, secondary, and university education.

This first report met with severe opposition. Many of the privileged groups who had for years been free to manipulate the educational facilities of Quebec objected violently to this threat to their power. They managed to delay, and almost succeeded in preventing, the establishment of the new Ministry in spite of the support of many groups and the work of the then Minister of Youth (who was slated to become the first Minister of Education), Paul Gérin-Lajoie, who exhausted himself barnstorming the province in favour of the new Ministry. Although he succeeded in selling the people on the necessity of a Ministry of Education, Gérin-Lajoie was forced to compromise with the objections of the episcopacy, the Fédération des Collèges Classiques, and other groups (French and English) who opposed the whole idea. The result was that the legislation that created the new Ministry (the much publicized Bill 60) appeared to many to be a retreat on the part of the government, although the Minister's co-ordinating powers remained intact.

The Commission's second report, presented in 1965, dealt with the pedagogical structure of the educational system and a possible program of study. In 800 pages, the Commission made more than 300 recommendations on nursery schools and kindergartens, the duration of primary and secondary and university education, the novel idea of establishing institutes as a sort of midway point between high school and university, and a complete overhaul of all programs of study and curriculum with definite suggestions as to methods of teaching.

The government accepted most of the recommendations of the Commission and undertook to change the school system at every level. Quebec's public schools are still all either Catholic or Protestant, and those who do not belong to either of these two religious denominations simply have to find a place in one of the systems.* Nor did the Liberal government find a satisfactory solution to the presence of a privileged private-school system (collèges classiques), which has for years blocked the progress of public-school graduates into university. Unless solutions are found to these important problems, many doubt that the educational reforms now undertaken will have real influence.

The Lesage government also recognized that the key to

* Before its defeat in 1966 the Liberal government had not tackled the problem of confessionality, and the policy of the new Union Nationale government, while not yet clear, appears less favourable to change than that of the Liberals.

Quebec's future lies in its economic development. The vigorous program aimed at what René Lévesque called 'la reconquête de notre économie', will undoubtedly continue through the sixties. More and more Quebec universities are producing the economists, engineers, and other professionals needed in industrial administration – areas traditionally dominated by English-speaking Canadians – and the proposed reforms in the educational system will further increase the supply. New organizations such as the General Finance Corporation and the Quebec Council of Economic Reorientation are encouraging French Canadians, traditionally cautious with their money, to invest in the economic future of their province.

The process of 'economic emancipation' has also been carried out through the nationalization of the private power companies, the establishment of a steel complex largely owned and financed by the state, immense hydro-electric developments such as the one on the Manicouagan River, the creation of an Industrial Research Council, and the curtailment of the powers and privileges of private companies that exploit Quebec's natural resources. The population on the whole seems to agree with the government that only by such careful economic planning can French-speaking Canadians realize the Liberal slogan *maîtres chez nous,* and they appear determined that political and constitutional barriers will not stand in the way.

With the move of René Lévesque and Eric Kierans into the ministries of Social Welfare and Health in 1965, the province shifted some of its strength to the battle against social inequality. It is still too early to speak of specific legislation, but it appears that Quebec's antiquated social welfare structure fragmented by racial and religious divisions and dominated by out-dated concepts of what constitutes 'charity' will soon disappear.

Fully realizing that the French-speaking Canadians of North America want to be sustained by close cultural ties with the French-speaking community of the world, the Quebec government in 1965 signed a cultural *entente* with

France. This international agreement dealt largely with the exchange of professors, students, and educational experts, and the establishment of a joint Permanent Commission of Franco-Quebec Co-operation. Later another agreement was signed dealing with other cultural exchanges, and it is hoped that in time similar arrangements will be made with other French-speaking countries involving not only culture and education but also technical aid and economic and industrial co-operation.

During the sixties, organizations like the Institut Canadien des Affaires Publiques and the Mouvement Laïque de Langue Française, reviews like *Cité Libre, Parti-Pris*, and the Dominican *Maintenant* have greatly influenced the re-evaluation of Quebec's traditional institutions, especially the legacy of clerical paternalism. Often with great foresight, they have highlighted the need for revolutionary changes and today there are few French-speaking Canadians in Quebec who are willing to let any traditional institution or constitutional limitation interfere with their *révalorization*.

Because part of this *révolution tranquille* involved relations with the federal government or with the English-speaking community at so many points, it was only natural that French-speaking Quebeckers should reassess the links that bind them to an entity called Canada. And although most French Canadians would look upon a separation of Quebec from the rest of Canada as an extreme solution to their problem of *l'épanouissement du fait canadien-français* in North America, nevertheless there were few of them who would not agree with the sentiments expressed in Raymond Barbeau's *J'ai choisi l'indépendance* and Marcel Chaput's *Pourquoi je suis séparatiste*. These two books, written at the beginning of the 1960s demonstrated the deep dissatisfaction of the French-speaking Canadian population.

The foundation of this dissatisfaction lies in the fact that the six million French-speaking Canadians of Canada form *une nation*; they are a people who share a common heritage, speak the same language, have their own political and social institutions, live in a geographical unit that by the will of both English-speaking and French-speaking Canadians has become a sort of reserve for French-speaking Canadians, and above all, possess *un vouloir vivre collectif* – a will to live as a distinct people in North America.

V

The question then arises, can Confederation as established in 1867, or as possibly reformed by 1967, satisfy the legitimate ambitions and claims of the French-speaking Canadians? The over-all answer seems to be no. Economically the French Canadians still count for little. English-speaking Canadians and Americans exercise a decisive influence on the everyday existence and standard of living of the French-Canadian people. Furthermore, many have accused the federal government of using the immense economic powers granted to it by the British North America Act of 1867 for the benefit of the English-speaking majority at the expense of the French-speaking minority.

Although a great number of French Canadians share these sentiments, they constitute an oversimplification of the economic situation. A study of Quebec's economic development shows that it has also been hindered by geographical considerations, by the fact that its natural resources have only recently been considered valuable, and by the neglect of Quebec's politicians, who were for years cajoled or bribed into selling these resources for a song. It is also true that Quebec's educational system has not been geared to the modern industrial and technological age.

Socially many French-speaking Canadians feel that they are considered second-class citizens. They live in what a separatist has called a 'ghetto confédératif', with the federal government (that is *les Anglais*) offering only token gestures such as bilingual cheques and sermons on national unity. French Canadians see further demonstrations of this discrimination in the fact that they are expected to be bilingual while their English-speaking compatriots need not be. The fundamental criterion of whether a French Canadian is competent is whether he is bilingual. This is true even though Quebec is the world's largest French-speaking area outside of France and Montreal is the world's second-largest French-speaking city. In the face of what amounts to racial and/or linguistic discrimination, it is not surprising that many French Canadians doubt that Confederation can provide them with the atmosphere they need for complete *épanouissement*.

Many French Canadians also see Confederation as a threat to French Canada's cultural evolution. Radio, television, movies, billboards, and even textbooks impose cultural values that originate outside Quebec. Moreover, the French Canadian must earn his living by using not only the English language but also 'English' methods, approaches, and know-how. Many fear that the end result of this avalanche of foreign influence will be assimilation for the French-speaking Canadian.

Surrounded as it is on an English-speaking continent, Quebec has a problem of cultural development that should be faced not only by the French Canadians but by all Canadians – for their country is supposed to be a bilingual and bicultural one. Yet the cultural needs of the French linguistic minority have been largely overlooked ever since Confederation. In the eyes of many Quebeckers it is imperative for Quebec to step in where Ottawa has failed and to link the province to the French-speaking community of the world. Quebec, in the sixties, has become French Canada's international voice.

The established structure of the national political parties is another matter about which the French Canadians have been increasingly concerned in the sixties. Some feel that the only positive action French-speaking Canadians can perform in Ottawa is to delay the inevitable day when the majority will have its way. This interpretation of French-Canadian power in Ottawa is no doubt an oversimplification, since it refuses to recognize that, in the past, Quebec has not been well served by its politicians. Inept and in many instances the dupes and supporters of clerical control of Quebec's political life and that of other vested interests, French-Canadian federal leaders have wasted their time and the little talent they had.

Yet, French-Canadian politicians at Ottawa have had to contend with the fact that although Confederation acknowledged the dual nature of the Canadian heritage, it did not enforce the recognition of equality between the two cultures across Canada. French was abolished as an official language in the west; there were angry quarrels over separate schools for Roman Catholics (and by virtue of this for French Canadians) in New Brunswick, Ontario, and Manitoba, and in the newer provinces of Alberta and Saskatchewan; the Métis leader Louis Riel was hanged; Canadians quarrelled about troops for the Boer War and about conscription in the two world wars. In all these incidents the limitations of French-Canadian political power at the federal level was apparent. And the story was still the same even when the Prime Minister was himself a French Canadian. In the light of this experience, it is difficult to conclude that Confederation ever meant there was to be a French-speaking Canada parallel to an English-speaking Canada. It only permitted Quebec to be a province *pas comme les autres.* Today the refusal of the English-speaking provinces to make constitutional or administrative arrangements to meet the linguistic, cultural, and educational needs of their French-speaking populations suggests to many that the pattern of the past is to be continued. And this means that to the majority of English-speaking Canadians French Canada is to be understood only in terms of the Province of Quebec. If this is true, Quebec City and not Ottawa is and must remain the pivot of French-Canadian life.

This anxiety about Ottawa's role in the daily life of the French Canadians was amply demonstrated by the important divisions in the Quebec wing of the federal Liberal party which characterized that party during the 1960s. On the one hand there was a group of politicians, known as the Old Guard, who seemed to be quite content to carry out Quebec's traditional political role in Ottawa. This meant accepting as inevitable French-Canadian minority status, being satisfied with minor cabinet portfolios, plus one prestigious but often powerless position, and presenting their party as the best guardian of French-Canadian 'survival'. International, economic, or broad social questions did not concern the Old Guard particularly. They preferred to immerse themselves in the routine decisions of party politics and to supervise the distribution of patronage.

On the other hand, the New Guard, made up of dynamic and active young men, rejected this traditional concept of the French-Canadian role in Ottawa. They saw the French Canadians as equal partners in the federal sphere with a vital and real role to play in the administration of the affairs of the country. Equal partnership to them meant that Canada is the product of an association between those Canadians whose language of expression is English and those Canadians whose language of expression is French. In practical terms, as Maurice Sauvé has demonstrated, this meant an equal division of at least the important economic cabinet portfolios between French-speaking and English-speaking Canadians. This was not the case during any of the federal administrations that succeeded each other in the sixties. French-speaking Canadians continued to be excluded from those portfolios that traditionally have been associated with the greatest amount of influence and power.

To explain Ottawa's inability to draw the new type of Quebecker in any significant number, two reasons may be given. First, it would appear that the standards of competence applied to French-speaking Canadians are rather different from those applied to English-speaking Canadians. Many French-speaking Canadians are at a great disadvantage in Ottawa if their command of English is limited. On the other hand many English-speaking members and ministers have absolutely no knowledge of French, and yet they get ahead successfully in government. Secondly, the delay in making Ottawa a truly bilingual capital with adequate educational and cultural facilities for French Canadians has deterred many able French Canadians from moving there.

If French Canadians are being told, in effect, to stay in Quebec, can they be denied the right to transform their province into an autonomous country? Many have asked themselves this question, and some have answered with militant nationalism. On February 23, 1963, this nationalism exploded into terrorism for the first time. At first through the Réseau de Résistance and then through the Front de Libération Québécois, commonly called the F.L.Q., bombs were planted in radio stations, military establishments in Montreal, the R.C.M.P. barracks, the Legion Hall in St. Johns, Quebec, Montreal's central Post Office building, and ten mail-boxes in residential Westmount; attacks were made on several national monuments; F.L.Q. slogans were painted on prominent buildings and on the home of the Lieutenant-Governor in Quebec City; and an attempt was made to derail a train carrying the Prime Minister. The first victim of these terrorist activities was a sixty-five-year-old veteran, W. V. O'Neill, who was killed instantly on April 20, 1963. On May 17 of that year Sergeant Major Walter Leja was seriously and permanently injured while dismantling a bomb that had been placed in a Westmount mail-box.

The purpose of these terrorists, who were in time arrested and sent to jail, was to destroy what they saw as the symbols of colonial control, such as the Royal Canadian Mounted Police and the armed forces; to eliminate the English-speaking communications network; and to sabotage any commercial or industrial establishment that did not use French as its main language or practised discrimination against French-Canadian employees. French-Canadian collaborators were also to be attacked by the F.L.Q. Although there have been other bombings since 1963, no large-scale terrorist activity has taken place. The militant nationalists have been concentrating on demonstrations and marches.

The climax of this more pacific type of nationalism was apparently reached during the visit of Her Majesty Queen Elizabeth II to Quebec City in the fall of 1964. Expressions of anxiety about the Queen's safety made by Raymond Barbeau and Marcel Chaput, two discredited members of the separatist movement, were taken seriously in English-speaking Canada, with the result that some believed that the

Queen might be attacked in the old city of Champlain. The federal government, which unwisely insisted on the visit, took intense security precautions. In fact, Quebec became an armed camp for her visit. Terrifying riots marred the Queen's visit, largely caused by panicking Quebec Provincial Police. The Quebec population, fearful of the thousands of police, preferred to watch on their television sets the lonely rides of the Queen through the streets of the city lined with troops and yellow barricades.

Le samedi de la matraque, as October 10, 1964, is called, with its spectacle of charging police and swinging clubs in the midst of demonstrators, accentuated French-Canadian resentment against those responsible for the visit. As for English-speaking Canadians, served by a sensational press which presented to its horror-struck readers photos of riots and empty streets, many decided that this 'French-Canadian nonsense' had lasted long enough. The visit that was to be productive of so much 'national unity' became instead a national nightmare which six million French Canadians would not soon forget.

VI

In the face of the vast transformation of Quebec that has taken place since the beginning of the 1960s, and the varied incidents and frustration the *révolution tranquille* has caused, a reassessment of Canadian federalism became inevitable in this decade. Since 1960, many solutions have been suggested and many steps taken in order to effect such an adjustment. In order to recommend 'what steps should be taken to develop the Canadian Confederation on the basis of an equal partnership between the two founding races', the federal government appointed a Royal Commission on Bilingualism and Biculturalism on July 9, 1963. The Commission, made up of an equal number of French-speaking and English-speaking Canadians, spent over thirty months travelling across Canada ascertaining the views of every sector of the Canadian community. At the same time, the Commission carried out a vast research program on bilingualism and biculturalism, or cultural diversity, in Canada.

In its preliminary report issued on February 1, 1965, the Commission concluded that 'Canada, without being fully conscious of the fact, is passing through the greatest crisis in its history.' The Commissioners believed that the source of this crisis lay in Quebec, and that the crisis itself had arisen because for the first time since 1867 the French Canadians of Quebec were seriously questioning the constitutional and political arrangements made in that year. Unfortunately this recognition of a state of crisis was not endorsed by important elements within the English-speaking community. Many instead tended to view French Canada's dissatisfaction as the expression of a lunatic fringe, as an exercise in emotionalism, or as the opinion of pessimists and radicals.

And yet no one appeared able to find a solution to resolve the crisis. The formulae of co-operative federalism and federal-provincial conferences only seemed to intensify the dissatisfaction of the French Canadians and the frustration of the English-speaking Canadians. Many longed to find the answers to two questions: What could reconcile Quebec, and what constitutional formulae would best meet her needs? Many solutions were put forward, but at the time this article was written none had been adopted and the entire discussion had degenerated into wordy debate.

The first and most clear-cut solution has been separatism. The complete separation of Quebec from the rest of Canada is a feasible remedy, not only because of the dissatisfaction of many French Canadians, but also because since the Second World War less developed and poorer nations than Quebec have achieved independence. The majority of French Canadians are separatists at heart, finding solace in the thought of *un état canadien-français* where they could really be *chez nous*. But most view it as the last possible solution.

Another solution that has been suggested is the maintenance of the existing constitutional *status quo*, but with a greater emphasis on provincial autonomy. However, this solution was no longer acceptable in the sixties. To satisfy the economic and social demands of the French Canadians and to carry out the projects that have already been proposed by the provincial government, it has been necessary (and will continue to be necessary) for Quebec to encroach seriously on the powers of the central authority.

Realizing that Ottawa will not allow any usurpation of its prerogatives and responsibilities, the government of Quebec has begun to talk officially of a particular status for that province. Particular status means many things to many people. For some, it implies the transformation of Quebec from a province of Canada into an associate state in Canada. This would probably mean that all legislative, executive, and judicial power would be vested in the Province of Quebec. After having negotiated an international agreement, Quebec would then delegate certain fields of jurisdiction to the central authority (Ottawa) and provide the sums of money necessary to administer them. It would be difficult for these delegated powers to be exercised through a democratic Parliament, and thus Quebec would have to send delegates to a Central Council. Others tend to modify this extreme position and suggest that the federal government and Quebec should arrive at a definite division of power with full autonomy for each in carrying these out. In this context, Quebec could still elect representatives to a central Parliament and thus maintain the over-all benefits of Confederation.

In this way, also, Quebec would not lose the free-trade area and the attraction of foreign capital that Confederation provides. Moreover, no one would need to suffer from a dislocation of Quebec's economy or an exodus of English-speaking business from Quebec. In return for these constitutional arrangements, Quebec would forgo independence, co-operate fully in the projects of the central authority, maintain the bilingual character of the province, and guarantee the educational rights of the English-speaking minority.

The sixties, however, showed that the solution of associate state was unacceptable to the majority of English-speaking Canadians, since it would mean revolutionary constitutional changes. Furthermore, many felt that it would deprive Canada of the powerful centralized authority needed to maintain a proper equilibrium between the component parts of the country and to enact measures to equalize Canada's vast economic and social differences.

As the debate continued, it gradually became apparent that what most informed people understood by 'particular status' was a constitutional affirmation of the distinctness of Quebec. Because of its very generality and lack of definition, it is considered the most useful formula for Quebec. Already Quebec is not constitutionally *une province comme les autres*. It has among other differences a Legislative Council and its own civil law, and the affairs of its government are conducted in both languages. Any new Canadian constitution will have to emphasize this peculiar character of Quebec.

The constitutional recognition of Quebec's particular position within Confederation would no doubt put an end to the anxiety that Quebec's constant opting-out has generated among English-speaking Canadians. Such a document would also recognize that Quebec fulfils its role best within Confederation through the full use of its constitutional powers, that it must be in complete command of them, and that it can either delegate them or accept intervention only in times of national emergency. Then no one need worry about concessions to Quebec or the dictatorship of the French Canadians.

Hand in hand with this type of particular status there would have to be accepted two suggestions that were frequently made during the sixties. When the quarrel over Quebec's off-shore mineral rights occurred in the summer of 1965, Mr. Lesage rejected the federal government's offer that the Supreme Court of Canada should decide what level of government owns the right to exploit the wealth that may lie off the Canadian coastlines. Since, in his mind, the Supreme Court was the 'creature' of the federal government (which alone names its judges), it could not serve as the final court for constitutional questions. Consequently, he espoused the view that Canada should be provided with a constitutional tribunal made up of judges named by both the federal and the provincial governments. How this court would function has never been made very clear, but one can assume that it would become a sort of arbitration board.

The second suggestion recognizes that Quebec and the other provincial governments do not live in a vacuum. Governmental action at any level is bound to overlap and the provinces often cannot carry out their responsibilities without Ottawa's co-operation. For these reasons it was suggested many times during the sixties that the provinces should be officially consulted before the elaboration of the federal government's policies in many fields of jurisdiction. This idea has provoked no great trauma. It is already part of the Canadian way of doing things.

VII

Throughout the early sixties, French-speaking Canadians asked themselves if Confederation could continue to serve their purposes, while their English-speaking counterparts wondered what Quebec wanted. Unable to obtain satisfactory answers to either question, both groups were for the most part anxious about the direction in which the debate was leading them. Few Canadians, however, felt that the dialogue had lasted long enough or that the time had come to reach satisfactory conclusions.

So far none have been reached. A persistent sense of injury still permeates French-Canadian thinking on the subject, and exaggeration and distortion still accompany the *phrases ronflantes* of the most militant nationalists. Quebec politicians continue to reassess the agreements they have reached with English-speaking Canada and to insist that in certain areas they must retain exclusive jurisdiction. Many of their people are thus encouraged to view Quebec as an isolated spot in the universe and not as part of a universal order with varied cultural elements under one constitutional roof. In fact in the sixties one became aware that most of Quebec's spokesmen no longer had either the desire or the will to develop a close relationship with English-speaking Canada.

On the other hand, the majority of English-speaking Canada spent little time in the sixties trying to understand what equal partnership meant, let alone doing anything about it. Many, of course, sympathized with Quebec's aspirations to reform the province and its institutions. There was not much difficulty there, for many people outside Quebec felt that Quebec was 'catching up' with them. The trouble occurred when Quebec challenged Ottawa's traditional role in Canadian affairs and at the same time began to look seriously at the plight of those French-speaking citizens who lived outside the frontiers of the province. Few people in English-speaking Canada wanted to hear anything about particular status for Quebec, and fewer still seriously thought of changing their provincial constitutions to provide schools and other facilities for the French-speaking population of their province. Such changes were not even made in New Brunswick, where 49 per cent of the population is now French-speaking. In fact, in that province the population has also split along linguistic lines over the government's bold plans to fight poverty. In Saskatoon, French-Canadian parents organized a strike to force the Roman Catholic School Board of that city to grant a few hours during which the language of instruction would be French, but for the moment at least it has not been successful. Elsewhere the story was the same, although Ontario announced a sort of cultural exchange program with Quebec in 1966.

So popular was anti-Quebec feeling in western Canada that Mr. Diefenbaker did not hesitate during the election of 1965 to capitalize on it to recover his political fortune. One wonders also if Mr. Pearson's inability to obtain a majority in this same election was not due to an anti-French backlash as much as to his own failures of leadership.

Yet through the uproar of the bigots and the fears expressed by moderates, some sane voices were still heard in the sixties. There were some in Quebec who believed that French Canada could not limit itself to the banks of the St. Lawrence, for the glory of New France was that a few men had opened a continent and made possible a country stretching from sea to sea. There were also some in English-speaking Canada who worked tirelessly to convince their people that a Canada that did not take into account the duality of its heritage, and adjust to it, would not long endure.

In the early sixties Canadians gave themselves a flag which is their own, and prepared for a World's Fair which is a monument to their past and a promise of their future. In 1967 they will celebrate not only the beginning of a constitutional reality called Canada, but above all their willingness to live and build together. This will demand a degree of generosity of spirit that was often lacking in the first half of this most critical decade.

PART TWO

12. The Human Community

JOHN PORTER

Canada for the last one hundred years, like the United States for almost twice as long, has been conducting an experiment in the creation of a new society – a new nation – in the vast regions of North America. The American experiment – we must concede the word 'American' to the United States – was begun with a revolution which had clearly stated aims. These goals have been repeated continually, not only in school textbooks and by Fourth of July orators, but by great leaders such as Lincoln, Wilson, and Roosevelt, who inspired the people once more to believe in and strive for 'the American dream'. These charter values of liberty and equality, particularly equality of opportunity, are recurring themes in American culture, and provide goals towards which society strives, and in the light of which progress can be measured.

Canada did not start with a revolution, and therefore, unlike the United States, the charter values that guide it are not clear. With its counter-revolutionary past, prolonged colonialism, and monarchical institutions, Canada has not rejected the old European forms as Americans are said to have rejected the 'European Father'. Consequently people are judged more in terms of what they have achieved than of what they might achieve. This conservative climate has been reinforced by the efforts of Canadians to distinguish themselves from Americans. Hence Canadians have rejected republicanism as being essential to the creation of a new nation.

Canada has been described by S. M. Lipset as élitist rather than equalitarian in its values; that is, Canadian values tend to stress the superiority of those in élite or leadership positions rather than the equality of all persons because they are human beings. This tendency to value the differences of status and aristocratic modes has been reinforced by the fact that Canada has two charter groups speaking different languages. The emphasis on the differences between people rather than on their similarities as human beings has led to the 'mosaic' rather than to the 'melting-pot' as the basis of social integration.

Yet Canada is a twentieth-century democracy based on an industrial economy. It is more similar to the United States than any other country in the world. Canadians as often as not compare themselves with Americans. Millions of them, in the course of time, have gone to live in the United States. It is not the task of this paper to engage in an extensive comparative analysis of the two societies, but if Canadians make any judgements about how they have done in their first century, they are likely to make them in terms of North American standards, by comparing themselves with the American experiment. The social scientist can do the same thing.

We can ask to what extent Canada has become a coherent society in the new world; to what degree has there been a democratization of its social institutions by the provision of opportunity, particularly educational opportunity, and to what extent has industrialization provided opportunities for upward social mobility. Industrialization and democratization of society are concomitant social processes. Both may be impeded by the orientation to conservative values, to traditionalism: both may be served, as in the United States, by the values inherent in revolutionary beginnings.

Canada, one hundred years after Confederation, is a modern, urban, industrial society. About three-quarters of its population live in towns and cities that the official census defines as urban, that is, a centre with a population of 1,000 or more. Only one-tenth of Canadians live on farms, a small proportion considering the importance of agriculture in the past and the still-lingering ruralism in social images and popular culture. The census definition of an urban community is not very satisfactory, but there are other criteria by which Canadians can be considered city-dwellers. About one-half of the people live within the seventeen metropolitan areas ranging in size from Montreal with 2.1 million population and Toronto with 1.8 million, to St. John's, Newfoundland, and Saint John, New Brunswick, with almost 100,000 each in 1961.

About two-thirds of all the people live in two of the ten provinces. Ontario has 34 per cent of the population and Quebec 29 per cent. The four Atlantic provinces combined have less than one-tenth of the population. Two of the Prairie Provinces, Saskatchewan and Manitoba, share between them a further one-tenth. Alberta and British Columbia, like Ontario and Quebec, are provinces of growing economic and political power and prestige in Canada's industrial epoch. Most of the ten years between 1951 and 1961 were ones of rapid economic growth, when the Canadian population increased by 30 per cent to reach 18.2 million. This growth was not uniform for all parts of the country. During the same ten-year period Alberta's population grew by 42 per cent, British Columbia's by 40 per cent, Ontario's by 36 per cent, and Quebec's by 30 per cent. All the other provinces grew at a rate less than the country as a whole. Saskatchewan's population increase for the decade was only 11 per cent.

Differential rates of growth between the provinces and regions of Canada, such as that of the 1950s, has been the pattern throughout the twentieth century, except that the rapidly growing regions and provinces have changed. With the exception of the stagnation years of the 1930s when the population of Canada grew by only 10 per cent, the Atlantic provinces have grown in population at a rate far less than that of the whole country, a fact that marked the decline of those once proud and vigorous provinces to the low status of economically depressed regions.

For the rest of Canada there have been in the present century two important phases in population growth and economic boom. The first was the rapid development of the West, particularly the wheat economy in the first decade of the century, and the second was the rapid development of the industrial areas of Ontario, Quebec, and British Columbia during and after the Second World War. In the first growth period between 1901 and 1911, the population of both Saskatchewan and Alberta grew by more than 400 per cent compared to 34 per cent for the whole country. Ontario and Quebec were regions of slow rates of growth compared to the West, until the census of 1931.

Although for the first thirty years of the present century the Canadian West was growing faster than the East, the country as a whole was receding from a predominantly rural and primary producing way of life. Every census from the first in 1871 to the latest in 1961 has seen a steady decrease in the proportion of the total population – from 80 to 30 per cent – who live in rural areas. Even as the West was developing its wheat economy and the plains were filling up with Canadian, British, and European settlers, the cities of both the East and West were growing relatively more quickly than the rural population.

Canadians often think of themselves as a rural outdoor

people, and both their popular and their high culture tend to emphasize this, but throughout the present century there has been an inexorable economic push towards industrialization and urbanization. The First World War was the point of no return in this process of social and economic development. It was the ordering of the economy to the needs of war that marked the Canadian lift-off to industrialization. After the stagnation of the years following the First World War, the economic requirements of the Second World War provided a powerful second-stage booster in the same direction.

The Canadian community – in so far as an industrialized society can be said to have any community features – is no longer a rural and primary producing one. Perhaps one reason the idea of ruralism remains is because of the romance and drama of some of the primary producing sectors of the economy, such as the exploitation of oil in Alberta, the extraction of iron ore in the Ungava peninsula, and the opening up of the northern territories. As these exploitations are portrayed in picture-book accounts of what Canada is like, they leave the impression that Canadians are primary producers achieving great feats in breaking through mountain and across tundra, and gouging out seaways, canals, and dams. Some Canadians are primary producers and take part in these feats, more often accomplished with foreign capital and skills than with indigenous resources. The typical Canadian worker lives in a city in housing ranging from slums to suburbs. He rides the bus or commuter train to work or drives his car along the freeways that penetrate deep into the hearts of the large cities. It is this process of urbanization that characterizes the present developing Canadian community. Consequently Canada takes on many of the features, both pleasant and unpleasant, of any industrialized 'community'. There are concert halls and art galleries, and in larger cities a genuine theatre. At the same time there are increased rates of crime, suicide, and alcoholism, which are more or less 'normal' for the types of social structure that industrialization brings.

The growth of the Canadian population from 3.5 million

in 1867 to 18.2 million in 1961 and an estimated 20.8 million in 1967 has come more from natural increase than from net migration. (The natural increase is the excess of births over deaths, and net migration is the excess of immigrants over emigrants.) This is because Canada has lost almost as many people through emigration as she has gained from immigration. Nathan Keyfitz, in calculating the Canadian demographic equation of natural increase and migration, has estimated that in the one hundred years between 1851 and 1951, 19.4 million were born in Canada and 8.9 million persons of all ages died, leaving a natural increase of 10.5 million. The number of immigrants for the same period was 7.2 million, but the loss through emigration was 6.5 million, leaving a net migration of only 700,000 over a century.

The loss from emigration is striking and surely is of consequence for Canadian social structure. Canada has received large numbers of migrants for a temporary stay who have gone on to other places, most often to the United States, but also many have returned to their former homeland. At the same time large numbers of Canadian-born have left the country for the United States. There has thus been a very great moving around of the population, some coming in, some leaving, and some moving from one province to another, for interprovincial migration has always been high as economic opportunity has shifted from one region to another. Still others have moved off the farms into the cities.

The scale of these demographic movements suggests a weakness of ties within the human community of Canadian society, and as well a weakness of attachment to the physical and natural surroundings which have both beauty and drama. A coherent social structure requires close human ties, a sense of belonging, and a feeling of being different from others. These social-psychological relationships are difficult to trace in Canada. Obviously many of the people now living in Canada, both native-born and immigrant, have strong kinship links with both the United States and Europe. Whether these family ties with former homeland or possible future homeland are stronger or weaker than ties within Canada we do not know. In the absence of any extensive studies of the social consequences of these demographic movements, we can only speculate that they have a weakening effect on Canadian social life. Quite possibly they could also have a conservative effect, for by and large it is the young who migrate. They leave behind an entrenched and tradition-bound generation less desirous of change and less perceptive of the need for change. If the adventurous and bold find greater opportunities elsewhere there is a drain on the scarcest resource of any society, its human talent. This condition could be creating for Canada a very great problem of leadership at all levels of its institutions.

This peculiar demographic condition is not all that impedes the cohesion of Canadian society. In the early 1960s, as the centennial of Confederation approached, the country's great historical French-English bifurcation became increasingly pronounced and the major issue around which political power-holders and power-seekers made their moves. The lack of cohesion of which we have been speaking applies more to 'English' Canada than it does to French Canada. It has been estimated that there were about 65,000 French in Canada in 1763. There are now more than five and a half million. This growth of population is attributable almost entirely to natural increase, since immigration from France or French-speaking territories has been negligible. In addition to their natural increase within Canada the French supplied an emigration to the United States (these became the Franco-Americans of New England) of about 800,000 between 1830 and 1930. French Canada has always been a society of high fertility. In 1950 the French birth-rate was 32 per 1,000 compared to 24.5 per 1,000 for the non-French population. However, the more that French Canada assumes the characteristics of an urban, industrial society the less is the gap in the differential birth-rates. The French in Canada have created a culture of their own by living predominantly within one province, and by being isolated in language from the rest of North America. This culture has been dependent upon natural increase rather than immigration for its survival.

Other parts of this French culture besides high fertility rates were being threatened by the industrialization of French-Canadian society. The traditional culture of French Canada has been outlined in a variety of sociological studies. Its recurring themes were ruralism, church-centred parochialism, authoritarianism in church and politics, and a rejection of worldly acquisition of skills and economic gain. Consequently class lines within French Canada were clearly drawn. A small proportion of the population was educated in the humanistic, church-operated classical colleges, but masses of the people were poorly educated and lacked the skills for a modern industrial technology. (Actually the difference between English and French Canada in this respect was only one of degree, since Canada has relied very heavily on skilled immigrants.) The French, moving off farms and out of rural areas into the industrial system, became grossly over-represented in the low-status, unskilled, poor-paying jobs. Moreover, the values of the traditional culture tended to make them submissive workers in mines, mills, and factories. Their confessional trade unions lacked the militancy of their English counterparts. At the top a relatively small, educated middle and upper class supplied recruits to political and church élites who lived in contented coalition with English leaders. The political regime, authoritarian and corrupt, of Maurice Duplessis was the high tide of this French-English class relationship. In the late 1950s and 1960s the so-called quiet revolution took place that was to bring one of the most curious social contradictions of modern Canada – a society's leaders claiming to safeguard their culture by in fact rejecting it. The values upon which the quiet revolutionaries were making their appeal – equality of opportunity, political and educational democratization, laicization if not secularization of many of the activities which the Church controlled – were of an alien culture with their origins in the French and American revolutions, neither of which had much influence on French Canada. Anti-authoritarianism in politics and rationalization and efficiency in economic life were among the revolutionary values acquired from outside.

French intellectual and political leaders began to protest, with values borrowed from other cultures, the low economic status of French Canadians, and insisted that this inferior class position could be remedied if they were masters in their own house. The conflict of interests with the rest of Canada was expressed in terms of ethnic rights, the right of a 'nation' to control its own destiny. But the movement could equally be interpreted as a revolt against the old culture, where French-Canadian élites ruled in coalition with the dominant English.

By 1960, then, Canada had failed to create a coherent society. The two major ethnic components of the population, the British and the French, continued to live in separate linguistic islands. In addition, many ethnic groups other than British and French, as they came into the country, were encouraged to maintain ethnic solidarity and separateness. The ethnic fragmentation of Canada has been one of the outstanding features of its social structure. If there is any Canadian ideology, if Canadians can be said to stand for anything in general (as in general Americans can be said to stand for the charter values expressed in their revolutionary beginnings), it would seem to be the doctrine of unity through diversity.

Canadians have sought to create a society made up of many mutually exclusive sub-societies which must find a way to live together within one nation state. Strength or unity through diversity may or may not be a sociologically absurd doctrine, but in Canada it has become so, as the divisiveness of ethnicity has been reinforced by the political divisiveness of the federal system. Provincialism in politics is associated in some respects with ethnic differentiation, and so by 1960 in response to this dominant ideology the locus of political power had shifted from the central government to the provinces. The rejection of strong instruments of central government, and hence the rejection of a strong Canadianism, would seem to be an about-face from the intentions of the original founders of the country. If Canada was to be a new nation with a new purpose it was to be one with hyphenated citizens, who were expected to keep their ties to the lands of their forefathers and to live with dual loyalties. Canada, in official documents, does not even recognize itself as a nation in the sense that 'Canadian' can be an ethnic origin, despite the fact that Canada has existed longer than many modern European nations whose people are considered to have an ethnicity, and who are recorded as such when they come to Canada.

The ethnic fragmentation, the cherished mosaic, has been the most important stumbling-block to a coherent society. All the ethnic groups in Canada are now minorities. The largest in 1961 were the British with 43.8 per cent of the total. In 1901 they were 57 per cent, but throughout the century their proportion has been declining. Many of the British retain in Canada the historic divisions of the British Isles, even though the majority, probably the vast majority, of them have never been near Britain. England, Scotland, or Ireland are still for large numbers of Canadians 'the old country', romantic ideas of which have been kept alive through voluntary associations promoting folk cultures and ritualistic activities such as Highland games, and St. Patrick's day and Orange parades. The transplanting of these rivalries and differences of the British Isles was an important contribution to ethnic pluralism. It is difficult to see how people whose ancestors sang 'Loch Lomond', or 'Saturday Night in the Old Kent Road', or 'The Harp That Once Through Tara's Halls', but who themselves have been Canadian for several generations, can be culturally different. But the fictions are maintained, and the cue is given to all other groups to do the same thing. Considered separately, the English become a minority of 23 per cent, the Scottish of 10.4 per cent, and the Irish of 9.6 per cent. That leaves the French as the largest minority with 30.4 per cent. All the other non-

British, non-French ethnicities made up, in their great variety, 25.8 per cent of the population. They were German (5.8 per cent), Ukrainian (2.6), Dutch (2.4), Italian (2.5), Polish (1.8), native Indian and Eskimo (1.2), Jewish (1.7). The remaining 8.5 per cent of the population were of many origins, although none of them made up more than 1 per cent of the total.

When members of a society are differentiated in some way, as Canada's ethnic groups are, it usually serves some sociological function or purpose. For example, the differentiation of men and women leads in all societies to appropriate social roles or tasks for each sex. Sex is, however, a visible biological difference. Often quite spuriously other visible differences—skin colour, for example—are taken to mean differences of other qualities such as intelligence, moral worth, and so forth. These erroneous ideas form the basis of privilege and exploitation, both of which are being broken down only very slowly on a world-wide basis in the latter part of the twentieth century.

Ethnic differences are differences in language and culture, and only to a minimal degree, as far as most of the European ethnicities are concerned, are there visible physical differences. Differentiation into ethnic groups can lead, like sex differences, to discrimination in the assignment of social roles. Some groups are believed to have particular qualities which suit them more for some social and economic activities than for others. One of the costs of cultural or ethnic pluralism seems to be that the diversity becomes structured into class arrangement, into higher and lower ethnic groups. It is not possible here to go into the extensive literature that debates the relative merits of 'melting-pot' assimilation or cultural pluralism. Pluralism means the creation of sub-societies and sub-cultures which often develop into a class structure. This class structure may not always be inevitable, but Canadian pluralism appears to have developed that way.

Ethnic differentiation results from conquest or from migration. In the first case the conquerors subdue the conquered and put them into inferior positions, often retaining the indigenous class structure as an instrument of rule. The British conquest of Canada kept intact some of the authority structure of New France, particularly the Church. In the second case, through immigration restrictions, the host society lays down the conditions of entry, selects those to come in, and determines what they should do. The idealist would ask if it must always be so or whether the principle of equality can ever assert itself over the ethnocentricity which leads to invidious distinctions. Unlike the American value system, which has always emphasized the idea of equality of peoples within a new nation, the Canadian value system has stressed the social qualities that differentiate people rather than the human qualities that make them the same.

Canada has always had its preferred and less-preferred sources of immigrants who, as they have arrived to work, have ended up at different levels of the occupational world. The British have always provided a large number of skilled and professional immigrants. On the other hand, Ukrainian peasants were important as settlers to take on the forbidding task of opening up the western prairies, as Italian peasants were an important source of construction labour in the period after the Second World War.

It is to be expected, particularly if they do not speak one of the two 'official' languages of the country and in addition have a low educational level, that newcomers would assume a low status until they, or what is more likely, their children, fitted more into the host culture. However, the entrance status of the various groups tends to harden and becomes perpetuated over generations. This condition leads to a particular distribution of the various groups in the occupational world.

In one study Professor B. R. Blishen derived from census data an occupational class scale based on average earnings and average years of schooling. In this way he ranked 343 occupations in the 1951 labour force. He then sought to show how the various ethnic groups in the labour force were distributed through this occupational class scale. He discovered that the British were over-represented in the higher-level occupations and under-represented in the lower. The French, on the other hand, were under-represented in the higher-level occupations and over-represented in the lower. There were relatively fewer British as the occupational scale was descended, and there were relatively more French and more of all the other ethnic groups. Jews were the only group who followed the British pattern. They were over-represented in the top occupational levels, because of the frequency with which they were found in the learned professions. This high occupational status represented a great achievement for the Jewish group, because many of the parental generation came to Canada as very poor immigrants and worked in low-status, factory occupations. The great emphasis on learning in the Jewish culture resulted in high educational levels for the second and third generations. Such a pattern does not seem to have been the case with the other non-British, non-French groups. This distribution of Jews in professional occupations should not, however, become confused with power, because Jews very rarely get to the very top positions in either the economic or political system.

With the growth of industrialization the French have consistently dropped in terms of occupational status; that is, their over-representation in low-status occupations has increased relative to all other groups with the exception of the Italians. Even in Quebec where the French made up about eight-tenths of the labour force in the 1960s the same differences in occupational levels were to be found. Thus the opportunities for advancement that came with the industrialization of Quebec were not equally distributed between the English and the French. There is little doubt that these marked differences in status levels were an important ingredient of the quiet revolution.

The relationship that is here being sketched between ethnicity and social class, as measured at least by occupational level, has been clear to any sophisticated observer. The French-English difference in the class structure has been a literary theme, and also the subject of important sociological studies such as E. C. Hughes's *French Canada in Transi-*

tion. One cannot live in Canada for long without noticing the social levels of the different groups, for among other things it leads to residential segregation, with particular groups living in isolated community-like sub-cultures. In large Canadian cities the British will be over-represented in high-status occupations, and certain other ethnicities, depending on the region, will service them from lower-status jobs. An interesting example is the low-status jobs occupied by the French in Ontario along the Quebec border where the French are over-represented among unskilled labourers and in restaurants, laundries, and other types of low-status service occupations. In other regions of Canada there are similar class-like characteristics of inter-ethnic relations, although the groups will be different because of their varying regional distribution. In 1951 about four-tenths of all those of European origin lived in the Prairie Provinces and one-third in Ontario, but only one-tenth lived in Quebec and the Atlantic provinces combined. Two-thirds of the Ukrainians and six-tenths of the Scandinavians lived on the prairies. Manitoba, Saskatchewan, and Alberta, with about one-fifth of the Canadian population, had more than two-fifths of those of European origin in Canada. Alberta and British Columbia, with about one-seventh of the population, had almost half of those of Asian origin. More than one-half of all Italians in Canada lived in Ontario urban areas.

In some respects this regionalism of ethnicity is a reflection of the different groups' attachment to agriculture. With the relative decline in the proportion of the labour force in agriculture some ethnic groups have moved out of this occupation more than others. In the 1960s the Germans, Dutch, Scandinavians, and East Europeans were over-represented in agriculture as they always have been in Canada. The British have been under-represented. The Jewish and Italian groups are almost entirely urban. It should be noted that with the dramatic fall from nineteen to twelve per cent of the male labour force in agriculture during the 1950s, no group had more than one-quarter in agriculture by 1961.

Canada had in 1961 an aboriginal population of about

192,000 Indians and 12,000 Eskimos, making up together a little more than one per cent of the total population. About three-quarters of all Indians lived on reserves. The Indians and their reserve system are administered by the federal government. To be an Indian for the purposes of the Indian Act, and thus to be entitled to the benefits or otherwise of the reserve system, the individual must have Indian paternity. Indian maternity and white paternity defines the individual as Métis. No one really knows how extensive this marginal group is, but some estimates are as high as 80,000. They are probably the most distressed of all Canadians. Many of them live on the edges of reserves, but are not of the reserves. Similarly they are rejected by the white communities when they seek a place in the white economy. The welfare and educational benefits provided the Indians are denied the Métis, since not being Indians they are the responsibility of the provinces in which they reside. Their low level of education makes it difficult to integrate them into the industrial economy. In their social no-man's-land they were perfect objects for the war on poverty which was announced in 1965.

Government officials make great claims about what has been done for the Indians, and professional anthropologists, more often than not, are extremely critical of government policies. Many Indians themselves place a high evaluation on their own cultures, and wish to retain within the reserve system their treaty rights. This attitude is, of course, consistent with the ideology of diversity. However, no assessment could ignore the fact that native Indians are, after one hundred years of the system, at the very lowest end of the the occupational ladder. Almost half of them, by far the largest proportion of any group, were in 1961 in low-level primary and unskilled occupations. Judged by the Blishen scale of 1951, 85 per cent were in the lowest two classes.

While Indians, from the time that treaties were made with them, have in the main lived in bands on reserves, the Eskimos have come into contact with white civilization much more recently. In earlier times they had only sporadic contact with fur-traders or white missionaries. In the post-

Second World War period of northern military installation and mineral exploitation they have increasingly been absorbed into the white man's economy, primarily as unskilled workers. Thus many of them have become transformed in a very short time from nomadic hunters to wage-earners living in settled communities and sending their children to school. The Eskimos have no treaties with the government of Canada, but are full-fledged citizens, although unlike their white fellow citizens they are the object of the paternalistic policies of a remote government department in Ottawa. Many observers have suggested that such a guided democracy has had the effect of destroying a proud people's native skills of living off the hunt and surviving in the most brutal climate in all the world. It is unlikely that those who express such conservative views would ever themselves want to live such a life, dependent on the caribou for their bodies' needs and the itinerant, dog-sledding missionary for their souls'. Obviously many of the Eskimos do not prefer it. Given time the Eskimos could be integrated into Canadian life, while the reserve system could prevent the Indian from ever becoming so integrated.

Although the transition to an industrial economy has been going on throughout the present century, the change was accelerated in the period following the Second World War. The development of an industrial economy brings changes in the occupational structure of the labour force. In 1901, 40 per cent of the labour force worked in agriculture. The proportion dropped slowly until 1951 when it was 20 per cent, but by 1961 it had dropped to 11.5 per cent. During the 1950s the off-farm migration was about 40,000 per year. In 1961 there were 481,000 occupied farms, a loss of 142,000 since 1951, and the farm labour force fell by 340,000. Saskatchewan, the centre of Canadian wheat production, felt the changes with particular force. It had lost 100,000 of its farm population in the four years preceding 1960. By 1961 only about one-third of the Saskatchewan population lived on farms, and the government estimated that something like

7,000 people would be leaving Saskatchewan farms each year during the 1960s. Although farming was of a different type in Quebec and Ontario, similar changes were taking place in the agricultural labour force and in farming as a way of life.

Across the country the number of farms declined, but the average size of farm increased from 279 to 358 acres between 1951 and 1961. As well, farming methods were becoming more scientific and more mechanical, and often involved large-scale corporate farming. With these changes farmers and farm managers required higher levels of technical and managerial skill.

Along with the decline of farming as an occupation has gone a relative decline in the importance of other primary occupations such as mining, logging, and fishing. There has been, that is, a shift out of primary producing occupations into more skilled occupations. The proportion of a society's workers engaged in occupations such as services and commercial activities compared to those engaged in the primary occupations is often taken as a measure of economic progress. If for comparative purposes the United States is taken as the most advanced industrial society, it had in 1955 14 per cent of its work force in primary occupations and 52 per cent in tertiary occupations. At the same time Canada had 21 per cent in primary occupations and 46 per cent at the tertiary level. A similar way of looking at the labour force as it changes to an advanced industrial level is to trace the changes in the proportion of those in the goods-producing industries with those in the service-producing industries. Again on this criterion the 1950s was a watershed period for Canada. In 1951, 58 per cent of the labour force was engaged in goods-producing industries, and 42 per cent in service-producing industries. By 1963 almost the reverse situation applied. Less than half the workers (45 per cent) were producing goods while more than half (55 per cent) were producing services.

Yet another way of measuring these changes is by examining the changing proportions of the labour force engaged in non-manual and in manual occupations. Between 1901 and 1961 the non-manual and service occupations rose from 23 per cent of the labour force to 50.5 per cent, while the manual occupations, including agriculture, fell from 72.2 per cent of the labour force in 1901 to 41.8 per cent in 1961. The agricultural occupations by themselves, as we have seen, dropped from 40.3 per cent to 11.5 per cent over the same period. Thus the manual occupations, excluding agriculture, remained almost steady, moving only from 31.9 per cent in 1901 to 30.3 per cent in 1961. Although it is difficult to measure, there is little doubt that at each of these levels the skill content of most occupations was more advanced than formerly. The non-manual white-collar occupations have grown because of the increased number of professional, managerial, and clerical personnel required as the economy becomes more industrialized. These components of the labour force were increasing at a rate greater than others.

Although it is not possible here to extend the analysis into the differences between the male and the female labour force over the period (we have had to consider the two parts of the labour force as one) it is important to realize that women have an important labour-force role in an industrialized economy. There is probably a dual process here: women can acquire as easily as men many of the skills that an industrialized economy requires beyond those for which they have been traditionally trained, such as teaching, nursing, stenography, and the like. They also become important second-income earners, so that their families can enjoy the higher standards of living that industrialization brings. There seems to be in all industrial societies an increased tendency for women to enter the labour force. In 1901 in Canada only 12 per cent of women of working age were in the labour force, that is, working for pay, while in 1961 the proportion was 30 per cent. In the 1950s and '60s the female labour force was growing at a faster rate than the male. Almost half the women who are working in the 1960s are married. The fact that the increase in the female labour force has been greatest for women over forty years of age suggests that the developing pattern is for women to return to the labour force when their major child-rearing activities are completed or have been handed over to other agencies such as the school.

It is important to consider some of the social changes that are associated with these basic changes in the economy and in the occupational structure. In very general terms, despite the nostalgia of some for the old ruralism, industrialization represents progress, particularly in terms of higher standards of living, and a more widespread appreciation of culture, lengthening of life, control of disease, reduction of the working day, and, most important of all, higher levels of education. But there are many other benefits as well. Philosophers, of course, will dispute the definition of progress in such empirical terms as here suggested, and others will point to increased rates of deviant behaviour such as crime, suicide, and mental disorders as evidence that industrialization brings a toll of human casualties. It is doubtful, however, that given a choice a majority of Canadians would want to return to the kind of life that went with earlier periods of industrialization or the old ruralism.

Industrialization represents a general upgrading of the labour force which has become richer in skills than formerly because of the increasing number of skilled and professional workers. Since low birth-rates prevail in the higher occupational groups, the skilled and professional classes, even if they replace themselves, do not supply enough recruits to fill all these emerging jobs. Consequently new skilled and professional workers either must be recruited from formerly unskilled lower classes, or they must be imported from some other society. Industrialization makes such demands for skilled technical and professional workers that all industrial societies have had to revolutionize their educational systems. Earlier phases of industrialization brought universal secondary education. In the present phase of industrial growth, further development of the system and even its survival as an independent entity depends on the provision of tertiary-level education, including not only university but various forms of technical sub-professional training beyond high school. It is possible, and this is in fact what Canada has done, for a society to rely so heavily on outside sources for skilled and professional workers that it can neglect, at least for a time, its own educational resources.

Industrialization, then, constitutes an opportunity for large numbers to move upwards in the class structure. This process sociologists call upward social mobility, that is, the condition in which individuals are better off or have higher status than their parents. Upward mobility is the social counterpart of the upgrading of the labour force. The educational level of the population, then, can be considered the single most crucial measure of capacity for industrial development. Educational purists are often upset at measuring the advantage of education in these practical market-place terms, but there is no basic conflict between the civilizing and humanizing effects of education and the role that education has in providing skills and technology. The long historical trend has been for these to work together to make for general social progress.

Industrialization has a further important social consequence. It cannot be fully exploited as a form of economic activity without a democratizing of the society, because it cannot rely on a system of privilege as the basis for recruitment to occupations. For example, if education is costly it becomes available mainly to those who can afford to pay for it rather than to those who could, because of their ability, make the most use of it. To survive and develop, an industrial society must search out and train its human resources, particularly in a period of intense international competition for talent. Migration statistics show for the last decade a tremendous transfer of skilled and professional workers from one country to another. To compete with other countries requires policies directed at the democratization of education. We will now try to assess Canadian achievement in the light of these requirements of industrialization and democratization.

By any measure Canadian educational systems were seriously inadequate for the great industrial development of the post-Second World War period. In 1951, at the threshold of this development, more than half of the men in the labour force (55 per cent) had no more than an elementary-school education. About one third had some high-school, and less than a tenth had some university or other tertiary-level training. Women in the labour force were better educated than men, and this is probably because there has been a much closer link between schooling and traditional female occupations. Even in the 20- to 24-year age groups of males in 1951 at least half had no more than elementary school. There was some improvement in educational levels by the time of the 1961 census, but the changes were minimal, a continuation of the slow trend of improvement of the last fifty years. There was no indication that Canadians generally or their leaders in particular were aware of the critical needs of the educational system. By 1961 the proportion of males in the labour force with elementary-school education only had dropped to 44 per cent. But for the important age group 20 to 24, who would be in the labour force for the next generation, the proportion with elementary school only was still as high as 31 per cent. This lower third had very poor prospects indeed in the complex occupational world of the 1960s and the future. It is doubtful that they even had the basic skills for retraining. A large proportion of this under-educated group were the off-farm migrants who ended up at the bottom of the new class structure that was developing in the large cities.

These educational deficiencies, as would be expected, were not uniform for all provinces, regions, or groups. Newfoundland in 1961 had 58 per cent of its male labour force 25 to 44 years old with only elementary education. New Brunswick had 56 per cent; Quebec and Prince Edward Island both had 51 per cent; Saskatchewan, 42 per cent; Nova Scotia, 41 per cent; Ontario, 39 per cent; Manitoba, 37 per cent; Alberta, 34 per cent; British Columbia, 22 per cent. There were important differences in the relationship between ethnicity and school attendance. In 1951 just half of the age group 5 to 24 years were in school. By 1961 the proportion had risen to 68.3 per cent. The ethnic distribution of those in school in this age group is striking. The Jewish group had 84.8 per cent, a fact which further confirms the high value that Jews place on education. In descending order they were followed by Asian, 73.6 per cent; British, 72.3 per cent; and Scandinavian, 69.1 per cent. Less than the national proportion of 68.3 per cent were the Dutch with 67 per cent; German, 65.6 per cent; French, 64.1 per cent; Italian, 61.7 per cent; native Indian, 54.8 per cent. All other European groups combined, as they were for this census tabulation, had 70.1 per cent.

The levels of education in Canada that have just been reviewed and the attitudes to education that must lie behind these statistics cannot be separated from another major divisive element in Canadian society, that is, religious differences. As though ethnic diversity were not enough, religious divisions impose additional strains on unity. Moreover, religion and ethnicity are often interwoven to constitute the vital components of religio-ethnic sub-cultures. In 1961, 46 per cent of the population was Catholic. Catholics in Canada, as elsewhere, have always claimed the right to control education for their children, and the subject has long been a contentious issue in Canadian politics. Education falls within the jurisdiction of the provinces, and provinces vary in the extent to which separate Catholic schools are supported through taxation. Whether Catholic schools raise money on their own or receive public funds, they have always been impoverished, relative to public, tax-supported schools. If the educational rights of Catholics are a liberty they are entitled to enjoy it would seem to be a liberty denied by inadequate financial support. In Quebec, where 88 per cent of the population is Catholic, the former low educational levels did not spring from constitutional or political disadvantage but reflected the traditional values of French-Canadian society. The low occupational levels of the non-charter ethnic groups in Canada are a reflection, not only of their minority ethnic-group status, but also of the fact that many of the groups are predominantly Catholic. The problem of providing a highly skilled industrial labour force is made more difficult because many values about education are imbedded in these religio-ethnic sub-cultures.

The inadequacy of the educational system to meet the demands of an increasingly complex work world was counter-balanced by a heavy importation of skilled and professional workers. Between 1953 and 1963, according to the Economic Council of Canada, 80,000 professional and highly skilled workers came to Canada from outside North America. About three-fifths of these professional and skilled workers were British, a fact that shows the tendency for the occupational level of the different ethnicities in the immigrant labour force to correspond to the occupational levels of the ethnic groups already in Canada. Large numbers of unskilled workers, for example, came from Italy during the same period.

Reliance on immigration for some professions is striking. Of all the physicians and surgeons working in Canada in 1961 almost 20 per cent had immigrated in the preceding five years. For engineers the proportion was 25 per cent, for architects about 34 per cent. Calculated in a different way, between 1953 and 1963 the number of engineers entering Canada was equal to 73 per cent of the number graduated by Canadian universities. For architects it was 141 per cent, for physicians and surgeons 53 per cent. In one estimate made by the present writer about one-third of all the new professional occupations that came with the industrial expansion between 1951 and 1961 were filled from immigration, and about one-half of all the new skilled and technical manual occupations were also filled from immigration.

Up-grading the skill levels of the labour force was taking place by heavy reliance on external recruitment, since Canadian educational systems were not geared to the needs of the industrial economy. This cultural lag reflected the low evaluation of education within the society. Canadian families were not transmitting positive attitudes and values about education to their children, and Canadian leaders were not putting the necessary emphasis on the need to stay in school. Nor were they investing enough resources in education.

These conditions applied particularly to tertiary-level education. Even in the 1960s Canadian university education was more expensive to students than it was in any other comparable industrial society. In 1962-3 in Canada, the charge to students through tuition income amounted to 26 per cent of university operating costs, compared to 9.9 per cent in the United Kingdom. A large proportion of this 9.9 per cent in the United Kingdom would have been met through state awards to students. In 1957-8 in a group of 364 publicly sponsored universities and colleges in the United States the proportion of costs paid by student fees was 8 per cent. For Canadian students the annual costs for a year at university were extraordinarily high, and the amount of money available for student awards was pitifully low. This persistent cultural lag in the full-scale development and democratization of tertiary-level education could be considered a principal defect of Canadian democracy.

Democratization of education, that is, the making of all levels and types of education available to all according to their talents, is essential to the release of a society's creative potential. The technical, scientific, and social problems of a highly advanced industrial society are so complex that no society can afford to waste its human resources but must engage in a constant search for talent. There is little doubt that had their educational systems been more developed Canadians would have experienced much more upward social mobility than they have. They would also be in a much stronger position to meet the international challenges of the mid twentieth century.

As well as a release of their creative energies societies require leadership. Modern challenges are such that no society can afford to recruit its leadership groups on the basis of privilege. The requirement of upgrading the labour force which has been referred to earlier had its counterpart in the opening up of all the top positions to those who have the necessary ability. In the past Canada's élite groups, its top leaders in business, politics, the civil service, and the educational systems, have been recruited from a narrow base of middle- and upper-class British. At times middle- and upper-class French, particularly in politics and the Catholic Church, have shared power with the British. But the rest of Canada's ethnic groups are scarcely represented at all in the top decision-making positions. Thus the educational system should be called upon in the future not only to supply the necessary skilled and professional workers, but also to supply the very ablest at the top of all major social institutions.

Only in this way will Canada offer equal opportunities for all and make the best use of its human resources. And, in addition, if the official ideology recognizes a Canadian ethnicity, rather than only European or others, then, even though bilingualism and biculturalism should spread, the society would be more coherent and less fragmented than in the past.

13. The Land's Wealth

RODERICK HAIG-BROWN

People, not resources, make nations. But North America grew because Europeans came in search of land and raw materials, and North American settlement everywhere has followed the discovery and exploitation of natural resources. Canada's first settlers were European fishermen, attracted by the cod banks of the western Atlantic, and fur-traders were almost everywhere her first explorers. Agriculture followed inevitably upon settlement, spreading to the Great Lakes–St. Lawrence Lowlands. Behind the agricultural land was forest land, another resource to support settlement. Gold brought the first rush of population to British Columbia. In time, with the completion of the transcontinental railway, the prairie grasslands became open to use and settlement.

Canada's development has left her with a population largely distributed within two hundred miles of the southern border – in fact about half the population of the country lives in the Great Lakes–St. Lawrence Lowlands, little more than one per cent of the total land area, and it is here that most of the secondary industry and a high proportion of the diversified agriculture is concentrated. Northward for another two or three hundred miles from the border, or roughly to the fifty-fifth parallel, the country's resources are fairly well known and to some extent developed. Northward again there is an immense land mass reaching almost to the North Pole, whose resources, with few exceptions, have not yet proved sufficiently attractive to overcome the tremendous difficulties of climate and distance. It may well be that the eventual use of this area will call for a wholly different pattern of development from those patterns that have proved effective elsewhere on the continent.

The early history of resource use everywhere on the continent was one of ruthless exploitation, based on what has been called 'the myth of abundance' – the belief that water, soil, forests, wildlife, and fisheries were inexhaustible. The first official Canadian interest in natural resources was expressed in Sir John A. Macdonald's 'National Policy', which followed upon Confederation. It was directed towards development of the renewable resources – agriculture, forests, and fisheries – and its co-ordinating symbol was the transcontinental railway. Reflecting the concern for agriculture, the Experimental Farm System was founded in 1886. First stirrings of Canadian thought for the natural beauties of the land are evident in the establishment of five national parks between 1885 and 1907: Banff (1885), Yoho (1886), Glacier (1886), Waterton (1895), and Jasper (1907), all of them accessible by railway. This was reflected again provincially in Ontario's establishment of Algonquin Park in 1894 and Quebec's reservation of the Parc des Laurentides and the Parc du Mont Tremblant in 1895. But it was not until the first years of the twentieth century that resource management on a broad scale became a matter of practical politics in the United States, when the ideas of men like Gifford Pinchot and John Muir, powerfully supported by Theodore Roosevelt, began to reach the public conscience. The new concept of 'conservation' was soon quite widely accepted in Canada, and in 1909 Sir Wilfrid Laurier's government created a 'Commission of Conservation' which existed for twelve years. During this time the Commission maintained committees on forestry, lands, fish and wildlife, water, minerals and fuels, and public health. It published much valuable material, encouraged resource inventories, and began to examine the interrelationships and ecological balances of the various resources. Altogether, under the chairmanship of Sir Clifford Sifton, it appears to have been considerably in advance of the thinking and practice of its times. It aroused the jealousy of certain government departments, possibly through overstepping its co-ordinating function. Sifton resigned in 1918 and some two years later the Commission was dissolved.

Rational development of resources was largely forgotten during the boom years of the 1920s. The depression of the 1930s, with the disastrous drought in the Prairie Provinces, aroused a new interest in intelligent management, and in some important respects the decade was an era of rebuilding. The Reconstruction Conference of 1945, working from the foundation of the Rowell-Sirois Report, recognized many important principles of resource management and gave sharp encouragement to surveys and research in all the renewable resources. It was followed by a somewhat tentative Federal Resources Conference in Ottawa in 1954 and the very ambitious Resources for Tomorrow Conference in Montreal during 1961, out of which has developed the Canadian Council of Resource Ministers, representing the federal government and all the provincial governments.

All this should lead to increasing sophistication in resource management, with emphasis on regional and river-basin planning, better-financed research, and long-range consideration for the good of the country as a whole. At the same time, pressure for development has never been greater than it is today, and the scale of many projects to be considered in the second half of the twentieth century is such that errors of judgement or surrender to expediency can mean waste and damage beyond anything so far experienced.

II

The early settler's first concern is for agricultural land – if he is to stay and thrive in the new land he must find soil to grow his crops. Even before the settler, the explorer often carried seeds and domestic animals, which he would put ashore in the hands of the natives against his later return. Apart from the sheer necessity of growing food, there was the land hunger of the European immigrant. Ownership of land was wealth, honour, prestige, and security to one who had been tenant or labourer, anything but owner, in his own country.

In very broad terms, this was the pattern of Canadian settlement and development. Some men, with large or small capital, came directly to farm. Others came to work at whatever they could find, to save money and take up land. Still others were brought by dreams of gold or other wealth, but many of these remained to establish themselves on the land. Though massive immigration from Britain and Europe did not really start before the end of the Napoleonic wars, most of the good farmland of the Atlantic provinces and the Great Lakes–St. Lawrence Lowlands was settled well before Confederation. Agricultural settlement had even reached across the Canadian Shield to become precariously established along the Red River in Manitoba. But it was not until after Confederation, with the Homestead Act of 1872 and the completion of the transcontinental railroad in 1885, that the great western prairie lands were really opened up. In the early years of the twentieth century settlers moved into them in tens of thousands, not only from Europe but from eastern Canada and the United States as well. By 1912, 184 million acres of farmland had been surveyed in the Prairie Provinces and in 1913 over 150,000 settlers came to the West.

While eastern settlement was solidly based on long experience and on mixed farming and special crops made possible by ready markets, there was little thought of the future in western settlement. There were empty spaces to be filled and a single-crop economy could do this as nothing else could. Wheat grew well, found a ready market, and demanded only limited agricultural skill and knowledge from its growers. All that was needed was to put more land into production as quickly and simply as possible. Swamps were drained, water-tables were lowered, and the protecting prairie sod was ploughed under. Winnipeg, Regina, Saskatoon, Calgary, and Edmonton grew and prospered on prairie grain. At the same time, important technical advances were achieved. In 1886, William Saunders had been appointed director of the newly established Experimental Farms Branch of the Dominion Department of Agriculture. The Central Farm was then, as it still is, at Ottawa and subsidiary farms were at Nappan in Nova Scotia, Brandon in Manitoba, Indian Head in Saskat-chewan, and Agassiz in British Columbia. In 1894, Charles Edward Saunders, a son of the director, working with a cross-strain made in 1892 by his brother Percy, developed the famous Marquis wheat; it was followed by other successful varieties such as Ruby, Garnet, and Reward. Such early-maturing, disease-resistant grains, together with mechaniza-tion of seeding and harvesting, increased the tempo of devel-opment and production. Summer fallowing was practised more and more widely from 1880. The result of this intense specialization was a steady decrease of soil fertility and quality, the effects of which were fully felt for the first time in the dry years of the 1930s.

Under the British North America Act, both federal and provincial governments may pass agricultural legislation, with federal legislation taking precedence. Unhappily this position has been heavily eroded by court decisions over the years and the federal power is now exercised only under special conditions amounting to emergency. Legislation recognizing the emergency situation in the western wheat-lands came in the Prairie Farm Rehabilitation Act of 1935, which, with the Special Areas Act of Alberta and the Saskat-chewan Land Utilization Act of the same year, began the difficult task of bringing large areas under controlled management, restoring grasslands for hay and pasture, and encouraging crop rotation in place of the old grain-and-fallow sequence.

Since that time, the P.F.R.A. has been broadened to cover extensive resettlement, the establishment of community pastures, and water conservation in many forms. It has been extended to cover several parts of British Columbia, providing assistance in diking and irrigation projects, and it is now a permanent stabilizing force in western agriculture generally. More recently it has been a major force in the St. Mary and Bow River irrigation project and various reclamation projects, including that of the reclamation of one and a half million acres in the Saskatchewan delta now under development by the Manitoba government.

The Maritime Marshland Rehabilitation Act of 1948 provides assistance to Nova Scotia, New Brunswick, and Prince Edward Island in protecting and developing extremely productive marshlands that are subject to tidal flooding. The Canada Water Conservation Assistance Act of 1953 provides assistance to the provinces in any major water conservation project that is beyond the normal financial capacity of the local governments involved. Three projects have been undertaken in Ontario—on the upper Thames River, the Ausable River, and the Humber and Don rivers. An extensive flood-control project on the Fraser River in British Columbia is under consideration.

The network of federal acts is perhaps the clearest indication that agriculture throughout Canada has passed the pioneer stage and is entering upon an era of careful planning, considered management, and sophisticated development. Over the past thirty years it has become clear that agricultural land of good potential is limited and, while there is a steady world demand for agricultural products, stable prices and regularly increasing costs ensure that only efficient farming methods on sound land can succeed.

During much the same time there has been a steady drift of population throughout Canada from rural to urban areas.

The family farm, it has become clear, is no longer the highly desirable thing it was once considered to be, and the farm family is no longer the secure unit of Canadian life, the goal of immigrant and native-born alike. In a highly industrial-ized civilization, with ready material wealth and generally high industrial wages, farmers and their children no longer find the individuality, the sense of property, and the other advantages of farm life sufficiently attractive. On the farm itself the cost of machinery and buildings and labour is high, and good farming practices call for substantial outlay. The modern farm is a significant capital venture.

These economic and social trends, which are by no means confined to Canada but reflect twentieth-century develop-ment everywhere, offer a still further opportunity for the efficient direction of Canadian agriculture and land use by both federal and provincial governments. The Agricultural Rehabilitation and Development Act (ARDA) of 1961, assented to by all ten provinces, provides the necessary legisla-tion for joint federal-provincial action in (1) alternative use of marginal or sub-marginal farmlands, (2) projects that will develop income and employment opportunities in agricul-tural areas, and (3) projects for the development and conser-vation of the soil and water resources of the country. Up to March 31, 1966, $43.6 million had been committed for ARDA projects; of this about $24.9 million had been spent. Some of the funds were spent on research projects, mainly involving inventories and potential rural developments, but the majority have been applied directly to rural development, alternate land use, community pastures, and soil and water conservation. Parliament has also established a Fund for Rural Economic Development of $50 million which is being administered by the Agricultural Rural Development Branch.

ARDA quite clearly reflects a major change in the nation's way of life and the national policy towards agriculture. The shift from rural to urban living is a fact and its causes are obvious. Yet agriculture remains, and always will remain, a vital part of the national economy, and it is therefore essential that farm incomes and living conditions be comparable to those of the cities. The way to this seems to be through larger and more efficient farm units, conversion of marginal farmlands to other uses such as forestry and watershed protection, planning and consolidation of rural communities, and steady improvement of services. At the same time, the general welfare of the country demands that every effort be made, through education, information, and the provision of opportunities, to ensure that those who leave agriculture find useful and satisfying employment.

There is, of course, new farmland still to be developed in Canada, mainly in the West. Total reserves of land considered potentially suitable for agriculture are usually shown as between 40 and 50 million acres, 24 million of which are in the Prairie Provinces, 10 million on the Canadian Shield, 4½ million in the Appalachian Region, 2 million in British Columbia, and 1 million in the Arctic and sub-Arctic. The total of agricultural acreage in the St. Lawrence Lowland–Great Lakes region is declining, partly through the withdrawal from marginal lands and partly through urban expansion. In the five years preceding 1961, decrease in total farm area in British Columbia and the six eastern provinces exceeded the increase in the Prairie Provinces by nearly 1½ million acres. The total number of farms in Canada has decreased from the high point of 732, 000 in 1941 to 480,000 in 1961.

Total farmland in Canada is considered to be a little over 170 million acres, of which rather more than 100 million are rated as improved farmland. Of the improved land about 60 per cent is likely to be under crops in any given year, about 40 per cent in pasture and summer fallow; of the acreage under crop, approximately 50 million will be in grain and fodder crops, 10 million in tame hay, and a little over 2 million in all other crops, including potatoes, tobacco, sugar-beets, vegetables, and fruit.

Canada is significant in world grain markets, producing about 6.6 per cent of the total crop of wheat, oats, and barley from about 5 per cent of the world acreage in an average year. She exports farm products worth about one billion dollars annually, including substantial quantities of beef cattle and meat, dairy products, tobacco, flax-seed, rape-seed, and oil-seeds, though wheat accounts for more than half the total value.

The federal government has operated experimental farms for a period of more than seventy-five years. At the present time there are nine federal Research Institutes engaged in basic work, with four Research Laboratories and ten Regional Research Stations. Twenty-six Experimental Farms and twenty substations are scattered through the provinces and territories.

The provinces support this federal work with agricultural services of various types, including extension departments that reach directly to the individual farmer. Agricultural training at university level is available in all provinces. Universities in Quebec, Ontario, and the four western provinces have degree-granting courses, and postgraduate facilities are available in most of them. While it is true that the necessity for intricate federal-provincial political arrangements has slowed Canadian development and prevented such natural growths as the U.S. land-grant colleges and the Co-operative Extension Service, the country has a strong frame of organization that can become much better co-ordinated. Under ARDA, research emphasis will shift from such matters as production, marketing, and home economics, to broad rural economic and social problems. Federal leadership should become stronger and at the same time more closely co-ordinated with provincial aims and desires.

Total mineral production in Canada, excluding fossil fuels, has increased from less than six million dollars in 1886 to well over two billion dollars today. In spite of its size, it has not been an easy increase; in fact it may well be true that more money has gone into the ground than has been taken out of it. The vastness of the country, difficulties of climate and transportation, the heavy overburden of forest and brush in many areas, have all combined to slow discovery and delay development. But the twentieth century is an age of minerals, and the years since the Second World War have seen a fivefold increase in Canadian production. There are good reasons to suppose that the remaining years of the century will see at least a comparable increase.

Canada has five main types of geological regions. The Appalachian region covers Newfoundland, Nova Scotia, New Brunswick, the Gaspé peninsula, and part of Quebec along the south shore of the St. Lawrence. The Plains regions include Prince Edward Island, the Hudson Bay Lowland, the St. Lawrence Lowlands, the great western plains through to the Arctic Ocean, and some of the Arctic islands. The Cordilleran Region covers the whole of British Columbia and the eastern slope of the Rockies. The Innuitian region extends from Ellesmere Island to Prince Patrick Island in the far north. The Canadian Shield runs from the Labrador coast, across northern Quebec and northern Ontario, around Hudson Bay and its islands, reaching massively across northern Manitoba and Saskatchewan to the Arctic Ocean and again to some of the Arctic islands. It is the main source of the country's mineral wealth, covers nearly half of the total land area, and remains only partially explored.

Gold brought the first rush of settlers to British Columbia just before Confederation (1858); coal-mining on a small scale began in that province a few years earlier and in Nova Scotia over a hundred years earlier. But in general, mining and minerals did not play a major part in the early settlement of Canada. The country's mineral wealth, for the most part, is of types that call for slow and painful discovery, costly and often risky exploration, and fairly sophisticated means of transportation. Development has grown with steadily increasing rapidity in the metal-hungry economy of the twentieth century and will inevitably continue to grow even more rapidly as technology makes new demands and at the same time provides readier access, more sophisticated means of search, and new methods of separating and recovering minerals.

The main burden of geological survey work has been car-

ried by the federal government ever since Sir William Logan
founded the Geological Survey of Canada in 1842. Formidable surveys were made on foot and by canoe during the
remainder of the century and the first two decades of the
twentieth century, and the major features of the land were
gradually revealed. In some instances important mineral
deposits, such as the Ungava iron-ore bodies, were found long
before they could be opened to use. After the First World
War float planes came to be used more and more, and by the
1930s exploration throughout the country, and especially on
the Shield, had become much more rapid and efficient. Air
photography proved a tremendous aid in mapping. In 1952
helicopters were first used in extensive reconnaissance of far
northern areas and it is now reasonable to suppose that the
enormous task of mapping the Canadian Shield will shortly
be completed.

This federal work is supported in all provinces by more
detailed geological exploration. Such modern techniques as
aero-magnetic surveys show anomalies that can be checked by
intensive ground exploration; this combination has already
yielded such important discoveries as the lead and zinc of the
Brunswick ore zone in New Brunswick in 1953, the American
Metal Company discoveries in 1954, and the Kennecot Copper Company and Texas Gulf Sulphur Company finds and
other discoveries in 1955.*

In addition to survey work, all provinces give important
assistance to prospectors and mining interests by technical
advice, identification of specimens, and assay work. Several
provinces conduct prospectors' schools and offer direct assistance by payment of grub-stakes or transportation or both.
Quebec, Ontario, Manitoba, and British Columbia have
special provisions for the construction of access roads and
trails to mining properties.

---

* Undoubtedly there are other and more recent discoveries, possibly
of equal or greater importance. A large iron-ore deposit was discovered under several hundred feet of limestone in Ontario, and the
Tasu iron-ore deposit (minor) in the Queen Charlotte Islands was
found through ground check of an aero-magnetic anomaly.

Though many mineral deposits were known and gold was important in British Columbia and the Yukon before the end of the nineteenth century, it was not until the start of the twentieth century that mineral production in Canada began to assume major proportions. The total value passed $50 million for the first time in 1900, doubled to $100 million by 1912, and reached almost $250 million in 1929, during a period of rapid growth after the First World War. Growth since the Second World War has been even more spectacular, rising from less than $500 million in 1946 to over a billion dollars in 1951 and over two billion dollars in 1962.

It is impossible to list all the major discoveries and developments that have played a part in this growth. Following upon the early gold discoveries in British Columbia, copper-gold was developed at Rossland and silver-lead in the Kootenays, where the great Sullivan mine still produces seventy-five per cent of the lead and nearly half the zinc mined in Canada. Nickel-copper became important at Sudbury, Ontario, in the late 1880s, and silver discoveries at Cobalt followed soon after. In 1909 the Porcupine gold-field was discovered, followed by the Kirkland Lake field in 1912; these two fields quickly made Ontario the leading gold-producing province and eventually raised Canada to her position as the second gold-producing nation in the world.

Growth continued steadily during the 1920s, with important copper properties at Britannia, at Copper Mountain, and near Anyox, all in British Columbia, coming into large-scale production. In Quebec, the Noranda copper mines were discovered in 1927 and the asbestos production of the Eastern Townships was increasing steadily. In Manitoba the Flin Flon copper mine began production in 1930 and the Sherritt Gordon in 1931. Pitchblende was discovered, also in 1930, at Labine Point on Great Bear Lake.

Although the thirties were by no means a time of general growth and optimism, the annual value of Canadian mineral production increased during the decade from about $200 million to $450 million, and the value *per capita* of population from $27 to nearly $50. It was the clearest possible indi-

cation of the strength and permanence of Canada's place in a
world making ever increasing and ever more complex use of
mineral resources. The scattered and diffuse nature of discovery gave firm promise that much could be expected of the
Pacific Cordillera and, especially, of the immense reaches of
the Canadian Shield.

This promise has been maintained and reinforced in all
the years since the Second World War. Gold discoveries at
Yellowknife in the Northwest Territories; high-grade asbestos and new copper discoveries in British Columbia; the
nickel-copper of Lynn Lake, Manitoba; uranium at Beaver-
lodge, Saskatchewan, and Blind River, Ontario; the massive
lead-zinc deposits at Pine Point on Great Slave Lake; development of great iron-ore bodies at Steep Rock in Ontario and
Knob Lake in Labrador – all indicate extensive mineraliza-
tion over a tremendous area. The Pine Point and Knob Lake
developments are especially interesting in that they justified
branch railways, 430 and 360 miles long respectively, thus
reversing the usual rule that remote resources wait upon the
availability of transportation.

Mining men are invariably among the first to point out –
and properly so – that undiscovered minerals are just that
– unknown as to location, quantity, quality, workability;
essentially non-existent except perhaps as geological possibilities or probabilities. The one and three-quarter million
square miles of ancient mountain roots that make up the
Canadian Shield are just rocks, some two thousand million
years old, with or without overlay of water or muskeg or
glacial drift, folded and faulted, scarred and altered, but no
more than that until shown to be otherwise by the miner's
difficult, costly, and hazardous techniques of search. A surface
showing of ore is that and no more until assays and stripping
and drilling have shown that it may be more. It is still not
a mine until far more extensive physical exploration has
proved a body of ore large enough and valuable enough to
support several years of operation; and during the years of
operation search must continue until the mine itself or available funds are exhausted.

One can consider, then, only the promise of favourable geology and favourable economic demand, but in these terms the possibilities of the Canadian Shield and, to a lesser degree, of the Cordillera seem immense. The Shield at present accounts for about seventy-five per cent of Canada's metal production, including more than ninety per cent of the gold, almost ninety per cent of the copper, over eighty per cent of the iron ore, and nearly all of the nickel, platinum, uranium, and cobalt. Yet most of the producing mines lie within three hundred miles of the Shield's perimeter. Geologists believe that this reflects relative accessibility rather than any geological peculiarity of this outer fringe. It follows, therefore, that the rest of this enormous area, having roughly similar formations, offers the mathematical probability of more or less similar discoveries.

It is generally considered that the exposed rock of the Cordillera has been fairly thoroughly prospected, except in the far north and in the more remote parts of the Coast Range. High elevations have limited exploration in many areas, and heavy overburdens of soil, gravels, broken rock, and forest have made prospecting very difficult in some of the more accessible areas. Again there is the mathematical and geological probability of significant new discoveries.

These probabilities are bound to be reinforced by the spread of settlement, by improved transportation, and by the steady growth of mechanical and technical skills and equipment. Finally there is the stimulus of constant increase in world demand for both metallic and industrial minerals and the likelihood of new uses and new demands, especially in the field of alloys. The main values of Canadian mineral production are in nickel, copper, iron, gold, uranium, asbestos, and zinc, with important quantities of lead, silver, platinum, salt, potash and sulphur. The annual value of a further fifteen minerals, including gypsum, cobalt, cadmium, magnesium, molybdenum, peatmoss, and barite, runs between one and ten million dollars. Smaller values of such metals as antimony, bismuth, columbium, tellurium, and tin must also be noted. This diversity is of considerable importance. Some minerals in limited demand today may become more important. Often recovery of a by-product mineral is of significance in the over-all operation of a mine. And the discovery of larger concentrations of at least some of the minerals is a clear possibility. Diversity may also be considered a factor in the stability of the industry as a whole.

Minerals are a wasting resource in the sense that they can yield themselves only once. Yet in a country with such immense mineralized areas as Canada has, the mining industry has great flexibility. New discoveries are a constant factor as the country opens under roads and settlement. Major discoveries permit the establishment of smelting and refining plants such as those at Trail in British Columbia, Flin Flon in Manitoba, Falconbridge in Ontario, and Noranda in Quebec. Steel mills using domestic ore, such as those presently planned in Quebec and British Columbia, are a further step in development. The final stage, in which the bulk of mineral production is put to use in domestic secondary industries, is dependent upon population growth or other readily available markets. In Canada today all these effects are operating in some degree and there can be little doubt that their total effect, in terms of mining discovery and mining operation, is cumulative. It is difficult to think of any nation in the world where mineral development shows greater promise of rapid and continuing growth.

About twenty-seven per cent of the total land area of Canada is classified as productive forest. The forest has been used since the days of earliest settlement and now supports a giant industry that accounts for thirty per cent of the country's total export trade, valued at over $1.7 billion annually. Ninety per cent of this total is in lumber, newsprint, and wood pulp. Canada is the world's leading exporter of lumber, and produces over half the newsprint of the western world.

The overwhelming bulk of this production is from the coniferous or softwood species that make up eighty-two per cent of the productive stands; about twenty of a total of some thirty species are commercially useful. The deciduous or hardwood species of commercial value are found chiefly in the central provinces and in the Great Lakes–St. Lawrence region, and to a lesser extent in the Acadian region of the Maritime Provinces. Sugar maple, beech, white elm, basswood, red ash, white oak, and butternut are among the important hardwoods. Predominantly coniferous forest reaches across the country from the Labrador coast to the Rockies and the Alaskan boundary in what is known as the Boreal forest region. White and black spruce and tamarack are characteristic of this region, mixed with balsam fir and jack pine in the eastern part and alpine fir and lodgepole pine in the west. British Columbia, with its high mountains and sharply differentiated rainfall areas, has four forest regions – Coast, Subalpine, Montane, and Columbian – in all of which conifers are predominant, from the Douglas fir, western hemlock, red cedar, and Sitka spruce of the coast to the alpine fir, lodgepole pine, and Engelmann spruce of the Subalpine region.

These immense forests are spread over nearly 1¾ million square miles. Almost one million square miles are considered to be producing merchantable timber and about two-thirds of this area is at present commercially accessible. The remaining 750,000 square miles, though not considered productive forest, have importance for water conservation, erosion control, and, in some areas, recreational purposes and the grazing of domestic stock.

The wide diversity of timber and terrain has naturally produced a great deal of variation in both logging methods and processing. In the east comparatively small timber and long, strategically placed rivers of fairly even flow favoured the use of horses and river-driving, and led to early development of the pulp-and-paper industry. The country's first wood-pulp mill came into production at Valleyfield, Quebec, in 1866, and was followed by mills at Sherbrooke in 1869 and Merritton, on the Niagara Peninsula, in 1887. By 1891 some twenty-three pulp-mills were in operation, seventeen in the province of Quebec, three in Ontario, two in Nova Scotia, and one in New Brunswick. Newfoundland, of course, was an important pulp producer long before joining Confederation, with large plants at Corner Brook and Grand Falls.

The first pulp-mill in British Columbia was built at Port Mellon in 1909 and is still in operation. An earlier paper-mill, built in 1894, was unsuccessful. Large trees and rapid, short-run rivers with wide fluctuation of flow encouraged early mechanization and extensive railway operations primarily for lumber production. Since the Second World War there have been rapid and important changes in both east and west. The power-saw has come into universal use, revolutionizing the basic woods operations of falling and bucking and greatly increasing output for manpower. The railways have given way almost entirely to trucks, and steam to diesel power. Ingenious and adaptable new machines on rubber tires or caterpillar treads have replaced the old steam donkey with its fixed spar-tree and heavy rigging, and, with well-planned roads, these new machines can reach out into timber stands previously considered inaccessible. Machines of the same type are rapidly replacing horses in the logging operations of eastern Canada and a steady increase of mechanization is to be expected in every phase of woods operations.

At least equal advances have been made in the use of wood during the post-war years. The trend, in both east and west, has been towards better planning of use. In British Columbia several large new pulp-and-paper plants have been developed and several more are in the planning or construction stage, both on the coast and in the interior. Generally these plants, some of which produce both kraft pulp and newsprint, are operated in co-ordination with sawmills, plywood plants and paperboard plants. Integration of this sort permits the use of inferior species and much smaller and lower-grade logs than simple sawmilling, and has materially reduced the enormous waste of the coast operations. In the east, sawmills are becoming larger and more centralized, with greatly improved machinery; this also is encouraging a trend towards large integrated plants which should result in much more efficient use of timber.

Forests are a provincial responsibility and this has led to

wide diversity in systems of tenure and management. Some ninety per cent of the timberlands of the country are still under Crown ownership, but the ten per cent under private ownership are, generally speaking, the most productive and strategically placed lands, producing about forty per cent of the total annual cut. British Columbia is generally considered to have the most advanced system of control and management in the Tree Farm licences that have resulted from the Sloan Commission reports of 1945 and 1955. The earlier railway operations called for substantial timber holdings by large companies. The Tree Farm system has permitted extension of these holdings by the inclusion of sufficient Crown land to sustain a large mill operation, provided that the entire holding is managed to balance cut against increment over a specified period. Other such holdings, consisting chiefly or entirely of Crown lands, have been granted to both large and small operators on the same basis of sustained yield. On the whole, this has worked strongly against the small operator, who cannot afford the long-term planning and capital costs involved and is now largely limited to contracting for the big companies or operating in the government-owned sustained-yield units known as public working circles. In spite of this seemingly successful effort at control, it remains true that the lower coastal forests are still being heavily overcut, while those of the interior are undercut.

Forest tenure in the eastern part of the country is much more varied, with thousands of small woodlot owners, as well as large-scale licensing of Crown lands. Legislation also varies widely among the several provinces concerned. Ontario has a particularly active replanting program under which some thirty or forty million trees are planted on Crown and private lands annually. Quebec and Ontario maintain outstanding forestry extension services. The Tree Farm movement attempts to interest private woodlot owners in sustained-yield management and has met with some limited success in the Ottawa Valley and in New Brunswick. Efforts have been made to discourage clear cutting (that is, total destruction of a stand rather than selection of mature trees) by such legislation as the Trees Act of Ontario, and the Small Tree Conservation Act of Nova Scotia. But it is extremely doubtful that any of the existing legislation really produces sustained-yield management on any effective scale.

It is not altogether surprising that forest management has not developed more strongly in Canada. Pulp and paper are and have been for some while the nation's chief export. In both east and west the forest industries are the backbone of the economy, and even today pulp-and-paper production is rapidly expanding to meet new markets – in fact, presently planned capacity may well exceed the demand of available markets in the near future, at least for some years. The immensity of the resource has always given an illusion of inexhaustibility and even today it can be pointed out that, according to available inventories, the allowable cut for the country as a whole is of the order of ten billion cubic feet, while the actual cut is only a little over three billion cubic feet. Unfortunately these figures obscure a maze of complexities that have an important bearing on the practical and economic aspects as well as on the wise and proper use of forest land. The land that is now being cut over and that has been cut over in the past is generally the most productive land, with the most favourable climate for regrowth; it is also the land closest to good markets, with the most useful and economical transport routes. Without this land in good heart and steady production, it is highly questionable that Canada can maintain her pre-eminence as a world exporter of lumber, pulp, and newsprint, even though normal improvements in transportation, machinery, and technology may permit expansion into new areas.

The federal government has no direct responsibility for forests, as it has for sea and inland fisheries, and no partial responsibility, as it has in agriculture. Although a federal Department of Forestry, with its own minister, was created in 1960, there is no clear federal forest policy and no strong federal leadership. So long as the present oversensitive attitude of the provinces towards the management and development of resources continues, there seems little likelihood that a strong federal attitude can be expected, and even less that it would be received with co-operation. Yet, left to themselves by virtue of the British North America Act, the provinces have scarcely achieved an impressive record. Almost without exception, they have tended to use the forests as a ready source of revenue for other purposes: as a means of attracting capital and providing wages, with little or no provision for research or management and, until recently, only nominal consideration for protection. Even a province such as British Columbia, whose boast it is that almost fifty cents of every dollar of income derives from the forests, is returning little more than a third of direct forest revenue and about one-eighth of total tax revenue from forest industries to its forests.

If the Canadian forest industry is to hold its high place in the Canadian economy and its relative position in world markets it is believed that the yield of Canadian forests must be doubled within the next quarter-century. Any such achievement seems highly unlikely without basic forest research on a scale not yet attempted anywhere in the country. There is at present, for instance, little real knowledge of forest ecologies or forest soils, and little work has been or is being done. There is no outstanding school of forestry in any Canadian university, though schools of forestry at the universities of New Brunswick, Laval, Toronto, and British Columbia do some research – the total research investment being shown at the Resources for Tomorrow Conference as $130,000 annually, a truly pathetic figure for an industry employing 300,000 persons with an annual payroll of $1.2 billion. At the same conference it was pointed out that the federal government of the United States employs nearly 1,000 professional research workers for 783 million acres of forest land, the United Kingdom 141 workers for four million acres, and Canada 323 for over a billion acres.

The inescapable conclusion is that Canadians have not yet learned a proper respect for their forests even as direct economic assets. Forests are, of course, very much more than this. In large measure the health of the forests is the health of the land. Properly managed forests are vital to soil and water conservation, serving even land where no trees grow; they can be managed to provide recreation, protect fisheries, grow perennial crops of wildlife, and provide valuable grazing for domestic stock.

It would be wrong to suggest that there has not been for some years past a growing awareness of these problems and others like them. But it has been slow growth, difficult to stimulate or encourage in a public increasingly insulated from the renewable resources by urban living. There can be little doubt that the provinces have largely failed in their responsibilities by preferring a ready source of revenue to sound forest management, by failure to encourage research, and by lack of imagination in developing public interest in the forests. Strong federal leadership is needed, especially in research and in the development of a clear-cut and effective philosophy of sustained-yield management. But no federal leadership, however enlightened and inspired, can succeed without a new order of thinking and a new sense of responsibility in the provincial administrations, where control of the resource rests. Education, still another provincial field, has an important part in this. No nation can expect outstanding achievement in forestry without outstanding schools of forestry in its universities, and no Canadian school of forestry is likely to become outstanding on present research budgets.

Canada has major fisheries resources on the Atlantic and Pacific coasts and lesser fisheries in the inland waters and the Arctic Ocean. All are fairly fully exploited and those of the Atlantic and Pacific coasts have been heavily worked over long periods of time.

It is difficult to differentiate in every case between a national and an international fishery. Inshore fisheries, those within enclosed waters or within the three-mile limit, are quite clearly national in the sense that vessels of no other nation can fish within those limits; but the fish stocks may, and often do, move out to offshore waters, beyond national control or protection. A nation may be protecting breeding and rearing areas of large stocks of fish that mature in the open ocean, exposed to the fishing operations of many nations. Or the advantage of nearness to the grounds and sheltered harbours may have established an ocean fishery that has been relatively secure from competition over a long period of history, only to be opened to other nations at some later time by advances in technology and transport.

Most of these things have occurred or are occurring in some degree in the saltwater fisheries of Canada. It follows, then, that management must depend to a large extent on the difficult field of international treaties and agreements. This is actually the case in several of the most important of Canadian fisheries, and the rapid improvement of technology in all the great modern fishing nations is steadily increasing the impact of international competition to the point where any stock not fully utilized is almost certain to be brought into question.

The cod banks of the western Atlantic have been an international fishery practically since their discovery by Cabot at the end of the fifteenth century; in the course of the sixteenth century they led to the first shore establishments by British and French fishermen and so to the first Canadian settlement. Today these same waters, off Newfoundland and Labrador and in the Gulf of St. Lawrence, still support an immense fishery, shared by vessels from Portugal, Spain, Norway, Denmark, France, Italy, Germany, Iceland, the United Kingdom, the United States, Russia, and Canada. This fishery is studied and supervised under the Northwest Atlantic Fisheries Convention of 1949 and regulated by the countries concerned on recommendations submitted by a commission established under the Convention.

On the Pacific coast, United States and Canadian fishermen have from the earliest times harvested the same stocks of halibut and salmon. Depletion of halibut stocks was recognized in the International Pacific Halibut Convention, subscribed to by the two countries in 1923. Common interest in certain salmon stocks was recognized under the International Pacific Salmon Fisheries Convention of 1930, for the purpose of protecting and managing the Fraser River sockeye salmon, extended to include pink salmon in 1956. A more recent form of competition, produced by the Japanese high-seas fishery for salmon of both Asiatic and North American stocks, is recognized in the North Pacific High Seas Fisheries Convention between Canada, U.S.A., and Japan, signed in 1952. Finally, the Great Lakes Fisheries Convention of 1954 between Canada and the United States is aimed at restoration of the seriously depleted fisheries of the Great Lakes.

This listing of international conventions, to which the International Whaling Convention and the North Pacific Fur Seal Convention could be added, gives some idea of the very large issues involved in protecting Canadian offshore fisheries. These are by no means the end. New nations have from time to time entered the Northwest Atlantic Convention. Russia without a doubt belongs in the North Pacific Convention. Fishing vessels are constantly being built larger, with more sophisticated gear and equipment, while mother ships, often with processing plants, reduce the need of shore-based installations. More and more nations are certain to reach out ever farther to search the seas for food for hungry populations.

The proposed Canadian twelve-mile offshore limit, especially if established beyond a line drawn from headland to headland on both coasts as has been suggested, would provide a significant measure of protection. But it would still leave many important fishing grounds along the continental shelf open to the fleets of all nations, and adequate means of international co-operation in management and control would still be necessary for the preservation of sustained-yield fisheries.

Canada ranks seventh among the fish-producing countries of the world and third among the fish-exporting countries. Atlantic cod and lobsters have long been important in the economy of the country, as have the five species of Pacific salmon. Both coasts have important herring fisheries, with annual catches of the order of 250,000 to 350,000 tons. Other significant species in the Atlantic fishery are haddock, flounder, redfish, mackerel, halibut, and several shellfish. After salmon and herring, the most important Pacific species is the halibut, with an annual yield of about seventy million pounds. Other groundfish have been neglected until fairly recently, but increasing numbers of draggers are now operating and some ten million pounds of sole are landed annually. Of the shellfish, crabs, clams, and naturalized oysters are the most important. Both coasts have stocks of some species that are at present little used, and further exploration may reveal others. Whitefish and lake trout are the most important species in the freshwater fisheries, with annual yields of twenty-five million and six million pounds respectively.

While most known stocks of the more valuable species are quite heavily fished and there is some local depletion, improved management, better distributed effort, and natural adjustment of stocks can still produce increased yields. At the Resources for Tomorrow Conference of 1961, W. E. Ricker predicted significantly increased landings by 1980 of such Atlantic species as cod, haddock, herring, flounder, mackerel, scallops, and oysters, and of Pacific sockeye, pink and chum salmon, Pacific halibut, herring, sole, crabs, and oysters. In fresh water, whitefish landings are expected to increase from twenty-five million to thirty-six million pounds.

Except in the province of Quebec, sea and inland fisheries are the responsibility of the federal government under the British North America Act. The federal government does in fact control and administer all saltwater fisheries except those of Quebec, but the provinces of Ontario, Manitoba, Saskatchewan, Alberta, and British Columbia administer their own freshwater species by agreement with the federal government.

Considering the size and diversity of the fisheries, the resource has been well protected and research has been outstanding. Management generally has been directed towards a free fishery, in which anyone could enter, and which has encouraged settlement on both coasts. For many Canadians, fishing has been and still is a seasonal or part-time occupation, combined with logging, farming, or trapping. Capital investment in processing plants has necessarily been fairly high, but in individual vessels and gear it has usually been low or moderate.

The effect of this policy on both coasts has been to emphasize labour rather than capital investment and has led to a static and unprogressive industry, highly inefficient in comparison with the development of other industries and consequently yielding a comparatively poor return to the individual fishermen. These effects have been known for some time. They are particularly severe on the east coast, where oportunities for other employment are few, long custom resists change, and long-established communities depend on the old ways. Poor returns make it impossible to find the necessary capital to permit expansion of operations and increased efficiency.

It has been pointed out that circumstances on the west coast are somewhat different. Here there is over-commitment of both capital and labour and correspondingly poor returns for both. In the salmon industry in particular there are enough boats and gear in the water to catch up every salmon that swims, and drastic controls have become necessary to protect breeding-stocks. In the course of a relatively short season (July to October) net fishermen are usually permitted to operate only two or three days a week. Here fairly drastic licence limitations would place less hardship on both communities and individuals than on the east coast and there is little doubt that some such system will shortly be adopted.

Prospects are not good for expansion on either coast unless Canadians build larger and better-equipped boats to compete with other nations fishing the offshore waters, or develop fisheries at present unexploited. While some larger and newer boats are coming into service on both coasts, the pace of change is slow and extensive development of new fisheries is unlikely without assured markets. The fishing industry, like the agricultural industry, calls for reduction and relocation of manpower and increased size and efficiency in its units of production if fishermen are to realize the same standard of living as other workers. This will not be achieved without strong and protracted government action and considerable expenditure of both funds and ingenuity.

There has been a phenomenal increase in fishing as a sport throughout North America during the post-war years. This is true of both freshwater and saltwater fishing, and in many parts of the United States the sports fishery catch of certain species has exceeded the commercial catch in both quantity and economic value. This is a factor of permanent and almost certainly growing significance. Inevitably, it will apply only to certain species and certain localities, but wherever it does apply the economic return of a sports fishery is so much greater than the return from similar quantities of commercially caught fish that the sports fishery must be very carefully considered. In some instances it should be possible to manage a sports fishery in such a way that it offers the alternative employment needed to reduce manpower in the commercial industry.

Though Canadian fisheries research has been of a high order under the Department of Fisheries and the Fisheries Research Board of Canada and in the universities, an enormous amount of fundamental research still needs to be done. Oceanographic research and general fisheries research on the high seas are essential, both for the discovery of new stocks and for the proper management of known stocks. Further basic research is needed for the proper management of the valuable anadromous (river-spawning) species, including the salmons of both coasts. There is real promise of increased production through stream control, stream protection, and the establishment of artificial spawning and nursing areas. High dams remain a constant threat to anadromous species and no useful solution is yet in sight. Stream pollution through municipal and industrial wastes and agricultural and forest spraying can be disastrous, but it is essential for the nation to bring these evils under control for many other reasons besides fisheries protection.

There is every reason to believe that the production of Canadian fisheries can be maintained and even increased under proper management, though the value of the fisheries in relation to the rest of the economy may be expected to decline. Some reduction of employment seems inevitable if living standards are to be improved and the industry itself is to be brought up to modern competitive levels.

Abundant energy is the most important single factor in modern technology. Until the turn of the century wood and coal, especially the latter, were the most important energy sources. Since that time oil, natural gas, and water power have gradually taken over. Since the Second World War the possibilities of nuclear power have become apparent and there can be little doubt that this source, unless the problems of realizing solar energy are soon solved, will become more important than all others combined.

Coal has been mined in Nova Scotia for more than two hundred years and that province is still Canada's major producer, though annual output has declined from nearly eight million tons in 1940 to slightly over four million tons. Coal discoveries on Vancouver Island played a considerable part in the early development of British Columbia. There are important coal deposits in the Interior Plains area of Saskatchewan and Alberta and in the Rocky Mountains between Alberta and British Columbia, but there are no known deposits of coal or oil in the Canadian Shield and discoveries are not expected as there was no abundance of plant or animal life in Precambrian time.

Canadian coal production has fallen from a maximum of over nineteen million tons annually to about ten million tons, but large reserves remain. The future of these is uncertain. Coal has declined in usefulness because it is costly to mine and transport and because it is no longer a valuable fuel in transportation. Strip mining of lignite deposits, however, can produce very cheap thermal-electric energy and some may well be used for this purpose. Gas production from deep deposits has not so far proved economically sound – cost is high and quality low. Some authorities believe that production of synthetic liquid fuels in competition with petroleum fuels may eventually be possible.

Although the geology of the Interior Plains has long been

known to be favourable for oil discovery, search was generally unsuccessful until the Leduc field was discovered in 1947. Since that time oil has been found throughout the length and breadth of the prairies from Manitoba to Alberta and northward into the Peace River country and the Northwest Territories. The possibilities of exploration have by no means been exhausted in this vast area and exploration has scarcely reached into the favourable areas of the Yukon and the Arctic. Alberta is the main producer, with Saskatchewan, British Columbia, and Manitoba following in that order. Exploration and discovery in Manitoba are showing signs of decline, but continue at a high rate in the other three provinces.

Natural gas was discovered by drilling at Medicine Hat as long ago as 1890 and further discoveries continued at a relatively slow rate before the middle thirties, by which time Alberta was producing about sixty per cent of the nation's total. After 1935 discoveries became more rapid and in the great exploration of the fifties and early sixties enormous quantities were proved or indicated to exist in Alberta, with large quantities in the British Columbia section of the Peace River and smaller but significant quantities in Saskatchewan. National production in 1962, almost entirely from the prairies, was more than thirty times that of 1937.

These spectacular fossil fuel resources are of major importance not merely to the provinces concerned but to the economy of the country as a whole. Canada is now an exporter as well as an importer of crude oil and a heavy exporter of natural gas. Oil pipelines have been established from Edmonton to Sarnia, to Vancouver and to the United States. Natural-gas lines also cross the border and reach eastward to Toronto and Montreal. Local industrial development has been stimulated by the availability of cheap energy, and important petro-chemical industries have been established. The petroleum fuels supply more than fifty per cent of a modern nation's energy needs; thus a surplus of a prime energy producer such as natural gas, properly distributed, can be a major factor in industrial growth.

Hydro-electric power has been of steadily increasing importance throughout the country since the turn of the century. Ontario has now developed its full potential of some 8 million horsepower, which must be heavily supplemented by thermal-electric installations. Quebec province, with turbine installations totalling about 13 million horsepower, has a further potential of almost the same amount. British Columbia, with about 4 million horsepower installed, has a further potential of 15 million, a substantial part of which will be realized by construction in progress on the Peace and the Columbia. Canada as a whole has a total installation of 27 million horsepower, with a potential of 75 million.

Until fairly recently, the role of hydro-power was largely one of isolated plants serving individual communities or interdependent plants serving limited areas of population. Modern energy demands have outdated these concepts and a modern industrial nation must inevitably think in terms of integrated transmission lines and over-all planning of sufficient sophistication to realize the highest possible yield from its energy sources. Direct-current transmission and other technical improvements, though not yet extensively proved in Canada, make this possible; power can be brought to settled areas from remote sources such as the Peace River in British Columbia and Churchill Falls in Labrador; it can be exchanged between watersheds and regions to take advantage of differences in climate and precipitation; ultimately, when a national transmission grid is established, it may even be possible to take advantage of changing load demands as they vary with time differences across the continent.

These practices and others like them are already put to use to a limited extent within limited areas. At present, because of its abundance in many parts of the country, hydro-energy carries a major part of the base load and meets intermittent peak loads by bringing additional turbines into operation. Most authorities believe that as energy demands increase it will become necessary, and desirable, to use thermal sources for base loads and to reserve hydro sources more and more for peaks of demand. This assumes the availability of economically priced thermal-electric power in large quantities. Large modern steam plants fired by coal, oil, or natural gas are, in fact, competitive with all but the most economical hydro sources, producing electricity at a cost of about four mills per kilowatt hour.

There is little question that nuclear energy is the most likely means in sight of developing large quantities of thermal-electric power. Using natural uranium or uranium dioxide, with heavy water as a reactor, Canada has made extremely important advances in this field since 1946. A successful pilot plant of twenty thousand kilowatts is in operation near Chalk River, and a full-scale plant, known as CANDU, is in advanced stages of construction on Lake Huron; it will supply 200,000 kilowatts and will be purchased by Ontario Hydro when in satisfactory operation. This unit is expected to produce electricity at six to seven mills per kilowatt hour, but addition of other units is expected to reduce the cost to between four and five mills. It is considered likely that large plants constructed on similar principles should be able to produce electricity at less than four mills by 1970.

All forecasts in nuclear matters are necessarily hedged about with extreme caution. The field is so new that un-expected difficulties may always arise, but at the same time possibilities of rapid and significant advances can never be discounted. It seems at present that CANDU is less costly and more versatile than reactors developed by other nations and its importance was clearly recognized by the great inter-national interest in the project shown at the conference on Peaceful Uses of Atomic Energy held at Geneva in 1964.

Canada is a competitive producer of heavy water and has the world's largest known reserves of uranium. These factors ensure maintenance of the very low fuel costs on which the expected success of large plants on the model of CANDU is based, and would seem to give Canada an assurance of abun-dant low-cost thermal energy strategically placed to support a national transmission grid. Strong possibilities of export of nuclear reactors, heavy water, and uranium fuel should materially assist further development.

In addition to the export of natural gas and some oil, Canada has recently accepted the principle of limited export of electrical energy. It would seem that the country is, by any standards, an energy-rich nation and that intelligent, well-integrated use of energy resources must prove a major factor in the economic growth needed to solve the current problems of population adjustment.

No resource is harder to define and assess than the recreational resource and, partly for this reason, none has been treated with greater carelessness and neglect. Canadians have accepted from the beginning a common property right in fisheries, wildlife, scenery, and wilderness, all those things that go to make up the recreational resources, and have insisted on right of public access. At the same time, they have felt that the country had almost unlimited surpluses of such things, which could, in the main, be left to look after themselves. A few parks were set aside, the last of the buffalo were protected, some attention, largely stimulated by United States interest, was paid to duck-breeding areas. Gestures of this sort were enough, it was felt, for resources that merely served the leisure hours of a few people and whose well-being all too often seemed to conflict with the honourable march of progress. You can't, Canadians were fond of saying, eat scenery.

The years since the Second World War have brought about some change in this thinking. It is now evident that increasing wealth and leisure, not merely in Canada but throughout the North American continent, are putting a tremendous strain on available recreational resources. Universal, independent automobile transportation, the immense popularity and adaptability of small boats, and the very real need to escape from the cities, all emphasize this trend. The economic returns from tourism, both domestic and foreign, have stirred the interest of even those governments which remain unresponsive to the more important social implications.

With this stirring of interest has come the usual belated recognition that the resources, after all, are by no means unlimited and indestructible, that pressures fall unevenly, and

that planning and management are essential. In many, perhaps most, parts of the country this recognition is too late.
Desirable lands close to heavily populated areas have been
alienated and can be recovered only with difficulty and at
high cost, if at all. Pollution has been allowed to affect lakes
and their surroundings and even salt water, and now must be
reduced and controlled. In some areas dedicated to recreational use, ill-planned recreational and commercial uses have
been permitted, to the detriment of recreational values.

Canadian practice in setting aside recreational lands has,
not unnaturally, tended to follow United States practice, with
some considerable delay. Federal practice, though far from
adequate, has tended to be more responsible and better conceived than provincial practice, but provincial jurisdiction
over land and resources effectively precludes further federal
expansion in the field except by invitation of the provinces.
Federal practice and policy has recently tended to become
firmer and more clearly defined while provincial practice, if
anything, has become more wavering and uncertain in the
face of commercial pressures. Much can be achieved at the
provincial level; but strong federal leadership is needed and
should be welcomed by the provinces.

Canada has an important and impressive though far from
complete system of national parks. The largest of these are
in the west and were established when railways were the chief
or only means of access. Banff, Jasper, Waterton Lakes, Yoho,
Kootenay, Mount Revelstoke, and Glacier, all established
between 1885 and 1920, provide excellent locations in the
Alberta Rockies and the British Columbia Selkirks. Elk
Island and the enormous Wood Buffalo Park, also in Alberta
(though the latter extends into the Northwest Territories),
are primarily game reserves. Riding Mountain Park is in
south-western Manitoba and Prince Albert Park is in central
Saskatchewan.

Without the 17,300 square miles of Wood Buffalo, a large
proportion of which is of questionable recreational value,
these western parks total over 11,300 square miles. The national parks of the rest of the country total only a little over 600

square miles and the largest of these, Cape Breton Highlands, accounts for well over half this small total. There is no national park in Quebec province; Ontario has only three small national parks, and there is no national park on the Pacific coast or in the British Columbia Coast Range.

The national system is supported in several provinces by large areas of provincial parks and wilderness areas, but often these are doubtful in status, poorly protected, and with limited development; there has been little planned effort towards proper protection of primitive ecologies or towards strategic location in terms of main population centres. Some experts regard many of the provincial parks as 'paper' parks, useful to quiet the provincial conscience but unable to command development *as* parks or to withstand pressure for industrial development within their boundaries. Nearly all provinces have, however, set up good numbers of small parks, campsites, and picnic-sites that serve, in some measure, immediate public demands.

The most critical weakness in provincial parks administration has been in the failure to develop and define a proper philosophy and policy of use and administration. The great provincial systems of Ontario and British Columbia, for instance, remain open to change of any kind by Order in Council, which may reflect little more than the whim of the minister and can at best reflect no more than the short-term view of the government in office. This is an extremely precarious situation for assets of such massive, and supposedly permanent, value. As recently as 1962 both the Minister of Lands and Forests and the Minister of Mines in Ontario proposed to allow prospecting in provincial parks, and were only prevented from doing so by public outcry. In British Columbia the public has been less successful, and recent Orders in Council designed to permit prospecting, mining, and logging in park areas previously protected from such activities, have fully revealed the illusory nature of the system.

This failure of the provinces has been placed in proper perspective by the statement of National Park Policy adopted by the federal government in 1964. The provinces have been caught badly off balance by the enormous post-war growth of interest in outdoor activities. In 1956 the provincial parks of Ontario were used by 61,000 campers. In 1965 they played host to 10 million. Increases of this nature, which will undoubtedly spread throughout the country, cannot be met by niggardly budgets and *ad hoc* policies. They call for advanced understanding of the most up-to-date parks philosophy, for clear statement of policy that looks forward in terms of decades, and for determined administration. Logging operations in Algonquin Park undoubtedly cause serious damage and loss, as will mining and other industrial activities in the parks of British Columbia. But failure to direct and control the ordinary recreational uses with foresight and imagination can cause even greater damage and losses beyond any possibility of recovery. The simple pressure of millions of human feet can change the whole nature of a sensitive ecology; high-powered outboards on the quiet waters of Quetico will destroy much more than quietude; bulldozers and blacktop over sand-dunes or glacial moraines cause destruction that can never be repaired.

Parks are important, but at best they can serve only a minor part of recreational needs and help to preserve certain vital aesthetic and scientific values. It is essential to realize also that a very high proportion of Canadian land area, perhaps as much as eighty per cent, is at present effectively inaccessible and will remain so for a long while; much of this land is muskeg or tundra, plagued by flies and mosquitoes in the brief summers and severely limited by climate through the rest of the year. Of the remainder a very high proportion is committed to farm or forest use, but it is these relatively close-in areas that offer the most useful recreational possibilities. This will call for multiple-use planning of an order beyond anything known in the country today, with careful preservation of marshes and wetlands, close protection of stream banks and lake edges, firm control of pesticide spraying and other pollutions, and well-planned access.

Wildlife is a major factor in recreational resources and Canada has an abundance of fine big game species of interest to the hunter, the naturalist, the camera enthusiast, and the simple observer. Seasonal migration draws birds from the whole continent and beyond. The fur trade, which fostered exploration and early settlement, has declined to a minor position and the annual value of wild fur trapped is little more than 10 million dollars. But the country still supports an abundance of fur bearers, including beaver, mink, musk-rat, squirrel, lynx, otter, marten, and ermine. The decline reflects low prices and the competition of fur farms and synthetic furs. Trapping remains important as a means of providing a livelihood, and therefore a continuation of settle-ment, in many remote areas. It is noteworthy that the decline in Canadian fur production since the Second World War reflects a decrease in world fur prices and a resulting decrease in the numbers of trappers, rather than any decline in the resource itself. Fur farming, which has accounted for a steadily increasing proportion of total Canadian production (from 31 per cent in 1940 to 62 per cent in 1959), has also been limited by prices that remain consistently low in the face of increasing production costs. It is debatable whether recovery can be hoped for through increased prices or the development of new markets, but if either or both these possibilities should be realized, Canadians will be in a good position with both wild and ranch species and the long Canadian tradition of fur production. It has been suggested that weakness in manufacturing and marketing may be par-tially responsible for the Canadian decline, but if this is the case it would seem that any marked increase in prices would produce rapid improvement. The present annual value of the industry is of the order of $25 million, which compares with the high year (1946) of $43 million.

Wildlife has strong aesthetic and sentimental value and, through its attraction for hunters and other tourists, very real economic value. Inevitably there is some retreat in the face of civilization and specialized land use, and management be-comes more and more essential as natural balances are upset. Research and constant vigilance are necessary, but the sur-vival of most Canadian species seems reasonably well assured for the foreseeable future. Close regulation is essential for the protection of a few species, such as the polar bear and the musk-ox and possibly some of the rarer sheep which can be readily threatened by grazing competition from domestic stock. Non-selective insect sprays are a real hazard to birds and small mammals, as they are to the whole ecological balance of the lands they are supposed to protect, but there is some sign that their use will be brought under much firmer control, even if it cannot be eliminated altogether.

The greatest danger to the recreational resources, including wildlife and game fisheries, is in the unsophisticated approach of politicians and the general carelessness of the public. Canadians, as a people, spend well over half a billion dollars annually on travelling abroad, and it must be assumed that they bring back important benefits by so doing. As against this, travel to Canada, chiefly from the United States, brings in over half a billion dollars. The recreational resources play a very important part in this vital exchange, besides filling their primary function of direct service to the people of the country. The attendance of people in the national parks alone has increased from about 1 million in 1947 to nearly 10 million in 1963 and the figures for many provincial parks are at least as spectacular. One need only watch the roads in summer-time, the sales of small boats and outboards, of camping, hunting, and fishing equipment, to understand that the urbanized Canadian is turning to the woods and waters with enthusiasm beyond anything felt by his forebears. It is an enthusiasm that will call for the most sophisticated attention of politicians and the best efforts of management.

In 1961 the population of Canada reached 18 million, representing an increase of 30 per cent during the previous decade. It is estimated that the population may reach 25 million by 1975 and 40 million by the year 2000. During the thirty years between the censuses of 1931 and 1961 there was a very sharp shift of population from rural to urban living: in 1931 54 per cent of the population lived in centres of population of one thousand or more, in 1961 nearly 70 per cent. This trend is expected to continue, possibly at an accelerated rate.

The task of developing Canada has been a vast one, materially inhibited by climate and by difficulties of terrain. Not the least of these difficulties was the Canadian Shield, covering nearly half the country, whose harsh and apparently barren nature restricted easy movement from the east, just as the massive mountains of the Cordillera barred access from the west. Modern transportation and technology have begun to reveal and release the very large mineral and pulp-timber resources of the Shield and other difficult parts of the country. This, more than anything else, accounts for the rapid increase of population since the Second World War.

Increased wealth and increased population is bringing about sharp changes in the Canadian way of life. A country rich in natural resources has advanced from the initial stage of producing raw materials into the secondary stage of elementary processing, and is now advancing rather rapidly into the third stage of manufacturing. At the same time the need for increased efficiency in primary production has set a premium on larger units of production and increased mechanization, while the attractions of urban life and its many services have become increasingly apparent.

But the country's economy remains and will remain based on its natural resources. Until now resource use has been extensive rather than intensive – that is, it has reached farther and farther into a virgin land to take whatever came most easily to hand. Often this has been destructive, not merely to the resource itself but to the land and water that produced it and upon which other resources depend. Both good and ill, usually unplanned and unforeseen, have resulted from this policy, but the total effect has been one of high-grading, in that the best has been used first; transportation routes have been extended, at high economic cost, and often the most accessible and productive land has been gravely impaired or placed altogether out of production.

Much of this was inevitable in the effort of opening a new land, and change is not easily achieved. Neither is the knowledge upon which sound and useful change must be based. In the renewable resources, fundamental research is still the major prerequisite to sound planning, but governments and industry remain reluctant to allocate the substantial funds needed, and universities generally have not been able to build up natural-resource schools to the high levels that are needed.

At the same time, much useful knowledge does already exist and extensive rehabilitation and improvement work could be undertaken in such resource fields as forestry, fisheries, and recreation. Intensive programs of this type would not only ensure maintenance of economic production against world competition in the future, but would offer alternative employment for manpower displaced by the effort to increase efficiency in the primary industries. In many instances the work could be based on existing communities or some consolidation of existing communities.

Federal leadership is essential to sound resource management, but the provisions of the British North America Act have made this difficult in all fields except fisheries and, to a lesser extent, agriculture. As the country becomes more closely integrated and interdependent, federal responsibility and leadership will become more and more essential. ARDA appears to be an instance where such leadership has been offered and accepted. Fuller integration of energy resources through national planning and a stronger measure of national control will sooner or later become essential. Conservation of water through pollution control and watershed management is primarily a provincial matter, but will not be achieved without strong federal leadership. The many schemes for redistribution of water through diversion that are at present under consideration are so gigantic in scale, and promise to be so overwhelming in long-term effect, that the national interest is certainly involved. The suggestion has already been made in the United States that water is a 'continental' rather than a national resource. There is no international law or precedent to support this view and there is no present information to justify the assumption that the Canadian population will not, in time, put the whole of the nation's

magnificent water resources to full use. This issue alone calls
for immediate, intensive study and a firm declaration of
national policy to set outside pretensions in proper perspective. It has been pointed out, for instance, that the capitalized
value of Canadian water to be stored by the Columbia River
dams, if used for consumptive purposes, would be approximately two and a half billion dollars, while the value of the
same storage for hydro-electric and flood-control purposes has
been assessed at slightly more than 500 million dollars.

Though the more accessible and more profitable resources
have been developed, and in some cases over-developed,
Canada remains a country with large undeveloped resources. Climate and difficulties of transportation are inhibiting factors, as is the lack of ready markets. Advance will
certainly be rapid over the next thirty or forty years, and if
the developed resources can be brought under sound management as new resources are coming into use, the position
should be a strong one. Close federal-provincial co-operation
and strong federal leadership are essential if full benefits are
to be achieved. There is reason to hope that the Canadian
Council of Resource Ministers, a direct outgrowth of the
Resources for Tomorrow Conference of 1961, may yield a
coherence of policy and action that the nation has not so far
enjoyed.

14. Industrial Development

O. J. FIRESTONE

Canada, with a population of some twenty million people, two-thirds of one per cent of the world's population, is one of the leading trading and industrial countries, with her goods and services sold all over the world.

Canada today is the world's fifth largest trading nation in terms of total exports and imports. She is among the eight leading industrial nations in terms of Gross Domestic Product originating in manufacturing, and the fourth on a per-capita basis – following the United States, Western Germany, and France, but ahead of the United Kingdom, the U.S.S.R., Japan, and Italy. As a result of great advances in industrial and trade development, Canadians have experienced for most of the postwar period a particularly rapid rate of economic growth, making it possible for them to expand their productive capacity substantially and at the same time enjoy a rising standard of living.

The range of Canada's manufacturing industries is broad: the processing of minerals and non-ferrous metals, the milling of wheat, the conversion of logs into pulp and paper, the production of synthetic materials, chemicals, iron and steel products, and a wide range of consumer goods and capital goods – both finished and unfinished goods, for final use or for integration into other production processes.

The industries provide jobs for about 1.7 million persons, or about one-quarter of all those employed in this country. The gross value of manufacturing production amounted to over $35 billion in 1965, equivalent to about two-thirds of Canada's Gross National Product valued at $52 billion. Net value added by manufacturing was of the order of $13 billion, equivalent to approximately 30 per cent of the Gross National Product. In terms of wages and salaries, manufacturing contributed about 29 per cent to total earnings. Putting it in general terms, Canadian manufacturing industries provide jobs for one out of four Canadians. One of every three dollars earned originates directly in Canada's secondary industries.

During the first half-century, primary industries, particularly agriculture, were the main sources of gainful employment and income. But the situation changed following the significant industrial efforts exerted during the First World War, with manufacturing becoming the single most important source of income earned in Canada. Still, in terms of number of persons working, agriculture was to remain the main source of employment for another two decades.

It took the Second World War to transform Canada's economic structure. This country came out of the war as a major industrialized nation with manufacturing by far the most important and most dynamic source of economic activity, employment, and income. Rising productivity made it possible to pay workers higher wages while at the same time the number of hours worked per week was reduced. Increased profits made it possible to reward management and investors adequately and to attract increasing amounts of capital for further plant expansion and productive improvements.

As workers were able to get higher wages and obtain better working conditions in manufacturing industries, other sectors of the economy had to follow suit in order to keep their work force. And sectors such as agriculture, which could not compete with the attractions and rewards of urban factory employment, lost large numbers of farm workers to cities and towns. Between 1945 and 1965 the agricultural labour force was reduced by about one-half – from some 1.2 million to a little over 600,000 – while employment in secondary industries rose from 1.1 million to 1.7 million.

Manufacturing industries have become the greatest spenders on improving their capital assets, surpassing public utilities, which in the past for most periods have made larger capital expenditures than any other sector. The distribution of capital expenditures in 1966 was as follows:

	Amount (millions of dollars)	*Percentage*
Manufacturing industries	2,696	18.5
Public utilities	2,663	18.3
Housing	2,216	15.2
Primary industry	2,013	13.8
Government departments	1,985	13.6
Commercial services and construction	1,712	11.8
Institutional services	1,261	8.8
Total	14,546	100

SOURCE: from *Private and Public Investment in Canada, Outlook 1966*, Department of Trade and Commerce, Ottawa, 1966.

The industries have developed largely to cater to Canada's domestic market. But increasingly they have striven to obtain a growing share of expanding export markets, although they have experienced setbacks from time to time. Still, about two-thirds of Canada's merchandise export trade, amounting to $8.5 billion in 1965, comprised fully or partially manufactured products. This represented about 17 per cent of the gross value of Canada's total manufacturing output; in other words, 83 cents out of every dollar came from sales to domestic consumers, with the other 17 cents being earned by selling abroad.

No other economic area produces as substantial a profit for Canadian and foreign investors alike. In 1964, for example, secondary industries generated corporation profits amounting to $2,133 million or 46.5 per cent out of a total of $4,589 million. The finance, insurance, and real estate sectors came next with $633 million or 13.8 per cent, followed by the wholesale and retail sector, with $585 million or 12.7 per cent, and mining (including oil and natural gas) with $557 million or 12.1 per cent. Transportation and communications produced corporation profits of $385 million or 8.4 per cent, while all other types accounted for the remainder of $287 million or 6.3 per cent.

But the contributions that manufacturing industries make are much more complex than profits alone. The very fact that they employ more people than any other sector of the economy, providing the greatest single source of income earned, means that they not only create output but also create the income that results in the demands for their products. Manufacturing industries represent also the most important single group of taxpayers, thus making an essential contribution to the fiscal soundness of the country.

This industrial prosperity has made it possible for Canadians to play a greater role in international affairs, politically, militarily, and economically, and at home to expand the range of government services in areas vital to human betterment and economic progress, such as education, health, and urban development. And, moreover, it has given Canadians a sense of achievement and inner strength to withstand internal discontent and international bickering.

One of Canada's outstanding social scientists, a great teacher, and a distinguished civil servant, O. D. Skelton, once observed: 'with Confederation a new stage in the industrial

development of the northern half of this continent began.'
In 1867 Canada had a population of 3.5 million people, a
labour force of 1.1 million, a Gross National Product of
about $420 million, and merchandise exports of some $50
million. (The data for 1867 are special estimates based
largely on two studies by the author. The estimates are of
necessity approximate and subject to a number of limitations.)

Manufacturing operations were of a simple nature. Canada was still waiting to realize the full benefits of the Industrial Revolution, which had made the United Kingdom a
great industrial and trading nation. Still, Canadian manufacturing industries provided jobs for some 170,000 people,
about 16 per cent of the 1,060,000 persons working. The
gross value of goods manufactured was of the order of $170
million and the net value added in manufacturing about
$85 million, equivalent to approximately 20 per cent of the
Gross National Product.

At the time of Confederation, the average person working
in manufacturing earned about $217 per year, or approxi-
mately 75 cents per day. He usually worked ten hours a day,
six days a week, and only some were able to shave off an hour
or two on Saturday.

In 1967, Canada's population approached 20½ million,
the labour force 7½ million, persons working 7¼ million,
Gross National Product $62 billion, and merchandise ex-
ports close to $10 billion.

Manufacturing industries provided jobs for about 1¾
million persons, or about 25 per cent of the total number of
persons employed. Gross value of manufacturing production
amounted to some $42 billion, and net value added by manu-
facturing was approximately $18½ billion or about 30 per
cent of the Gross National Product.

The average hourly wage in manufacturing in 1967
amounted to about $2.25, with the number of hours worked
per week slightly above 40, on the basis of a five-day week.
Employees were usually given two weeks' paid holidays and
numerous other fringe benefits.

Over the last century the general price level in Canada has risen about fivefold. This meant that the average Canadian working man had to earn five dollars in 1967 for every dollar his ancestor earned in 1867 to be able to buy the same quantity of goods and services – though, of course, he would have the benefit of the considerable improvement in the quality of goods and services that has occurred over the last century. Allowing then for price changes, the average Canadian working in a factory in 1967 would have real earnings four times those of his ancestors in 1867, not counting the fringe benefits, shorter hours of work, better working conditions, and the higher quality of goods and services he would be able to buy with his earnings. Thus in terms of human satisfaction he would be considerably better off than can possibly be portrayed with crude statistics reflecting a century of economic progress.

Over half a century ago a senior Canadian civil servant wrote an economic treatise to lend substance to Sir Wilfrid Laurier's famous pronouncement, 'The twentieth century shall be the century of Canada.' This was the conclusion offered: 'There will be in Canada as in other industrial countries occasional years of depression when little progress will be made, but the development of the manufacturing industry will keep pace with the general growth of the country.'

As the record of achievement over the last century shows, this forecast was not optimistic enough.

At the time of Confederation about sixteen per cent of the labour force were working in what may be described as very simple fabricating activities, catering largely to local markets and drawing on native raw materials, mainly lumber. Secondary industries of some significance at the time of Confederation included the manufacture of agricultural imple ments, furniture, matches, machinery and tools, woollen goods, and boots and shoes, along with shipbuilding, flour milling, sugar-refining, salt-works, and brewing and distilling. These industries contributed in total about twenty per cent to the national income of the nation.

Canadians had embarked on Confederation full of great hopes and expectations of building a great nation occupying half a continent, with a comprehensive transportation network moulding the country into an integrated economic unit. This would create a rapidly expanding domestic market for the new industries that were expected to spring up to meet the requirements of a growing and more prosperous population living increasingly in urban communities.

Economic conditions were in fact favourable in Canada between 1867 and 1873, and the continental railway system was built linking together the scattered pockets of economic activity across the country. But by the end of 1873 the boom broke and was followed by world-wide depression. In the United States it involved a sharp cut-back in building and railway construction, and in Great Britain a severe contraction of credit and a steep decline in foreign trade. The fall in prices and in international lending brought an abrupt check to economic expansion in new countries. In Canada the first effect was a decline in the demand for lumber. Between 1873 and 1879, exports of forest products fell by one-half. The prices of manufactured goods fell more rapidly than those of agricultural products, but by 1876 the country was generally enveloped in a depression that grew slowly worse until 1879. By then both the price level and the physical volume of exports had fallen by twenty per cent from the peak of 1873.

In general, the three main factors deterring Canadian economic growth and industrialization during this period were these: a persistent decline in international prices that reduced considerably the proceeds from Canadian exports; a significant drop in international lending, which aggravated the existing shortage of capital even further; and a low level of investment in most sectors (with some exceptions, e.g. railway building), as business had little incentive to expand capital facilities in view of uncertain market prospects and unsettled economic conditions.

The depression lasted twenty-three years, with some temporary improvement around 1882 and 1883, but with no definite economic upturn taking place until after 1895.

While the depression continued, the agitation for increased protection of Canadian secondary industries grew. Tariff levels of manufactured products had been comparatively low in Canada between 1867 and 1878. Canada had begun to rely more and more on exports to the United States. The choice now faced was either to obtain greater access to that market or to pursue a more nationalistic policy and develop industries to cater to the domestic market, protected increasingly from competition of products imported. Canadians were aware that the former policy would bring greater long-term benefits to Canada, because they would then enjoy the benefits of international specialization, and that the latter policy would slow down the rate of economic growth and would bring repercussions in the United States.

An election was fought in Canada in 1878 on the issue 'Reciprocity of Trade or Reciprocity of Tariffs'. This was one of the deciding reasons for the pro-tariff Conservative win in that year. Trade negotiations ensued for the reciprocal removal of tariffs on industrial products between Canada and the United States, but to no avail. In 1879, then, the Canadian government embarked on a policy of vigorous tariff protection designed to foster Canadian industrial development on a broad scale. The policy that was to transform the economy and make a great nation was impressively labelled the 'National Policy'. This policy continued in existence until 1896 when, with a change to a Liberal government, the great tariff wall that had been built up was gradually dismantled.

After 1896 and particularly following the turn of the century, manufacturing expanded in most of the important categories: the provision of capital equipment, the production of goods for general consumption, and the processing of natural products for export. The program of railway construction, the growth of cities and towns, the equipping of western farms, and the extension of community facilities in both East and West gave a great impetus to the production of capital goods. The iron and steel industry particularly made rapid progress.

The period after 1900 has been described as one encompassing the most vigorous industrial growth in the country's history. The ventures of the previous thirty-odd years were by comparison little more than experiments and beginnings. A few industries lagged behind and failed to fulfil their promise, but the majority entered on a career of continued and quickened expansion. A steadily enlarging home market – thanks to the thousands of immigrants who moved into the farmlands of the West – was combined with a flow of capital from the investors of Europe and the United States to maintain expansion on a continuing basis, with boom conditions creating new problems. New mining discoveries brought an increasing processing industry, particularly after important finds of non-ferrous metals and iron ore in Ontario.

There was further industrial development based on forest resources, with governments taking increasing interest in the conservation of forests and their greater economic use. Pulp-and-paper production can claim the record among Canadian manufactures for phenomenal growth. In the census of 1871 it was not mentioned. In 1881 five mills were reported, employing sixty-eight men. It then began to grow, but the increase was moderate until the twentieth century. Then it quickly passed its older competitors, until at the end of the First World War it ranked among the first two or three dominant manufacturing industries in the country.

While no other manufacture showed that impressive a development, many grew with notable rapidity, especially those not far removed from the extractive stage, with ample natural resources to give them an advantage over foreign competitors. In these industries the Canadian producer became dominant at home and a prominent exporter to world markets. Old and flourishing industries that had developed as a direct consequence of expansion in agriculture were meat packing and flour milling, the latter keeping pace with the extension of wheat acreage.

Among textiles, cotton manufacturing expanded, but woollen production faced difficulties because of British competition. Other industries that made significant progress during this period produced farm implements, rubber, chemicals from domestic mineral products, and automobiles. Last but not least was an industry that was to give the great impetus to further development – the generation of hydro-electric power, which for Canada was destined to play as great a role in economic development as coal did in an earlier age in Great Britain.

The period between 1900 and the outbreak of war in 1914, and again after the end of the war until about 1924, witnessed a profound change in the size of the business unit. A process of consolidation was at work and reached its climax in the four years 1909-12, when 275 firms were reduced by various mergers to 58. The principal industries affected were pulp and paper, lumber, machinery, iron and steel, milling, canning, brewing, boot and shoe, bread, jewellery, and meat packing.

Foreign capital played an increasing role during this period. British capital invested between 1900 and 1914, primarily in industrial and mining developments, has been estimated at $300 million. During the same period between $600 million and $700 million came from the United States, to be invested largely in industry.

The figures for 1900 to 1910 illustrate the great growth during this period of broadening and diversification: persons employed in manufacturing rose from 443,000 to 510,000 or by 15 per cent; gross value of production about doubled from $556 million to $1,152 million, and productivity in terms of output per man-year rose by better than 40 per cent – the greatest productivity increase achieved in a century of industrial development in Canada.

The outbreak of the First World War found Canada in a deepening recession. Unemployment was rising, exports were declining, and industrial capacity was increasingly unused. But the threat of the recession's becoming a serious depression faded quickly as military requirements for men and materials created demands that could only be met by making more effective use of manpower and creating additional industrial and agricultural productive capacity.

The decline in exports from Europe and the high cost of shipping enabled Canadian manufacturers to obtain a larger share of the home market. Although the munitions orders were but a temporary factor, they had important long-run effects: the demands imposed resulted in a considerable increase in technical and operational efficiency. Munitions also forced a much-needed diversification, particularly in the iron and steel industry which had been highly specialized to supply the requirements of railway building and heavy construction.

The capacity of the steel industry, essential to Canada's broadening industrial base, was nearly doubled: from 1¼ million ingot tons in 1914 to 2¼ million ingot tons in 1919. In fact, the level reached after the First World War was so high that little further change occurred in steel capacity until the outbreak of the Second War.

Either newly created or greatly expanded during the First War were the aircraft and shipbuilding industries. From a very modest beginning in 1917, the aircraft industry in the course of two years turned out some three thousand training planes for British and Canadian forces. Shipyards were greatly expanded and produced close to one hundred ships, half of them steel and the other half wood, the total tonnage being about 350,000 dead weight tons.

When the war came to an end the Canadian manufacturing industry employed some 586,000 men on a year-round basis, turning out a gross value of production estimated at $3.2 billion. The net value added amounted to about $1.3 billion, equivalent to over 25 per cent of the Gross National Product. The gross value of manufacturing production in 1918 was about 2½ times what it had been in 1914; allowing for the considerable rise in prices, the increase in real terms was about one-third. Even more important was the significant growth in skills and managerial experience that Canadians had acquired under the pressure of a major military effort.

As the Royal Commission on Dominion-Provincial Relations put it: The Canadian manufacturing industry emerged from the War with a more dominant place in the domestic market, with an enlarged productive capacity, and with much improved and diversified facilities. The outlook for economic growth and further industrial development after 1920 appeared to be encouraging.

One of the dramatic changes contributing to rapid expansion and further diversification came from the realization on the part of American industry that the Canadian market had grown sufficiently to make it economically feasible and financially attractive to set up branch plants in this country. These could also serve those foreign markets that could be reached more advantageously from Canada, particularly other British countries that accorded Canada preferential tariffs.

Many millions of dollars poured into Canada in the 1920s to build up the motor-car industry, the metal processing and fabrication industry, the chemical industries, and the electrical-equipment and machinery industries. Also rapidly expanding, and somewhat dependent on foreign capital, were the pulp-and-paper industry, the non-metallic product industry (largely needed to cater to the building boom of the late 1920s), and the farm-implement industry. The expansion was so rapid that manufacturing investment in volume terms reached a peak level in 1929 that was not matched by anything that had happened before or that was to happen in the next decade and a half, including the period of the Second World War and the years of reconstruction following it.

Close to 100,000 additional jobs opened up, offering workers wage-rates higher than in most other sectors of the economy. Total employment in secondary industries reached 666,000 in 1929, a level not reached again until Canada was fully engaged in the major industrial effort required by the Second World War.

By 1929 Canadian manufacturing industries turned out a

great variety of processed materials and fabricated products never produced before. Gross value of production approached the $4 billion mark, greater by about one-quarter in value and more than one-half in volume than the level right after the First World War.

But then late in 1929 came the crash followed by the Great Depression. In the short space of four years, industry laid off some 200,000 men – one out of three. Many of those who kept their jobs were working part-time and drawing wages barely adequate to eke out a living.

The output of manufacturing declined to $1.9 billion by 1933, a drop of one-half in value terms and one-third in volume terms. Many factories closed their doors while others kept on going, not knowing how long they could keep losing money or when their creditors or bankers would force them into bankruptcy.

Slowly, starting in 1934, the economic situation started to improve, little by little, partly as a result of a more favourable external economic environment as world trade took a turn for the better, and partly because levels of employment, income, and living standards had dropped so low that economic conditions could not get much worse. Business had cut back investment to such reduced levels and structures and equipment had deteriorated to such an extent that additional capital expenditures were called for if business was to continue to operate.

While government economic policies were not as effective as their framers had wished – and some of the beneficial results of measures taken by the federal government were nullified by economic policies pursued by provincial governments moving in the opposite direction – they did contribute to some stabilization of economic conditions and to a gradual return of confidence on the part of the business community and individuals.

Capital expenditures started to rise, and so did exports. Jobs became more plentiful and wages and salaries began to climb. Demand for manufactured products expanded and factory owners were only too happy to oblige.

When the Second World War started, the Canadian manufacturing industry had almost recovered the ground it had lost in the preceding decade, though it was still operating significantly below capacity. By 1939, some 658,000 Canadians had factory jobs and manufacturing output was valued at $3.5 billion.

American participation in Canadian industrial development had only been partially slowed down during the depressed years. With the introduction of the British Empire Preferential System in 1932 it became increasingly advantageous for American manufacturers to serve markets within the British dominions and possessions (it was the British Empire then) from their Canadian subsidiaries. Thus they proceeded to build up those Canadian subsidiaries and establish new ones. For it mattered little to American firms whether they made their money in the United States or from their subsidiaries operating in Canada, as long as they made money, and by selling from Canada they could overcome the hurdles of the rising tariff walls so typical of the 'beggar-thy-neighbour' trade policies that beset the irrational international community of the 1930s.

The Second World War hit the North American continent with unexpected force – Canada being drawn into the conflict long before the United States, but both countries being wholly unprepared militarily, economically, and industrially. Pearl Harbor was a heavy blow to American pride, but it also aroused the wrath of an economic giant who did not know his own strength. Intensive industrial integration followed on a continental scale, with Canada and the United States working more closely together than at any time in their history. Under the direction of governments, Canadian and American industry developed production-sharing arrangements, accompanied by a substantial exchange of research information and technical and managerial know-how.

With Western Europe overrun by Nazi hordes, with the

United Kingdom reeling under tne destructive onslaught of continuing air-raids, and with the U.S.S.R. being pushed farther and farther towards the east and losing most of her industrial regions to the victorious German armies, North America became the economic and industrial bastion of the free world.

Expansion of productive capacity was particularly striking in such manufactures as tools, electrical apparatus, chemicals, steel, aluminum, and other non-ferrous metals. New factories were built, shipyards constructed, and armament assembly-lines installed. Entire new industries were created to produce, for example, roller bearings, magnesium, and artificial rubber. Some industries, such as aircraft production and shipbuilding, with relatively small employment before the war, attained such a large war-time employment that the process amounted to the creation of a new industry rather than the expansion of an old one. Advances were made in the production of finished goods and equipment, some of which were of a type quite new to Canadian industry and which had previously been imported – optical glass, high-octane gasoline, and penicillin and sulfa drugs. At the height of the industrial war effort in 1943, about three out of every five persons employed in Canadian manufacturing industries worked on war orders.

Industry's adaptation to meet military demands required still greater diversification and increased skill and technical knowledge, more complex machinery and more closely integrated processes than anything that had previously been known in Canada. But even in purely statistical terms of capacity and output the growth was remarkable. Between 1939 and the war peak, output of steel increased by approximately 120 per cent and of aluminum by about 500 per cent. One new development, the production of synthetic rubber, commenced with an annual output of 3,000 tons in 1943, which rose to 45,000 tons in 1945.

Fully fabricated war equipment and munitions were also turned out in large volume. From 1939 to 1945 some 816,000 mechanized transport vehicles were produced in addition to over 50,000 armoured fighting vehicles. Canadian ship-yards in the same period built over 4,000 naval ships and approximately 400 ocean-going merchant vessels, the latter involving some 3.7 million dead weight tons, in addition to substantial ship-conversion and repair work. The aircraft industry produced in the same period over 16,000 military planes. The chemical industry turned out some three billion pounds of chemicals and one billion pounds of explosives. This tremendous output of munitions and war equipment, valued at about $10 billion, was used only in part by Cana-dian forces, with a large proportion, about 70 per cent, being made available to the Allies.

The creation of this war-time industrial structure ab-sorbed substantial resources of the country. Between Sep-tember 1939 and August 1945, new business investment in buildings, structures, machinery, and equipment is estimated to have exceeded $4.5 billion, of which some $3.5 billion was either directly or indirectly associated with the war effort. A substantial portion of this investment program was either financed or encouraged by the government. Up to V-J Day, the Canadian government spent more than $700 million on industrial plant expansion, of which about 75 per cent comprised wholly owned Crown companies and the remainder was war equipment and installations added to private industrial plants. In addition, through a variety of fiscal measures, the Canadian government encouraged pri-vate industry to spend an extra one billion dollars on plant expansion serving military purposes.

At the peak of the war effort in the fall of 1943, persons engaged directly or indirectly in war work, mainly in indus-try, numbered 1.2 million, declining to about 600,000 when the war ended on August 14, 1945. During that year manu-facturing industries employed over 1.1 million people, about 70 per cent more than in 1939. The gross value of manufac-turing output in 1945 amounted to $8.2 billion, about two and one-third in value terms and about one and three-quar-ters in volume terms of what the industry had produced in

1939, involving a much greater variety and technically more complex fabricated items, comparable in quality in most instances with the best produced in the United States.

When the Second World War ended there existed in Canada a wide-spread concern about the future – the possibility of rising levels of unemployment and economic adversity of the type experienced after the First War and in the 1930s. But instead – with remarkable alacrity and comparatively little dislocation – Canadians realized the task of converting their war-time industrial structure to one geared to meet rising civilian demand. The problem was one of inflation rather than one of recession. The conversion to a peace-time footing was fully completed by the end of 1947, and Canadian industry was ready to push back new technological and economic frontiers.

Two developments gave a further spurt to manufacturing expansion from 1950 onward. First, the intensive search for new supplies of minerals and other natural resources after the end of the War brought a number of important discoveries – crude oil, natural gas, iron ore, non-ferrous metals, and a number of minor metals – which gave a major impetus to capital-goods-producing industries. The chemical industry became increasingly diversified. Discoveries of oil and natural gas in Alberta were important enough to develop despite the distance to the principal markets. The rapid economic expansion of the West created new demand for manufactured products. Thus, gradually, the handicap of great distance from markets and materials, which industries in the Prairie region had hitherto experienced, diminished in importance.

Secondly, the outbreak of the war in Korea in mid 1950 led to the establishment of a three-year defence program of some $5 billion. Three industries in particular received great stimulus from the rearmament program – the aircraft industry, which produced jet aircraft complete with engines; the electronics industry, which produced a variety of new items, from radar equipment to one-mile infantry-pack radio sets, which were later supplied in increasing quantities to the United States and other NATO allies; and the shipbuilding industry, which revived after several years of decline following the end of the war and drew increasingly on equipment-producing industries to fit out, power, and arm the new naval vessels.

Manufacturing industries that had expanded because of the rearmament program proved adaptable to many civilian uses. The outstanding example is the comparative ease with which a television industry was established. It assumed increasing importance toward the end of 1952 as progress was being made toward the establishment of a national television network.

Reconstruction and conversion of secondary industries following the end of the Second War had taken two and a half years. This period was followed by a decade of continued economic growth, only temporarily interrupted by two recessions of comparatively short duration and minor in terms of economic dislocation – 1948-9 and 1953-4. By and large the period 1945 to 1957 was one of high levels of employment, of income, and of industrial development. In fact, Canada's manufacturing industries continued to expand more rapidly than the economy as a whole, both in terms of contribution to national income and in terms of employment.

The next four years, 1957 to 1961, were a period of slow growth, with the labour force expanding more rapidly than employment opportunities, and higher levels of unemployment than at any time since the depressed 1930s. What aggravated a difficult economic situation even further were large balance-of-payments deficits, greater than anything Canada had ever experienced before, leading to an exchange crisis followed by devaluation of the Canadian dollar in mid 1962.

This, plus substantial increases in imports, affected manufacturing adversely. Some plants closed down; others went on part-week production schedules. Those that continued to operate on a regular basis cut back their expansion plans. Employment in secondary industries actually declined between 1957 and 1961 by 6 per cent, while the general employment level rose by 6 per cent. Canada still had on an average 466,000 persons unemployed in 1961, equivalent to 7.7 per cent of the labour force.

After reaching a low point in the down-swing phase of the business cycle in February 1961, the Canadian economy resumed its upward course. Strong expansionary forces came into play, largely the result of heavy capital spending by business and of rising export trade, supported by increased domestic demand for goods and services. Rapid economic growth followed, bringing to Canada the longest expansion phase in peace-time history, six years in a row with further growth indicated for the years following Canada's first centenary celebrations.

Accompanying this rapid growth in the economy as a whole, and in fact contributing substantially to it, was the significant increase in manufacturing activity. Employment in secondary industries rose between 1961 and 1967 by over one-third and gross value of production by over one-half. Manufacturing industries had re-established their role as a dynamic factor in Canadian economic growth.

Canadian manufacturing industries had come of age in the 1920s. No more did they feel dependent primarily on meeting local and regional needs, or rely on the forced pace of providing supplies serving military efforts. They began to look increasingly to international markets, and such industries as the pulp-and-paper companies and the farm-implement manufacturers became leading exporters of fully manufactured products.

Canadian industries up to the First World War had relied on exporting less than 10 per cent of the value of their output; in most years of the 1920s they about doubled this proportion. In 1920, some 17 per cent and in 1930 about 15 per cent of total Canadian manufacturing production was exported, notwithstanding in the latter year the beginning of the depression.

During the 1920s, fully and chiefly manufactured pro-

ducts made up between 40 and 50 per cent of total exports
as against between 30 and 40 per cent in earlier decades, and
'fully and chiefly manufactured' meant a much greater
degree of processing and fabrication.

During the 1930s, the proportion of Canadian manufactured products exported dropped substantially as foreign
markets shrank even more than the domestic market. Even
by 1939, fully or chiefly manufactured items comprised only
about 11½ per cent of the value of total domestic production, equivalent to 43 per cent of total exports.

The war, of course, pushed the exports of manufactured
products to new peaks as Canadian industry supplied large
quantities of munitions and military and civilian supplies
and equipment to the Allies and other friendly trading
nations. This heavy flow subsided as the war came to a close.
Still, even in 1945, the proportion of manufactured products
in the total value of domestic production was 22 per cent,
and the proportion in terms of commodity exports was 55
per cent.

But the pattern changed considerably after 1945. Initially
Canada continued to export large quantities of manufactured products, helping the war-devastated countries of
Europe in their postwar reconstruction and supplying other
countries with capital goods and production materials. But
within five years most of the nations had recovered from the
ravages of the war, and resumed their positions as important
industrial and trading nations, particularly Japan and the
countries of Western Europe. Hence, Canadian secondary
industries that had not felt strong international competition
for over a decade had to adjust themselves to a new international trading climate. International division of labour,
low cost of production, high quality, adequate financing,
and proper servicing had become the basis of the new international trade in manufactured products.

However, good fortune offered new opportunities. Important resource discoveries – crude oil and natural gas, iron
ore, non-ferrous metals and non-metallic minerals – accompanied by a strong push forward in the pulp-and-paper

industry, all contributed to raising materially Canada's exports to world markets. Sales of wheat and flour overseas expanded by leaps and bounds, and Communist countries became Canada's best customers. Canadian exports to the United States, including both raw and processed materials, rose rapidly, partly because of the growing dependence of the U.S. economy on basic materials from abroad, and partly because of a deliberate policy of using natural resources on a continental scale – for example, bringing more Canadian crude oil to the north-western and Pacific Coast states.

Thus, with the world clamouring for Canada's natural-resource materials and foodstuffs, and with the international tariff system continuing to encourage the importation of materials in raw or processed form rather than in fabricated form, Canadian manufacturing industries found themselves faced with a situation they had not experienced for half a century. During the late 1940s and the 1950s, Canadian manufacturing had again found it necessary to rely on the Canadian market to absorb more than 90 per cent of its production, with exports of fully manufactured products less than 10 per cent of total output, dropping in some years to as low as 7 per cent. The proportion of manufactured products to total commodity exports, which had been up to 50 per cent during the 1920s and around 55 per cent at the end of the Second War dropped to range between 35 and 40 per cent in the period up to 1960.

Manufacturers then began to realize that they had been losing ground in world markets, as far as the export of fully manufactured products was concerned. Not that this was anything new – but what *was* new was the realization that unless industry could put its house in order, increase productivity, lower costs, and acquire expanding markets both at home and abroad, Canada was destined to fall behind most other industrialized countries in the world. Further, successive Conservative and Liberal governments made it clear to Canadian industry that it could not rely on government to bail it out by increased protection on a significant scale. Canada and other nations had started gradually to dismantle trade barriers, with the objective of encouraging increased international division of labour. In this changing international environment and changing climate of policy, Canadian industry had to adjust itself and compete effectively.

The 1950s and the early 1960s were characterized by Canadian industry continuing to fall behind in international trade, particularly serious since world demand for industrial products expanded by leaps and bounds. Here was one of the eight leading industrialized nations of the world in terms of absolute value of its manufacturing operations, and among the first four nations on the basis of value of manufacturing output per capita – losing ground steadily.

Was it due to the manufacturer's being content to cater mainly to domestic market where competition was less fierce? Was it due to the Canadian dollar's being overvalued, making it difficult for Canadian manufactures to hold their own in international markets? Was it due to a failure of Canadian trade negotiators to obtain adequate trade concessions from the main markets of the world on a *quid pro quo* basis? Was it due to the manufacturing industry's not keeping pace with the technological and scientific progress and new design developments abroad? Was it due to a lack of incentives for Canadian producers to increase their output as much as their main foreign competitors did and fight for expanded sales opportunities both at home and abroad?

Probably all these factors contributed, though some assumed greater weight than others. For example, when Canada devalued the dollar from a premium level over the American dollar to 92½ cents (U.S.) in mid 1962, significant improvements in the competitive position ensued: the downward trend was gradually reversed, and exports of fully manufactured products rose again both in absolute and in relative terms.

The problems confronting Canadian manufacturing industry have been assessed by the Economic Council of Canada in these terms:

The postwar reductions in trade barriers, together with other

underlying economic forces, have particularly encouraged
a much more rapid growth of world trade in manufactured
products and processed materials.

Canada simply did not keep pace with world trends. Two
other developments marked the international trade pattern
of the 1950s and 1960s.

First, there have been much more rapid rates of increase in
such product groups as machinery, transportation equipment, chemicals and plastics, and much less rapid rates of
increase in such other groups as textiles and clothing and
primary products. Second, the expansion of world trade has
become increasingly concentrated among the industrially
advanced countries, and there has been a relative decline in
the importance of trade between the industrially advanced
and the economically less developed countries. . . .

Canada has been adversely affected by the shift in the structure of international trade. . . . Countries which export
mainly manufactured products have had an improvement in
their so-called terms of trade during this period, while
countries such as Canada, which export mainly primary
products and industrial materials, have experienced a deterioration in their terms of trade. This deterioration in
Canada's terms of trade, which represents a reversal of the
trend of the previous two decades, may also partly reflect the
reduction in the exchange value of the Canadian dollar.
Thus, for Canada, a larger volume of exports was required
in 1963 than in 1953 to finance a given volume of imports.

The key element in explaining the setbacks experienced
by Canadian manufacturing industries in world trade – and
also affecting their competitive position in the domestic
market as Canada gradually reduced tariffs on manufactured
products in the postwar period – was a continuing inability
of these industries to raise their productivity at a rate comparable to the rate in other industrialized nations. Of nine
industrialized countries in Western Europe and North
America, seven had greater productivity increases in manufacturing industries than Canada over the period 1950-60.
Only the United Kingdom had fallen behind Canada.

But British industries did achieve a decided improvement in the 1955 to 1960 period, while Canadian industries continued to slip. In that five-year period, productivity increases in Canadian manufacturing industries were one-fifth those of France and Western Germany, and one-third those of the United States and the United Kingdom. Obviously such a situation could not continue without change for any length of time without disastrous effects on Canadian economic growth and standards of living.

Canadian manufacturing industries responded to the challenge by embarking on the largest capital investment program in their history. Between 1962 and 1966, they invested close to $10 billion in expanding and improving their capacity, over 50 per cent more than they had spent in the preceding five-year period. Results began to show: in 1965, industrial-output volume rose seven per cent over 1964, with employment in manufacturing up approximately three per cent. The increase in output per man-year was thus of the order of four per cent, a better record of achievement in a single year than the industry had been able to realize during the preceding decade. Gradually, Canada started to export greater quantities of fully manufactured products and the proportion of total domestic output turned upward again.

In this effort to increase exports of highly fabricated products, the manufacturers had the full support of the federal government. The government advocated strongly the removal or reduction of tariffs on fully manufactured products among the major trading nations of the world, and proposed substantial financial assistance, particularly in the area of export financing, along with significant fiscal incentives to expand and improve production facilities and to increase exports of processed material and fabricated products, the last being accompanied by vigorous trade promotional efforts.

Canada supported fully the United States in what became known as the Kennedy Round of Trade Negotiations. The key objectives of Canada's trade policy in these negotiations were explained by the Minister of Finance in these terms:

These negotiations will be more concerned with manufactured products and we must keep clearly in mind that the expansion of efficient secondary industries is necessary to provide adequate employment opportunities for Canada's growing labour force. For this reason we shall be looking for those particular tariff reductions abroad which will open up new export markets for the products of our secondary industries. This will help them to achieve better economies of scale, which are vital to the attainment of cost efficiency.

For three-quarters of her first century as an independent nation Canada has welcomed the inflow of foreign capital and its participation in the industrial and general economic development of the country. In most areas of economic activity, Canada did not impose restrictions on the inflow and outflow of foreign capital. Funds could go into any secondary industry or natural-resource sector that foreign investors wished. Such capital was treated equally with domestic capital, a privilege accorded to foreign investors unmatched in any other industrially developed country in the world.

Foreign capital was attracted by the high return for funds invested, by the ease of transferring dividends and repatriating capital, and by the liberal character of fiscal policies pursued by Conservative and Liberal governments alike, as far as the treatment of foreign investment was concerned. Large and increasing amounts of foreign capital moved into Canada, most of it, since the end of the First World War, going into industrial and resources development.

Even though Canada invested what for this country were significant amounts abroad, her external net international indebtedness increased by leaps and bounds over the last few decades. The result was that foreign investors took overwhelming control over secondary industries and natural-resource development, with the greatest proportion exercised by U.S. corporations and investors. The claim has been made that foreign investors, particularly American industries, have moved into those sectors that bring the greatest rewards for risks taken, the implication being that Canadians have to be content to place their savings in safe and conventional forms or in the less profitable industries. But new evidence has become available with the publication of the first report under the Corporations and Labour Unions Returns Act suggesting that this claim is not quite borne out. The 1962 report provides details for nineteen sectors of manufacturing activity in Canada. Of these, eleven industry groups showed greater foreign ownership while eight groups showed greater Canadian ownership.

The inflow of foreign capital has brought many benefits to domestic industry and to Canadians generally. American industries in particular, in sending capital to Canada, not only wanted an adequate return on their investment but also were interested in acquiring a long-term stake in the economic growth of the host country – whether this included access to raw materials, access to energy resources, or access to markets.

They were primarily interested in the *continuing* success of their subsidiaries. They re-invested large amounts of their earnings in the country and they sent additional capital to Canada when this was required to finance further expansion and integration of operations. With this capital came American management and American skill, as well as, in a number of instances, assurances of markets either in the United States or overseas.

Canadians were thus able to expand their manufacturing industries more rapidly than they could have done on their own savings and their own initiative. And further, Canadians were able to increase the productivity of their manufacturing operations – in many instances either up to the level of performance achieved in the United States or close to it, sometimes even exceeding it – because they were able to draw freely on American scientific and technological progress and managerial experience. This applies to some extent also to foreign investment coming from overseas, though its impact and non-financial contribution to Canadian industrial development was less in the last half-century than the contribution made by American investors.

While the benefits were fairly readily observable, the disadvantages were less apparent, though, in the views of some, just as real. While some complaints were being voiced about American-controlled industries in Canada not behaving as 'good' Canadian corporate citizens, there were fewer complaints about foreign control from other countries. Little concrete evidence was presented to substantiate such claims.

But the public's uneasiness about growing foreign control became more pronounced, particularly in the decade commencing with the mid 1950s, when figures released indicated that foreign investors had achieved majority control over most of Canada's key economic sectors, particularly manufacturing and mining. It represented not so much a concern about the lack or the inadequacy of opportunities for Canadians to participate in these foreign-controlled businesses – though this was one factor – but rather in an innate aversion to economic control that could lead to political control and interference in Canadian national affairs.

Politicians were slow to sense this growing public uneasiness. Canadian-American economic and political relations had, by and large, remained friendly for many years, and there appeared little that the U.S. government could do to help Canadians in the dilemma they were facing. For as long as Canadian laws freely permitted the inflow of U.S. capital, and as long as American private investors chose to direct a large portion of the capital available for investment abroad to Canada, the matter of limiting inflow of foreign capital, the manner of prescribing its participation in Canadian industrial and resources development, and the ways and means of encouraging Canadian investors to acquire a greater stake in that development, were largely domestic matters for Canadians to resolve.

Gradually both major political parties in Canada recognized this basic truth. Principles and policies were evolved, which in their broad outlines had striking similarities. To quote John Diefenbaker when he was Prime Minister of Canada, leading an overwhelming Conservative majority in Parliament:

We have had to import capital on a large scale. . . . This continued inflow of capital into Canada has desirable and undesirable features. We like the higher and accelerated rate of growth and development it makes possible. We do not like to have a large proportion of many of our major industries owned or controlled outside Canada. . . .

We have made it clear that we expect foreign concerns operating in Canada, or Canadian subsidiaries of foreign companies, to carry on operations as Canadian businesses. We expect them to make available a fair portion of their equity securities for purchase by Canadians; to include Canadians on their Boards of Directors; to make proper disclosure of their Canadian operations; to employ competent Canadians in senior management and technical positions; to conduct a fair share of their research in Canada; to purchase their requirements within Canada if those are available on competitive terms; and not to be denied by those in control a fair opportunity to sell their Canadian products in export markets.

Three years later, Walter Gordon, the Minister of Finance in a Liberal minority government, had this to say about Canadians' relying too greatly on the savings of other nations:

There is a clearly recognized danger that if deficits continue at this rate, they will lead to a growing measure of control of our economy passing abroad. There is a danger that in allowing these deficits to continue we are sacrificing our birthright, the birthright which our forefathers laboured so hard to hand on to us.

The Minister then proceeded to present to Parliament a number of fiscal measures designed to encourage foreign-controlled companies to offer Canadians at least 25 per cent equity interest in their firms. While some of the fiscal proposals were alterered as the debate about their merits and demerits continued both within and outside Parliament, the actions taken by the Canadian government were symptomatic of its desire to search for ways to lead Canadians out of the dilemma.

An unforeseen development, however, was to offer some possible assistance from an unexpected source. The U.S. balance of payments had been deteriorating for several years. When mild measures of exhortation to American industry and investors were not fully effective, the U.S. government presented a set of guide-lines with the specific objective, among other things, of reducing the capital outflow for direct investment abroad. Canada, which had been receiving the largest share of U.S. capital going to a single country, was likely to be more significantly affected than most other nations.

Faced with the possibility of a reduction of capital inflow from the U.S., Canada protested to Washington. One point particularly at issue was that Canadian subsidiaries were affected by U.S. directives given to American parent companies. And so, at a conference of the Joint United States–Canadian Committee on Trade and Economic Affairs, Canada obtained a clarification of what was regarded as an important matter of principle. United States authorities re-emphasized the view that 'United States subsidiaries abroad should behave as good citizens of the country where they are located'. This was a diplomatic way of saying that the American government had no intention of interfering in Canadian domestic economic affairs.

This announcement was followed shortly by the tabling in the House of Commons on March 31, 1966, of a statement of guidelines set out by the Canadian government to cover 'principles of good corporate behaviour for subsidiaries' of foreign companies operating in Canada. This twelve-point program, put forward by the Liberal Minister of Trade and Commerce, Robert H. Winters, encompassed all the essential points presented six years earlier by the Conservative Prime Minister, with some changes in wording and emphasis.

Of these twelve points, two are singled out here for brief reference, to indicate the problem any Canadian government faces. Point 9 of the guide-lines called for 'a Canadian outlook within management' including the 'promotion of qualified personnel and inclusion of a major proportion of

Canadian citizens on its Board of Directors'. Point 10 called for providing 'opportunity for equity participation in the Canadian enterprise by the Canadian public'.

The first report under the Corporations and Labour Unions Returns Act throws some interesting light on the dimensions of the problems to which the two points apply. There were in Canada 217 large corporations operating in the manufacturing and mining fields, each with assets of $25 million and over. Their total assets amounted to $19.3 billion. Of these, 138 companies, with assets of $12.8 billion, were 50 per cent or more non-resident owned. Only the remaining 79 companies, with assets of $6.5 billion, were less than 50 per cent non-resident owned.

Many of the Canadian citizens who were members of boards of directors of foreign-controlled companies were merely nominal members; they included frequently the Canadian lawyer and accountant representing the interests of the foreign subsidiary and the parent company in Canada. Hence Canadians have a long way to go to obtain a major say in the management of the big industrial corporations that largely shape Canada's economic destiny.

What opportunities do Canadians have to participate in the equity of the 217 giants? During the period 1958 to 1962, eighteen of the 217 offered voting shares to the public. Of these eighteen, nine were owned largely by Canadian residents; the degree of non-resident ownership here ranged from 3 to 17 per cent. The other nine were largely owned by non-residents, with one being 57 per cent owned by non-residents, another 68 per cent, and the remainder between 80 and 95 per cent. The eighteen corporations offered shares to the public that would represent approximately 15 per cent of the equity at the end of 1962. This amount would be slightly over 2 per cent of the equity of the 217 corporations with assets over $25 million each.

Two per cent is a long way from the 25 per cent that the former Minister of Finance described as a desirable goal of Canadian participation in foreign-controlled Canadian industrial and resources development.

Have Canadians pursued their struggle to industrialize their country in a haphazard and improvised fashion with little direction or definite purpose, or have they evolved a philosophy of industrial development based on sheer necessity to build up an economically and politically independent country? The traces of such a philosophy are faint, but the broad outline is recognizable.

All through Canada's first century as a nation, governments have taken a firm hand to encourage the growth of secondary industries in this country, to foster their productivity and viability, to spur them on to greater competitiveness both at home and abroad, to spread their benefits and to distribute them regionally so as to achieve a more balanced economic growth of the country as a whole.

All through that first century Canadians have been trying to achieve continued economic growth of a type and at a rate that would bring the greatest benefits to the nation as a whole. In this process they became preoccupied with this argument: were greater economic benefits to be derived from pursuing liberal trade policies and concentrating mainly on the development of their natural resources and such secondary industries as were competitive in world markets, or should they encourage the growth of the whole range of manufacturing industry to become a 'fully' industrialized nation?

Even before Confederation, and continuing thereafter for a hundred years, the argument centred around whether Canadians should remain a nation of 'hewers of wood and drawers of water', or find their true destiny in expanding manufacturing industries and pursuing a course of nationalism whatever the cost. This argument has been conducted latterly along more sophisticated lines, under the veil of pious endorsement of liberal trade principles.

What those engaging in this eternal debate are apparently overlooking is that shaping the pattern and direction of Canadian economic development is not just a matter of choice made by sectors of self-interest, by armchair strategists, or by improvising politicians – but a matter of economic circumstances and economic forces that vary over time and are subject to strong domestic and international influences, both economic and political.

The whole pattern of Canada's economic development over the last century provides ample evidence that the choice Canadians had to make was not the simple black or white one of whether to remain 'hewers of wood and drawers of water'. What they had to decide was the degree to which they could balance the expansion in secondary industries with the growth of primary industries and, in the twentieth century, with a significant expansion in tertiary industries (the service sector). It was through this balancing of expansion in one sector with the growth in another sector, through the balancing of development of one region with improvements in another region, through the balancing of increases in income levels of the majority of the population with the support of income levels of those less well endowed, that Canadians were able to make their greatest economic and social progress.

While Canadians have always been a self-reliant and energetic people, and for most of the century have preferred less government to more government, on the subject of industrial development there has been less public controversy about government participation than on any other major economic, social, or political issue facing the nation. As a result, governments have formulated a variety of economic policies and taken numerous steps to foster and achieve continuing industrialization of the Canadian economy.

The very act of Confederation in 1867 brought into focus the ambitions of a fledgling nation: to create a strong, more integrated, and more unified economic base on which to build a confident and prosperous nation through developing the vast natural resources of half a continent and through speeding up the process of industrialization.

All through Sir John A. Macdonald's National Policy, in the latter part of the nineteenth century, through the period of liberal trade policies of Sir Wilfrid Laurier in the early twentieth century, through the great tariff-raising contest in the R. B. Bennett era of 1930 to 1932 when increases in the general level of duty on the bulk of imports approximated 50 per cent (exceeding in broad terms the increases of even the National Policy), to the period after the Second World War when successive Liberal and Conservative governments subscribed to the principle of Canada's joining other countries in the gradual freeing of international trade – all along, politicians have striven to encourage, strengthen, and broaden Canada's industrial development. Some of these measures became fully effective only after considerable delay. Other policies proved to be successful shortly after their implementation, such as the building up of a huge industrial war machine during the Second World War and its smooth, effective conversion to peacetime industrial uses in the years 1945 to 1947. Still other policies did not go beyond declarations of hope and exhortation to business to act in the national interest, sometimes accompanied by ineffective government action, such as the efforts to increase the financial stake of Canadians in foreign-controlled industries.

The outstanding strengthener of Canadian industry, and a great nation builder in an economic sense, was an engineer turned politician, Clarence Decatur Howe, an American by birth who made Canada his home and who devoted all his adult life to making this country strong. Minister of the Crown in the federal government from 1935 to 1957, he held eight portfolios: Railways and Canals, Marine, and Transport before the war; Munitions and Supply during the war; Reconstruction, Reconstruction and Supply, Trade and Commerce, and Defence Production after the war.

His economic achievements are legendary and his direct contributions to building up Canadian industry more numerous than those of any Cabinet Minister before or since. C. D. Howe was once asked: 'Has the Canadian government a long-term industrial development program?' He replied in the affirmative, adding:

> Our program, though, may be less distinct and [less] publicized than that of some other countries. We do not tie our

program of industrialization to a particular period of time like some of the four or five year plans which have become so fashionable today. Our program is a continuing one because we consider further industrialization of the Canadian economy as one of the important factors contributing to a continuing high level of employment and income, with which a rising standard of living for the Canadian people is intimately associated. To this end we are devoting all the means at our disposal.

C. D. Howe was the first Minister to lay down some of the basic principles that could usefully guide government in developing policies to encourage Canada's long-term industrial development. Briefly these included:

1. Canada is a free-enterprise economy and the initiative for industrial expansion rests with private individuals and firms.
2. The government will endeavour, through its policies, to create a climate within which private initiative thrives and industrial expansion is encouraged.
3. The government will take the initiative and do what it can to co-ordinate the efforts of governmental, business, and other interested groups in achieving full and effective utilization of industrial expansion in the interests of all citizens in the country.
4. If industrial expansion and economic development is hampered by the lack of intiative, the government, where the national interest demands, will take appropriate action.

In essence, C. D. Howe's philosophy reflected a great deal of the pragmatism that has been so typical of Canadian economic policy formulated during the last century: Let private enterprise do the best job it can do in building up industry and let it reap the appropriate rewards for risk and initiative. Let government help private business any way it can to do a better job itself. But if individual initiative fails or is unwilling to proceed with industrial development clearly called for as being in the national interest, then government intervention must take place, preferably indirectly, but if necessary directly.

When Canadians needed a synthetic-rubber industry during the Second World War, C. D. Howe approached a number of companies to suggest that they build up such an industry. He offered financial and other government assistance, but there were no takers. The Canadian government then established the Polymer Corporation. This company, founded in 1942, has become in the postwar period one of the most successful business corporations in Canada, operating as a Crown company, producing synthetic rubber and a wide range of chemicals. Drawing on substantial research achievements and a high rate of productivity, this company competes successfully in world markets and produces profits that are the envy of many a large private corporation in Canada.

Some of the measures taken by the federal government to encourage Canada's industrial development in the postwar period were these: setting up of the Industrial Development Bank to provide credit, not obtainable from commercial sources, to industries, particularly small enterprises; providing fiscal incentives such as tax concessions and accelerated capital-cost allowances to establish new industries and to modernize and expand existing industries; offering export-credit insurance and financing to increase sales abroad of products manufactured in Canada; giving assistance to encourage more industrial research and improved design; subsidizing specific manufacturing sectors; and granting tariff concessions for infant industries. A new department of government was established in 1963, the Department of Industry, specifically charged with the responsibility of fostering the establishment, growth, efficiency, and improvement of manufacturing industries by programs (1) to assist the adaptation of manufacturing industries to changing conditions in domestic and export markets and to changes in the techniques of production; (2) to assist manufacturing industries that require special measures to develop an unrealized potential or to cope with exceptional problems of adjustment; and (3) to promote the development and use of modern industrial technology in Canada and to improve the effectiveness of participation by the Government of Canada in industrial research. In addition, the Department has an Area Development Agency, which has been established to formulate and implement programs to assist economic development in designated areas.

Other measures taken by the federal government were designed to help certain specific high-productivity industries to become even more efficient through a very large expansion of the markets they were serving. The outstanding example was the special arrangements worked out with the U.S. government and the automobile industry for Canadian subsidiaries to share, on an equal basis with their American parents, access to the whole North American market for automobiles and production parts. Other far-reaching measures proposed by the Canadian government included the establishment of a Canada Development Corporation whose functions, as outlined by the Minister of Finance, include:

> Financing the initial development, or expansion of large-scale industrial projects in Canada, and to provide financing, including refinancing, for large Canadian enterprises which might otherwise be led to seek funds outside Canada, with a consequent loss of ownership and control to non-residents. The Corporation would be expected to invest in projects and enterprises which are likely to contribute to the sound economic development of Canada and to be profitable in the long run.

While the federal government has determinedly pursued policies to foster Canadian industrial development over the century – at times encouragingly effective and at times frustratingly ineffective – provincial governments have come more into their own, as far as industrial development is concerned, in the last half-century and particularly since the end of the Second World War.

Three factors have contributed to the increasing importance of provincial governments in the field of industrial development. Many government measures relate to problems facing specific industries located in Canada's major urban centres, problems that are related to the 'property and civil rights' clause of Section 92 of the British North America Act and are therefore the direct concern of provincial governments. Provincial governments have offered to train labour, build plants, construct adequate transportation facilities, and open and expand regional and local markets. And finally, the fiscal strength of provincial governments since the Second World War has improved greatly, partly as the result of Canada's great prosperity and partly as the result of popular demand for increased decentralization; hence provincial governments can now assist industry through direct means such as the building of industrial estates and through indirect means such as industrial development loans. They have also provided low-cost energy sources and industrial research.

What did industrial development mean to Canadians during the first century of their nationhood? It represented, as to all young nations, a highly desirable objective: Canadians planned to speed up the process of economic growth, and to become a 'developed nation', because they wanted material welfare and political independence. What Canadians had to learn early in their economic history and throughout the century was that industrial development not only brought blessings but also required sacrifices and hard toil – with one generation doing the toiling in the hope that the next generation would get the benefits. But the next generation would find itself in a similar situation, and the fruits of labour of industrialization remained more of a promise for the future than a realization for the present.

This is not to deny that industrial development did not bring many benefits to Canadians during the first century. It did: more jobs, higher incomes, improved standards of living, a sense of national achievement and ability to play a greater role in international affairs. These results were achieved not because of industrial progress alone but because Canadians were able to achieve reasonably balanced economic growth over the last century. Industrial progress was accompanied by improvements in the food-producing and natural-resource industries. This was blended with the rapid expansion of the service sector, which served both the industrial and the resource development of the country as well as providing an improvement in the quality of living – essential if economic progress is to be equated with human progress.

Industrial development is even more vital for political reasons. If Canadians want to remain an independent and viable North American nation, living as they do next to two giant neighbours – the U.S.A. and the U.S.S.R. – then they must build up their economic and industrial strength on a continuing and internationally competitive basis. In this uncertain world, economic growth and industrial development are essential to Canada's national survival.

15. Unions and Co-operatives

EUGENE A. FORSEY

Canada at Confederation was basically rural and agricultural. Only about one-eighth of its people lived in places of 5,000 or over. What the 1871 census called the 'agricultural class' made up about a quarter of 'all classes'. It was over twice as large as the 'industrial class', and nearly twice as large as the 'industrial' and 'commercial' classes put together.

Canada today is overwhelmingly industrial. Over half its people live in places of 5,000 and over. Farmers and farm workers make up less than ten per cent of the labour force. Union members alone outnumber the 'agricultural class' more than two to one, and this though unions have succeeded in organizing only about thirty-five to forty per cent of those eligible for membership.

Not less striking is the growth of organization among both farmers and workers. At Confederation, there were scarcely any farmers' organizations, unions were few and scattered, co-operatives were almost non-existent. There were farmers' associations in New Brunswick, the Eastern Townships of Quebec, and here and there in Ontario, but no shadow of a central organization. There were one British trade union and five American, besides purely local Canadian unions in each of the four original provinces and on Vancouver Island; there was one local central organization. Now we have a Canadian Federation of Agriculture, with affiliated provincial organizations in every province but Newfoundland, representing about eighty per cent of the farm population. We have the Canadian Labour Congress, a national federation of unions with over a million members, with provincial federations in every province and local labour councils in over a hundred cities and towns. We have the Confederation of National Trade Unions, with about one-tenth as many members as the C.L.C., almost all in Quebec. We have the Co-operative Union of Canada, for English Canada, and the Conseil Canadien de la Coopération, for French Canada, working closely together, and between them grouping an astonishing variety of co-operative enterprises. There are now close to 5,000 credit unions, with nearly 3,000,000 members and assets of over $1,500,000,000, and almost 3,000 marketing and purchasing co-operatives, with about 1,700,000 members and a total annual business of about $1,500,000,000.

Why did these movements spring up? Why have they persisted and grown?

The farmers' movement arose partly from the perennial deep-seated rural suspicion of being outsmarted and exploited by urban interests; partly from the feeling that unorganized farmers will not get the legislative measures agriculture needs; partly from the belief that organized farmers can save money by doing their own buying and selling, eliminating the urban 'middleman'. With the growth of industrialism, farmers felt confronted by an unholy trinity of manufacturers, banks, and railways. They had to fight the manufacturers, whose tariffs and 'monopolies' raised their costs and restricted their markets. They had to fight the banks (and mortgage companies) to keep themselves from being swamped by debt and crippled by high interest-charges. They had to fight the railways to get fair treatment and fair rates. They had also, in the West, to fight the Grain Exchange and the elevator companies. The individual farmer was helpless in the face of such opponents, and the farmers' movement arose out of the consciousness of that helplessness.

The labour movement arose out of a similar consciousness of the helplessness of the individual wage-earner. In classical economic theory, the free, individual employer confronted the free, individual worker. Each was the best judge of his own interests, and they struck an individual bargain which gave each exactly what was right for him and for the community. But the workers soon found that the 'free' employer was freer than the 'free' worker. The employer knew more. He had more money. He could afford to wait till hunger drove the worker to accept his terms. Within the factory, he was an absolute monarch: the worker had no rights, only privileges. The employer gave, and the employer took away. He got as much as he could for as little as he could.

The worker needed higher wages and better working conditions. He needed constitutional government in industry. He needed to make the employer a limited monarch, still managing the plant, but within limits laid down by an industrial constitution, the collective agreement, which would give the worker rights and the means of enforcing them.

The worker also faced some of the same problems as the farmer: the tendency of protected manufacturers to raise prices, of banks and mortgage companies to charge all the traffic would bear.

Workers faced also one problem farmers did not. There was no legislation prohibiting farmers' organizations or penalizing their activities. There was legislation prohibiting unions or penalizing their activities. In 1872, the year of the historic Toronto printers' strike, unions in Ontario and Quebec were still 'conspiracies' at common law, and the law was invoked to crush them.

Long before Confederation, workers in England at Rochdale, Lancashire, had decided that unions and collective bargaining were not enough; that what was needed was a radical transformation of the industrial system. Workers should build their own non-profit system, side by side with private enterprise, but with the hope of eventually superseding it. They should organize to do their own buying and their own producing of the things they needed, through 'co-operatives', in which every member would have just one vote (no matter how much capital he put in), and from which every member would get dividends in proportion to his 'patronage' or purchases (not the amount of his share in the society's capital).

These 'Rochdale principles' became the corner-stones of a world-wide co-operative movement. Canadian farmers and workers alike were not slow to recognize the possibilities of using co-operatives as one way to freedom and prosperity.

The real beginnings of the farmers' movement came in 1872, when the farmers of Stanstead, Quebec, invited the American 'National Grange' to set up a branch there. Within three years, the Grange had spread to other parts of the Eastern Townships and to Ontario, Nova Scotia, and New Brunswick. A Dominion Grange came into being, and by 1877 had won virtual independence. By 1879, there were 766 local Granges, with 31,000 members, mainly in Ontario but also in Quebec, the Maritime Provinces, and Manitoba. From then on, the order declined. In 1907, it merged with the Farmers' Association of Ontario to form the Dominion Grange and Farmers' Association, which expired in 1913. At one time or another, the Grange had at least one local in every province except Saskatchewan.

A second American farm organization, the Patrons of Industry, entered Ontario in 1889. Within a year, lodges had been set up in three counties and a Canadian section incorporated. Almost at once it became independent.

The Patrons grew even faster than the Grange, but declined faster still. Within five years, they had 50,000 members; by 1902 they had practically disappeared. The Ontario organization had spread into Quebec and the Maritime Provinces, and the American order had organized a Manitoba association, which soon became independent.

With the opening up of the prairies, the centre of gravity in the farmers' movement shifted to the West. The new organizations were purely Canadian, though both American and Old Country immigrants played a considerable part in them.

Dissatisfaction with the working of the Manitoba Grain Act led to the organization of the Territorial Grain Growers Association in 1902 and the Manitoba Grain Growers Association in 1903. In Alberta, in 1905, a local of the Territorial Grain Growers and one unit of the American Society of Equity united to form the Farmers' Association of Alberta. What was left of the American Society became the Canadian Society of Equity. In 1909, the Farmers' Association and the Canadian Society formed the United Farmers of Alberta.

In 1907, the Manitoba organization, the Saskatchewan (formerly Territorial) Grain Growers Association, and the Alberta Farmers' Association formed an Interprovincial Council of Grain Growers' and Farmers' Associations. Early in 1910, this, with the Ontario Grange, formed the Canadian Council of Agriculture.

The United Farmers of Ontario was formed in 1914; in 1918, the United Farmers of New Brunswick; in 1919, the Fermiers-Unis de Québec; in 1920, the United Farmers of Nova Scotia and the United Farmers of Prince Edward Island. The U.F.N.B. and U.F.N.S. were admitted to the Canadian Council of Agriculture in 1920, the F.U.Q. in 1923. In British Columbia, attempts at organization by the American Farmers' Alliance and the Grange had petered out; the first real organization was the United Farmers of British Columbia, founded in 1917.

No provincial organization calling itself United Farmers now remains. But the national farm organization – succes-

sively the Canadian Council, Chamber, and now Federation,
of Agriculture—has for many years covered substantially the
whole country, and includes not only the provincial federations but many organizations in particular branches of
agriculture and most of the large farm co-operative organizations. During the 1940s and 1950s, an insurgent farm-union
movement sprang up in the four western provinces and
Ontario, with new organizations in Manitoba, British
Columbia, and Ontario. Only the Ontario and Manitoba
unions are now outside the Federation, but the five Farm
Unions still have their own National Union. The Quebec
farm organizations have been affiliated with the Canadian
Federation for well over twenty years.

Canadian unions existed as early as 1814, but a labour movement got started only a few years before the farmers' movement. There was no American central organization Canadian
workers could call in, so they had to do the job themselves. In
1863, Hamilton unions formed a Trades Assembly. In 1871,
six Toronto craft unions (five international, one local) did
likewise. Ottawa followed suit the next year; St. Catharines
soon after. In 1873, the Toronto Assembly called a convention of Canadian unions, which established the first national
central organization, the Canadian Labor Union. In practice
this was an almost purely Ontario affair.

   The depression of the 1870s was fatal to the C.L.U. (which
held its last convention in 1877) and to the Toronto Trades
Assembly (which expired the next year) and the other local
central organizations. But many of the individual unions survived, and, with the adoption of the National Policy and the
building of the C.P.R., began to grow. The building trades
showed a marked expansion. The railway unions spread
west and east from Ontario. The Nova Scotia coal miners,
in 1879, formed the first regional miners' union in America.
An American national organization, the Knights of Labor,
which included both skilled and unskilled workers, entered
Canada effectively in 1881 and spread rapidly. Five of the six
unions that had formed the Toronto Trades Assembly, and a

dozen new ones (mostly craft), set up the Toronto Trades and Labor Council (1881), which under one name or another has functioned ever since; and in December 1883 this body summoned a national convention. With a single break (1883-6), the national centre has functioned regularly ever since: first as the Canadian Labor Congress in 1883, then as the Trades and Labor Congress till 1956 when it merged with the long-alienated Canadian Congress of Labour to form the present Canadian Labour Congress.

The earlier Congress, like its predecessor, was at first a purely Ontario organization. The first delegates came from craft unions, unions of unskilled workers, and assemblies of the Knights of Labor. At the second convention, the craft unions were hopelessly outnumbered by the Knights, who had a majority also at the conventions of 1887, 1888, 1891, and 1893, and formed a substantial minority in most other years till 1897.

The more genuinely national character of the new central body was evident in 1889, when it met in Montreal, with Quebec well represented. Until 1898, however, conventions were made up almost entirely of delegates from the two central provinces. It cost too much to send delegates from the Maritimes or the West, unless the convention happened to be held there. Workers who, like one delegate in 1883, got $8.50 a week clearly could not build rich unions; total revenue of the Congress even in 1896 was only $255.26. The first delegate from British Columbia appeared in 1890, from Manitoba in 1895, New Brunswick in 1897, Prince Edward Island in 1900, and Nova Scotia in 1903. In 1905, there were no Maritime delegates at all and only five Westerners in a total of 139. Indeed, except when the convention met outside Ontario or Quebec, till 1906 one or other of those provinces usually had a clear majority of the delegates. Representation varied markedly with the place where the convention was held.

Until the late 1890s, relations with American trade unionism presented no problem. Most of the unions in Canada were either locals of internationals chartered by the American

Federation of Labor or local assemblies of the Knights of
Labor. The Trades and Labor Congress confined itself
almost wholly to seeking legislative changes, and till 1896
seems to have had no contact with the A. F. of L. In that year,
the Congress complained to the Federation about the
application of the American Alien Contract Labor Law to
Canadian workers. The Federation replied by suggesting the
T.L.C. send a fraternal delegate to the A. F. of L. convention.
This the T.L.C. did not do, but in 1898 it invited the A. F.
of L. to send one to the T.L.C. convention, and in 1899 the
two began the exchange which still continues.

So far, harmony. But the Congress was poor. It had no
office and no full-time staff. (These came only in 1902, with
'a stenographer and a typewriter' and 'two desks and a chair'.)
From 1897 on, the Congress kept trying to get the international unions (or the A. F. of L.) to turn over the dues paid
to the A. F. of L. on Canadian membership, a problem finally
solved by getting the internationals to affiliate their Canadian
membership direct. Meanwhile, in 1897, the A.F.of L. started
making a grant (initially $100) to the Congress.

Till 1902, the Congress constitution had always provided
for representation of the Knights of Labor, and from 1895 for
national unions as well as international. By 1902, however,
the internationals had become so strong, and the Knights so
weak, that the former were able to get the constitution
amended to eliminate the Knights and to forbid recognition
of any national union where an international existed. In
effect, this meant exclusion of any organization 'dual' to an
A.F.of L. union.

The T.L.C. did not, however, by any means accept the
subordinate role that the Federation repeatedly tried to
impose on it. The Federation persisted, right down to 1955,
in chartering local unions in Canada. It tried to deny the
Congress the right to charter local councils, and succeeded in
1939 in forcing it to expel all the C.I.O. unions, though only
after a struggle; but a similar attempt, in 1946, to force
expulsion of the Machinists collapsed. (The Congress president was himself a Machinist.) After this, the Congress set

up a full-scale series of departments and an organizing staff, and otherwise made plain the status it felt it did and should enjoy as a fully autonomous Canadian trade-union centre.

None of these disputes, however, really disturbed the basic harmony between Congress and Federation. The Congress, made up overwhelmingly of international unions whose American members were affiliated to the Federation, never faltered in its allegiance to international unionism. It knew that in most industries international unions alone had the staff, experience, and money to do the job that had to be done.

Meanwhile, however, the Canadian labour movement had been 'by schisms rent asunder, by heresies distrest'. The unions expelled by the T.L.C. in 1902 promptly formed the National Trades and Labour Congress, which in 1908 became the Canadian Federation of Labour. In 1919, after the Winnipeg general strike, many unionists in the West, attracted by revolutionary industrial unionism, broke away from the T.L.C. and formed the One Big Union. Between 1901 and 1921, small local Roman Catholic unions (some of them former Knights of Labor assemblies) sprang up in Quebec under the fostering care of the clergy, and in 1921 formed the Canadian and Catholic Confederation of Labour (now the Confederation of National Trade Unions, 'deconfessionalized' but still almost purely Quebec and French-Canadian). In 1927, the Canadian Federation of Labour and other national unions formed the All-Canadian Congress of Labour, dedicated to national and industrial unionism (a single union for all workers, skilled and unskilled, in a given industry, instead of separate unions for each craft). By 1935, purely Canadian unions of one kind or another, including the Workers' Unity League (Communist), made up nearly half of the total union membership. Within a few years, however, international unionism reasserted its predominance, and for many years now about seventy per cent of all Canadian unionists have belonged to internationals.

The great debate in the United States in the 1930s over the relative merits of craft and industrial unionism found only faint echoes in Canada. But when the T.L.C. expelled the Canadian branches of C.I.O. unions, these at once formed a Canadian Committee.

Through all this, the four railway-running trades (conductors, trainmen, engineers, and firemen) remained unaffiliated with any central body, though all of them had occasionally sent delegates to T.L.C. conventions. They co-operated with each other and with the two T.L.C. railway unions in a Dominion Joint Legislative Committee. In the last few years the two largest, the Trainmen and the Firemen, have affiliated with the C.L.C.; the Conductors have dwindled to very small proportions, and the Engineers have voted to affiliate with the C.L.C.

In 1940, the All-Canadian Congress and the Canadian C.I.O. united in the Canadian Congress of Labour which from the first enjoyed complete autonomy both for itself and for the Canadian sections of C.I.O. unions. The C.C.L. organized the mass-production industries, pioneered in labour research, workers' education, and labour public relations, and, though never as big as its rival, eventually had as many members as the whole movement had had in 1939. Till 1953, almost annual resolutions of both C.C.L. and C.L.C. in favour of unity came to nothing, since the A. F. of L. and C.I.O. were at loggerheads and the T.L.C. could not admit unions dual to A. F. of L. unions. Once the American organizations agreed to discuss unity, this obstacle disappeared, and in 1956 the T.L.C. and C.C.L. united as the Canadian Labour Congress. Within a year, what was left of the One Big Union also joined. For a time it looked as if the Catholic unions too would come in, but this fell through. By 1966, the only considerable bodies still outside the C.L.C. were the C.N.T.U.; the United Mine Workers; the Communist-dominated Mine, Mill and Smelter Workers and United Electrical, Radio and Machine Workers; the Locomotive Engineers; the Teamsters; and the Seafarers – the last two having been expelled from the C.L.C.

The Canadian co-operative movement has its roots in both the farmers' and labour movements. The farmers' organizations, almost from the beginning, went into business themselves in various co-operative enterprises. Coal miners in Stellarton, Nova Scotia, under the leadership of a British working-class co-operator, opened a co-operative store in 1861, and at least nine more followed in that province before 1900. One lasted till 1905, when it was burned down; but it was succeeded almost at once by the British Canadian Co-operative Society, which still flourishes. The Canadian Labor Union, in 1876 and 1877, adopted resolutions strongly supporting co-operatives, which one of the leaders called 'the panacea for all the evils of the workingman'. Co-operatives were a cardinal tenet of the Knights of Labor, and its Canadian assemblies established several co-operative businesses (all short-lived). The T.L.C., under the leadership of immigrants bred in the British union–co-operative tradition, repeatedly passed resolutions endorsing co-operatives, as did the C.C.L. later.

The first really big development in co-operatives, however, came with Alphonse Desjardins's founding of the *caisses populaires* (credit unions) in Quebec, in 1900. The second, the grain growers' co-operatives in Western Canada, began with the launching of the Grain Growers' Grain Company in 1906. This, after tribulations well nigh incredible, became a large, highly successful enterprise. It was followed by co-operative elevator companies in Saskatchewan (1911) and Alberta (1913); and in 1917, the Grain Growers' Grain Company and the Alberta Co-operative Elevator Company merged to form the United Grain Growers Limited.

About the time the western developments began, several co-operative stores had been started in southern Ontario. In 1909, George Keen, one of the leaders there, summoned a meeting at which was founded the Co-operative Union of Canada. By 1911, this had member organizations in Ontario, Quebec, Nova Scotia, Saskatchewan, and British Columbia. Reorganized in 1943, it now includes provincial co-operative unions except in Alberta and Quebec, and seven interprovincial co-operatives.

In Ontario, co-operation among farmers on a large-scale began in 1914 with the United Farmers' Co-operative Company Limited (now the United Co-operatives of Ontario). In Quebec, the Coopérative Fédérée, founded in 1922, is now a large and flourishing organization. Co-operative sales of farm products in the two provinces now run to well over $200,000,000 annually, and co-operative purchases of farm supplies to well over $100,000,000.

A second wave of farm co-operation hit the prairies in the mid 1920s, resulting in the formation of wheat and other 'pools', which, after spectacular successes, nearly foundered in the Great Depression. Massive government help pulled them through, and the three wheat pools, with the United Grain Growers, are now the largest grain-marketing co-operatives in the world, though the Wheat Board has taken over some of their original functions. The prairies also boast the largest group of consumer co-operatives on the continent, the first consumer-owned petroleum refinery, and one of the world's few co-operative farm-implement companies. Co-operatives market well over half a billion dollars' worth of prairie farm products.

Recurrent in the history of the farmers' and labour movements have been attempts to get together for common ends, notably legislative or political. The initiative usually came from labour, understandably enough. Labour was for many decades much the weaker: it needed the farmers' help much more than they needed its help.

From the beginning, labour had a long list of legislative proposals. In 1874, Ottawa elected the first Canadian Labour M.L.A. In 1876 and 1877, the C.L.U. was calling for independent political action. The Knights of Labor also favoured it. The Canadian Labor Congress, in 1883, unanimously endorsed it. Throughout the 1880s and 1890s there were sporadic attempts, almost all unsuccessful, to elect Labour members to the Ontario and Quebec legislatures and the Dominion House, and the T.L.C. repeatedly renewed its endorsement of direct political action. In 1886, it approached the Grange to secure united action on the Factory Act, and to get its opinion on no less than twenty-one questions of public interest. The replies were not encouraging.

The Patrons of Industry, however, were eager for political action. They ran a candidate in the 1891 Dominion election, forty-three in the Ontario election of 1894 (electing seventeen), and twenty-nine in the Dominion election of 1896 (electing three). The T.L.C. seized the opportunity to renew the attempt at farmer-labour co-operation. In 1893, the Congress, the Patrons, the Grange, the Knights of Labor, and the 'Social Problems Conference' worked out a common platform, and the Congress set up a committee to meet with the Patrons for 'a union of the labor forces (rural and urban)'. In 1894, it actually provided for Patron affiliation, though this was rescinded in 1895.

The Patrons fizzled out politically after 1896, but the Congress kept talking about a Labour Party and (occasionally) about farmer-labour co-operation; and local labour organizations kept running occasional candidates. Two labour members, one the Congress president, Ralph Smith, were elected to the Dominion House in 1900, and a third candidate was barely defeated. In 1906, a second Congress president, Alphonse Verville, was elected M.P., and the Congress adopted what became its political action policy for the rest of its life. The provincial executives were to summon conventions to set up Labour parties, and then to step out of the picture, having recommended the T.L.C. 'Platform of Principles' as the new parties' platform. The result was the foundation of Labour parties in Ontario, Quebec, Nova Scotia, Manitoba, and British Columbia. Nothing much followed till towards the end of the First World War.

In 1916, the Canadian Council of Agriculture drew up a Farmers' Platform. In 1919, the United Farmers in New Brunswick and in Ontario won two Dominion by-elections. The U.F.O. also won forty-four seats in the Ontario legislature, the Labour Party eleven, and the two formed a coalition government. In 1920, the western farmers' organizations, with the U.F.O. and the U.F.N.B., formed the National Progressive Party; Progressive and Progressive-Labour candidates won two Dominion by-elections; fourteen independent Farmer members were elected to the Manitoba legisla-

ture, seven Farmer and four Labour (co-operating) to the
Nova Scotia legislature, and seven Farmer to the New Brunswick legislature. In 1921, the U.F.A. won a sweeping victory
in Alberta and formed a government that included a Labour
minister; and the Progressives elected sixty-five members to
the Dominion House (thirty-seven from the prairies, twenty-
four from Ontario, one from New Brunswick, and three from
British Columbia). The Progressives took all but six of the
prairie seats, and Labour three of the rest. Their combined
forces outnumbered the Conservatives by eighteen. In 1922,
the United Farmers of Manitoba won a resounding victory
and formed a government. In 1923, the Saskatchewan Grain
Growers elected sixteen members to the provincial legislature.

The Progressives soon began to disintegrate. The Ontario
Farmer-Labour coalition was overwhelmingly defeated in
1923, and both parties ceased to be of any importance. The
Manitoba Farmers' government gradually faded into Liberalism. The U.F.A. government in Alberta was drowned by the
Social Credit tide in 1935. Farmers' parties in the rest of the
country virtually disappeared, and the various Labour parties, provincial and local, attained only very limited success,
chiefly in Manitoba.

The United Farmers of Canada, Saskatchewan section, had
co-operated with labour in setting up a provincial Farmer-
Labour Party, which, with the U.F.A. and various small
Labour parties, in 1932 launched a national farmer-labour
party – the Co-operative Commonwealth Federation (C.C.F.).
From 1941 on, both labour congresses devoted considerable
attention to promoting labour-farmer co-operation, but only
insurgent farmers' organizations showed much disposition to
co-operate, and the results were not impressive. The C.C.L.,
from 1943 till it merged with the T.L.C. in 1956, officially
endorsed the C.C.F., but usually without much visible electoral effect. The C.C.F. held power in Saskatchewan from
1944 to 1964.

In 1961, the Canadian Labour Congress and the C.C.F.
jointly launched the New Democratic Party, which absorbed
the C.C.F. The Congress itself did not affiliate, though unions

representing about a fifth of its membership have done so; farm and co-operative organizations have held aloof. The new party's performance in both Dominion and provincial elections has been disappointing.

The farmers' and co-operative movements are now solidly established, without serious divisions, and making steady, if unspectacular, progress. Labour has organized practically all the railway workers (a dwindling number) and a good half of all manual workers in manufacturing and other goods-producing industries. But it has scarcely touched most of the white-collar workers or workers in the growing service-producing industries. It is still divided: the C.N.T.U. is a formidable force in Quebec, where, moreover, French-Canadian nationalism raises problems within the C.L.C. itself. And though the C.L.C. is completely independent of the A.F. of L.–C.I.O., friction with that body, and with some of the big unions that belong to both, can still arise.

At Confederation, Canadian unions were at best barely legal; small, weak, scattered, and without any apparatus of co-operation; distrusted, despised, or hated by most of those in authority; cabin'd, cribb'd, confin'd by all manner of restrictions. Their members worked long hours for low wages and under bad conditions; social security was undreamt of. Now unions are not only legal: collective bargaining, once anathema to the respectable, is compulsory. The unions are big and strong, and they have local, provincial, and national federations. They are still perhaps distrusted by those in economic authority, but not despised, and seldom hated (at least openly). Their members generally work forty hours a week or less, for wages that are generally the second highest in the world, and usually under reasonably good conditions. They have a whole series of social security measures. Canadian unions can thus look back on a record of impressive achievement.

16. Transport

K. W. STUDNICKI-GIZBERT

The two main themes in Canadian transport are the application of new technologies to the needs of a growing and changing economy and the strengthening of Canadian unity. The use of transport, especially railways, as a means of national policy has led to the development of east-west transport systems and has often resulted in diverting commercial flows from the United States to Canadian centres or ports.

Considering the small populations and limited financial resources of the provinces of British North America, the scale on which railways were projected even before Confederation is most impressive. The construction of individual railway lines was pursued with great vigour: during the 1850s railway mileage increased from 66 to 2,065, and by 1867 there were approximately 2,500 miles of track in operation in Canada and the Maritime Provinces. These were built at the cost of over $150 a mile, which at that time represented a huge investment financed partly locally but largely from England. Almost from the start, most of the railways got into financial trouble; the Grand Trunk Railway being the chief problem. Almost from the start railway problems became a source of bitter political controversies. Revenue expectations of the early railways were not realized; local traffic development was not fast enough to provide economic volume of traffic, and the railways, like the canals before them, failed to attract any substantial volume of American traffic. The large influx of capital and labour caused by railway construction led to considerable stimulation of economic activity as well as to inflationary pressures and consequent dislocations. However, the changes brought by the railways were profound, and their role in making Confederation possible cannot be over-estimated.

Confederation was followed by the construction of the Intercolonial Railway, as the obligation to link the old province of Canada with the Maritimes by rail was explicitly written into the British North America Act. After its completion the line was not commercially successful, although the connection with the Grand Trunk Railway and thus with central Canada created a 'national system'. The line suffered from traffic volumes too low to generate revenues that would cover the high costs of construction, equipment, and operation, especially since these costs were to some extent inflated by inefficiencies during the construction and early operating stage.

The greatest transport dream realized after Confederation was the transcontinental railway. As the construction of the Intercolonial was conditional on the union of the Maritimes with Canada, so the construction of the Pacific railway was the condition of British Columbia's joining the new nation. Of course, without the transcontinental railway system, political and economic absorption of the Prairies by the new Dominion was not feasible.

The admission of British Columbia into Confederation and the fears of possible inroads by United States railways provided the incentive to start the C.P.R. as soon as possible. Even so, a decade passed before actual construction of the railway began. It took those ten years to carry out surveys over the large tracts of unknown country, and to sort out different financing projects. There was rivalry between competing financial groups, and bitter political controversy.

After the agreement with Canadian Pacific was signed, the progress of railway construction was rapid; here the credit is due not only to the dynamic group that managed Canadian Pacific Railways, but also to the government of the day, whose support enabled the company to overcome its financial crises. In 1885 the line was completed and opened for through traffic on June 28, 1886.

The following figures illustrate the progress made in Canada during the period 1875-85: the total number of miles in operation increased by 137 per cent from 4,331 to 10,273, as compared with the 94 per cent increase from 2,240 to 4,331 miles during the previous decade (1865-75). The total capital invested in Canadian railways increased from $318.6 million in 1875 to $625.6 million in 1885 or an increase of $307.0 million of which $117 million, or 38 per cent, represented the assistance by different levels of government. The extent of the effort expended in creating the railway system can be illustrated by the fact that the federal government's assistance to railway construction represented, on the average, 25 per cent of total federal expenditures during this decade. This is quite comparable with the current efforts of the developing countries to accelerate economic growth through transport investments. A survey of planned transport expenditures of underdeveloped countries indicates that transport investments amount to from 16 to 46 per cent of total public expenditures, in most cases falling within the 22-30 per cent range. The Canadian experience of the 1870s and '80s matches this pattern very well.

The rapid development of the West led to expectations of

even greater expansion, which appeared to be limited only by the availability and cost of transport. It appeared logical to think of the expansion of railway networks in terms of a new and competitive system. The beginning of this century witnessed the establishment of two such competitive national systems – the Canadian Northern and Grand Trunk Pacific.

The second national system, the Canadian Northern Railway, was established in 1899 by private interests with the assistance of the Dominion and Manitoba governments, through the amalgamation of three smaller companies. The new company expanded both west, from Manitoba through Edmonton to Vancouver, and east, to Ontario, Montreal, and the Maritimes. As G. R. Stevens describes it: 'Immigration was at its peak; in 1911-1912 more than 700,000 settlers arrived in Canada. Most of them sought virgin land and the Canadian Northern provided the key to that quest. As early as 1909 it was handling one third of the grain traffic of the prairies, and in 1911 it added a thousand miles of tracks to its holding.'

The third transcontinental system was the Grand Trunk. The Grand Trunk directors, operating a regional network in Ontario and Michigan, feared the railway would be strangled by the expansion of the C.P.R. and American railways unless it could take part of the new western markets. They shared Laurier's dreams of accelerating the already rapid development of the West and the northern timber and agricultural areas in Ontario and Quebec, and they responded to pressures for expansion from New Brunswick. Even if the concept of a second transcontinental railway could be defended on the grounds of fast economic development of the country, the creation of a third can be explained only by political factors and the strong personalities that became involved in the promotion of the rival schemes.

The First World War with its consequent cessation of rapid development, rising costs, and financing difficulties, made the collapse of the two new transcontinental systems imminent. For a short time government subsidies allowed the continuation of their operation and made the comple-

tion of the railways possible; soon it became obvious, however, that nationalization provided the only feasible means
of keeping the second transcontinental railways network in
operation. The Canadian Northern take-over in 1917 was
simpler than the nationalization of the Grand Trunk; the
compensation of the latter's shareholders led to bitter arguments before the arbitration boards and commissions. Only
in 1920 was the take-over of the Grand Trunk system and
its amalgamation with the previously nationalized Canadian
Northern Railway and the government-owned Intercolonial
begun. The management of the new railway – Canadian National – was faced not only with the problems in integration
of formerly rival systems, the costly overhaul of the facilities
whose maintenance had suffered through war-time shortages,
and heavy burdens of interest charges, but also with the
political pressures to which the national railway was exposed.

The creation of the Canadian National was not a pre-
meditated act to establish an integrated national system. On
the contrary, the prevailing sentiments were against public
ownership – 'railways were as much a curse to politicians as
politicians were to railways.' The partial nationalization of
Canadian railways was an unwanted but logical consequence
of the overbuilding of railway lines and heavy public investment in commercially unsuccessful private enterprises.

The establishment of the Canadian National system provided a chance to rationalize the whole Canadian railway
network, even if such a rationalization proved unpopular
in many areas enjoying excessive railway service because
of the past rivalry of the competing railways. A full-scale
rationalization would imply the government take-over of
C.P.R. lines, a possibility seriously suggested in 1921 by
Lord Shaughnessy, then chairman of the Canadian Pacific.
At that time, the combined mileage of Canadian National
and Canadian Pacific was 35,452 miles, of which thirteen
per cent, according to Lord Shaughnessy, were superfluous.
Shaughnessy's suggestion was rejected, not only because of
the terms of the proposal (which were a matter for negotiations) but also because of the horror of a huge railway mono-

PUBLIC INVESTMENTS IN PRINCIPAL CANADIAN RAILWAY
SYSTEMS AS OF JUNE 30, 1916

System	Total investment (thousands of dollars)	Public investment as % of total
Canadian Pacific	530,789	43.0
Canadian Northern	494,762	60.3
Grand Trunk	424,169	6.6
Grand Trunk Pacific	192,312	59.5
National Transcontinental	159,882	100.0
Intercolonial & P.E.I. Rlws.	125,731	100.0

NOTE: Grand Trunk Pacific branch lines (public investment of
$13,469,000) not included.

SOURCE: G. R. Stevens, *Canadian National Railways*, Toronto, 1962.

poly and the fear that such an organization would become,
in Sir Clifford Sifton's words, 'a monster of patronage and
political power'. Ironically enough, a few decades later the
railways' monopoly was broken by new highway competition, and the need for railway co-ordination was written into
an act. Branch-line rationalization became one of the main
recommendations of a Conservative-appointed royal commission, and the radical solution proposed in 1921 by the
C.P.R.'s chairman has not been seriously considered.

The development of modern highway transport dates from
the introduction and wide public acceptance of the internal
combustion engine. Although the first motor vehicles appeared at the turn of the century, their importance before
the First World War was negligible. In 1915, there were
95,000 motor vehicles registered in Canada, of which about
500 were commercial vehicles: the motor-vehicle fleet almost
trebled between 1915 and 1918 and the number of commercial vehicles increased to about 15,000. This explosive
growth continued throughout the period between the wars:

from 277,000 in 1918, to 1,500,000 in 1940. In the post-war
period the growth was resumed: the number rose from
1,497,000 in 1945 to 2,872,000 in 1951, and to 5,256,000
in 1960.

The increasing acceptance of motor vehicles and their
rising number forced the development of the highway network. Initially, because of the limited operating radius of
motor vehicles, road traffic was of a predominantly local character, which was reflected in the local rather than the national
or regional character of the highways. The system planning
approach on the provincial level and the construction of the
Trans-Canada Highway are post-Second World War developments. In the period between the two World Wars highway construction was mainly aimed at improving and extending local road networks to meet the demand of the growing
number of vehicles and greater average vehicle mileage.

The economic effects of highways have been all-pervading
and, therefore, extremely difficult to identify. The effects of
the establishment of the railway systems can be generalized
in terms of economic development, the opening of our new
territories for settlement, and the economic and political
unification of the country. The Canadian highway network
grew out of the improvements and extensions of local, or at
the best regional, systems; no new previously inactive areas
were opened for development; the effects of long-distance
highway transportation or long-distance road travel on national economic, social, or political unity have been confined
to recent years. At the same time there is no facet of economic
or social life that has not been significantly changed by highway development. Residential and industrial location patterns have been transformed. Highway transport and the
shift to less bulky energy sources (from coal, requiring heavy
bulk carriage, to electric power transmission and oil) gave
industry – light industry in particular – greater freedom to
locate with respect to supply sources and thus strengthened
the relative attractions of locations near the main market
centres. In short-haul passenger transport, the dependence
on railway transport has lessened, thus permitting the growth

of large but lower-density urban centres. Suburban sprawl
and ribbon developments along the highways are some of the
visible consequences. Equally important have been the problems of local public passenger-transport systems faced with
competition from private automobiles, and with inefficiency
because of the low population-density of suburbs geared to
private automobile service.

The financial consequences of the high and sustained rate
of highway construction have also been serious, especially
since the main burden of meeting the demand for new roads
and streets has to be borne by provinces and municipalities.

HIGHWAY EXPENDITURES, SELECTED YEARS

Year	Total expenditures on roads, bridges & ferries (millions of dollars)
1919	22.2
1923	56.1
1927	59.4
1930	96.4
1933	44.4
1935	59.5
1938	103.0
1946	144.5
1950	284.4
1955	513.8
1960	1,067.3

SOURCE: Dominion Bureau of Statistics, *Highway Statistics* (Annual) and
Road and Street Mileage and Expenditure (Annual).

The improvements and the extensions of the highway network and the improvement of the motor vehicle brought the
expansion of highway transport. The introduction of mul-
tiple-axled vehicles and the tractor-trailer combination made
long-haul road transport economical. From purely local
cartage and feeder operations the trucking industry devel-

oped to a point where it could compete with the railways for the increasing range of traffic. Between 1947 and 1952 road transport overtook the railways in terms of tons hauled, but, because of the differences in the average length of haul, the railways in the 1950s were still responsible for more than fifty per cent of the total ton-miles produced by all modes of transport in Canada. Even so, the monopoly of the railways was broken in most of the traffic markets, including markets for long-distance movements. In the late 1950s some of the average lengths of haul for interprovincial truck traffic exceeded the 1,000 miles mark.

Railway development was significantly affected by the promotional activities of the governments and, later, by a comprehensive system of rate regulations. The development of trucking was little affected by *direct* intervention of the governments, although it could not occur without rapid growth of highway expenditure. The regulation of the industry has been in the hands of the provinces; even when the Privy Council decision declared in 1954 that Canada's entire international and interprovincial trucking industry was under federal jurisdiction, the Motor Vehicle Transport Act of 1954 left the administration of economic regulations of the industry in the hands of the provincial boards. It is most likely that the division and the lack of uniformity of the regulatory responsibilities, combined with heterogeneity of weight and traffic regulations, have adversely affected the development of the industry.

Almost from the beginning of the railway era, railway rates were a matter of governmental concern and subject to state regulation and influence. Since 1888 railway rates have been regulated successively by the Railway Committee of the Privy Council and the Board of Railway Commissioners for Canada (1903), which in 1938 was reorganized and re-named the Board of Transport Commissioners. However, some of the most important railway rate issues have been dealt with as government policy decisions incorporated in Acts of Parliament.

The history of Canadian railway rates is highly complicated; the two main themes are the increase in railway costs (especially labour costs), and the increase in transport competition, which resulted in a growing number of competitive rate reductions. The interaction of these two forces further complicated the rate structure and tended to favour the regions where the competition was keenest–central Canada–allegedly at the expense of the peripheral provinces. The governments attempted to counteract this tendency through mandatory rate equalization and regional and general subsidies, while freezing the important western grain rates. The problem of railway rates was deemed important enough to be the subject of major inquiries by three royal commissions since 1948.

Between 1946 and 1958 the Board of Transport Commissioners authorized a number of general rate increases, raising the maximum level of railway rates by 197 per cent during this period. However, for competitive reasons the railways were forced to introduce competitive rates and certain charges which effectively decreased the average tariff level. The comparison of the indices of maximum permissible railway rates and average railway revenue per ton-mile illustrates this phenomenon.

It may be noted that both indices show a high correlation up to 1950; since 1951 the average revenue per ton-mile index increased by only 15 points as compared with a 56-point increase in the index of maximum permissible railway rates. This coincides with the intensification of road-rail competition. It would not be correct to assume that the competitive check on railway rate increases is now confined to central Canada, although this was largely the case in the early fifties.

The over-all problem of railway rates and subsidies was considered by the (MacPherson) Royal Commission on Transportation (1959-61). The Commission, recognizing the now all-pervading effects of competition in transport, recommended a different approach to the problem; it called for heavy but decreasing subsidies related to uneconomical parts

MAXIMUM PERMISSIBLE LEVEL OF RAILWAY RATES
AND THE AVERAGE REVENUE PER TON-MILE

Year	Maximum permissible level of railway rates	Average revenue per ton-mile
	(index: 1946 = 100)	
1946	100	100
1947	100	105.2
1948	121	122.9
1949	131	130.2
1950	145	144.8
1951	162	141.7
1952	170	143.8
1953	198	155.2
1954	198	158.3
1955	198	152.1
1956	212	146.9
1957	220	158.3
1958	220*	156.2

* The last permissible rate increase took effect on December 1, 1958.
SOURCES: Industrial Traffic League, *Circular No. 3776*, 1959, and Dominion
Bureau of Statistics, *Railway Statistics* (Annual).

of railway operations (branch lines, passenger services) and
subsidies on low-rate grain movements. Other proposals
would increase the rate-making freedom of the railways. In
effect, the Commission adopted the principle that in the
long run all the necessary adjustments in the transport scene
can be effected through the workings of a competitive price
mechanism; the purpose of the subsidies thus becomes either
to ease the transition period or to bear the costs of using
the transport industries as an instrument of national economic policies. The Commission distinguished between
'national transport policy', or policies related to the structure
and functioning of transport industries, and the use of 'transport as a means of national policies'; this distinction played
a significant role in framing the Royal Commission's recommendations. There are two questions to be answered in
assessing the Commission's recommendation: first, is it true
that the basic structure of the Canadian transport industries

is sound and that all the necessary adjustments can in fact be
made through the workings of the competitive price mechanism?; and second, is the distinction between the 'National
Transportation Policy' and the policy of using 'transportation
as an instrument of national policies' valid? Considerably
more investigation than the research done so far is required
to answer the first question. Regarding the second problem, I
consider the distinction made by the Commission to be not
only meaningless but likely to lead to erroneous policy conclusions. In fact, these two fundamental assumptions are
mutually contradictory. A national transport policy – as distinct from general development policies using transport as an
instrument, and from *ad hoc* actions aimed at the solution of
a particular problem or problems – can only be justified either
if major long-term structural maladjustments exist which can
be eliminated through consistent state action, or if, in the
absence of state action, serious structural maladjustments
are likely to arise. Even then it would have to be established
that Canada needs a 'national transport policy' while it does
not need a 'national ice-cream production policy'. The
answer, of course, is that transport affects national and
regional economic development to a vastly greater extent
than ice-cream production: that transport can be used as an
instrument of developmental policies and the ice-cream
industry cannot. Otherwise, the national (or regional) interest in transport is related to its usefulness as an instrument
of national (or regional) development policies with which it
can be co-ordinated. In other words, the Commission could,
but need not, have been right about the relative absence of
structural maladjustments which competition could not
cure. If it were right, its reasoning based on the distinction
between 'national transport policy' and 'policy using transport as an instrument' was invalid, but this distinction could
have also been invalid if the Commission was wrong in its
first 'fundamental assumption'.

The competitive developments in transport industries
present an opportunity of developing a more efficient and
flexible transport system; at the same time, however, the

problems of readjustments, created by the new market situation, to the increasing pace of technological progress present a new set of problems which are likely to require new policy approaches.

Air transport in Canada performs two distinct transport tasks: first, as a mainline aviation function, it provides the means of rapid communication between the widely spread centres and between Canada and other countries, and second, it provides modern transport services in the frontier or northern parts of the country where the establishment of efficient surface transport services is difficult or economically unjustified. These two different tasks have been reflected almost from the beginning in different organizations of the two branches of the industry.

The early development of mainline aviation in Canada was handicapped by the lack of suitable equipment – which was reflected in high operating costs and low service reliability – and the financial problems of the depression and post-depression years.

The development of frontier aviation preceded the air transport developments in the populated parts of the country, with the mining industry providing the main stimulus for its development. As early as 1926, a year-round air transport service was introduced into the newly discovered Red Lake mining district of north-western Ontario, though the use of aircraft in northern resource exploration work can be traced to the early activities of the Laurentide Company in 1919. By 1929 nearly all the isolated mining districts of northern Canada enjoyed air service. The increase in gold exploration during the depression years led to further expansion of the industry, but in the late 1930s the growth of frontier aviation was halted partly because some mineral exploration areas entered the production stage which justified the development of surface transport, and partly for the reasons "internal" to the aviation industry itself – financial weakness of the smaller firms and subsequent dislocations due to the consolidation by larger corporations.

Unlike frontier aviation, the mainline air services operated in competition with surface transport and required
direct government support for their development. The
basic decision to develop mainline air services was taken in
the late 1920s, partly as the result of the fear that this market
might become dominated by U.S. companies, and partly because of the traditional policy to develop an all-Canadian east-
west transport system. In 1928 the first inter-city airmail services were started (in the early stages of the industry's development airmail was the usual means of promoting air services)
and the construction of the 'Trans-Prairie Airway' began.
As an economy measure, both airmail services and the airway construction program were virtually halted during the
depression. However, the airport construction program was
resurrected in 1932 as an unemployment-relief measure. The
serious program to create a transcontinental air transport
system had to wait until the late 1930s, with the establishment of the Department of Transport (1936). After an unsuccessful attempt to organize a partially private and partially
publicly owned airline, Trans-Canada Air Lines was founded
by Act of Parliament in 1937 and began operations in 1938.

After the dislocations of the war years, the Canadian civil
aviation industry was re-established and assumed its present
pattern. The mainline or transcontinental trunk services are
operated by Air Canada (formerly T.C.A.), with a limited
degree of competition provided by Canadian Pacific Airlines
(C.P.A.) and some regional carriers. The Canadian scheduled
international services are provided by Air Canada (Europe,
North America, West Indies) and Canadian Pacific Airlines (Orient, Australia, Hawaii, South America, Southern
Europe, and the Netherlands), and non-scheduled international services are provided by both corporations, as well
as a number of independent charter operators.

The secondary scheduled services are maintained by a
number of regional carriers, each enjoying a degree of local
monopoly. All but one (Eastern Provincial) originated by
independent carriers taking over parts of Canadian Pacific
Airlines' regional services and developing them into regional

systems. The largest regional network (in British Columbia and the Yukon) is still operated by Canadian Pacific. In practically all cases, the regional carriers must rely on revenues from non-scheduled operations – northern charter activities related to national defence, exploration, and administrative functions, as well as international charter. These tend to fluctuate widely.

Small and medium-sized aircraft charter and non-scheduled operations are conducted by a number of small, independent carriers. These services are of the greatest importance in the northern country, although recently some executive charter operations have been successfully developed in the metropolitan areas.

All air transport activities are strictly regulated by the Air Transport Board. In practice this tends to restrict competition and stabilize the rates. In spite of this policy of 'stabilization through regulation', the non-scheduled sector of the industry suffers from wide revenue fluctuations due to factors beyond the industry's control (defence programs, mining booms); at the same time, the scope of the operations of frontier aviation tends to be progressively diminished by the northern extension of surface transport systems. In spite of this, aircraft still perform the key functions in northern exploration and development.

The development of trunk-line aviation has revolutionized long- and medium-haul passenger movements and become the main medium of public transport over longer distances. In this way, air transport has made an important contribution to the unification of the country and changed the structure of nation-wide organizations, increasing their ability to control the local operations of their national head-offices by allowing speedy visits by their executives. To a very large extent these developments have been 'technology-induced' – each generation of aircraft being followed by larger, faster, and more economical aircraft to permit progressive reduction in rates.

Although the airlines are not directly subsidized, they benefit by indirect subsidies provided through state-owned (or state-subsidized) airports and navigation systems which operate at heavy losses. The logic of insisting on strict balance-sheet or profit-and-loss-accounts discipline in the operations of a nationally owned airline, while exempting from such discipline government-operated airports, is rather questionable, especially in view of the commercial characteristics of airport operations, and the fact that by assuming the deficits on airport activities the Canadian government subsidizes not only Canadian but also foreign carriers. This double standard also results in over-investment in airport facilities, often induced by motives of local pride, intercity competition, or purely political factors.

The success in opening up the western areas of Canada through the construction of suitable transport facilities was followed by the idea of opening up northern Canada. The first northern railway was the Hudson Bay Railway line constructed to provide an additional route for prairie grain to the overseas markets. The railway was first proposed in the 1880s, and construction started in 1906. After some interruptions, the line was finished in the late 1920s and the first grain shipments were exported through Churchill in 1931. As an alternative route for the export of Canadian grain, the Hudson Bay Railway suffered from the difficulties of navigation through Hudson Bay. Later, the existence of this railway provided an incentive for mining development in Northern Manitoba (Hudson Bay Mining Company developments at Flin Flon), and in more recent times the line was extended to exploit nickel deposits at Lynn Lake and Thompson.

Another important northern railway was the Northern Alberta Railway, built to open up the wheat-producing areas of the Peace River country. It was constructed with private capital, and was later taken over by the Province of Alberta, coming eventually (1929) under the joint ownership of the C.P.R. and the C.N.R. The discovery of rich mining deposits at Pine Point and the growing interest in the development of the north led recently to the construction of a railway line connecting Peace River with Great Slave Lake.

The two major provincial railway systems aimed at the
development of the northern areas are the Pacific Great
Eastern, originally serving the interior of British Columbia
and recently extended so as to be economically viable, and
the Ontario Northland, connecting North Bay with the mining areas of Timmins, Noranda, Cobalt, etc., and Moosonee
on James Bay.

In Quebec the railways connecting the Chibougamau
copper-mining area with the C.N.R. system, and the iron-
ore companies' railways Gagnon–Port Cartier, and Sept Iles–
Schefferville, are the most important northern railway lines.

Following the development of a modern highway system
in southern areas of the country, development roads began
to be constructed in the northern regions. The first and most
important was the Alaska Highway, which was built for
military reasons but provided the valuable land transport
link between the Yukon and the Peace River country. The
other great northern highway is the Mackenzie Highway,
connecting Peace River with the Mackenzie–Great Slave
Lake water system. The Mackenzie Highway started as a
winter road in 1938 and was subsequently improved. It was
completed as a year-round road to Hay River shortly after
the Second World War, and extended to Yellowknife in 1961.
It was recently reconstructed to a good standard gravel road.

> There is no question but that road transport is now an
> important means of transport in the north. It replaced water
> transport as the dominant method of moving freight in the
> Yukon during the mid-fifties, and it has also played a grow-
> ing role in linking the Yukon with Southern Canada. Truck-
> ers using the Alaska Highway have greatly diminished the
> remoteness of the Yukon and have had a favourable effect
> on the cost of living in that region. . . . Road transport has
> also had a considerable impact on the southern fringes
> of the Mackenzie District of the N.W.T. With the excep-
> tion of petroleum movements from Norman Wells to
> Yellowknife, and some dry cargo movements to small, out-
> of-the-way points, it has made seasonal water and tractor
> train operations almost obsolete in the vicinity of Great

Slave Lake since the Mackenzie Highway was extended to Yellowknife in 1961. Consumer goods prices and business costs – particularly inventory costs – fell markedly with the advent of road access. This was a consequence not so much of a fall in transport rates as of a great improvement in speed and regularity of service, plus the fact that good transport was available the year round.*

Transport, especially road transport, improvement as a means of opening up the Canadian North has been expanded under the 'Roads to Resources' program, the Development Road Program in the Yukon and Northwest Territories, and the construction of the Pine Point railway. Important as those projects are, it is incorrect to see in the history of the opening up of the West by the railways a parallel to development strategy in the North. The Canadian West was an agricultural region; the resources were ubiquitous and an area development could take place within the network of a transport system. The Canadian North is mainly a region of point development; the available resources (other than forests) are highly localized in specific points, their location being outside human control. This fundamentally changes the ways in which the country can be opened up through transport investment. This point was summarized in the report of J. Anderson-Thomson of the Great Slave Railway Commission:

> There seems to be some confusion or loose thinking regarding this matter of a development railway . . . [which] would help in the development of mineral resources in that part of the Precambrian Shield. . . . Now a railway can help in the development of farming, ranching, lumbering or even musk ox farming on the Tundra. . . . Unfortunately, however, such does not apply to mines whether precious or base metal. These cannot be developed from a small beginning to become a major producer, and the Precambrian Shield could be criss-crossed with a veritable network of railroads, and they would not add one ton of ore to an ore deposit. . . .

* E. R. Weick, *Road Transport in the Pioneer North*, Canadian Transportation Research Forum, Quebec, 1965, pp. 9-10.

The St. Lawrence–Great Lakes waterways system, which played the key role in the settlement of central Canada, acquired new economic significance with the construction of the St. Lawrence Seaway and the improvement of the St. Lawrence Ship Channel.

The idea of developing the St. Lawrence waterways system to accommodate ocean ships can be traced as far back as the beginning of this century. However, the first concrete proposal was the report of the Wooten-Boten Commission in 1921. Following this report and the subsequent investigations, the Canada–U.S.A. St. Lawrence Deep Waterway Treaty was signed in 1932 but failed to be ratified by the U.S. Senate. Interest in the project continued, the government of Canada being keenly interested in the navigation aspect of the project and the governments of Ontario and New York State having a primary interest in the power development. In 1951 the Canadian government took a decisive step in bringing the project closer to its realization by passing the acts creating the St. Lawrence Seaway Authority and giving the Province of Ontario the authority to develop the hydro-electric potential. This action was soon followed by the signing of a treaty between Canada and the United States in 1954, the main provisions of which were: (a) the hydro-electric power was to be developed by the Province of Ontario and the State of New York; (b) the construction of the waterway – deepening of channels and lock construction – was left to the federal governments, each being responsible for works in its own section; (c) provisions for the setting and revising of tolls were made to cover the maintenance and amortization costs. In 1959 the Seaway was officially opened. The construction costs were well over $1,000 million; the costs of power developments amounting to approximately $600 million, and the costs of the navigation projects to $460 million ($330 million was the cost of the waterway to Canada).

The most important commodities transported through the Seaway are: grain (about thirty per cent of the total traffic); mineral products – iron ore carried between Sept Iles and steel-production centres (forty-five per cent of the total traffic, two-thirds of this being to steel-production centres located in the Great Lakes region); manufactured products (about twelve per cent of the total traffic); fuel oil, forest products, etc., providing the balance of traffic.

The new traffic generated by the Seaway put further strain on the other parts of the Great Lakes–St. Lawrence waterways system, especially the Welland Canal, the capacity of which must be considerably expanded. The shipping lines had to make substantial adjustments to take full advantage of this development. Thus the effects of the Seaway on the industrial heartland of Canada and the organization of the grain trade, significant as they were during the first five years of the waterway's operations, are likely to be even more profound after all the necessary adjustments are made.

Less dramatic than the Seaway construction but also of major importance was the improvement of the navigation on the St. Lawrence river. The St. Lawrence Ship Channel, extending from about forty miles below Quebec City to the foot of the Lachine Canal at Montreal, was widened and improved. The widening of the channel, further development of the aids to navigation, and the increased effectiveness of ice-breaker operations, resulted in the greater attractiveness of the Port of Montreal and the extension of the navigation season.

SEASONS OF OPEN NAVIGATION ON THE
ST. LAWRENCE SHIP CHANNEL

Year	First arrival from sea	Last departure for sea
MONTREAL HARBOUR		
1945	April 9	December 3
1950	April 18	December 7
1955	April 5	December 16
1960	March 21	December 16
1962	March 12	December 19

SOURCE: Dominion Bureau of Statistics, *Canada Year Book* (Annual).

Although the effects of the extension of the navigation period on the Port of Montreal have undoubtedly been beneficial, these developments have had adverse effects on the traditional winter ports of Canada: Saint John, New Brunswick, and Halifax, Nova Scotia. The concern about the possible decline of these ports and the economic effects this would have on the Maritime economy has not been without influence on governmental thinking about further improvements that might eventually achieve year-round navigation on the St. Lawrence. The technological progress that may make such a development feasible would put into focus the conflict of regional interests. Winter navigation on the St. Lawrence would further strengthen the central region and would possibly weaken an already economically weak region of Canada.

Natural-gas and oil pipelines are the newest and most specialized Canadian transport industry. Their development followed the oil discoveries in western Canada and had a profound effect on the pattern of energy supply and the growth of industry.

The most important oil pipeline systems are the Interprovincial (Redwater, north-east of Edmonton, to Port Credit near Toronto) and the Trans-Mountain (Edmonton to Vancouver). A specialized pipeline to carry natural-gas liquids was also constructed from the Alberta-Saskatchewan boundary to Winnipeg.

Parallel with pipeline oil transportation, a system of pipelines for the movement of natural gas has been constructed. The most important lines are: the Trans-Canada pipeline (from the Alberta-Saskatchewan boundary to Montreal); the Alberta-California pipeline; and the Westcoast Transmission line from the Peace River district to Vancouver and the west coast states.

With the exception of the Northern Ontario section of the Trans-Canada pipeline, the pipelines were constructed by private enterprise. As a result of the growing concern over the national energy policy and the extent of American control over the industry, the National Energy Board was established in 1959 to be responsible for the regulation of the construction, operations, and rates of the pipelines, as well as for the control of the export of gas and petroleum.

If Canada has become a distinct economic unit it is largely because the country has successfully developed a national transport system. All regions of the nation are now linked by rail, highway, and air transport with profound effects on the country's industrial development, marketing patterns, and inter-regional population movements. The pipelines connect oil- and gas-fields of the West with the industrial heartland. The St. Lawrence–Great Lakes navigation system is the most important inland waterway anywhere and a significant factor balancing the disadvantages of the long hauls involved in serving a large continental mass.

Considering the distances involved and the relatively small population, the effort necessary to create the national transport systems was immense, and largely justified the description of Canada as a 'high-overhead economy'. As with any other large overheads, the burden of the transport systems tends to decrease – in relative terms – with the growth of the economy, but given the geographical framework of the Canadian economy it is not likely ever to become negligible. This in itself provides a powerful reason for continuing efforts to increase the efficiency of the national transport systems.

The efficiency of the national transport system is likely to remain the key factor determining Canada's economic growth. In this field technological, economic, and political problems are interrelated. Technological progress makes possible significant improvements in high-density-traffic railway operations, but to obtain the full benefits of new developments, the railway system must be radically streamlined. This, in turn, produces serious problems of readjustment: further radical reduction in the railway labour force; elimination of hundreds of miles of low-density lines (thus depriving some of the smaller communities of railway services); and, eventually, elimination of duplications. These are serious decisions, with considerable social and political implications. The spectacular development of highway transport during the last decades and the extension of the economic length of haul—a factor of considerable significance in creating larger national or regional markets—has been made possible by increased size and improved design of vehicles. Highway transport, like any other transport system, can only be as efficient as its weakest link. In order to achieve the full advantages of a true national highway transport system a co-ordination and standardization of operational and economic regulations as well as of user taxation systems is necessary. A co-existence of ten uncoordinated and completely autonomous regulation and user tax authorities is an obvious absurdity in view of the growth of inter-provincial, long-haul movements; unfortunately this absurdity is firmly established in the B.N.A. Act.

With the increasing accent on regional development, the approach to some of the problems of transport planning acquires a new dimension. If transport can be used as an instrument of economic development, including regional development, then transport investment planning, subsidy, and taxation policies must logically be fitted into regional development planning. Transport developments undertaken because of the faith that they will somehow have general beneficial effects—without measuring these benefits or co-ordinating transport effort with other development policies—are just another version of the 'cargo cult' which makes the primitive tribes construct mock airports in the jungle hoping that 'cargo' will mysteriously arrive.

17. Communications

WILFRED KESTERTON AND
JOHN S. MOIR

The function of transportation is to carry things – the function of communications is to carry ideas. Because of Canada's continental dimensions and natural geographic barriers, both transportation and communications have played a more important role in our national development than in most countries. Across the vast territorial expanse from the Atlantic to the Pacific the Canadian people are spread in a narrow ribbon close to the American border. Complicating the physical problems are the external factors of two cultural pulls – eastward to Europe and southward to the United States – and the internal factor of language division. The awesome challenge to Canadian communications is to act as the lifeline of cultural unity by linking, through time and space, the separated parts into a truly national society.

On July 1, 1867, when George Brown's Toronto *Globe* hailed 'the gladsome midsummer morn' of Canadian nationhood, the press of British North America was already 115 years old. Only a few pre-Confederation newspapers, born after John Bushell began the *Halifax Gazette* in 1752, lasted into the new nation's first century, and fewer achieved importance. But these participated in and chronicled a growing nationhood for years before they disappeared: *Le Canadien*, established in Quebec in 1806 and brought to greatness after 1822 by Etienne Parent; the Montreal *Herald* (founded by William Gray, 1811); the *Acadian Recorder* (Anthony Holland, 1813); the *Nova-scotian* (George Young, 1824); *La Minerve* (Ludger Duvernay, 1826); the Charlottetown *Examiner* (Edward Whelan, 1847); and *Le Courrier de St-Hyacinthe* (J. P. Guité and A. De Grandpré, 1853). Still flourishing are the lively Montreal *Gazette* (Fleury Mesplet, 1778); the Brockville *Recorder* (Chauncey Beach, 1820); the Belleville *Intelligencer* (George Benjamin, 1834); the Ottawa *Citizen* (William Harris, 1844, begun as the Bytown *Packet*); the Toronto *Globe and Mail* (George Brown's *Globe*, 1844); the Hamilton *Spectator* (Robert Smiley, 1846); and the *London Free Press* (William Sutherland, 1849).

Some of the power with which such newspapers entered the Confederation period derived from improvements in their mechanical production. The first manufacture of paper in British North America in 1830 and of iron presses there in 1833, the gradual adoption of power presses after 1840, and the use of Morse's magnetic telegraph to gather news after 1846, all contributed to their viability.

While journalism was becoming firmly entrenched in the East, a new generation of pioneer editors was anticipating the Confederation vision of a nation stretching from sea to sea. H. C. Williston and Columbus Bartlett* set up the *Victoria*

---

* Williston and Bartlett were Americans from California; but before the year was out, journalists with a clearer British North American connection had founded newspapers. The Nova Scotian Amor de Cosmos established the *British Colonist* in December. It is the only British Columbia paper from 1855 to still survive.

Gazette and Anglo-American in 1858, and William Bucking-
ham and William Coldwell started the *Nor'-Wester* at Fort
Garry in 1859. After Canada's first Dominion Day, journal-
ism expanded with an expanding nation. Printer-editors
came with railway and homesteader to the empty prairies and
with gold-hungry prospector to the Canadian north. P. G.
Laurie brought the pioneer Battleford *Herald* to future
Saskatchewan in 1878, and Frank Oliver began the pioneer
Edmonton *Bulletin* in future Alberta in 1880. In 1898 the
Allen brothers' *Klondike Nugget* and G. B. Swinehart's
Midnight Sun arrived in Dawson City in almost a dead heat.

Canada's newspapers formed no nation-binding network
when the country was young. In the East even the biggest
journals were fairly modest undertakings. In the West,
spotted about the country in pioneer isolation, they were
primitive productions fashioned with a shirt-tail-ful of type
on an easily portable Washington press or one of its near
cousins. Whatever those papers could contribute to the 'one-
ness' of Canadians was weakened by their infrequency of
issue and small circulation: three years before Confederation there were only twenty-three dailies in British North
America, most of them small and all in the East.

During the rest of the nineteenth century Canada's newspapers grew in number, size, and frequency of printing. One
hundred and twenty-one dailies served 570,000 subscribers in
1900, *La Presse* of Montreal leading the field with 66,500.
By then the news they brought was increasingly up-to-the-
minute. There was steady growth in their circulation, plant,
capitalization, and personnel. This progress derived largely
from new press inventions. Electrically driven rotary presses,
stereotyping, slug-casting of type, improved newsprint manufacture, and better folder attachments and inks increased
efficiency and promoted growth. There was nothing particularly Canadian about these inventions; the improvements
were borrowings from other lands. But when the Leggo
brothers reproduced a photograph of Montreal's new Custom
House in the *Canadian Illustrated News* of June 3, 1871,

they showed that in half-tone photo-engraving at least Canada could take a lead.

The impact of nineteenth-century technological change was intensified by such post-1900 innovations as the teletype, the teletypesetter, plastic photo-engravings, and improved colour processes. Inventions like these played a major part in transforming Canada's press. Newspapers needed time-saving equipment to serve a readership vastly increased by population growth, greater literacy, and wider, easier access to distribution. The dependence here was mutual. If enlarged readership could be served only by staggeringly expensive equipment, that equipment could be paid for only by vastly enlarged readership. This meant that, to survive, dailies often had to capture all or nearly all the potential readership of their area. The result was circulation battles in which the losers died and the survivors grew huge and strong. A decrease in the number of newspapers, a centralization of dailies in large urban centres, an increasing concentration of control in the hands of fewer and fewer publishers and owners, were all part of the process. Just as the quasi civil-servant editor dominated eighteenth-century journalism and the 'personal' journalist the nineteenth, the capitalist publisher became the most important newspaper figure in the twentieth century. The one-newspaper city has replaced the multi-newspaper town of earlier days. After a century of Confederation, French and English general-interest dailies have declined to about 100 from a peak of 138 in 1913. With diminished numbers, those dailies now serve more than four million subscribers, more than seven times the circulation of 1900. It is small wonder that the *Toronto Daily Star* subscriptions could exceed 420,000 in 1951 and the paper be valued at $25,000,000, or that *Le Nouveau Journal* could still fail in Montreal in 1962 even though $3,800,000 had been spent on it during its nine months of publication.

Under modern economic conditions strong newspaper groups have taken over an increasing share of Canada's press. The Southam organization, Free Press Publications, the

Clifford Sifton group, and the Thomson Company owned forty-four of Canada's dailies in early 1966 and commanded forty-two per cent of daily circulation. Outside Canada the Thomson newspaper organization is one of the most powerful in the world. No Canadian group is a chain of the same pattern as Hearst's monovocal papers. But taken together Canada's four major groups are making it increasingly hard for independent new-comers to gain a foothold and for individual entrepreneurs to maintain their place in the world of daily journalism.

The modern Canadian newspaper flourishes in a libertarian climate. It emerged in early pre-Confederation days from restriction and even domination by government, when victories in the political and religious areas and such press triumphs as Joseph Howe's acquittal in his famous libel trial removed the shackles of officialdom. In recent times the press or its champions have won new battles for the same cause over the Alberta Press Act and Quebec Padlock Law. Some critics think newspapers have now become too independent. Aware of the growing strength of Canada's large press groups, they have called for measures more appropriate to the theory that says government should be the 'residuary legatee of responsibility for an adequate press performance'. But the prevailing libertarian philosophy is that the due process of law, invoking legislation enacted mainly during the late nineteenth century as Newspaper and Libel Acts, is sufficient to ensure responsible behaviour by the newspaper press.

During Canada's first century the periodical press has not enjoyed the same strength as its newspapers. While modern trade publications have become tough and durable, both consumer and belletristic magazines have shown themselves to be weak and ephemeral. Promising ventures such as the *Canadian Monthly and National Review*, launched when Canada was a few years old, proved no more enduring than the admirable *Literary Garland* of pre-Confederation times.

In 1961 the O'Leary Commission reported that three out

of four general-interest magazines bought in Canada were American publications, that the number of Canada's general-interest consumer magazines had dwindled to five, and that two of these were in a precarious state. Canadian publishers attributed many of their difficulties to the 'overflow publications', 'split runs', and 'Canadian editions' produced by their American exploiters. 'Overflow publications' are surplus copies of magazines dumped on the Canadian market at non-competitive prices after the domestic market has paid basic costs; 'split runs' are American magazines in which Canadian advertising has been substituted for American advertising; 'Canadian editions' are American magazines containing Canadian advertising and a small insert of Canadian editorial matter. To rebut criticism of such devices, American publishers attributed weaknesses in the Canadian industry to the inferiority of the Canadian product. They said that advertising wrested from American periodicals by government measures would go to other media rather than to Canadian magazines. They said that the strength of American publications in Canada contributed strength to the Canadian periodical publishing industry generally. Any weakening of the American hold on the Canadian market, so they contended, would produce a virtual monopoly for the Maclean-Hunter consumer magazines and would probably cause many of that company's weaker rivals to disappear.

The Commission agreed, in the main, with the Canadian publishers. The measures it recommends to protect and encourage an indigenous periodical press are comparable to the help the government has given to the C.P.R. and the CBC. No such artificial aid seemed called for in the case of Canada's newspapers; yet aid was given to both magazines and newspapers. By an income-tax bill enacted in June 1965, advertisers who placed advertising aimed at the Canadian market in a non-Canadian newspaper or periodical were not allowed to use such advertising as an income-tax deduction after January 1, 1966. The Act defined a Canadian publication as one in which at least three-quarters of the voting shares were owned by Canadians. Implication of the clause was that it would so increase advertising costs that it would drive advertisers away from foreign magazines and thereby discourage foreign ownership. Not that the newspaper, published by conventional methods and even with the aid just described, could focus Canadian thinking and contribute to a sense of identity for Canadians as *The Times* of London or the *Guardian* of Manchester could do for Englishmen. Distances in Canada are too great to permit a 'national' newspaper to be printed and distributed in the ordinary way.

Instead, newspapers have made their contributions through the wire services they use, The Canadian Press and United Press International of Canada. Nation-wide in operation, these two agencies make it possible for Canadians in all parts of the country to be equally well informed through fast and comprehensive news of their region, their nation, and the world.

The Canadian Press grew out of the Western Associated Press in 1917, being first called the Canadian Press Limited and taking its present name in 1923. It is a co-operative news-gathering agency of which nearly all Canadian dailies are members. Its head office is in Toronto and its other bureaus are in Halifax, Quebec City, Montreal, Ottawa, Winnipeg, Edmonton, Vancouver, New York City, and London, England. Staffers serve in St. John's, Saint John, London, Windsor, Regina, Calgary, Victoria, and Washington, D.C. An exchange service with Reuters and the Associated Press gives it access to world news. It introduced its French-language service in 1951. It also serves the CBC and most private radio and television stations. Some weeklies also use CP material.

United Press International of Canada began in 1922 as British United Press, British Commonwealth subsidiary of the American organization, the United Press. Merger of the parent company with the International News Service in 1958 to form United Press International caused a reorganization of the Canadian unit. Although it changed the credit on its news reports from BUP to UPI, British United Press remained the official name of the company until 1964, when it adopted its current name. Like its parent, it is a private agency; that is, it depends upon the writing of its own reporters for all copy. The Canadian organization operates chiefly in Canada, although it has a branch office in London, England, and correspondents elsewhere. Montreal is headquarters for UPI of Canada, while it has bureaus in Halifax, Quebec City, Ottawa, Toronto, Winnipeg, and Vancouver. The company furnishes a news report, a telephoto service, a sports wire service, and a television film service.

If press agencies have diminished regionalism and given Canada's newspapers a commendable national quality, they may also have contributed a uniformity less praiseworthy. Syndicated material and wire-service news stories may have imposed a conformity of pattern generally regarded as a major flaw of modern North American journalism. The price paid for the immeasurably better service the 1967 newspaper gives may be an accompanying loss of newspaper character and personality. The trend may have contributed to the general blandness that Canadian journalism acquired when circulation-hungry newspapers, anxious not to offend potential readers, abandoned narrow partisanship and took the public-service approach to policy.

As Canada moves into its second century, the 'facsimile' newspaper may strikingly affect the character of Canadian journalism. The *Globe and Mail* began experiments in wire transmission of newspapers in 1960, but suspended them, at least temporarily, by 1963. If facsimile does make possible simultaneous publication in each main region of Canada, the national newspaper thus produced will hardly weaken the trend toward press uniformity. But the new process may well join Canada's railway network, the CBC, and The Canadian Press in contributing to Canadian unity and identity.

Samuel Morse's electromagnetic telegraph was a generation old in Canada when Confederation was born. Canadians had been quick to see the advantages of the telegraph for business and the press, and enterprising Torontonians put the first Canadian commercial line into operation less than three years after Morse transmitted his first telegraph message in 1844. In rapid succession lines were built linking Buffalo, Toronto, Montreal, Quebec, and New York City, and in 1848 telegraph systems were opened in Nova Scotia and New Brunswick. The telegraph revolutionized Canadian communications by carrying messages in minutes over distances that postal communications had previously spanned in days or even weeks.

The early creation of small rival companies was followed by consolidation. By 1861 the Montreal Telegraph Company had bought out all competitors in central Canada, only to have its monopoly challenged by the Dominion and the Great North Western telegraph companies in 1868 and 1880. Again the need for economy led to consolidation of all these lines in 1881, but in that interval the Dominion Telegraph had finally joined the central provinces to the Maritimes with sinews of copper, almost a decade after statesmen had proclaimed the political unity of British North America.

Scarcely had the merger of 1881 been achieved when a new rival appeared in the C.P.R., the first railway telegraph system allowed to operate in competition with commercial telegraph companies. Before the C.P.R.'s 'steel of empire' linking the Atlantic coast to the Pacific was one year old, 336 C.P.R. telegraph offices were operating in Quebec, Ontario, and the West. Four decades later the second transcontinental railway was operating the Canadian National telegraph system, which included lines formerly belonging to the Great North Western, the Grand Trunk Pacific, the Canadian Northern, and the National Transcontinental railways.

From their inception, telegraph companies in Canada showed a strong bias towards consolidation rather than cooperation in answer to Canada's challenge of distances and widely dispersed population. Although nine telegraph companies are still operating in Canada, the C.N. and the C.P. are giants that nearly monopolize the domestic telegraph field. After the First World War the Dominion Government Telegraph Services was established with 9,300 miles of poled line and 400 miles of cable to serve the remote areas of the lower St. Lawrence and the Yukon (economically unattractive to commercial companies), but since 1931 these lines too have been operated by the C.N.R. By 1964 Canada possessed 49,730 miles of poled line, one of the largest per-capita telegraph systems in the world.

The second revolutionary step in communications came less than a decade after Confederation when Alexander Graham Bell converted telegraphy into telephony. On August 10, 1876, he transmitted the world's first long-distance telephone message from his home near Brantford to Paris, Ontario, a distance of eight miles, but via sixty-eight miles of rented telegraph lines. The first Canadian telephone exchange was opened in Hamilton just two years later, but it was not until 1888 that satisfactory two-way conversations by telephone were achieved through technical changes in the equipment. Today Canadians make more telephone calls per person than any other country, and come third after Americans and Swedes in the per-capita ratio of telephones.

The American Bell Telephone Company, incorporated in 1880, was able to buy up all Canadian telephone patents and lines in 1882 because unimaginative Canadians refused to invest money in this Canadian invention, and the expansion of telephone communications then proceeded rapidly under American management. Within one year the Bell Telephone Company was servicing 4,400 subscribers on forty-four exchanges, was operating 600 miles of long-distance lines, and had linked Windsor to Detroit by the world's first submarine telephone cable.

The Bell Telephone Company initiated the development of telephone systems in all Canadian provinces except British Columbia, where the B.C. Telephone Company has provided a majority of services. In Nova Scotia and New Brunswick the Bell Telephone Company sold its lines to private companies in 1888; on the prairies the company's systems were bought by the provincial governments of Manitoba and Alberta in 1908 and by the Saskatchewan government in 1909.

Canadian submarine telegraphic communications have from the outset been allied to land telegraphy in function and development. As early as 1852 a cable was laid from New Brunswick to Prince Edward Island, and four years later another joining Newfoundland and Cape Breton was established as the first stage of a transatlantic system. In 1857 these Canadian cables were bought by an English company which proceeded to land the first transatlantic cable on Newfoundland on August 2, 1858. When this cable failed, the famous *Great Eastern* was employed in laying transatlantic cables to Newfoundland in 1866. After three more cables had linked the Old World to the New, the Anglo-American Telegraph Company acquired a monopoly of them in 1883, only to be challenged in turn by the Commercial Cable Company, which opened a rate-war with the older Anglo-American system.

Later submarine cables gave Canada communication lines to Bermuda and the Azores, but the greatest achievement was the establishment of a long-discussed link with Australia through New Zealand in 1902, tied in turn to the Australia–Great Britain cable. This Pacific cable was a government project undertaken jointly by Canada, Great Britain, New Zealand, and Australia, and was operated by the Pacific Cable Board until 1929 when it was sold to the newly-formed Imperial and International Communication Company. In 1949 the Canadian government created the Canadian Overseas Telecommunications Corporation which, as part of its operations, took over various telegraph cable systems across the Atlantic and Pacific and to the West Indies. The latest telegraphic refinement was added in 1956 – Telex, a teleprinter switching system giving direct teletype service on both submarine and land lines across Canada.

Although Canada was an early participant in transoceanic telegraph systems, not until 1956 did she get her first direct telephonic cable link with Europe. This cable – a joint Canadian, British, and American undertaking – provided sixty telephone circuits that can also be used for telegraphy. A similar direct telephone cable system to Australasia was completed in 1963.

Though young by comparison with the newspapers, moving pictures are the oldest of the mass media introduced by the electric age. The first public demonstration of Edison's Kinetoscope in New York in 1894 was given by the enterprising Holland brothers of Ottawa. Picture shows were offered in Vancouver in 1898 and what was probably Canada's first movie house was opened later in that city. But it was not until 1907 that a theatre specifically designed for the showing of moving pictures opened in Montreal. At the same time the first chain of movie theatres was being established, soon to claim Canada-wide coverage through its fifty houses. The great boom in movie viewing, however, came after the First World War when the Famous Players chain was created in 1920. A similar wave of expansion followed the Second World War when the Arthur Rank interests entered Canada.

The persuasive impact of the moving picture as a cultural mass medium has been acknowledged in the establishment of boards of censors for the Dominion and for eight of Canada's ten provinces. With power to regulate the content of individual films and the audiences to which they may be shown, censorship in Canada is undertaken and defended on moral or religious grounds – political ideologies have never concerned the censors. Although no evidence has ever been adduced that movies have debased Canadian morals, Canada continues to rank as a 'most censored nation' with regard to its viewing of movies.

As a medium of education in Canadian schools, movies were generally rejected until safety film had been introduced and until experience in the Second World War showed their real potentialities for instruction and propaganda. Numerous film libraries were soon established by government agencies and by private educational organizations. As a means of combining education with recreation, the showing of movies by film societies expanded rapidly. Film societies first appeared in the 1930s, but since 1945 interest has been so keen that now more than one hundred such societies are affiliated with the Canadian Federation of Film Societies. The Federation is a division of the Canadian Film Institute (formerly the National Film Society of Canada) which, since 1935, has operated as a repository for non-theatrical films, as a clearing-house for information about films, and as an agency for the evaluation of films.

The introduction of television, a potent rival of the movie houses and their new relation the drive-in theatre, was viewed with dismay by theatre owners, who predicted an early and complete demise of their form of film viewing. Although theatre attendance did decline drastically during the 1950s, the worst predictions were not realized as a hard core of viewers continue to patronize the movie theatres, attracted in part by habit, in part by promotional gimmicks, but more especially by some better-quality films produced specifically to meet the challenge of television.

Granted that moving-picture films can reach and influence large numbers of viewers, the question remains to what extent have films served Canada as a *Canadian* cultural medium. Early film production in Canada – mostly docu-mentary – was extensive because of low costs, and as late as the 1920s it still seemed possible that Canada might develop an indigenous theatrical-film industry. Attempts to produce full-length or feature films in Canada involved, however, ex-tremely high costs. The full-length silent *Carry On Sergeant*, made at Trenton, Ontario, cost half a million dollars. Already Canadian actors, technicians, and directors were finding greater opportunities in Hollywood, and to add to the diffi-culties of Canadian companies, their American rivals con-trolled most of the Canadian theatres. For the Canadian film industry the Great Depression marked the end of attempts at feature-length production and forced it into making shorts and documentaries, the one field where the Canadian indus-try has been able to hold its own over the years. On the eve of the Second World War the National Film Board was estab-lished as a government agency to produce such films, which would interpret visually one region of Canada to another.

As the Board began to produce a significant number of documentaries depicting a wide variety of aspects of national life, Canadians discovered their own image thanks to the

Board. The Canadian film industry had found a *métier*, but still it required government action to do what private capital had been largely unable to undertake. The war-time demand for shorts and documentaries encouraged private industries to enter this field once more, and by 1950 thirteen companies were producing films in Canada, mostly on industrial or on short subjects. Continued Canadian dependence on Hollywood for theatrical productions, however, contributed significantly to the nation's dollar shortage in the immediate postwar years. To offset this economic imbalance, major American picture companies combined in 1948 in the 'Canadian Co-operation Project' to promote tourism in Canada by giving the country greater foreign exposure through newsreels and travelogues. Despite repeated efforts a theatrical film industry still failed to develop, and Canadian talent continues to flow towards the United States.

An indirect compensation for Canada's colonial status in the empire of the silver screen has been the sophistication of Canadian audiences, which in turn has forced the struggling Canadian companies to strive for and frequently reach Olympian heights of quality. Still, the Canadian film industry remained too long without honour in its own country. Crawley Films' *The Loon's Necklace* received honours at the Edinburgh International Festival of Documentary Films before it got the premier award in the Canadian Film Society's first film festival of 1949. Further recognition of the unique if limited scope of the Canadian film industry has come in the frequency of awards at film festivals outside of Canada, so that the industry's efforts – and Canada's image – were perhaps better known and appreciated abroad than in Canada.

But a brighter day was dawning for the Canadian film industry as television, the enemy of the theatrical movie houses, became both patron and dependant of a first-rate film industry that could produce documentaries and short theatricals of the highest artistic and technical quality. Until the introduction of video-tape, films alone could offer scope and flexibility in television programming. This development reduced opportunities for local talent and postponed further the growth of feature-length film-making as a self-sustaining Canadian industry. Evidently artificial aid seemed called for: in June 1966 Parliament voted to establish a corporation with a fund of $10 million to promote activities in this field. The money was to be used for investment in individual feature-film productions and for awards for outstanding film accomplishments in Canada. In the stipulation that films so aided must have 'a significant Canadian creative, artistic, and technical content', there was evidence that the motion picture continued to be regarded as one of the media of communication able to contribute to the Canadian sense of identity.

Few components of the national life have provided stronger cement for the Canadian mosaic than has Canada's broadcasting system. The organizers of the first radio network hoped to foster national identity and strengthen Canadian nationhood. Their philosophy has permeated all subsequent broadcasting developments. It has been reaffirmed by Royal Commission and recurrent parliamentary committee report. The propriety of moulding the system to serve Canadian culture and Canadian self-expression has been an unfailing ingredient of the constant discussion and controversy that have marked broadcasting's short history.

Like Bell's telephone, radio had close connections with Canada from its very inception. From Signal Hill, St. John's, Marconi sent his first experimental message, the single letter S, winging across the Atlantic in 1901 to inaugurate the electronic century. Later Marconi selected Cape Breton for the first transatlantic radio station. The Canadian government set one precedent for future radio development by requiring licences for all wireless telegraph stations in 1905. Until the outbreak of the First World War, however, radio telegraphy remained a purely commercial medium, although the 1913 Radio Telegraph Act presciently included 'radio telephones' in its definition of wireless, when vesting control of the whole medium in the Minister of Defence.

As a supporting arm in war, radio never showed its real capabilities until the last 'Hundred Days' of rapid advance in 1918, but observers agreed that radio, especially radio telephony, was no toy. Voice radio possessed the potential to become a mass medium that could revolutionize the economy and culture of a country; and for a country of Canada's continental dimensions radio could annihilate space, like its forebear the telegraph, and also reach a mass audience.

The first wireless telephony transmitter licence was issued to the Marconi Wireless Telegraph Company experimental station XWA in Montreal in 1919. When provision for licensing private commercial broadcasting stations was made in 1922, thirty-four stations began operating within the year, providing radio communications in every province except Nova Scotia and Prince Edward Island.

At this early stage the private radio industry was concentrated in the large urban market areas, and as late as 1931 half the Canadian operating wattage was located in Montreal and Toronto. At this time, too, Canadian broadcasters encountered interference from stronger American stations using every wave-length of the limited broadcast band. A Canadian-American agreement to assure Canada of six clear channels was nullified by an American court decision that governmental allocation of wave-lengths was *ultra-vires* in a free-enterprise economy. Canada participated in the 1927 Washington Conference, which provided for the first frequency allocations under the International Telecommunications Union, which Canada had joined in 1906. Two years later in Ottawa, Canada joined Cuba, Newfoundland, and the United States in trying to regulate frequency use in North America. Despite a further agreement in 1932, interference from American transmitters continued, and was compounded by strong Mexican stations that jammed Canadian channels in the evening. Not until the Havana Convention was implemented in 1941 could Canada be certain of a fair share in hemispheric frequency allocations.

Private broadcasting in Canada even during the 1920s was being publicly criticized in terms now familiar to Canadian ears. Too much time was devoted to advertising, insufficient use was made of live programming and of Canadian talent, private radio did not provide east-west communications, and this with the increasing use of American programs threatened Canadian cultural unity. Canada seemed to be facing 'cultural annexation' by the United States. To take account of such considerations and to forestall the chaos of unregulated advertising experienced by the United States when it began network broadcasting in 1926, the Aird Royal Commission investigated the radio communications situation in 1929. Although noting divergent views, the Commission recognized Canadian unanimity on one basic point: 'Canadian listeners want Canadian broadcasting.'

The Aird Commission's recommendation for nationalized radio in the national interest was shelved temporarily by the onset of the Great Depression, by the Conservatives' 1930 election victory, and by Quebec's challenge to federal authority over the field of radio – a threat removed only in 1932 by Privy Council decision. But public pressure for a national broadcasting system did not decrease, and Parliament responded by creating the Canadian Radio Broadcasting Commission.

The Canadian Radio Commission, as established, was intended to be a cultural cement in the process of nation-building. It did praiseworthy work in bringing many Canadians together in their common attention to such events as the Christmas Day broadcasts and the Moose River mine disaster. But in 1936 less than half the Canadian people were covered effectively by Commission broadcasting. Nation-wide coverage obviously required time, experience, and money, and only time was available in quantity throughout the depression.

Moreover, as the dependent creatures of government, the Commission and its chairman, Hector Charlesworth, were subjected to the haphazard interference of Cabinet and back-benchers alike. They suffered constant acrimonious criticism, especially because the Commission through its power to regulate every aspect of private radio in Canada became prosecutor, judge, and jury over its rivals' operations. This unenviable role left both the Commission and the Corporation which succeeded it open to charges of dictatorship until regulatory functions were transferred to the Board of Broadcast Governors in 1958.

The Broadcasting Act of 1936 replaced the Commission with the Canadian Broadcasting Corporation. The Act gave the CBC greater independence and more clearly defined responsibility by making it answerable only to Parliament through a single Cabinet Minister.

The achievements of the new broadcasting body were substantial and commendable. A network of stations made highly varied programs available to nearly all parts of Canada. The war years, 1939-45, proved the real value of a national radio network in creating a sense of community in the nation. A French-language network and a second English one were established during the war, and the first relay station was built to meet lack of local radio communication. A Corporation achievement of a different kind has been its success in winning a disproportionately large share of international awards, particularly for programs in the public-service and 'cultural' fields.

Another public communications development had equally happy results. Throughout the years between the two world wars, the Canadian government relied heavily on the technical knowledge of its Signal Corps in radio matters both operational and advisory. Beginning in 1923, the Corps built and maintained a radio system servicing both government agencies and business throughout the Northwest Territories, a network that eventually comprised twenty-four stations stretching from Aklavik to Churchill before it was turned over to the Department of Transport in 1960. In addition, the Signal Corps has provided communications at various times for the R.C.A.F., for the airmail service and the Post Office, for the Hudson Strait expedition and for the Atlantic and Pacific coasts, and has also been a source of technical experts to attend international conferences.

If the depression delayed the growth of national, publicly owned radio, it also hampered the development of private broadcasting. But the postwar decade saw both a rapid proli-

feration of private radio stations and the financial embarrassment of the CBC. Originally intended to be self-supporting,
the CBC found itself unable to meet the cost of expanding its
facilities through the limited income from receiver licences.
From 1951 on it became dependent on parliamentary subsidies and in 1953 those unprofitable licences were abolished.
At the same time, the advent of CBC television brought
voracious demands on the public budget.

From one standpoint the introduction in 1952 of the new
medium of television was a major accomplishment. Canada
adopted television more quickly than any other country in
the world. By the end of 1955 she had become the world's
second television country in terms of programs, number of
stations, network service, extent of coverage, and per-capita
ownership of sets. Montreal became the world's fourth and
Toronto the fifth largest TV production centre, and in terms
of sets-in-use and production of programs the Corporation
provided the world's largest French-language television
service.

Despite such achievements economic difficulties encouraged criticism of the system. The CBC's so-called highbrow
planning was widely resented. Private stations and their
sympathizers felt it was unjust to force the taxpayer to subsidize the CBC. Above all, the role of the Corporation as both
regulator of and competitor to the private stations was loudly
denounced. Many who objected to the comparative independence of the CBC called for a more authoritarian control
of the publicly owned Corporation; others, by contrast, felt
the CBC should be made freer of potential parliamentary
influence by being provided with funds on a more regular
basis than that of the parliamentary grant.

The urgency of such issues led to the appointment of the
Royal Commission on Broadcasting in 1955 (the Fowler
Commission), thus implementing a recommendation by the
Massey Commission in 1951. Although the philosophy of
national, publicly owned broadcasting was defended by the
Fowler Commission, it did recommend the separation of the
CBC's operational and regulatory functions, an end achieved

by the creation of the Board of Broadcast Governors in 1958.

What the B.B.G. is required to regulate is a mixed system of government-sponsored but politically independent broadcasting side by side with the American type of privately owned and operated stations. In the field of radio the dualism has become generally harmonious. Private radio has proved itself quite happy to leave network broadcasting to the CBC: this is because it is local advertising that sustains the local stations, national advertisers (except for spot advertisements) having transferred their advertising to television. In such a non-competitive situation the complementary programming favoured by the Fowler Commission is readily possible.

The situation is different for television. Because national advertisers pay such large sums to use the new medium, private stations have moved quickly to establish their own network. Known as Canadian Television, it was created by the link-up of eight Canadian cities in 1961. CTV has not had it all its own way in seeking the national advertiser's dollar. Despite the complementary roles envisaged for the privately owned CTV and the publicly owned CBC, a rather unexpected commercial competition has grown up between the two bodies, partly as a result of the Conservative government's rejection of the Fowler proposals to replace annual parliamentary grants by a long-term system of financing. By granting funds according to a tacit philosophy of 'making up the operating deficit', the same government implicity supported the Fowler recommendation that the Corporation adopt more aggressive measures to earn much of its own revenue.

The situation has placed the CBC in an ambiguous position: it is asked to contribute to Canada's cultural identity, yet much of its creative energy has been dissipated by enforced competition with CTV. Neither CBC nor CTV seems to like the arrangement. Heated controversy over Grey Cup telecasting rights in 1962 stopped just short of open defiance of the B.B.G. by the CBC. The Corporation is openly dissatisfied with Board policy regarding CBC affiliates and has challenged the B.B.G.'s right to regulate the CBC. CTV and independent private stations have condemned the Board's fifty-five per cent Canadian content rule as artificial and unrealistic. Both press and public have criticized the B.B.G. for many of its licensing decisions. Dissatisfaction of this kind led to another study of Canada's broadcasting troubles. R. M. Fowler, who had been chairman of the Fowler Commission, headed a Committee that reported in 1965. After condemning the existing broadcasting situation in wide-ranging detail, the Fowler Committee made many recommendations intended to improve radio and television and to enable them to play a more decisive part in the strengthening of Canadian nationhood. Most controversial of its proposals was that one regulatory body, the Canadian Broadcasting Authority (Régie des Ondes), should replace the B.B.G., and should direct, supervise, and control the whole broadcasting system. The Authority was to be given coercive powers where needed, and the CBC was to be shorn of much of its strength. Reaction to the controversial recommendations and to the Report as a whole suggests that there is still no imminent likelihood that broadcasting will completely fulfil its early promise as a contributor to national harmony.

The technological achievements of communications of the past century have virtually annihilated time and space, the twin continent-wide dimensions challenging the Canadian people. But the failure to exploit this revolution has left Canada still without a sense of national unity. Provincialism and parochialism remain much stronger forces than Canadianism. The person-to-person nature of telegraph and telephone really exclude those means of communications from consideration as mass media. The newspaper can never entirely succeed in becoming national in scope because of its inherent physical structure. The challenge then of mass-media communications upon which a viable Canadianism must be founded becomes the responsibility of films, radio, and television. They and they alone must provide the life-blood of a cultural unity, in the broadest sense, for the Canadian people.

18. Science
and Medicine

WILLIAM CARLETON GIBSON

The story of Canadian science
and medicine since Confederation goes from the days of
isolated nuclei of scholars scattered across the country, to the
1960s, when we have great institutions throughout Canada
dedicated to teaching, research, and practical applications
both industrial and clinical. A half-century of hobby research has been followed by fifty years in which career research has been accepted in principle, though the principle
has been slow in its application.

The high point in the development of pure science was
probably reached during Rutherford's spectacular years at
McGill conducting research in nuclear physics. In medicine
the climax of Canadian achievement was reached when
Banting discovered insulin in 1922. Since then medical

research has become recognized as of national importance. But two wars were required to put research in the pure sciences on a par with those in medicine.

Canada's development in science and medicine has been retarded by proximity to the United States. We have often been willing to have our science 'second hand', and many Canadian subsidiaries of American companies have done no original research themselves, depending blindly, instead, on the development program of the parent company. 'Contract research' centres have developed in the U.S.A., and some Canadian companies send their problems south for investigation, often by scientists trained originally in Canada.

Two pre-Confederation university appointments set the stage for the scientific development of the country: of Henry Holmes Croft to Canada's first Chair of Chemistry at Toronto in 1842, and of Sir William Dawson to the principalship of McGill University in 1855. They and their contemporaries, though weighed down with a heavy load of purely undergraduate teaching, managed to train a generation of dedicated men who, in turn, prosecuted research and produced more trained people in science.

Visitors to the campus of the University of Toronto have often wondered what went on in the slate-covered 'round house' of the original King's College (later the Senate Chamber). This was Croft's laboratory, which he had patterned after the Abbot's Kitchen at Glastonbury Abbey! Croft's early writing appeared in Canadian and British journals. Staking out claims for science in Toronto kept Croft busy, for no twenty-three-year-old professor, though recommended by the great chemist Michael Faraday, was likely to be suffered in silence by the President, Archdeacon (later Bishop) Strachan. As W. Lash Miller has put it, 'Anticipating Huxley by a dozen years, Croft has a set-to with a bishop; but Croft's bishop was a much more dangerous antagonist than Huxley's – he was, in fact, Croft's president. When the row was over, the University was secular, the bishop gone, and Croft Vice-Chancellor.'

William Dawson was literally to lead McGill University in Montreal out of the wilderness. Once the will of James McGill had been untangled, and the University had begun with a Medical Faculty, the Governors looked to the British Isles for a principal. The Queen's representative in Canada, Sir Edmund Walker Head, the unsung architect of our later Confederation, was consulted. He 'both startled and disappointed' the Governors of McGill by suggesting Dawson, a Nova-Scotia-born man, thirty-five years old and still working on his M.A. degree from Edinburgh.

The mixture of grit and vision that William Dawson brought to the Burnside farm was what McGill needed, rundown and forlorn as it was, and with depressed Governors straining to see 'some man of mark in England'. Dawson made McGill, and gave science and medicine a great lift in Canada, simply because he was not too proud to take his coat off and do the work himself. He planted the great trees that grace McGill today, indexed the earliest library books, built up the geological collection from his summer fieldwork. More important, Dawson continued to be a great teacher as Professor of Geology and Paleontology. Even at age twenty-two, Dawson numbered among his admirers the great geologist Sir Charles Lyell, Darwin's mentor. It is little wonder that Dawson, on the basis of his scholarly achievements, became the President of the American Association for the Advancement of Science, and of the British Association. Canadian science benefited from his teaching, his research, and the educational philosophy he held to in establishing McGill as a university for all of Canada. Medicine and science he backed to the full.

But Dawson, like Croft, was ahead of his time. He established a School of Engineering, a Chair of Practical Chemistry, and early work in scientific agriculture, only to see them suspended for lack of financial support. Dawson wrote prophetically at the time: 'For my part I am not ashamed of them. . . . There is not one of them which is not important for the material progress of the country; and there is not one of them which by us, or others, will not be at length success-

fully carried out. I do not despair of any of them.' Their
eventual role in Canada's development proved how right
Dawson was. He had a 'do-it-yourself' philosophy that was
utterly foreign to the older establishments in Europe. At
the University of Edinburgh, Dawson had seen the fringes
of the continental view of higher education, but he rightly
judged that Canada could not wait for a very gradual development of its colleges. Instead, he plunged in, proclaiming
science as the ingredient that would help to build up the
new country, rich in untapped resources. It was fortunate
for Canadian science that William Logan, the Montreal-
born director of the Geological Survey of Canada, had been
able to endow the Chair of Geology and Paleontology which
Dawson was to hold for so long at McGill.

Meanwhile, in an entirely different part of the country,
agricultural science was setting out on its remarkable new
adventure. At the age of eighteen, William Saunders, in
London, Ontario, was founding a pharmaceutical manufacturing firm. It was not long before he became the initiating
force in the new Ontario College of Pharmacy. He then was
made Professor of Materia Medica in the University of
Western Ontario's Faculty of Medicine, which opened in a
cottage in 1882. Within four years Saunders was named to
direct the Dominion Experimental Farm in Ottawa; there
he embarked on experiments in the development of new
varieties of economically important plants, and within a year
had a remarkable chemist, Frank B. Shutt, at work.

From the cereals research came Marquis wheat, which was
magically to enlarge the area of Canada's wheat-growing
lands. The research was directed by William Saunders's son,
Charles, with the co-operation of farmers in the West, such
as William Moir Douglas of Indian Head, Saskatchewan.
From Shutt's chemistry laboratory came the early work on
fertilizers and myriad problems of crop production, much
of which is today embodied in the Science Service of Canada's
enterprising Department of Agriculture. The tradition
established by the Saunders family, father and son, is still a
sure guide.

Once again, the provision of a nucleus, in this case the Dominion Experimental Farm, led to the rapid development of a corps of well-trained scientists in the public service. The universities of Canada, again with the stimulus of Dawson at McGill, Abbé Léon Provancher, and Abbé Ovide Brunet of Laval, brought instruction in botany to a high level. Plant geneticists have continued to hold an important part of the stage – from the earliest days of William Saunders and his apple-breeding to President Thompson of the University of Saskatchewan and Leonard Huskins of McGill. The grain-rust research paid handsome dividends for Canadian farmers. Sound genetic foundations in this field were laid by J. H. Craigie (on rust fungi) and by Margaret Newton (on mutations in rust).

In 1945 Dr. Henry Marshall Tory, in discussing the returns from research, said: 'The saving in one year ($25,000,000) as a result of the rust control research project was sufficient to repay to Canada the total cost of the National Research Council from its foundation to the present time.'

In the field of physics, two complementary centres of research activity began at McGill and the University of Toronto almost simultaneously. At the former, the twenty-seven-year-old Ernest Rutherford and his students changed our world through researches into radioactivity. At Toronto, John Cunningham McLennan was destined to develop a strong school of physicist disciples across Canada.

Rutherford, born on a New Zealand farm, was at work in the Cavendish Laboratory when Principal Peterson and Professor Cox visited Cambridge. With Frederick Soddy, Rutherford was brought out to Montreal to the fine new physics laboratory set up by Sir William Macdonald. Rutherford was the right man at the right place. The Curies had just reported to the French Academy on the isolation of radium, and Röntgen's X-rays were only three years old.

Onto this well-set stage Rutherford emerged, and not long after completing his ninth year at McGill and returning to Cambridge, he received the Nobel Prize. He introduced measurement into the field of radioactivity and opened the door to the alchemist's dream of the transmutation of the elements. As we look back from the position of Canada's Centennial year, taking for granted the fission of atoms for power and heat, we little realize that it was in Rutherford's laboratory at McGill that Soddy developed today's chemistry of the radioactive elements, including their planned disintegration; that Howard T. Barnes measured the heat given off by such processes; and that Otto Hahn had his first inkling of chain reactions, which his pupils, in turn, produced in his Berlin laboratory in 1939, using uranium 235. How prophetically did Rutherford write in 1921: 'Each atom, though it is quite incommensurable, has in it the power of a thousand horses, . . . infinite material power is at our fingertips awaiting release.' Norman Shaw has written: 'Undoubtedly Lord Rutherford may claim sole responsibility for the greatest outburst of original research in Canada, and the subsequent influence of his personality and works is beyond assessment.'

The thirty years that Sir John McLennan spent in the Department of Physics at the University of Toronto were crowded with discovery and development as two generations of future physicists were trained for a new country. Many of the things we take for granted today were developed in the McLennan laboratory – encompassing such fields as spectroscopy, low-temperature work on liquid oxygen and liquid helium, and radiation physics. McLennan's successor, E. F. Burton, and his pupils in turn played an important role in the development of the electron microscope. Astronomy in Canada was deeply indebted to the early Toronto teacher-researchers. Atmospheric physics and Canadian meteorology stem from these laboratories.

In the field of psychology the first laboratory on British soil was set up at the University of Toronto in 1889 by James Mark Baldwin, a graduate of Princeton who had studied in Germany with Wundt, the apostle of the new 'physiological psychology'. Within a year Baldwin could boast an equipment grant from the Board of Governors of $1,451, and within two years he was able to bring from Leipzig one of

Wundt's early pupils, August Kirschmann.

Within twenty years the Toronto laboratory had become the rallying-point for men such as G. S. Brett in the history of psychology and E. A. Bott in applied psychology. The latter worked for years on motivational problems in rehabilitation – urgent as the war-wounded came home. The end of the First World War saw, at last, the emancipation of psychology in many Canadian universities from the opinionated but dead hand of philosophy. In the more liberal institutions psychology laboratories had been able to develop under the noses of benign philosophers. However, it is instructive to see the ebb and flow of teachers and texts in colleges strongly dominated by theological considerations; in one such, in 1875, Herbert Spencer was the 'demon' to be replaced; by 1880 it was John Dewey; the replacement finally settled upon was Aristotle.

By 1940, however, a great transformation had been wrought, and psychologists from every university in Canada sought to aid in the war effort. Naturally, in such an encounter, psycho-physiological problems and questions of personnel selection were given a high priority. William Line in the Army, S. N. F. Chant in the R.C.A.F., and E. S. W. Belyea in the Navy commandeered large numbers of Canadian graduates in this field. D. O. Hebb's classical work at McGill on the behavioural changes resulting from loss of brain tissue was applied to aid the unprecedented number of survivors of war-time head injuries. Rehabilitation studies pioneered by Bott a generation earlier were expanded by him and by C. R. Myers with the R.A.F. overseas.

Since the war, psychological research has become an integral part of Defence Research Board activities, both at the Defence Medical Research Laboratories near Toronto and in the extra-mural programs in Canada's universities. The National Research Council and the Mental Health Division of the Department of National Health and Welfare have also financed much of the psychological research in Canada in the thirty-year period preceding our Centennial. However, it is sobering to reflect on the fact that by the time

Canada reached its hundredth birthday more than half of the research support in this field was coming from United States sources.

Medical science in Canada's hundred years since Confederation has been replete with great teachers, but not, to the same degree, with innovators. The years before Confederation could boast of Jacques Cartier's successful cure of scurvy in 1535, by extracts of evergreen needles and bark. Michel Sarrazin (1659-1735) was to become Canada's first scientist, surgeon, botanist, physiologist, and anatomist. However, by the time William Osler graduated in medicine at McGill University in 1872, there was still only the barest suggestion of medical research. As Osler could testify, the scourge of smallpox kept physicians so busy that little time was available to any physician for such airy things as research. But, with the $600 per year which he received as physician to certain smallpox wards in Montreal, Osler purchased several microscopes. With these he gave the first demonstrations to students in his course in histology and physiology, subjects he had studied in Rudolf Virchow's laboratory in Berlin and with Burdon Sanderson in London. Osler pressed for compulsory vaccination against the smallpox that he saw daily. In the years 1872-80, Montreal alone counted 4,911 dead from this disease.

Part of Canada's medical history, an ugly part, is embodied in the following account by Canada's well-known medical historian and public health figure, Dr. J. J. Heagerty, of militant anti-scientific outbursts in Montreal during these years:

> From 1875 to 1885, a great deal of antagonism to vaccination had been aroused . . . notably by a well-known physician, Dr. Coderre. The antagonism to vaccination became so intense that riots frequently occurred, the troops were called out and, as a result, compulsory vaccination could not be carried out. Vaccination fell into disrepute and very few of the inhabitants were vaccinated during the ensuing years, so that the major part of the population was unprotected.
>
> In this year [1875] over three thousand people filled the

city hall at Montreal and overflowed into the surrounding streets to voice their protest against compulsory vaccination. From year to year this opposition was kept up, and in the year 1885 culminated in riots. Rioting began in Montreal on the 28th of September, 1885, at the close of a week when 226 of the 245 [smallpox] deaths for that week had been among French Canadians. A howling mob of anti-vaccinationists assembled that night and took possession of the streets. The crazed bigots wrecked the east end branch of the Medical Health Officer's department, tore down placards from vaccination stations and from infected houses, assaulted the City Hall itself and, after being driven off by the massed police, broke in and wrecked the Health Offices, smashing the windows and throwing quantities of disinfectants and placard posters into the street.

Chief of Police Paradis was attacked and badly beaten by the mob, who threatened next night to burn down the house of the mayor and that of a French-Canadian alderman who supported vaccination. Mayor Beauregard rose from a sick-bed to try to quell the riots. The house of Dr. Laporte, another civic medical officer, was set on fire. The rioters broke into the office of the *Montreal Herald* and gutted it.... During the hubbub Mayor Beauregard was actually arrested by order of a French-Canadian senator, because the Mayor had forcibly taken possession of the Montreal Exhibition grounds for a smallpox hospital.

On leaving McGill in 1885, Osler served as Professor of Medicine at the University of Pennsylvania for four years; some of his McGill students followed him there, to work under him in their summer vacations. One such was Henry Esson Young, from Huntingdon, Quebec, whose eventual career as Minister of Health and Education was to improve the life of all future generations in British Columbia. His influence on the public health movement in Canada was to be as great as that of Osler in Britain.

When, in 1889, Osler became established as Professor of Medicine at the new Johns Hopkins Medical School in Baltimore, even more Canadians sought him out as their teacher. Space permits only a brief reference to two pairs of brothers,

Thomas and John McCrae of Guelph, Ontario, and William and John MacCallum of Dunnville, Ontario. After completing his Arts and Medicine degrees at Toronto, Thomas McCrae went to Johns Hopkins for his postgraduate training. Following closely on Osler, he became an outstanding internist, Professor of Medicine at Jefferson Medical College in Philadelphia, and eventually a well-known textbook author. He influenced the careers of countless fellow Canadians.

John McCrae, the 'soldier poet', was two years younger than Thomas. Having taken degrees in Arts and Medicine in Toronto he served as a resident physician at Johns Hopkins in 1899, and then became Assistant Pathologist to the Montreal General Hospital. Within a year he was off to the Boer War as an artillery officer. On his return he took up his pathology and poetry-writing again, until the World War in 1914. Off he went again – this time as a medical officer. Early in 1915 his poem 'In Flanders Fields' appeared in *Punch* and made him immortal. The trench-warfare phase of Canadian medicine is so rarely mentioned that it may be well to recollect it; in McCrae's diary entry for May 27, 1915, we read:

> Day cloudy and chilly. We wore our greatcoats most of the afternoon, and looked for bits of sunlight to get warm. About two o'clock the heavy guns gave us a regular 'black-smithing.' Every time we fired we drew a perfect hornet's nest about our heads. While attending to a casualty a shell broke through both sides of the trench, front and back, about twelve feet away. The zig-zag of the trench was between it and us, and we escaped. From my bunk the moon looks down at me, and the wind whistles along the trench like a corridor. As the trenches run in all directions they catch the wind however it blows, so one is always sure of a good draught. We have not had our clothes off since last Saturday, and there is no near prospect of getting them off.

William G. MacCallum was the son of a family doctor, and studied classics at the University of Toronto. In the summers he studied botany and served as an apprentice to his father. It was not any surprise, therefore, when he applied to enter Johns Hopkins Medical School, but he asked for, and eventually received, second-year standing in the four-year course; on graduation in 1897 he was to lead his class.

While still a medical student he showed the entire sexual cycle of the malarial parasite in the blood, using birds. When Sir Ronald Ross, the authority in this field, read MacCallum's little paper he remarked, 'I have ever since felt disgraced as a man of science.'

MacCallum's next discovery, made after his training in pathology, was the role of the parathyroid glands in tetany. These minute 'oat-seeds' embedded in the thyroid were shown to regulate the level of calcium in the circulating blood. Some years later, another Canadian, J. B. Collip, was to identify and purify the active principle now known as 'parathormone'.

John Bruce MacCallum graduated in medicine at Johns Hopkins in 1900 after publishing six original scientific papers. He was to publish a total of thirty scientific contributions before tuberculosis ended his life at thirty. Perhaps his greatest contribution to knowledge was his undergraduate research on the development of the spiral muscles making up the wall of the heart.

When, in 1909, Osler was speaking before the Ontario Medical Association in Toronto on 'The Treatment of Disease', he remarked prophetically: 'As our knowledge of the pancreatic function and carbohydrate metabolism becomes more accurate we shall probably be able to place the treatment of diabetes on a sure foundation.' A short twelve years later, Frederick Banting, assisted by a graduate student, Charles Best, working through the heat of a Toronto summer, began an historic series of experiments on the ability of pancreatic extracts to lower the blood sugar and hence to help diabetics.

Banting had returned as an orthopaedic surgeon from the First World War, and while waiting for a practice to develop in London, Ontario, was given a bread-and-butter teaching job in the Department of Physiology of the University of

Western Ontario. One night while preparing a lecture for his students, Banting read an article on stones in the duct of the pancreas and their effect on the scattered islet cells first described by the medical student Langerhans in 1867. At 2 a.m. Banting jumped out of bed and scribbled in his notebook his plan of campaign: 'Ligate pancreatic duct of dogs. Wait six or eight weeks. Remove residue and extract.'

Banting drove on relentlessly to discover the secrets of the pancreas. By December 1921, he was able to report to the American Physiological Society meetings in New Haven that he and Best had been able to isolate a potent hormone, which they called 'insulin' because it was derived from the islet tissue of the pancreas. This hormone would restore to normal the blood-sugar level of diabetic dogs. The presentation by Banting was so painfully halting that no one could have been blamed if the main point of his communication had been missed. But Professor J. J. R. Macleod, Toronto's professor of physiology, now added Collip and Noble to the team, and the work of purification of the extract began. Even before the substance was safe for human injection, patients began to arrive in Toronto in the last stages of diabetes, and when the Nobel Prize for medicine was awarded to Banting and Macleod in 1923, an avalanche of patients descended on Toronto.

From the vantage point that he now occupied Banting made a most statesmanlike contribution. A foundation was set up to aid young researchers across Canada. The Banting Institute became Canada's hive of industry in the medical field as students and scientists tackled the limitless problems of disease. When the ultraconservative voices in society asked why Canada should even be in this field, Banting would roar, 'It is not within the power of the properly constructed human mind to be satisfied.'

As Banting travelled during the thirties, given honours wherever he passed, he came to the sad but inescapable conclusion that once more he was going to be caught up in war. In 1938, fortunately for Canada and for the Allied cause, he started to develop on a large scale such specialties as aviation medicine. When war came in 1939 the Banting Institute on College Street was already bursting with research activity. The corps of men trained by Banting, Best, and their associates was to power the research effort of the National Research Council of Canada in war medicine. In this it was joined by the recently opened Montreal Neurological Institute under Dr. Wilder Penfield, the brain surgeon.

Penfield had come to McGill University in 1928 from the Presbyterian Hospital of Columbia University's Medical Center in New York. As a pupil of Osler at Oxford he had many affinities with McGill, and he proceeded to design Canada's first university-owned hospital, the property of the Board of Governors of McGill. In 1934 the Institute was opened, combining hospital services with clinical investigation, and with basic research laboratories of the kind Penfield had known when a pupil of Sherrington at Oxford, and of Ramón y Cajal in Madrid.

The Institute was built by friends of the University, and the research endowed with a capital sum of $1,000,000 from the Rockefeller Foundation. Twenty-five years later Dr. Alan Gregg was able to say that the returns on this investment, in terms of men trained and discoveries made, were the highest he had known in his long association with the Foundation.

Penfield, the naturalized Canadian, took the lead in many war-time scientific projects, and his pupils studied such military-medical problems as motion sickness, decompression sickness, air-ambulance transport of head injuries, concussion, and increased intracranial pressure. His pioneer work on blood substitutes in the First World War had taught Penfield the urgency of such problems. In postwar years the study of epilepsy due to penetrating wounds of the brain became part of the research program. This was eventually expanded to include the surgical removal of brain scars resulting from birth injuries. Today the enlarged Institute draws physicians and surgeons from around the world and reminds Canadians of the high standard of medical science at their disposal.

Embedded in the fabric of Canada is the life and labour of Dr. Henry Marshall Tory. In the first century of our Dominion's existence no one has set the stage for Canada's scientific development as he did. Born three years before Confederation, he lived eighty-three useful years. Educated at McGill in theology and mathematics, Tory brought a combination of Methodist evangelism and Maritime hard-headedness to all his projects. After a distinguished career in education, he was, in 1923, appointed by the government to the National Research Council. The Senate had previously, in a disgraceful display, killed an excellent bill designed to provide a National Research Institute. After this catastrophe in Parliament, Dr. Tory faced a long up-hill grind with the early, under-financed N.R.C., but he was the right man at the right time. His first major achievement was probably his work in the basic-refractories industry, which gave the country the largest basic-refractories industry in the British Empire, exporting some fifty different products to thirty countries.

By 1935 Dr. Tory had the National Research Council running in high gear and hoped to be able to finish up some of his best-loved projects. However, on May 29 he was told by the arch-detractor of his early Alberta days, the Right Honourable R. B. Bennett, that his services would not be required by the Government of Canada after May 31. As Tory's biographer, E. A. Corbett, says: 'It is unlikely that there have been very many occasions in the history of Canada when a distinguished public servant has been so shabbily treated.' At age seventy, however, Dr. Tory could afford to be rid of such pitifully short-sighted masters.

The appointment of Tory's successor, Major-General A. G. L. McNaughton, to the Chairmanship, in such circumstances, was not given the popular acclaim that it deserved. He initiated research in radio and ballistics, having already, in 1926, developed a cathode-ray direction-finder with Colonel W. A. Steele of Ottawa. Upon McNaughton's recall to the Army in October 1939, to take command of the First Canadian Division, the Chairmanship of the N.R.C. passed

to the capable hands of Dr. C. J. Mackenzie, Dean of Engineering at the University of Saskatchewan.

The years of pioneering by Dr. Tory were now to pay
handsome dividends to Canada. Mackenzie found a budget
of less than one million dollars per year and a staff of three
hundred. In a few months he had been given a budget of
seven million dollars and a staff of two thousand. Twenty-
one new laboratories were opened, including one for explosives research at Valcartier, a nuclear laboratory at Montreal,
the atomic energy plant at Chalk River, and radar and aeronautics establishments at Ottawa. Twenty Associate Committees were set up, co-ordinating the work of one hundred
sub-committees.

A Crown corporation known as Research Enterprises Ltd.
was set up to make optical equipment, but was soon thrust
into the radar-manufacturing business also. Private citizens,
by now convinced of the value of research in the war effort,
contributed $1,300,000 as a 'no-strings attached' fund to
serve as a memorial to Sir Frederick Banting, tragically
killed in an air crash while *en route* overseas.

The Canadian contributions poured forth: microwave
fire-control instruments; the proximity fuse which was to
change the course of the war; anti-chemical-warfare clothing;
de-icing and defrosting modifications to aircraft.

An N.R.C. 'jammer' was developed to disorganize the
radio-controlled glider bombs of the German air force. The
proximity fuse came into its own in the Ardennes in December 1944. It was used with great success against Japanese
naval bombers, and against the V-1 'buzz bombs' over the
United Kingdom. The chemical industry of Canada contributed its leading researchers in the field of explosives with
the result that RDX, with twice the effect of TNT, was
developed economically. The submarine pens at St-Nazaire
and Lorient and the battleship *Tirpitz* all felt its blast. In
Toronto Dr. G. F. Wright developed a flashless propellant,
DINA, for use at night.

The uranium mine opened at Gilbert La Bine's discovery
on Great Bear Lake in 1930 had been closed in 1940 by the

war. It was secretly re-opened in 1942 as the atomic-bomb project gathered momentum. Since 1940 N.R.C. scientists had been bombarding uranium in a pile built by Dr. George C. Laurence. A British group came out to Montreal to work in 1942, to find the heavy-water supply of Free France awaiting them. As a result of the Quebec Conference the great Chalk River atomic development was started, 130 miles west of Ottawa.

Meanwhile the armed forces were hard at research and development too. The rubber-tracked 'weasel' was developed for an invasion of Norway and found its greatest use at Monte Cassino, Normandy, and the Scheldt. Because the great French field experimental station in Algeria had been lost, a new and vast one was set up at Suffield, Alberta. All manner of chemical problems were worked on there, and in addition flame-throwers were perfected on its proving-grounds. The projection of burning gel fuels was similarly developed for use in Holland. Fungicides were produced for tropical equipment.

The navy had the advice of Dr. R. W. Boyle, director of N.R.C.'s Division of Physics and Electrical Engineering. He had had a brilliant research career in the First World War in anti-submarine detection devices. Now he brought this to bear on the problem of magnetic mines, in association with Dr. J. H. L. Johnstone and Dr. G. H. Henderson of Dalhousie University. Demagnetizing was accomplished by an energized cable around each ship, later known to the public as the 'degaussing belt'.

Ingenious devices were developed to meet the paralysing menace of German mines. Deep-water trials of detectors for midget submarines were carried out at Whitecliffe Point, B.C. Navy research on the Nazi acoustic mine and torpedo paid large dividends. Other projects covered such fields as the controlled floodlighting of ships at dusk to minimize the silhouette effect, the making of potable water from sea-water, the design of self-inflating life preservers for unconscious seamen, and the search for gas-detecting paints. Early experimental work produced high-altitude breathing equipment for fighter pilots, new methods of penicillin production, and an anti-typhus vaccine which won Dr. James Craigie the American Typhus Commission medal.

The enduring effect of all this war-time scientific activity was to convince Canadians that there was, in this country, adequate research ability. The day of dependence on 'second-hand' ideas was over, and an air of self-confidence pervaded university campuses and research institutions. The development could be charted in budget figures for government research alone, and these showed a world of difference in thirty years: from $100,000 in 1920 to approximately $40,000,000 in 1950.

The postwar researchers followed up a number of ideas unearthed in six years of battle. Arctic research was organized by an Advisory Committee under Dr. H. L. Keenleyside, the Deputy-Minister of Mines and Resources. Ice-breakers, radio communication, medical research, and Arctic air navigation soon became important areas of activity. By 1952 Defence Research Medical Laboratories opened a permanent building at Downsview, Ontario.

One of the greatest discoveries in Canada's history was made by a scientist working on a Defence Research Board grant – Dr. Murray Barr of the Department of Microscopic Anatomy at the University of Western Ontario. This superb histologist found, in the course of research on anoxia and the nervous system, that there is a distinct and constant difference between the cells of male and female animals. This has triggered a vast amount of research around the world on the sex chromatin in cells of all body tissues. It ranks in scientific importance with the discovery of insulin.

Other Canadian developments in biology are best exemplified by the Connaught Laboratories. This integral part of the University of Toronto was set up in 1914 to produce enough diphtheria anti-toxin for the whole of Canada. Its history ever since has been characterized by similar activities on a mass scale. Colonel Albert E. Gooderham's farm was deeded to the University as a mark of appreciation of his friend the Duke of Connaught in 1917. At this Dufferin

Division there will soon be located a complex of sixty buildings in all. The Connaught's future was assured when it undertook the production of insulin for the country following Banting's great discovery. The list of triumphs in biological products of great purity includes heparin, injectable liver preparations, tetanus toxoid, and human blood serum.

Penicillin production during the Second World War owed a lot to the Connaught research and technical staffs. More recently, the development by Parker, Morgan, and Morton of a synthetic medium for the artificial cultivation of tissue cells in order to grow the virus of poliomyelitis has led to the Connaught's great reputation in the polio-vaccine enterprise. Rhodes and Farrell made possible, by their efforts, the production of sufficient Salk vaccine to conduct the historic field trials in the United States in 1954. The successive directors, R. D. Defries and J. K. W. Ferguson, have given a most practical impetus to first-class research and its early application in Canadian life.

A very important field in which Canadians have made major contributions is that of anaesthesia. In 1929, Professor G. H. W. Lucas of the University of Toronto introduced cyclopropane. It was an isomer of propylene which had been investigated by Velyien E. Henderson and W. Easson Brown in 1924. In the 1930s H. R. Griffith of Montreal introduced curare, the South American muscle-paralysing drug, to achieve relaxation with minimal anaesthetic dosage.

In the forest industry Canada has had a long tradition of university-based research. In 1913 a Forest Products Laboratory was installed at McGill by the Dominion Forest Service. In 1927 this was replaced by an Institute built on the McGill campus by the Canadian Pulp and Paper Association. Its operations have been directed by a tripartite board representing the Association, the federal government, and McGill University. In its forty-year history it has seen researchers from all parts of Canada engaged in pure and applied research.

In the field of industrial research, Canada's contribution has been remarkably high. In railway engineering, mining,

chemicals, and pulp and paper, Canadian scientists and
engineers have been particularly inventive. Ernest A. Le-
Sueur of Ottawa pioneered new processes of electrolysis
using a porous-diaphragm type of cell. He was also able to
solidify acetylene. Further developments in the use of acetylene resulted in oxyacetylene welding producing tempera-
tures up to 7,000 degrees Fahrenheit, and eventually in new
types of high explosives for war-time use, including cordite
in the First World War and RDX in the Second World War.
Acetylene work by a Canadian team also resulted in large-
scale production of acetone for the acetate yarn industry,
especially in the United Kingdom.

Thomas L. Wilson of Woodstock, Ontario, experimenting
with lime and coal in an electric furnace, produced calcium
carbide, which formed acetylene gas when placed in water.
Out of this developed a great industry, the Union Carbide
Company. The Dow Chemical Company was formed by
Herbert H. Dow of Belleville, Ontario, who like LeSueur
had pioneered in work on electrolytic cells.

Provincial governments have set up their own research
councils, often for applied work, the earliest being Alberta
(1919) under Dr. Tory's stimulus. Ontario followed in 1928,
British Columbia in 1944, and Nova Scotia in 1946. An
example of 'pure' research conducted within one of these
establishments, however, is to be seen in Vancouver in the
work of Gobind Khorana on enzymes.

Laboratories located not on campuses but within industrial plants have often collaborated fruitfully with highly
sophisticated research laboratories at universities. In the
pharmaceutical industry, as an example, the early work of
Collip at McGill found an outlet in the Ayerst Laboratories
in Montreal where, in 1930, a female sex hormone was
developed to be taken by mouth. Another commercial 'first'
from this sharing of ideas was the hormone resembling that
from the anterior pituitary, also developed by Collip.

The Centennial of Canada's Confederation finds many
'research parks' being assembled, such as the Sheridan model
near Oakville, Ontario. University-based parks are only pos-

sible where adequate lands remain available for long-term rental. Thus the University Endowment Lands at Point Grey, adjacent to the U.B.C. campus, are about to be developed for the financial benefit of the three public universities of the province. The M.I.T.–Harvard–route 128 research development and the Stanford University farm-rental arrangements for clean industry have caused many industrial corporations to re-site their applied and basic research laboratories. The next hundred years in Canada's economy will probably be greatly affected by such developments.

In 1962 Canada's satellite, Alouette, was launched with dual radio antennae seventy-five feet in length. Today the de Havilland research group near Toronto is hoping to increase the length tenfold. With no lunar pretensions, Canadian scientists have nevertheless been able to develop on their own a rocket that can reach a point 180 miles from the earth. The Aerospace Institute of the University of Toronto has in hand today a broad spectrum of research studies, from air turbulence to noise and metal fatigue.

McGill University has for many years had a space-medicine research program. To this has been added a Space Research Institute under Dr. Gerald Bull. The High Altitude Research Project (HARP) has caught the popular imagination, though it has always had its detractors at Ottawa. One of the field laboratories is at Highwater, Quebec, where a 16-inch naval gun is part of the apparatus. The range station is in Barbados, where missiles and vehicles (Martlets) are shot at an initial velocity of one mile per second out of a 119-foot gun mounted vertically. The eventual program for orbiting satellites will complement the present researches on high-velocity winds in the ionosphere. Trails of space vehicles are presently photographed simultaneously from tracking stations in Grenada, St. Vincent, Tobago, and Trinidad, the 'smoke' being produced by tri-methyl aluminum interacting with atomic oxygen.

In conclusion, one senses a new direction to Canada's research efforts in science and medicine as our Centennial approaches. New sources of power developed at Chalk River by Atomic Energy of Canada, Ltd. (a Crown corporation set up by the National Research Council in 1952) are now available to Canadians and to our neighbours abroad in this shrinking world. For years NRX was the most powerful atomic reactor anywhere. It produced cobalt 60, which Canada presented to many emerging countries for medical use. Masterful engineering has produced a new type of power station (CANDU) capable of generating one thousand megawatts, the key feature being its capability for limitless extension. Safety is ensured by the use of fuel rods encased in individually pressurized tubes, which are surrounded by moderator fluid in an unpressurized tank. Because of this unique system, refuelling of individual tubes can be done while the rest of the reactor produces energy smoothly and continuously. Again Canada's friends benefit, as India builds four CANDU plants and Pakistan orders a replica. At Pickering, Ontario, a 266-million-dollar power plant of the same type is at present being constructed for the metropolitan Toronto area. Within eight years of our Centennial it is estimated that one half of all power stations being built will be run by atomic energy.

Medical research in Canada is in an analogous position, as it shares its findings with other nations. The rise of voluntary agencies to support medical research in Canada's universities is at last being paralleled by a Medical Research Council financed with federal funds. The reach to our neighbours by groups such as the Connaught Laboratories and the Muscular Dystrophy Association (with its support for key researchers abroad as well as at home), and by teams of physicians serving overseas through Medico or Canadian University Service Overseas – all these bring Canadian science to a new stage in its development. International engineering careers beckon to Canadians, both to the researcher at home and to the applied scientist abroad. McGill University is but one of Canada's many ambassadors as it applies scientific knowledge to social and nutritional problems in Barbados. There is scarcely a university in Canada that has not loaned some of its faculty for scientific programs abroad under UNESCO, F.A.O., the World Health Organization, and the Colombo Plan.

As Canadian scientists approach the threshold of a bright new century they can take quite literally now the injunction of John McCrea, the physician poet: 'It will be in your power every day to store up for yourselves treasures that will come back to you in consciousness of duty well done ... things that having given away freely you yet possess.'

19. Education

GEORGE E. FLOWER

At the end of Canada's first century as a nation, more than one Canadian in four is a full-time student or teacher. Add to these over a million more who are enrolled part time in some organized form of adult education, and the uncounted numbers, estimated to be also over a million, taking part in employee training programs and seminars operated by business and industry, and it is clear that education has become Canada's largest national enterprise. Over the years we have come to regard more and more institutionalized schooling as a birthright for all the children of all the people. Each year a higher proportion of the high school age group is to be found in high school, of the college age group in college; and our schools and univer-

sities are under constant pressures to take on new tasks, to
set up new programs, to serve purposes not served in those
settings before. Why?

The fact seems to be that Canadians, to use a phrase of
John W. Gardner's, increasingly turn to education as the
servant of all their purposes. A century ago any formal education was largely a privilege for the few; now substantial
formal education is a normal expectation for all. Thoughtful Canadians no longer look on education as a kind of consumer good, something it is pleasant to have if you can afford
it; rather they regard it as an investment—an investment,
on the one hand, for the individual student in his future, but
also, and perhaps more important, a capital investment for
the future development of the nation. Not even the most
dismal economist any longer doubts that trained manpower
is the essential component of economic survival. By 1967
Canadians are saying (though our behaviour and our words
may not always agree) that Canada simply cannot afford *not*
to provide educational opportunities appropriate to the full
measure of the potential abilities of each individual citizen
of tomorrow. So education in the Canada of 1967 is vastly
different from education in the Canada of 1867, when—not
to deny that there were giants in those days too—a discharged
non-commissioned officer who could find nothing better to
do could almost always find a job 'keeping' a one-room
school, and when appointment to the faculty of a college of
the day was as often as not a refuge for a man of the cloth
who had failed in successive parishes.

The purpose of this essay is to discuss a few of the problems and opportunities in education facing Canadians in
1967. I hope some of the major achievements and accomplishments will shine through, and can be taken for granted.
For the state of Canadian education today is a mixture of
certainty and uncertainty. Certainty, on the one hand, that
education is supremely important, is the servant of all our
purposes; uncertainty, on the other, as to precise purposes
and programs and procedures and ways and means. Such

certainty and uncertainty has led to no fewer than thirteen major royal commissions on education across the country in the last fifteen years.

The most fundamental questions are always the most difficult to answer. What are Canada's goals in education? Education for what? A glib answer, of course, is 'for everybody'. Canada has moved a long way toward providing universal education at public expense. The public provision of education without fee, to the end of high school, has with one or two exceptions been generally accepted as axiomatic; and now we talk – and to an increasing extent act – to ensure that post-secondary education is not denied able students because they cannot pay for it.

But 'Education for what?' is a far more searching question than that. Until relatively recent years education in Canada has really been education for more education. A central concern of the elementary school was preparation for the secondary school. The secondary school was largely an academic sausage-machine, preparing students for liberal arts and science at the university. Those who did not measure up to that kind of a program simply dropped out. That was fine in its day, when dropouts could be absorbed readily in the labour market as successful and productive members of society. But now all youngsters, not just the academically inclined, must remain in school longer; and it has long since become obvious that a single-track school program, with single-track standards in that program, will not do for all youngsters; for in such a program many children will fail to learn, and therefore learn only to fail.

It is not too much to say that formal education until recent decades has been designed largely as education for the *academically best* of our children and young people. Canadians are now thinking more in terms of education for the *best in each youngster*, whatever his individual interests and capacities and potential contribution to society may be. Instead of trying to fit the individual to a standard course of study, the emphasis is shifting towards fitting a course of study to the individual.

Curriculum is slow to change, in part because of a typically Canadian refusal to embrace wholeheartedly the Cult of the New. In trying to decide between something old and something new Canadians often have the uncomfortable feeling that they may be comparing the well-known worst of the old with the hoped-for best of the new. It has been said, probably with some justification, that a good deal of the curriculum at the university level, quite apart from the schools, is a monument to the special interests of deceased faculty members.

Nevertheless the last quarter especially of Canada's first century has seen many sweeping changes in education in the direction of recognizing and meeting the differing needs of individuals. Let three examples suffice.

The first is the rapid expansion of vocational and technical education. This came none too soon. In the face of alarming unemployment, manpower studies as of 1960 indicated that while there was a major surplus of unskilled labour, at the same time there was a serious shortage of skilled and semi-skilled workers. In fact, in the five years from 1955 to 1960 we actually imported more skilled and semi-skilled workers as immigrants than we turned out from all our vocational and technical programs put together. This was the emergency that resulted in massive federal financial support to the provinces for vocational and technical education and re-education, and since 1960 development has been rapid. Of course changes in the amount of vocationally oriented education highlight the brute problems of what kinds of vocationally oriented education make sense. So quickly are business and industry changing that Canada's Director of Employment Services says the great majority of youngsters now in secondary schools will graduate to types of employment for which job specifications do not even exist at the moment. How are the schools to provide realistic vocational education for vocational specialties still largely unknown? Organizing vocational and technical education that will be stimulating to the individual and profitable for society is a tall order. Canada's answer at the moment – and it seems to be a sound one – is to emphasize a combination of general, liberalizing education together with concomitant studies leading to vocational literacy in various technical and service fields.

What of post-secondary formal education? The problem of numbers is increasingly evident here as well. In 1955-6 only one in twelve of the age group eighteen to twenty-one was continuing his studies full-time; it is estimated that by 1970-1 the proportion will be better than one in five. This will mean a tripling of enrolment between 1959-60 and 1970-1. My personal estimate is that the figure will be substantially higher than that, as it has been for some years in the United States. How can these students and Canada best be served? In traditional programs in a multiplication of expanded colleges and universities, most of them fighting to stem the tide of numbers by continually raising admission requirements? By setting up new and differing programs in those colleges and universities, in non-traditional fields and with differing entrance requirements and standards at differing levels? Or in new types of post-secondary institutions, offering shorter programs than the universities and with different entrance requirements? The answer to date has been, and doubtless will continue to be, a combination of all three. But several provinces have established growing networks of junior or community colleges and technological institutes, to make two or more years of terminal and often vocationally oriented post-secondary education more readily available to all who may profit from it. The four most populous provinces – Quebec, Ontario, Alberta, and British Columbia – are cases in point. Whether such institutions should offer the first two years of a university-degree program as well as a variety of non-university vocational and technical programs remains a hotly debated issue, with plans in Quebec and Alberta tending to emphasize the former, those in Ontario and British Columbia tending on the whole to de-emphasize it.

A third example of widespread progress in Canadian education toward meeting the differing needs of individuals is a renewed emphasis on quality education. There have been times when thoughtful observers have wondered whether, in our concern to provide education for all, we may have lost sight of what Whitehead called 'the habitual vision of greatness'. Was there danger that the effort to provide education for everybody left very little energy and resources for sufficiently challenging the most capable – whether they be the most capable at plumbing or philosophy, machinery or medicine? Perhaps. But the varied educational program, succeeding the single program which covered good, bad, indifferent, bored and interested, handicapped and gifted, has meant that from elementary class to graduate school it has become possible to be increasingly demanding, with increasingly higher standards of excellence. Canada's college degrees today represent a higher level of achievement than ever before; so do school certificates from whatever program the youngster may have graduated. There will always be those who claim that Johnnie can't read, or that this year's crop of graduates is not up to those of the Good Old Days. Such claims simply do not stand up to careful scrutiny.

Variety is one of the most distinctive characteristics of arrangements for the organization and control of education across Canada. Yet at least one major factor has remained constant over the century, and with pervasive effects: education is a provincial matter, guaranteed as such under the British North America Act.

The language of the Act is strong. 'In and for each Province the Legislature may exclusively make Laws in relation to Education. . . .' As C. E. Phillips writes in *The Development of Education in Canada*,

> Each of the British colonies which later became part of Canada had taken some state action to assist education before they had entered into any permanent union. Education was therefore a provincial prerogative before Confederation and continued to be so thereafter. The autonomy of the federating provinces in this respect was ensured by constitutional guarantee chiefly as a safeguard of religious

privileges in education but partly to maintain vested political interests in a field which had already become an important function of government.

Control of schools has continued to be guarded jealously as a provincial right by all provinces; Canada is the only federated democracy in the world without some kind of a federally supported co-ordinating national education agency. It is scarcely possible to speak of Canadian education; it would be far more accurate to speak of education in Canada's ten provinces and the Territories. Each of the provinces has created local school districts under local education authorities, to which it has delegated certain powers and responsibilities for the actual operation of schools. In practice, then, education at the school level is a provincial-local partnership. What shall be taught, by whom, to whom, under what conditions—these are all provincial matters, worked out under provincial regulations through local school boards.

On the whole this arrangement has worked well for Canada. It has kept the schools relatively close to the local people whom they serve; it has permitted localized and provincial values to show through in the school operation—be they emphasis, for example, on a particular type of technical education in an industrial centre within a province, or varying degrees of commitment among provinces to religious instruction in the schools. But what has been lacking is some desirable measure of federal or interprovincial co-ordination in education: some degree of planning in the national interest. I am not referring to the perennial complaints of letters-to-the-editor that children of families moving from one province to another, or even from one school district to another within the province, have to adjust to differing school programs; why not some standardized program? they ask. There is sound evidence to suggest that widely standardized programs tend to stagnate, because of the difficulty of introducing wide-scale change. More important, though: since change is the single future element of which we can be certain, surely one of the most useful things that can be done in schools is to make youngsters adaptable to change. From this point of view youngsters who are moved are privileged, rather than disadvantaged.

What I am referring to is some co-ordination of education from province to province from the broader point of view of the national interest. If people are our most precious national resource, then the maximum development of those people is vital to Canada as a whole, and not only to its component parts. Surely there needs to be some national planning to ensure as far as possible that sound schooling exists in every part of every province; that appropriate educational opportunity is available for every youngster, wherever he happens to live; and that finances are at hand to underwrite the necessary standards.

The 'Provincial Fact' is so strong in education that the establishment of any major office of education by the federal government seems highly unlikely. Nevertheless, involvement of the federal government in education continues to increase, on the grounds of national interest and because of concentration of fiscal ability at the federal level. A recent count showed at least twenty-nine federal agencies directly involved in service of some kind to elementary and secondary schools. The problem is that such federal involvement tends to be based on temporary and immediate needs rather than on long-term considerations; some problems deserving national attention are neglected, because the federal government's role in education is clearly limited. And when the federal government does act, in the words of the Executive Secretary of the Canadian Education Association, 'there is not always the consultation between competent school authorities and the federal authorities which would make the operation as effective as it might and deserves to be.'

One solution to this problem is interprovincial co-operation in education: to rely on a strong interprovincial agency, instead of a federal agency. Progress has been made in this direction through the Canadian Education Association, which is maintained by the ten provincial governments and major city school systems. Since 1960 the provincial ministers of education have met regularly as a Standing Committee, with the staff of the Canadian Education Association serving as a secretariat. Through this Standing Committee the provinces have been developing common policy on matters such as school-leaving examinations, educational television, and machine processing of comparable data on education; the Committee and the Canadian Education Association also serve to work out a relatively united front for dealing with the federal government on educational matters. Certainly through the Canadian Education Association as well as other national organizations such as the Canadian Teachers' Federation, the Canadian School Trustees' Association, and a variety of professional specialist associations, at least a wide range of information now flows readily back and forth from coast to coast. While all this is promising, there remains a long way to go before there will be truly adequate direction in educational matters of common concern to the provinces, and hence to Canada as a whole. The answer may lie in marked expansion of the resources and activities of the Standing Committee of Ministers.

I have been referring principally to the organization and control of elementary and secondary education. The colleges and universities are in a somewhat different position. Historically they have developed largely as self-governing institutions, not directly under the control of any civil government. They too have active national organizations: not only the many scholarly societies in the various disciplines and the increasingly vocal Canadian Association of University Teachers, but also the Association of Universities and Colleges of Canada, which, as a creature of the colleges and universities and with strong leadership, serves to represent the institutions nationally. As universities have come to depend increasingly on government grants for financial support, however, and as numbers of new institutions have been chartered by the provinces, the influence of governments on university policies has become increasingly obvious. Does a provincial government have the right to control the universities, as it does the schools? This idea has not gone unchal-

lenged. President Claude Bissell of the University of Toronto
has spoken and written forcefully of three basic freedoms on
which he believes the universities must stand firm: the freedoms to determine who shall be taught, what shall be taught,
and who shall teach. These imply a fourth freedom: the freedom of a university to allot its financial resources as it sees fit.
At the same time there has developed on Canadian campuses
a groundswell of demand on the part of academic staff for
a representation on governing boards, and a more active
voice in the control of the institutions of which they are a
part.

The extent to which university authorities can or should
continue to remain absolute masters in their own house is
an open question. Society now depends on the university–
more than it ever dreamed of depending even twenty-five
years ago–to prepare both generalists and specialists for posts
of leadership in all walks of life. Moreover, society has to
be–and to a considerable extent is, judging by increased
government grants to universities–willing to pay the necessarily high costs. Ontario now has a Ministry of University
Affairs, as well as a Ministry of Education; Quebec now has
a Conseil d'Education Supérieur. Presumably something has
to give, and is giving. In Britain H. C. Dent is able to write:

> The Universities entirely accept the view that the Govern-
> ment has not only the right but the duty to satisfy itself that
> every field of study which in the national interest ought to
> be cultivated in Great Britain is in fact being adequately
> cultivated in the University system, and that resources which
> are placed at the disposal of the Universities are being used
> with full regard both to efficiency and economy.

Whatever changes in the control of universities may occur,
it will be vital to ensure that sound scholarship is not sacrificed to political expediency.

In the United States, the separation between Church and
State in education is definitive, but that has never been the
case in Canada. The churches have been active from the

start. The British North America Act restricted the powers
of a provincial government in education only in that it could
take no action which 'would prejudicially affect any Right
or Privilege with respect to Denominational Schools which
any Class of Persons have by Law in the Province at the
Union'. The result is that five of the ten provinces – Newfoundland, Quebec, Ontario, Saskatchewan, and Alberta –
have had and continue to have publicly supported schools
identified with various religious denominations. In Newfoundland and Quebec all schools have been frankly confessional, with direct provision for considerable control by
several denominations in Newfoundland, by Roman Catholics and Protestants in Quebec. In Ontario, Saskatchewan,
and Alberta, separate schools exist – that is, schools under
denominational influence and 'separate' from the ordinary
publicly supported schools. Various compromise arrangements exist in practice in the remaining five provinces except
British Columbia; moreover, some form of religious instruction is to be found in the ordinary publicly supported schools
of all provinces except British Columbia.

Public support for denominational schools has always
been a sensitive and delicate question in Canada, intimately
associated with provincial autonomy in education. There
are those who insist that the process of education is insepar-
able from religion in at least some of its aspects, and that it
therefore follows that freedom of religion involves freedom
for religious education on terms just as favourable as those
surrounding any other schooling. They argue that it is far
more important, far more in the spirit of individual freedom, that a child and his parents should have the option of
religious instruction or none at public expense than, say,
Geometry II or Office Practice I. Others believe that it is not
possible to do justice in public schools to the wide range of
religious convictions of parents and their youngsters, and
that whatever can be done in the schools is both inadequate
and divisive; therefore the lesser of two evils is to operate
strictly non-sectarian schools at public expense. Let other
schools exist, but as private schools financed privately. My

personal view tends toward support for the non-sectarian public school, opposing tax funds for denominational instruction. But it must be admitted that the people of the five provinces where public support is granted to denominational schools—and these five embrace three-quarters of our population—regard their plans as working reasonably well, and as providing a desirable measure of individual freedom in the vital area of conscience and conviction.

Nevertheless there are signs of a relative decrease in the influence of churches on public education, and a corresponding increase in the influence of civil government. Far-reaching changes in the structure and operation of education in Quebec in the last few years may justly be interpreted as representing a relative decline of clerical influence; a similar reversal of the dominant church role in college- and university-level education across the country can also be documented. It would seem to be a safe prediction that the formal education of Canadians, in their second century, will be considerably further removed from direct church influence than was the case in their first century.

The trend toward increased size in organizations of all types in western societies is so evident as scarcely to need documentation. Government is now Big Government, and becomes bigger and more complex every year; the business partnership becomes the corporation, and corporations become united industrial empires; the corner store has all but given way to the large chain. The same forces have been at work on local school systems. They too become larger with each passing year. In the last thirty years a wholesale shift has taken place in local school organization in Canada: from horse-and-buggy district to motor-car area. This reflects a number of factors, such as the trek to the cities and the advent of instantaneous communication and near-instantaneous transportation; but in particular it reflects an insistent popular demand for a much wider range of educational opportunity than is possible within the limited resources of a tiny school district with few pupils and fewer specialized staff.

Essentially, the deliberately planned larger unit, which is now to be found in some form in every province, is a means of combining under a single local authority a number of smaller school districts. The object is to provide more adequate financing and facilities, with more effective professional leadership and broader curriculum, to ensure better education than would be possible in independent smaller units. It should be noted that school district reorganization is really never completed: before one cycle of reorganization is finished, another begins. One might well ask, too, whether many of our reorganized larger units are not still too small to achieve to the full the potential advantages of larger size. Today in Canada there are about 5,500 functioning local school authorities; Britain, with a little less than three times our population, has only one local education authority for every thirty-seven of ours.

Relatively large as that figure of 5,500 functioning local school authorities in Canada appears to be, however, it is only one-third the number actually in existence twenty years ago; and small school districts continue to be merged into larger units. In Ontario, for example, further reorganization of rural elementary school districts cut by half the 1965 total of 3,400 school administrative units in the province. At the same time in Quebec, under 'Operation 55', fifty-five regional school boards were established to blanket the province where 1,200 had existed before.

But the fact remains that many of our schools are still too small. Dr. James B. Conant, in reporting on his well-known study of secondary education in the United States, stated that one of the greatest single stumbling-blocks to excellence was inadequate size. 'The enrollment of many American public high schools', he concluded', 'is too small to allow for diversified curriculum except at exorbitant expense.' There is Canadian evidence to support the same conclusion. As for the smallest school of all—the one-room school—each year sees the number declining. At that, almost one-quarter of our 24,000 schools today are one-room schools. In view of sparsity of population in many parts of the country it

seems likely that we shall have to make do with at least some
one-room schools for many years to come. But evidence has
long since demonstrated that the one-room school is far too
small to be anything other than second-best.

But new situations create new problems. Whereas once
we were concerned with how small is too small in a school
district or a school, now we begin to wonder how big
is too big. Is there a point of bigness beyond which we should
not go? May we suddenly waken to the situation where school
systems by force of circumstance have grown so large as to be
virtually unmanageable; so large that the individual pupil—
and teacher—and even school—is literally lost within some
mammoth school system purportedly serving one or another
of the sprawling megalopolises that seem destined to take
over the country? This becomes a difficult problem in all our
major urban districts, with a core city economically and
socially interdependent with its suburbs. It would appear
that traditional patterns of school-district organization may
no longer hold; what is needed is some scheme whereby the
fiscal advantages of very large size may be obtained, without
losing the personal and operational advantages of smaller
size. Mr. H. Carl Goldenberg, reporting as a one-man Royal
Commission on Metropolitan Toronto, offered some promising plans for a two-tier system of local school government for
the metropolitan area that may move a considerable distance
toward obtaining the best of the two worlds of large-size and
small-size school systems. He recommended a single metro-
wide board of education with over-all financial powers, along
with a series of local boards responsible for day-to-day operation. At any rate, as Canadians face their second century, they
will have to solve many far-reaching problems of how best to
organize school systems—and universities, for that matter—
in the face of inevitably larger size than they have ever known
before.

It is true that quality merchandise is rarely found in the
bargain basement. As education has increased in quality, so
has it increased in cost. In 1967 Canadians will need to invest

not only more dollars on education than they have ever invested before – probably well over \$4 billion, but a higher
percentage of gross national product than ever before – perhaps upwards of eight per cent. Where does the money come
from? For schools the sources are mainly three: provincial
grants, which have been steadily increasing in proportion
until the national average now is almost fifty per cent of
current operating costs; the federal government, largely
through the provinces, to the tune of about eleven per cent;
and local revenues – mainly real estate taxes – of about forty
per cent. For post-secondary education the chief revenue
sources are provincial grants – about forty per cent; federal
moneys, including funds from such agencies as the Defence
Research Board – about twenty-five per cent; student fees –
a further twenty per cent; and the remaining twenty per cent
from endowment, gifts, and miscellaneous sources.

Two marked trends can be noted in recent years in school
and college financing alike: increasing dependence on provincial governments for financial support, and also – both
directly from federal sources and indirectly through federal
payments to provincial governments – increasing contributions from the federal level of government. Both these trends
seem likely to continue, not only because the fiscal squeeze
on municipalities is greater than on the two senior levels of
government, but also because only a senior level can effect
equalization of educational opportunity by taxing on some
standard basis across the larger jurisdiction, then making the
proceeds differentially available to various parts of that jurisdiction, depending on their need.

Is education costing more than Canadians can afford? It
seems clear that the upper limits of taxation are not absolute
in economic terms; the limits are more psychological. We
can raise and spend much more for education or for anything else, if we want to. A question of public values is involved. While the gross national product is a notoriously
weak basis for international comparison, it remains one of
the most usable; and while Canadians devote six or seven per
cent of our gross national product to education, many other

countries devote more. The United States runs about seven per cent, Britain the same. The U.S.S.R. is over fifteen per cent, and some of the emerging nations of Africa, attempting to crowd two centuries of development into two years, run a startling forty to fifty per cent.

It is notable, too, that in one sense Canadians are actually spending less on education in publicly supported schools today than they have done in the past. This becomes clear when expenditure is expressed in terms of dollars per pupil per billion dollars of gross national product. In 1931 Canadians spent $14 per enrolled pupil per billion dollars of gross national product; in 1941 the figure was down to $7.20; by 1961 it had climbed back to $11.10; and for 1965 it was an estimated $12.36. Not infrequently, too, people point to newer school buildings and complain of education's 'edifice complex'. While school building costs have soared since the Second World War, studies indicate that, space for space, they have risen only half as much as has the cost of office buildings, only two-thirds as much as that of housing, and less than one-third as much as highway costs or wages for unskilled labour. Edifice or not, school planners have made the building dollar go farther than anyone else.

In 1959 one in forty-two of the total civilian labour force was a teacher; by 1964 it was one in thirty-five. Bearing in mind that teachers are a relatively highly educated group, the serious question arises as to whether we will be able to continue to spare an annually increasing proportion of that highly educated group to teaching. At present the situation is especially critical at the college level. It is estimated that by 1970 colleges and universities in Ontario alone will need 330 per cent of the total full-time teaching staff they had as recently as 1963. The earned doctorate is the basic qualification sought after for college teachers; to provide the needed number of additional college teachers for Ontario *alone* in 1970 would actually require eleven times the total number of Ph.Ds earned at *all* Canadian universities in 1963, leaving not a one for business, or industry, or government, or anything other than teaching in an Ontario college or university.

Many avenues are being explored to meet this crisis in staffing. Graduate schools are rapidly expanding, with increasing numbers of substantial scholarships and fellowships available. The degree of Master of Philosophy—a new degree designed for the college teacher and involving a somewhat shorter period of study than the Ph.D.—has appeared. Teaching salaries in schools and universities climb steadily, the better to compete with other occupations. School systems and universities continue to make tempting offers to well-qualified potential staff from abroad—although their shortages, too, are catching up with us. Undoubtedly there is and will be robbing of Peter to pay Paul, with colleges luring away many of the best-qualified teachers from the schools.

But I doubt that any of this is enough. The danger is that, not finding qualified people wanted and needed for the supremely important task of teaching, schools and colleges accept what they can get—people with lesser qualifications. What then can be done?

Three additional possibilities suggest themselves. First, in this day of lengthened life expectancy, let us also lengthen the normal span of productive work life for teachers. Can we much longer afford to retire highly skilled professional workers at the traditional age of sixty-five? Why not sixty-eight? Or seventy? Secondly, let schools and colleges make more use of part-time teachers, whether economists with a bank, chemists with an oil company, or mothers unable to work full-time but happy to teach two days a week in a neighbouring school. Thirdly, I believe we must break away from our traditional thinking as to how teaching shall be carried out, to take advantage of new ways of making more efficient use of the teachers we now have. What of television, and taped lectures, and laboratories not only for language, and self-instructional devices of all sorts, including computer-assisted instruction? While such devices cannot replace the teacher, they can re-place him. They can free him from much repetition and routine work with students, to multiply his usefulness in the more creative aspects of teaching. Professor Sidney Pressey of Ohio is said to have wondered aloud, plaintively, why a modern classroom should be any less well equipped than, say, a modern kitchen. All this, of course, requires a new approach to class size. The tendency has been to think that smaller classes are clearly preferable to larger ones, and that one teacher working with a class of twenty-five to thirty is about right. Such an all-purpose ratio, of course, is nonsense. A class of even two pupils may be too large for some purposes and in some circumstances, whereas in others a class of two hundred or even two thousand may be quite small enough. What is needed is greater flexibility of organization, and greater flexibility in thinking about such matters on the part of both professionals in education and the citizens who pay the bills.

An inevitable conclusion from careful reading of the social history of Canadians in their first century is that, increasingly, we have become truly a learning society. The trend of development in education has by no means been constant from decade to decade or even from one part of the country to another, but it has nevertheless been moving steadily upward. At this particular moment in our history, we are caught up in a veritable fountain of development; seldom has there been a people more education-conscious than are the Canadians of 1967. The problems, of course, are legion: problems of program, of purpose, of personnel, of organization, of control, of finance. But ways are being found, and will be found, to overcome these problems.

From the point of view of education – and therefore of the well-being of the nation – Canada's second century looks bright.

20. Religion

JOHN S. MOIR

The pattern of Canadian religious life was already firmly established and easily discernible in 1867. Canadians of every province were a staunchly church-going people for whom religion was a vital aspect of everyday life. The religious fact of Canada at Confederation (as basic in 1867 as it had been two generations before and is a century after) was pluralism. The province of Quebec was overwhelmingly French and Roman Catholic, its complexion unchanged by the missionary efforts of several Protestant denominations. The Roman Catholic, Anglican, Methodist, and Presbyterian communions together comprised eighty-five per cent of the population of the young Dominion, while the Baptists, Lutherans, and Congregationalists together added another 8½ per cent. The smaller Protestant sects and the pagan native population accounted for the remainder.

From their European mother churches the Canadian denominations had inherited their theology, organization, and forms of worship. The larger Protestant churches were numerically strong in Canada because they were strong in Britain, but each had assumed from the North American environment a more democratic hue in its institutions and practices. Anglicans and Methodists in Canada had generally accepted a greater lay participation in church life than was known 'at home', and the Canadian Synod in connection with the Church of Scotland led the imperial van of that communion in 1862 by permitting instrumental music at public services! Despite the claims of past historians, the frontier did not create either the civil or the religious forms of the New World, but the frontier did add an undeniable leaven to the Old World culture.

One noteworthy feature of Canadian religious life was the popular acceptance of voluntaryism – the legal separation of Church and State – a feature derived mostly from the American precedent. After the prolonged and spasmodic conflict stretching over two generations, the attempt to establish an Anglican state church had ended in 1854 with the secularization of the Clergy Reserves. But in fact Church and State, if separated in theory, continued to be related in a way unknown in the United States. Without exception the Protestant churches in Canada believed fervently in the nineteenth-century ideals of individualism and self-help, and with their Roman Catholic brethren shared a puritanical approach to moral and social issues that has often been credited to or blamed on the ever-present frontier. In Canada the churches have not hesitated to act, individually or collectively, as pressure groups urging the state to pass social and moral legislation. Theologically the Christian churches were conservative, deriving their beliefs from contemporary or past European schools, and it has continued their lot until the present to be recipients rather than creators of theological thought, another characteristic facilely explained by references to the frontier or immaturity.

But one element of nineteenth-century European thought was (and continues to be) notable by its absence from Canada, namely a genuine anti-clericalism. The nearest approach to anti-clericalism in Canadian history was the small and ineffective Parti Rouge in Quebec, whose anti-clericalism was in fact a most pale, even transparent, reflection of the anti-clericalism they professed to admire in Old France. This absence of anti-clericalism probably reflects the predominantly rural outlook of Canadian society, an outlook still prevalent well into the twentieth century.

In contrast to their American brethren, the Canadian churches had not needed to face the burning issue of slavery – an issue which had threatened the unity of that nation and which had turned the unity of several denominations into 'a house divided'. By the date of Confederation not only had the Canadian churches escaped America's 'irrepressible conflict' and its sordid 'carpet-bagging' sequel, but most had gone a long way towards identifying themselves with life in the new Dominion by suppressing 'old country' issues that had no place in the New World. Thus, Presbyterianism was ripe for a union that would reverse the Scottish Disruption of 1843. Among Anglicans there were no just grounds for the complaint raised by the Tractarians in England about political interference with the Church. And the subtle differences of evangelicalism that had split British Methodism were irrelevant on the spiritual frontier of British North America.

Probably the most important factor favouring denominational union was the creation by 1867 of a Canadian-born and largely Canadian-educated ministry. In proportion as the Canadian churches ceased to think and act as colonial dependants of affluent mother churches overseas and learned to rely on their own spiritual and physical resources, they prospered in their self-reliance. The historical importance of the Wesleyan Methodists in pre-Confederation days had been due to their spiritual and institutional independence, marked by autonomous status in 1828 and by the opening of their own college in 1836. Of all the British-based English-speaking churches the Church of England was the last to achieve this *nationalist* as opposed to *imperial* status, and even now traces of 'Englishness' are still evident in its habits of mind and personnel policies.

In 1867 the Methodist and Presbyterian communions were on the eve of national unions that would largely complete their 'Canadianization'. The Church of England had further to go psychologically in this direction, although legal and structural autonomy already existed. Because of its international organization the Roman Catholic Church in Canada was as a whole less able to identify its interests directly with Canadianism, but, paradoxically, the Roman church in the Province of Quebec formed an integral part of the French-Canadian concept of *la nation*. This linguistic-religious connection had not prevented co-operation between English and French Roman Catholics on the separate-school issue before Confederation, but after 1867 there was growing evidence of internal friction within that church stemming from 'national' or linguistic rivalries.

Of the three smaller Protestant communions – Baptist, Congregational, and Lutheran – none achieved numerical significance either before or after Confederation. The Baptists in Canada, strongest in the Maritime Provinces thanks to the continuing influence of the late-eighteenth-century 'New Light' revival, were nevertheless divided in every province into two branches – the General or Free Baptists (more liberal in their doctrines and practices), and the Particular Baptists (more Calvinistic in theology and literalist in forms of church government). Congregationalism, virtually obliterated in the Maritime colonies by 'New Lightism' and political repercussions from the American Revolution, was, in the age of Confederation, concentrated almost entirely in urban or semi-urban areas of Quebec and Ontario, and even there it was weakened by its late arrival and its lack of any centralized organization. Yet the numerical insignificance of Congregationalism was more than offset by the public achievements of its members at large, and especially of such leaders as the scientist, teacher, and theologian, the Reverend Adam Lillie.

Like the Orthodox churches in this century the Lutheran

communion in Canada suffered from the outset all the disabilities of an 'ethnic' or national church in a foreign land. That ethnicism which in the nineteenth century identified Presbyterians with Scots, or Anglicans with the English, was partially dissolved for those two communions by the fact that English was the tongue of both Church and State. But until the First World War forced Lutheranism to depreciate its Germanism by making all things German politically and socially undesirable, the Lutheran Church provided linguistic protection for German culture in Canada.

To the Christian churches in Canada Confederation provided both a challenge and an opportunity. Here before them was a political example of strength through union. Inspired by the heady ambitions of the lay nation-builders, the churches aspired to emulate Confederation by submerging the religious controversies that had embittered the pre-Confederation era, and by expanding their organizational structures to coincide with the political boundaries of the new nation. Thus Confederation led directly to the national union of all Presbyterians in 1875 and a similar intra-denominational union of three Methodist bodies in 1874 (completed a decade later by the inclusion of the remaining Methodist groups). The Roman Catholic and Anglican churches also shared in this post-Confederation expansion by the establishment of dioceses in the newly acquired Canadian West, and by subdivision of existing bishoprics in the settled East. In the political sphere Confederation had the undesirable effect of projecting the stresses and strains within the separate colonies into the national political arena. Similarly, in religious matters, Confederation led to the perpetuation of old colonial issues, such as separate schools and the Orange-Catholic rivalry, but now agitated as national rather than purely sectional issues.

In the first decade of the Dominion's life the Roman Catholic attack on liberalism that had begun in 1864 with the *Syllabus of Errors* was largely confined to the province of Quebec. The Ultramontane movement defended the absolute authority of the papacy. It was led by such as Bishop

Bourget of Montreal who did not hesitate to issue through the *Programme Catholique* a list of approved politicians and to deny the sacraments to any person voting for the Liberals. But Louis Riel's execution of Thomas Scott, an Ontario Orangeman, during the Red River uprising of 1869-70 aroused the slumbering anti-Catholicism of Protestant Ontario. The fateful decision to hang Riel after his second rebellion, in 1885, ultimately cost Sir John A. Macdonald his political support from Quebec.

In Quebec Honoré Mercier was quick to use Riel's death as the rallying-cry that joined the issues of provincial rights and religious hatreds into political success at the provincial polls. Once in power, Mercier unwittingly proceeded to fan the flames of religious discord by his legislative settlement of the Jesuit Estates issue. Since the Conquest the disposition of the property of the Society of Jesus in Quebec had been a constant source of conflict, and Mercier's invitation to the papacy to act as arbitrator between the various claimants was an open invitation to Canadian Protestants to oppose this 'interference' of a 'foreign ecclesiastic'. D'Alton McCarthy, Macdonald's heir-apparent as Conservative leader, promptly organized the Equal Rights Association which, when it failed to block the Jesuit Estates settlement, turned its attention against the separate schools of Manitoba. The Manitoba School Act of 1890, by ending all public aid to denominational schools, created in Manitoba the unitary, nondenominational system of primary education that Ontario had been unable to maintain intact before Confederation.

It was within the power of the federal government to re-establish by remedial legislation the separate schools in Manitoba – and thereby to satisfy the loud complaints of Quebec and the bishops against discrimination. To such a remedial bill the Conservative government at Ottawa was pledged when it fell from office in 1896. Paradoxically the new Liberal government headed by Wilfrid Laurier, a French Roman Catholic, refused to interfere with the provincial educational rights of Manitoba. The Manitoba school system was not adopted in Saskatchewan and Alberta despite pressure to exclude separate schools. But the Liberal victory of 1896 was the death-knell of ultramontanism in Canada and henceforth Liberalism was accepted without religious reservation.

The first half-century after Confederation presented the Christian churches in Canada with a variety of problems, some affecting all denominations, others peculiar to particular churches, but all related in some degree to national growth. The national policy of peopling the newly-acquired West and developing an industrial society in the East offered to every church the challenges of providing spiritual welfare to two new groups. Settlement on the prairies required the mobilization of resources through such bodies as the Catholic Church Extension Society, and the speedy creation of new parishes, dioceses, conferences, and synods. Different, but in some ways more demanding, were the religious circumstances of a rapidly urbanizing and industrializing society in Ontario and Quebec. Here the problem was not the geographical extension of established forms of organization, but a basic reorientation of attitudes to meet the social problems of an industrial working class, the appearance of trade-unionism, and the physical growth of churches in an affluent, capitalistic society.

When the churches turned to the problems posed by urbanization and industrialization, they all relied on the moralistic approach developed by advocates of laissez-faire to meet the European Industrial Revolution two generations before. The ideals of freedom of contract, non-interference by government, personal liberties, and individual conversion were to the churches sufficient justification to preserve the *status quo* against the threat of collective action by trade-unionism. Thus the Toronto Printers' strike of 1872 was denounced by the three largest Protestant churches for the same reasons that the Roman Catholic bishops condemned the Knights of Labor movement in the 1880s.

The passing of two generations, however, brought a profound change of attitude towards the social consequences of industrialization. The turn of the century saw the establishment by all the major Protestant denominations of boards of social and moral reform to keep a watching brief on such issues as temperance and Lord's Day observance. These parallel movements culminated in the organization of the interdenominational Christian Social Service Council of Canada in 1907, the same year that the publication in the United States of Rauschenbusch's *Christianity and the Social Crisis* gave form to the Social Gospel movement.

This general desire for the application of the Gospel to the social needs of men – the protection of the unprotected, by reorganization of the social order where necessary – found fertile ground, particularly in the Methodist and Anglican churches. The Rev. J. S. Woodsworth and Canon C. W. Vernon were leaders whose influence extended far beyond their own churches, while the Rev. Salem Bland, an inspired teacher and author, influenced generations of university students in Winnipeg and Toronto. The Social Gospel movement – a way of thinking rather than an organization – had its greatest success in the depths of the Great Depression in the founding of the C.C.F. party, but in its early years its pervasive influence affected Canadian politics indirectly through the pressure tactics of the churches.

One external force that rippled the surface of the churches in Canada was the wind of religious modernism blowing out of Europe. Canadian churches had been interested if distant observers of the clash between theologian and scientist, but the new gospel of scientism and the German discipline of higher criticism only reached Canada a generation after Confederation when the churches had been conditioned for the impact. Modernism disturbed the Canadian churches only slightly and at different times. Thus the Roman Catholics, Anglicans, and Presbyterians accommodated themselves to the 'new learning' with little difficulty; conservative Methodists exhausted their conservatism in the persecution of Professor George Workman at the turn of the century; the Baptist communion split on the issue as late as 1955; while fundamentalist sects generally rejected the whole movement.

Confederation undoubtedly inspired the Methodist and
Presbyterian unions in the decade after 1867, but the prerequisites of union – physical, psychological, and sociological
– already existed in 1867. 'Church' attitudes were replacing
'sect' attitudes as the churches accommodated themselves to
a materialistic society, and paid their own homage to affluence
and respectability by replacing frame chapels with 'sermons
in stone'. The inevitable sectarian reaction in favour of 'old-
time religion' and 'other-worldly' values appeared in such
form as the Holiness Movement which bit deeply into Methodist membership. The new sectarianism drew strength not
only from the less sophisticated, less affluent rural areas, but
also from the new urban proletariat of unskilled industrial
workers whom the 'respectable' churches seemed bent on
ignoring. The Free Methodists, the Salvation Army, and
similar groups offered hope to the socially disinherited.
Paradoxically the opening of the West, which had challenged
the churches, also re-created the frontier conditions that had
earlier favoured sectarianism in the East. Sectarian movements from eastern Canada and from the American mid-
West produced on the Canadian prairies greater religious
diversity than in any other region of the country.

Out of the Canadian West at the turn of the century came
the final impetus that created the United Church in Canada,
a unique experiment in interconfessional union. When the
Presbyterian and Methodist unions were created in the after-
glow of political Confederation, leading churchmen like
Principal Grant of Queen's, who were also nationalists, voiced
hopes that greater church unions, possibly including the
Roman Catholics, would follow and that a truly national
Canadian church might yet appear. To the Christian desire
for the reunification of Christ's splintered church was added
the practical need to reduce wasteful overlapping in the vast
western regions.

Throughout the 1880's the larger churches participated in
unofficial discussions of church union initiated by the Church
of England. By 1899, when the Presbyterian Church announced its readiness to co-operate with other churches in

new fields, the religious climate of Canada was ripe for further union. Seizing the opportunity, a new arrival from Scotland, Principal Patrick of Presbyterian College, Winnipeg, addressed the Methodist General Conference in 1902 on his own initiative in favour of organic church union. The spirit of union took hold and in the movement thus dramatically begun, the Congregationalists, Baptists, and Anglicans were subsequently invited to join, though only the Congregationalists took up the challenge.

By 1911 a Basis of Union had been adopted by the three churches. This Basis of Union received almost universal approval from Methodists and Congregationalists, but about one-third of the Presbyterians registered their dissent. Besides the traditional Presbyterian resistance to any change in doctrine and polity, basic differences of class and social outlook between Presbyterians and Methodists underlined the hostility of some Presbyterians towards union, especially in wealthier urban areas.

After an open rift in 1916, an uneasy truce between Presbyterian unionists and anti-unionists was declared for the duration of the First World War. The infectious nationalism of war-time experiences failed to mollify the anti-unionists, and it was soon apparent when the union question was re-opened in 1921 that no compromise was possible. Successive anti-unionist appeals to the courts and legislatures of the country against the absorption of the Presbyterian Church only intensified bad feeling. The anti-unionists' strength also increased, and the consummation of union in 1925 left more than a third of the Presbyterians outside the union to form a new church. But the physical dynamic of the Presbyterian Church in Canada had been broken by the union and successive censuses have recorded the steady decline of the new Presbyterian Church of Canada.

The United Church was intended by its founders to be the nucleus of a national church. That high aim has not been achieved. Although the Union is viewed by some as a *fait accompli* (reflected in the past tense of its title, the *United Church*), the early unionist sense of mission for union among

POPULATION OF CANADA BY MAJOR RELIGIONS

Denominations (with % of total population)

	1871	1911	1931	1961
Total population	3,689,257	7,206,643	10,376,786	18,238,247
Anglican	501,269 (14.1%)	1,048,002 (14.5%)	1,639,075 (15.8%)	2,409,068 (13.2%)
Baptist	243,714 (6.8)	384,152 (5.3)	443,944 (4.3)	593,553 (3.3)
Lutheran	37,935 (1.1)	231,883 (3.2)	394,920 (3.8)	662,744 (3.6)
Mennonite-Hutterite	[see Baptist]	44,972 (.6)	88,837 (.9)	152,452 (.8)
Methodist	578,161 (16.3)	1,079,993 (15.1)	entered United Church	—
Presbyterian	574,577 (16.2)	1,121,394 (15.6)	872,428 (8.4)	818,558 (4.5)
Congregational	21,829 (.6)	34,215 (.5)	entered United Church	—
Roman Catholic	1,532,471 (42.9)	2,841,881 (39.4)	4,102,960 (39.5)	8,342,826 (45.7)
Greek Orthodox	—	89,323 (1.2)	102,529 (1.0)	239,766 (1.3)
Ukrainian (Greek) Catholic	—	—	186,879 (1.8)	189,653 (1.0)
Not stated	126,853*	32,490 (.5)	16,042 (.2)	—
United Church	—	—	2,021,065 (19.5)	3,664,008 (20.1)

*Includes pagan natives of Manitoba.

Christians has been continued in efforts towards understanding through discussions with Anglicans and others. The passing of two generations has blended into the United Church many divergent characteristics inherited from the three founding churches. As Canada approaches its hundredth birthday, the United Church of Canada presents a picture of greater internal unity than does its political counterpart, the Canadian nation.

Throughout the First World War, the Christian churches found no difficulty in supporting the 'holy war' against the 'Huns'. It was generally and confidently assumed that God was on the side of the big guns of the Allies and few individuals questioned the righteousness of the slaughter in Flanders' fields. But the national idealism engendered by the war at least convinced many churchmen that out of this bloodbath must come a new society—a Christian democracy—in which just price, fair wages, equal opportunity, and social security for all would be ensured. Instead, the end of the war ushered in the 'Roaring Twenties' when 'emancipation', materialism, moral degeneration, social unrest, and unbridled self-interest became characteristics of a generation. In the face of the 'Red scare' and labour unrest churches were uncertain in their policies to reconcile the divergent interests of an industrialized society. The few outspoken clergy who supported the working men in the Winnipeg general strike of 1919 heard themselves denounced as 'revolutionaries' by their own churches and sometimes charged with sedition by the civil courts (as J. S. Woodsworth was when he quoted Isaiah in defence of the strikers). A decade was to pass before the onset of the Great Depression transmuted the idealism of the social gospel into lay politics through 'New Deal' programs and the Regina Manifesto of the C.C.F.

The churches and the state both fumbled for constructive policies to meet the social disaster inflicted on Canada by the depression. As material resources dwindled, salaries of clergymen were reduced, foreign and home mission fields struggled for physical existence, and expansion programs inaugurated

during the prosperous twenties ground to a halt. The down-
town mission for relief of the migrant unemployed seemed to
be the most successful response of the churches to the challenge of the depression. The Roman Catholic Church experi-
mented with back-to-the-land settlements in an attempt to
salvage family life for urban unemployed. But the fact that
Quebec, where the church was strongest, remained predominantly rural until the 1940s retarded the Roman Catholic
Church's initiative in meeting industrial problems. Consequently such church-sponsored movements as the Antigonish
co-operative venture were generally confined to rural areas
and to the problems of independent producers—Catholic
trade-unionism had to await the Second World War and the
rapid industrialization of Quebec before it became an effective force.

The social impact of the depression finally forced the
churches to face the urgent issues of the Industrial Revolution. One answer was found by shifting the emphasis from
personal evangelization to collective religious witness. The
basic re-interpretation of the role of religion in Canadian
society begun by the depression was extended by the Second
World War from the national to the international context.
This time the problem of finding a justification for war
bothered more Christian consciences than it had in 1914-18,
and the advent of the nuclear age, with its threat of instant
and total destruction, meant that the problem did not end
with the Second World War. In every church clergy and laity
alike find themselves divided on such international issues as
disarmament and co-existence, or Canadian membership in
the 'nuclear club'.

The Roman Catholic, Lutheran, and evangelical churches
have gained most from the post-Second World War immigration boom, while the larger Protestant churches suffered a
relative decline. The war also created a renewed interest in
interdenominational co-operation and church union. Although the United Church accepted an Anglican invitation
in 1943 to further union discussions, the old problem of the
episcopal succession underlined their continuing separation.

After the war the Anglican Church found a larger field of endeavour within world Anglicanism, while the United Church's urge to greater union was diverted from its nationalistic goal by the ecumenical movements of the World Council of Churches towards the goal of international Christian unity.

One group of churches that has participated in Canadian religious life in a very limited degree is the Orthodox communion. Because as ethnic or national churches they are closely identified with the culture of their mother country, they have in Canada encountered two major problems – language and political affiliation. In an English-speaking environment, they perpetuate the mother tongue because language and religion formed essential parts of their Old World nationalism. The public education system and the general social milieu make the mother tongue of each ethnic church a foreign language to the children of immigrants, so that a church whose service is expressed in terms of an Eastern European language and culture offers little but sentimental attractions to the new generation of Canadians.

Secondly, the establishment in Eastern Europe of Communist governments who treat national churches as spoils of war has forced the ethnic churches in Canada to choose between continuing connection with a 'Red' church or severance from their cultural roots. In Canada the Russian Orthodox church, which had previously received aid from the Imperial Russian treasury, was split by the Communist Revolution into an *émigré* church preserving pre-Revolutionary ties and a 'living church' of those prepared to accept the severely circumscribed position of the mother church under Bolshevik control. When the U.S.S.R. became the comrade-in-arms of the Western Allies during the Second World War, an abortive attempt at reunion in Canada ended in further divisions over recognition of the Communist-appointed Patriarch of Moscow.

The Ukrainians in Canada – numerically the largest group of Eastern Europeans – are divided by their Russian, Austrian, or Polish origins and by their religious affiliations,

being either Orthodox, or Uniate (in communion with
Rome). Inspired by the creation of an independent Ukraine
at the time of the Russian Revolution, a Ukrainian Greek
Orthodox Church was formed, but it was torn by internal
dissension over foreign relations until 1948 when the church
was declared 'autocephalous' or autonomous. The smaller
Greek, Romanian, Armenian, Georgian, and Albanian Orthodox churches have been happily free of such international
political difficulties.

The European tradition of 'state orthodoxy'–where the
state finances the national church in return for political
support–has hampered the physical growth of Orthodoxy in
the politically and religiously free climate of Canada. Many
Orthodox members who opposed state orthodoxy in Europe
have been attracted to sectarian groups in Canada. The
Orthodox churches in Canada have generally stood apart
from other Christian churches because of the Orthodox belief
in their unique status as the only 'true church' and because of
their cultural ties overseas. Lacking any centralized organization, they have remained weak and dependent, in a position
similar to that of the British churches during Canada's colonial era, but with the added problem of language which
prevents 'Canadianization'.

Like the Orthodox church members, the Jews–largest of
the non-Christian religious groups in Canada–have faced
linguistic and cultural problems in accommodating to the
New World. After Confederation the Canadian Jewish population was greatly enlarged by refugees fleeing persecution
before 1914 in Eastern Europe and in Nazi Germany during
the 1930s. These refugees followed the established pattern of
Jewish settlement in Canada by joining the urban commercial and manufacturing interests–eighty-five per cent live in
Canada's four largest cities–and have contributed to Canadian culture and economic development far beyond their
numerical ratio. The synagogue, in its dual role of a house of
prayer and an educational centre, has preserved the Jewish
language and culture, but in the workaday world the Jews
have fitted easily into Canadian political and social life.

Canadian Jewry has supported the Zionist movement for a national Jewish homeland since 1892, and has given the state of Israel both moral and physical assistance since its creation in 1948.

A century after Confederation the Christian churches still show marked signs of conservatism that emphasize personal conversion and salvation. The Protestant churches in particular seem devoid of any philosophy of society or the group with which to meet the basic economic and social challenges as exemplified by the welfare state. Such a comprehensive philosophy does exist within the Roman Catholic Church but obviously does not receive acceptance by all of the varied interests within that communion. Generally speaking the Christian churches in Canada have been content to follow the leadership offered by lay forces in facing the problems created by an industrialized and urbanized society. In contrast to the churches, the sects possess and practise a general philosophy of life, but their emphasis on the 'disinherited' ties them closely to a single class outlook and preserves thereby their sectarian character. The twentieth century has witnessed the influx into Canada of numerous American sects, particularly in the Canadian West, where 'Bible Bill' Aberhart drew strong support from 'other-worldly' sects to his 'this-worldly' political party, Social Credit.

From the days of Champlain and Maisonneuve Canada's religious history has been closely identified with missionary enterprises. First as a French colony and later under the British administration, the northern half of the continent comprised a huge mission field for the European mother churches. Early missionary enterprises had two aspects—the conversion of the original inhabitants and the spiritual succour of the European settlers. By 1867 the European churches in Canada had largely passed from the mission stage to that of economic self-sufficiency, but missions to the native Indians and Eskimos, now under exclusively Canadian management, continue to this day as an important function of the churches.

Roman Catholic missions to the Indians dated from the

earliest days of New France, and Anglican missions arrived with Britain's Iroquois allies fleeing from the American Revolution. In the first half of the nineteenth century the Methodists operated an extensive system of mission schools in Upper Canada. West of the Great Lakes these three churches began Indian missions long before Confederation, and were joined by the Presbyterian James Nisbet in 1866. The colony of British Columbia became a mission field after the gold-rush began in 1858. But in the post-Confederation period these missions achieved an established geographical pattern still much in evidence. The Presbyterian and Methodist missions were largely confined to Plains Indians living on reservations, while Roman Catholic missions, mostly Oblate, work with the less sedentary inhabitants of the West, Northwest, and Arctic. Anglican missions have shared the Northwestern and Arctic fields, but with intensive work in the James Bay and Hudson Bay regions as well. The Church of England responded rapidly to the challenge of the Northwest, and established no less than four bishoprics there in 1872-3.

In their native missions the Christian churches have been confronted with two basic and related problems. Legally the native population remains a collective ward of the state, and all church mission policies must be framed in conjunction with governmental policies and practices. By the time of Confederation the churches and the state had achieved an uneasy alliance and an uncertain division of responsibilities regarding the welfare of the native peoples. The line separating physical from spiritual welfare defies definition, but church and state have generally managed a compromise arrangement that permits mission work to continue. The second problem of missions is basically the relationship between two civilizations, the one advanced, the other retarded. In the Canadian context the question is one of integration v. apartheid. Will the interests of a stone-age culture be served best by segregation, or by integration with a European-style industrialized civilization? Both policies have been tried with varying degrees of success, but the most recent trend is towards integration by slow stages.

Another type of home mission, a product of urbanization and industrialization, has been the service centres operated in various large cities to accommodate the physical and spiritual needs of foreign sailors, the unemployed, or residents of a depressed urban area. Such city-centre missions and settlement houses have usually represented the inspired work of a single founder, and have frequently drawn interdenominational support. Because these institutions provided such physical comforts as lodging or recreation areas, their religious function appeared to be secondary, and such recent developments as government-sponsored hostels, urban renewal projects, community centres, and, above all, the rising standard of living and the flight to suburbia, have reduced the need for such missions which performed heroic works among the socially and religiously uprooted victims of the Depression.

As for foreign missions, the interest of Canadian churches had barely been awakened before 1867. With the remarkable exception of the Nova Scotia Presbyterian mission to the New Hebrides which began in the 1840s, the participation of Canadian churches in the great wave of nineteenth-century missionary enthusiasm that caught up the Western world was only through cash contributions. Greater prosperity and the Presbyterian and Methodist unions that followed Confederation led, however, to extensive and direct involvement of these two denominations in foreign missions.

As in the missionary enterprise in Western Canada, personalities and personal interests proved a decisive factor in choosing a foreign mission field. Presbyterian missionaries frequently operated isolated and individual missions, but the Methodist missionary enterprise was more concentrated, particularly in Japan and West China. The West China mission of the Canadian Methodist Church was one of the largest enterprises of any single Protestant denomination anywhere. In Japan Canadian Methodists co-operated with their American brethren, as did Canadian Congregationalists in Angola, and both fields were continued by the United Church after 1925. The Anglican Church having concentrated most of its missionary work in the Canadian North, did not enter foreign mission fields on a significant scale until the present century, when mission workers were sent to India, Pakistan, Japan, and China. Baptist missions in India were originally undertaken in 1866 in co-operation with American Baptists, but soon became independent, and before the turn of the century the Baptists had added Bolivia to their mission fields.

Canadian Roman Catholics were late in entering the field of overseas missions, probably because, like the Anglicans, they were absorbed by work in the Canadian northland. The Sulpicians have operated missions in Japan and one group of Cistercians has in recent years assisted the work of its original congregation in South Africa. The Brothers of the Holy Cross have active missions in India and Pakistan, while the English Congregation of the Grey Sisters have during the present century operated missions in China, Japan, and the Dominican Republic. The first Canadian branch of the Missionary Sisters of Our Lady of Africa was opened in 1903. Many of the other religious orders of both men and women have missionary connections through their parent organizations, having settled in Canada originally in a mission capacity. In addition to the overseas missions of the major churches, smaller Canadian denominations have undertaken missions in Africa and Latin America during the present century, and have contributed surprisingly large numbers of personnel and large amounts of money to their chosen fields.

Canadian interest in foreign missions has drawn heavily on the support of student, juvenile, and women's groups. Under the inspiration of Dwight L. Moody's mission-preaching in the 1880s, the Student Volunteer Movement was organized, and several new Canadian fields were opened before the close of the nineteenth century. The S.V.M. led to the strengthening of numerous missions which until that time had operated primarily as individual undertakings. The Presbyterian,

Methodist, and Congregational Women's Missionary societies were each organized during the decade 1876-86.

During the past quarter-century Canadian interest in overseas missions has declined noticeably as a result of the financial difficulties caused by the Depression and later because of the political upheavals connected with the Second World War. Missions in Japan and in Japanese-occupied territories which closed in 1941 have not regained their former strength because of the anti-mission bias within newly emerged Asian nations. In many Asian countries new indigenous churches have taken over the works previously performed by the missionaries. In China virtually all Christian missions have been abandoned since the Communist Revolution. Similarly in Africa, missions have frequently been identified with colonial status by the nationalists, or elsewhere, as in Angola, have found themselves in violent opposition to the policies of the European rulers. Today foreign missions of the Christian churches of all countries find themselves at the crossroads of nationalism and colonialism, and either or both directions may yet prove to be dead ends for their undertakings.

Canadian society seems in the past one hundred years to have settled into a comfortable pattern of religious pluralism. Individual churches at times appear to be social agencies rather than religious communities, an appearance stemming largely from a too-close identification with the rising standard of Canadian living. Spasmodic outbursts by 'angry young men' against this worldliness have not as yet led to any general revolution in the Canadian religious way of life. Future change is more likely to come as a result of such modern non-Canadian forces as the lay movement, the liturgical revival, and ecumenism.

21. Sport

JACK BATTEN

Failure is the word that Canadians use most frequently to describe their country's performance in sports, at least in international sports, in the last years of Canada's first century. And it is hockey, Canada's own unique contribution to sport, that has brought them to this sorry characterization. Hockey sets the tone for all the other sports in Canada, and around the world in the 1960s, Canada's hockey wasn't up to Russia's standards or Sweden's and barely even with Czechoslovakia's. Canadian teams were also well beaten at the Olympic Games of 1960 and 1964, and they haven't brought home a world championship since the tournament of 1955 when a rugged, rowdy band of rejects from the National Hockey League, playing as the Penticton Vs, just managed to defeat the rest of the world. This sorry record

606

has left Canada's sporting enthusiasts standing sadly in humiliation.

And since sport is the most ephemeral of social activities, one that rarely permits a glance backwards at past achievements, these recent failures run deep enough to obscure for Canadians what is, in fact, a very accomplished and exciting sporting history. Canada, if the truth be recognized, enjoys a tradition in sports that would not shame an older and more populous nation. It has, after all, among a great many other triumphs, done these things: produced one world heavyweight boxing champion – Tommy Burns of Hanover, Ontario, champion from February 23, 1906, to December 26, 1908; staged annually the oldest continuously run stakes race in North America – the regal Queen's Plate, first run in 1859; founded a sports giant rivalled in success and profits perhaps only by the New York Yankees – the Toronto Maple Leaf Hockey organization; provided the stadium, spectators, and inspiration for the most thrilling and significant running race in the twentieth century – the John Landy–Roger Bannister mile run at the British Empire Games in Vancouver in 1954; invented one game, hockey, inherited another, lacrosse, and refined a third, Canadian football; given birth to an incredible number of world-class athletes in almost every sport played by civilized man, not excluding sculling (Ned Hanlan), ladies' high jumping (Ethel Catherwood), middle-distance running (Bill Crothers), rifle shooting (George Genereux), and high-powered speedboat racing (Bob Haywood). All this from a country whose population in a hundred years barely reached twenty million.

It's a record filled with pride, the kind of pride that set Canadians industriously at work, as the centennial year approached, to repair the one giant flaw in it. In the 1960s, professional hockey governors, national magazines, concerned citizens, and the Prime Minister himself came forward with schemes and advice, and criticism of other experts' schemes, to restore Canada's supremacy in world amateur hockey. By 1964, a hockey centre had been created in Winnipeg, where a group of young men were to be schooled, in hockey and academic subjects, over the following four years, with the ultimate objective of a victory in the Olympic Games of 1968. It seemed, at last, a fine plan, and, Canadians agreed, it might just make 'failure' obsolete as a description of their country's sports record.

The games that Canadians were playing in 1867 and in the years before the turn of the century seem to have been more rugged, rougher, and even more heroic than the sports that are played today; and the athletes of those years have themselves left an impression to succeeding generations of men bigger than life-size. Some Canadians did devote themselves to the more sedate sporting pastimes, like cricket and golf. English soldiers brought their cricket bats and balls to Canada as early as the mid eighteenth century and by 1835 matches between groups of players from Hamilton, Toronto, and Montreal were annual events. Golf was introduced into the country in the 1860s and on November 4, 1873, the first golf club, the Royal Montreal Golf Club, was organized. But these sports were the exceptions, and far more Canadians were attracted to athletic competitions that were filled with exciting, raw, elemental action, sports that more closely matched the frontier flavour that life in those days offered.

The favourite sport of Confederation years was lacrosse, a game that eventually fell into decline because it was *too* bloodthirsty. It was followed in popularity by sculling, a magnificently difficult test of endurance, and by such other he-man activities as long-distance running, snowshoe racing, and paddling—anything that required men to drain themselves of all their energy in one long, sustained, all-out effort. Even the tug-of-war was regarded in those years as a highly serious sport, and winning teams could count on the same kind of acclaim from the country that a century later was reserved for Grey Cup football champions. A team of Scottish-Canadians from the Ontario town of Zorra, for instance, won renown across Canada in the autumn of 1890 when they out-pulled a team of behemoths from Chicago at the Fall Fair of the Embro and West Zorra Agricultural Society and thus became the tug-of-war champions of North America.

Another esoteric sport requiring a good deal of muscle that a number of Canadians played in the same years was, of all things, polo. The polo capital of Canada was southern Alberta, where the sport was taken up in the 1880s by a group of cattle ranchers. At first their equipment consisted of broom handles and cricket balls, but by the mid 1890s they were sufficiently well equipped and organized to keep a league of seven clubs in constant action. The High River Polo Club emerged as the league's dominant team, and in the early 1900s it won both the Canadian and American championships. Polo's popularity in the West continued for a dozen years into the twentieth century, but with the coming of the First World War it lost its best players and its audience appeal, and after 1918 it never again returned to the glorious days when High River produced the continent's champions.

But lacrosse was the first sport of the country in the hearts of most Canadians in the Confederation years. It was, for one thing, a distinctly Canadian sport, conceived and refined by the Canadian Indians a few decades before the white man arrived in North America. The Indians called it 'baggata-way', but whatever the name, the soldiers and settlers from Great Britain and France were attracted immediately to the rugged, free play of the game. However, on at least one occasion, the Indians turned their innocent game into a weapon against the new, white North Americans. That happened on a June day in 1763 when two teams of Indians — one Ojibway, the other Sacco — were invited to play an exhibition game outside the British garrison at Fort Michilimackinac. The game was hotly played and an absorbing spectacle — too absorbing for the British, who were caught entirely off guard when on a pre-arranged signal one player lofted the lacrosse ball inside the Fort's open gate and all the players, plus a couple of hundred Indian spectators, rushed after it, armed with the tomahawks and knives they had concealed in their clothing. For the British, the game ended in a tragic massacre.

But by 1867 Canadians were sufficiently reconciled to

lacrosse and to its Indian inventors to send an eighteen-man team of Caughnawagas on a Confederation-year lacrosse tour of the British Isles. And on July 1, 1867, the feature sporting attraction in Toronto was a lacrosse match between the Toronto Club and a team from the Six Nations Indian reservation. The match attracted more than five thousand fans, a magnificent crowd for those years.

Lacrosse continued its popularity well into the twentieth century. Some of its finest players were athletes who were more famous in other sports, men like the Montreal Canadiens hockey player Newsy Lalonde, and Ted Reeve of the Toronto Balmy Beach football team. But it rapidly declined in crowd appeal when a rough style of play began to predominate over the speed and grace of well-played lacrosse.

The greatest and most popular athlete in Canada in the years before 1900 was not a lacrosse player but a sculler: the redoubtable Ned Hanlan of Toronto. Hanlan may be the closest Canada has come to producing an unbeatable athlete. He rowed 350 official races and scored the incredible number of 338 victories. He took on the world's best amateur scullers and defeated them all. He was probably the first athlete of any sport who was entitled to call himself 'champion of the world'. With no more amateurs to conquer, he turned professional in the late 1870s, and by rowing for large purses and larger side bets, he made himself a modestly wealthy man.

As a professional, besides whipping his opponents, Hanlan had to overcome some instances of inspired skulduggery, since sculling, especially two-man matches, attracted the gamblers, fixers, and hoodlums who have always been a part of the sports scene. Professional sports were not as meticulously run in those days as they have been in recent years, and gamblers were offered lots of opportunity to ensure that their bets were safe. On one occasion, Hanlan was rowing in a five-mile match race against an American named Courtney on the Potomac River in Washington on May 19, 1880. This race drew a crowd of forty thousand, including a number of Senators and Congressmen, since Washington had declared a holiday in honour of the great Hanlan. Gamblers planted a third rower at the half-way point in the race, out of sight of the crowd, to ensure, in some way too devious to fathom, that Hanlan wouldn't win the race. The third man set out when he had a half-mile lead over Hanlan, but it wasn't enough. Hanlan, rowing with a magnificent sweep, overtook him easily, and then, for the second time that day, he passed Courtney who had taken a short cut and lopped nearly a mile off the race's true course. Hanlan won something like five thousand dollars in that afternoon's work and added yet more lustre to his name.

Sculling had always been popular in Canada in its early days, but it was probably Hanlan's example that inspired the long line of Canadian singles rowing champions that brought distinction to the country. In 1904, Lou Scholes of Toronto won amateur rowing's most coveted race, the Diamond Sculls at Henley, England, and in later years he was succeeded as Henley champion by three other Canadians: Joe Wright in 1928, Jack Guest in 1930, and Bob Pearce in 1931.

In the same way, a couple of decades later, it was probably the example of a short, slender, determined young man from Hamilton, Ontario, that established the tradition for Canada's distinguished marathon runners. The young man was named Bill Sherring and his great triumph came on May 1, 1906, when he won the marathon race in the Fourth Olympic Games which were held, appropriately enough, in Greece. Sherring's endurance and skill, if not his Olympic victory, were matched in later years by a number of Canadian runners, men like Tom Longboat, an Onondaga Indian from the Caledonian reservation near Bill Sherring's home town of Hamilton, and Gérard Côté, the cigar-chewing postman from Quebec.

The team sport that replaced lacrosse in the affections of most Canadians, and the sport that is today most closely identified around the world with Canadians, is, of course, ice hockey. Hockey was invented by a group of students at McGill University who about 1875 refined the popular pastime of knocking a ball around a sheet of ice into something resembling a scientific sport. The first organized hockey game, as nearly as hockey historians can make out, was played in Kingston, Ontario, in 1885 between teams from Queen's University and the Royal Military College. Or, at any rate, Queen's displays in its gymnasium the puck that it *claims* came from that first game.

The popularity of hockey, as a healthy game for young Canadians and as an interesting, exciting spectator sport for older Canadians, spread rapidly, especially after 1893 when Frederick Arthur, Lord Stanley of Preston, the Governor General of Canada, presented a trophy named after himself to be competed for by the best amateur hockey teams in Canada. Seventeen years later, in 1910, the National Hockey Association, a newly formed professional league, took possession of the Stanley Cup and it has remained to this day the symbol of professional hockey supremacy in the world and the most famous sporting trophy in Canada.

Competition for the Stanley Cup helped to bring some unity and organization into professional hockey, to make it a national sport, but hockey didn't really enter its modern period until the late 1920s when cities in the United States were introduced into the National Hockey League (successor to the old National Association). This expansion coincided with the entry into the sport of sportsmen-entrepreneurs like Conn Smythe of the Toronto Maple Leafs and Leo Dandurand of the Montreal Canadiens. They set out to convert hockey into an even more exciting spectator sport than it had been in its early days, something that would appeal to the less-expert American fans as well as to Canadians. They introduced several rule changes—for instance, permitting forward passing in all three ice zones—that speeded up the game, and they instructed their coaches to make more frequent player switches so that the pace would never lag and bore the fans.

At the same time, Smythe undertook to turn hockey into a social as well as a sporting occasion. He built a new arena, Maple Leaf Gardens, that was the last word in smart comfort, and he encouraged businessmen to bring their wives to the

games and to make a hockey night a special event for business
customers. With Smythe in the lead, the NHL became spec-
tacularly successful: crowds and profits soared, and the game
became as much a part of the North American sporting scene
as baseball and football. Smythe's team was the basis of the
most powerful and profitable sports organization that Canada
has known. Since the Gardens opened in 1932, it has paid out
more than three million dollars in dividends, and the Maple
Leaf team has acquired the status of a national institution.

The finest Canadian athletes of the between-wars period, the
model sporting heroes, contrasted sharply in style with the
early Canadian champions. They weren't rugged, durable
heavyweights, like Ned Hanlan or the great lacrosse players;
they were more inclined to grace and speed and cleverness.
And they were probably best typified by three men of those
years: Jimmy McLarnin, the boxer, Sandy Somerville, the
golfer, and Percy Williams, the sprinter. All three shared the
same personal characteristics – modest, dedicated, honest –
and, as athletes, all three possessed what sports fans are fond
of calling 'class'.

McLarnin showed his class in the way he moved around the
ring; he was the master of boxing's classic punch, the left jab,
and he had perfected all the inside arts of the sport – how to
slip a punch, how to use the ropes, how to tie a man up in a
clinch. He learned his skills from an old carnival fighter from
England named Charles 'Pop' Foster, who took McLarnin off
a newsboy's beat on the Vancouver waterfront in the early
1920s when he was only twelve years old. In fourteen years as a
professional, McLarnin fought and beat thirteen world's
champions and became himself the welterweight champion
of the world on two occasions in the mid 1930s. The boxing
writers thought enough of McLarnin to elect him to Boxing's
Hall of Fame in 1950, joining a select circle of only fourteen
men, most of them former heavyweight champions. Long
before 1950, McLarnin had retired to California with his
bank account and his brains firmly intact.

Percy Williams was the master of the fast start. He was a

100-yard and 200-yard specialist, and his ability to accelerate
rapidly and apparently float to the tape made him great.
When he sailed for the Olympic Games in Amsterdam in the
summer of 1928, he was totally unknown to world track. He
was barely known in Canada, and then only as a twenty-year-
old Vancouver high-school runner. That made his victories,
in the space of three days over the world's toughest fields in
the Games' two glamour events, the 100-metre and 200-metre
sprints, the most stunning surprise of the Olympics – perhaps
of any Olympics. And, in the kind of universal uproar that
only a spectacular sports upset can create, Williams astounded
and cheered his country. When he returned to Canada, he
was greeted in a succession of celebration parades from
Quebec City to Vancouver, where a day's holiday had been
called in his honour. Williams's period of fame was intense
but short; in 1930 in the finals of the 100-yard dash at the first
British Empire Games, held in Hamilton, Ontario, he pulled
a muscle in his thigh and never quite recovered. He entered
the Olympics again in 1932, but this time he missed qualify-
ing for the finals in either of his specialties and – declaring
rather sadly that he'd 'never really cared for track' – retired
from competitive sport.

C. Ross 'Sandy' Somerville, the third great athlete of the
1918 to 1939 years, had a touch of the patrician about him.
He belonged to the classic era of amateur golf, to the days
when the 'gentlemen' golfers hadn't quite yielded to the pros
as the masters of the game. Somerville, who came from
London, Ontario, wasn't the only fine Canadian amateur;
there were also, among others, the remarkable Thompson
brothers, Frank and Bill, of Toronto, each of whom won the
Canadian Amateur Championship against American opponents. But Somerville was decidedly the best. His greatest
victory remains to this day the most important moment in the
history of Canadian golf. It came in 1932 when Somerville
was twenty-nine. He had at that point already won the
Canadian Amateur four times, but he seemed jinxed when
he approached the tournament he wanted most to win – the
American Amateur. Winning it put a golfer in the class of

Bobby Jones and Francis Ouimet, the supreme golfers of this period, but Somerville had never lasted in that competition past the second round of match play.

In 1932, Somerville deliberately tuned his game to reach a peak in late August when the American tournament was to be played at the Five Farms Country Club near Baltimore. His strategy worked: he breezed through to the finals on the impetus of a game that was as sharp and controlled as the American spectators had ever seen. In the semi-finals, he overwhelmed a golfer named Guilford, nicknamed 'Siege Gun' in honour of the power of his game, by the lopsided margin of seven and six. The finals proved a much tougher test; there Somerville met John Goodman of Chicago, who was later to be called the 'new Bobby Jones', and at the twenty-seventh hole, Somerville found himself two down. But the turning-point came at the thirtieth, a difficult dog's-leg par five, when Somerville played a long gambling tee shot across the tops of a grove of trees. He made his gamble, took the hole, broke Goodman's spirit, and won the match and the American Amateur Championship, two and one. No Canadian had won it before; none won again until Gary Cowan of Kitchener, Ontario, triumphed in the 1966 tournament.

These three – McLarnin, Williams, and Somerville – were not the only world-class athletes that Canada produced in the 1920s and 1930s. Perhaps in achievement they were matched by George Young, the only man to negotiate the swim from Catalina Island to the California mainland; by Torchy Peden, the brave king of the six-day bicycle races; by Ethel Catherwood, the Olympic ladies' high-jump champion of 1928; by some of the professional football heroes of the 1930s, men like the miraculously elusive runner of the Winnipeg Blue Bombers, Fritzie Hansen, or the Toronto Argonauts' hard-nosed plunger, Red Storey. But McLarnin, Williams and Somerville were matched by none of the others in Canada and by few in the world for the grace and skill they brought to their sports.

And by the same yardsticks, perhaps the most remarkable

team of those decades wasn't a football or a hockey team, but
a ladies' basketball team. It was the Commercial Graduates
Basketball Club, more familiarly known across Canada in
those years simply as the Edmonton Grads. The Grads began
modestly enough, as the ladies' champions of Alberta in 1915.
But from there they never stopped going: from 1922 to 1940,
with very few changes in personnel, they were, by a decisive
margin, the best team at their sport in the world. They
won ninety-six per cent of the games they played during that
period. They were, for almost all of those years, provincial,
regional, national, and North American champions, and with
no more leagues to conquer on this continent, they made
periodic barnstorming tours around the world. They played
twenty-seven games against all comers from all countries and
they out-scored their opposition, on the average, sixty-nine
points to eleven. No overseas team, needless to say, ever
defeated them. Only one thing did succeed in beating the
Grads: lack of opposition. By 1940, some of the ladies felt
they had beaten everyone in sight who was worth beating, and
they decided they would have to disband. In that last year
they won twenty-six basketball games and lost none.

The post-1945 years brought with them an age of enormous
expansion in sports. Shorter working hours, the spread of
television, and easier transportation combined to create a
wider sports audience, people who for the first time found
themselves captivated by the spectacle of men displaying
their mastery over games. The entrepreneurs of sport took
remarkably effective advantage of the commercial possibilities the new audience presented. New leagues were formed
and old ones expanded; stadiums and arenas were built in
unprecedented numbers; and the ability to perform well at a
sport suddenly became for young men and women a quick
route to undreamed-of wealth.

For the most part, the new golden age of athletics was
dominated in Canada by professional sports. The National
Hockey League began to turn the greatest profits in its history, and professional golf acquired an enthusiastic and large

following for the first time, especially in the mid 1960s when a young pro from Toronto named George Knudson emerged as Canada's finest golfer since the days of Sandy Somerville. Professional football blossomed in the 1950s into an immensely successful spectator sport – and also introduced a new phenomenon into Canadian athletics: for the first time, 'imported' players, in this case Americans, became national sports heroes. Men like Indian Jack Jacobs of Winnipeg and Sam 'The Rifle' Etcheverry of Montreal replaced hockey players in the affections of many fans. Boxing, wrestling (which is actually one part athletics to three parts dramatics), horse racing, minor-league hockey, soccer, basketball – all of them professional sports – found for themselves in the post-war years interested, dedicated fans in large numbers. Even baseball, the most American of games, attracted new Canadian interest. Canada, indeed, produced a handful of fine baseball players of its own – Ron Taylor, for instance, of Leaside, Ontario, the first-line relief pitcher for the St. Louis Cardinal championship team of 1964, and Pete Ward, son of a Montreal Maroon hockey player, who was the regular third baseman on the Chicago White Sox team of the 1960s.

Perhaps the most dramatic fact of the post-war sports boom was its *national* impact. In the first forty years of the twentieth century, most professional sports, with a few isolated and impermanent exceptions, were confined to central Canada where the promoters could confidently expect to find audiences, arenas, and profits. But with the boom in Canada's economy west of Ontario after the war, professional sports, following the money, moved across the Prairie Provinces and into British Columbia. And, for the first time, sports became less satellite and more national in character. Football, with teams from Montreal to Vancouver, offers the most obvious example of this important new change; from 1950 to the present, the west has moved rapidly to a new position of equality with the east, on the field *and* at the box office. And this pattern has been repeated in most other major sports. The Maritimes, however, where there has occurred no economic boom, has lagged behind the rest of the country in its

sporting significance. Professional sports – except for the
occasional boxing promotion usually built around a local
favourite – has had relatively little impact on the four eastern
provinces.

But with all the emphasis on professionalism, perhaps the
single most popular Canadian athlete of the post-war years
was the most amateur of performers, a lady figure-skater,
Miss Barbara Ann Scott of Ottawa. Lady athletes tended to
monopolize Canada's public attention in the late 1940s and
early 1950s; besides Miss Scott, there was Marilyn Bell, whose
dramatic swim across Lake Ontario in August 1954 made her
an overnight celebrity, and Marlene Stewart, who won almost
all the golf championships open to ladies in North America
and Great Britain. Miss Scott reflected everything that is
valuable in the spirit of amateurism in her dedication to
athletic excellence for no reason except the pleasure and
accomplishment of excellence. But at one point in her career
her amateur spirit was unfairly tested – and the uproar that
resulted across Canada was probably unmatched until the
squabble over the pipeline debate in Parliament blew
through the country a few years later. It happened in 1947,
after Miss Scott's first victory in the world figure-skating
championships, when Ottawa presented her with a car as a
sign of the city's affection and respect for her. Miss Scott had
hardly taken the wheel of her new present when the world
figure-skating authority ordered her to return it on penalty of
disqualification from future amateur competition. Canada
was outraged and for a while it appeared that Miss Scott was
the only Canadian who kept her dignity. She returned the car
and resumed her career. She won the Olympic title and the
world title for the second time, both in 1948, and when she
returned home, Ottawa again offered her a new car as the
city's gift. This time, with no more question about sacrificing
her amateur standing, she accepted the car and kept it.

Canada's sports life can't be measured solely in terms of its
champions and its superior players. Spectator sports tell only
part of the story about a nation's athletics. The other yard-

stick is participation, and as *participators* in sports, Canadians
have been remarkably active in their one hundred years. The
Encyclopedia of Sports, a bulky 1,007-page volume that offers
a nearly overwhelming collection of data on all of the world's
sport, says of Canada that 'No country in the world is more
devoted to sports. . . . Canadians enjoy watching contests, but
not even England, with *its* intense devotion to sports, is more
eager for actual participation in sports than are Canadians.'
  Over the years, with the gradual increase in leisure time,
Canadians, like all North Americans, have devoted more and
more of their time to sports until today only jobs and families
occupy more of most Canadians' hours. For instance, half a
million Canadians are now active golfers; by 1965 they were
attacking the turf of 750 golf courses, two and a half times
as many as there were in 1955. Almost as much as golf,
Canadians like bowling, both the lawn and the indoor five-pin
varieties, and in the winter, they ski and they curl – tirelessly.
Twenty-five years ago, the hills around Collingwood, Ontario, were just that – empty hills; but in 1967, these hills
are the favourite winter playground of an average of ten
thousand skiers per week-end, and the situation is the same
on British Columbia's Grouse Mountain, in Quebec's
Laurentians, and on every slippery winter hill in between.
  But in purely numerical terms, the outdoor activity most
Canadians prefer is just *getting* outdoors: a million-odd
Canadians consider camping the best of all sporting activities, and they have 2,038 federal, provincial, municipal,
and private camping-grounds to choose from across Canada.
These range from Banff Park's Tunnel Mountain camp-
ground, which has space for 950 camp sites, to the two-tent
grounds in the Georgian Bay Islands National Park. Altogether, Canada has eighteen national parks, covering some
29,000 square miles. Sadly, not all of the parks are meticulously kept up and some of them have taken on the appearance of honky-tonk slums around the edges. But for the most
part Canada is ideal camping territory, from Long Beach on
the west side of Vancouver Island, the only place in the

country where a motorist can enjoy an unobstructed view of
the Pacific, to Terra Nova Park in Newfoundland on the
shores of the Atlantic.

Whatever their roles in sport – spectators, participators,
professional champions, amateur dabblers – Canadians are
demonstrating, at the end of their first one hundred years,
that they are very like citizens in most other parts of the
world. They are, like these others, simply entranced with the
spectacle of athletic motion. The spread of sports in Canada
since the end of the Second World War is a reflection of their
spread on an international basis. For the mid twentieth century, whatever other age it may be in the world's history
books, is undoubtedly the Age of Athletics. The great champions of sport no longer emerge from a handful of Anglo-
Saxon countries; now they come from all kinds of previously
unlikely places – boxers from Nigeria, badminton players
from Malaya, sprinters from Cuba, long-distance runners
from Kenya.

Canada's future record in sports will be judged, inside
and outside the country, against this broader international
background, and that's the compelling reason, it seems to
most Canadians, why Canada must regain its old position of
dominance in world hockey. Within the country's borders,
most Canadians are excited by their professional football and
hockey teams, by the fine golfers and boxers, and by all the
other individual performers; and most Canadians are proud
of these players' and teams' native achievements. But now, in
the heady challenging atmosphere of *world* sports, Canadians
need to show off a champion of all champions, a champion
that is most likely to come from our hockey teams. And that,
to most Canadians, is the task that lies ahead in the next
century of Canadian sports.

22. From Villages to Cities

NORMAN PEARSON

Canada has crammed into the ten decades since Confederation a vast transformation of environment that took as many centuries in most parts of Europe. The buildings which characterized the historic regions of Canada, the architecture which had such diversity and traditional roots, and the original planning of settlements—all have been virtually wiped out, or submerged, or changed out of all recognition, in the urban and industrial revolution of the twentieth century. The traces that remain indicate not one world but several different worlds, which have risen and then in their turn been swept aside in the tidal waves of change. In central Canada, it is not uncommon to find a city which is only as old as our Confederation but which has had four or five city halls, of which not a trace remains, except of the latest. In almost every region of Canada, places that were thriving in 1867 have passed away, their former presence now scarcely suspected; new developments attest to the gaps in local historical knowledge, as bulldozers clearing the path for housing unearth Indian burial grounds, or the graves of former heroes. Places that confidently expected great expansion are now quiet backwaters, and every decade new towns are established. The landscape, even in the wilderness, bears witness to the transforming power of the new nation, for good or ill.

When Canada was pieced together, it was not so much one identity as a collection of beginnings, a series of landscapes, of embryo cultures. For the Maritime architecture and busy harbours of Nova Scotia and New Brunswick, the end of reciprocity with the United States and the beginning of the shift to steam scarcely seemed prognostic of disaster: the signs of the nineteenth-century industrial revolution of coal and iron and railways began to be evident in the gracious villages, in the network of small towns supplementing the older mines, and in the lumbering and fishing of the frontier regions on the rivers feeding the string of settlements around the shore. Areas now desolate were once cheerful little farms, and the process of grubbing out woodland continued. Many of these little areas were curious mixtures of Georgian architecture, family silver, and pioneer farming; still others were, as in Cape Breton, secret hamlets with the sea-trade as their window on the world. In the St. John Valley, the river was, as it had always been in the valley of the St. Lawrence, a roadway linking white-painted colonial settlements, each with its church in rhythmic sequence. But the prosperity of Halifax, the proud city of wooden urban architecture with its fine stone central area, was destined to give way to the poverty, crowding, and slums that resulted from the changed economy. There were frequent fires, as in 1877 when two-thirds of the central peninsula of Saint John was utterly destroyed. Crowding was already in evidence. In the mining areas and industrial centres, poor housing and bad working conditions combined with waste and destruction of landscape in a manner that would have been familiar to European industrial regions. But in general, the landscape, as prints and paintings and vivid descriptions indicate, was one of prosperity and a degree of graciousness. The cities were proud of their progress, and the countryside of the advanced state of its husbandry.

In the roaring lumbering towns of Maine and the Madawaska a curious local identity emerged, showing a true frontier region where the architecture blended the folk traditions of Quebec and the influences of New England classicism. Not until the Intercolonial Railway came in the 1870s was the isolation touched, and the picturesqueness remains today.

Beyond the bare hills of St. Louis du Ha! Ha! the long river-based civilization of Quebec was much as it had always been. The characteristic pattern of long strip-farms, the ribboning of settlements along the St. Lawrence, was seemingly stable and enduring. The settlements from the fortress Quebec to the great *entrepôt* of Montreal were linked daily by the river craft and annually by the joyous fires of St. Jean Baptiste and the tocsin of church bells from steeple to steeple. The rooflines designed to handle heavy snowfall and the transmuted domestic architecture of fieldstone French farmhouses gave this scene a beauty which in Europe frequently characterized Canada for decades afterwards.

Montreal was already a distinctive and bustling city at Confederation, and as intensely developed as most European cities of the day, but in its own vernacular. Industry and the strong financial district, suburban expansion, and tangled communications come down to us in the pictures of a truly urban place. Quebec City, at that moment beautiful in its medieval form, was bursting its confines, and the harbour was a forest of wooden ships.

In the Ottawa Valley, the half-built wilderness Westminster that was to become Ottawa formed a gothic fringe on the crude and primitive frontier town. All up the valley the ruthless lumbering went on, and farms that are now poor and deserted were just then being carved out of the bush.

For Upper Canada, the scene at Confederation was that of

a fully developed landscape all along the valley of the St.
Lawrence. In Kingston, the citizens were concerned about
saving some of the town's old French character before the
stone Georgian buildings, now in their turn being engulfed,
threatened it. Niagara-on-the-Lake, the former capital, was
quietly sinking into tranquillity while Niagara Falls boomed
into a tourist town. Toronto, a predominantly Georgian city,
relatively compact and still human in scale, vied fiercely
with upstart and ambitious Hamilton for pride of place,
while swampy Dundas, dying as the head of navigation on
the Great Lakes and bypassed by new Welland canals, vege-
tated. To the west, Berlin (now Kitchener) with its own
distinct German culture, was expanding in a trim Mennon-
ite countryside.

A highly developed agriculture and a pattern of small and
prosperous market towns, with the steadily expanding networks of turnpikes, stagecoaches, and railways, ran parallel
to the older industrial development based on water power
and river access. The pioneer cities of Galt, Guelph, and
Goderich were serving the new hinterland of the Huron
area, and from this base, Ontario was pushing northward
into the rich lumbering country.

Settlers pushed northward too, but into an area which
hitherto had known only the voyageurs from the Ottawa
River, Lake Nipissing, the French River, and the North
Channel to the fur and wood centres of the old Canada.
Recent Indian treaties had thrown open Manitoulin Island
to settlement, but the hinterland was still much as it always
had been, with forts, fur posts, and lumber camps situated
in the more accessible areas, and the mining of copper at
Bruce Mines.

In the great grasslands that became the Prairie Provinces
there were scattered log or stone forts, trading-posts, block-
houses, and the camps of nomadic Indians. For the Red
River settlement and the Métis country to the west, the main
link was with the Minneapolis country, and the creaking
ox-cart and the turf or wooden farm-house were the only real
evidence of the work of man. Hidden in this vast region were

the relics of the era of exploration and scattered at strategic points the palisaded posts of the great fur companies.

In the western Cordillera and on the Pacific coast it was a landscape in sharp contrast to the strip-farms of the Métis or the Scots settlements on the Red River. Isolated, with the hinterland scarred by the lumbering and gold-mining in the Cariboo country, the colony seemed poor compared with the expansive U.S.A. The coastal settlements and scattered farms were usually small, and the architecture varied from the primitive to the classical and gothic of colonial society. Vancouver was not established as an urban settlement until Granville was founded in 1874 and it did not receive its name until 1886, when most of the town disappeared in a great fire, and was hastily rebuilt.

In 1867, the Indians were in fact the only people in many parts of Canada: on the Pacific, the Maori-like lodges and totems of the sea peoples; on the prairies the skin wigwams of the Athabascan and Sioux; in the northern woodlands, north to the hostile and static Eskimo civilization, the many nations in their bark lodges; and in the Grand River the urban Mohawk; while the Micmac and the remnants of the allied tribes added to the heritage of their Maritime regions. It is an irony that in all likelihood the name Canada itself derives from an Indian word meaning 'town', and yet the last vestiges of urban Hochelaga and the palisaded villages of Huronia and Iroquoia were virtually forgotten at the beginning of modern Canada.

The greater part of the land, in what was to be one of the largest countries in the world, was virtually untouched, and these almost separate and distinct worlds were to remain so for many more years. The first thirty years after Confederation, Canada was plagued by periods of severe economic depression, and while the original confederation of 1867 (one tenth as large as the Canada of the present day) was expanding and being linked by the railway and the telegraph, there was little change in many areas, except for the worse. By the 1890s the Maritimes and urban centres in Ontario and Quebec experienced some deterioration and crowding. Between

1890 and 1895 more people left Canada than entered it.
Then dramatic change came, with the expansion of the railway and the use of federal power to shape the development
of the west. But the decline of the sailing ship and the separation from New England left the older centres of the Maritimes in a position as marginal as their geographical circumstances. The great features of the next phase of the cultural
landscape of Canada were the railways and the free land of
the west. The significance of confederation was slow to be
appreciated, but it dramatically reshaped half a continent.

The first railways simply supplemented the water-transport
system, like portages around rapids. In the 1830s the Montreal–St. Jean and Montreal–Lachine lines were built, and by
the 1850s the Grand Trunk line linked Quebec and Detroit.
By 1885 the Canadian Pacific was completed across the country, and from 1867 to 1914 there was a spate of railway building that revolutionized the face of Canada.

In the Maritimes the railway was hailed as the means by
which cities would become of metropolitan stature, but
though such small market towns as Amherst became engineering centres, the geographical advantages of Montreal and
Toronto eventually cut off their expansion. For a period,
when steam coal was in world demand, the new mining
towns such as Glace Bay boomed in a growth that added
standard artisans' dwellings, bunkhouses, and even renovated
wooden row-housing to the buildings of the older civilization.
In Stellarton, New Glasgow, Dartmouth, and many smaller
places, the company housing and the company store, later to
be so much despised and feared, appeared on the scene, serving mine or steel works or sugar refinery. The compact cities
of good proportion and white-painted Maritime architecture
were now overshadowed by the fiendish pictures of Doré's
industrial revolution, but in wood rather than in stone or
brick. The belching chimneys, the blackened façades, the
gridiron streets of a Sydney or a New Glasgow were added to
the gradual decline of the marginal highland farms, and all
the familiar world was changed. Mining, quarrying, and

smelting and the shifts of population were the first phases. As the west was opened, the increasing urbanization of Ontario and Quebec drained off capital and in due course halted this industrial revolution almost in full flight. The building of power stations at Niagara signalled the end of the smoky settlements of industry and slums, and in a few decades only the wreckage remained. When western agriculture and the urbanization of Upper Canada were established, even the hinterlands were affected, and in time the Acadian dikes on the lowlands of Fundy were neglected, to be restored only after half a century. The net result was to slow down change in so much of the region that outside the larger centres, it seems almost a museum of the nineteenth-century city- and town-scape.

In Quebec the effects were marked. Though now oddly silent and limited, St. Jean was a typical railway boom town; when the Champlain and St. Lawrence system linked up there in 1836 it greatly reduced the travelling time between Montreal and New York, and for a few years it was a rapidly expanding terminus city. This pattern was repeated in various regional centres as the railways marched onwards. Gradually Quebec City came to be an industrial as well as a government town, and paper mills began to be seen on the rivers draining into the St. Lawrence. Montreal began to expand rapidly and in a few years added the electric commuter railway (as had Sydney, under the influence of Boston), to establish the basis for a metropolitan pattern of suburbia. Slowly the great river was bridged, and these links were strengthening factors when the railways pushed across the Shield to Lake Superior: for when the west was opened up, the hinterland was as much that of Montreal as of Toronto. There began the great engineering works on the Seaway which eventually led to the relocation of towns like Iroquois and Morrisburg, and the steady accumulation of population in the valley around Montreal. The city began to see itself as the Paris of Canada, and the principal public buildings reflect this faithfully.

The rural village in the greatest part of Quebec remained

virtually in the same romantic form which was eventually to
be in marked contrast to the cosmopolitan Montreal urbanization. The log cabin was everywhere in old Canada.

In Ontario the railway had created the basis for the indus-
trial-agricultural order that preceded Confederation. When
the lines had been built across the rocky Shield around Lake
Superior, first in a strand and then in a steadily expanding
web across the prairies, both central Canada and the west
were transformed. Ontario agriculture was changed by the
sudden influx of vast armies of immigrants who in a few years
turned virgin land into acres of grain. Towns like Brantford,
Galt, and Hamilton, manufacturing farm and railway machinery, suddenly boomed. New suburbs appeared in gridiron
patterns with rows of standard but generally detached houses,
and some brick terraces were created. In Toronto the immigration led to a great variety of industries, and gradually, as
in Montreal, the towers of the financial districts began to
climb like the chimney stacks of industry to change the skyline. At Confederation the church and the Georgian house
and square were dominant; by the turn of the century that
city was almost gone, and the skyline would have done credit
to a cartoon of the progressive city of commerce, Manchester-
style.

The market towns reached their peak of development; the
landscape of rural Ontario has ample evidence of the prosperity of this last phase, but the scene was to change as the
new farmlands and the end of land clearances combined,
forcing marginal areas to dereliction. Much land was virtually plundered, cleared of trees only to be abandoned
again, and many current conservation problems derive from
this era of misplaced confidence.

The real change was a shift in settlement. For one thing,
the railway led to mineral finds. At this point the gap between
the Red River and old Ontario was rapidly filled in with a
series of developments. At the same time, the extension of
lumbering into hitherto untouched areas added a temporary
impetus to the boom. Thus places like Port Arthur and Fort

William resulted from railway rivalry, and each built public buildings and hotels for populations that have yet to materialize. The counterpart in the west was the unprecedented creation of cities like Winnipeg, Regina, Calgary, and Edmonton from the dusty plains. Dreams of steamboats on the Nelson-Saskatchewan river system, and various speculative land booms sought to spread cities miles out into the plains.

But there was a solid and real change in northern Ontario and in the prairies, and it was perhaps best symbolized by the large provincial buildings: in Regina, the legislature was built in a ploughed field when the city hardly existed and had scarcely a tree. All over the west and the north there were examples of the confident architecture of expansion and settlement: and the grain elevator which was the cathedral of the prairies was later to inspire Le Corbusier to his denunciation of all existing architecture as false. This functionalism, like the basic gridiron and chessboard settlement patterns of the surveyor and the military and civil engineer, was well done, which was an amazing performance when one realizes the speed of change. Perhaps later expansion was not handled so well. Some of the great planned cities, like Prince Albert, did not expand, but others like Winnipeg became in a few decades great symbols of the new Canada: polyglot and untraditional, with every known language spoken on the streets by immigrants who became participants in the adventure of nation-building. Winnipeg was built, like Regina, on grain: to outsiders it might be physically crude and standardized, but it was made vigorous and colourful by the many forms of architecture on its wide Portage Avenue. The prairie city spread out across the plains and came to an abrupt end. It had well-defined edges and it was repeated regularly across the plains in a thousand variations on the gridiron plan: railway, grain elevator, public building, and railway hotel. Some like Winnipeg or Moose Jaw were built on flood plains and suffered disaster after disaster. Some like Saskatoon were to become places of beauty when the rivers were controlled and bridged; others, such as Regina, were to create painfully, tree by tree, an island of greenery in the arid land.

The mineral and lumber development of the north was forceful and, in many areas, simply repeated the errors of all such exploitation. The evils of the polluted air, the derelict landscape, the poisoned waters, and the shacks of the company town or the railway change-point were evident, like the moon landscape that emerged around Sudbury, or the bald erosion that followed some of the ruthless lumber operations. But some areas were more fortunate. Sault Ste. Marie and the Algoma area, between 1887, when the railway arrived, and 1905, were the scene of Francis H. Clegue's exploitation of water power, wood pulp, and iron ore from Michipicoten. A city rose which became wealthy and reasonably attractive – in marked contrast to the single-function mining towns. Some of these remain a standing rebuke to Canadian society. The Nickel Belt towns gradually evolved to an urban form, and in time some of the worst features of mining were mollified. Other areas such as Porcupine, Cobalt, Larder Lake, and Kirkland Lake (1890-1905) are in themselves amazing testimony to the problems of building settlements in such terrain. Kirkland Lake has filled in several lakes with waste; Porcupine was for years thirty-two miles by canoe and trail from the railway.

The railway changed the solid market-towns of Ontario and Quebec and created the western cities with their broad streets and open skies. These changes were then modified again by the streetcar. Most large cities were attenuated, and suburbs were created within the web of radial tracks; the phenomenon of the urban region became evident in the way Sir Adam Beck's electric railways linked Hamilton and the many surrounding towns like Oakville, Brantford, and the older places in the Niagara Peninsula, in a constellation that was to be later vastly augmented by the motor car. Attempts were made in the gridiron cities like Toronto and Winnipeg to build radial railways: loops were built in Toronto, where the belt line led to the creation of many pleasant inner suburbs and to a diversity in the structure of the older city as industry and commerce followed. In Montreal the commuter railway and the streetcar created a European complexity; while Toronto resembled an American city in the central area and an English town in the outskirts. In Winnipeg and Edmonton emerged the prairie metropolis, free-standing, and symmetrical as a jewel. Vancouver began to spread to the encircling mountains. The strip commercial area and the apartments, still disguised as mansions, began to change the urban landscape. Vast over-subdivision occurred on the outskirts, and congestion appeared at the core. The hated rows of terrace houses began to appear in the heart of the city, and as housing fell behind the pressures of immigration, colourful, crowded, polyglot areas, with their own churches and shops and social clubs, appeared all over Canada. The streetcar city reached out into the countryside and the speculator built new towns which were gradually absorbed by the city. In the general rush, parkland was often overlooked.

There were some thoughtful practitioners of the art of city-building. With Confederation had come the new parliaments in Toronto and Quebec, and Ottawa suddenly began to look like a permanent place. In Montreal, the Olmsted plan for the Mountain gave the metropolis a secure bastion which remained for decades the finest urban park in Canada. National pride eventually redeemed the battlefield sites in Quebec from the hands of speculation, and in time thirty-five miles of parkland on the Niagara Frontier were set aside and beautified, straight across the river from the desolation in the United States. The genesis of a National Parks system came in the reservation of great tracts of mountainous lands in the Rockies against the general rape of resources.

In 1867 Ottawa had covered 1,829 acres and the population was 18,000. In the early days it grew quite haphazardly from the military construction yard of Bytown and the lumber centre of Philemon Wright in Hull. In 1884 Sir Wilfrid Laurier wrote:

I would not wish to say anything disparaging of the capital,

but it is hard to say anything good of it. Ottawa is not a
handsome city and does not appear to be destined to become
one either.

In 1899 the Ottawa Improvement Commission was set up,
but even then it was a voluntary body and until 1902 did not
have the services of a professional planner or architect. It
took until 1927 to establish the Federal District Commission
and to begin making a national capital plan, but the process
of beautification paved the way for the later dramatic
changes.

The early Canadian cities such as Dartmouth, Halifax,
Dundas, Toronto, or Niagara-on-the-Lake had had greenbelts, but they were largely misused and not fully appreciated
until 1957 when Ottawa achieved a permanent greenbelt.
For the most part the cities struggled with bricks and mortar
and boulevards until the impact of the Chicago and Beaux-
Arts traditions led to movements for creating the 'City Beautiful'. Grandiose avenues and monumental boulevards were
a substitute for the control of the city fabric as a whole, a
watered-down version of what Haussmann did for Napo-
leon III in Paris, or what Daniel Burnham created on Lake
Michigan in Chicago. Today a few streets remind us of this
epoch, which died in the problems of the motor age.

Canada continued to be remade by power and by the techniques of communication and transport. Bell's telephone
system and the expanding hydro power put poles and wires
on the streets, and this tangle of street furniture was not
helped by the streetcar wires and signs which gradually
emerged in response to the developing city, and then dis-
tracted the attention of the automobile driver. The landscape was remade by dams and roads; and the prairie landscape, under the impact of mechanization and monoculture,
became in time a dust-bowl. The stage was set for rural
depopulation and urban sprawl. The Great Depression complicated this evolution by bankrupting municipalities, stop-
ping expansion, and leading to the dispersal of the planning
profession and the decay of public works in many localities.

The seeds of future urban renewal and housing problems were broadcast. But even in this age the signs were evident that the car and the plane would remake the Canadian scene more drastically than any change since the completion of the railway and the subsequent waves of immigration and settlement.

The first signs were evident in the gradual disappearance of the crafts and skills that had been used in the old villages since their establishment. The bakeries and the smithies eventually gave way to the urban bakery and the city service station. In the older areas of coal-mining the new freedom of movement led by 1925 to the death of the 'company store'. When liquor prohibition killed the hotels and new paved roads were built, most small communities, oriented to the river or lake or the railway, began to change, and many disappeared altogether.

The advance of hydro-electric power coincided with the end of the old milling industries; the advent of the car led to the destruction of the electric railways; in a mistaken belief in progress most communities destroyed the commuter lines they would need in a few decades. The freedom of movement led to long ribbons of development and highway commercial uses outside every town. The sharp edges between town and country began to blur as the villages around the large cities were absorbed; and as the farms became mechanized and industrialized the marginal lands were gradually abandoned. In some areas the same generation which had seen the land cleared watched the trees return. Speculators put sidewalks and hydrants in fields decades ahead of the need for them and there was gross over-subdivision of land. The really favoured locations began to pull ahead of the cities of lower rank; in the nineteenth century Hamilton and Toronto competed; in the twentieth, Toronto pulled ahead and attracted the head offices and the enterprise capital.

The major cities embarked on bold plans, and the air was full of talk of garden cities and ring roads and ceremonial entrances to cities. Major expressways were planned and the

Commission of Conservation published reports that seemed to pave the way for a national land policy. But with the depression many of the visions became minor schemes. In Ottawa, it took another thirty years to get the railways moved from the central area. In most of the major cities some attempt was made to keep alive an advisory planning function, but it is clear that almost until the Korean war, planning in Canada was a dying art. The lack of continuity and the failure to establish research and a statutory planning system have yet to show their full consequences, but some results are beginning to be evident in today's cities.

The aeroplane led to many changes. In the west, it rapidly became the means by which cities stayed in contact and explorations were made in the north. It was to become a challenge to the railways as a link between the provinces. Gradually airports were established and for the first time national communications became easier. When the Trans-Canada Highway was begun in the 1920s, it was clear that several decades would be needed to complete it; when it was opened on September 3, 1962, a great chain of national and regional airlines had already blazed the trails across the land and north into the mineral storehouse. As the roads and the airports advanced, there began the erosion of the prairie elevator-railhead towns and the market towns of the east. The extension of pipelines and trucking and the centralization of functions in the larger towns resulted in many smaller places losing their significance.

The war induced a permanent change in Canada and marked the transition from agriculture to industry, from a rural to an urban nation. It created prosperity and mobility and demands for change; it worsened housing conditions in the larger towns and caused a spate of construction of temporary buildings which remained decades later.

Immediately after the war, the federal government recalled Jacques Greber who had in 1937 redeveloped an axial composition in Elgin Street and Confederation Square in Ottawa. The government also commissioned a National

Capital Plan, building on the 1903 plan by the landscape
architect F. G. Todd, and the 1922 plan by Noulan Cauchon.
By 1950 in co-operation with E. Fiset and J. Kitchen a plan
was evolved, and in 1951 it was adopted by Parliament. This
plan was then carried out by the Federal District Commission
and its successor, the National Capital Commission, and has
altered the city with parklands, new scenic arterial roads,
and the decentralization of public buildings within a 41,000-
acre greenbelt. Railway relocation and redevelopment gave
hope that the capital of 700,000 people expected in 1980
would evolve to a graciousness unsuspected in the early days.

In the east, few other cities had such care. The west had a
stronger planning tradition and was able to make advances
in statutory planning, based on the then advanced legislation
of the 1920s in Nova Scotia and Ontario. In most urban areas
there was virtual chaos in the first period of the postwar
boom. The Ottawa greenbelt remained almost the sole example in Canada, and cities with old colonial commons
tended to misuse their heritage of greenery. Solid stone
buildings of European design were torn down during the
motor-car age and the international glass-fronted office building replaced older forms of architecture. Such buildings
were frequently torn down before their time. The loss of
records of this period is grievous: a book recording colonial
architecture in Ontario noted in 1964 that many of the best
architectural examples were destroyed even while the record
was being assembled. Century-old wooden houses were frequently burned by the suburban fire-brigade for practice,
and it took considerable local agitation before the environs
of the Stoney Creek battlefield were preserved from housing
development. Upon a bewildered and unprepared nation
burst a period of intense growth. Scarcely had the planners
drawn up schemes for satellite towns and greenbelts than
gridiron subdivisions for housing engulfed the greenbelts.
The net result of three decades of the 'garden city' movement
in Canada was the curved street, the suburban house, and the
combined school and park site. Forecasts had envisaged attractive combinations of local shops and community facili-

ties; the changing patterns of retail trade caused shopping
centres to be built on the outskirts of communities. The
suburban style was everywhere and housing was mainly confined to the small single-family house. This did give healthy
and open living; but frequently communities out-ran their
services, and the septic-tank suburb resulted. All too frequently the change was a selective process, leaving the lower-
income people captured in the inner suburbs, which became
walled in by the new developments.

Concurrently, the expansion of manufacturing and secondary industry favoured the larger areas and the six or
seven major cities advanced rapidly. In expanding so quickly
they suffered traffic congestion and deficiencies in public
services. Planners discovered that they must now move war-
time housing, relocate markets, and redevelop worn-out
manufacturing areas. Gradually they rediscovered the slums
and realized the impact of growth on the central areas, which,
in layout and functional characteristics, were frequently
outmoded.

When the stability of the industrial change was recognized, some smaller communities, deprived of their airfields
and munitions works, declined, while those not based on
defence expanded. Substantial immigration completely
changed the character of a city such as Toronto in a decade:
it became a metropolis, and like Montreal more cosmopolitan
and sophisticated, and with its special localities, for example,
of Italians or Portuguese. For a time such cities as Toronto,
Edmonton and Montreal were perhaps the fastest-growing
in the world. The old forms of government showed the
strain and by 1953 Toronto had developed a metropolitan
government. Similar forms of government were beginning
to be evident in Vancouver, Winnipeg, Montreal, and Halifax.

Canada now has a young population, and the addition of
about one million people a year has had direct and indirect
effects. First came the frantic building of houses for newly
married couples, and then an expansion of lakeside cottages
as the mobile new families sought recreation. Then came the

wave of building primary and later secondary schools; this was followed in the 1960s by the creation of new universities, and institutes for technical training and the re-education of people whose skills had been made obsolete by changing technology. All this was accompanied by the gradual broadening of the housing stock as larger houses, then the duplex, the semi-detached, and finally the row house (renamed the garden apartment, town house, or maisonnette), came to be succeeded by a wave of apartment building in both central and suburban areas.

The 1950s saw the building of a great number of new frontier towns, mostly in the north, that were connected with mineral exploitation or great engineering works. New communities were generally planned and organized with concern for human values. With the building of the Distant Early Warning Line came the impetus to rebuild Aklavik, and so Inuvik was created, with sewers and services in 'utilidors' above the permafrost into which old Aklavik was sinking. Places like Coppermine and Frobisher Bay were included in visions of Arctic cities under domes, with glass towers and urban gardens. Distant towns like Whitehorse grappled with the problems of integrating military and civil settlements. In the Mid-Canada line the Eskimo saw radar stations and camps open and then in a decade close down as the missile replaced the bombing plane. Mines such as Rankin Inlet opened, trained the Eskimo, and then left him in a broken world.

The planned towns of the northern frontier had their vicissitudes, but gradually stabilization and the arrival of a road or a railway integrated them into the economy. Many of these towns were indistinguishable from suburbs to the south, and in so far as this is the acceptance of a national minimum of civilized environment for all Canadians, it is an advance; against this must be balanced the loss of a regional form in architecture.

The expansion of the great cities promises to use up vast areas of good farmland in the next few decades, but this comes at a time when a smaller number of farmers on less

land produce more food than ever before. The result has
been the passing of the pioneer landscapes of the Okanagan,
the prairies, old Ontario, Quebec, and the Maritimes, reflected in the collections of antiques and the creation of
memorial pioneer villages. This loss of craftsmanship and
tradition has had serious effects on architecture. There are
a few strong regional patterns, but the loss of a tradition of
design and the virtual extinction of historic crafts has standardized architectural and building methods. This, coupled
with the years of chaotic urban growth, has frequently submerged form in the metropolitan *milieu*, despite new civic
buildings and many fine individual examples. Most cities are
simply echoing Manhattan and building skyscrapers on nineteenth-century streets.

The major change of the next century is already apparent,
in the prospect of building within a few decades as much
physical environment as has been built during the total history of Canada. The new Canada will be seen in the outline
of two vast cities, each of five million people, centred around
Montreal and Toronto and spreading laterally along the St.
Lawrence Valley which produced them. It will be seen in
the cities exceeding one million, centred around Vancouver,
Winnipeg, and Ottawa, and in a few other large cities. It
exists already in the physical surroundings that are a summary of the sweeping changes of the past century. The only
constancy is change. We have gone from villages to cities,
from the frontier to the space age in our first century and we
shall, in the next few years, change our environment even
more profoundly.

23. Literature in English

LOUIS DUDEK

It is clear . . . that Canada has produced a goodly number of talented writers; but she has not yet produced a single writer of the very first rank.' So begins the concluding chapter of Desmond Pacey's *Creative Writing in Canada*, the best short survey of our literary history.

It could be argued, however, that since Yeats, Shaw, and Joyce are Irish writers, and T. S. Eliot and Ezra Pound American, England itself in this century has perhaps not produced a writer of the very first rank. (I don't know how successfully, but it could be argued.) Auden is a heavy candidate; as for most others, they could be knocked off as easily as Canadian ducks. Then, has Soviet Russia – population 221 million – produced a writer of the very first rank? (Gorki . . .

Sholokhov . . . Pasternak . . . Not one of these is a Tolstoi or a Dostoevski.) Have Spain or Italy? Greece? Poland? Norway? Why should Canada be more favoured than nations as old and revered as these?

I ask the question merely to shake up our stereotyped notion of literary grandeur, which assumes that major writers are turned out by the dozen in any respectable civilized country (which is certainly not the case), so that we may place our real achievement in a larger perspective. In the first place, one must enter into the subject to see how interesting it is. Every literature, even the greatest, is paltry and dull to those who know nothing about it. But assuming that we are interested, what do we expect of literature in Canada, and how do we view it in relation to the great past of English literature or of French literature?

Canada is not a primitive country. It is not a young nation except in a political sense. Its literature does not begin with animal fables, proverbs, folk ballads, or primitive epics. On the contrary, it begins with decadent romantic lyric and the lees of late-eighteenth-century sentimental poetry imported from England. The problem of Canadian literary development has not been one of growth from primitive roots, but one of sloughing off an imported tradition and of discovering the language, the subject matter, and the form natural and true to Canadian needs.

A constant problem in the search for expression, in the midst of migration from the old world to the new, has been the certification of the true Canadian. Who is in fact a Canadian writer? Canada is often a stopping-off place for migrants who go to settle elsewhere, or die young (Robert Service, Louis Hémon); it is often a visiting-place for writers from abroad who live here for a while and then go back (Patrick Anderson, Malcolm Lowry); it harbours writers who have come late, in their full manhood (Heavysege, Kirby, Grove); it is a mere nesting-place, a first home, for native writers who leave when they grow up to spend their lifetime somewhere else (Bliss Carman, Gilbert Parker, A. J. M. Smith). Occasionally they come back, like Charles G. D.

Roberts, to spend their last years here and to reap the honours that we have prepared for them as prodigal sons.

If the local raised to universal expression is the essence of literature, how can such writers be considered Canadian? To what extent are they Canadian? The answer to this question depends on our conception of national literature. If a national literature is simply the literary product of a community of people possessing a variety of character and talent—not the expression of some mythical racial entity or national over-soul—then all these migrant writers are Canadian in so far as they contribute to our literary history, in so far as they add something to the development of a language, a characteristic subject matter, a sense of form that mirrors the life of this community. The most relevant, of course, are those who are born and bred here, who express the environment and conditions of life in hitherto unseen ways, derived from the daily round and formed from early childhood; but all who enter into the stream of Canadian life and add to its current interest are part of the literature of Canada.

Obviously many of the writers who come and go, or who arrive late in their development, have served to provide us with important transfusions from the great cultures of Europe. These imports serve to underline the simple fact that literature in Canada is not merely a native growth, springing from primitive conditions, but a late branch from the well-developed literatures of England, of France, and of Europe in general. It is a cultivated sprig that has been transplanted to a new environment, either to perish or to adapt and change until it can become a new species.

This is the value of tradition. Necessary and indispensable as a parent, Europe is the mother country of Canada. But tradition is something to be transformed, so that the new growth may be a fresh creation, an individual. The growth of such a national literature is not a metaphysical emanation, as Herder and Fichte assumed in the gusts of German idealism; it is not the voice of a racial soul, but the work of a human community composed of diverse individuals, united

in time and place. Pushkin was part Ethiopian in racial
origin; Dumas's *père* also was part Negro; the Rossettis were
part Italian; Proust was Jewish on his mother's side; Emile
Zola was half-Italian; Joseph Conrad was Polish. The idea
of racial and national purity belongs really to the Nazi
ideology; it does not apply to any nation or to any national
literature. So too in Canada: Lampman, though born in
Canada, was part Pennsylvania Dutch, Grove was Swedish,
Drummond was Irish, Mair was a Scot, Klein and Richler
are Jewish Canadians, Nelligan was of mixed Irish and
French-Canadian descent; yet all these belong to the Canadian family. Half the bulk of our national literature, in fact,
is French in language and tradition, yet it is Canadian. I
think of our literature and our political life as the work of
a team in which there are large proportions of English,
French, Irish, and Scots, and a goodly proportion of other
assorted strains, all co-operating towards the common good.
Just as the spirit of co-operation results in high achievement
for the group, so the national idea serves to unite the energies
of the Canadian people in the direction of self-realization.

An early writer like Oliver Goldsmith (Canadian-born
grand-nephew of the author of *The Vicar of Wakefield*), in
his long poem *The Rising Village* (1825), attempts to describe Canadian life and environment but succeeds for the
most part only in giving us descriptions reminiscent of
eighteenth-century England:

> Beneath some spreading tree's expanding shade
> Here many a manly youth and gentle maid,
> With festive dances or with sprightly song
> The summer's evening hours in joy prolong . . .

Or for prose style, we can study Frances Brooke, an English-
woman writing in Canada in the period after the fall of
Quebec:

> You have nothing against you, Ned, but your modesty; a
> very useless virtue on French ground, or indeed on any
> ground: I wish you had a little more consciousness of your
> own merits: remember that *to know one's self* the oracle

of Apollo has pronounced to be the perfection of human
wisdom. Our fair friend Mrs. H—— says, 'Colonel Rivers
wants nothing to make him the most agreeable man breathing but a little dash of the cox-comb.'

In the first stage of our literary development, before Confederation, almost all our writing, but for one important exception, was of this colonial, derivative kind.

The exception is Thomas Chandler Haliburton, whose
book, *The Clockmaker; or, The Sayings and Doings of
Samuel Slick, of Slickville*, was published in 1836. This book
is astonishingly precocious in its bold handling of language
and its literary skills. Haliburton was a native-born Nova
Scotian of Loyalist descent, educated at Windsor, N.S., and
trained for the bar. He pitched upon dialect humour, a
branch of American writing then coming into vogue, and
developed it with great success. The book won him a reputation in England and in the United States as well as in Canada. The dialect is a literary creation but it does seem to have
local traits of style, and it has the freedom of a frontier literature in its rough-and-ready humour. This work, of truly
local origin, no longer smacks of the drawing-room and of the
British quarterly as does the work of the immigrant writers
of the same period.

The difficulty of finding a native form for literature may
be demonstrated in Charles Sangster (1822-93), the first
poet of some rank who was born and nurtured in Canada
and who wrote out of purely Canadian experience. In
The St. Lawrence and the Saguenay (1856) he composed
Spenserian stanzas with sedulous care; but like all imported
mannerism, his treatment did not convey the reality of the
local subject matter, and his sense of form was entirely
mechanical:

> First, the sweet Idyls from the shepherd vales,
> Where Peace and rural Happiness abide;
> Bird-hymns and wild rejoicings in the dales,
> Where the swart Peasant cheers his rustic Bride;
> Anthems from solitary plains that glide
> To where the death-dirge wails along the sea;

> Low chantings from the stars, and far and wide
> The Minstrel Breezes, meeting playfully,
> Rehearse their wanderings in Canzonet and Glee.

This is no proof that the Spenserian stanza cannot be used in Canada, or in the Himalayas for that matter. Later, James Reaney will play like a true virtuoso on the metrics of Spenser's *Shepheardes Calender*, and Service will whack away in Kipling's metres; but in Sangster the borrowing is still slavish and the form oddly archaic.

An important progressive stage of development came with the late-romantic flowering of the 1880s and 1890s, in the poetry of Carman, Roberts, Lampman, and D. C. Scott. If we compare the writing here with that of Sangster, Heavysege, or Goldsmith in the earlier period, we find an achieved gracefulness and naturalness in the use of refined style that suggest a much surer, more educated literary standard and a much easier adjustment to local experience and feeling. Charles G. D. Roberts's flowing hexameters, formalistic as they are, speak with an easy grace that seems to stand in convincing relation to a known reality:

> Here where the road that has climbed from the inland
>   valleys and woodlands,
> Dips from the hilltops down, straight to the base of the
>   hills, —
> Here, from my vantage-ground, I can see the scattering
>   houses,
> Stained with time, set warm in orchards, meadows, and
>   wheat . . .

Bliss Carman may still flaw his best poems with poeticisms or sentimental coyness – 'some wonder-thing' or other 'wilding things' – but in general he too has found a natural voice. Duncan Campbell Scott's directness, especially in his Indian poems, and Archibald Lampman's detailed, conscientious descriptions of nature, confirm the achievement of this group of poets.

The form of poetry, too, became acclimatized during this period, in Roberts's *Songs of the Common Day* (1893) and

Carman's *Low Tide on Grand Pré* (1893). This is difficult to prove; one must sense it in the example

> There is something in the autumn that is native to my blood,
> Touch of manner, hint of mood;
> And my heart is like a rhyme,
> With the yellow and the purple and the crimson keeping
> time . . .

(Bliss Carman, Songs from Vagabondia, 1894)

The key to these mysteries lies in the marriage of content and form: when we find that the poet's feeling and thought are perfectly expressed in the traditional form he has adopted, we say that he has made it his own. This is clear in Lampman's 'Heat', 'Among the Timothy', 'In October' – truly fine Canadian poems; in Carman's most famous poem, 'Low Tide on Grand Pré', in his 'Vestigia', 'The Eavesdropper', 'Windflower', and other poems. Less so in Roberts's 'Tantramar Revisited', where the hexameters are somewhat too consciously drawn out and smoothed over to express his melancholy, nostalgia, and regret over time and change. (The theme is common to Carman and Roberts at their best.) This generation of poets was, however, trying to domesticate traditional English metres, as they found them in Swinburne, Tennyson, Rossetti, and Arnold, to the Canadian environment. In the 1890s Canada produced four minor romantic poets who laid the groundwork for a native literature by their effective use of literate English in their own Canadian context.

The same pattern can be seen in the fiction, although it was much slower in developing than the poetry. Our early historical novels, in their imitation of Sir Walter Scott and Victor Hugo, are almost absurd in the Canadian context. As late as Mazo de la Roche (1927) the form of the novel was still an artificial import. Leacock's sketches, on the other hand, like much of comic literature, were a breakthrough, by means of parody and amusing innovation, to a freedom of form and attitude.

A cautious propriety in style and form was the bane of

Canadian writing in this late-romantic generation. The transitional period that followed was marked by two notable signs of growth and coming maturity: the spirit of revolt, in the form of parody, iconoclasm, even vulgarity of style; and professionalism, or the capacity to produce popular literary entertainment in substantial quantity. Neither of these features is a proof of lasting literature; both are signs of growth in a culture. They are necessary steps toward adult maturity and independence of mind.

Bliss Carman had already begun turning out a popular strain of poetry with his *Songs of Vagabondia* beginning in 1894. His cousin Charles G. D. Roberts, in the meantime, was catering for the middlebrow with books of popular fiction. Carman produced some threescore volumes of poetry, and Roberts published dozens of titles of popular animal stories in this way. The principle is well described in Roberts's verses explaining why he left Canada:

> Your poet's eyes *must* recognize
>   The side on which your bread is buttered.
>
> You've piped at home, where none could pay,
>   Till now, I trust, your wits are riper,
> Make no delay but come this way,
>   And pipe for them that pay the piper.

In fact, both Roberts and Carman lived most of their adult lives outside of Canada as professional writers, working for a market that was much richer abroad than at home.

In the same way, in the vein of popular literature, L. M. Montgomery wrote *Anne of Green Gables* (1908) and a score of serial books continuing a lucrative stream of fancy. Ralph Connor produced some thirty novels beginning with *Black Rock* in 1898, followed by *The Sky Pilot* the next year, and *The Man From Glengarry* in 1901. Stephen Leacock's numerous books, including the best, *Literary Lapses* (1910), *Sunshine Sketches of a Little Town* (1912), and *Arcadian Adventures With the Idle Rich* (1914), were obviously exploiting a rich vein of popular entertainment literature. Literary values in this kind of writing always tend to become obscured: the pastime pleasures blur the more austere virtues, and critics must remain forever nonplussed. Leacock, however, is still read by hundreds of thousands for the laughter, kindliness, and simple pleasure his books contain. Mazo de la Roche's *Jalna* in 1927 brought to a grand finale this middle-class literature of appeasement. (Her book was in its twenty-eighth printing by 1958, with numerous translations and a circulation in the hundreds of thousands.) The dozen or so Jalna books that followed are of course more of the same profitable ore, like serialized soap-opera (which Jalna very much resembles) or Little Orphan Annie in the comic strips.

Yet it is some achievement to have succeeded with popular literature of this kind in Canada. The style and technique of these writers is professional in its skilful handling of melodrama, humour, pathos, and suspense. The writing is no longer charged with absurd mannerisms and stylistic effusions as were the earlier Canadian novels, William Kirby's *The Golden Dog* (1877) and John Richardson's *Wacousta* (1832). The new popular literature was skilful, unaffected, and capable of genuine effects of evocation and comic catharsis.

In poetry, too, the turgidities of Charles Mair (*Tecumseh*, 1886) and the honest striving of Lampman and D. C. Scott were followed by the very popular books of Robert Service (*Songs of a Sourdough*, 1907, *Ballads of a Cheechako*, 1909) and of William Henry Drummond (*The Habitant, and Other French-Canadian Poems*, 1897). Here a brutal, declarative style, in Service, and a humorous native dialect, in Drummond, combine to break down the proprieties and conventions, and make appeal to a less-demanding, less-pretentious audience. Service hit it right down the line:

> The pallid pimp of the dead-line, the enervate of the pen,
> One by one I weeded them out, for all that I sought was—
> Men.

Service wrote rousing, popular verse. His books sold widely, in England, in the United States, and in Canada. The two

most successful poems, 'The Shooting of Dan McGrew' and
'The Cremation of Sam McGee', are popular favourites still
recited with zest by Service admirers.

But this revolt was also destructive to the old forms of
poetry. The break with traditional formalism is pre-figured
in Tom MacInnes, beginning with *Lonesome Bar* in 1909.
He wrote *ballades, villanelles*, and all the French forms
popular in England about 1900, but with an irreverence that
suggests a disrespect for these pretty arrangements. In a
poem for Walt Whitman he calls for poets 'Resistant, uncon-
forming, singular', who will follow Whitman in literary
iconoclasm. Just so, Robert Service parodies the formal
poetry of Carman in the Prelude to *Rhymes of a Rolling
Stone* (1912):

> I sing no idle songs of dalliance days,
> No dreams Elysian inspire my rhyming;
> I have no Celia to enchant my lays,
> No pipes of Pan have set my heart to chiming.
> I am no wordsmith dripping gems divine
> Into the golden chalice of a sonnet;
> If love songs witch you, close this book of mine,
>   Waste no time on it.

(Bliss Carman's *Pipes of Pan* volumes appeared from 1902 to
1905.) Service, of course, hammers away in the old traditional metrics. But there is a huge difference between
this use of metres, with all its recklessness and verve, and
Carman's and Lampman's careful, formal writing. Where
Lampman could take pride in Roberts's use of the hexameter,
or in 'the elegiac distich of Tibullus and Ovid', Service succeeds as a rough, popular versifier. He is no respecter of
forms, but in fact a barbarian from 'the Wild', who rhymes
merely for gross effect.

William Henry Drummond, using the romantic ballad
for comic purpose, was also damaging the high-serious attitude toward that form which the romantics still observed.
Compare the ballad as written by Carman with one by
Drummond:

> On the long slow heave of a lazy sea,
> To the flap of an idle sail,
> The Nancy's Pride went out on the tide;
> And the skipper stood by the rail . . .
>
>   (Carman, 'The Nancy's Pride')

> On wan dark night on Lac St. Pierre,
>   De win' she blow, blow, blow,
> An' de crew of de wood scow 'Julie Plante'
> Got scar't an' run below—
> For de win' she blow lak hurricane
>   Bimeby she blow some more,
> An' de scow bus' up on Lac St. Pierre
>   Wan arpent from de shore.
>
>   (Drummond, 'The Wreck of the "Julie Plante" ')

The language of Drummond's habitant poems is the language of plain people, but in this case a dialect based on genuine French-Canadian character. True, there was no such dialect in actuality. Drummond created a literary language out of the faulted speech of French Canadians speaking English, yet he made this a vehicle for a most affectionate picture of that people at the turn of the century, and he expressed his own Irish humour and feeling through these poems. At the same time, unawares, he loosened the straitjacket of literary puritanism and made it possible to free language for the expression of real life and human character. The poems of William Henry Drummond are still read and widely admired. And like all the popular writers, including Leacock, he leaves the question pending that Kipling asked in 'The Conundrum of the Workshops': 'It's pretty, but is it Art?'

The abundance of dialect writing in this period really has a two-fold meaning for literature: it is a liberation from the standards of conventional cultivated English (what Lampman once praised in an essay on Roberts as 'a high degree of culture' and a 'scholarly gift of expression'); and it is the liberating self-parody of a pioneer world giving itself the first foretaste of self-confidence and identity, if only in a comic guise. Canadian literature up to about 1920 may be described as 'timorous and humorous'; after this we get boldness, and even brutality–in fact, the more boldness and brutality the more cheers. But this whole process is one of self-assertion and growing self-confidence; and dialect humour, in Haliburton, Drummond, Leacock, and Richler (or in French in Jean Narrache and recently in the writers of 'Joual'), is one of the solvents and catalysts.

In this direction, Canada moved from parody to authentic realism in fiction, first in novels of farm life, then in novels set in the city. We have Robert J. C. Stead's book *Grain* in 1926, documenting life in Manitoba, and Frederick Philip Grove's *Settlers of the Marsh* (1925) and Martha Ostenso's *Wild Geese* (1925), the first examples of prairie realism in Canadian fiction. Later examples are Sinclair Ross's *As For Me And My House* (1941) and W. O. Mitchell's *Who Has Seen the Wind* (1947). All these writers concentrate on small-town or farm life in Canada, characteristically on the limitations and human poverty of the environment; yet they raise their subject matter by their fidelity to truth, and often (as with Grove) achieve a mythical largeness through the sense of tragedy against the great background of open nature.

In the modern stage of Canadian poetry, which may be said to begin with E. J. Pratt (*Newfoundland Verse*, 1923), literary language takes on a hard realistic ring, and comedy acquires a sharp edge. Pratt wields a slapstick vocabulary of assorted learning, of bio-geology, theology, and world geography; he plies an academic wit on moral and human problems; but the language is always downright and direct, hammering away at themes of epic proportion. Pratt is a problem for the critic, of course: his subject is the large mythological-biological drama of life, and his form the long narrative poem in traditional metres. (In this, he is nearer to Masefield and E. A. Robinson than to Eliot and the moderns in twentieth-century poetry.) The metrics and the form of Pratt's poetry are about as anachronistic as his extinct dinosaur Tyrannosauros Rex, but they have been resurrected to take part in a great moral battle of the present: the dilemma of man's savage animal nature pitted against the humanistic demands of Christianity in an age of scepticism and war.

In the modern poets who follow, beginning in the late 1920s, we find a naturalness of style, in the colloquial vein, that parallels the natural speech of T. S. Eliot, the mature Yeats, and W. H. Auden in the 1930s. A. J. M. Smith, whose central aim is aesthetic purity, writes still in a style somewhat stiffened by the consciousness of literary models; but his colleague F. R. Scott scatters his sparks of wit with great conversational verve:

> Note, please, the embryo.
> > Unseeing
> It swims into being.
> *Elan vital,*
> Thyroid, gonads et al.,
> Preserve the unities.
> Though endless opportunities
> Offer, arm joins shoulder.
> Ego forms. It grows bolder,
> Meets fellow anthropoids
> In cell-groups. Avoids
> Behaviour that's odd –
> Like questioning God . . .

In the same way A. M. Klein, Montreal's expressive Jewish poet, lets himself go with great exuberance and euphoric freedom. In Klein, as in Irving Layton a decade later, this freedom with language leads to a certain barbarism of idiom and vocabulary; but the result is in general authentic poetry of a time and place.

But the best example, perhaps, of natural language perfectly adapted to the purposes of poetry, is to be found in the Toronto poet Raymond Souster. Here a perfectly relaxed style of unmarred genuineness reveals a personality and carries a verdict on modern life that will probably remain the best poetic expression of the last quarter-century in Canada:

> . . . scarlet flame of Dosco's
> open hearth behind the jail; stench of coke-ovens;
> poverty naked as the Newfie girl under her cheap dress

that November; smell of fish and ocean
at North Sydney piers; lobster on the half-shell
in Cormier's; the movie where a hundred was a crowd . . .

This is not to say that a highly charged or even esoteric language may not be possible in Canadian poetry—as it obviously is, witness Margaret Avison or James Reaney—but that the language of common speech is the modern touchstone, and in Canada it amounts to an assimilation of poetry to local reality.

In prose, a parallel success in developing an adequate language of fiction may be seen in the novels of Morley Callaghan and Hugh MacLennan. Callaghan has been accused of looseness and carelessness, but his main virtue as a writer is in the flow and the energy of his spontaneous style. Unlike Hemingway, to whom he has often been compared, he is not laconic and stoical, but emotive and compassionate, nearer to D. H. Lawrence than to any other modern writer in English. In contrast, Hugh MacLennan is graceful and supremely rational, clear and direct as Henry Fielding, yet at the same time at ease in his time and place, and as much a representative Canadian as Lester Pearson or René Lévesque. In these two writers Canadian prose has found an authentic style, on native grounds, that equals that of the poetry, and leaves the field well prepared for the literature to come.

The experimental leanings of modern poetry may be seen on a close examination of F. R. Scott, A. J. M. Smith, A. M. Klein, and Earle Birney, our poets of the 1930s and 1940s. Smith displays short Imagist poems of the classical Greek variety, *vers libre*, and Eliotic mixtures of tone and imagery, as well as exotic experiments with language and arrangement. The same features appear in F. R. Scott with somewhat less artifice; but here, too, the extreme of experiment is a patterned arrangement or rational structure into which the poem is fitted. Both poets, however, are concerned with liberating the form of poetry from traditional prescriptions.
   A. M. Klein is equally enterprising, even to the point of

making language experiments; as also is Earle Birney in the far west of Canada. Klein is sentimental, nostalgic, and exuberant, so that his experiments are vitalized by feeling; yet the most daring experiments fail here too, because in this case the mannerism is imposed upon the material:

> O city metropole, isle riverain!
> Your ancient pavages and sainted routs
> Traverse my spirit's conjured avenues!
> Splendor erablic of your promenades
> Foliates there . . .

The same may be said of Birney's 'Anglosaxon Street' and 'Mappemounde', both in the linguistic exotic vein. Later in Birney's development, actual typographic experiments appear that are far more successful. In fact they are technically the most interesting poems written in Canada in this century.

Experiment, of course, in a tradition-bound country like ours, is an attempt to break out of the routine and the mechanical; it is often only the beginning of a search for the creative principle of form. Once experiment has been attempted, we can go on to more integral and organic forms of poetry, new forms that emerge out of the demands of the materials and are therefore the only adequate ones for the poem in question. Now the language and the subject matter of imagination can combine in the shaping of a poem as an organic improvisation, to be perfected and completed as a memorable verbal unit. We have this kind of poetry in Raymond Souster, in a number of poems by Irving Layton, in James Reaney's first book, *The Red Heart*, in Alfred Purdy, in Alden Nowlan, and in several of the younger poets now writing in Vancouver, in Toronto, and in Montreal – John Newlove, George Bowering, Frank Davey, Harry Howith, Michael Gnarowski, and others. Out of these the next few permanent names will emerge. There is a prolific outpouring of new poetry in Canada at present: from a modest beginning in the late 1920s, the modern movement grew to a compact group of poets in the 1940s, with magazines

in Montreal, Vancouver, and Toronto; and it has further
expanded since into a widespread interest and activity
among young people in every part of Canada.

The experimental novel has not yet appeared, however; in
the main the traditional lines of the realistic novel are still
being explored. But there are some interesting examples of
new technique in fiction among the young writers. Sheila
Watson's *The Hook* and Leonard Cohen's two recent novels
are suggestive departures. The caricaturist techniques of
Mordecai Richler are also waywardly inventive.

Urban realism, large moral issues, and political awareness
have appeared only recently in Canadian fiction. First, in
the 1930s novels of Morley Callaghan and in the novels of
Hugh MacLennan, then with extraordinary abundance in
a number of brilliant writers: Robertson Davies (whose
setting is Kingston, Ontario), Brian Moore (a newcomer
from Ireland), Colin McDougall (*Execution*, 1958), Herbert
Steinhouse (*Ten Years After*, 1958), Mordecai Richler,
Ethel Wilson (the Jane Austen of British Columbia–*Swamp
Angel*, 1962), Earle Birney (who has written two novels),
John Buell (*The Pyx*, 1959), Adele Wiseman (*The Sacrifice*,
1956), and Jack Ludwig (*Confusions*, 1965). A good number
of the new writers are dedicated to the task of stirring Canadians out of their complacency–a program that may even
become a bit of a bore–but they have written some very
lively books, holding up a mirror to the tragedy and comedy
of local human frailty.

Among these new writers, Mordecai Richler, Robertson
Davies, and Brian Moore especially present attractive facets
of the new Canada. In Richler the vulgarities of urban life
and speech are parodied and caricatured without stint or
mercy in a style of inexhaustible comic catharsis. His work
presents many fascinating themes, in its subject matter,
style, and narrative pace; but perhaps its most revealing
aspect is the radical break with his own Jewish culture that
he portrays. In this, Richler has moved from a certain provincialism of viewpoint, such as we find, for example, even

in A. M. Klein, toward a ruthlessly awakened vision and a world perspective. His Montreal novels, *Son of a Smaller Hero* (1955) and *The Apprenticeship of Duddy Kravitz* (1959), are essential counterparts of his European novels with their larger political themes, *The Acrobats* (1954) and *A Choice of Enemies* (1957).

Robertson Davies's light satirical novels set in the fictitious town of Salterton (a comic mirror-image of Kingston) have a similar relation to the staid conventions and rigidities of English Canada. His *Diary of Samuel Marchbanks*, with its sequel, reveals an erudite wit and satirical humour which, like all satire, may harbour a secret affinity with the very foibles it castigates. The novels, *Tempest-Tost* (1951), *Leaven of Malice* (1954), and *A Mixture of Frailties* (1958), entertain brilliantly with a galaxy of toy-box characters drawn from Canadian life, acting in situations that bring out their best points of innocent absurdity. Robertson Davies would free us from parochialism, from old tics and hardened habits; he is a learned and highly entertaining caricaturist who raises the level of intelligence without yet releasing any fearful genii of chaos or creativity.

Brian Moore, an Irish writer from Belfast, settled in Canada for a while; like Malcolm Lowry, who lived and wrote here for some fifteen years, he will probably be a 'Canadian writer' until international fame takes him entirely out of our domain. One senses from every page of his writing that this is Irish brogue ('Coffey had to cut his entertaining to a duck egg for lack of spondulicks') not the plainsong of common Canadian. But *The Luck of Ginger Coffey* (1960) is set in Montreal and develops the significant theme of a New Canadian responding to the new life, so that it bears strongly on Canadian literature.

Ginger Coffey's response to Canada moves from blanket clichés of rejection, through personal setbacks, to a partial rediscovery of the possibilities of love and a new life. From 'Canadians were terribly slabbery . . .', 'Everybody bullshits out here . . .', 'this gassy Canuck beer . . .', 'Money is the Canadian way to immortality . . .' and 'Just a poor clutch

of Arctic-bound sods . . .', he moves through mortification
and degradation to the significant question: 'What did it
matter? . . . And in that moment he knew that, sink or swim,
Canada was home now, for better or for worse, for richer or
for poorer, until death.' The parable of Ginger Coffey is that
of many New Canadians who must suffer and bend their
spirit in a new country: 'Wasn't he, too, a man who would
always be a stranger here, never at home in this land where
he had not grown up. Yes: he too.' This is the difficult
reversal, where Canada now—such as it is—has its own character and alien identity, which the stranger must learn to
adopt and accept.

So the movement of Canadian literature has traced a line
from vague echoes of England—the horns of elfland—in the
earliest literature, through the romantic idea of nature con-
veyed in terms of Canadian landscape in the nature poets,
to sentimental humanism, and finally urban realism and
actuality. The recent urban fiction is still limited by a
typically Canadian self-disparaging strain of satire, a feature
we also find in the poetry, so that our writers have not yet
opened their art to universal human issues. But this is clearly
the hope for the poetry and prose of the future.

No doubt this is one possible meaning in the so-called
'archetypal' school of criticism and poetry in vogue at present, a trend that has been much stimulated by the writings
of Northrop Frye in Toronto. Professor Frye has had a
marked influence on Canadian poetry and prose, and his
reputation is of world scope, so that his work adds a new
dimension to Canadian writing. The archetypal theory, a
branch of modern criticism he has developed further than
any other critic, raises the concrete to the mythical and
universal. In its marriage with native realism, as we find in the
poetry of James Reaney and Eli Mandel, it clearly enlarges
the Canadian perspective.

Canadian scholarship, indeed, presents a special branch
of literary activity which has followed the general pattern of
our growth and development. From such early eccentric

discourses as those of Archdeacon W. T. Leach in the middle of the last century (*On the Nature and Duties of the Military Profession* and *On the Hypothesis of the former existence of a great Fresh Water Inland Sea within the Continent of America*) we have moved to solid examples of formal scholarship at the turn of the century, such as James Cappon's *Roberts and the Influences of His Time* (1905), and then to profound original achievement, in the work of Gilbert Norwood (*Greek Tragedy*, 1920), Pelham Edgar (*Henry James*, 1927), A. S. P. Woodhouse (*Puritanism and Liberty*, 1938), and more recently Barker Fairley (*Study of Goethe*, 1947) and Northrop Frye (*Fearful Symmetry*, 1947).

More clearly the level of important scholarship is marked by the appearance of impressive historians of Canada, critics and bibliographers of Canadian literature, and writers on Canadian social and economic problems. This may seem provincial, but it is in fact more realistically cosmopolitan than the study of antiquities alone would be. Writers like H. A. Innis, Frank Underhill, Donald Creighton, J. B. Brebner, J. M. S. Careless, A. R. M. Lower, and (on a more popular plane) Bruce Hutchison, Thomas Raddall, and Thomas B. Costain, are clearly the measure of maturity in native scholarship, writing on Canada with an authority to equal the works on European literature, world history and politics, philosophy and art.

In the larger fields of literature, Canada has produced such impressive world scholars as Northrop Frye, George Woodcock, Watson Kirkconnell, Malcolm Ross, Kathleen Coburn, George Whalley, Hugh Kenner, Charles Cochrane, G. G. Sedgewick; as well as Karl Stern, Hans Selye, N. J. Berrill, and Marshall McLuhan, in various scientific and special areas of knowledge. These clearly relate to the important work in Canadian literature that has been done in recent years by A. J. M. Smith, E. K. Brown, W. E. Collin, Desmond Pacey, Carl F. Klinck, R. E. Watters, Roy Daniells, and others. Indeed Canadian scholarship has reached a very high development, corresponding directly to the growth of Canadian society.

To those who know and read the work of the Canadian past and present, it is clear that we have produced a large and fascinating body of literature. We have grown from pioneer conditions, where mere survival, the struggle to till the soil and to weather the seasons, have occupied us for many generations. With the coming of prosperous society and the rise of cities, we succeeded at the turn of the century in producing books that many could read with pleasure, books that were read widely in Canada and abroad, and are still read. In terms of Canadian society, this was a happy moment of fulfilment. The gentility of the romantic poets, the humane conservatism of Stephen Leacock, the fictitious manorial life depicted by Mazo de la Roche, the convivial civilized humour of Drummond and Pratt, all these mark a period of cultural ascendance for English life in Canada. The characteristic culture of Victoria, British Columbia, or of Toronto before the Second World War, provided the ideal social background for this literature of congenial warmth and gentility.

What has happened since, and is happening now, is in effect a social change that is inevitably reflected in literature. The ruling order has been shaken by the resurgence of a maturing French culture and by the emergence of other ethnic groups who have brought a new vitality and colour to Canadian life and Canadian writing. The former middle-class hegemony has been shaken from within by an upsurge of energy from the redbrick strata, in Canada as well as in England. This is a social change of great consequence. It has acted mainly as a revolt against gentility – as it did somewhat earlier in America – but this promises a much deeper positive change in the spirit of life and literature. In the end, let us hope, it will result in a higher type of creative impulse, more rousing energy, and a more genuine sense of art and form. Canada may or may not be a melting-pot, but it is in fact a parti-coloured country. And the future of Canadian literature lies in the direction of many-sided freedom of development and of large human awareness, not in any narrow view of national identity. It is in this direction that our literature has been moving for the first hundred years of its history.

24. Literature
in French

JEAN BASILE

A curious country. Because of
its geographical situation, its political context, and its ethnic
origins, the combination of influences acting upon French
Canada was such as to give it every opportunity of producing
its own distinctive literature. To the west was English Canada, which was preoccupied with the culture of the continent; to the south the United States, which, while still
attuned to the European scene, was a melting-pot for twenty
different cultures; and, to the east, France, with its most
natural of influences, that of kinship and language. But from
the beginning French Canada had been cut off from France.
Its future – indeed its very existence – was to depend to a far
greater extent on its desire to survive and on its political
development than on literature. As it happened, the three-

fold pressure from which could have emerged a new culture
served only to work against it: such is the usual state of language minorities.

In 1884, two years after the appearance of the poetical
works of Octave Crémazie, the year of the publication of
Laure Conan's excellent *Angéline de Montbrun*, which was
the first French-Canadian psychological novel, Crémazie's
favourite correspondent, the abbé Casgrain, was to declare:
'French-Canadian literature is an accomplished fact.' This
judgement he based upon the work of four precursors: François-Xavier Garneau's *Histoire du Canada* (1836), the poetry
of Crémazie, Philippe Aubert de Gaspé's *Les Anciens Canadiens* (1853), and, finally, his own work as Quebec's first
literary critic.

Before this: nothing, or almost nothing. It was in 1820
that Michel Bibaud founded the first French-Canadian
literary magazine, and two years later that he published the
first two anthologies of the poetry of Quebec: a few accounts
of travellers—whether French or French-Canadian no one
knows—among these sixty thousand peasants who were cut
off from home for half a century, from 1763 until 1815. This
event is a most important one, for it crystallized a dream:
that of remaining French. The first to remember the dream
and attempt to make it come true were the men of letters.

French-Canadian literature *is* an accomplished fact.

Following the example of Michelet, François-Xavier Garneau, 'in his reassessment of Quebec's historical development, placed his focus upon the great family of the People in
order to refute the contempt of the British for a nation they
considered devoid of either history or literature'. Crémazie,
from exile in France where he spent his last days, sang of his
country in a rather ostentatious way and with a rhetoric
which is entirely that of the Empire. More acceptable on a
literary level, the work of de Gaspé managed to retain its
local charm without deserving the pejorative label of 'merely
regional'. If one work must be singled out as authentically
French-Canadian, it is *Les Anciens Canadiens*. In this it was
to remain unique for many years.

Despite the publication in 1865 of Pamphile Lemay's *Essais poétiques*, nothing had really been achieved by 1867; there was still everything to be done if French literature was to survive in North America, for it seemed doomed at that moment to lose itself in oblivion or suffocate in the English clutch.

Twenty years later, the sonnet had become the dominant form. In 1887, Louis Fréchette published *La Légende des peuples*, a work where the influence of Hugo is strongly marked and which was itself unsuccessfully imitated by William Chapman in *Les Feuilles d'érable* (1890). Pamphile Lemay continued to sing of the peasant's rustic customs, as did Alfred Garneau in 'La Tristesse des lieux' and 'L'heure exquise', poems that were not published in collected form until 1906. *Les Floraisons matinales* of Nérée Beauchemin appeared in 1897. Intimate in mood, his poems may have glorified the delights of attachment to the soil: at any rate they opened the way for an entirely new group of poets who enlisted at the very beginning of the twentieth century in the struggle against 'decadence'.

As for prose: with the exception of Laure Conan—a genuine writer who, probably unconsciously, sketched a cruel and moving picture of Quebec in her own days in *Angéline de Montbrun*—and Pamphile Lemay (*Contes vrais*, 1899), it could be said to have been slumbering. We find from the very beginning of French-Canadian literature this neglect of prose in favour of poetry: a serious indication of either the lack of creative imagination or the uncompromising Puritanism which, as in Geneva, killed the theatre. Very likely both.

For fresh inspiration, we must look to the work of a journalist, Arthur Buies, an unconventional character who in 1868 founded a newspaper that was to run for less than a year, and wrote in it columns of irrepressible satiric wit before turning to geography and publishing *Le Saguenay et la vallée du St-Laurent* (1880). In the period of literary dullness at the end of the nineteenth century he stands out as a brilliant exception because of his unceasing assertion of principle, his energy, and his non-conformist sincerity.

It was not, in fact, until Jean Charbonneau founded the 'Montreal Literary School' in 1895 that a true literary movement emerged such as had not really coalesced even around the writers who had previously grouped themselves under the name 'The School of Quebec'. More of a gathering than a coterie, the Montreal School had no well-defined program. It was at once Romantic and Parnassian, symbolist, even neo-classical. All the French influences and fashions of the day co-existed in it without harm to each other. Poetry first, and then prose, gave it an impetus that was to continue until our own times. Within its tolerant atmosphere, a paralysed and bed-ridden Albert Lozeau could produce emotional poetry in *L'Ame solitaire* (1907), *Le Miroir des jours* (1912), *Lauriers et feuilles d'érables* (1916); Charles Gil could write lyrically; Albert Dreux could experiment quite skilfully with the free-verse form. To our modern eyes, however, it is Louis Dantin who appears to have been, if not the greatest, at least the most unusual person in the School. An unfrocked priest, he lived as an exile in the United States where he wrote a considerable body of novels, poetry, and criticism. Obsessed by religious problems, he wrote poetry of very high quality which was collected in two volumes, *Le Coffret de Crusoë* (1932) and *Poèmes d'outre-tombe* (1962). His critical approach was international in nature, and his work as a critic remains outstanding, perhaps the best in French Canada. A good deal of research into his life and work is at present in progress.

A touching detail entirely to Dantin's credit is that this exceptional man fostered the literary birth of another poet, Emile Nelligan, whose work he collected, prefaced, and published in 1903. In Nelligan we recognize a true poet, certainly the greatest of his time. His work, conceived within the three-year span from 1896 to 1899, is a brilliant cry springing from universal sources. It modernized French-Canadian poetry through its successful fusion of purely humanistic aspirations and hitherto unformulated but unchanging French-Canadian characteristics.

Ah! comme la neige a neigé!
Ma vitre est un jardin de givre.
Ah! comme la neige a neigé!
Qu'est-ce que le spasme de vivre
À tout l'ennui que j'ai, que j'ai!

His appearance on the French-Canadian literary scene was
that of a fallen angel. In 1941 he died of the madness which
he seems to have sensed approaching, and which had indeed
manifested itself as early as 1899. His thought was 'couleur
de lunes d'or lointaines'—colour of distant golden moons.
Emile Nelligan represents the first turning-point of a new
poetic sensibility.

Not all the poets belonged to the Montreal School: some,
more independent, preferred to work alone. Of these, René
Chopin revealed a good mastery of his verse form in *Le
Coeur en exil* (1913) and *Dominantes* (1933). But he was
less inspired than Paul Morin, who definitely made his mark
on the history of French-Canadian literature. Neo-classical
in spirit, Morin's work extends over three volumes—*Le Paon
d'émail* (1911), *Poèmes de cendre et d'or*, *Géronte et son
miroir* (1960)—each one exemplary in its technical virtuosity;
but the tone of his poems, while always remaining pure,
seems nowadays outdated.

Other poets, followers of Nérée Beauchemin rather than
Crémazie or Fréchette, condemned both the intricate rhyme-
schemes of the latter and the 'decadence' of the former to
advocate a more direct kind of poetry. In 1931 Robert
Choquette published *Metropolitan Museum*, a historical
meditation of high artistic merit in which the poet portrays
his desire to live as a young American but one who writes
in French—and he was the first perhaps to write French in
such a determined and lucid manner. Previously Alfred
Desrochers had published *À l'ombre d'Orford* (1920), which
is remarkable for its hearty, virile sense of communion with
the land of Quebec.

The novel meanwhile continued to languish under an
apparently unshakable curse. The year 1914 did, however,
mark the appearance of Louis Hémon's *Maria Chapdelaine*,

a novel that came from France but seemed to capture intimately the inner reality of French-Canadian life. Four years later, Albert Laberge – like Arthur Buies a quite exceptional person – published *La Scouine*; but the sixty copies of this novel, having stirred up a few private eddies of interest, went largely unnoticed. On the other hand, the publication in 1934 of the violent satire *Les Demi-Civilisés* by Jean-Charles Harvey created a scandal, even though the author's aim had been merely to combat in the French-Canadian novel its tendency to moralize and to preach nationalism. For the French-Canadian novel did exist, if only in the didactic novels of Lionel Groulx: *Rapaillage* (1916), *Chez nos gens* (1920), and especially *L'Appel de la race* (1922). In these Groulx adapted his gifts as a historian to the style of the French-Canadian 'conteur' or story-steller. *Au Cap Blomidon* and *L'Appel de la race acadienne* are two of his poorer novels and contributed less to French Canada than his historical work and his nationalist theories: for it was mainly through these that he acquired in the thirties his incomparable reputation and the sway he held over an entire generation of thinkers. A body of over thirty books ensured the dominance of this historian, whose theories on the individuality of the French-Canadian nation seem to us nowadays still quite moving, if rather out of date.

The years between the wars, however, saw a consolidation in the position of the novel. Three works published in rapid succession by very different men broadened a tradition that had derived mainly from *Maria Chapdelaine* and rapidly made up the missing ground so that the novel could also become resolutely modern.

The philosophy of *Menaud maître-draveur* by Félix-Antoine Savard (1937) still leans heavily on *Maria Chapdelaine*; but the novel is distinctly original in style and treatment, and it embodies what is perhaps the first successful use of a prose language that is neither bastard nor pure French, but truly Canadian. In *L'Abatis*, Savard undertook to write a poetic narrative in a flexible form and this also marked another step forward.

Léo-Paul Desrosiers's *Les Engagés du grand portage* (1938) is the climax of an unremarkable life's work. But what a climax it is! Desrosiers's style, no less than the story itself, explodes with a primitive force unparalleled in French-Canadian literature.

And lastly, the richest of these novels— *Trente Arpents* by Ringuet (1938), which without a doubt marks the end of the generation of writers who attempted to give literary substance to the rustic novel. In its description of the nobility and the decadence of a dynasty wedded to the soil, it sums up and defines a French-Canadian archetype in such a way as to defend it from further scorn. Ringuet is probably the last of his line: he is no less important for that. If the French-Canadian novel can also record a turning-point in sensibility, then *Trente Arpents* stands at the very point of change.

This would have been the appropriate moment for l'Abbé Casgrain's historic phrase—which came, after all, only a century too soon. Poetry was at this point firmly established and forward-looking. The novel had regained a tone it had not possessed since *Les Anciens Canadiens*. Criticism had two great exponents in Camille Roy, who was closer to Brunetière than to Ste-Beuve and who exerted a considerable influence on the students at Laval, and Louis Dantin, whose tragedy it was to have to deal most of the time with authors of lesser talent than his own.

There can be no doubt that the rise of the new consciousness transcended literature: it was visible in all other fields of endeavour. The masterpieces of the essay form had not yet been produced, but a tradition of historical discipline had been fostered, diversified, and developed by Lionel Groulx, and by Thomas Chapais, whose courses on the history of Canada were published gradually from 1919 to 1934. Nor must another source be forgotten: that of journalism, which has not yet been properly assessed, even though this so-called 'inferior' form was eminently suited to a country whose existence had from its inception been a perpetual struggle.

The scene was now set for the third literary resurgence

which was to confirm the progress of French-Canadian literature towards its greatest truth and originality. Poetry, the
true native genius, came to be dominated by four writers
who eclipsed all their forerunners except Nelligan. At this
point, the general practice of using French authors as standards of reference became no longer necessary. The new
French-Canadian poetry was able to stand on its own, assert
its personality, and consolidate its indigenous quality and its
strength.

Akin to Rimbaud in the brevity of his work and life (but
not in other ways), Saint-Denys Garneau can claim a place
in the foremost ranks of contemporary French-Canadian
poetry on the strength of his two books, written in 1935 and
1938: *Regards et jeux dans l'espace* and *Solitudes*. His
poetry, in which an atmosphere of sadness and of an all but
accepted solitude is deepened by tragic premonitions of
approaching death, becomes an almost spiritual experience.
It is a token of his exceptional sensitivity and expresses itself
in a fluid form with a very distinctive inspiration. Having
declared 'Do not disturb me, I am profoundly occupied,'
this French-Canadian *enfant du siècle* was to die while still
in his thirties, leaving behind him a life's work the full scope
and importance of which has not yet been determined, but
which is being studied and analysed by a host of research
workers.

More mature in form but less directly moving, the poetry
of Alain Grandbois appeared slowly over a span of years.
Republished in one volume in 1963 by Les Editions de
l'Hexagone, the poems in his three books (*Les Iles de la nuit*,
1944, *Rivage de l'homme*, 1948, *L'Etoile pourpre*, 1957)
represent what is no doubt the most considered and the surest
body of work in the poetry of Quebec. His poetry too is
informed by the theme of death – and anguish – but this is
tempered by the unceasing quest for love and happiness of
a man who is consciously enriching his old age.

Rina Lasnier is still producing impressive poetry of perfect aesthetic unity. In both *Les Madones canadiennes* (1944)
and *Le Chant de la montée* (1947), she reveals her unrivalled

skill in the use of imagery that is never inorganic to the poems. Highly accomplished on a technical level, she writes love poetry which expresses accurately the sensuality of a love that shades into mysticism.

As early as 1942, Anne Hébert, the fourth member of this brilliant group, established her poetic reputation in *Les Songes en équilibre*. But her second volume of poems, *Le Tombeau de rois* (1953), followed by *Poèmes* (1960), brought confirmation of her autonomy and her desire to explore the beauty of renunciation through imagery that is sometimes mysterious, sometimes pregnant with reality.

These four leaders, who represent a poetical theory deriving in an increasingly direct way from their native Quebec, who create through detail an archetypal whole, and who are moved rather than influenced by French experience, reveal very often a lyrical power that is fundamentally North American. This can also be said of Gilles Hénault, whose budding poetical work is a lyrical revolt full of curses and cries (*Voyages au pays de Mémoire*, 1960, *Sémaphore*, 1962); of Gatien Lapointe, who in *Ode au St-Laurent* (1963) combines pure lyricism with a rather down-to-earth awareness of his kinship with the land; and, indeed, of all the poets in the 'Hexagone' group to which Gastron Miron, himself a poet of rare achievement, lends his unwearying support. Amongst these poets still in the middle of their literary careers can be distinguished Roland Giguère, whose work is idyllic in mood, Fernand Ouellette, brilliant and dream-like, Pierre Trottier, who, in his treatment of the same theme of death, is the only one to make successful use of imagery that is mischievous or darkly ironical, and a few others as well. Rather off the beaten track, the poetry of Jean-Guy Pilon is often opulent and wide in scope; it embodies the poet's struggle to reconcile human hope and inescapable destiny. Pilon already has to his credit five volumes of poetry that is rich in its all-pervasive music: *La Fiancée du matin* (1953), *Les Cloîtres de l'été* (1955), *L'Homme et le jour* (1957), *La Mouette et le large* (1960), *Pour saluer une ville* (1963).

This sense of kinship with North America allied to a traditionally French sensibility has perhaps been represented best by an essayist and literary critic, Jean Le Moyne. A profoundly religious thinker in contact with the most progressive sources of modern Catholicism, imbued with French culture yet receptive to American literature and modes of thought, Le Moyne successfully portrays, in a series of critical studies and particularly in one on the Canadian woman, one of the first truly modern profiles of the French Canadian. In a lighter mood of reminiscence or reflection, Pierre Trottier draws another such profile, which confronts the French Canadian with Racine as well as with Lawrence Durrell (*Mon Babel*, 1963). Father Ernest Gagnon in *L'Homme d'ici*, attempts on the level of the essay form to renew the fundamentally religious concept of a nation under stress. A more modest approach is that of Jean Simard, who, in two *Répertoires*, deals in an absolutely simple way with everyday things and, rather like the French moralists, undertakes to describe rather than analyse the present situation. This is the sage who is never given to very exalted flights, but whose prose is full of good nature and charm and, although it may occasionally slip into indulgence, always remains elegant and clear.

Resolutely unconventional, Paul Toupin in *Souvenirs pour demain* (1960) attempts to force French-Canadian literature into the mould of the literary confession. A critic of society, whose false values he rejects because he finds them incompatible with the quest for personal fulfilment, he is, on the basis of his three plays, *Brutus* (1950), *Le Mensonge* (1952), and *Chacun son amour* (1955), one of the founders of French-Canadian drama—a genre which in the previous hundred years had managed to produce nothing but minor works. The single exception is *Tit-Coq* by Gratien Gélinas (1948). This play, of uneven achievement but of strong appeal for the public, marked a collective movement that is likely to rekindle the interest of the public in the kind of French-Canadian theatre that provides it with what it most desires, a picture of itself. Marcel Dubé is undoubtedly the

most gifted of the French-Canadian playwrights. Four plays
have more than proved his generosity and strength of expression. And yet in none of these plays (*Zone*, 1953, *Le
Temps des lilas*, 1958, *Un simple soldat*, *1958*, *Florence*,
1960), nor even in his latest play, *Les Beaux Dimanches*
(1965), has he produced an outstanding work of the first
order, for they are all of them spoilt by awkward or tedious
scenes that emphasize rather than conceal an almost completely morbid vision of the world, recalling in this one
point the theatre of Tennessee Williams. In *Le Gibet* (1960),
and *Les Violons d'automne* (1962), Jacques Languirand
attempts, perhaps rather artificially, to use a more modern
symbolism, but he does not succeed in making it his own.
His latest play, *Klondyke* (1965), takes up in the manner of
a Brecht play the strands of a Canadian epic – the gold rush –
but under this false pretence expresses mere banalities. In
Françoise Loranger's *Une Maison un jour* (1965), a new
voice is heard, melancholy and very Chekhovian, still clumsy,
but distinctive in tone.

While poetry was engaged in a search for a rigorously French-
Canadian style, supported in this by a few precursors and by
critics whose primary aim was no longer systematic comparison, the novel at about the same time in the fifties was
also undergoing an upheaval. Did the resounding success of
Bonheur d'occasion represent the appearance of a literary
audience that had at last become firmly established? Perhaps. In any case this novel, published in 1945, is certainly
superior to all other French-Canadian novels in its delicacy,
its strength of treatment, its brilliance and beauty. No doubt
Gabrielle Roy's talent had the advantage of appearing at the
ripe moment. But it is likely that the novel's strength was
such that it would have imposed itself in any circumstance,
as *Maria Chapdelaine* had done thirty years before. From
then on, the progress of the French-Canadian novel can
almost be charted by the appearance of this one novelist's
books: in 1950, *La Petite Poule d'eau*, which represents
more than just another stage; in 1954, *Alexandre Chênevert*,

which, while more accomplished in form than *Bonheur d'occasion*, has lost the earlier novel's touching ambivalence; in 1955, *Rue Deschambeault*, where the more introspective style is a new breakthrough. Finally, back in Quebec after her stay in France, Gabrielle Roy published *La Montagne secrète* (1961), a strange book in which a confession seems to emerge only to be re-absorbed into the pattern of the novel.

There are no other comparable novelists: not Germaine Guèvremont, despite her *Marie-Didace* (1947); nor André Langevin, who, after writing *Poussière sur la ville* (1953) and *Le Temps des hommes* (1956), stopped abruptly on a road that had promised to be long and fruitful, as though these two works had exhausted within him all possibility of renewal; nor André Giroux, who is able to create characters and construct plots but whose work fades away after *Au-delà des visages* (1948) and *Les Gouffres a toujours soif* (1953). Yves Thériault is the only one to achieve a peak in French-Canadian literature with his novel about Eskimo life, *Agaguk* (1958). An extremely gifted writer with a sure and generous feeling for language, but uneven in his inspiration, he introduces into his numerous works—only a few of which, however, deserve to be remembered—a direct, healthy, but rather conventional eroticism which tends at weaker moments to become something of a set formula.

The work of Claire Martin, after Gabrielle Roy the most gifted of the French-Canadian woman novelists, is sometimes rather shaky in form; but its aim is to seize upon a new aspect of the reality of French-Canadian womanhood, no longer from the exterior but through a fundamental commitment of the writer (*Quand j'aurai payé ton visage*, 1962, *Avec ou sans amour*, 1958, *Doux-amer*, 1960). Jacques Ferron, in *Contes pour un pays incertain* (1962), introduces sophisticated satire and handles folklore and paradox with consummate skill; his distinguished arrogance has rallied many young authors around him. Jacques Godbout is at the beginning of a body of work which is quite unconventional, and resolutely international in interest. In poetry, Paul Chamberland, a writer who is patriotic without being domi- nated by Hugo, revitalizes his genre through his fine freedom and pure sense of poetry, in *Terre-Québec* (1964) and *L'Affi- cheur hurle* (1965). Finally, Marie-Claire Blais, in each suc- cessive novel, has asserted herself as a prototype of Nordic sensibility, quite distinctly French-Canadian even in the company of Chekhov, O'Neill, and Colette; in work that is allusive and of an almost sadistic simplicity, she successfully creates a lunar world with all the ambiguity of the classics, which can impose their painful presence while belonging to all time.

The central dilemma of French-Canadian literature, for many reasons, is the problem of language—a problem that constantly threatens to stifle it and yet gives it at once its strengths and its weaknesses. Crémazie had discussed the question with Casgrain in a letter that appropriately enough quotes from a lecture given by David H. Wayne in the Uni- versity of Montreal. Quebec, theoretically a province with only one language, is the unfortunate possessor of a double language, the demotic and the learned (if such a title can be given to international French). The conflict created in the writer by this dilemma is easy to imagine. It is a dilemma that each generation, right down to our own time, has in some way or other tried to resolve.

As early as 1918, Marcel Dugas, speaking for the Montreal School, stated: 'The French language exists; the Canadian does not.' To this, Henry Bernard, a critic of the period, replied: 'The French language used by everyone else is not the one we French Canadians use.' The linguistically inter- national speech of Paul Morin and René Chopin offers a sharp contrast to the Canadianism of poets such as Alfred Desrochers and Robert Choquette. From language it is but a step to theory, and to the kind of profession of faith made by Claude-Henri Grignon who, while claiming that only the

demotic Canadian can be of interest to the world, takes care
to print the Canadian expressions he uses for that purpose
in italics!

Language, unfortunately, is not the exclusive property of
literature. This may be a cliché nowadays: it was perhaps
not quite such a cliché for the writer twenty years ago.

It was not until the recent waves of revolt against the
English elements in Canada, and the parallel revolts against
the 'bourgeois' aspects of life in Quebec, that the problem
was confronted in its totality by a small group of very young
writers publishing in the extremist review *Parti pris*. Their
works, written in Montreal slang, adopted a temporary position for a direct Canadian language as the only one capable
of liberating the creative imagination that is indispensable
for any form of committed art. A young critic called Gérald
Godin has perhaps best summed up that movement by saying: 'French is an ideal for the future – slang is the present,
without losing sight of the future.' In practice the few
attempts that have been made, for example by the two
budding writers Jacques Renaud in *Le Cassé* (1965) and
André Major in *Le Cabochon* (1965), although they did
arouse some degree of interested curiosity, did not carry the
approval of the public, which interpreted them as retrograde
rather than progressive steps in French-Canadian literature.
The statements of Paul Chamberland, who belongs to the
same group, are more ambiguous. Like Grignon, he declares
that he writes well when he writes badly. Claude Jasmin,
who is only too willing to play the role of the *enfant du siècle*,
has a more independent, less sectarian manner; it is nevertheless similar in that it creates a kind of bastard but effective
style, racy and vivid, which is thought to be American but is
really nothing at all – as in *La Corde au cou* (1961), *Délivrez-
nous du mal* (1961), *Ethel et le terroriste* (1964), and *Pleure
pas Germaine* (1965). His world is not without interest; but
the incoherence of his form restricts him within a narrow
compass from which it is difficult to see him ever breaking out.

Yves Berger, a French writer and publisher who is particularly well informed about French-Canadian literature,
recently said: 'It seems to me that we are presently witnessing
the re-birth – perhaps indeed the birth – of French-Canadian
literature.' It has required four precursors, political and
social events, polemicists, historians, critics, twenty different
individuals, and a strong dose of faith and courage to arrive
at this result.

Whereas the abbé Casgrain, anticipating the new school
of French-Canadian critics in his optimistic and patriotic
declaration, could state that 'French-Canadian literature is
an accomplished fact', Gilles Marcotte was much more
cautious when he entitled his essay on literature in Quebec
'Une Littérature qui se fait' ('A literature in the making')
published in 1962. A hundred and twenty years were needed
to produce that change. In fact, the contradiction is only an
apparent one: French-Canadian literature does exist as a list
of names – and yet, can one really deny, in the light of the
uninterrupted literary production of the last hundred years,
that an instrument of thought is still indeed in the making?
A hundred years is not a very long time to establish a tradition. It will be necessary to repeat that truism for some time
yet, even though we hasten to add that writers such as Nelligan, Saint-Denys Garneau, Gabrielle Roy, Jean Le Moyne,
and the others certainly deserve the recognition they aspired
to in the literary world. Nevertheless the question remains
whether their work – even when it has established precedents,
or created an internal impetus the repercussions of which
may just now be beginning to appear – can be said to have
given rise to a truly literary phenomenon, and to have set
down lines of thought for the guidance of an entire nation.
We read and admire this or that poet or novelist; it even
happens that we discover some further resonance in his
work. But unquestionably we still turn for our real suste-
nance to Camus, Mauriac, Bernanos, or Gide. Is this the
result of a puritanical atmosphere that does nothing to encourage, or even reacts against, exploration of the unknown
paths of the future? Is it because the population is just too

small to produce sufficient writers to carry on, or because, more simply, the size of the reading public, despite its daily growth, still remains fatally restricted? Who can tell? What is certain is that François-Xavier Garneau is not Michelet, Nelligan not Baudelaire, Saint-Denys Garneau not Rimbaud; what is no less certain, however, is that after a half-century of more or less skilful imitation, sometimes brilliantly transposed, creative imagination is just beginning to appear. It is a fact that what has been sadly lacking is genius: collective rather than individual genius. Perhaps, as the critic Guy Sylvestre has pointed out, we need a Dante to solve all the problems at once. There has been no Dante.

Although the product of a homogeneous nation (and that is still its greatest chance of success), French-Canadian literature is made up of exceptions. There is now, however, a combination of circumstances promoted by a revival in the nation's thinking: a convergence of profound aspirations hitherto incompletely expressed, an increasing awareness in the writer of his responsibility as an actor and a witness within a society that has other problems besides mere survival. And French-Canadian literature can be seen to be expanding daily along non-conformist lines, overthrowing one after the other the obstacles that had proved stumbling-blocks for even the greatest of the earlier generation of writers. A liberalizing atmosphere, a consciousness of great diversity without the old motto 'French Canada will have a Catholic literature or none at all': the entire evolution of French-Canadian society reveals itself as a resurgence of activity attended by a re-awakening of interest in the independent public and even in the world of international letters.

It seems that from now on the French-Canadian writer will be reconciled with himself. The public is with him, willing to listen to anything at all providing it relates to the public. More than ever, everything has still to be done; everything is possible. The same optimism existed a hundred years ago. An American offshoot of Latin greatness, no nation aimed at universal genius more than the French-Canadian nation. None is more deserving of success.

25. The Performing Arts

THOMAS HENDRY

If one set out to design a country whose geographic, ethnic, economic, and political configurations would all conspire together to render the establishment and expansion of the performing arts all but impossible, one could do worse than to accept Canada as the model.

Vast distances separate the centres of population able to support the sophisticated organisms that theatre, opera and ballet companies, and symphony orchestras must be; our French founding fathers were cut off from their roots in Europe at just the moment when the struggle for survival was easing and the harsh northern soil was becoming ready to accept and nourish the seeds of culture; the Scots who rushed in to run the newly acquired snowbound northern empire

675

were men in whose tradition the building of fortunes and universities, not opera houses and theatre companies, satisfied the noblest of aspirations; the successive waves of immigration that lapped periodically at the quays of Montreal and Halifax bore to our shores millions from the British Isles and Europe whose peasant and proletarian traditions were quickly abandoned but who brought with them little collective memory of the essentially middle-class experiences of the performing arts. Divided by language and religion, we erected barriers at regular intervals along our frontier civilization in the form of provincial boundaries; we imprisoned education within narrowly regional walls and prohibited any possibility of a national experience on the part of our young people in the acquiring of appreciation of the arts. Burdened with memories of European economic, political, and religious inhospitality, we turned uncritically to English and American concepts of the responsibilities of the State, flung the cultural baby out with the political bath-water and eagerly affirmed the individual's right to go to the grave without ever having seen and heard live theatre, opera, ballet, or music performances. Finally, when we did set up a national system of mass communications in the CBC, we ultimately divorced English from French in a form of cultural apartheid that effectively prevented any healthy, competitive cross-fertilization between our two principal traditions.

Despite all this, somehow or other we have managed to found and sustain four major professional symphony orchestras, four major professional dance organizations, two professional opera organizations, and a dozen continuing professional theatres. In its time, our radio drama was recognized as among the best in the world; our serious dramatic work on television occupies from time to time a similar niche. Certain of our symphony orchestras and dance companies are regularly welcomed abroad with more enthusiasm than we ourselves frequently accord them; our Stratford Festival theatre company, when it travelled to England in 1964, created a world-wide dramatic impact in re-introducing the use of the open stage; in terms of supplying individual talents to be taken up by the more organizationally sophisticated we have become to a considerable degree an artistic Scotland for the world. Canadian singers are taking the place of Canadian hockey players as the classic Canadian cultural export; Canadian dancers cross the Atlantic to study and are snapped up in England; our actors and writers save up their tiny CBC cheques and buy one-way tickets to Hollywood, New York, London.

These unwilling expatriates can take heart, however, from the good news that the market for Canadian-produced opera, ballet, theatre, and serious music has grown in fifteen years from fewer than one hundred thousand persons to about half a million 'regular' attenders – those who turn up at least six times yearly to some manifestation in this area, be it the Canadian Opera Company on tour, Les Feux-Follets in the Place des Arts, the Manitoba Theatre Centre, or a Toronto Symphony concert. Visitors and casual or one-time attenders swell the total somewhat but provide little in the way of cohesive audiences on whose interest serious work may be based.

Things *have* changed. This can be seen if one compares conditions now with those of the twenties or thirties. Gone are those days of interminable and regular Farewell Tours by British artists; of Donald Wolfit and his company paddling their way across Canada like Mayfair voyageurs, offering glittering bits of Shakespeare as barter to the nervous natives; of Little Theatres drearily discovering the easily discernible parts of Ibsen and Shaw; of endless music festivals and lectures; of Chautauqua and the Minneapolis Symphony for unwilling school kids; of boring stock companies, and elocutionists executing any poetry that came their way; of the last pale shadow of the Ballet Russe de Monte Carlo blowing across the land like the slipper-shod and doomed crew of a choreographic Flying Dutchman; of a continent's hitting its cultural apogee every Saturday afternoon when the Met came on the radio; of Manitoba-Moorish neighbourhood cinemas where one received, besides an awareness of how low the film art could sink, gifts of disastrous dinnerware designed to lure one back; of Teachers' Societies doing *Macbeth* and vice versa. All, thank God, are no longer with us. And our half-million regular-attending compatriots share our knowledge.

What changed things?

After the Second World War Canada was blessed with an immigration wave from Europe that was largely bourgeois in its values and background, and in its ranks were contained most of the people destined to provide us with the leadership we have so sadly lacked. Not only artistic directors and performers came out of this benevolent invasion; many of those destined to shape the thinking of our boards of directors turned up at this time. Previous to their coming, a Canadian's awestruck view of a truly cultured compatriot was based on the fact that the Favoured One, despite his Canadian residence, had actually seen an opera in Milan, a ballet in London, a play in New York, had actually eaten an éclair in Budapest, watched a parade in Berlin, heard a quartet in Warsaw, a symphony in Amsterdam.

Suddenly there were people in our midst who had done more than merely visit these cultural Nirvanas: they had lived their entire lives in London, Milan, Budapest, Berlin, Warsaw, or Amsterdam. And now here they were – obviously sane, educated, sophisticated – in Canada, *even though they might have gone to New York*, our own North American cultural home, our multi-purpose Mecca. The decision of these people to choose Canada caused many of us to question our existing values. Added to that – since they were middle-class, dynamic, and vocal – was their chastening appraisal of the cultural wilderness in which they found themselves here in Canada, and their eagerness to do something about the sad situation. Its grip on the national structure never before challenged on cultural grounds, the native-born middle class, which had survived the depression and consolidated its economic position during the Second World War, began to pull up its cultural socks and to utilize some of the imagination it had heretofore channelled almost entirely into commerce.

To the chorus of discontent were added the voices of many of our returning servicemen who brought back an awareness of the richness of European cultural life. This awareness persisted, since the Second World War did not produce the disillusionment with things European that had accompanied the experience of the 1914-18 war. The returning soldiers, sailors, and airmen went to university and infected an entire generation of Canadians with a view of life that could not possibly have existed in Canada during the thirties. They showed discrimination, they talked favourably about the good things of life in Europe, they denounced the less-good things, and because of the essential camaraderie of military life, they talked about the British, the French, and the Germans as people in the end no better and no worse than Canadians. As a race, we began to shake off those feelings of inferiority we had nourished since colonial days – a development vital to the rise of cultural manifestations requiring collective agreement and action.

We still sent overseas for our music-festival and drama-festival adjudicators; we still maintained in our heart of hearts the fiction that Things Were Done Better in London or Paris or New York; but superficially at least, we began to realize that there were potential cultural leaders among us worthy of our support.

The postwar ferment in the performing arts that I have so sketchily suggested here led to the typical Canadian Establishment reaction to any potentially messy situation threatening to get out of control: we established a Royal Commission to look into the matter. In 1949, Vincent Massey began the heroic work of sorting out the aspirations of those active in the arts, of providing some sort of comprehensible framework of attitude within which many Canadians could place these strange, troubling, half-formed, but urgent feelings of need.

After two years of examining the Canadian cultural scene and noting the great gaps in the lines where the banners of the legions of the arts, letters, humanities, and social sciences ought to have been proudly waving, the Massey Commission gave that most Canadian of advice: it recommended that a Committee be formed to deal with the situation. To be sure the Committee, in the view of the

Commission, ought to have a rather grand name – the Canada Council for the Encouragement of the Arts, Letters,
Humanities and Social Sciences – but a committee it would
be, none the less, composed of private citizens operating at
arm's-length from government, modelled largely – even to its
name – on the Arts Council of Great Britain. Conservative in
its administrative approach, the Massey Commission turned,
in Canadian terms, rabidly revolutionary in its final para-
graph where, for all to see, it recommended that 'the Council
would find it possible to perform its varied duties effectively
with an annual budget which would constitute a very slight
charge upon all members of the Canadian population'. There
it was in all its radical splendour: a recommendation by an
impeccable Royal Commission that state aid to the arts be
part of Canadian governmental policy. Six years later, on
October 11, 1957, Queen Elizabeth II gave approval to its
official seal, and the Canada Council was in business, with
Brooke Claxton, who had steered a successful legislative
course for the enabling Act of Parliament, ensconced as the
Council's first full-time chairman.

The Council's first grants came at a crucial moment for the
performing arts; the expectations that had their first flowering with the publication of the Commission's Report in 1951
were beginning to fade along with the hopes aroused by the
immediate success of the Stratford Festival which had begun
in 1953. The performing arts had been declared by a Royal
Commission to be a perfectly respectable, indeed a desirable, field of Canadian endeavour. But beyond the comfort
they could take from the Commission's generous words, the
European-born artistic leadership that was arising throughout the country, to match the few Quebec leaders who had
returned from training abroad, could find little substance on
which to base a lifetime of hard work. In a tightly structured
country, in sociological terms, no possibility of structure had
been provided in terms of cultural values.

The Council's assumption of its task altered all this immediately. Overnight a new standard of artistic values was
imposed, if that is the word, on a receptive artistic com-

munity. Certainly success in New York and London was, and has remained, the final test of Canadian artistic excellence. But to an extent the existence of the Council made possible a certain 'repatriation' of standards.

Overnight, the Canada Council grant became the Good Housekeeping Seal of Cultural Approval in Canada, and artistic enterprises were quickly divided into two groups: the fortunate excellent few – or so they seemed – who received a grant; the aspiring many who sought aid in vain. Over the years, familiarity and frequency have robbed the Canada Council grant – *per se* – of its original semi-magical powers, but in general the Council and its Secretariat have remained the most reliable of Canadian critics in the area of the performing arts. Could this perhaps explain slightly why we have in Canada so few professional critics of any reasonable stature? In the Council we have a body able, by distributing or withholding support, to effectively back up its appraisals. Viewed against this background, the opinions of our critical writers are of minor and insignificant interest indeed, in the final analysis, to our performing artists.

One must bear in mind when viewing the artistic ferment of the fifties from the relative placidity of the sixties that during the previous decade television was hewing a revolutionary path through the settled Canadian response to artistic manifestations. When the Idiot-Box Insurrection was over, the land lay strewn with dead and dying cinemas, which until the fifties had housed the largest collective response to the performing arts. Old habits died and, in terms of social patterns, nothing took their place: when the novelty of television wore off, a significant minority looked around for something else to do. In attracting this wandering eye, the performing arts found a small, but committed, audience.

The Massey Commission, in its summing up of the cultural state of the nation and its recommendations as to desirable social activity to repair many of our deficiencies, gave conscious stimulus to an already existing phenomenon – the rise of the non-profit arts organization.

The patron saints of the performing arts in North America

had been, until then, rugged New York individualists like Tony Pastor, Florenz Ziegfeld, Kermit Bloomgarten, Billy Rose, and David Merrick – men who made and lost millions in the performing arts in much the same way that individualistic entrepreneurs make and lose millions in stock markets and grain exchanges every day. They were businessmen like other businessmen and their *raison d'être* lay in specialized opportunities for profit.

The Massey Commission suggested that the Canada Council ought to support the work of voluntary organizations (i.e., non-profit organizations) across the land. The precedents of the past, which saw state subsidies flowing to such frank profit-seekers as railroad companies and farmers, were discarded when consideration of means to develop and extend the arts was the topic under discussion. Benevolent or not in its effect, this thinking is still very much with us and to this day has inhibited the development of state support for a feature-film industry in Canada. To apply the non-profit criteria certainly solves a great many discretionary dilemmas, but it is doubtful that in *all* cases state support of frankly profit-seeking endeavours ought to be withheld. It would be easy enough to work out formulae with respect to profit-sharing or reimbursement of support, and it is suggested that as the development of the arts in Canada continues, a wider application of the present gentle trend in this direction – support to publishing houses and art galleries notably – will include currently excluded areas of activity.

It is in the non-profit mould, however, that each of our opera, ballet, theatre, and symphonic organizations has been formed, and it is likely that future organizations will continue in this pattern.

One significant change is likely: because within the confines of North American individualism continuing financial support from the private sector – individuals and corporations – has been an uneasy tenant. Each year fund-raising committees scream ever louder that the demands for support have crossed the threshold from reasonable to absurd. Significantly, the screams of protest have grown louder as state subsidies have mounted and private support has become, in percentage terms, an ever-diminishing fraction of total performing-arts revenue.

Several voices have been raised, of late, advancing the sacrilegious view that private fund-raising is a most inefficient way of financing opera, ballet, theatre, and music; and that returns are, in general, abysmal when compared with the energy expended in their collection. Further, performing-arts leaders have begun pointing out that the advantages of long-range planning are denied them under the present year-to-year, hand-to-mouth system of subsidization and support.

Under our present conditions, audiences have grown from less than one-half of one per cent of our population to almost three per cent. If this figure is to be raised to even the dismal target-level of five per cent, advanced as desirable by the Rockefeller Brothers Foundation report, then vast changes in thinking and methods will be necessary. In thinking of ways to enlarge the effect of the performing arts perhaps it is as well to consider where we've been before becoming too concerned with where we're going.

Theatre began in North America on November 14, 1606, at Port Royal, when Marc Lescarbot presented the first performance of a water-pageant depicting part of the career of Neptune. By 1694, theatre aficionados and clerical authorities were involved in bitter dispute over the presentation of Molière's *Tartuffe* in Quebec. Amateur activity in music and theatre were two of the chief comforts of frontier life, and by 1825 the Theatre Royal had been opened in Montreal and was playing regularly in French and English. On this stage in 1842, Charles Dickens made his debut as an actor. Throughout the second half of the nineteenth century, home-grown repertory theatre was offered in Toronto in addition to tours by the 'greats' of European and American theatre. This tradition continued into the 1920s, even into the vaudeville pattern, and it was not unusual to see Sarah Bernhardt on the same bill with a champion prize-fighter. The pattern that has sustained Ed Sullivan for fifteen years kept vaudeville afloat for more than thirty. In the large cities, as the twentieth century began, the foundations of our securely based symphony orchestras were well and truly laid. Accepted as 'respectable' from the beginning, the symphonies have clung, until recent times, to a tradition of exclusiveness. Even now, though they are the oldest, most established, and certainly one of the most expensive of our performing-arts organisms, the symphonies have lagged far behind the theatre in expanding their audiences.

Despite the existence of stock companies in the major cities, the seeds of our present theatrical crop were sown in the Little Theatre during the twenties. The stock companies were generally composed of expatriate Americans or Britishers, and when their audiences dried up – thanks to the talking film and radio – they folded their theatrical tents and stole silently back to their homelands. The amateurs, with whom they had shared an uneasy coexistence, remained. Out of their aspirations came, in 1932, the Dominion Drama Festival, which was designed to provide a national structure and sets of standards for the many groups from sea to sea. For about twenty years the Dominion Drama Festival held within its confines almost the only continuing indigenous Canadian production activity. Even now it is probable that many more Canadians each year see amateur plays than see professional productions.

In ballet, hardy pioneers began arriving from Britain and Europe, Gweneth Lloyd arrived in Winnipeg during the thirties and founded the Winnipeg Ballet Club, which later became the Winnipeg Ballet Company and later the Royal Winnipeg Ballet. Later arrivals – Celia Franca who came from England in 1951 to found the National Ballet of Canada, and Ludmilla Chiriaeff who arrived from Switzerland in 1952 destined to begin Les Grands Ballets Canadiens – swelled the ranks of artistic directors. In 1958, Winnipeg-born Arnold Spohr took over the direction of the Royal Winnipeg Ballet and remains to this day the only native-born Canadian occupying such a position.

But if the traditional 'high' culture – opera, ballet, serious music, the drama – has received a cold welcome in the True

North, the opposite has been the case in mass art. Long-playing records, movies, television, and radio were – at birth – clutched to the Canadian bosom where in cheer and approval they have dwelt ever since. Beginning with our very first radio stations, the listeners and viewers have shown a marked preference for material of U.S. origin. Dick Van Dyke is in a very real sense one of the spiritual heirs of Amos 'n' Andy both in the U.S. and in Canada. An awareness of this subversive taste in Canadians was certainly one of the motivating factors in the work of the Canadian Broadcasting League at the close of the twenties. As a broadcasting equivalent to the building of the C.P.R., we erected a defence against penetration from the south by creating what eventually became the CBC. And to whom did we look for assistance in our efforts to lay out an intangible trench-system along the undefended frontier? To Britain, naturally. Men like Tyrone Guthrie, in cramped studios in Montreal, sent out the first of the clarion calls to Canadian cultural identity disguised as radio dramas and paid for by, of all people, the Canadian National Railways.

The activity of the Canadian Broadcasting Corporation / Radio-Canada, initially in radio and later in television, provided the opportunity for performing talent. Without radio and television to provide supplementary earnings for their personnel, symphony orchestras would even now simply not exist in Canada. English-speaking acting talent would gravitate even more quickly than it does now to the U.S. or Britain, and it is doubtful if a community of French-speaking theatre artists would exist at all. It was out of the pool of radio talent that Tyrone Guthrie drew his first Stratford casts; even now, Montreal actors sandwich stage appearances between all-important television and radio commitments. Radio and television made a Canadian theatre inevitable, but their development had aspects of doubtful value. Because of costs, radio and television production facilities must be centralized. In Canada, it is in Toronto and Montreal one finds the great preponderance of production facilities; it is in Toronto and Montreal that one finds ninety to ninety-five per cent of

Canadian talent. If an actor is not born there, it is to Toronto or Montreal he must inevitably go.

As a result, drama with anything like a regional flavour has been rendered impossible. Further, the growth of regional performing-arts organizations has been slowed by the necessity of competing, in the case of the best talent, with the vastly greater material resources of television and radio as concentrated in Toronto and Montreal. Something of a love-hate relationship has evolved between the performing-arts organizations and the CBC: they find it difficult to live with, and impossible to live without.

Certainly such playwrights as we have – and we don't have many – learned their trade and still earn most of their income in broadcasting studios supplemented by occasional forays into legitimate theatre. For composers the same holds true. CBC commissions to composers have far outnumbered those given by our orchestras and other musical organizations.

Certainly a way will have to be found out of the present employment-pattern cul-de-sac if regional development in the performing arts is to continue. Historically, the presence of a small metropolitan pool of talent has made broadcasting activity possible; expansion of broadcasting activity has created further employment opportunities and the talent pool has enlarged; the existence of the large talent pool is then used as a justification for further centralization of broadcasting activity. As populations grow, the number of cities able to support conservatories of music, which can offer necessary supplementary income to musicians, increases; Ottawa has already been suggested in this regard as a place of co-operation between its University and National Arts Centre towards the establishment and maintenance of a chamber Orchestra. As repertoires grow and seasons lengthen for our regional theatres, the planning for permanent companies becomes more and more intensive; eventual independence of the need for broadcasting income seems to be the answer here, as it is already for our dance organizations and the artists they employ. Only opera, because of its need for the enormous resources that only metropolitan regions offer, seems to be relatively permanently confined to present patterns. Of the various forms, legitimate theatre seems to offer the most exciting opportunities for proliferation, since it is the least costly to support and maintain and at the same time offers the best potential for wide popularity.

One wonders how quickly the missing teeth will be added to the smile from across the footlights. Saskatchewan lacks a professional theatre but could easily support one designed to fulfil truly provincial responsibilities. In the Maritime Provinces, summer programs of theatre, often of very high quality and in the case of the latter exclusively Canadian, can be found in Halifax and Charlottetown. The answer here is obviously some sort of regional theatre capable of creating audiences, on a touring basis at first, in the principal cities of the region. Newfoundland, because of its unique population pattern, its enormous material potential for growth, and its long history, offers opportunity to anyone capable of designing a theatre company suited to the very unique needs of the island.

The imminent establishment of a government support fund for a Canadian feature-film industry is a source of hope to potential producers. Reception to modest Canadian films like *Nobody Waved Good-bye* has proved that Hollywood has no monopoly on appeal. In the past, cinema effort in French and English has centred itself directly or indirectly on the National Film Board. Already this is changing as Canadian private financing, guided by film-makers like Budge Crawley and Harry Horner, begins to participate in the essentially international film market.

Someone has remarked that the next great phase of human progress will centre on the civilization of the corporations. Those most in need of the message are the corporations owning private television stations. The public tolerance born out of gratitude for those offering technological development will in time wear thin, and public responsibilities appropriate to private-enterprise opportunity will be more and more sharply defined. The present sterile pattern in private television, modelled as it is on the barbaric practices of private radio, will surely in time defeat its own purposes and force reforms. There *must* be a limit to the number and frequency of commercial messages carried; unless by some tragic mischance public taste becomes permanently debased during the present anarchic outpouring of junk, surely one day the public will rise up in wrath to demand something, *anything*, of genuine value from our privately owned centres of broadcasting. Applications are already on file in several regions for provincially owned 'educational' television channels. If, by some miracle, these regional outlets are programmed imaginatively, they could offer a bright, competitive hope for what is now a generally cheerless picture. Certainly the CBC will demand and obtain higher annual grants in order to be able to lessen its dependence on the American and British producers of much of the inferior material at present cluttering up our national air-waves.

In the performing arts themselves, the chief obstacle to major expansion lies in the present starvation of leadership. The European-born or European-oriented leaders who arose in Canada out of the debris of the Second World War are, to a man, hard at work and creating international reputations for themselves. If the classic pattern is followed, certain of their number will sooner or later depart for greener pastures abroad. If the search for artistic leadership may be compared with gold mining, it is fair to say that the day of picking up the easily identified nuggets is over. Now a much more intensive process of sifting, involving ever-smaller-mesh screens in the pans, is beginning. Barring unforeseen political upheaval in the next few years, it simply ain't gonna rain Europeans any more. As our present leaders reach international status and depart, we will have two courses of action open to us. The first, which has already been adopted by the symphony orchestras, will be to simply replace one departing artistic leader of international reputation with another artistic leader of international reputation, sustaining the one with the same apparatus that sustained the other: a Canadian-born, Canada-oriented, more or less permanent management. Under this system genuine long-term planning – as in the case of professional football teams, which suffer from the same problem –

becomes a function of management rather than of artistic leadership. This, in turn, leads to a certain conservatism of outlook that could prove inhibiting to the growth of audiences, as it has already with the symphony orchestras. In these, the resident Canadian management becomes, in football terms, the coach; international artists like Ozawa or Mehta become the star quarterbacks who lead the team to seasonal triumph but do not stay long enough to basically influence patterns of growth.

The other course open is much more expensive but, in absolute terms, by far the more desirable and productive of the two. It consists of arranging our organizational patterns in the performing arts so as to offer the maximum opportunity to young Canadian talent – talent that has grown up in an easy and natural relationship to the art it eventually seeks to serve. To fully exploit this line of opportunity, a great increase in subsidy will be required, coupled with much more action on the part of subsidy-giving bodies. Present support traditions in the arts are largely based on the awareness that a significant leadership was present in Canada and able to absorb support, more or less productively, on a relatively grand scale. The art of the subsidy-giver has become the art of choosing the correct recipients from among the potential élite clamouring for the support dollar. An artistic Establishment has arisen, given status by the national recognition implicit in national subsidy. To some it is the Rat Pack, to some the Cultural Mafia. The very first lists of Canada Council grants back in 1957-58 and 1958-59 largely determined its shape and membership. It includes managers like Pierre Béique (Montreal Symphony Orchestra) and Walter Homburger (Toronto Symphony), but accords them a special but different status from that assigned to those who are artistic directors as well as genuine leaders. The latter group treat each other more or less as equals, avoid territorial disputes, and in general operate largely in the manner of a benevolent cartel. Sir Tyrone Guthrie, thanks to his establishment of the Stratford Festival, has become the non-resident, irreverent patron saint of the group.

Generally democratic in outlook, this group accepts un-ashamedly the concept of relative equality in assessing the influence of its members. Most Equal are those who were leading artistic groups *before* the Canada Council got into business. A special or Very Most Equal status is reserved for Michael Langham because of the success with which he built upon Guthrie's pioneering efforts at Stratford; other Most Equal members include John Hirsch of the Manitoba Theatre Centre, Celia Franca of the National Ballet, Herman Geiger-Torel of the Canadian Opera Company, Jean Gascon and Jean-Louis Roux of Le Théâtre du Nouveau Monde, and Arnold Spohr of the Royal Winnipeg Ballet. Almost Most Equal status goes to the aforementioned Messrs. Béique and Homburger, to Leon Major of Halifax's Neptune Theatre, to Mavor Moore (who, although he has produced longer than any Most Equal member, is a late-comer to the current non-profit field), to Murray Davis, formerly of Toronto's Crest Theatre, to Victor Feldbrill of the Winnipeg Symphony Orchestra (who loses points for not having founded his organization), to Meredith Davies (the conductor of the Vancouver Symphony, who loses points simply because he lives in Vancouver), and to recent arrivals to the subsidized non-profit field, like Malcolm Black of Vancouver's Playhouse Theatre Company, Jean Roberts and Marigold Charlesworth, formerly of Canadian Players Foundation, Yvette Brind'Amour and Mercedes Palomino of Montreal's Le Théâtre du Rideau Vert, and Ludmilla Chiriaeff of Les Grands Ballets Canadiens. Fairly Equal status is enjoyed by Edward Gilbert, who is taking over from John Hirsch in Winnipeg, by Irving Guttman of the Vancouver Opera Society, and by Michel Cartier, director of the recently professionalized Les Feux-Follets. A special status is reserved for rugged individualists like Gratien Gélinas, who would probably be characterized by club members as Most Outspokenly Equal, and for composer Lou Applebaum, Most Advisingly Equal. Non-resident privileges are extended to a certain few, headed up by Douglas Campbell; these, although (a) they were in the business before Canada Council began, and (b) founded an organization (in Campbell's case, Canadian Players), have moved on to greener and broader fields in other lands.

The Rat Pack is frankly pragmatic, is outspoken among itself, tight-lipped when dealing with those outside its ranks; it welcomes those as members who show talent, a knack for leadership, and the precious ability to attract subsidy support. It tries not to appear exclusive, but when its members meet, a stranger has only to sit down among them and he will cause a complete and discernible change in the tenor and intensity of discussion by his presence alone. Similarly, music, opera, ballet, and theatre leaders tend to form sub-clans, to speak most frankly only in the presence of others like them. An exception to this rule is Herman Geiger-Torel, who is welcome in all groups.

All of these men and women are growing older and better known in their professions. For some, during the next few years, the call to foreign stages, new challenges, will prove irresistible. At the moment, no likely successors are in view. All are aware of the problem of succession; only in a few instances are solutions being sought.

If prospects are a bit bleak on the organizational level, the picture is different on the level of the interpretative artist. Emma Lajeunesse, who became Mme Albani, created the classic Canadian pattern when in 1866 she left Canada, became famous, and in 1883 returned to her homeland as thousands cheered. International reputations and Canadian adulation (if this word can be applied to our mildly expressed approval) have become the lot of artists like Maureen Forrester, Glenn Gould, Lois Marshall, Zara Nelsova, Harvey Hart, Norman Jewison, Stanley Mann, Teresa Stratas, Frank Peppiatt, John Aylesworth, Ted Allan, Bernard Braden, Arthur Hiller, Norman Mittelman, Raymond Massey, Jon Vickers, Arthur Hill, Kate Reid, Lloyd Bochner, Christopher Plummer, Sidney J. Furie, Barry Morse, Deanna Durbin, Yvonne De Carlo, Monique Leyrac, Gilles Vigneault, Jack Carson, Melissa Hayden, Lorne Greene, and even Pinky Lee. Alas, once they have made their names abroad they are gener-

ally lost to us, priced out of our modest market. We get them
on the way up and on the way down, and sometimes in
between.

How can a cultural region like Canada sustain a large pack
of artists of excellence? In this age of international art is there
such a thing as a Canadian artist, anyway? Is Maureen Forrester less Canadian because she has moved to Philadelphia?
What about Jon Vickers, who resides, but rarely works, in
Canada? Surely if we are to keep our performing artists as
residents, we will have to be originators of mass culture –
long-playing records, recorded radio and television drama,
feature films. Artists tend to live near their place of work.
Our population of interpretative artists of the first rank
deserves a national effort aimed at providing them with an
economic reason for staying in Canada.

Our record of original creation poses a problem to which
we ought to give infinitely more attention. A few recent and
intemperate words on this topic by Canadian playwright Len
Peterson are worth quoting as we contemplate the Centennial
construction of new theatres in at least a dozen cities and
wonder just what will come to occupy their stages during the
Second Century:

> What am I doing here? The question most of us in the
> Association of Canadian Television and Radio Artists are
> asking, if we haven't already fled on this eve of Canada's
> bilingual schizophrenic birthday. The citizenry of the coun-
> try are pouring increasing sums into the subsidizing of the
> performing arts in Canada and increasingly the writers,
> actors, singers, dancers and models find themselves unem-
> ployed! What game is this? The longer the CBC, for instance,
> is in business, the more programs it imports. The number of
> native artists employed by the private radio and television
> stations is in inverse ratio to the lavish promises made to get
> licenses. The rough, tough, American recording and film
> industries continue to smother any development in both
> fields in Canada. The Centennial Commission and Expo '67
> are apparently having trouble finding much for native talent
> in the performing arts to contribute beyond bits in safe,

safe, safe, non-controversial pageants (along with the Indians), though Crisis is the Royal Guest at our Birthday Party. Our theatre patrons, managers, directors, and producers pride themselves as much as ever on their dedication to the importation of performers and vehicles from outside the country. And so it is, and so it goes, on and on. Next item on the agenda: to bury the Fowler Report. Why do we fear ourselves so much? – so much that during the entire 150 years of the French Régime there was no printing press in Canada – so much that today we import annually as much in printed material as the U.S.A., Britain, France and Belgium *in toto* – so much that our radio, television, film, theatre, recordings and concert hall are all one-way foreign streets.

Enough! An end to this subservience! This second-class citizenry! This maggoty parasitic existence! This boobism! This down-grading by too many politicians, patrons, producers and civil servants of this nation and its right to be heard.

Enough! Our artists must take the lead in speaking for the nation. We must become the warriors, the clowns, the adventurers and the conscience of Canada. The CBC, the N.F.B., the private radio and television stations, the theatres and movie houses, and the recording companies can best serve Canada by serving its artists. They are soulless without artists, and without a majority of Canadian artists they are foreign invaders.

Enough! We, as artists, must demand action, freedom and standards! The performing arts' outlets belong to us! They exist to serve the nation, *by serving us*. We are no other nation's creatures, houseboys, camp-followers, serving 'the man' Uncle-Tommishly. Such is the role of ACTRA: to act as the collective voice for the performing artists in this fight.

No native art: no community, no country.

If we are to continue to exist, the slight protests in Quebec recently are but a gentle whisper to what we must shout for, work for, fight for. And get. That we may use our talents to rouse this nation into being.

Such is my stand.

Certainly there are aspects of Mr. Peterson's *cri de coeur* with which one may quarrel. It is an attitude that, in the wrong hands, could lead to a Canadian equivalent of the blind alley of Socialist Realism. It is also an attitude that seems, through qualitative discrimination, to suggest that one form of expression is in some way better than another. This view is in direct opposition to the more realistic, and in the end less snobbish, awareness that if the North American continent has something to offer the world in terms of cultural leadership, that something lies in our ability to make cultural manifestations available to everyone in our society conveniently and, in many cases, reasonably cheaply.

The attic-dwelling Bohemian with his long-playing records, the suburban television addict, the matron at her opera, the Yorkville mods with their carbon-copy Beatles, the coffee-house poetaster, the starry-eyed young balcony-dweller at the ballet, the bearded habitué of the Humphrey Bogart film festivals, the shirt-sleeved coke-drinker at the band concert, the symphony-lover, the theatre season-ticket-holder, the FM radio owner, are all participating actively and immediately in a culture whose range makes the repertoire of the Ed Sullivan show look narrow and constipated. Surely the essence of this pluralistic approach to cultural participation lies in the essentially fruitful experience we are passing through as we apply our North American genius for distribution to the problem of the individual's alienation from his culture.

Our task is not to cut down the number and variety of cultural experiences available to an individual but to apply ourselves to the creation of a climate where the attainment of excellence becomes possible in each of many areas, and where individual lack of audience-participation on economic grounds becomes a thing of the past. We want to have everything we have now *and* Canadian plays, music, television, radio, ballet, and opera.

As organizations grow, so grows conservatism within them; one million dollars is exactly one hundred thousand dollars more timid than is nine hundred thousand dollars. Organizationally we *have* developed. Amazingly. Do we really need to defend what has been created by painting everything with the conformist camouflage out of the tin labelled Accepted, Masterpiece, Recognized, Approved, O.K.? Are we permanently in the business of turning out reprints of the Old Masters? Are we *never* to paint pictures of our own?

In Quebec they have learned—however incoherently the lesson may reside in many an average mind—that cultural expression, original creation, and what I would call the persistent survival of identity go hand in hand. If Quebec represents a minority who, though threatened with submersion, have managed to retain an identity within Canada, and if Canada as a whole represents a minority fighting a dwindling battle to retain its identity in North America, then perhaps the rest of us may learn a lesson from Quebec.

Are we willing to choose the clumsy original—even now and then—in preference to the sure-fire *Hamlet*, the currently chic Frisch, the socko-biz Molière? Are we willing to spend more than token amounts to permit our composers to leave their commercial-concocting long enough to learn their business, or would we be wiser to put the money into two or three more Stradivarius-toting interpreters of Bach? Are we willing to pump enough money into something capable of building a really involved ballet audience among the young who make up such a huge percentage of our population, or should we continue to operate on the basis of referenda taken at the Mausoleum Club? It takes an Act of Parliament to export water; how about an embargo on emigration by potential playwrights? Man cannot live by down-stream rights alone! Pollution of the Great Lakes is punishable by law; pollution of the air-waves creates fortunes.

We're old enough to know better. After all, our second hundred years begins any day now. Let's be brave and take a look in a Canadian mirror, if we have one. If we don't, let's buy one and *then* let's take a look. The chances are we might get to like what we see.

There is something to be seen already, as a matter of fact, in the work of playwrights like Marcel Dubé, Jacques Languirand, Eric Nicol, Gratien Gélinas, Jack Gray, Len Peterson, Mavor Moore, and John Coulter; there is something to be heard in the music of Healey Willan, Harry Somers, Jean Papineau-Couture or François Morel, Roger Matton or Harry Freedman; there is a good deal to be experienced in the choreography of Brian Macdonald, Grant Strate, James Clouser, Ludmilla Chiriaeff, Michel Cartier.

Sooner or later we'll get over our obsessive ancestor-worship in the arts and realize that in their work all of them—Shakespeare and Molière, Tennessee Williams and Arthur Miller, Bernard Shaw and Sean O'Casey, Euripides and Giraudoux—gave us a precious gift: the gift of freedom to do something else.

We've been slow to take up this gift of freedom; slow to give audiences something Canadian they could feel excited about.

One hundred years of effort have proved that the performing arts *can* take root in our northern climate; they've proved that as individual artists Canadians are as good, pound for pound and given reasonable opportunities, as artists anywhere; they've proved that a tiny minority *will* become a faithful audience. The task of forming the performing arts into a widely meaningful area of Canadian experience remains for the second hundred years.

It's not a bad challenge, as challenges go.

26. Painting and Sculpture

HUGO MCPHERSON

Canada's first century has ended with an unprecedented surge of vitality in the visual arts, but though natives and visitors alike sense the new atmosphere of energy and experiment, it is not immediately clear just how our cultural Victorianism has emerged into the market-place of 'Pop' culture. Yet that is where we are – in the Pop age, the electronic age. The social élite who gave us marble museums that were more awe-inspiring than pleasing, today begin to look like high-camp figures; and an alert new audience is demanding that art become a living element of the daily scene. There is an intelligible pattern of development from the artful politics of Sir John A. Macdonald's era to today's vigorous politics of the arts – an organic progression, in the critic's view, from great grandfather to Dada to

697

Pop. Twenty years ago, American 'action painting' finally forced us to see the work of art as an *event*, rather than a mimetic imitation in the Aristotelian sense. The long dominance of easel-painting, in which the artist self-consciously set out to create a likeness of a subject, was broken, and then the new technology of communications smashed the picture frame itself, and distributed art images everywhere in such varied forms as film, colour prints, transparencies, television images, and so on. At the same time, a flood of images from points as diverse as Australia, Scandinavia, and Japan became part of the ordinary Canadian environment. (The centre pages of *Time* magazine are perhaps the most familiar illustration of the new situation.) Visually, Marshall McLuhan's 'global village' had apparently arrived.

In this new atmosphere of 'instant information' it became popular for artists, architects, and critics to say that an 'international style' had triumphed, and that regional and even national idioms were *passé*. This facile half-truth was particularly appealing to Canadians, because their visual arts had never managed to produce a national school or national style, despite the exhortations of patriots; and now it appeared that the problem of style had conveniently disappeared.

What had really happened, however, was something very different. First, the impact of international art released Canadian artists from the closet-culture of a nationalist view of art. Second, the break with the easel-painting and picture-frame conceptions of art led artists to redefine their social role: they were no longer making 'pretty' pictures or stating rational propositions in paint; they were persons actively at work in a community, shaping its environment and its way of understanding. And third, the problem of style had not been solved at all. If the informed artist was now confident enough to experiment with a bewildering variety of styles and materials, the problem of which style to adopt became more important than ever. The real language of the age was, by 1960, the New York style, and a growing number of Canadian artists, including an important group from Quebec–*les plasticiens*–found that they could use that idiom easily, though they kept their own accent and vocabulary of forms. Moreover, after decades of existing on colonial fringes, many Canadian artists were happy at last to have a seat close to the throne.

Thus neither the efficiency of communications nor the artist's redefinition of his role can solve the obsessive problem of style. As Professor A. R. M. Lower has argued repeatedly, Western society is dominated by 'centres of consciousness'; and if the centre does not happen to be Halifax or Calgary, then the artist there adjusts his style to, or at least compares it with, the style of the presiding centre. This remains Canada's situation in the visual arts today; and there is no lack of miff-making patriots to decry it as fresh evidence of American imperialism.

But if this sounds depressing, the question of *content* in our visual arts is reassuring. Artists who have lived and developed in a particular community will see experience from the vantage-point of their formative years, even though their first adult act may be to rebel against their background. In Canadian art the prevailing subject has always been land-scape, and this vision of a huge, brilliant, and menacing terrain still dominates the Canadian imagination, still shapes the statement of our artists. With some artists – Borduas and his group – the landscape has become interior or psychic, but the palette and the colours could not be mistaken for the work of an English painter or the Spaniard Tapies. In other painters such as British Columbia's Jack Shadbolt, Gordon Smith, and Donald Jarvis, the natural history of the region provides an enduring substructure for daring explorations in colour and form. And even such intransigent artists as Mashel Teitelbaum and Gordon Rayner divide their work between summer seasons devoted to country subjects and winter seasons when they ponder the urban spectacle. William Ronald and Harold Town, both of whom have under-stood the lessons of cubism and abstract expressionism, began with Canadian landscape and still reveal their debt to it, while such new Canadians as Gershon Iskowitz celebrate their discovery of Canadian forms and colours in lyric, semi-abstract compositions. The same is true of sculptors: Robert Murray, now living in New York, and Peter Sager, who has spent fifteen years in London, both use Canadian names in their titles to indicate the origin of their themes. In 1967 the Canadian content of our visual arts is stronger than ever, but the dream of a national style is as outmoded as the political slogans of the early part of the century – 'Canada First' and 'Canada's Century'. The styles of Canadian visual art will be as varied as the painters' temperaments, but the subject-matter will have the kind of congruity that Ralph Waldo Emerson called for a century ago when his republic was about seventy-five years old: it will speak for a particular time and place in whatever language the artist regards as viable. Today we have a few more tongues than the Boston Brahmins of 1860 knew; and we are bound to get a visual 'literature' in many dialects – a variety of images that mingle the insights of many societies with the fresh Canadian terrain and consciousness. The 'original relation to the universe' that Emerson called for is now being achieved in Canada; but it will be more international than Emerson could have understood.

How did this peculiar and exciting situation come about? To return to the origins of Canada's visual arts is less an aesthetic study than an exercise in social history, but the study is nevertheless rewarding, for self-understanding depends in part on knowing where we come from. M. Guy Viau begins his monograph on modern painting in French Canada by discussing *la tradition mourante* – a dwindling current of domestic crafts, sculpture, and portrait-painting which in pre-Confederation days served the community's religious, aesthetic, and social needs. Sculpture was its most accomplished art: sweetly and blessedly sincere, sculpture served the church and the seigneurie well; but its influence did not extend into the Protestant austerities of Upper Canada, though the crafts and polite painting appeared in new communities across the land. In retrospect, that pre-Confederation period when artisans and artists were produc-

Painting and
Sculpture 1867 - 1967

1. Cornelius Krieghoff: The Hunters, no date / oil on canvas 14¹/₂ x 17. *Owner unknown*

2. *Aurèle de Foy Suzor-Coté:*
Indiennes de Caughnawaga, 1924
bronze 17¹/₄ x 22
The National Gallery of Canada,
Ottawa

4. Maurice Cullen: The Old Ferry,
Louise Basin, Quebec, c. 1907 / oil on
canvas 23³/₄ x 28³/₄
The National Gallery

3. Homer Watson: In The Laurentides,
1882 / oil on canvas 26 x 42
The National Gallery

5. *J. W. Morrice:* Landscape, Trinidad,
c. 1921 / oil on canvas 26 x 32
The National Gallery

6. *Tom Thomson:* Black Spruce and
Maple, c. 1916 / oil on panel 8³/₄ x 10¹/₂
The Art Gallery of Ontario

7. *F. H. Varley:* Self-portrait, 1919 / oil on canvas 24 x 20
The National Gallery

8. Clarence A. Gagnon: Village in the Laurentian Mountains, c. 1925
oil on canvas 34½ x 51. *The National Gallery*

9. *J. E. H. MacDonald:*
The Solemn Land, 1921
oil on canvas 48 x 60
The National Gallery

10. Emily Carr: Forest Landscape (1), no date / oil on paper 36 x 24. *The National Gallery*

11. A. Y. Jackson: Early Spring, Quebec, c. 1926 / oil on canvas 21 x 26
The Art Gallery of Ontario

12. *Frances Loring:* The
Hound of Heaven, 1918
bronze 39″ high
*The Pollock Gallery,
Toronto*

13. Arthur Lismer: Lily Pond, Georgian Bay, 1948 / oil on aluminum
12¹/₂ x 16. *The Art Gallery of Ontario*

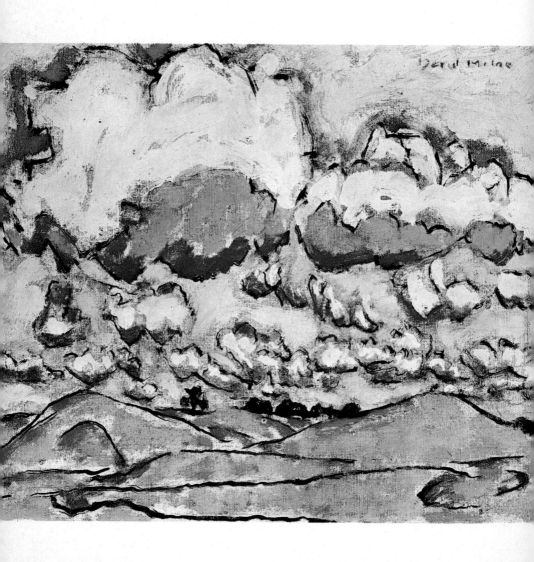

15. *L. L. FitzGerald:* Williamson's Garage, 1927 / oil on canvas 22 x 18
The National Gallery

14. *David Milne:* Clouds, c. 1931
oil on canvas 18 x 22
The National Gallery

16. *Jean-Paul Lemieux:* Visiteur du soir, 1956 / oil on canvas
31¹/₂ x 43¹/₄. *The National Gallery*

17. Paul-Emile Borduas: Sous le vent de l'île, c. 1948 / oil on canvas
45 x 58. *The National Gallery*

18. Jean-Paul Riopelle:
Pavane, 1954 / oil on canvas,
triptych 9′ 10″ x 6′ 7″,
9′ 10″ x 4′ 11″, 9′ 10″ x 6′ 7″
The National Gallery

19. *Alfred Pellan:* L'Affût, 1956/oil on canvas 35 x 51
The National Gallery

20. *Alex Colville:* Children in a Tree, 1957 / egg
tempera on canvas 19¹/₄ x 28
The C.I.L. Art Collection

21. *J. W. G. (Jock) Macdonald*: Nature Evolving, 1960 / oil on canvas 44¹/₂ x 55. *The Art Gallery of Ontario*

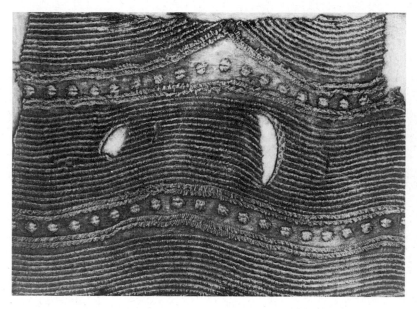

22. *Albert Dumouchel:* Premier labour, 1964 / relief print 20 x 27
Hart House Collection, University of Toronto

24. Jack Shadbolt: The Bush Pilot in the Northern Sky, 1963 / oil
18' x 37'. *Edmonton International Airport*

23. Goodridge Roberts: Lake Orford, 1945 / oil on canvas 30 x 40
The National Gallery

25. *Gerald Gladstone:* Female Galaxy in Recline,
1965 / welded steel 36" high x 60" long x 36" deep
Courtesy of the artist

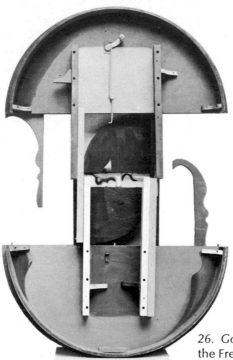

26. *Gordon Rayner:* Homage to
the French Revolution, 1963
painted construction 70 x 46
The Art Gallery of Ontario

27. *Ted Bieler:* Wall relief, 1965-6 / concrete, two entrance walls, each wall approximately 36' high x 24' long x 12' deep
Expo Administration and News Building, Montreal

28. *Gordon Smith:* Blue Painting, 1959 / oil on canvas 22 x 33
Mr. & Mrs. C. R. B. Salter

29. *Robert Murray:* Pointe au Baril I, 1963 / cedar and iron painted maroon 12$\frac{1}{2}$' high. *Mr. & Mrs. Paul Arthur*

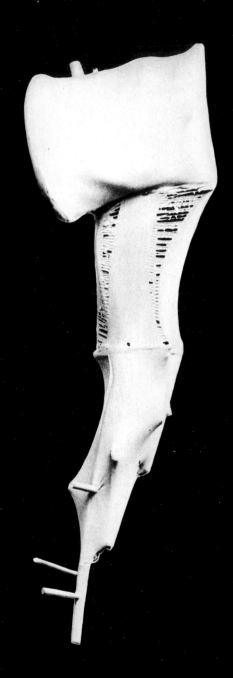

30. *Les Levine:* Hanging Environ, 1964 / sprayed
wood and canvas construction 61″ high
The Isaacs Gallery, Toronto

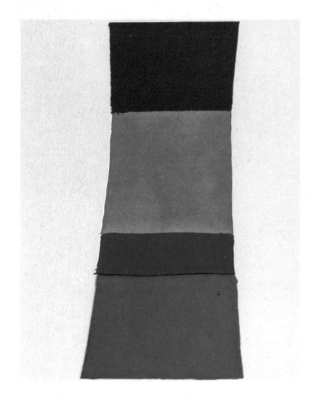

31. Jack Bush: Nice Pink, 1965 / a serigraph from the
folio "Five Colour Prints" 26 x 20¹/₂
The David Mirvish Gallery, Toronto

32. *Sorel Etrog:* The
Complexes of a Young Lady,
1961-2 / bronze 9' high
Mr. & Mrs. S. J. Zacks.
On loan to Hart House,
University of Toronto

33. *Jack Nichols:* Clown and Prince, 1962 / lithograph 19¹/₂ x 15
Courtesy of the artist

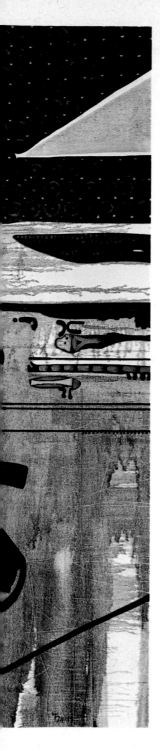

34. *Harold Town:* Sashay Set, 1962,
from the series "Tyranny of the Corners"
lucite and oil on canvas 81 x 74¹/₂
The National Gallery

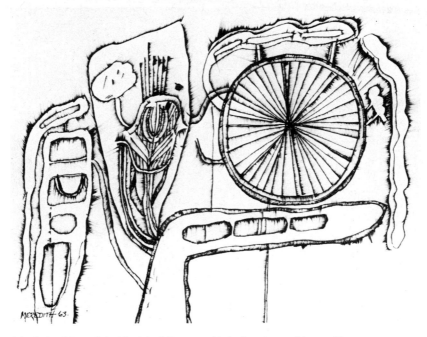

36. *John Meredith:* Untitled II, 1963 / ink drawing 10$^{1}/_{2}$ x 14$^{1}/_{2}$
The Isaacs Gallery

35. *William Ronald:* Mural,
1965-6 / acrylic and oil, 100' in
circumference
St. Andrew's-by-the-lake
Rectory, Ward's Island,
Toronto

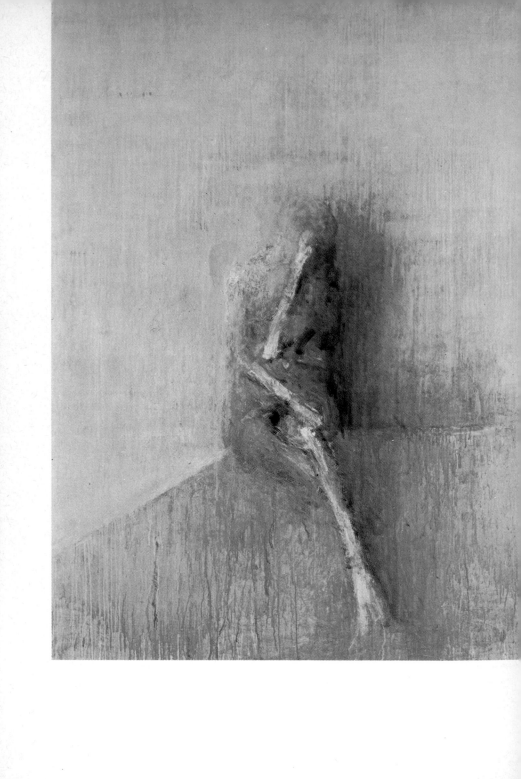

37. *Graham Coughtry:* Corner Figure, No. 13, 1961 / oil and lucite on canvas 78 x 54. *The Isaacs Gallery*

38. *Robert Hedrick:* Landscape, 1959 / oil on canvas 36¹/₂ x 48¹/₂. *Mr. & Mrs. Percy Waxer*

39. *Jean McEwen:* Entrelacs rouges, 1961-2
oil on canvas 39 x 60. *The National Gallery*

40. Greg Curnoe: Being Tickled, 1964
oil on plywood 34 x 48
The David Mirvish Gallery

41. *Michael Snow:* Five Girl-Panels, 1964 / enamels, approximately
54 x 120. *The Isaacs Gallery*

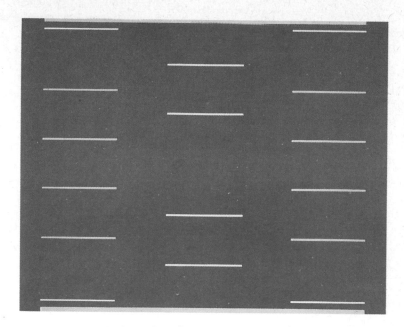

42. *Yves Gaucher:* Signals 3, 1966 / acrylic on canvas
48 x 60. *Gallery Moos, Toronto*

43. *Kazuo Nakamura:* Blue Reflections,
4 Horizons, 1965 / oil on canvas 31³/₄ x 27³/₄
From the Imperial Oil Collection

ing decorations and furnishings for their homes and churches takes on a special lustre; the national attitude towards such work has changed from a barely tolerant acceptance of its quaintness to pride in its unsophisticated directness. Early-Canadian is now sought after in much the way that Early-American is prized in the United States. This new interest in our own past is strong proof that Canadians have at length developed a sense of place that supersedes the old nostalgia for Europe. Evidence of another kind is the current interest in Eskimo and Indian artifacts, and the new impulse to regard *their* cultural history as an important element of Canadian consciousness. Canada is newly aware of its individuality, and with that recognition *la tradition mourante* is undergoing a rebirth: wood-carvers (Anne Kahane), tapestry makers (Micheline Beauchemin), potters, and iron-makers are today doing exciting work; and if they owe something to Denmark and Israel and France, they have inherited more than a little from the Canadian past.

The next step in the growth of the visual arts is difficult to describe, because in many ways it looks like a step backwards. As the nineteenth century progressed, a surprising number of artists emigrated to Canada, bringing with them the sensibilities and styles of their European experience. In 1867 the most prominent of these were Cornelius Krieghoff (whose work was recently described by an angry Quebec art historian as 'croûtes dans le style de Düsseldorf'), and Irish-born Paul Kane, who combined tableaux of exploration and Indian life with the aristocratic manner of Sir Joshua Reynolds and others. In the early Confederation period another current developed: since there was no adequate art-training program in Canada, talented young Canadians were sent to Paris or London to complete their studies. (A few got to New York, where they encountered the indigenous academic realism of the Hudson River School.) Probably the classic example of this situation in Canadian painting was Homer Watson of Doon, Ontario (where a summer art school now flourishes). Watson, in such early work as his diploma painting for the Royal Canadian Academy, *'Les Laurentides'*, showed something of the same fidelity to atmosphere and place that distinguishes the Hudson River group in New York; but by 1900, after visits in England, he succumbed to the Constable style, and sacrificed both his personal vision and style to a romanticism that had little to do with Canadian pioneer reality.

In these years the painter survived by teaching and doing commercial work—a situation that persisted until 1950 and after. Sculpture, for lack of facilities and a market, was moribund. And artists bravely attempted to assert their identity, and to be *seen* occasionally, by organizing societies —the Montreal Society of Artists, 1847; the Ontario Society of Artists, 1872; and the Royal Canadian Academy, 1880, sponsored by Queen Victoria's daughter Princess Louise (wife of the Governor General, the Marquis of Lorne, and herself a polite painter).

Until recently, the temptation to scorn both the pretensions and the slavish imitativeness of this period has been strong. It left Canada with Robert Harris's earnest portrait of the Fathers of Confederation (1883)—a work no better or worse than American political portraits of the century—and Louis-Philippe Hébert's Queen Victoria Monument in Ottawa—a work no better than similar monuments in Calcutta or Bombay, though surely better than the Albert Memorial in Kensington Gardens, London.

But for Canada, as for America and Latin America in this period, the recognized trail for the artist led back to Europe; it was a route paved with economics and bordered by sentiment. There were no signs pointing to Montreal or Toronto, or even New York. The bare fact is that the works of Kane, Krieghoff, and a number of their increasingly realist followers (plus a few primitive artists) constitute the best record that we have of Canada's past. Uprooted or restless Europeans, as Krieghoff's current prices reveal, have become Canada's rarest 'old masters'.

The really significant transition – and it came very slowly – was from a visual art that reported Canadian experience in borrowed styles to an art in which *subject* and *manner* visibly confronted each other to produce works of fresh energy and genuine originality. The genesis of this change rose out of French Impressionist experiments, and came to Canada through the work of Maurice Cullen, Aurèle Suzor-Coté, and James Wilson Morrice, the first native-born 'old master'. Both Suzor-Coté and Cullen adapted Impressionist techniques of creating light to the peculiar atmosphere of Canadian weather; and both rejected in their subject-matter the temptations toward drama and romance that made so much painting of the age appear contrived and false. Cullen was the more subtle of the two, and though his concern with atmospheric effects of snowfall and lamplight is excessive, such works as 'The Old Ferry, Louise Basin, Quebec' (1907) have great solidity and integrity. Suzor-Coté was less dedicated to a personal vision, and when he turned to sculpture, some of his work was disturbingly derivative: as Robert Hubbard has pointed out 'Caughnawaga Women' (*c.* 1924) clearly owes its inspiration to the Swedish sculptor Carl Milles. Morrice, though influenced by Whistler, the Impressionists, and Japanese art, was primarily absorbed by problems of colour and form and their interrelations. His ability to see the structural contours of a scene gave us a classic image of 'The Ferry, Quebec' (1909); and in such later works as 'Landscape, Trinidad' (1921) he exhibits a Fauvesque colour sense that reveals one of the influences on the Group of Seven. Morrice, however, was far enough beyond the domestic problems of Canadian art that we remember him best as a gentle Fauve, the friend of Matisse.

Then – with Fauvism and the intricate decorative effects of Art Nouveau's twining plant-forms safely a part of the Canadian artist's imagination – a group of eight young artists came together in Toronto, fired with a desire to paint the wildness and beauty of Canada, and to express their vision in an idiom native to the vast *terrain inconnu* that they took for their subject. This was the Group of Seven, so named in 1920 after the untimely drowning in northern Ontario of Tom Thomson, their most spectacular member. This group was probably the greatest blessing and the greatest disaster that could have befallen Canadian art.

First, the blessing. In a country where the artist felt himself an outcast on 'the ragged fringes of the universe' (Scott Fitzgerald's phrase for the American mid-west in 1920), the new group provided an embattled focus of energy and inspiration; a few critics decried their barbaric colours, bold compositions, and vigorous brushwork as 'The Hot Mush School'. But Canadian nationalism was strong, and the Seven had created the most original and powerful definition of their land that Canada had known. Ranging in subject-matter from Tom Thomson's brilliant impressions of northern lights and autumn hills to A. Y. Jackson's rhythmic analyses of winter landscapes, Lawren Harris's stark patterns of the Rocky Mountains, and J. E. H. MacDonald's and Arthur Lismer's close-up confrontations with vegetation, these canvases presented Canada in the same way that Whitman and Thoreau might have hoped to see America presented. The landscape is alive; and the painter's encounter with its brutal power is a battle, rather than the polite and banal observation of a visitor from abroad. The work of this group, indeed, produced a national image that has no parallel in American painting. Robert Hubbard has shown that part of the Group's inspiration came from Scandinavian paintings which were exhibited at the Albright Museum in Buffalo in 1912, but the Seven assimilated influences without losing their personal vision. Not surprisingly, a good deal of their best work consists of oil sketches done on board, cigar-box lids, or birch panels. The spontaneity and stripped-down forms of many of these sketches look forward unconsciously to the abstract 'action painting' of the fifties.

Second, the disaster. Nationalism, no doubt, was the only impulse that could have persuaded a conservative and indeed ignorant public to accept the work of the Group of Seven; but if we recall that Picasso, Braque, Kandinsky, and others were already developing their approaches towards cubism before

1910, the work of the Group of Seven looks like a small and provincial aftermath of Les Fauves. That kind of comparison, however, is finally irrelevant, for Canada is both an ocean and an age away from France, though the gap is closing supersonically. The Seven produced a body of painting that is central in the evolution of Canadian society; within another generation it will be recognized as an extraordinary achievement in a society so young. Nevertheless, the achievement of the Group exerted a paralysing effect on the visual arts in Canada for a full twenty-five years. By 1933 the remains of the original group was transformed into a much larger organization, the Group of Canadian Painters. And this new, nationwide fellowship (though a few of its members were interested in international developments in art) apparently felt no keen challenges either at home or abroad. Its annual exhibitions, like those of the Ontario Society of Artists and the Canadian Academy, were full of watered-down echoes of the Seven: in some, the palette of the Seven became grotesque and posterish; in others the bold composition became crude and stereotyped; and from all sides imitative imaginations and minor talents emerged to elaborate the original inspiration. But the significant moment had passed, and there were no new leaders.

The large artists' organizations, by the end of the Second World War, seemed to have outlived their usefulness as guides to fresh ideas. What remained were isolated individuals and small groups whose work would at once confirm the failure of a 'national' style, and suggest the growing depth, richness, and diversity of the Canadian imagination. The most striking of these were two isolatoes, Emily Carr and David Milne, in English Canada, and two passionate crusaders, Alfred Pellan and Paul-Emile Borduas, in French Canada.

Emily Carr, in 1927, saw the work of the Group of Seven as 'a world stripped of earthiness, shorn of fretting details, purged, purified'. However inaccurate that description, their work inspired her to paint anew the forests of British Columbia in a style that approaches the ecstatic vision of the mystic.

The trees of the great rain-forests spiral up in vibrant brush strokes, and light filters through the thin layers of paint with a kind of bursting radiance. Emily Carr had probably met California's Mark Tobey in Victoria, and learned something of his feeling that the particular tangle of crowds, if we can see it from a cosmic distance, becomes a graceful and inspiring calligraphy. In any case, this sense of landscape rhythms has influenced a whole school of West Coast painters. Jack Shadbolt, now the senior member of the group, makes constant comparisons between the earthy and human forms of a landscape and the larger patterns of geological structure, or views the landscape as emblematic—a host of flags seen from an aeroplane. In a different way, Gordon Smith sees shoreline details as landscape; Donald Jarvis finds that trees resemble assemblages of people; and John Korner sees Vancouver in grid-like plaques of colour that hover between close observation and the colour patches of a climatologist's map.

David Milne, though as much a recluse as Emily Carr, is much harder to define. I regard him as the most impressive painter that Canada has produced, perhaps because, as Keats said of Shakespeare, he must have 'led a life of allegory'. Milne was apparently detached from national, political, and social issues; he simply saw his experience in terms of space, form and colour; these were his drama; and his work, whether landscape, still life, or studies of urban forms, somehow rises above time. Yet his compositions observe with an uncanny accuracy the worlds in which he lived, and they range without the smallest fanfare from joy to melancholy to still contemplation. Milne, who exhibited in the celebrated Armory Show at New York in 1913, should now be prescribed study for aspiring young artists.

French Canada neither needed nor shared significantly in the outburst of the Group of Seven; they had lived with their landscape for a long time. In the thirties and forties, moreover, Quebec was in many ways a 'closed' and defensive society; but its intellectuals were strongly attracted to France. Its artistic breakthrough came when Alfred Pellan and later Paul-Emile Borduas went to Paris and brought home the theories and images of contemporary French art. Alfred Pellan was in Paris during the thirties, and returned to Montreal with a bag of surreal and abstract goodies that rocked the provincial academies. His vision, which owed a good deal to Miro and Léger, confronted the public with brilliantly coloured images of the unconscious – personal myths of sex, music, machinery, wine, dance – images that inspired such followers as Leon Bellefleur to paint vivid but somehow austere *paysages intérieurs*. By 1948, Paul-Emile Borduas's anarchistic manifesto 'Refus Global' went beyond the surrealism of Pellan and created another academic scandal. Borduas and his followers called themselves *automatistes*, a term that suggests the source in the subconscious of their abstract compositions. This style, rich in colour and sensual in its handling of paint, influenced such varied artists as Albert Dumouchel (like Pellan and Borduas an influential teacher), Ulysse Comtois, Jean McEwen, Jean-Paul Mousseau (who carried the idiom into illuminated plastic sculpture), and a dozen others. In Borduas's own work, the style led to increasingly narrow colour schemes and deceptively simple composition. In some of his late canvases, plaques of black and white play against each other in a kind of ultimate symbolic chess game. In the work of Jean-Paul Riopelle, Borduas's most brilliant pupil, *automatisme* became a special kind of action-painting in which wedges of variegated pigment, applied with a palette knife, produce vibrant tapestry-like compositions reminiscent of stained glass.

The work of these painters and their followers marks Canada's first real *rapprochement* with contemporary international art; yet their work possesses an individuality that speaks of Canada – of that obsessive and ineluctable landscape that still pervades the Canadian imagination. In finding the means to naturalize the international idiom, however, the Quebec group reached an audience abroad. Borduas was known in Europe and America when he died in 1960; Pellan had a retrospective exhibition at the Musée d'Art Moderne in Paris in 1952; and Riopelle is regarded by the French as one of theirs.

In English Canada the decisive shift away from the complacent provincialism that grew out of the Group of Seven came only after 1953 when J. W. G. (Jock) Macdonald and a number of other abstract painters, including Jack Bush, Harold Town, William Ronald, and Kazuo Nakamura, decided to exhibit as a group under the name of Painters Eleven. Their manifesto vigorously asserted the autonomy of the artist's vision and the value of experiment. The group ceased to exhibit as a unit following a show of their work at the National Gallery, but by then they had made an important point: if the traditional artists' societies would barely tolerate advanced and experimental painting, the new generation (by no means all of them youthful) would create their own forum. Fortuitously, the moment for protest was ripe, for small commercial galleries began to appear in Toronto and Montreal at an astonishing rate, and artists, no longer held down by the caution of societies and museums, were creating an exciting new scene for a growing and responsive audience.

There was greater diversity in this decade than Canada had ever known. In Quebec, Jean-Paul Lemieux and Goodridge Roberts continued to produce their distinguished landscapes. In Toronto, Albert Franck, Jack Nichols, and William Kurelek followed their unique figurative talents, and Joe Plaskett sent back romantic canvases of Paris interiors. But the chief orientation of the younger artists was New York, and the great teacher Hans Hofmann was perhaps as influential as the native Jock Macdonald in helping young artists to find their personal direction.

Before describing individual painters, however, I must observe very briefly a number of complementary developments that give the new scene its air of space and adventure. The Canada Council, founded in 1957, has awarded hundreds of arts fellowships that have taken artists abroad; it has helped museums to increase their collections of Canadian art; it has brought together artists from many disciplines to discuss their problems and needs ; and it has helped, along with provincial governments, to finance the handsome art magazine *Vie Des*

Arts, and *Canadian Art,* which is known internationally for
the excellence of its design. Corporations such as International Nickel and C.I.L. have begun collecting contemporary
Canadian art; and architectural commissions, including
sculpture and murals for government buildings, have become
a normal part of the artist's activity. Most federal agencies
now devote one per cent of the cost of new buildings to works
of art, and the government may launch a similar program for
buildings already in existence. The Secretary of State's
Department is planning new schemes to project Canadian
art abroad. In 1966 the country's leading art schools were
under strong attack to update curricula and methods of
instruction.

Meanwhile, new kinds of summer schools and workshops
are multiplying, for artists find that if they cannot go abroad,
they can import artists of international reputation to work
informally with small groups. For example, as a result of the
workshop at Emma Lake, Saskatchewan, at which Barnett
Newman and Clement Greenberg have been among the
guests, a group of prairie artists—Ronald Bloore, Kenneth
Lochhead, Arthur McKay, and sculptor Robert Murray—
very quickly found an audience in the United States and
Canada. Painter Alex Colville, the distinguished 'magic
realist' from New Brunswick, shows most of his work in New
York—for him the most convenient art centre. Vancouver, as
much involved in West Coast American art movements as
with Eastern Canada, launches a far-out program in sculpture
by importing a gifted young American, Iain Baxter, to the
University of British Columbia. Such new flexibility and
mobility promises a brave new world for the visual arts.

At this point, Toronto remains the most influential art
centre in English Canada. Jack Bush works there, though he
has resigned from artists' societies and is very close in technique to such younger American painters as Jules Olitski
and Kenneth Noland; the quiet, satiric wit of some of his
compositions, however, could only come from a country that
has long debates over flags and national anthems. Harold
Town, the most intellectual of Ontario painters, remains in

Toronto; and William Ronald has returned after making his vivid colour sense and rhythmic abstractions from natural patterns well known in New York. Town, in his autographic colour prints, has created one of the most original statements of his generation, and he goes on to explore a great variety of media without losing the flashing, ubiquitous consciousness that informs all his work. Kazuo Nakamura, the most tranquil of the Ontario group, continues to alternate between still landscapes and quietly-textured abstractions that resemble ideal, cosmic relief-maps.

A comparable diversity and power is seen in the work of a half-dozen others, most of whom (like their colleagues in Quebec) began as painters, but who have done experimental work in film, sculpture, constructions, graphics, music, and even recitation. Michael Snow, who now works in New York, is probably the most avant-garde of the new generation; his 'Walking Woman' works, which are his anchor-image in exploring the whole field of perception, may one day be as well known as Marini's men on horseback. Graham Coughtry has imported the melancholy terror of Francis Bacon and the underground passion of Spain to create a new Canadian image of figures-in-space. Robert Hedrick, Dennis Burton, Richard Gorman, and the rangy Gordon Rayner (who has created powerful new images of Ontario's northern landscape) compound the diversity in striking ways. But the same vitality crops up everywhere. In London, Ontario, Pop painter Greg Curnoe has added a new title to the hit parade, printed across a canvas with a child's lettering-set: LOVE DOESN'T LAST LONG, BUT THINKING ABOUT IT DOES. Vancouver's Roy Kiyooka has expressed his West Coast vision in monumental hard-edge paintings with the subtlest of colour combinations. Yves Gaucher (Montreal's most intellectual artist) has done superb intaglio prints, and explored the possibilities of optical painting with a religious intensity. Richard Lacroix has established a printmakers' atelier in Montreal which may serve as a model for others across the country.

Sculpture in Canada appeared for a long time to have died with the last of the totem-pole carvers and Quebec's religious craftsmen. In the past, Canada had no good foundries for bronze casting, and no architects or patrons who believed in monumental sculpture for public spaces. The result has been a series of polite and often sentimental historical monuments in towns across the nation that had no relation to the space in which they appeared – statues of Robert Burns, or Wilfrid Laurier, or successive chiefs of the Ontario Hydro Commission. Sculptors such as Frances Loring and Florence Wyle, trained at the Art Students' League in New York, were reduced to having only small works cast and leaving larger projects in plaster. And because there was no real market for sculpture and no cultivated audience, sculpture lingered through a long generation with pseudo-Rodinesque profundities, pseudo-simplicities in the Art Nouveau manner, and works that in homage to the Cunard Line should be known as 'Queen Mary modern'. But in the fifties, largely because of the belated influence of the Bauhaus, architects began to think of sculpture not as decoration but as a necessary and even central part of the environment. The sculptural import of Japanese gardens was studied; the possibilities of fountains were considered for the icy Canadian climate; and builders began to realize that architects, sculptors, painters, and ceramicists should all co-operate in the conception of a building or public complex.

It would be optimistic to say that this development has gone very far in Canada, but it is an established idea and promises much for the future. For example, Jack Shadbolt painted what is probably the most important mural ever produced in Canada for Edmonton's International Airport. The architects installed a rank of telephone booths immediately below it, painted an improbable lilac. Even more disastrous, sculptors have had so little experience in coordinating their work with architects that many of our new public sculptures are radically out of scale with their sites. But a new *entente* between artists and architects is in the making, and some of the results are already visible in the administration building of the World's Fair, Expo '67, in Montreal (architect, Irving Grossman; sculptors, Ted Bieler, Armand Vaillancourt, and Ulysse Comtois).

The real breakthrough for the new sculptors is that they have found new media suited to the age and to the materials of modern architecture. The leading materials are welded steel (including a steel that forms a protective coating against the weather); varieties of cement that can be cast in wax or styrofoam moulds; and plastics that can be bonded with other materials, coloured, and adapted to almost any form or architectural requirement. In this field, such young men as Ted Bieler, Gerald Gladstone, Jean-Paul Mousseau, Gord Smith, Yves Trudeau, Arthur Handy, Iain Baxter, and Robert Murray are in the vanguard. The promise of their work is one of the most exciting in Canada's art, for they have already shown us the possibilities.

But what of the future? As Canada ends its first century, there is strong evidence that the cultural lag that has kept it apart from the international scene has closed. Canadian art has been primarily concerned with doing its homework— finding out what Canada is and how it relates to the larger community of nations. From now on, everything depends on the ability of the artist to make clear his view in the global schoolroom. But one final point must be made. As we enter deeper and deeper into the Pop age, our concern with the visual arts and communications must grow. Our artists are ahead of us in recognizing that the visual arts are interdependent, and that combined art-communication forms will dominate in the decades ahead. The 'happenings' and 'environmental constructions' that increasingly absorb our artists today may now appear as a form of play; in fact, they presage the realities of the next generation. And in exploring the possibilities of that world, Canadian artists are in the *avant garde*.

27. The Structure of Government

NORMAN WARD

The chief concepts in the structure of Canadian government were largely settled before 1867. The British North America Act, which determines the basic outlines of government at all levels, is one of the youngest major parts of the Canadian constitution. The separation of Church and State (except in Quebec), the separation of the judiciary from both the legislative and the executive branch, the monarchical and cabinet systems wedded to a Parliament drawn from a British model, the use of the common law (again except in Quebec), and the departmentalization of civil administration under ministers—all were established norms in Canadian public life before the Charlottetown Conference was even planned. To them can be added a number of historical factors of profound influence:

the absence of a military tradition, the presence of a tradition of public enterprise in the satisfaction of economic needs, the use of two languages in the legislature of the Province of Canada, and the practice of proceeding by orderly means as the usual method in the settlement of disputes, are among the most significant. The parts that all these played naturally varied in the different colonies that became Canada, but their over-all significance was everywhere the same: the structure of the government of Canada had to meet certain fairly fixed standards, yet be flexible enough to adapt itself first to the original purposes of Confederation, and then to the endlessly changing circumstances of a growing nation blessed with great spaces, diversified resources, and peoples of differing national origins. The result is a structure that is of the essence of pragmatism, and owes about as little to any consciously held body of doctrine as a living institution can.

In this, it may be said, one finds the hallmark of the English-speaking peoples, and it is true that the dominant forces in shaping the government of Canada, where they were not uniquely Canadian, were British and American. From the British, Canada borrowed the silhouette of the government at Ottawa and in each provincial capital, and much of the nomenclature by which its parts are designated. The resemblance to British models can be misleading, for Canada developed some of its key governmental practices concurrently with the British, and Canadian practice is therefore often only superficially the same. From the Americans we borrowed the federal system (thinking that we built better than *they* knew) and, after experimenting first with British devices, much of the system of municipal government, particularly in urban centres.

Since both British and American influences were worked out on Canadian soil, the result is always uniquely Canadian; but other forces too, neither exclusively British nor American, have affected the Canadian structure. The colonial governments of all the original provinces, for example, had no real counterparts elsewhere, and the Province of Canada after 1840 developed a constitution so exceptional as to be unworkable. The Prairie Provinces, in their turn, originally represented an attempt to export the government of Ontario westward, particularly at the municipal level. The hand of the French Canadian, which had much to do with the shape of the federation decided upon in the 1860s, exerted direct influence in many other ways too: for example, at the point where parishes became units of local administration; in the adaptation to Canadian purposes of the cabinet, the Speaker-ship of the House of Commons, the civil service; and generally in any area sensitive to the persuasive powers of representation. (The crisis that Canada faces at its centennial is in part a failure of a representative system, viewed in its broadest sense.) And finally, as is common with occupied territories, Canada's aboriginal tribes had almost no influence on the structure of government, except in the indirect production of the machinery necessary to the administration of their affairs by others.

Anyone who was unfamiliar with federal systems, and who looked dispassionately at the structure that has resulted from all the foregoing factors could hardly fail to be impressed by its complexity. It is most intricate where it probably appears to most Canadians the simplest – in local government. It is not merely that the ten provinces, each having exclusive jurisdiction over municipal affairs, have developed ten different systems which often use familiar words (such as city and county) to denote quite different entities. The proliferation of local authorities in any well-developed community in Canada, largely following American practice, almost defies description. The typical Canadian city has, like its British counterpart, an elected council; but unlike its British counterpart, it will probably also have a separately chosen school board, hospital board, parks board, library board, police board, playgrounds commission, and half a dozen other bodies necessary to the protection, health, and welfare of its citizens. This diffusion of responsibility, needless to say, militates against clear-cut lines of authority, but it is a well-established element in Canadian government and no strong opinion for its reversal exists. Rural local government is of course much simpler, except in the increasing number of areas where urban populations have spilled over into formerly uncluttered countryside, requiring in extreme cases the application of the federal principle in such experiments as Metropolitan Toronto. By contrast, all the provinces except Nova Scotia and New Brunswick have large districts (ranging from roughly fifty to ninety-five per cent or more of their land area) that are so thinly settled that they require no municipal organization whatever. The government of these sparse areas, combined with that of the Northwest Territories, is actually another category of Canadian government, about which little is generally known.

Local government in Canada, which is everywhere equated with local self-government, gives general satisfaction, as the regularly low turn-out of electors at the polls attests. If traditional party lines were drawn in municipal politics, as is common in Britain and the United States, the electors' interest might be greater, but the parties and the municipalities might both suffer from the intrusion of irrelevant issues into local affairs, and the inevitable problems of local patronage, for few municipal governments have trustworthy merit systems for their civil services.

On the other hand, local governments in Canada already suffer from a variety of circumstances over which they have no real control: the mandatory duties imposed on them by the provinces and the less obligatory services expected of them by their citizens have generally been rising in number or in cost or in both; but their main source of revenue, from which they average around eighty-five per cent of their income, remains based on a single item – property – which is not nearly as flexible as the things it is expected to pay for. Two flexible factors do affect municipalities: their boundaries and the grants they can hope to get from senior governments to assist in the pursuit of a variety of desirable goals. Unlike the Dominion and the provinces, whose boundaries are sacrosanct, the boundaries of local areas are not fixed; hence, the pressure to meet problems of both cost and administration by creating larger units of local government, especially for schools, hospitals, and roads, is everywhere in evidence, and is met by pressure from those who have a vested interest in the *status quo*. Commonly this pits a province, to whose government municipal affairs is just one more portfolio, against the municipalities or pressure groups based on the municipalities, with the result that provincial-municipal relations are plagued with many of the arguments that bedevil Dominion-provincial relations.

There is one important difference: in municipal affairs the province not only has the last word but can, if necessary, dictate a unilateral settlement of any dispute. The provinces are senior to the municipalities not only in authority but in age. The fond myth of the democrat – that sturdy local self-government gives rise to democracy at higher levels of government – was nowhere true historically in Canada, though in Upper Canada the United Empire Loyalists, fresh from well-organized communities south of the border, agitated at length and finally successfully for representative institutions. Elsewhere progress was historically slow, and even occasionally resented; and in virtually every instance it was imposed from the top down.

The colonies and in due course the provinces, within which all local development took place, occupy a special position within the structure of Canadian government – a position that has varied greatly over time, and even at any one time among the separate provinces. As colonies or parts of colonies, they all had their own peculiar backgrounds which need not be recapitulated here. As provinces, and hence as member states in a federal system, they might be presumed to be equals, except that they are not. They entered Confederation by a variety of routes, and on varying terms; even the four charter members started off with unequal representation in the Senate, which was supposed to be their special guardian. Only Quebec was obliged to be officially bilingual. Those that came in later did so sometimes as whole entities with their own constitutions, while others were created out of territories under Canada's jurisdiction and given constitutions by statute. (None, it should be noted, entered Confederation by conquest.) Some were permitted to grow in size after joining, while others remain fixed at their original boundaries. (In general, Canadians decided for unexplored reasons that all provinces should be as large as possible.) Some controlled their own natural resources from the beginning, while the Dominion controlled those of the Prairie Provinces until 1930. Some came in as unilingual states, while Manitoba and the Territories were originally constituted as officially bilingual. Obviously they all differ enormously – in size, wealth, population, and influence within the Dominion. They have played varying roles as laboratories for political experiments whose results had a wider application: the rise of Social Credit in Alberta and of the Co-operative Commonwealth Federation in Saskatchewan are well known; the fact that many important changes in the national election system were first tried out in the provinces is not. Some of the provinces have dabbled with American devices like direct legislation, while others have clung more firmly to the British model.

The one thing they appear to share in common is their form of government, and broadly speaking they do. But it is not really parliamentary government on the traditional British model, except in a superficial sense. There is in each province a Lieutenant-Governor, who since 1892 has been by judicial decision a representative of the monarch as well as the appointee of the Dominion government. Each province has a premier who is in some instances called 'prime minister'; each has a cabinet and a legislature (unicameral everywhere except Quebec) to which the cabinet is responsible. In each is a system of courts whose organization is provincial but whose judges above the rank of magistrate are the appointees of the Dominion, which also pays them. The similarity of these façades is misleading if one concludes that the provinces all have the same system of government; they are ten separate adaptations of one original model, and a model sometimes imperfectly understood. Yet the provinces all share one departure from the model: their legislatures are hardly ever in session, normally meeting for a consecutive five to ten weeks each year, and then being prorogued to leave the executive free of scrutiny for upwards of nine months. Though there is an observable tendency for legislative sessions to lengthen, particularly in the larger and more complex provinces, provincial government in Canada is essentially executive rather than parliamentary government – a phenomenon which is, of course, accentuated when one party stays long in office. Though all the legislatures, in accordance with British practice, vote the funds for public expenditures, only three have anything approaching an independent Auditor General who reports regularly, as an officer of the legislature, on the executive's management of the money.

Except for a handful of constitutional powers (such as the appointment of the Lieutenant-Governors), there are few formal links connecting the provincial structure of government with the Dominion's. Informally, at any given moment there will be in existence several dozen advisory and consultative committees that will include representatives from both jurisdictions and cover almost everything from civil defence to setting the dates of the annual duck-hunting season. Nor is there any instrument by which any province can influence the Dominion's structure, as the Dominion appoints Lieutenant-Governors. The Dominion was not set up to be in any sense merely the agent of the provinces. Apart from this, the structure of the federal government is superficially much like that of the provinces', with the overriding consideration that in the national government, in addition to all the added prestige of being national, there is only one of each institution instead of ten. There are undoubtedly far more Canadians aware of the fact that the Queen is the Queen of Canada than that she also has a representative in each provincial capital, and that provincial laws are enacted in her name.

Paradoxically it is at the Dominion level that one encounters the greatest difficulty in assessing precisely what the Crown means within the structure of government. The legal and constitutional position is reasonably clear. The Queen's title for Canada has, since 1952, specifically mentioned the country by name, though giving it second billing to the United Kingdom; and the Governor General has since 1926 been the monarch's personal representative chosen on Canadian advice, rather than an emissary sent out by the British to represent not Her Majesty, but Her Majesty's Government. A series of controversies, notably in 1873, 1878, 1896, and 1926, has laid down the broad lines of conduct that can lead a Governor General into trouble. Yet the Queen is an absentee Queen, and her resident representative is clearly not a monarch, selected as he is for a short term by men in public life from among men in public life. The result is a further paradox: while the monarchy and its *alter ego* are such as to satisfy the most ardent 'loyalists' and those who prize the British connection, they do not do so in a way that aggravates more than the extremists among the republicans. In many parts of Canada, indeed, one receives the impression that some citizens are unaware that Canada is a monarchy at all – a suspicion which the appointment of Canadians as Governors General has done little to allay. At least two official booklets, issued through the Department of Citizenship and Immigration for the edification of those seeking to become citizens, have omitted the Queen altogether in their description of Parliament.

On the other hand, one can hardly have much doubt that Canada's structure of government includes a prime-ministership. The governor's cabinet became the prime minister's cabinet before Confederation, but it was Confederation which settled that the office of prime minister would thereafter be held by one man instead of shared by two, one English-speaking and one French, as in the former Province of Canada. Even before that, the acquisition of responsible government in the late 1840s had ensured that whoever held office would wield enormous power, and that among those who held office the one who chose all the rest would wield the most power. A number of individual ministers in Canadian history have expressed dissatisfaction with their chief and have variously resigned or been otherwise disposed of; it took half a dozen strong ministers, acting in concert, to unseat the weakest prime minister we ever had, in 1896. The prime minister's mandate has been strengthened in recent decades by his choice as party leader in a national convention, a phenomenon that has enhanced the position of all party leaders; only the C.C.F.-N.D.P. has machinery for changing a leader once chosen, and in the other parties the unhappiest of caucuses has only rebellion open to it as a means of action.

Given that one of the prime purposes of Canada's form of government is to contribute to the maintenance of some semblance of national unity, the prime minister's position is also enhanced, rather than weakened, by that unique Canadian device of making the cabinet representative of as many provinces, regions, and language and religious groups as is possible at any one time. It is true that this has always given Canada a larger cabinet than strict administrative efficiency would require, and one by-product of that has been the development of an informal inner cabinet whose members have an influence that belies the constitutional theory that all Her Majesty's advisers are equals. It is true too that the prime minister's choice of colleagues is limited, and often severely limited, by the requirements of a representative cabinet. If a province returns to Parliament only one member of the prime minister's party, the leader's choice is reduced to deciding whether the province is to have a minister or not. It is rather a Canadian specialty, indeed, that able men have often to be passed over for lesser men from the right place, ethnic group, or religion – a rivet in the Canadian structure of government that helps hold firmly in place the democratic belief that almost anybody can run the country.

But the representative cabinet frees the prime minister from having to pay attention to a vast amount of regional detail that is best left to individual ministers, just as the Governor General frees him from much time-consuming ceremonial. The clearest example of this is in Quebec, where local affairs have until recently been delegated *in toto* by English-speaking prime ministers to French-speaking lieutenants; and if the lieutenants are weak, the whole structure of the cabinet, and thus the party, is weak, as the Conservatives in particular have discovered more than once. Quebec is the outstanding example of one of the chief activities that Canadian government imposes on a prime minister – the endless juggling of personalities and interests in his representative cabinet. The structure of government gives a prime minister a freer hand than one might suppose from the superficial facts, for if he is a good juggler he can maintain his own position almost indefinitely. Thus Sir John A. Macdonald, in his unbroken reign from 1878 to 1891, put thirty M.P.s and senators through fifty-seven cabinet appointments in a ministry of sixteen portfolios; and Mackenzie King contrived to lose in succession, from the same cabinet, ministers who severally supported and opposed conscription.

The cabinet's status as a miniature Parliament has inevitably had its effect on the other institutions with which it comes in contact. Like democratic executives everywhere, government in Canada, with remarkably few changes in its actual structure, has adapted itself to the demands of modern society by the simple device of adding indefinitely to the power of those who already hold power. The cabinet has met the demands by accepting the power, incidentally systematizing its own affairs with reforms that have given it a secretariat, parliamentary undersecretaries, and a committee system. The Governor General, as the unavoidable accompaniment of responsible government and the democratization of the franchise, has been elevated to the rank of constitutional monarch. The Senate, too, has become less important for what it does than for what it represents; and of the Senate it must be added that the outlines of what it represents can easily become blurred. Originally the key compromise in a plan that based the House of Commons on representation by population, the Senate's position as champion of the regions and provinces was from the first undermined by the immediate transfer of that role to the cabinet, by the debilitating effects of life appointment which left the Senators without electorates, incentive, and clear responsibilities, and not least by the natural acceptance of the fact that the cabinet was responsible only to the House of Commons, the only place where proposals for public expenditure could be initiated.

Apart from that last proviso, the Senate has virtually the same powers and privileges as the House of Commons; but the central fact of its existence is that it has rarely acted as if it had. The chief reason for this is unquestionably that the Senate is recruited in the main from people who are entitled to reward, and is thus full of members who sit there for what they have done, rather than for what they show promise of doing. Sociologically, without doubt, the Senate is interesting: with its special qualifications of age and property-owning, it stands perhaps for some dim primal urge to give a special place in government to the wise old headmen who can raise a benevolent hand to check the hot-headed democrats in the other place. It has sometimes done that, for the Senate has always contained able and opinionated men; many of whom, it must be added, continue to work hard at enterprises unrelated to the Senate but useful to groups and bodies corporate who need a voice close to the throne. The Senate's debates, freed of concern over what anybody may think about them, are commonly of a high order, and the Senate has to its credit some fine studies undertaken by its committees, not to mention the many thousands of divorces it facilitated before the establishment of a divorce commissioner in 1963. As long as it exists some Canadians will find satisfaction in urging its immediate reform; this has been going on almost since Confederation, but no one has thought of a feasible way of reforming the Senate without making it a rival of the House of Commons, and reforms that will not do that have not seemed worth pressing for. Actually, without changing a single rule or statute, the Senate could reform itself by undertaking more, and it is significant that no one in the cabinet or the House of Commons encourages it to try.

The Senate's loquacious legislative partner, the House of Commons, enjoys a singular historical distinction which it has never really shaken off. In the 1860s when the grand design was being planned, the House of Commons and its functions were taken completely for granted. Once representation by population and the use of English and French were conceded, little that was contentious arose concerning the House. The main elements in its written constitution had been settled with the surrender of the initiative in financial legislation to the executive, a development that had preceded responsible government in the Province of Canada, but followed it in the Maritimes. Everybody by the 1860s knew what an elected assembly was and what it was supposed to do, and everybody knew that in the event that any doubts arose one could always look to Westminster to see what was going on there.

It is only a slight exaggeration to say that the House of Commons has been taken for granted ever since. The House of Commons of the 1960s resembles the House of the 1860s more closely than any other major political institution resembles its century-old counterpart. The role of the individual member has changed, for with the rise of a relatively non-partisan civil service and of technical standards for government contracts, he is no longer the local broker in the vast distribution of patronage through which Canada was largely governed down to the First World War. The House has changed its procedure several times, normally in the direction of facilitating the flow of government business rather than improving parliamentary scrutiny of public affairs or protecting the rights of minorities. The franchise has been widened from a moderate property qualification for males only, to universal suffrage, and women have been admitted to the House and Cabinet. They find, as do their male compatriots, that in the surveillance of an unbelievably complex administration which employs much delegated legislation, and of which barely one-half is directly under a responsible minister who can be got at in the House, they have exactly the same tools as their predecessors of 1867: no research assistance, no expert committee staffs, no members' reference service in a national library; just themselves. The invention of the typewriter has brought one amenity – stenographic services.

The House of Commons has changed little in other ways.

Ontario and Quebec began with a large majority of the membership, and the acquisition of six new provinces since 1867 has not materially changed their dominance. The majority of Quebec's members, reared in backgrounds largely if not wholly foreign to the basic British common-law concepts that surround Parliament, have always interpreted their roles differently from their English-speaking colleagues. With some notable exceptions they have not, for example, been seized with the necessity for an effective committee system, nor overly exercised about those niceties of parliamentary principle that arise from time to time in disputes such as the pipeline debate of 1956. They have always appreciated Parliament as a forum, but less as a forum *per se* than as one within sight and sound of the executive from which favours can be sought. The structure of Parliament adapted itself so readily to the settlement of all those problems that can be met by concessions and favours that there arose no need for parliamentarians to understand what lay behind them, and the Quebec renaissance of the late 1950s and 1960s, despite its massive significance, was for a long time virtually unheralded in the House of Commons.

Legislatures, by their very nature, do not lend themselves to adaptation by *ad hoc* arrangements, partly because any *ad hoc* arrangement that seems to work – such as the division of the Speakership and the Deputy-Speakership of the Commons between members from the two great language groups – quickly becomes permanent. In a sense, the revival of committee work that began during the Second World War, and quickened perceptibly when Mr. Diefenbaker had to find employment for his huge majority in 1958, is an *ad hoc* arrangement that, given the feeble tradition behind it, could disappear with a change in circumstances. In the meantime, the House of Commons has been building, through its committees and the consideration of estimates by committees, an important new liaison between Parliament and the public service, for the House has been using those committees to examine the public service.

That institution bears in Canada an added burden to the normal load of administering under political direction the affairs of state; it is also another element in the maintenance of national unity, and as such must be representative of Canada's major groups. That it has been inadequately representative, particularly in its upper levels, is demonstrable, for most of those parts of the public service that do not depend on English theory depend on American theory, and in neither case have administrators, in the main, found the kind of competence they are seeking among French Canadians. The merit system, whose adoption (from 1908 to 1918) was an event of great significance to Canadian government, itself points up a basic difficulty. To English Canadians, who adapted the system from British sources, merit means ability to do a job in the immediate pragmatic sense regardless of language, though in fact, under the circumstances, English would be *assumed* to be the language in most cases; to French Canadians, though ability to do a job would not be ruled out as irrelevant, merit *includes* bilingualism.

The failure of the national public service to be bilingual, though there are growing pressures that will make it much more so, has been circumvented at Ottawa in part by an efficient and little-known agency called the Bureau for Translations, an absolutely essential instrument of government worth mentioning because so few Canadians ever hear of it. It is a striking comment on the public service of Canada, and its relations with citizens, that in an average year the Queen's Printer publishes approximately four times as many texts in English as in French, and the difference is one that has been lessening. That statistic is probably as valid an indication as any of the degree to which a bilingual Parliament has permitted the construction of a unilingual public service.

Here a line – or several lines – must be drawn, for some departments have been more sensitive than others to the nature of the society in which they exist, and all the departments as a group are probably more sensitive than many of the Crown corporations. This may reflect the position of the departments under ministers whose constituencies, for administrative purposes, may be the whole Dominion; that at least is more likely than the possibility that it results from the ubiquitous presence of 'treasury control', a system of financial management uniquely Canadian in that the Treasury Board (a subcommittee of the cabinet) and the Department of Finance between them assertively assist all the departments in the preparation of their annual budgets and the subsequent issuing of the money for purposes approved by Parliament. The Crown corporations are largely outside the orbit of treasury control (and some of them are all but beyond the ken of Parliament itself), and are worthy of note because together they comprise roughly one-half of the public service (in a country where ministerial responsibility is assumed to be the key to good government) and, while not unique in themselves, have been employed for federal purposes uncommon in English-speaking North America. The public business enterprise in Canada is as old as Confederation, and some municipalities and provinces have pioneered in using public devices for electrical utilities, transportation systems, and (on the prairies) telephone services. The structure of Canadian government owes much to the ancient willingness of Canadians to use public funds to build railways, canals, and harbour facilities, and later, as the needs of the country changed, to use public funds to possess railways, airlines, ships, radio and television networks, uranium mines, and synthetic-rubber plants. For all these and similar purposes the Crown corporation outside the direct political control of a minister has seemed to be the appropriate device, though other reasons for their establishment include a desire to remove a controversial or highly technical matter from politics, to establish a unit that is financially independent, and to attract into public administration businesslike men who would balk at becoming mere civil servants.

The Crown corporation is in every instance an *ad hoc* solution to a pressing problem, and as such gives evidence of the inventiveness of Canadians when it comes to circumventing supposedly established principles, and even the constitution itself. The complexity of the Canadian scene is such that no simple and rigid structure of government would have any chance of being successful. The country has always needed not only *local* government, in the widest sense, but also shadowy areas where no permanent government exists but into which a committee or a royal commission can be thrust to investigate, to create or plumb public opinion, or to prepare the public for a decision which the government is ready to announce as soon as a respected and carefully selected authority recommends it. Consultative and advisory committees are born every year, destined to give representation to nascent interests and to keep the prime minister and his colleagues, or individual departments and agencies, in touch with the public pulse on weighty matters. Despite the overwhelming importance of Dominion-provincial relations in Canada, no federal department to cope with them has existed since 1873, when the portfolio of the Secretary of State for the Provinces was abolished on the improbable grounds that its incumbent had not enough to do.

The main single reason for the failure to re-establish the portfolio is undoubtedly that Dominion-provincial relations concern such high policy that they have had to remain in the hands of the prime minister and (primarily) his minister of finance. The result has affected the form of government in two ways: the Dominion-provincial conference, which meets irregularly and treats a wide variety of topics, is none the less a permanent part of Canadian political machinery; and one of the most important subjects in Canadian politics is discussed and its problems settled outside of Parliament, at the top executive or diplomatic level. There is, indeed, no association outside the party organizations which combines members of the several legislatures as such, and Canadian M.P.s are as likely to meet their provincial counterparts at a session of the Commonwealth Parliamentary Association in Africa or Asia as in Canada.

Dominion-provincial relations do not lend themselves to ready generalizing, but a good deal can be said about the constitutional framework within which they take place. The British North America Act enjoys three distinctions that

surely set it apart from the rest of the world: for a century it
has remained as a statute of *another* country; during that
period it had no single acceptable method for amendment;
and the two major groups who together comprise most of
the Canadian population have never agreed on what it
represented when it was written.

Whether it was just another constitution which, in sound
British tradition, naturally omitted all reference to such
things as the prime minister and his cabinet – which everybody of course knew about – or whether it was a compact
between two peoples – again not mentioned because *that* was
understood too – the British North America Act certainly
intended to establish an approach to a federal system – a
quasi-federal system, it has been called – in which the Dominion government was to be paramount. The grant of
powers to the federal Parliament is sweeping. The federal
authority was given control over what were in 1867 crucial matters affecting the provinces: the appointment of
Lieutenant-Governors, judges of the higher provincial courts,
and senators representing the provinces in Parliament; the
reservation and disallowance of *any* provincial legislation
within a year of its passage; and the passage of remedial legislation by Parliament under certain circumstances affecting
separate schools in a province. The grant of powers to the
provincial legislatures was a limited list, which did not
include the monopoly of so much as one field of taxation.

Almost every relevant factor has since Confederation
worked to turn this part of the structure of Canadian government upside down. The decision to make each province a
miniature responsible government inevitably led to cen-
tralism within each province, and hence to rivalry with the
Dominion. The decision to have a few large provinces instead
of many small ones has minimized the Dominion government's opportunities either to dominate the provinces, or
to play them off against each other; the two largest, paradoxically, cannot be played off against each other without
endangering the Dominion. The development of the welfare
state and the invention of the automobile have in wholly

unforeseen ways added to the powers originally given to the provinces. The mere problem of space makes Ottawa remote from much of Canada and enhances the importance of provincial capitals, a truism to which urbanization around the main cities of Canada has in recent years given an added fillip. The patterns of migration and settlement, the exploitation of provincial resources, and the rise of powerful industries based on them, have all contributed to what right-thinking English Canadians of nationalist bent consider a subversion of the constitution.

And to these comprehensible economic and political elements must be added the mysteries of judicial decision, which by the 1920s had reduced Parliament's main (and originally sole) grant of power to a highly specialized instrument that could be used only in emergency operations, with the courts deciding what an emergency was; while the powers of the provinces were at the same time steadily extended, generally under 'property and civil rights', a phrase whose scope in popular meaning, as well as in legalistic meaning, has grown. Occasional and sporadic reversals of these trends have been observable from time to time, and the statute of 1949 which made the Supreme Court of Canada the last court of appeal for Canadians has given considerable heart – not without justification in recent years – to those who read the British North America Act as if it means what it says. But even English-Canadian commentators on the Act disagree about what it says.

If the Supreme Court is to emerge as a champion of Parliament's power, it will not only become regarded as something it has never been, a 'political' court and a subject of controversy; it will also be going contrary to what seems to have been a satisfactory interpretation of the constitution for a large number of Canadians. For though a handful of academics and national politicians have long spoken almost with awe of the interpretations of the British North America Act that have been issued from time to time by the courts, not even the feeblest of public opinions has been aroused to support them. And on the positive side, those actual changes in the text of the act that have taken place have revealed no compelling urge among Canadians to reverse the courts' reversals by constitutional amendment. The provincial governments, including even those eccentric enough to believe that a strong national government is a good thing nowadays – a peculiarly English-Canadian notion – have not gone out of their way to bring one into being. The revision of our original quasi-federal structure into a genuine federal structure, in short, seems to have been acceptable to the great mass of Canadians.

The one genuine and extensive source of complaint about the revised structure has been that provincial revenues have never kept up with provincial obligations, a fact which, second only to relations between the French-speaking and the English-speaking, has put greater strains on federalism in Canada than any other single factor, and produced another great series of *ad hoc* devices variously designed to shore up the weakest provinces, exploit to the full the direct taxes permitted the provinces, take from the rich and give to the poor, maintain certain minimum national standards in sundry areas affecting the citizen, and lure the provinces into enterprises that the Dominion was interested in but the provinces could not afford; and all this while the Dominion retained the monopoly of 'any mode or system of taxation' assigned it by the constitution. The depression of the 1930s put one kind of strain on this structure; the two world wars another; the welfare state a third; and the rise of theories about the use of national fiscal policy to manipulate the economy agreeably yet a fourth. The tangled snarl of Dominion-provincial financial relations cannot be summarized here: it has involved a wholly flexible structure in the sense that everything anybody can think of has been tried, a wholly rigid one in the sense that no permanent solution has ever been sighted. The renaissance in Quebec has added strains that are new in kind but familiar in form. The Canadian constitutional structure includes an uneven distribution of responsibilities and tax sources that reaches down to the smallest municipalities, which understandably find it difficult to persuade their provinces to be yet more generous with them, as the provinces in turn are always urging the Dominion.

The citizen who views the complex network of Canadian government with the somewhat less than Olympian detachment of a taxpayer might on occasion be justified if he compared himself to a passenger on one of his forefathers' superannuated sailing barques: though it is in no immediate danger of sinking because it is loaded with lumber, when in trouble it could none the less ship a lot of water and be uncomfortably full of holes, and even appear frequently to be on the verge of breaking up; yet the same ship in calm water sails as smoothly as any other. It has often been said of Canada that it is a difficult country to govern, thanks to problems of space and the thin thread of its population strung across the country; of language, race, and religion; of deep economic inequalities among the provinces; and of being overshadowed by husky friends. Since this is so, the structure of its government can be considered a success only if it survives; and government in Canada has so far operated well above the survival level. Its founders in 1867 introduced no startling innovations but built on known foundations. Their successors have contrived to alter the structure, but always on the same foundations. The structure they have produced is one in which the strait-laced observance of constitutional niceties must often give way to a principle invented on the spur of the moment. It is one that makes almost insatiable demands on the supply of able men for both politics and administration. It has never proven itself adaptable to a rigorous penny-pinching attitude on the part of those men, virtually all of whom have been ready to recognize that they work in an enterprise in continual need of expert repairs; and repairs cost money whether expert or not.

For all these reasons, and others, no part of the government of Canada can be said to have become a national monument. The parliamentary tradition, for example, is weak rather than strong; but Parliament has many rivals, including not only the ten provincial legislatures (all of which now maintain governmental operations larger than those of the entire Dominion at Confederation) but also Dominion-provincial conferences and the federal cabinet, which are key parts of the Canadian representative system. Even within Parliament the Speaker of the House of Commons is not a grand national figure as 'Chief Commoner', but a relatively minor actor, generally destined to play his role briefly and then give way to another deserving recipient, probably from the other language group. The monarchical symbol is strong, but Canadians do not uniformly regard it in the same way, and it is itself divided between a Queen who lives abroad and a Canadian in Ottawa. And so on. Whichever of our political institutions one selects, one will at once find it sharing the limelight, if it is in the limelight at all, with others.

Paradoxically, the inability of Canadians to find in their government the equivalent of, say, the American presidency, or the Crown in Britain, does not result from a relative unimportance of government in Canada, or a relative lack of it, but rather the contrary. From the days of the earliest French colonists, Canada has never suffered from under-government, and her citizens, including the vaunted pioneers who settled the west, have always wanted government to be not too far away. The structure they have erected might win few prizes for polish or general proficiency, but it has one saving grace which is almost a credo in the mind of every successful practitioner who has ever been involved in it: it works, and it works in the presence of different peoples devoted to the same country, but not necessarily to each other.

28. Social Services

ALBERT ROSE

In the last two decades of the first century of Confederation, Canada has frequently been referred to as a 'welfare state'. These allusions have been made most often, however, by those who oppose further extension of intergovernmental programs of social welfare and health services. The basis of the reference was the proliferation of tax-supported programs inaugurated after 1940, and the fact that the proportion of Canada's net national income devoted to the social and health services reached 9.4 per cent in 1957 and increased to 12.5 per cent in 1963. By comparison, the proportion in the United States in the latter year was 8.5 per cent.

In retrospect, the process that provided the opportunity for serious debate throughout the post-war period began long before the onset of the Second World War and may, indeed, be traced back beyond the date of Confederation. The assumption of responsibility by Canadian society to meet the needs of its less fortunate members through the resources of local, provincial, and federal governmental agencies was, however, substantially limited prior to the onset of the Great Depression (1929-39) to cases of outright destitution or medical indigency.

Until recently it was assumed by most students of the subject that the services and policies usually envisaged within the meaning of the twentieth-century term 'social welfare' simply did not exist in Canada during the second half of the nineteenth century. R. B. Splane has demonstrated that this assumption is not valid and that, in fact, a great many activities were undertaken in the fields of charities and corrections before and during the first third-century of Confederation, out of which emerged the modern concepts of social policy. He concluded, 'It would appear, indeed, that a kind of practical humanitarianism always found a significant degree of expression both in public and in private endeavours.' Clearly, however, there is a vast difference between the practical expression of philanthropy within a society dominated by the laissez-faire principles of the Manchester School and the ideology of what J. S. Morgan has described as 'the socially responsible state'. The acceptance of social policies which led in Canada to the substantial assumption of public responsibility is, for the most part, a development of the last forty years.

In terms of public interest in welfare matters, of the involvement of the various levels of government in Canada, and of total and per-capita expenditures on social welfare by the public authorities, the year 1929 does seem to provide a real dividing line. Prior to 1929 the social services under public auspices were largely confined to the provision of modest amounts of money intended to relieve destitution. In the event of a personal or family crisis, such as the illness and consequent unemployment of the breadwinner, or in the event of a catastrophe such as fire or flood, the local authority might provide a short-term payment to help the family meet the impact of the emergency. Such assistance was not given as a matter of right, nor planned in relation to the needs of the destitute, whose hope of additional assistance, if required, lay in the existence of voluntary charitable organizations, often under sectarian auspices.

The onset of a long period of deep economic depression did not effect radical change in this picture quickly in Canada, or result in any major comprehensive legislative attack upon social insecurity, such as the Social Security Act of 1935 in the United States. Rather, the dismal and dreary progression of years of economic stagnation, of incredibly great unemployment, and of dire poverty for a very substantial proportion of Canadian families did serve to awaken the nation to the sheer lack of public and voluntary services to meet human needs in an industrial society. The gaps in the social services were evident as never before. The shortage of personnel – trained and untrained – to help individuals and families to survive in a period of peace-time became obvious, not merely to those in need but to the relatively well off as well. The nature of the changes taking place in Canadian as in all Western societies began to be understood and examined in the sphere of government as well as in the private business community. The Royal Commission on Dominion-Provincial Relations, 1937-40 (the Rowell-Sirois Commission) was the logical and inevitable consequence of these social and economic concerns. Its recommendations helped to lay the foundation for the constitutional, political, economic, and administrative participation of the federal government, in partnership with other governments, in the expanded provision of social welfare and health services.

Twenty-five years later the array of programs designed to provide specific categorical and general assistance to persons and families in Canada is impressive. In some respects the nature and variety of the services provided, such as family allowances and hospital insurance, are well ahead of provisions in the United States. In other respects, as in old age pensions and survivors' insurance, Canadians have not been so well served. Nevertheless, there has developed in Canada a series of intergovernmental arrangements and administrative techniques scarcely visualized in 1939.

In the early 1960s, however, the so-called 'shared program' – in which the federal government sets national standards and provides a substantial proportion of the funds required and the provincial government administers the program and provides the balance of the funds – has been disowned by the government of Quebec as an obstacle to the attainment of mastery within its own sphere. The federal government has permitted Quebec to 'opt out' of some thirty federal-provincial programs on the understanding that sums of money equivalent to the federal contributions will continue to be made available from the federal treasury to enable the province to undertake its own programs. Other provincial governments have suggested that they would welcome a similar arrangement. This, plus increasing demands upon the provincial governments in the fields of education and the social services, and their growing acceptance of social responsibility, threatens seriously the entire centralized administrative and financial structure built since 1946.

It is a great source of satisfaction for Canadians to observe that the Gross National Product (total market value of all goods and services produced) was more than $52 billion in 1965, where in 1933 the comparable figure was slightly less than $3½ billion. The fact that these are over-all national figures must be emphasized. The truly significant questions are concerned with the distribution of the total national income, as between the various factors of production and between the several geographical regions in a country like Canada. Has the high level of economic activity and prosperity since 1939 brought commensurate gains to the Canadian people? What is the impact of very rapid change upon Canadian families and family life? The major elements of change must be recorded and the evidence weighed carefully.

The increase of seventy per cent in our population in less than twenty-five years is, in the view of the specialists in demography, phenomenal. Moreover, such increase is not, as some people believe, largely due to immigration from abroad, which has amounted to 2½ million persons since 1945. It is primarily the result of one of the highest birth-rates in the world and a decreasing and relatively low death-rate. Births in Canada are now approximately 425,000 per year and exceed deaths by more than 300,000. Together with immigration (less emigration) they account for a net annual increase in the Canadian population of about 350,000 persons.

By 1957, it was reported that one-third of the total Canadian population was under 15 years of age, that is, about 5½ million children. Today the proportion is about the same but the number is about 6½ million; by 1967 it may be 7 million. We are all aware that the full tide of this flood of children has engulfed our elementary schools, has reached our high schools, and will, by the late 1960s, more than double enrolments of the early 1960s in Canadian universities, despite the retention of high standards of admission. At the other end of the age distribution Canadians are tending to live longer in substantially increasing numbers. Nearly one in every eight Canadians is now over 60 years of age and one in every twelve is over 65 years of age. In absolute terms this means that more than 1.6 million persons are at least 65 years of age and about 2.4 million are at least 60 years old. Those over 70 numbered one million for the first time in 1965.

The major implications of these facts concerning the two extremes in the Canadian age distribution are quite simple. The proportion of Canadians in the most productive years – ages 20 to 59 – is less than 50 per cent. For the first time in our history half the population, generally speaking, must support the other half. This ratio of productive to dependent persons in our society has been decreasing since 1929 but will probably remain as it is for two or three decades, in view of the rapidly increasing numbers of both young people and old people in this country. It is recognized, of course, that many persons under 20 are employed, and that many persons over 60 continue to be productive even beyond 70 years of age.

A further implication of increased population is little understood, particularly by those who deplore the fact that the numbers requiring assistance and the total cost of providing social services has increased substantially in the prosperous Canadian society of the 1950s and 1960s, by comparison with the situation in the depressed 1930s. The sheer numbers make it inevitable, without any increase in the rates of such phenomena as child neglect, mental retardation, illegitimate birth, and juvenile delinquency, that the child welfare agencies, both voluntarily and publicly sponsored, will be under very severe pressure. Similarly, services for the elderly, including institutional facilities and housing programs, and hospitals for chronically ill are literally years behind in meeting justifiable requests for assistance and placement.

Canadians are now, for the most part, city-dwellers and increasingly are to be found within the seventeen census-designated metropolitan areas. A good deal may depend, of course, on the census definition of 'urban' and 'rural', but there can be no question of the direction of the trend. In the census of 1901, 65 of every 100 Canadians were considered 'rural' dwellers; by 1931 the rural-urban ratio was almost 50-50; by 1951, 54 of every 100 Canadians were designated 'urban' dwellers, and the ratio today is probably 71-29 in favour of urban residents. In the census of 1961 it was 69-31.

More particularly, much of our population growth is occurring within a very few metropolitan cities. In Canada the increase in total population from 1951 to 1961 was 30.2 per cent, but the increase in the seventeen census metropolitan areas was more than 54 per cent. In 1961, 45 per cent of the Canadian population lived in these metropolitan areas. The Report of the Royal Commission on Canada's Economic Prospects, 1955-1980 (the Gordon Commission) suggested that nearly two-thirds of our population of some 27 millions will reside in these cities by 1980, and nearly four-fifths of all Canadians will be urban dwellers. During the 1950s, when the residents of metropolitan areas increased in number by more than half, the population of the central (core) cities in these areas rose slowly or not at all, while outside the central cities in the vast suburbs the increase was phenomenal. Our urbanization, therefore, has been a suburbanization for the most part.

The ramifications of these urban concentrations of population are widespread and of profound significance. There is no doubt that the urban industrial society collects and deposits its needy persons and families in very substantial measure at the heart of the metropolis. The urban core deteriorates along with its residents, and the combination of slum environment, personal disability, and family disorganization has proved to be one with which the social and health services are unable to cope. Human need tends to be concentrated in the urban central city within the metropolitan area, and research in many North American cities has shown that a very small proportion of families (as few as 6 per cent) absorbs a very substantial proportion of all services available (as much as 50 per cent).

In this era of rapid population growth, urbanization, and industrialization, a high degree of mobility seems to be characteristic of our mode of living. In part, this tendency is implicit within the organization of modern industry and commerce. The main implications of frequent family movement upon the individual, upon family life, and upon the community are largely unexplored. It is known, however, that for some individuals and families there are profound effects – upon children, parents, and grandparents. Nevertheless, the report of a study conducted by the School of Social Work, University of Toronto, in 1957, points out that 'we can scarcely ignore the potential significance in this connection of the high premium which our society places on upward economic and social mobility.'

Not all mobility is upward, however, and the relatively needy move about as much if not more frequently than those in better circumstances. When they do make such moves and apply for assistance – counselling or financial aid – they may encounter residence regulations that deny welfare assistance to those who have not resided in the municipality or province for a period of one year or more, depending upon the provincial legislation or local stipulation. Moreover, in the large metropolitan areas encompassing a dozen or more municipalities, frequent movement across boundary lines is the cause of a good deal of headache and heartache for those in need and for the social agency staffs who seek to serve them. The required funds and personnel are not clearly available for persons or families who in effect claim no municipality as their home.

At the end of the Second World War the labour force in Canada numbered approximately 4,500,000 persons. By 1957 the comparable figure exceeded 6,000,000 and it is estimated that more than 7,000,000 Canadians were employed in 1965. The annual increase in the labour force depends upon a number of factors, including the availability of jobs, but it is at least 100,000 persons in years of economic recession and may exceed twice that number in more prosperous years. It is clear that our national economy has been required to provide about 2½ million additional jobs since 1946. To a substantial degree we have succeeded in this tremendous task, although there have been several periods of severe unemployment.

Almost one in four Canadians in the labour force is a woman. This proportion has been remarkably stable since the mid 1950s, although it had increased steadily during the war and early post-war years. Approximately one-half of these women are married (the proportion was less than one-quarter in 1955), although it is not known how many of these married women have children. Employment opportunities for women continue to expand rapidly. During the last quarter of 1963 nearly 1,900,000 women were at work in Canada and the statisticians made particular mention of the increased numbers of married women seeking employment. The number of employed women had increased nearly 7.5 per cent over the last quarter of 1962.

Working wives make up at least 12 per cent of the labour force: that is, nearly 850,000 persons. In a major research project carried out in the mid 1950s by the Women's Bureau of the Canadian Department of Labour in co-operation with the eight schools of social work in Canada, the prime reasons given for seeking employment were economic. Married women said they worked to help pay for a house or to save for a house, to pay for automobiles, television sets, and costly vacation trips. While some of those interviewed felt that there were social and emotional components in their employment as well, and that they might be better mothers as a consequence of working, few ventured beyond the need to satisfy tangible elements in the family standard of living.

The employment of adolescents in recent years is an additional phenomenon replete with disturbing implications for the society and its social services. In 1961 the Social Planning Council of Metropolitan Toronto warned young entrants to the labour force that they were probably destined for a life of unemployment. This statement noted that in the years 1935-9 about 5,000 young Canadians aged 15-19 entered the labour force each year; the prospect for the later 1960s was 100,000 new entrants per annum. Some 35 per cent of Canadians in this age group were in the labour force in the early 1960s, that is, were available for and actively seeking employment. Unemployment among them was more than twice the national average and more than three times the average for adult married men. The typical pattern revealed in research interviews with unemployed adolescents runs in these terms: they leave school, they say, to assist the family financially; they are currently unemployed; they are being supported by their families or have left them to subsist alone. Social agencies find it extremely difficult to reach such youths even to offer help.

Income is the lifeblood of our economic and social system. Canadians, in recent years, have produced goods and services with a market value about ten times greater than in the best years of the 1930s and about sixteen times greater than in the worst years of that dismal decade. Even when we take into account the fact that total population is 70 per cent greater and that prices have tripled since 1939, it is probable that per-capita purchasing power has doubled in the twenty years since the close of the Second World War. Income per capita in simple dollar terms has quadrupled and is approaching

$2,000 per annum. Average hourly wages and average weekly earnings in the leading Canadian industries have more than tripled, and a substantial proportion of the labour force earns far more than the national average. Interestingly enough, it has been possible for many workers to achieve these higher wages for a considerably shorter working week. On the average, in 1944 industrial workers worked a little more than 46 hours per week; by 1950 this average was just over 42 hours; by mid 1958 the average working week in industry in Canada was 40.7 hours. Today, in some industries, the average is less than 40 hours.

Higher incomes and a shorter working week should mean, surely, increasing opportunities for the use of greater leisure time and a whole series of implications for family living. What it does appear to mean for an increasing number of families is a second job for father on a part-time basis on the week-end or his day off. While there are no reliable statistical data on this point, the tendency is unmistakably clear. Moreover, the continuously higher cost of providing a reasonably adequate standard of living for the larger Canadian family of recent years has meant that one income – that of the principal wage-earner – is insufficient. The social implications emanating from the employment of the married woman, particularly the working mother, are as yet relatively unknown.

Western industrial society is, once again, in the grip of a revolution that will, without doubt, alter a great many aspects of our lives and indeed our way of thinking about certain aspects of life. As one writer has expressed it, 'As the machine generated changes in industry and society, so automation will alter our consumption of leisure and our concepts of work, and may give living a new character.'

The prime concern of the social services at this stage is with those who are threatened with more or less permanent but unpaid leisure. It is clear that those jobs that have been commonly filled by the unskilled and least educated in the society are scheduled to disappear in increasing numbers. Moreover, many jobs now held by persons who consider themselves skilled or at least semi-skilled, and by persons who

consider themselves in managerial capacities, will disappear
during the next decade or two. It is not unreal to visualize the
possibility that many workers will require re-training two or
more times during their working careers. While there are
new jobs being created at the same time, in part by the computers themselves, these are often not capable of being filled
by those displaced in the first instance and, as has been noted,
are very often in the categories filled by women.

Work has always been one of the principal sources of status
in our society. 'The kind of work that we do, to the extent
that it can be readily identified and given a meaningful label
by our associates, gives us, in great measure, our place in
life.' The several industrial revolutions since the eighteenth
century have weakened this relationship to the point that,
increasingly, status comes primarily from the things that
money can buy. Moreover, work satisfaction, which is bound
up with the degree to which a worker can exercise his judgement on his job, will necessarily diminish even further, as
automated procedures reduce or eliminate man's role in
production.

It is frequently stated that the Canadian standard of living
is 'the third (or second) highest standard of living in the
world'. What is meant by this statement is a simple fact –
Canadians do have per capita more goods and services available for consumption than the people of any other nation,
with the exception of the United States and Sweden. We have
so many automobiles that our transportation facilities are
close to strangulation in urban traffic; almost every family has
a television set (where reception is possible), and many have
more than one set; most of our families abound in radios,
washing-machines, clothes driers, mechanical refrigerators,
and smaller appliances. Food and clothing are abundant in
Canada. Housing is far more abundant than fifteen or twenty
years ago but remains in short supply for those families in
the lowest two-fifths of the income distribution. The health
conditions of Canadians are generally satisfactory and our
standards of medicine and public health are relatively high.
Millions of Canadians have joined voluntary or governmen-

tal prepayment programs to meet the very high costs of illness and hospitalization.

From the point of view of those who work in the social welfare and mental health services particularly, the fundamental question that must be posed at this point is, simply: Are Canadians and Canadian families relatively happy, relatively well-adjusted, relatively more able to avoid social breakdown than in past decades? By 'social breakdown' is meant the inability of an individual or family to function in society in what is considered an acceptable mode of living and behaviour without the help of some voluntarily or publicly provided service. Needless to state, there are no measures of absolute happiness and the well-adjusted state may be one which none of us would prefer. Nevertheless, some of the facts concerning social need in Canada merit examination, lest we be carried away in our joyful flood of automobiles and appliances.

It is fairly commonplace now to state that we live in an industrial, as opposed to an agricultural, society; that the typical citizen is an employee of a relatively large impersonal corporation which hires him for a specific job at a specific hourly or weekly rate. Our citizen lives and works in an urban centre, most often in the midst of a metropolitan area. He is paid for the job he performs, in cash at the market rate of remuneration and without reference to his marital status, number of dependants, and other financial obligations. It must be obvious that any interruption in the regular rhythm of the cycle of work, wages, expenditures, and payments is a matter of grave concern to the individual and particularly to his family, if he has one.

The classic exposition of the causes of poverty in this kind of society was made by Sir William Beveridge in 1942. This classification is well worth reproduction if we are to understand the nature of poverty and its meaning for those responsible for policy decisions in the fields of social welfare and health. Beveridge wrote in his *Report on Social Insurance and Allied Services* that there are eight primary causes of need: unemployment, that is, the inability of a person dependent on and physically fit for employment to obtain work; disability, that is, the inability of a person of working age to pursue a gainful occupation because of illness or accident; loss of livelihood, that is, by a person not dependent on paid employment, such as a professional person or self-employed shopkeeper; retirement, by virtue of age; marriage needs of a woman, which would include the needs associated with marriage, maternity, cessation of a husband's earnings through unemployment, disability, or retirement, widowhood, legal separation, and incapacity for household duties; funeral expenses, that is, of self or dependants; childhood, that is, the expense of rearing and educating children, including the neglected, deserted, or truly orphaned child; and physical disease or incapacity, that is, of self or dependants. To this list should be added, at least, *mental retardation*, intelligence sufficiently below the normal that the individual is unable to earn enough income to provide a minimum adequate standard of living for himself or his family.

It is clear, then, that the question 'Who are the poor?' has no simple answer. If we may put the point in another way, the simple answers are generally based upon simple prejudices. For example, the 'poor' are still frequently thought to be lazy, shiftless, wasteful persons who are either so devoid of energy that their earnings are nil or substandard or highly irregular, or so devoid of intelligence in their spending habits that the product of their labour is largely wasted or does not redound to the benefit of their families. The fact is that there are few such people in our society today, and those who might fit the description of permanent indolence are often persons with a profound emotional sickness or those who are alcoholics, drug addicts, and the like.

Despite the recent concern and attention to the nature and cause of poverty, many people find it difficult to accept the fact that there is poverty and social distress in the affluent society. They will, for the most part, concede the unfortunate adversity of some families and some individuals – the widowed mother with dependent children; the chronically ill head of a household; the mentally retarded child; the elderly person without family. It might be said that there is fairly general agreement on the nature and misfortune of 'the dependent poor', those dependent upon public or charitable funds for basic support. For all the rest who may be considered as poor, however, the responsibility is regarded not as that of the state and its total citizenry, but primarily as that of the individual and members of his family. Even when the problems do not necessarily include a need for money but involve relationships between people, within the family, and within the community – marital difficulty, parent-child conflict, juvenile delinquency, personality disorders, mental illness – there is not widespread understanding and support.

A consideration of the nature and role of the social services in a federal country like Canada at once raises questions and issues of a constitutional, political, economic, social, and administrative nature. From a constitutional point of view it is eminently clear that most social welfare provisions have been interpreted to be the responsibility of the provincial governments under Section 92 of the British North America Act, which assigned 'property and civil rights' to the provinces. A constitutional amendment was required before the government of Canada inaugurated a system of unemployment insurance in 1940. A further amendment was required before the introduction of the Old Age Security Act in 1951. Similar action was essential when a contributory old age and survivors' insurance scheme was to be added to our social security system in 1965. Many of the major public measures have taken the form, however, of federal legislation which offers grants or partial payments in support of assistance to certain categories of disadvantaged persons if and when the provincial governments pass complementary legislation.

Since 1940 the provincial governments have found themselves with financial resources inadequate to the tremendous responsibilities which are theirs in an industrial urbanized society. The federal government, on the other hand, with more flexible sources of revenue, does not have the basic constitutional responsibilities. While the provinces have not always enthusiastically welcomed the advent of these so-called 'shared programs', they did not resist the development of intergovernmental arrangements until the 1960s. Most have now adopted the viewpoint of the Province of Quebec that 'sharing' should be restricted simply to the financial contribution required from the federal government. In this view, administration in all aspects should be determined at the provincial and local level.

In order to comprehend the nature and extent of public participation in health and welfare measures, we must look at the present governmental programs from two points of view or systems of classification: the level of government or governments involved, and the method of providing the social or health service. It must be pointed out that most governmental schemes are designed to maintain or improve the income of a disadvantaged person or family. There may be trained social workers on staff in administrative or supervisory positions or even in a specialized counselling service attached to the program, but the basic objective is to meet physical or essential needs rather than psychological or emotional needs. The following exposition is based upon a classification by level of government:

FEDERAL PROGRAMS

1. *Family Allowances* (The Family Allowances Act, 1944)
In recognition of the fact that wages and salaries are not related to the size of family, an amount of $6 or $8 per month (depending on the child's age) is paid to the mother on behalf of each child under the age of 16. Date of inception was July 1, 1945.

2. *Youth Allowances* (The Youth Allowances Act, 1964)
A payment of $10 per month is made on behalf of each youth aged 16 or 17 to encourage young people to remain in school so that they may further their education and their eventual opportunity in the labour market. Date of inception was September 1, 1964.

3. *Old Age Security Allowances* (The Old Age Security Act, 1951)

An allowance (at present $75 per month) is paid to every person over the age of 70 who has resided in Canada for 10 years.* Date of inception was January 1, 1952.

In these three wholly federal undertakings the benefits are paid by cheque one month after formal application has been made. No means test is required to prove need.

4. *Canada Pension Plan (1965)*

In March 1965 the federal parliament passed Bill 136, 'An act to establish a comprehensive program of old age pensions and supplementary benefits in Canada payable to and in respect of contributors'. This legislation, known as the Canada Pension Plan, has many features that constitute new departures in Canada's social security program. The plan came into effect on January 1, 1966, and requires that each employee and each employer contribute 1.8 per cent with respect to the employee's first $5,000 of annual earnings, less an exemption of $600. The full pension will be available in 1976, and in the meantime lesser amounts will be paid to those who retire. In addition to the retirement pension, the current Old Age Security Pension of $75 per month will be paid. The Canada Pension Plan is so constructed that it will be adjusted to changes in the general wage level and in the cost of living. The benefit scales are related to the standard of living attained by each individual contributor rather than to the assumption of a minimum standard supported by a single flat-rate payment. For the first time in Canada the program includes a provision for the widows and surviving dependants of deceased family heads.

5. *Unemployment Insurance* (The Unemployment Insurance Act, 1940)

A weekly benefit is paid to a person who is unemployed, is seeking work, and is available for work. The scheme is

*The age at which the allowance is paid is to be reduced progressively to age 65 over the five-year period beginning 1966.

financed by weekly contributions from employees and employers, which are equal in size and vary in amount in relation to the size of earnings. Persons who earn more than $5,400 per annum are not covered. Provided that he has paid in a specified number of contributions, the beneficiary can draw benefits for a specified number of weeks – a limit that has varied from time to time from 26 to 52 weeks. The federal government assumes the cost of administration and may have to supplement the fund, which dropped from more than $900 million in 1957 to less than $100 million by 1963.

6. *Veterans' Programs* (various pieces of legislation)
The Department of Veterans Affairs administers several schemes including War Veterans' Allowances to needy veterans and their dependants on a means-test basis; pensions to widows of veterans killed in action or as a result of warfare; and pensions to disabled veterans. Federal hospitals are maintained in several major cities and many veterans qualify for medical care, rehabilitation services, and other benefits.

FEDERAL-PROVINCIAL PROGRAMS

1. *Old Age Assistance* (The Old Age Assistance Act, 1951)

2. *Allowances to the Blind* (The Blind Persons Act, 1951)

3. *Disabled Persons' Allowances* (The Disabled Persons Allowances Act, 1954)
An elderly person who is 65 to 69 years of age, a blind person who is 21 years of age or over, a person who is totally and permanently disabled and is 18 years of age or over, may qualify for a monthly allowance of $75 upon examination of his means. These programs are financed on a 50-50 basis in the case of elderly and disabled persons, and 75-25 by the federal and provincial governments respectively in the case of allowances to the blind.

4. *Hospital Insurance* (The Hospital Insurance Act, 1958)
In each Canadian province that passed the enabling legislation, every person enrolled in the program is entitled to

standard ward care, diagnostic, laboratory, and X-ray services, and drugs and medications while in hospital. In general, the federal government pays half the total cost, premiums are paid by individuals or families at rates set by the individual provincial Hospital Services Commission, and the provincial government pays the balance of the cost and the costs of administration.

5. *Canada Assistance Plan* (proposed 1965)
The development and enactment of the Canada Pension Plan during the winter of 1964-5 made it inevitable that a thorough examination of federal-provincial programs of public assistance would be required. In April 1965, in an Address on the Speech from the Throne, the Prime Minister described the major features of a so-called Canada Assistance Plan. The Plan will encourage a co-ordinated approach to public assistance in place of the present system of support under four federal statutes: the Old Age Assistance Act, the Blind Persons Act, the Disabled Persons Act, and the Unemployment Assistance Act. 'The Plan will facilitate the development of a comprehensive general assistance measure which, while recognizing the varying requirements of different groups, would meet these requirements within one programme and within one administrative framework.'

FEDERAL-PROVINCIAL-MUNICIPAL PROGRAMS

1. *General Welfare Assistance* (The Unemployment Assistance Act, 1958)
The provision of general assistance or 'relief' to those who do not qualify under any of the aforementioned categories of financial assistance, or whose unemployment insurance benefits have expired or require supplementation to provide a minimum adequate standard, is offered by municipal governments in all provinces except Newfoundland (where it is provincially administered) through an intergovernmental program. In Ontario, for example, the financial responsibility is split 50 per cent federal, 30 per cent provincial, and 20 per cent municipal, with the costs of administration locally

financed. In other provinces different proportions pertain,
although the federal share does not exceed one-half of the total assistance granted. The regulations governing the amount
of assistance and the manner in which family budgets are
determined are, of course, the responsibility of the province.
Benefits vary with size of family and age of persons, from
province to province, and between municipalities.

PROVINCIAL PROGRAMS

1. *Mothers' Allowances* (first Act in Manitoba, 1916)
In each Canadian province there is legislation providing for
a monthly grant for a mother with dependent children, and
who is widowed, or deserted, or whose husband is incapaci-
tated or incarcerated. The amount of the grant varies with
the size of family and from province to province and depends
upon a means test.

2. *Workmen's Compensation* (first Act in Ontario, 1914)
In each province there is legislation governing a program of
compensation financed by premiums paid by employers.
Premiums depend upon the safety record in the specific
industry. In the case of an industrial accident or an injury
suffered while in insured employment, the worker (or his
widow and dependants) may receive a proportion of his previous income – for life in some cases – as well as the essential
medical care, rehabilitation services, appliances, and so on.

3. *Mental Health Services*
Perhaps the most important provincial activity in the health
and welfare field is the mental health program. At any given
time in Canada during the mid 1960s more than 65,000
persons were hospitalized for treatment of a mental illness.
Thousands more attended out-patient clinics. The whole
field of mental health – mental hospitals, mental hygiene
clinics, child guidance clinics – is among the most costly of
provincial responsibilities in the social services.

4. *Services for the Elderly*
The provinces share in the capital and operating costs of

homes for the aged (particularly in Ontario) and provide grants on a per-capita per-diem basis to support persons in privately sponsored institutions financed by charitable contributions. Many provinces participate in federal-provincial housing programs for the elderly.

In addition to their responsibility for the administration of general welfare assistance, the larger municipalities in Canada are engaged in a variety of services, which differ from place to place. Municipalities, for example, maintain homes for the aged in Ontario and elsewhere, maintain hospitals for the chronically ill, and provide allowances to convalescent tuberculosis patients.

It can be noted, too, that the basic techniques of providing financial benefits are not identical in the various programs under governmental auspices. This is the second major system of classification referred to previously. Three main approaches can be identified: the universal transfer system, social insurance, and public assistance.

Universal transfer programs, such as Family Allowances, Youth Allowances, and Old Age Security Allowances for those over 70, are so described because every person who qualifies on the basis of age or some other criterion receives the allowances more or less automatically. Moreover, payments are made from general tax revenues and constitute a transfer from those who, generally speaking, pay taxes and do not qualify for payment, to those who receive the benefits by virtue of social need and who, for the most part, do not pay taxes. The key is income redistribution without a means test.

In 1951, following the deliberations of a joint legislative committee of the Senate and House of Commons, the government of Canada chose, as its social policy in the field of old age, to pay a flat-rate benefit to every Canadian over 70 years of age who fulfilled the simple residence qualification. At that time, clearly, the development of a social insurance program to meet the needs of retirement appeared, to responsible elected and appointed officials, to be too complex and too demanding in its administration. Fifteen years later the op-

posite decision has been taken. The weaknesses of the flat-rate
benefit available under a universal transfer system – the inadequacy of the retirement pension, the political opportunism evident whenever the amount of benefit was raised, the
inability to relate the amount of the pension to an assessment
of an adequate standard of living for older people – led to the
introduction of the Canada Pension Plan, which is fundamentally a wage-related social insurance program built on
top of the former old age security program. This decision
represents a fundamental change in Canadian social policy
and, since the plan includes benefits for survivors and for
dependent persons, represents a broad new approach of
partial consolidation of several aspects of the social services.

Social insurance programs, such as Unemployment Insurance, Workmen's Compensation, and the like, require payment of premiums by employers and/or employees. The
benefits are usually related to earnings and contributions,
and, in some measure, actuarial principles underlie the
amounts of contribution and benefit. The contributor in
effect 'insures' himself against the risk of unemployment or
accident, builds a credit for himself in time of need, and
considers that he is entitled to the benefit as a matter of right.

Public assistance programs, such as Old Age Assistance,
Mother's Allowances, General Welfare Assistance, are provided directly to persons who qualify for assistance on the
basis of need. The distinguishing characteristics are the establishment of specific categories of social disability and the
granting of assistance only after means have been established
through an assessment of assets and income, if any. Funds are
provided through general tax revenues.

In our western industrial society a great many voluntary
efforts have been directed over the past two centuries towards
the establishment and support of health and social welfare
services. Historically, these may have begun as the charitable
interest of one person or one family of wealth or prominence,
or of a group of persons, interested in alleviating the distress
of a particular group of disadvantaged persons described as

'the poor', or 'fallen women', or 'juvenile delinquents', or 'discharged prisoners', or whatever. The role of various churches and religious institutions has been of paramount importance in many of these developments. In the Province of Quebec until very recently the social services were almost entirely in the hands of the Church.

From the personal charity and religious conviction of individuals or families it was but a short step to the creation of social or health agencies, such as the Family Service Association or the Neighbourhood Workers' Association, the Jewish Family and Child Service or the Baron de Hirsch Institute, the Protestant Children's Homes, the Catholic Family Services, the Big Brother and Big Sister Associations, the Victorian Order of Nurses, and the St. Elizabeth Visiting Nurses Association. In other areas of interest there developed the Y.M.C.A., the Y.W.C.A., and the Y.M.H.A. In Ontario and elsewhere, from the example of the Society for the Prevention of Cruelty to Animals, there emerged the organizational design for the Children's Aid Societies, intended to prevent cruelty to children. Settlement houses sprang up in the crowded downtown areas of most urban centres and provided the first English-language classes for immigrants, the first well-baby clinics in co-operation with the public health authority, and the first lending libraries, as well as recreation programs for all age groups.

Until the 1920s each of these relatively new or old organizations, for the most part, conducted an annual campaign among its supporters for operating funds and often for capital funds as well. The first Community Chest in North America had been founded in Cleveland in 1913 to coordinate the raising of funds for many services through a central organization. In the 1920s there developed federations in Montreal, Toronto, and elsewhere under sectarian or so-called non-sectarian auspices, with such titles as the Council of Catholic Charities, the Federation of Jewish Philanthropies, and the Federation for Community Service. In Toronto these were combined during the Second World War, and by 1946 there emerged the Community Chest of Greater To-

ronto, now the United Community Fund of Metropolitan
Toronto. Annual campaigns by these federated fund-raising
agencies to meet the operating costs of local and national
services numbered 116 in 1962 and raised nearly $40 million.
The total estimated expenditure in the private sector is of the
order of $125 million.

It is in these private voluntary agencies (so called because
they do not receive tax funds for the most part and are
directed by a board of volunteers) that professional social
work is practised in great measure. Although professionally
trained social workers are found in the public programs, they
constitute a more substantial proportion of the staffs of the
voluntary agencies. A national study of the supply of and
demand for social workers was carried out by the Research
Division of the Federal Department of National Health and
Welfare between 1951 and 1954. The study revealed the
existence of about 3,000 social work positions in Canada in
those years, with annual losses of about 25 per cent of incum-
bents through death, retirement, and transfer to another field
of work. No reliable estimates have been published in recent
years but it is known that the number of job opportunities
has expanded considerably. Eight schools of social work have
been founded to date in Canada, all affiliated with major
universities and offering graduate degrees only (Master of
Social Work, and the doctorate). These schools, with a total
enrolment of about 500 students in the mid 1960s, are unable
to graduate sufficient students to meet the demand for social
workers, and as a result many jobs are filled by persons
without social work training in the traditional form. New
graduate schools and some undergraduate courses will be in
operation by 1967.

The principal fields of service within the private agencies
are usually described as family welfare, child welfare, medical
social work, psychiatric social work, school social work, group
work, community organization, social welfare administration, and research. Some of these fields are well developed
in Canada, others are not. In the first five of these fields of
service the method of working is known as social casework –

the practice of a professional relationship between a coun-
sellor and an individual or family. The objective is to help
the person to help himself, to muster his resources and act to
solve his problems. The social group worker works with
groups of children or adults to enable the individual to meet
some of his needs within a group setting such as a recreation
program. The community-organization worker works with
citizens' groups, neighbourhood associations, business
groups, and community leaders to plan for the development
of appropriate and adequate services in the community.
Organizations such as the Canadian Welfare Council, the
Ontario Welfare Council, and various local social planning
councils seek to foster and facilitate social welfare planning
within the community and the larger society.

Poverty in Canada during the last quarter of the first century
of nationhood has been limited, for the most part, to persons
and the families of persons who have suffered one of the
major setbacks enumerated by Beveridge. Although poverty
is not a general problem in Canada, perhaps 6 per cent of the
population are so lacking in the basic material essentials of
living that they require financial assistance, through public
or voluntary services, to enable them to achieve a subsistence
level. An additional substantial group the exact size of
which is unknown is so close to the poverty line that fundamental insecurity is characteristic of their lives.

The 'dependent poor', then, are those individuals and
families who experience gross and long-term poverty from
which there is little prospect of escape. Without attempting
to list the infinite variety of possibilities, the following groupings include the greatest majority of Canadians in dire
poverty:

The unemployed – Persons who have exhausted their unemployment insurance benefits may apply for general welfare
assistance, formerly described as 'unemployment relief' or
just 'relief'. Since 1958 assistance has been extended to em-
ployable persons as well as to unemployables. In January

1964 there were 736,748 persons in receipt of assistance, including dependants. Most of this large number are not yet chronic in their unemployment. A reasonable estimate of those who have become physically or emotionally incapable of employment would be 75,000 to 100,000 persons. Together with their dependants they may number 250,000 Canadians in poverty.

The disabled—Those in receipt of Disabled Persons' Allowance numbered 53,103 persons in Canada as of March 31, 1965.

Widowed or deserted mothers with dependent children—At March 31, 1964, there were 46,235 widowed or deserted mothers in receipt of Mothers' Allowance from the various provincial governments. In these families were some 123,791 children.

Unmarried mothers—A substantial proportion of unwed mothers require financial assistance as well as counselling provided through tax-supported or privately financed services. The majority place their babies for legal adoption after confinement but some retain the child and attempt to support it.

Illegitimate live births in Canada are approximately 4.5 per cent of all births and in 1961 amounted to nearly 21,500 births.

Children in care of Children's Aid Societies or Institutions—Children who are neglected, deserted, abandoned, or otherwise removed from their parents for various reasons cited in the appropriate provincial child welfare legislation (for example, the Child Welfare Act, Ontario, 1954) will be found, in most cases, in the care of specialized social agencies or in institutions.

In Ontario, at December 31, 1961, children in the care of Children's Aid Societies numbered 14,041. Ninety per cent of these children were legally permanent wards of the societies. Total figures for Canada, including those in institutions, are not available, but a moderate estimate would be 50,000.

Families of Offenders – The families of persons committed to prisons or reformatories are usually in receipt of Mothers' Allowance in the respective provinces.

Blind persons – Those in receipt of Blind Persons' Allowance at March 31, 1965, numbered 8,586.

Mentally defective persons – Those retarded persons who are unable to support themselves and are dependent upon public assistance are probably accounted for in large part in previous categories.

Aged persons – Those elderly persons unable to obtain gainful employment and to support themselves and/or dependants include a very large proportion of those in poverty in Canada.

At March 31, 1965, the number of persons in receipt of Old Age Assistance in the age group 65-9 was 107,354. The percentage of recipients to total population in this age group in Canada was about 21 per cent.

At the same date 993,582 Canadians over 70 were in receipt of Old Age Security. They may or may not be substantially dependent upon the allowance. It may safely be assumed that between 40 and 50 per cent have little or no additional income.

The mentally ill – Those persons who are sufficiently disturbed to be hospitalized number more than 65,000 at this time in Canadian history. Few are self-supporting or able to support their families at this stage in their illness. The mental health services are able to return a substantial and increasing proportion to the community, but little is known of their readjustment in economic and social terms.

The 'dependent poor' in Canada may thus include as many as 1,000,000 persons who are, by definition in this analysis, supported in whole or in substantial part by public and private welfare resources. Whether this is considered a significantly large segment or a significantly small segment of our total population (nearly 6 per cent) depends upon one's judgement and one's expectations for an industrial urban society.

This group does not include the so-called 'low-wage earner', the individual whose income is beyond the levels permitting eligibility for general welfare assistance but is not sufficient to enable him to provide a minimum adequate standard of living, including decent and adequate housing accommodation, for himself and his family. The dimensions of this group, which may be described as 'the self-supporting poor', cannot be stated precisely. Does the group include all of those families and persons above the public assistance level but falling within the lowest third of the income distribution, as some believe? In each family this will depend upon many factors: the age of the head of the household, the educational and vocational level of adults or parents, the size of family, the geographical location in the nation, and other influences. Their main characteristic is one of 'near dependence', and any serious interruption in the flow of income, any serious health problem or disability, will quickly push them into the clear category of those in poverty.

As yet in Canada there has not been sufficient research to delineate and document the extent of poverty more clearly. A reasonable estimate might be that the 'self-supporting poor' group is at least twice as numerous as the group in dire poverty, that is, at least two million persons. Canada's 'poor', then, may number a total of 3,000,000, as many as one in six or seven persons.

The fundamental need for financial assistance is clearly encompassed by the notion of social need, but social need may certainly exist without the need for money. In our late-twentieth-century society there may be a few families without some serious social disability affecting a family member or the intra-family relationships. Nevertheless, most people manage to maintain sufficient stability to function, in the community and within the family, in an appropriate fashion. How many seek help from private practitioners and from the social services is not precisely known: in the former case, for obvious reasons; in the latter case, because there is no uniform or consistent reporting of simple statistical data on a national scale.

An intricate network of social welfare and health services has been developed in Canada, for the most part since 1940. Canadian society has tended towards the creation of what might be termed 'the socially responsible state'. A great variety of public and private services have been established to ensure that those who suffer the risks of an industrial urban society receive basic support and guidance to help them solve their own problems by the exercise of their own strengths and resources.

One method of measuring the tremendous strides that have been made is to examine public expenditure on the social and health services and to adjust the figures to take population growth into account. It is known that until the 1920s annual expenditure was of the order of $2 per capita. When the depression arrived in 1929 Canada was totally unprepared to meet widespread want. The depth of distress was reached in 1933 when approximately 15 per cent of the population of some 10½ millions and up to 30 per cent of the urban work force were supported by public relief. The total public contribution to relief, from the inception of federal grants (cost-sharing) in 1931 until its end in 1941, was $1 billion.

During the two decades of post-war prosperity public expenditures have grown enormously as all governments have sought to provide a full measure of social security consistent with the encouragement of a free-enterprise economy. Population growth has, of course, played an important part in the expansion of expenditures, along with the slowly and steadily increasing level of prices and incomes. By the fiscal year 1956-7, expenditures of all levels of government on health and social welfare reached $2,004 million, about $125 per capita. Eight years later, in 1963-4, total expenditures had grown to $4,087 million, an increase of over 100 per cent, and per-capita expenditure reached $215. The distribution of total expenditure among the various levels of government was approximately 69 per cent federal, 28 per cent provincial, and 3 per cent municipal. The health programs require a growing proportion of government expenditures in health and social welfare combined. In 1956-7 health programs accounted for $470 million or 23 per cent; by 1963-4 these outlays amounted to $1,365 million or 34 per cent of the total.

Nevertheless, there are major gaps to be filled and serious deficiencies in Canadian social and economic policies to be remedied before the welfare services can perform their proper role of assisting all Canadians to achieve a reasonably secure and healthful existence. The first prerequisite of social welfare remains, as Beveridge pointed out long ago, the maintenance of a healthy economy and full employment. Most welfare programs are designed on the assumption that most people can take care of themselves most of the time and provide an adequate standard of living. When this is not the case, as in the 1930s and in recent years of severe unemployment, the social services are unable to bear the brunt of gross need. A very few years of 7 per cent to 11 per cent unemployment, from 1959 to 1961, virtually exhausted the what seemed to be huge Unemployment Insurance Fund in Canada.

The second prerequisite of welfare, as Morgan has emphasized, is the provision of health services that bring all the resources of modern medicine – preventive, curative, and rehabilitative – to every citizen when he needs them, and without barriers of cost. 'The case loads and the budgets of welfare services, public and private, are today loaded with the price of unavailable and inadequate health care.' In 1964 a Royal Commission on Health Services, initiated by a Conservative government in 1961, reported to a Liberal government. (The Liberal party had included health insurance in its platform in 1919; a Liberal government introduced a Draft Bill on Health Insurance in 1944, and proposed a comprehensive health service in 1946.) The Royal Commission of 1961-4 recommended a sweeping national health service program well beyond the expectations of the protagonists of such a scheme, and to the dismay of the medical and dental professions. At a Federal-Provincial Conference in July 1965 the federal government announced that it would implement the major recommendation of the Royal Commission by initiating a system of medical care insurance in co-operation with the provinces.

Social welfare, in an urban industrial society, demands a third essential prerequisite—the provision of good living conditions. Canada's record in the field of public housing and urban planning is among the most dismal one can discover in the Western world. If we are to live in cities, the urban centres must be replanned and redeveloped without the sacrifice of human considerations to physical and economic objectives. If we are to live in metropolitan areas, then planning must be regional in scope and method.

The system of social welfare and health services developed in Canada is now broadly supported by all major political parties at the national level. Some critics insist that this phenomenon is evidence that the welfare state corrupts both conservatives and liberals alike, and leads all political parties to bribe the electorate with their own money. It is interesting, therefore, to note that one leading Canadian Conservative political ideologist has written recently:

> Because of the welfare state the popular majority now has more to gain by conserving than by innovating. The first interest of the worker who has a guaranteed pension is to make sure that its value is not watered down by inflation. The first interest of the citizen who has hospital and medical insurance is to make sure that it is not nullified by the destruction of medical standards or the driving away of doctors. The first interest of the man who has won adequate leisure time is to make sure that the income he needs to enjoy it is not gobbled up by increased taxation. . . . The proper mission of conservatives is not to uproot the welfare state, but to educate the popular majority to their true conservative interest, for which the welfare state is partly responsible. The new affluent majority must start to think as payers of taxes as well as receivers of benefits. . . .

One yearns to meet the members of this popular affluent majority who have not previously thought of themselves as payers of taxes.

29. The Fighting Forces

GEORGE F. G. STANLEY

Speaking in the Legislative Assembly of Canada, on February 9, 1865, D'Arcy McGee said, 'Another motive to union . . . is this, that the policy of our neighbours to the south of us, has always been aggressive. . . . The acquisition of Canada was the first ambition of the American Confederacy, and never ceased to be so, when her troops were a handful and her navy scarce a squadron. Is it likely to be stopped now, when she counts her guns afloat by thousands and her troops by hundreds of thousands?'

The idea of British North American union was born of the threat of invasion and nurtured by the Fenian raids. It was therefore natural that Canadian interest in military matters should run high in 1867, and that Sir John A. Macdonald's senior colleague, Sir George Etienne Cartier, should take the portfolio of the Minister of Militia in the first federal cabinet. It was an indication of the importance attached to defence matters by the government and by the people.

In 1868 Cartier introduced the first Militia Bill into Parliament. In many ways it was no more than a continuation of the Act that had governed military policy in the pre-confederate province of Canada. It relied upon the volunteer principle, which had supplanted the system of compulsory enrolment during the 1850s. The *levée-en-masse* paid lip service to the idea of universal military service; but it was a theoretical obligation only and was never invoked. In addition to the new Act, which authorized a volunteer force of 40,000 (later 45,000), the government constructed the Intercolonial Railway as a military road linking the Maritimes and the St. Lawrence provinces, divided the country into nine Military Districts, encouraged the organization of new volunteer regiments, most of them infantry and cavalry, and spent $1,500,000 annually on defence during the early years of Confederation.

The first call upon the services of the Militia came in 1870. Following the Riel troubles in Manitoba, the government decided to send a military force to Fort Garry. The expedition was commanded by a British officer, Lt.-Col. Garnet Wolseley, and included a British unit, the 60th Rifles, and two specially recruited Militia battalions from Quebec and Ontario. The expedition's role was essentially one that has become more familiar in recent years – that of keeping the peace – although some of the men who joined it seemed to think otherwise. The 60th returned promptly to Montreal; but the Militia remained on duty at Fort Garry until 1871.

The return of the 60th was in accordance with the policy of the Imperial government which had, in 1868, resolved to eliminate the garrison system in North America. British political leaders viewed with alarm the changing balance of power in Europe after the German victory of 1870, and the high cost to the British taxpayer of maintaining troops in

North America. When the Treaty of Washington removed most of the sources of friction between Great Britain and the United States, the British government felt that it could, without imperilling the security of Canada, return the colonial garrisons to their home stations. However, in view of the special interests of the Admiralty in the Royal Naval Dockyard in Halifax, and subsequently in Esquimalt, small garrisons were left at these naval bases.

To fill in the gaps created by the withdrawal of the British troops in 1871, the Canadian government organized two batteries, one at Quebec and the other at Kingston. These were the first permanent Canadian military units since the days of the fencible regiments during the War of 1812. The duties of the batteries were to man the guns of the fortress of Quebec and to provide instructors for the Militia artillery. The economic depression that hit Canada in 1873, combined with an easing of the pressures on Canada by the United States, postponed further expansion of the permanent force until 1883, when a new Militia Act authorized the formation of an Infantry School Corps (later the Royal Canadian Regiment) and a Cavalry School Corps (later the Royal Canadian Dragoons), and raised the establishment of Canada's miniscule regular army to one thousand officers and men. Meanwhile, however, steps had been taken in 1874 to establish the Royal Military College of Canada, whose graduates were expected to provide officers both for the Militia and the permanent force. Subsequently commissions in the British regular army were made available to graduates of R.M.C.

In 1867 the command of the Canadian armed forces rested with a 'General Officer Commanding'. Canadians were not yet ready to forego the colonial attitude that a Canadian was incapable of holding such an appointment, and so the commanding general was a British officer. This system, however, rarely worked well. The British G.Os.C. were seldom officers of any distinction; they were unfamiliar with the problems of a part-time military force; and they did not, as a rule, have any experience of colonial conditions or appreciation of colonial sensitivities. From 1874 to 1904 eight different officers held the appointment of G.O.C.; of these, four had serious differences of opinion with their Ministers, two were removed from their appointments, and one left Canada with his reputation suspect. The first G.O.C., Major-General Edward Selby-Smyth (1874-80), was probably the most successful, although some mention should also be made of Major-General Ivan Herbert (1890-5), whose reforms in training and administration led to a considerable improvement in the Canadian forces, both from the standpoint of efficiency and from that of morale.

Home defence was the fundamental role of the Militia. However, in 1884, the first officially organized contingent of Canadians was sent overseas to assist Great Britain. Some years before, in 1868, a number of French Canadians had volunteered to serve in the Papal Zouaves against Garibaldi, but these men were in no way the responsibility of the Department of Militia. Those who were sent to Egypt in 1884 were largely civilians. They were hired to handle the boats carrying Wolseley's force on its way to rescue General Gordon in Khartoum. Their officers were, however, drawn from the Militia. After the Wolseley expedition, proposals were advanced that Canada might wish to contribute troops for further British operations in the Sudan. The Canadian Prime Minister, Sir John A. Macdonald, not an enthusiastic imperialist, rejected the proposals and stated that 'reciprocal aid to be given by the Colonies and England should be a matter of treaty deliberately entered into and settled on a permanent basis'.

Far more important than the Sudan, as far as Canadians were concerned, was the Métis and Indian rising led by Louis Riel in the North-West Territories in 1885. The defeat of the North-West Mounted Police and Militia at Duck Lake, and the terrorizing of the white inhabitants by Cree Indians at Battleford and Fort Pitt, made it imperative that a force should be sent at once to the West. Militia regiments were mobilized, and under the command of Major-General F. B. Middleton, pushed forward from the main line of the Cana-

dian Pacific Railway against the three centres of resistance.
Engagements were fought with the Indians at Cutknife and
Frenchman's Butte; but when, after an initial reverse at Fish
Creek, General Middleton captured Riel's headquarters at
Batoche, the rising collapsed. The operation occupied about
two months and cost the country $5,000,000. It was the first
military operation organized and fought entirely by Cana-
dians without the assistance of Great Britain.

In 1898 a detachment of Canadian troops was sent to assist
the Mounted Police in maintaining order in the Yukon. But
their activities were completely dwarfed in the public mind
by the dispatch of Canadian troops to South Africa. In 1899,
the 2nd (Special Service) Battalion, Royal Canadian Regiment, under the command of Lt.-Col. W. D. Otter, sailed
for Cape Town to become part of the British 9th Division
in Lord Roberts's army. The Prime Minister, Sir Wilfrid
Laurier, had with some reluctance taken the decision to
commit Canadian troops. He felt that his hand had been
forced by the G.O.C., Major-General E. T. H. Hutton. However, once having sent the first contingent, he was prepared
to follow it up by sending additional troops, including artillery, mounted rifles, and a field hospital, as well as providing
two battalions of infantry to take over British garrison duties
in Halifax and Bermuda. All in all, some 8,372 Canadians
were mobilized for service during the South African War,
at a cost of $3,000,000. The Canadians served with British
formations and were paid by the Imperial authorities, with
the differences between the British and the higher Canadian
rates of pay being made up by the Canadian government.

The Canadians bore themselves with distinction in South
Africa. The Royal Canadian Regiment participated in the
grim fighting at Paardeberg in February 1900, and marched
triumphantly through the capitals of the Orange Free State
and the Transvaal several months later. Other Canadian
units served under Major-General Hutton in the East Transvaal and under Major-General Redvers Buller in Natal.
Four Canadians earned the Victoria Cross, one of whom,

R. E. W. Turner, lived to command a Canadian division during the First World War.

One of the by-products of Canadian participation in the South African War was a sense of pride and national identity. This feeling on the part of Canadians became even more apparent several years later, when the G.O.C., Major-General the Earl of Dundonald, challenged the authority of the Minister of Militia, Sir Frederick Borden. That the issue was one of political patronage in the Militia, in which Dundonald was basically right, did not alter the fact that the G.O.C. was the servant and not the master of the civil power. It was not up to him to thrust the question into the arena of party politics. The result was that he was dismissed, and a new Militia Act in 1904 placed the policy-making power in the hands of the Militia Council, a body comprising the Minister, his deputy, and the military heads of the four branches of the staff. Brigadier-General Percy Lake was the first Chief of the Canadian General Staff. A British officer of consummate tact and wide military experience, he held the appointment until 1908, when he was succeeded by Brigadier-General W. D. Otter, the first Canadian to hold the senior military appointment in Canada.

From 1870 onwards, the growing power of Germany had aroused apprehensions in Great Britain, particularly when the Germans began to expand their trade, to acquire colonies, and to build ships to protect both. The possibilities of a German invasion were frequently discussed, and in the years following the South African War, when Great Britain felt herself isolated and friendless, efforts were made to tighten the bonds of Empire. The Colonial Office, under Joseph Chamberlain, emphasized the advantages of imperial centralization, and sought to bring about not only closer commercial but also closer military ties between the various parts of the British Empire, including Canada. This appears in the proposals advanced at the early Colonial (later Imperial) Conferences for the establishment of a special Imperial Army reserve to which the colonies might contribute

contingents, according to their means and population, and
for colonial contributions to the Royal Navy.

In almost every instance these proposals were received
coldly by the Canadian political authorities. Canadians did
not want to lose their own identity or abandon control over
their own men. Moreover, the split between French and
English Canadians on matters of imperial policy made it
essential for every Canadian government to walk warily in
this matter of imperial centralization. Thus it was that Sir
Wilfrid Laurier, with a realistic approach to Canadian politics, preferred to establish a Canadian navy rather than
provide ships for the Royal Navy. Sir Wilfrid's Naval Bill
of 1910 passed Parliament, in spite of the opposition of those
whose sympathies were imperial and those whose outlook
was isolationist. However, the change of government in 1911,
when Robert Borden succeeded Sir Wilfrid Laurier, halted
the complete implementation of Laurier's Act, and all that
Canada acquired to start the Royal Canadian Navy was a
brace of obsolete British warships.

The British did not press the Imperial Army reserve idea.
They accepted the fact of colonial autonomy in military as
well as political matters, and from 1907 onwards laid emphasis on standardization of training, equipment, and organization. Canadian officers went to England for their advanced
military education and the Imperial General Staff organized
local branches for each colony.

At the same time, the Canadians took steps to build up
their own Militia. Staff training for Militia officers was
instituted, and new corps were formed. Between 1904 and
1914, the Canadian Medical Corps, the Canadian Ordnance
Corps, the Canadian Corps of Signals, the Canadian Corps
of Guides, the Canadian Army Pay Corps, the Corps of Military Staff Clerks, and the Canadian Officers Training Corps,
as well as new companies of engineers and army service
corps, were added to the Canadian military establishment.
Armouries and rifle ranges were also constructed at this
period, and plans were drawn up both for a general mobilization and for the mobilization of an overseas expeditionary

force of one infantry division and one cavalry brigade involving 24,000 men, including first-line reinforcements. How effective the proposed force was likely to be was revealed when two Imperial Inspectors-General visited Canada in 1910 and 1913. The first, Sir John French, found little of which he could approve, except the Royal Military College and Petawawa camp; the second, Sir Ian Hamilton, gave high praise to the men in the ranks of the Militia and the members of the various rifle associations. His strictures were directed against the inadequacies of their training and the shortage of their military stores.

On August 4, 1914, when Great Britain declared war on Germany, Canada possessed a small, partly-trained, partly-equipped Militia force between 50,000 and 60,000 strong. It possessed the facilities necessary for producing its own service rifle, the Ross, and for producing small-arms ammunition. It also possessed a navy of two ships, one on each coast. And that was all. The defence forces lacked ships, guns, equipment, and trained staff officers. But they had enthusiasm, the enthusiasm of amateurs.

In 1914 Canadians never questioned the idea that when Great Britain was at war Canada was also at war. There was no thought of neutrality. On August 1 the Prime Minister offered Canadian assistance to Great Britain. On August 6 the offer was accepted. Orders were issued for the mobilization of Canadian troops. However, the plan, so carefully prepared by the General Staff, was never followed. The Minister of Militia, Sam Hughes, took matters into his own hands. He ignored the existing Militia units and issued a call for volunteers for a Canadian Expeditionary Force. When the recruits, 35,000 of them, assembled at Valcartier, they were allotted to numbered battalions. During the remainder of the war, when new battalions were required or reinforcements were urgent, the Militia Department authorized the formation of additional numbered battalions. Most of the officers of the first contingent had had Militia experience; but many of the men themselves were completely without any military training. However, they were given several weeks on the parade square and on the rifle range and then embarked in troop transports and sent to Great Britain early in October 1914. Here they received further training on Salisbury Plain and in February 1915 were sent into action in France.

During 1915 a second division was raised, and then a third, fourth, and fifth. The last, however, remained in existence only a short time as a reinforcement division. In 1916 the first two divisions were brought together as a corps under the command of Sir Julian Byng; one year later he was succeeded by the Canadian, Arthur Currie. A man of no professional training other than that obtained in the Militia, Currie emerged as a natural soldier. In three years he rose from the command of a Militia battalion to the command of an Army Corps of four divisions and handled it in a way that won the esteem of his professional contemporaries. Even more significant to Canadians was the fact that Currie successfully resisted all efforts to split the Canadian Corps and to send part of it to Italy after the disaster of Caporetto. He knew his men. He knew that the Corps depended for its cohesion, for its morale, upon its sense of national identity and its knowledge that it was Canadian.

When the war ended in 1918, Canada looked back with pride and some amazement upon its military achievements: 628,462 men had been enrolled in the army, and 424,589 of them had served overseas; 5,468 men had entered the Canadian navy; and another 24,095 had, in the absence of a Canadian air force, served in the Royal Flying Corps. The price of the war was the lives of 60,661 of the country's young men. That they had served with distinction is clear from the fact that seventy Canadians received the Victoria Cross.

The Canadian troops had scarcely landed in France in February 1915 when they found themselves hurled into one of the major defensive battles of the war. Assigned a position in the Allied lines at Ypres, they encountered the first German gas attack on April 22. The French African troops, who were on the Canadian left flank, broke and fled in terror, thus opening the way for a German breakthrough. In spite of the burning effects of the gas, the Canadians closed the gap and saved the situation until the arrival of reinforcements. Then, with scarcely any rest, they were thrust into the ill-prepared offensives at Festubert and Givenchy. Again, in 1916, the Canadians demonstrated at Mount Sorrel and St. Eloi those qualities for which they were already famous: courage, steadfastness, resolution, and a certain fatalism. Late in the same year they moved into the region of the Somme, where the British had been battering away at the German defences for several months. Hitherto the Canadians had been thought of largely as good defensive soldiers; but in their action at Courcelette they acquired the reputation of being first-class shock troops. 'For the remainder of the war', wrote Lloyd George, 'they were brought along to head the assault in one great battle after another. Whenever the Germans found the Canadian Corps coming into the line, they prepared for the worst.'

The Somme offensive foundered in mud and barbed wire, and the Canadians returned to the relatively quiet sector of Artois. Here they spent the winter in minor raids and in preparing for the Allied spring offensive. The Canadian role in this operation was the seizure of Vimy Ridge. All four divisions participated. On April 9, 1917, the Canadian troops carried out their task with precision and success. 'The grandest day the Corps has ever had,' wrote the officer commanding the 1st Division. After fighting for some weeks on the plains of Lens, the Canadians were then transferred to Flanders. Here they shared with the British the misery and the mud that was Passchendaele. The Canadian divisions (with the exception of the Motor Machine Gun Brigade) did little fighting during the German spring offensive of 1918; but in the last hundred days of the war, from the first great battle in August at Amiens to the entry into Mons on November 11, they broke through the Hindenburg Line and spearheaded the drive towards the German frontier. Canadian troops also served in north Russia at Archangel and Murmansk, and in Siberia.

It was unfortunate that the cost of this mighty achieve-

ment should have included the abandonment of the system
of voluntary enlistment and the opening of a breach between
the French- and English-speaking peoples of Canada that
the ensuing years have never quite managed to close.

The end of the First World War saw a return to traditional
Canadian policies as far as matters military were concerned.
Following the recommendations of a special committee
headed by General Sir William Otter, the Canadian government went back to the volunteer Militia as the backbone of
the defence system. There was to be a small permanent force
comprising two cavalry regiments, three infantry battalions,
and several batteries, with the necessary quota of engineers,
signals, and other services; but the main defence force was
to be a Militia of eleven infantry divisions and four cavalry
divisions. A small, non-professional Canadian Air Force was
formed, which was to be used for civil purposes, such as
forest-fire patrols and transportation; there was also a small
naval establishment of two destroyers and two war-time submarines, supplemented by an equally small Naval Volunteer
Reserve.

One useful reform was, however, instituted. In 1922 Parliament adopted a measure establishing the Department of
National Defence, bringing the three services under the control of one civil head. Major-General A. G. L. McNaughton
would have liked to have achieved complete unity of the
three services under a single military command; but the
resistance offered by the head of the Naval Service, Commo-
dore Walter Hose, postponed the integration of the armed
services in Canada for another generation. The granting of
autonomy in 1938 to the R.C.A.F., which had hitherto been
under the Chief of the General Staff and had been looked
upon as part of the Militia establishment, firmly established
the three-service system.

At the same time, plans for the defence of Canada were
drawn up. Defence Scheme No. 1 was based upon the possibility of war between Great Britain and the United States.
The belligerency of the American republic over Venezuela

in 1895 and Alaska in 1903 had not been forgotten, and invasion from the south had always been the traditional threat to Canadian security. However, in 1922, by the naval Treaty of Washington, Great Britain surrendered naval superiority in the North Atlantic to the United States; thus the likelihood of Canada receiving reinforcements from Great Britain or protection from the Royal Navy ceased to exist. This fact, together with the sincere but naïve belief of Canadians in the League of Nations and the idea that war as an instrument of international policy was obsolete, accounts for the limited financial appropriations for defence purposes during the 1920s. The Permanent Force was never recruited up to strength; and the Non-Permanent Militia was never provided with new equipment. The advent of the economic depression in 1929 necessitated still further retrenchment in defence appropriations. Training at summer camps was virtually eliminated; firing practice was restricted; technical personnel were dismissed; and disbursements for defence purposes fell to just over $14,000,000 in the year 1932-3.

Changing world conditions led, however, to a change in Canadian policy. The political and diplomatic success of Hitler in Germany, the occupation of Manchuria by Japan, the invasion of Ethiopia by Italy, and the general impotence of the League of Nations had the effect of disposing Canadian opinion, public and governmental, towards increased defence expenditures. In 1931, the Chief of the General Staff, Major-General A. G. L. McNaughton, urged a reexamination of the Canadian defence forces in the light of the world situation. He pointed out the lack of balance in the various arms of the Militia and proposed the conversion of a number of infantry and cavalry regiments to artillery, armour, and other more essential units. The government accepted McNaughton's suggestions, and in 1936 the reorganization was put into effect.

At the same time, an effort was made to re-arm the three services to enable them to fulfil the role they might be expected to play. Defence Scheme No. 2 dealt with the

maintenance of Canadian neutrality in the event of a war
between the United States and Japan, and emphasis was
therefore placed upon the installation of new defence works
on the west coast. Greater reliance was also placed on the air
force. The R.C.A.F. (the 'Royal' was added in 1923) was
provided with increased funds and new equipment. Then,
when the centre of gravity of the international crisis shifted
from Asia to Europe, so too did the emphasis of Canadian
defence policy change from the Pacific to the Atlantic. New
shore defences were erected on the east coast, and the R.C.N.
was strengthened with new destroyers and mine-sweepers.
Special attention was also given to Defence Scheme No. 3,
which provided for the organization of a Canadian Field
Force (later the Canadian Active Service Force), a Corps
Headquarters, and two infantry divisions, for dispatch overseas to assist Great Britain in the event of a European war.
The proposed expeditionary force was not made known to
the general public, but it was known to and approved by
the Minister of National Defence, Ian Mackenzie.

On September 10, 1939, when Canada declared war on the
German Reich, it possessed a regular army of under 4,000
men, a Militia of about 50,000, an air force of 2,400, and a
navy of 2,000 – a pitifully small number with which to make
war. Even more pitiful was the equipment, much of which
was obsolete or inadequate in quantity and quality. But at
least Canadians were prepared psychologically for war even
if they were not ready materially.

Both the R.C.A.F. and the R.C.N. played a notable part
in the War of 1939-45: the former was responsible for the
operation of the British Commonwealth Air Training Plan
in Canada as well as providing officers and men for No. 6
Bomber Group and squadrons of 83 Tactical Group in
Europe; the navy bore the brunt of the Battle of the Atlantic
in the western approaches, where German submarines were
active in the Gulf of St. Lawrence and the river itself.

However, it is not unfair to say that Canada's main role
during the war was on land, if only because of the greater
numbers involved. Eight divisions were mobilized in Canada

during the war, five of which served overseas. Of these, two were armoured divisions. In 1942 an Army Headquarters was formed under Lieutenant-General McNaughton. He remained commander until 1943 when he was succeeded by Lieutenant-General H. D. G. Crerar. In all, 730,625 Canadians saw army service between 1939 and 1945. Add to this the 220,000 who served in the air and the 99,000 who served at sea, and the total is over a million men. The fatal casualties were rather less than those of the previous war. The total for all services was 41,700, of whom 22,964 were army personnel. It was a remarkable effort for a nation of only twelve million people – all the more remarkable when it is recalled that ninety per cent of these million were volunteers.

Conscription was introduced in 1940, by the National Resources Mobilization Act. At first the service of conscripts was limited to home defence. However, in 1942 a national plebiscite extended conscript service to overseas; but it was not until 1944 that 13,000 of these men were sent beyond the shores of North America. Only 2,500 of them ever reached the fighting line.

For several years the war in Europe was simply one of waiting. Excepting several small raids and the ill-fated attack upon Dieppe in August 1942, Canadian troops did not see action until the 1st Canadian Division was sent to the Mediterranean in the summer of 1943. Here, as part of General Montgomery's Eighth Army, they took part in the conquest of Sicily and in the drive up the Adriatic coast of Italy. After the bloody battle for Ortona in December, the Canadian troops moved to the Liri Valley for the assault on the Hitler Line. They did not take part in the occupation of Rome but were moved back to the Adriatic shore to join in the offensive against the Po Valley during the latter part of 1944. Early in 1945, the 1st and 5th Canadian Divisions were returned to the command of First Canadian Army in north-west Europe.

The other Canadian divisions, the 2nd, 3rd, and 4th, landed in Normandy in June and July 1944. Owing to the retention of the troops of 1st Corps in Italy, a British corps, a Polish division, and small Belgian and Dutch formations were placed under General Crerar's command. Following the capture of Caen, First Canadian Army was heavily involved in the fighting that took the British troops to Falaise and closed the gap on the German Seventh Army. Then, on the left flank of the Allied forces, the Canadians advanced rapidly through northern France to Belgium, to find themselves engaged in the difficult operations over flooded land that led to the clearing of the Scheldt Estuary and made possible the utilization of Antwerp by the British and American armies. In February 1945, First Canadian Army pushed through the German defences in the Reichswald and Hochwald. Once across the Rhine, the Canadian troops drove rapidly northwards in the direction of Bremen, to cut off the German troops still in Holland. In this last phase of the fighting, the arrival of the Canadian troops from Italy made it possible for First Canadian Army to fight as a complete Canadian formation of two corps, as General McNaughton had originally envisaged.

In addition to the war in Europe, Canadian troops shared in the futile defence of Hong Kong in 1941, in the occupation of Kiska, and in garrison roles in Newfoundland, Gibraltar, Iceland, Jamaica, and Bermuda. Plans were drawn up for Canadian operations in Greenland, St. Pierre, the Canary Islands, and northern Norway, but these were not carried into action. In 1945 arrangements were made for a Canadian division to serve against Japan; but the collapse of Japanese resistance in August 1945 rendered this force unnecessary.

Canadian military policy after 1945 was vastly different from that after 1918. In the interval Canada had achieved independence of Great Britain, had played a role in international affairs as a member of the League of Nations, and had contributed to the winning side in two world wars. It was the difference between childhood and maturity; between a colony and a nation. The factors that governed the military reorganization of 1945 were the recognition by the Canadian government of the intimate relationship of military policy and foreign policy, and the determination that its foreign policy should be based upon maintaining the world organization that replaced the old League of Nations, and preserving friendly relations with Canada's powerful neighbour, the United States.

The first change was in the emphasis placed upon the permanent forces. In 1946, it was announced that the establishment of the three regular services would be 51,000, of which 25,000 would be soldiers, 10,000 sailors, and 16,000 airmen. No longer were the regulars merely to serve as instructors for the Militia. They were to be maintained in a state of readiness that would make it possible for them to take the field where and when required. As the international situation grew worse the numbers of the regulars were increased until, in 1954, they reached 116,000. This increase necessitated additional units, and in 1953 two Militia regiments were activated and a new unit, the Canadian Guards, was formed. Additional armoured units were added to the regular army by activating Militia units from Manitoba and New Brunswick.

At the same time greater attention was given to training and education. A large tract of land at Gagetown, totalling 440 square miles, was acquired for formation training purposes. In 1948 the Royal Military College was re-opened to provide a university education for officer cadets; and this was supplemented by junior colleges at Royal Roads and St. Jean. The Canadian Army Staff College was opened at Fort Frontenac in Kingston, sharing the buildings with the National Defence College, for senior service officers and civil servants. The R.C.A.F. Staff College was opened in Toronto. Moreover, a new branch of the defence staff was organized in 1947, the Defence Research Board, whose Director was given equal status with the heads of the three fighting services. As a result of these changes, defence expenditures increased from $387,611,688 in 1946-7 to $1,775,000,000 in 1955-6 — a far cry from the small sums devoted to defence needs in the 1930s.

The up-grading of the regulars was accompanied by a declining interest in the Militia. In 1954, Militia training was limited to civil defence, or national survival as it was called. This had little appeal to the militiamen, and there was a drop both in numbers and morale. During 1964 a committee, headed by Brigadier E. R. Suttie, re-examined the role of the Militia. As a result of the committee's recommendations, a large number of Militia units were disbanded and the over-all strength was reduced to 30,000 men. At the same time, however, plans were made for more realistic training to enable the part-time soldiers, sailors, and airmen to train with the latest items of equipment and to practise current operational techniques alongside their regular force counterparts. The 'Saturday night' soldiers were thus restored to their earlier role as a fighting reserve for the regulars and as an aid to the civil power in the event of a national emergency. This last was a role that they had filled in 1948 in British Columbia when the Fraser River flooded, and again in 1950 during the Red River flood in Manitoba.

The increased regular military establishment in Canada was inspired, in the first instance, by the conviction that world peace was best kept by collective action. In 1949, Canada played a leading role in the North Atlantic Treaty and agreed to contribute troops to a joint military force in Europe under NATO command. In 1951 a Canadian infantry brigade group was sent to Germany, where it was quartered, on a rotational basis, at Soest. A Canadian air division of twelve (later eight) squadrons was also placed at the service of NATO with its headquarters at Metz in France. In January 1952, the Supreme Allied Command Atlantic was set up at Norfolk, Virginia, under which vessels of the R.C.N. have been periodically placed for combined training. The acceptance of a 'strike role' for the air division and the need to increase the fire power of the brigade group with rockets led the Canadian government to enter an agreement with the United States with regard to the availability of nuclear weapons. This move was accompanied by a political crisis in Canada, where opinion generally was against the extension of nuclear arms. But in 1964 the agreement was concluded and the troops in Europe, with the exception of the air squadrons stationed in France, were equipped with atomic warheads.

In 1950, as a result of the North Korean attack on South Korea, the United Nations authorized the creation of a U.N. command to direct military operations against North Korea. Canada contributed three destroyers and long-range air transport under the R.C.A.F. Troops were also enlisted and despatched to South Korea where they served, under Brigadier J. M. Rockingham, as a component of the Commonwealth Division. In 1951 the 2nd Battalion of Princess Patricia's Canadian Light Infantry gained a U.S. presidential citation for their defence of Kapyong. In all, some 22,000 Canadians served in Korea between 1950 and 1953.

The year after Korea, Canadians were called upon to undertake a new type of action, called 'peace-keeping'. In 1954 Canada was invited to contribute men to the Truce Commission in Vietnam, Laos, and Cambodia. Two years later, in 1956, Canadians participated in the formation of the United Nations Emergency Force in the Middle East, to supervise the frontiers of Egypt and Israel. Until 1959 this force was under the command of a Canadian officer, Major-General E. L. M. Burns. In addition to these tasks, Canadian soldiers served with the U.N. Military Observer Group in Kashmir; from 1960 to 1964 Canadian signallers and airmen served under the U.N. auspices in the Congo; and more recently (1964) Canadian troops were sent to maintain the uneasy peace between the Turks and the Greeks in Cyprus. This task of keeping the peace has gained Canada considerable prestige; and it seems clear that government policy is now, to a large extent, based upon preserving the image of Canada as a kind of international policeman, marching, flying, and sailing the international beat.

Another marked change from the pre-Second War period is the close collaboration between Canada and the United States. This collaboration began in 1940 with the Ogdensburg Agreement and the establishment of the Permanent

Joint Board on Defence. The co-operation of the war period continued after 1945, with arrangements made for interchange of personnel for training, standardization of equipment, and movement of American aircraft and ships over Canadian territory and through Canadian waters with the minimum of formality. This was followed up, after the detonation of the Russian atomic bomb in 1949, with the construction of three transcontinental radar lines: the first (Pinetree), extending from Vancouver to the Peace River, down through the northern United States, and across Ontario and Quebec to Newfoundland; the second (Mid-Canada) along the 55th parallel; and the third, the Distant Early Warning (DEW) line along the northern fringe of the continental mainland. The purpose of these lines was to give warning of the approach of hostile aircraft so that they might be intercepted before reaching the large American industrial and defence centres. The construction of the DEW line brought a large number of American service personnel into Canada and raised questions of how far Canada should go in surrendering territorial sovereignty for the dubious protection afforded by a soon-to-be-obsolete radar line. In March 1966 the Mid-Canada line was abandoned. The 1,000-mile section in the Hudson Bay area was regarded as redundant with improvements in the Pinetree line farther south.

The organization of the North American Air Defence Command (NORAD) in the autumn of 1957 raised similar problems of national sovereignty and Canadian control over her own aircraft. In order that a Canadian voice might be heard at Colorado Springs, a Canadian officer, Air Marshal R. Slemon, was appointed deputy commander. Three squadrons of R.C.A.F. planes were assigned to NORAD command. That Canada was not completely at the mercy of the American commander at NORAD is shown by the fact that, in October 1962, the Canadian government refused to place the R.C.A.F. component in a state of emergency alert when it looked as if open war might break out between the United States and Cuba. Also under the command of NORAD are the two BOMARC missile squadrons located at North Bay and La Macaza. Considerable criticism was directed against the BOMARCs on the grounds of their unreliability and short range and their need for an atomic warhead. However, following the agreement with the United States, the BOMARC missiles were equipped with nuclear explosives in 1964.

Perhaps the most promising development in Canadian military policy since 1945 has been the merging of the three services, army, navy, and air force, into a single defence force. The first tentative efforts in this direction in the pre-war period were thwarted by inter-service jealousy. However, after 1945, the government returned to the idea of a single Minister and single Department of National Defence. This was followed by the establishment of the cadet colleges on a tri-service basis in 1948 and by the formation of the Committee of the Joint Chiefs of Staff. More positive steps were taken with the formation of one Chaplain Corps and one Postal Corps for the three services.

Brooke Claxton, as Minister of National Defence, was interested in extending this policy of integration; but he concentrated his efforts on co-ordination rather than unification. It was not until the appointment of Paul Hellyer as Minister in 1963 that integration was taken up seriously on the highest political level. The Royal Commission on Government Organization found the maintenance of three separate services uneconomic and inefficient, and the Minister decided that the services should be brought under a single unified command. The integrated control of all aspects of planning and operations would produce a more effective posture for Canada and result in savings both in manpower and money. The first step was to reduce the size of the command structure. Where previously there were eleven commands – two navy, five army, and four air force – by 1966 there were only six: Mobile, Maritime, Air Defence, Materiel, Air Transport, and Training. At Canadian Forces Headquarters in Ottawa, integration was virtually complete by 1966.

The new policy was not put into effect without strong

protests from both military and political opponents. Several senior officers, particularly in the navy, voiced their convictions that the independence of each service was the foundation of its *esprit de corps*. But the Minister, despite objections and resignations, went ahead with the implementation of his plans. Air Chief Marshal F. R. Miller was appointed Chief of the Defence Staff, and in May 1965 Mobile Command, embracing all army formations in Canada, all tactical aircraft, and a small naval component, was formed under the command of Lieutenant-General Jean Allard, with headquarters at St. Hubert in Quebec. A year later General Allard succeeded Air Chief Marshal Miller as Chief of the Defence Staff, and Lieutenant-General W. A. B. Anderson took charge of Mobile Command. But if the integrated command structure could be said to be working satisfactorily, there were still many serious problems to be solved as Canada moved into 1967, before the ideal of a single unified Canadian Defence Force could be said to be achieved.

In 1869, Sir John A. Macdonald wrote prophetically, 'It will be a century, before we are strong enough to walk alone.' It appears that he was right.

30. Foreign Affairs

GÉRARD BERGERON

Can we really speak of Canada's 'international relations' or of Canada's 'foreign policy' before 1945? More than forty years had to elapse after 1867 before we got even a nucleus of a Department of External Affairs – the usual title of 'foreign affairs' being too much of a luxury. Canada was a ripe sixty years of age before it ventured to establish its first diplomatic mission in the capital of its only immediate neighbour, the United States. It took us another decade to begin to develop our own diplomatic service. And one is tempted to think that had it not been for two world wars, Canada's participation in world affairs would have grown even more slowly.

The Canadian outlook that began with Confederation was most succinctly described many years ago by a perceptive foreign observer, André Siegfried. 'Canada's foreign policy rests on three basic concerns, relatively simple and easy to summarize,' he wrote. They are: 'in international relations, the assertion of Canada's distinctiveness as a political entity; protecting the country against any threat from outside the Americas; and the bolstering of economic interests including natural resources and exports. Wherever we look, we always come back to one or the other of these three propositions.'

In this sense, Canada's foreign policy since Confederation has been based more on anticipation of the future than on recognition of the reality of the present. Its history has been less a record of achievement than a record of becoming. The political entity born on the first of July, 1867, has lived; but it has done so in a state of gradual becoming, and this amounts to saying that it has never remained for long the same. In 1867 the four original provinces were no larger than today's single province of Quebec. The 'completion of Confederation' was not fulfilled until 1949 with Newfoundland's entry. And, after one hundred years, Canada's entity is as precariously perched on the horns of its original dilemma as it was in its first uncertain days.

The events that led up to July 1867 do not need to be recalled here – except for one pre-eminent fact that gave them unity and significance: the Canadian federation was set up *against* the United States. It was an attempt to gather and somehow to hold together the scattered British American colonies so as to establish a viable claim to the northern half of the continent as a separate entity outside the United States, and an entity capable of withstanding the inevitable pressure of expanding American power. The old province of United Canada seemed to offer a firm nucleus for such a confederation, but only two other colonies were on hand at its foundation: New Brunswick and Nova Scotia. There was no exultation or glory in the event. Ideology and style were starkly absent.

> No popular patriotism brought forth the new creation, no
> revolutionary faith. The life of the new Dominion was at

first as drab, as empty and as devoid of great ideals as had been that of the struggling provinces. Only the eye of faith, and the great visions of its few founders, kept it together. Only by tediously slow degrees did the loyalty and love of its inhabitants show indications of centring on it, rather than on the far-off motherland. Compared with the United States, *élan* was lacking. Yet it might be said of that country, too, that no great popular wave of feeling had greeted its union. It was July 4, 1776, not September 17, 1787, that was celebrated in that country: the revolutionary idea, not the tame job of constitution making. Canada was to wait another 64 years for its 'Independence' day and when it came, it stole in so quietly that few people were aware of it, and fewer still would think of celebrating it. Some peoples are born nations, some achieve nationhood and others have nationhood thrust upon them. Canadians seem to be among these latter.*

Having had neither a war of independence nor a burning of the Bastille, Canadians needed time to recognize themselves. As A. R. M. Lower has written:

The name 'Canadian' was automatically extended to cover New Brunswickers and Nova Scotians, but to these latter it was something not a little repugnant and they clung to their own. In the old province of Canada itself, it was not allowed by the French to 'les Anglais' and on many among the latter, it sat uneasily, for they still talked of 'home' and preferred to think of themselves as Scotch, English or Irish. It was to be years before the name Canadian came to have content and to be worn proudly.

Nevertheless, the new Dominion of Canada began the patient game of fitting its jigsaw pieces together – but still as an enlarged colony under the protection and tutelage of its mother country. Thus neither the freedom that comes from independence nor the self-assertion that stems from power was involved in this process, though the new Dominion did maintain the internal self-government, or responsible government, that had already been granted to its member

*A. R. M. Lower, *Colony to Nation*, Longmans, Toronto, 1946, pp. 325, 327.

colonies. Still, if this Canadian federal state did not have control of its own external policy, the staking out of its claim across the continent and the consolidation of its territories very much involved the field of external relations. In effect, it was constantly affected by the formidable fact of United States power to the south, and it sought to utilize British imperial power as a guarantee for its own existence and gradual development on the American continent.

Britain itself, at this time, was really seeking to lessen, if not remove, its North American commitments. Therefore it looked with favour on the establishment and consolidation of the Canadian union, which could take over responsibilities in America and keep the northern territories out of the sweep of United States power. At the same time, the fact that these territories were legally British colonial possessions meant that the imperial power was involved in their entrance into the Canadian federal union. And so, much of the history of Canada's making good its continental claim is the story of the transfer of territories from British to Canadian charge. It is in this sense that one should see the relation between the expansion of the young Canada and the subject of external relations. It was essentially a transfer of title, facilitated by the existing imperial title and stimulated by concern over American influence reaching northward, that spread the Canadian union out across the map beyond its original components, from Atlantic to Pacific and from the lower Great Lakes to the Arctic islands.

Even as the Confederation of 1867 was being founded, negotiations were under way with Britain for its extension westward. It was an imperial statute, the Rupert's Land Act of 1868, that provided for the absorption of the vast north-western lands into the Dominion, and in 1870, when terms had been agreed upon to compensate the Hudson's Bay Company for the loss of its chartered monopoly, the western plains and the Hudson Bay regions were added to the union. The initially small province of Manitoba was also erected at the Red River, out of the north-western territories, and when a military expedition was dispatched to Red River in 1870, it went less to suppress the Riel uprising there (already settled by agreement in the Manitoba Act) than to indicate that Canada meant to uphold its claim in the face of efforts by American expansionists to swing the territory towards annexation by the United States.

Negotiations then brought in the Pacific lands of British Columbia in 1871, and the Atlantic colony of Prince Edward Island in 1873, both as Canadian provinces but also very much on their own terms as self-governing communities. Then in the 1880s the Arctic islands were turned over by Britain to Canada – though in this direction the Canadian claim in the polar region would still not be fully recognized internationally until enforced in 1925.

By 1896, therefore, when the federal Conservative party finally fell from office after dominating the first era of the Canadian union under John A. Macdonald's leadership, Canada's continental domain had been firmly marked out. Later, in 1905, the new provinces of Alberta and Saskatchewan would be established within it, and Newfoundland, of course, would join in 1949. But to all intents, Canada had staked out its claim on the map by 1896 when the federal Liberals under Wilfrid Laurier took over power. Indeed, its claim had been made more than a mere political expression by the completion of the Canadian Pacific Railway in 1885, providing a link between the settled east and British Columbia and laying the basis for the effective occupation of the empty western plains.

In this piecing together of Canada, external or foreign relations had played a vital part. Indeed, this was clearly evident to the political figures who were at the time coping with the shaping of Canada out of adjacent masses of land. They were up against, were even running counter to, the clear north-south patterns of North American geography. That was the first of the huge historical challenges successfully countered by the men of Confederation. With centennial hindsight, we can see the building of railroads and canals, the Pacific scandal, the Riel affair, as more than matters of domestic policy, even though they do not clearly

belong to the field of international relations as we understand them today.

Our External Affair, the Foreign Relation *par excellence*,
was, of course, the Republic south of the border. Trying to
heal its Civil War wounds, to weld its own north-south rift
into a new unity, still incomplete after a century's existence,
busy with its own vast internal empire and fast-rising industrialism – the United States usually paid scant attention to
the northern fringe of British provinces that had twice
refused to share its own revolutionary brand of independence. Nevertheless there were important topics frequently
under consideration in Canadian-American relations, such
as the yet unsettled line of the Alaska boundary, American
involvement in Canadian Atlantic fisheries, or the Canadian
quest, by offering reciprocity, for free admission into the rich
American market. At the same time, Canada as a colony,
even if internally self-governing, was constantly concerned
with its relationship to Britain. The establishment of the
Canadian High Commissioner's office in London, the colonial conferences that, beginning in the 1880s, discussed
imperial defence and trade relations, the evolution of Canada's responsibility for its own military defence at home,
were all aspects or attributes of a growing involvement by
Canada in its external relations before 1896. None the less,
the essence of Canadian external concern in the period
remained the establishment and confirmation of Canada as
a transcontinental state in North America.

Having established its claim to the northern half of the
continent, Canada had to show that it could weld the sprawling territory into a workable unit. Benefiting from favourable world economic conditions after 1896, Canada was able
to attract a vast influx of immigrants to people the empty
West, and of capital to finance the growth of its economic
base. In seeking immigrants and trade it reached out to
countries previously ignored, and thus cautiously put a toe
into the stream of world affairs. The First World War pulled
Canada much farther into the depths than it was prepared
to go. The country emerged from the war with a consider-

ably enhanced international status, and spent several years in working out a theory to fit the established fact.

However, relations with Great Britain and the United States remained by far the most important of Canada's external concerns. The economic background must not be overlooked; without it events would undoubtedly have run a very different course. As J. B. Brebner expressed it:

> During this expansive quarter century [1896-1920], the economic triangle of buying and selling, investing and dividend-paying, migration and production, into which Great Britain, the United States, and Canada poured their efforts, became the mightiest thing of its kind on earth and seemed destined to remain so. Individualism was still practically unbridled, so that competition was the order of the day, but the three areas proved to be complementary in so many ways that they co-operated in spite of themselves.*

Thus Canada, during this stage, instead of merely relying on the protective superiority of the United Kingdom as in the past or replacing it by the growing power of the United States, established the corner-stone of its foreign policy: the need for basic agreement between the two great English-speaking nations. The domestic implications of this policy, however, remain unresolved, as 1911 demonstrated: after winning four successive elections, Laurier was defeated on the issues of reciprocity and a Canadian navy.

The Laurier government, during its fifteen years in power, formed a link not only between two centuries but also between the absence of a foreign policy and the impossibility of having one. Canada's position was ambiguous; it was pioneering – unconsciously for the most part – the new concept of an emerging nation. Paradoxically, the colony was to win its emancipation in the process of being loyal to the mother country's concerns. The strains on a precarious national unity that accompanied participation in a purely imperialistic venture – the Boer War – left a deep impression on Laurier. In all attempts to establish a more tangible

*J. B. Brebner, *North Atlantic Triangle*, Yale University Press, New Haven, p. 225.

imperial unity his role was essentially negative – he resisted imperial pressures, but without advancing a Canadian Declaration of Independence. Despite the great loyalty he inspired, there remained a suspicion among many of his English-speaking followers that he was too French, and among his French-speaking compatriots that he was too English. The man was of sufficient stature to overcome great obstacles but these ambiguities were to be fatal in the end. In this he resembled another French-Canadian Prime Minister who, half a century later during the Suez crisis, attacked the 'supermen' guilty of yielding to what Laurier, in his time, had castigated as 'the vortex of militarism, the curse and blight of Europe'.

The Tory-Nationalist alliance that defeated Laurier was, in its turn, unable to agree on the form any Canadian contribution to imperial defence should take. However, when the British Empire found itself at war with the Central European empires, there was not a second's official hesitation in Ottawa: Canada was at war; in the existing constitutional framework there was no alternative. The natural unwillingness of French-speaking Canadians was overwhelmed by what has since been called 'the enthusiasm of patriotic ignorance'. Laurier himself had not forgotten his basic distinction between peripheral conflicts and those that threatened Great Britain's existence, and as leader of the Opposition he loyally supported the government's policy of participation. The Tory Prime Minister, Robert Borden, on his side, cast off many of his earlier colonial habits – a fact overlooked in too many of our histories. The war provided a great stimulus to Canadian national pride and to economic development; it was also a grim and sobering experience. There was criticism of British handling of the war effort and Canada increasingly demanded a voice in making policy. In 1909 a small Department of External Affairs had been established, but it was only in 1917, with Canadian participation in the Imperial War Cabinet, that the Canadian government for the first time had access to information that made the formulation of policy in international affairs more than an illusion. While

Borden did not reject the idea of a 'single voice' in foreign affairs, he believed that Canada and the other Dominions must have a part in deciding what that voice said.

At the end of the war Canada was almost a sovereign country, together with the other Dominions, among whom it was, in a sense, the youthful and dynamic leader. Sovereignty came by way of self-government: the Dominions could, directly or through London, amend their constitutions; their parliaments legislated without the mother country's interference; their military and naval forces were under their own control; and they were free to establish their own tariff policies and their own immigration programs. Even the supremacy of the Imperial Parliament had no practical effect, since the Imperial government carefully refrained from getting involved in matters that only affected the Dominions. Of greater importance was, thanks to Borden's insistence, the individual representation of the Dominions at the Peace Conference and, as a consequence, their full participation in the League of Nations – even though, in a last concession to the imperial idea, their signatures to the Versailles Treaty were grouped under the heading of the British Empire. This curious procedure was not the result of pressure from London, but rather came at the insistence of President Wilson. During a stay in London, Borden wrote in his diary on December 1, 1918, barely three weeks after the armistice: 'I am beginning to feel that in the end and perhaps sooner than later, Canada must assume full sovereignty. She can give better service to G[reat] B[ritain] & U[nited] S[tates] & to the world in that way.'

'. . . perhaps sooner than later . . .'

But independence must be paid for, and the greater its extent, the higher the price. Domestically, the war had come close to irrevocably tearing the nation's fragile unity along the lines of abrasion between Canada's two main cultural groups. Outside the country, the splendid North Atlantic triangle was gradually losing ground to a bilateral relationship between Canada and the United States as American investment in the Canadian economy rapidly increased.

This was, of course, more the direct consequence of participation in the war than a result of any increased independence that may have stemmed from it.

A half-century after its birth, at the close of the dramatic world struggle, Canada still had no true diplomatic service and still laboured under an ambiguous legal status. In first playing a significant international role, it had been drawn into a process much greater than itself, and not by deliberate choice. Emerging from colonial status, it promptly sought shelter in a twenty-year bout of isolationism to re-make its national unity and to pursue its economic development – at least for the first half of the period. In the thirties the Great Depression shrouded the country in economic paralysis – again a process much greater than itself.

These years between the wars witnessed the formal change-over from Empire to Commonwealth, an event marked in 1931 by the passing of the Statute of Westminster. Having obtained more than just an international status under the Statute, Canada came to recognize its international role, and proceeded to establish its diplomatic service; and so it was finally led into an international position as a middle power and as a potential leader) or, in the eyes of the more optimistic, as an actual leader) among the world's middle powers. During this quarter of a century Canada passed from the blindest continental isolationism to the broadest form of generous internationalism. This new international dimension was again achieved at the cost of yet another serious blow to national unity, in the conscription crisis, and by means of an inevitably closer partnership with the United States in the defence agreements of 1940 and the economic agreements of 1941. Canada's destiny thus seemed to fall into a repeating pattern: each decisive step towards emancipation was marked by a domestic crisis that jeopardized the country's very cohesion; and at each such stage, help was forthcoming from abroad to ensure short-term survival – but at the cost of ever-more-heavily mortgaging the future. Other things being equal, however, this is the common condition of all states who, on the international scene, must dance to the tune played by another piper.

The twenties saw two phenomena: the constitutional emancipation of Canada within a new Commonwealth, and at the same time the provinces, acting like true federal states, acquiring a growing degree of independence within a renewed federalism. The internationalism that grew out of the Versailles Treaty, and the new continental isolationism, were the dialectical poles of the first constitutional phenomenon. All this occurred during a period of government instability in Ottawa in the years 1921 to 1930. Four elections gave us four Prime Ministers, and during half the decade the government's life hung by a thread.

The two years that followed the peace treaty were a period of inactivity – 'a pause in Empire Constitutional development'. The next two years saw an attempt to revive the Empire's unity in matters of foreign policy and to keep the Imperial Cabinet alive. But a strong contrary wind was already blowing, and decentralization overwhelmingly carried the day in the Report of the 1926 Imperial Conference. The process was one that had already been quite evident in policies from the Dominions. These are Canadian examples: the Chanak incident in 1922, with Canada's decision not to support Lloyd George in his threats against Turkey; the signature of the Halibut treaty with the United States in 1923 without endorsement by the British Ambassador; the *de facto* recognition of the U.S.S.R. in 1922, followed by official recognition in 1924 (ten years before Washington was ready to take a similar step); in 1925, Canada's refusal to commit itself under the Locarno treaty.

After the war Canada clearly affirmed its independence of the two collective systems to which it belonged. In the League of Nations, Canada several times attempted to reduce the scope of Article X of the League Covenant dealing with collective security, and almost succeeded. A French-Canadian Minister-Plenipotentiary, Rodolphe Lemieux, clearly expressed the straightforward logic of the new Canadian nationalism: 'In military matters we are governed also by

and from Ottawa, and not by and from London; and we do
not want to be governed by and from Geneva.' In the 1925
elections Mackenzie King's position on the relationship with
Great Britain was almost identical to that long held by Henri
Bourassa, and he voiced it not only in Quebec but in Ontario
as well. These two currents ran along parallel lines, though
apparently without influencing each other: while upholding
its international 'coming of age', Canada was also vehemently
on guard against contamination from Europe. Somewhat
self-righteously, it recommended to Europe the supposedly
magical formulas of the Rush-Bagot Agreement and the
International Joint Commission. The 1926 Imperial Conference worked out the now classical definition of those historically unprecedented political entities, the 'Dominions':
'they are autonomous communities within the British Empire, equal in status, in no way subordinate to one another
in any aspect of their domestic or external affairs, although
united by a common allegiance to the Crown, and freely
associated as members of the British Commonwealth of
Nations'. Canada could now conduct its own independent
foreign policy, though in association – a free association,
fully mindful of the country's internationally independent
status – with what was to become the Commonwealth.

The effective founding of our diplomatic service came in
the period between the Balfour Report and the Statute of
Westminster. Our first Legation was opened in Washington
in 1927, after having been talked about for some forty years!
The Balfour Report removed any possible legal obstacles to
such a step; but since the end of the war, the North American
partnership had functioned without awaiting any formal
diplomatic expression. On the other hand, the United States'
economic influence was being increasingly felt in Canada.
There is no easy way to free oneself from having been born
one side of a triangle.

Canada's foreign policy in the thirties (such as it was) is
not something to be particularly proud of. But let us not
condemn it too strongly. From the Manchurian incident to
the Munich disgrace the policy of the three great Western

democracies – France, Britain, and the United States – cannot precisely be called glorious. Like everyone else, we were far more concerned over the sad drabness of the great and desperately long Depression than over the rise of European fascism and Japanese militarism. There, threats were so remote that their consequences did not seem inevitable. Obviously, this was merely hiding one's head in the sand. Hugh Keenleyside has described the hypnotic atmosphere of the sittings – one can hardly call them debates – in the nation's highest forum during these years:

> . . . the governments of the day, especially under Prime Minister Mackenzie King, consistently blocked all attempts to establish a tradition of informed debate on international affairs in the Canadian Parliament. The Prime Minister almost invariably delayed the introduction of the External Affairs estimates until the tired and impatient days at the end of the Parliamentary session. He would then make one long, prolix speech saying in effect that Canada had no responsibility for the sad state of the affairs of the world, that in any case these conditions were no threat to Canadian security, and that the best thing Parliament could do would be to say little and to take no sides. . . . As to policy the Prime Minister would commit himself to nothing except that in case of a crisis arising 'Parliament would decide.'*

During the 'angry thirties', Canadian diplomacy was little more than a half-secret prerogative of the Prime Minister, and was conducted in an almost furtively possessive way. Mackenzie King's statements provide material for a black record of the shortcomings and evasions of a policy of hesitant self-protection. But such an indictment would be artificial, if not unfair. King's 'now you see it, now you don't' style of leadership was as much of a trademark in international as in domestic policy. What does bear looking into, however, is the fact that his 'policy' and his rather special 'style' may have uniquely fitted the facts of life in a country that had nearly come to internal grief during the first world

*Hugh Keenleyside, *The Growth of Canadian Policies in External Affairs*, Duke University Press, Durham, N.C., 1960, pp. 6-7.

conflict and might irreparably fall apart were another war
to break out. There is still a third dimension in the over-all
world picture, which cannot be arbitrarily ignored: the
leaders of those Western democracies that most closely participated in the course of events were no more signally graced
by lucidity or courage. And so, in 1936, King could say with
more than just superficial common sense: 'After all we are
but 10 million on the north end of a continent, and we should
not strive to over-play our part . . . ; after all . . . there is such
a thing as a sense of proportion in international affairs.'
With today's hindsight, it would be difficult not to accept the
judgement of one of his biographers, MacGregor Dawson.

> King's tactics enabled him to secure and retain office – the
> indispensable first step. . . . He was too willing at times to
> yield his own judgment when confronted with opposing
> opinion. He was slow to admit that he had a duty to exert a
> moderate pressure in the direction in which he believed the
> country should move.

Canada did not declare war on the Axis powers until September 10, 1939, and then separately from Westminster;
thus was brought home the fact that the Dominion was not
automatically at war merely on the strength of Britain's
involvement. Between August 25 and September 9, the
Canadian government had carefully picked its way amidst
a hailstorm of events. The King Cabinet refused to take a
definite stand for or against the Conservative position, which
favoured a declaration of war and the sending of an expeditionary force; nor would it side with or against a group of
French-Canadian Liberal M.P.s with nationalistic tendencies who favoured Canada's abstention from any 'foreign
war'. The Prime Minister opted for a policy of 'aggressive
neutrality' which would allow him to backtrack or advance
according to the fluctuations in the two mainstreams of
Canadian public opinion. It was up to Ernest Lapointe to
dispel the last shreds of French-Canadian resistance by a two-
part argument: first, in the present circumstances, Canada
could not remain neutral; second, our participation would

have to rule out any form of conscription. On the first point, Lapointe said bluntly: 'No government could stay in office if it refused to do what the large majority of Canadians wanted it to do.' With respect to the second, he committed himself forcefully:

> The whole province of Quebec – and I speak with all the responsibility and all the solemnity I can give to my words – will never agree to accept compulsory service or conscription outside Canada. I will go farther than that: When I say the whole province of Quebec I mean that I personally agree with them. I am authorized by all my colleagues in the cabinet from the province of Quebec . . . to say that we will never agree to conscription and will never be members or supporters of a government that will try to enforce it. . . . May I add that if my friends and myself from Quebec were forced to leave the government, I question whether anyone would be able to take our place. . . . And those in Quebec who say that we will have conscription, in spite of what some of us are saying, are doing the work of disunity, the work of the foe, the work of the enemy. . . . I will protect them against themselves.

That is how far French Canadians were prepared to go – provided, however, that conscription for overseas service was *not* introduced. The 1942 plebiscite, called to free the government from its promises, brought out with statistical coldness the fact that the two Canadas confronted each other in radical disagreement on a vitally decisive question. But it was not until November 1944 that the conscription crisis came to a head. In quick succession King lost two of his ministers for opposite reasons. Tensions throughout the country were extreme. The 'race' issue was again marked by a bitterness that recalled the worst days of 1917-18. In the decisive vote itself, the government managed to get a comfortable majority of 143 to 70, with C.C.F. and Social Credit votes making up for Quebec Liberal defections. The closeness of victory and the country's unprecedented economic prosperity; the obvious fact that the decision to introduce conscription was taken reluctantly and *in extremis* – all these factors carried us to the end of the war without irreparable disunion. And as Brebner has already said:

> Canadian national unity after 1939 was largely a formal unity for it involved the difficult task of persuading the English-speaking majority to exercise their imaginations and their tolerance instead of their prejudices in thought, word, and action where French Canada was concerned. No one on either side expected miracles, but the thoughtful knew that every minute gain in conscious collaboration was worth far more than years of lip service toward making Canada more of a nation.*

The joy of victory erased unfortunate recollections on both sides. Canada's unity had been chipped but not broken. Energy could now be devoted to the consolidation of peace, to forging prosperity – initially through the temporary measures of 'reconversion'. Internationally, Canada had acquired a 'reputation' and was a little drunk on the glory – as not infrequently happens to beginners.

But amidst general light-heartedness, the more attentive Canadians did not forget the Canadian-American *tête-à-tête* launched by the Ogdensburg agreement on joint defence in August 1940, and followed by the Hyde Park agreement in April 1941 dealing with economic co-operation. Thoughtful observers already knew what such agreements entailed, and were apprehensive over what they were likely to entail in the future.

By definition, international relations are conditioned from the outside, or at any rate determined to a large extent, by the way they are looked at in any given moment. While unquestionably a new period began for Canada in 1945, characterized by the gradual and practical evolution of a real foreign policy, it is only arbitrarily assumed here that the period will come to a close in 1967. This latest chapter of the history of Canada's international relations is short; it spans a mere twenty-two years, of which only nineteen have gone by at the time of writing. It is, however, the most signi-

*Brebner, *op.cit.*, p. 319.

ficant politically, the most crowded by important events. Never has Canada's involvement on the world scene been as intense, as continuous, or as wide-ranging, and backing up Canadian involvement we now have an effective and growing diplomatic service functioning in all parts of the world.

The immediate postwar situation promoted basic agreement among all Canadians on the essential lines of our foreign policy. We agreed that the Iron Curtain should not shift farther west; that Europe's – and particularly Great Britain's – economic rehabilitation was essential; that decolonization should proceed without either excessive damage to vested interests or marked increases in Communist influence; and, more recently, that we would take part in helping the world's underdeveloped areas – without unduly jeopardizing our much-vaunted standard of living. The United Nations was too large and too vague a mechanism – but still indispensable – for Canadians to become divided on the subject, however much they may have been disappointed in their initial expectations of the organization's effectiveness. There was no longer any Empire – for us, at any rate – and the Commonwealth, no longer British, was on the decline; French-speaking Canadians who at an earlier stage had insisted that Canada join the Pan-American Union were now less keenly aware of our absence from the Organization of American States, since the modern concept of Commonwealth solidarity was leaving us a very free hand in this and other such matters.

NATO appeared on the scene in time to force nostalgic imperialists and rabid anti-imperialists to turn their attention elsewhere, if they did not want to look too outdated. In NATO we were on an equal footing with both our motherlands, and also with several other states whose populations and economies were more nearly comparable to ours. Above all, we would not be alone, face to face, with the American colossus. The original Canadian conception of NATO looked to an improved economic relationship among the partners, not just to a defence arrangement; but in this we were disappointed.

In the United Nations, Canada from the beginning made every effort to play a constructive role. Ironically, it has often been in areas where the great power veto (which Canada so vigorously opposed) seemed to frustrate hopes of effective action, that the Canadian role has been most useful. Our talent for compromise in the behind-the-scenes negotiations has received little public recognition but has served to enhance our reputation among many of our fellow members. For a time we thought of ourselves as a middle power like India, Australia, Brazil, or such strategically located or economically developed countries as Sweden, Yugoslavia, Israel, or Egypt. With the emergence of the many newly independent states of Asia and Africa we, like others, have had to climb down from such lofty views. Yet our vanity has not been too badly hurt, since international agencies have given us tasks that can only be done by medium-sized powers – the Armistice Commission in Indo-China, the United Nations Emergency Force in the Middle East, and so on. From the Korean War to the Cyprus expedition the old anti-militaristic reflex of French Canadians has been inactive, both because the commitments themselves were worth while and because the volunteer system for service was maintained.

Some mythical elements of our foreign policy survive, but the old habit of seeing ourselves as a useful go-between or a bridge between London and Washington is gradually disappearing. According to John W. Holmes:

> Insofar as Canada acted as interpreter to the United States since the last war, the role was that of interpreter not of the British ally but of the non-aligned within the Commonwealth. Canada accepted with enthusiasm the new perspectives of the Commonwealth after India and Pakistan joined in 1947. Canada used its influence to see that the Commonwealth's evolution as a multi-racial organization was not frustrated by nostalgic imperialism. Having itself recently embarked on a broader field of international policy, Canada found in the Commonwealth association with new Asian, and later African, states a source of perspective on world

politics and an asset in diplomacy. Having experienced the transition from dependent status to independence and the frustrations of limited power, Canadians were able to comprehend with sympathy the neuroses of independence and the instinct to neutralism in these new nations. Although rejecting neutralism for themselves, Canadians accepted sooner than Americans the wisdom of non-alignment for weak countries.*

Canada's international relations since 1945 can be roughly divided into two parts: our bi-lateral relations with the United States, and our relations with the rest of the world, including the principal international organizations such as the U.N. and NATO. There is an arbitrary element in this division, however. In our relations with the rest of the world, our position is always affected by the weight or attraction of our only continental neighbour who also happens to be one of the two leading world powers. In the cold-war context, our situation is not unique; possibly our geographic position makes us more acutely aware of it. A number of questions have arisen that are not directly involved in the basic antagonisms between the two blocs — Kashmir, Israel, Algeria, the Congo, Cyprus. Even in such issues, as in our contributions to such bodies as the U.N. and NATO, Washington's point of view and decisions (and London's to a lesser extent and on fewer issues) are often given more consideration than the basic facts of the issues as such.

But we still have that problem, and now increasingly the other problem of living with each other in Canada. These twin perplexities are fundamental to the future of Canadian foreign policy and even to the future of Canada itself. Confederation came into being in defiance of the United States, as we recalled at the outset; and so it remains. This is not primarily a problem of politics or of diplomacy in the usual technical sense. Nor is it a question of forces pulling in opposite directions; by and large the pull is in the same

*'The Relationship in Alliance and in World Affairs' in J. S. Dickey (ed.), *The United States and Canada,* for The American Assembly, Prentice-Hall, Inc., Englewood Cliffs, 1964, p. 113.

direction and toward the same objectives. So the latent antagonism comes down basically to the glaring disproportions between neighbours – to the great and growing imbalance that promises an uncertain future. The artificial, indeed the anti-geographic, character of the North American nations remains.

Pan-Canadian nationalism, having acquired a taste for self-assertion on the international scene, tends to verge on anti-Americanism, systematic if not virulent. Nothing is more irritating to an American – an irritation that, being a good neighbour, he generally manages to disguise – than this natural Canadian reflex to worry over the growing Canadian economic dependence on the United States, without taking into account the attendant advantages, or to fret over Canadian sovereignty (that very abstract concept) being jeopardized by joint defence arrangements, without taking into account the benefits of added protection. Brebner has compared the two countries to Siamese twins who cannot separate and live. For a truer picture, we should perhaps add that one of the twins has grown out of all proportion, has a gigantic appetite, is self-assertive, with a tremendous power drive enhanced by the belief that he is the defender of liberty throughout the world; meanwhile, the second twin asks for no more than to remain a good little boy with no very great aim in life.

All in all our foreign policy is quite presentable and defendable. It gives us cause neither to blush nor to boast. If one may venture a general criticism, it would be that too much weight is being attached, *a priori*, to inhibiting elements, to our limited tactical possibilities, to reasons that call for patience, care, and excessive caution. On the credit side is our ability to adjust with some skill and wisdom to situations created by others. It would never occur to us to trigger off new situations. At times we tend to be amazed at the consideration shown to us by others. There are even certain trophies that historical perspective may permit us to appreciate better: St. Laurent's part in the birth of NATO and Pearson's role in the Suez crisis. Were it not for the occasional embarrassment between ourselves and the United States, we might be able to say that 'all is for the best in the best of all possible worlds'.

Our foreign policy, legally sovereign and fully independent, nevertheless leaves us little room for manoeuvring or for real choices. We are among the manipulated rather than the manipulators. Past masters at the art of adjustment, we are also skilful in finding, after the event, Canadian rationalizations for our choices and for our political commitments, and in virtuously tying them in with broader, more universal values. We neither indulge unduly in righteous moralizing nor overplay our irreproachable record – that comfortable refuge of so many on entering adulthood. But we have proved fairly successful as mediators and as peace-keepers – especially as there is a natural tendency for others to think of us whenever an opening occurs in such jobs, for which there are never very many applicants. We do not easily deceive ourselves about our position. In the combination of mediator and realist, there may be a natural and effective role for Canadians to play abroad.

INDEX

Abbott, John, 122
Aberdeen, Lord, 123
Aberhart, William, 254, 601
Acadian Recorder, 526
Advertising, growth in 1950s, 322
Aeronautics Act, 247
Affari Vos (encyclical), 127
Africa, new nations, 327
  educational expenditure, 583
Agricultural Rehabilitation and Development Act, 356, 416, 418, 447
Agriculture
  Alberta farmers support Social Credit, 254-6
  British embargo on live cattle (1893), 113
  changes in 1800s, 63
  collective action of wheat farmers, 152-5, 216
  Conservative high tariffs, 242
  crops, 417

decline of labour force, 398, 400-1, 451, 487
depression and drought, impact of, 239
drift to cities, 415-17
dry-farming techniques of U.S. immigrants, 142
and early settlements, 410, 413-14
ethnic groups, 398
Experimental Farms, 411, 414, 418, 549, 550
exports, 113, 417-18
farm machinery, 63, 65, 316
farmers' organizations, 191, 210-11, 488-92, 499-500
farmers' parties, 190-2; *see also* United Farmers – of Alberta, etc.
federal aid, 244
first agricultural schools opened, 63
grain elevators' pricing agreements, 153

grain-growers' pooling of wheat sales, 216
improving conditions in early 1890s, 113
legislation, 414-15, 416-17
losing place to industry, 210
main source of employment to 1939, 450
marketing legislation, Ontario (1930s), 256
modernization of approach, 416-17
new strains of wheat, 414
no share in prosperity, 139
production (1950s), 315-16
prosperity during First World War, 192
provinces' role, 418
Quebec colonization, fallacy of, 165
recovery (1923-4), 216
resource management, 412, 414-15, 416-18
revolt (1890s), 116-17
shares in prosperity (late 1920s), 234
'Siege of Ottawa', 155
some tariffs lowered, 128
total farmland, 417
underdeveloped lands, 417
and Union Government, 192
U.S. capital investment in Canada (1890s), 129
western farmers' grievances (1880s, 1890s), 89, 112, 130
western farmers' protest against tariffs, 154-5
wheat, 142, 150, 216, 230, 234-5, 244, 315, 332, 361
Wheat Board, 208-10, 215-16, 244
Air Canada, 247, 515
Air Transport Board, 516
Alabama affair
Canada suggested as reparation, 46
claims settled by Treaty of Washington, 47-8
Alaska
Canadian hopes, 131
trouble in Panhandle, 130-1
U.S. purchase of, 45-6, 74
Alaska Highway, 518
Alberta
becomes province, 39, 159, 789
claims for provincial rights, 264
coal-miners' strike, 158
C.C.F. progress, 253
farmers' government, 211, 219, 500

federal control of natural resources, 142
homogeneity of socio-economic structure, 254-6
junior colleges, 572
percentage of Asiatics, 398
population, 387, 388
Press Act, 529
prosperity from minerals, 341
research council, 564
and Rowell-Sirois Report, 265-6
separate schools, 159-62, 373, 578, 591-2
settlement of Peace River country, 221
Social Credit, 254-6, 259
Special Areas Act, 414
takes over Northern Alberta Railway, 517
Alberta-California pipeline, 522
Alberta Co-operative Elevator Company, 497
Alderson, E. A. H., 179
All-Canadian Congress of Labour, 495
Allan, Hugh, 56-7, 60
Allan, Ted, 691
Allard, Jean, 784
Aluminum Company of Canada, 315
American Civil War, 3, 31
dangers to B.N.A., 26ff.
effects on B.N.A., 10-11, 20, 25-7
St. Albans raid, 26
American Federation of Labor
v. C.I.O., 496
and T.L.C., 156, 493-5
American Federation of Labor–Congress of Industrial Organization, 501
American Protective Association, 120
Anderson, Patrick, 640
Anderson, W. A. B., 784
Anderson-Thomson, J., 519
André, Fr., 95
Angers, A. R., 122, 123, 124
Anglican Church
character in 1920s, 227
in 1867, 586, 588
foreign missions, 604
initiated talks on church union (1880s), 594
lingering British influence, 588-9
native missions, 602
numbers (1871-1961), 596
post-Confederation expansion, 590
and religious modernism, 593

secularization of Clergy Reserves, 587
union discussions with Uniteds, 598-9
in world Anglicanism, 599
Anglin, Timothy Warren, 93
Anglo-American Telegraph Company, 535
Anglo-French Supreme War Council, 291
Annexation
Continental Union movement, 117
reciprocity as first step toward, 53, 110, 111, 117, 176
and U.S. commercial policy, 107
and U.S. purchase of Alaska, 45
Anti-Confederates
collapse of, 30-2
strength in Maritimes, 24-5
Applebaum, Lou, 690
Archibald, A. G., 39
Architecture, 326, 621-38 *passim*
at Confederation, 622-4
regional patterns, 638
Armed Forces, 764-84
Boer War, 768-9
British G. Os. C., 766-7
corps, new formations, 770-1
criticism of, by Sir John French, 771
First World War, 771-4
integration, 783-4
Korea, 781
Militia, 774
NATO role, 780-1
in Newfoundland, 306
'peace-keeping', 781
post-First World War, 774-5
post-Second World War, 778-84
second Riel uprising, 767-8
Second World War, 287-91, 776-8
Wolseley expedition, 767
Arts
art galleries, 326
and Canada Council funds, 324
non-profit organizations, 682-3
performing, 675-96; ballet, 684; Canada Council, 680-1, 682; and the CBC, 685-6; mass culture, 684-5, 692, 694-5; Massey Commission, 679-80, 681, 682; symphonies, 684; theatre, 683-4
revolution of the 1950s, 323-6
visual, 326, 697-712; development in Canada, 700-1; Group of Seven, 226, 703-5; recent developments, 708-9
Asia, rise of nations, 331

Asselin, Olivar, 133
Association of Universities and Colleges of Canada, 576
Atomic energy, first power station, 314-15
Atomic Energy of Canada Limited, 566
Australia, and new concept of Commonwealth, 329
Avison, Margaret, 652
Ayerst Laboratories, 564
Aylesworth, John, 691

Baldwin, James Mark, 551-2
Balfour Declaration, 232
Balfour Report, 796
Ballet, 684
Bank of Canada, 244-6, 254
Banks, tightening of credit, 208-9
Banks, N. P., 45
Banting, Frederick, 223, 556-8
Banting Institute, 557
Baptist Church
branches, 589
and Church Union, 595
in 1867, 586, 589
foreign missions, 604
'New Light' revival, 589
numbers (1871-1961), 596
split over religious modernism, 593
Bardeau, Raymond, 370, 375
Barnes, Howard T., 551
Barr, Murray, 562
Bartlett, Columbus, 526
Baxter, Iain, 709, 712
Beach, Chauncey, 526
Beauchemin, Micheline, 701
Beauchemin, Nérée, 661, 663
Beaverbrook, Lord (Max Aitken), 151-2
Bégin, Archbishop, 127
Béique, Pierre, 689, 690
Bell, Alexander Graham, 66, 534
Bell, Marilyn, 618
Bell Telephone Company, 534
Bellefleur, Leon, 707
Benedict XV, Pope, 180
Benjamin, George, 526
Bennett, Charles, 42
Bennett, R. B., 237, 264, 481, 559
becomes Prime Minister, 238
converted to necessity of federal powers, 266
election campaign (1930), 238
fear of revolution, 248
handling of delegations, 248

ill-prepared to cope with depression, 242
at Imperial Conference (1930), 243
at Imperial Economic Conference (1932), 243
New Deal program, 260-1
and police-state measures, 249-50
and Stevens Commission, 260
tied to rigid monetary framework, 242, 244, 247-8
unpopularity, 248
Bennett, W. A. C., 311, 342, 362
Berger, Yves, 673
Bernard, Henry, 671
Berrill, N. J., 657
Berton, Pierre, 311
Best, Charles, 223, 556, 558
Bethune, Norman, 329
Bibaud, Michel, 660
Bieler, Ted, 712
Bilingualism
  departments and Crown corporations, 726-7
  empty gestures, 371
  essential to nation, 382
  failure of public service, 726
  in House of Commons, 724
  lack of, in national capital, 374
  in legislature of Province of Canada, 714
  national problem, 372
  in provinces, 717-18
  Queen's Printer, 726
  and racial discrimination, 371-2
  royal commission, 376-7
  undermined by Manitoba Schools Question, 121 ff.
Birney, Earle, 652, 653, 654
Bissell, Claude, 577
Black, Malcolm, 690
Blaine, James G., 106
Blair, Andrew G., 104, 126
Blais, Marie-Claire, 671
Blake, Edward, 51
  Aurora speech, 50
  breaks with free-trade Liberals, 105
  and C.P.R. contract, 86-7
  doubts about unrestricted reciprocity, 110
  and Riel execution, 98
  silence in 1891 campaign, 110
  weaknesses, 91
  West Durham letter, 118
Board of Broadcast Governors, 334, 542, 544-6

Board of Railway Commissioners for Canada, 510
Board of Transport Commissioners, 510
Bochner, Lloyd, 691
Boer War
  Canadian Army contribution, 768-9
  Canadian participation, 373, 791
  implications for French Canada, 133
Borden, Sir Frederick, 769
Borden, Robert Laird, 312, 770
  becomes Prime Minister, 177
  and Canada's place in the Empire, 201
  and Canadian involvement in First World War, 792-3
  character, 177
  coalition government, 188
  conscription policy, 188-9
  female suffrage bill, 198-9
  loses Quebec support, 177
  on Naval Services Act, 169
  and Ontario Regulation 17, 187
  problem of shortage of reinforcements, 187-8
  retirement, 202
  visits England and France (1917), 188
  and western separate schools, 160, 161
Borduas, Paul-Emile, 699, 706-7
Bott, E. A., 552
Bourassa, Henri, 136
  allied with Conservatives on colonization, 166
  belief in Canadian biculturalism, 166
  on Canadian participation in Boer War, 169
  champions rights of colonists, 166
  and Laurier's compromise on western separate schools, 162, 166
  and Monk, on schools question, 166-7
  on Naval Service Act, 170, 175
  on Ontario Regulation 17, 187
  opposes police-state measures, 249
  Quebec colonization policy, 165, 166
  resigns over participation in Boer War, 135
  withdraws from federal politics, 166
Bourget, Bishop, 79, 95, 101, 164, 590-1
Bowell, Mackenzie, 119, 122, 123
Bowering, George, 653
Boyle, R. W., 561
Bracken, John, 297, 307
Braden, Bernard, 691
Brebner, J. B., 657
  on Canadian-U.S. interdependence, 804

on economic triangle, 791
on national unity, 800
Brett, G. S., 224, 552
Bright, John, 33
Brind 'Amour, Yvette, 690
British
in Blishen's occupational scale, 396-7
percentage of population, 394
skilled and professional immigrants, 396, 407
British-Canadian Co-operative Society, 497
British Colonist, 526
British Columbia
architecture, 625, 638
Asiatics, percentage of, 398
becomes province, 40-1, 789
boom (1890s), 112
and Canadian Northern Railway, 505
claims for provincial rights, 264
Columbia River treaty, 362, 448
commercial orbit of U.S., 86, 112
conscription mutinies, 296, 301
Co-operative Commonwealth Federation, 241, 253, 340, 342
disappearance of Liberals, P.C.s, 342
election (1966), 345n.
forest regions, 425
forestry – control and management, 427
gold rush, 7, 410, 419, 421
junior colleges, 572
Liberal program (1930s), 256
lured into Confederation, 140
mineral resources, 419, 421, 422, 424
mission field, 602
need for Pacific railway, 503-4
political action for workers, 115
population, 5, 387, 388
and Prairie Farm Rehabilitation Act, 415
promised transcontinental railway, 41
prosperity from forest resources, 341
railway as condition of Confederation, 55
railway loan guaranteed by Great Britain, 49
railway problems under Mackenzie, 57-60
relief-camp workers' march on Ottawa, 249
research council, 564
settlement of Peace River country, 221
Social Credit *v.* C.C.F., 342

threat of secession, 86
uncertain future (1867), 32, 40
U.S. commercial control contested, 129
and U.S. purchase of Alaska, 45-6
University Endowment Lands, 565
water conservation projects, 415
British Columbia Telephone Company, 534
British Empire, becomes Commonwealth, 232
British Empire Games, 607, 614
British Empire League, 132
British Expeditionary Force, 288
British Isles; *see also* Great Britain
early emigration to B.N.A., 5
emigration to Canadian West, 143
rivalries transplanted, 394
British North America Act
agricultural legislation, 414
amendment of, 232-3, 263, 264-7, 302, 337, 355
denominational schools safeguarded, 578
discrimination against Quebec, 371
education a provincial matter, 573
enactment, 32
fisheries, 433
forest resources, 429
highway transport a provincial matter, 524
intentions re federal-provincial relations, 729
Intercolonial Railway, 503
judicial decisions concerning, 263-4, 730
limited effects in depression, 236, 250
natural resources mainly provincial matter, 447
Old Age Pension amendment, 300
part of constitution, 713
powers given to provinces, 341
Property and Civil Rights clause, 80-1, 103, 484-5
social services, 747
and Statute of Westminster, 267
Unemployment Insurance amendment, 254, 266, 300
British United Press, 531-2
British War Cabinet, 291
British War Office, and McNaughton, 289
Broadcasting Act, 542
Brooke, Frances, 642-3
Brown, E. K., 657

Brown, George, 8, 9, 256, 526
    and Canada First movement, 50
    at Charlottetown Conference, 19, 20
    defeat (1861), 12
    efforts to restore reciprocity, 49-50
    heads committee on constitutional re-
        form, 16
    mission to London, 28
    proposes coalition (1864), 16-17
Brown, W. Easson, 563
Bruchési, Archbishop, 127
Brunet, Abbé Ovide, 550
Buckingham, William, 527
Buell, John, 654
Buies, Arthur, 661-2, 664
Bull, Gerald, 565
Bulletin (Edmonton), 527
Bureau, Jacques, 218
Bureau of Translations, 726
Burns, E. L. M., 781
Burns, Tommy, 607
Burton, Dennis, 710
Burton, E. F., 551
Bush, Jack, 708, 709
Bushell, John, 526
Butler, Benjamin F., 35, 43
Byng, Sir Julian, 179, 772
    insists on King's resignation, 218

Cabinet, 721-2, 723, 724, 733
Cahan, C. H., 268
Caisses populaires, 497
Callaghan, Morley, 226, 231, 652, 654
Campbell, Alexander, 90
Campbell, Douglas, 690
Canada
    achieves sovereignty, 793
    decline of influence in world affairs,
        331
    fourth most powerful nation, 326
    geological regions, 419
    internationalism, 327-8
    problems of governing, 732
    role as middle power, 331, 794
Canada, Province of
    Coalition (1864), 16-17
    constitutional reform, 8-9, 14
    delegation to London (1864), 28
    development of government, 724
    dualism, unworkable principle of, 8-9
    political form, pre-Confederation, 8
    population (1861), 4
    pushes Confederation, 17-19
    and St. Albans raid, 26
    unworkable constitution, 714-15

Canada and Its Provinces, 139
Canada Assistance Plan, 356-7, 751
Canada Banking Act, review of, 231
Canada Cement Company, 151
Canada Central Railway, 60
Canada Company (railway), 60
Canada Council, 311
    creation, 323, 679-80
    direction of funds, 324
    first grant recipients, 689
    non-profit criterion, 682
    performing arts, 680-1
    visual arts, 708-9
Canada Development Corporation, 484
Canada East, discussion of Quebec
        Resolutions, 23
'Canada First' movement, 50, 69, 74
Canada Pacific railway company, 56-7
Canada Pension Plan, 354, 357-8, 749,
        754
Canada Temperance Act, 67
Canada West, approval of Quebec
        Resolutions, 22-3
Canadian and Catholic Confederation
        of Labour, 495
Canadian Annual Review, 138, 207-8
Canadian Army Staff College, 779
Canadian Association of University
        Teachers, 576
Canadian Bar Association, against the
        Padlock Law, 258-9
Canadian Broadcasting Authority, 545
Canadian Broadcasting Corporation,
        312, 542-5
    contribution to the arts, 323
    establishment of, 542
    microwave network, 319
    and national purpose, 246
    opportunities in performing arts,
        685-6
    in Peking, 329
    and private stations, 247
    separate French network, 676
    served by Canadian Press, 531
    television, 319, 543-5, 688
Canadian Broadcasting League, 685
Canadian Car and Foundry, 151
Canadian Citizenship Act, 302
Canadian Civil Liberties Union, 259
Canadian Conference of the Arts, 323
Canadian Congress of Labour, 341, 492-
        3, 496
Canadian Corps (First World War), 287
Canadian Council of Agriculture, 192,
        491, 499

Canadian Council of Resource Ministers, 412, 448
Canadian Education Association, 575, 576
Canadian Expeditionary Force, 178, 288, 771
Canadian Federation of Agriculture, 488, 491-2
Canadian Federation of Film Societies, 536
Canadian Federation of Labour, 156-7, 495
Canadian Film Institute, 536-7
Canadian Film Society, 538
Canadian Forum, on nationalism, 233, 253
Canadian Illustrated News, 527
Canadian Labor Union, 492, 497, 498
Canadian Labour Congress, 252, 488
  formation, 341, 493
  friction with C.N.T.U., 501
  and N.D.P., 500-1
  and railway unions, 496
  united with T.L.C., 496
Canadian Manufacturer, on tariff reductions (1893), 119
Canadian Monthly, 529
Canadian National Railways, 220-1, 506
  new image, 320
  and Northern Alberta Railway, 517
  problems faced, 506
  and radio drama, 685
  reorganized, 245-6
Canadian National Telegraph, 533, 534
Canadian North, *see* North, the
Canadian Northern Railway
  collapse, 220
  establishment, 505
  line to Great Lakes, 146-7
  nationalization, 506
  public investment (1916), 507
  at Saskatoon, 141
  two-way traffic – immigrants and wheat, 505
Canadian Opera Company, 325
Canadian Overseas Telecommunications Corporation, 535
Canadian Pacific Airlines, 515
Canadian Pacific Railway, 220, 337, 789
  building line to B.C., 86-8
  completion, 504
  Crow's Nest Pass freight rates, 215, 216
  difficulties of getting under way, 504
  financial difficulties (1880s), 87-8

government take-over suggested, 506-7
and growth of trade unions, 492
heavily Conservative, 1891 election, 111
importance to nation, 108, 140, 319
Manitoban protests over freight rates, 89
monopoly in west, 104
and Northern Alberta Railway, 517
opposed by news agencies, 88
political bargaining for parliamentary support, 92
political neutrality lost, 135
preferential rates on oil, 130
progress (1880s), 70
public investment (1916), 507
and radio, 246
Regina-Saskatoon branch line, 140-1
route chosen, 87
and second Riel uprising, 89, 96, 767-8
subsidy for Crow's Nest Pass Line, 128-9
success of, important to government, 88
threat to Grand Trunk, 505
unable to handle wheat harvest, 145
in west, 142
western farmers' suspicion of, 146
Canadian Pacific Telegraph, 533
Canadian Players, 325
Canadian Press, 531
Canadian Pulp and Paper Association, Institute at McGill, 563
Canadian Radio Broadcasting Commission, 246, 541-2
Canadian Radio League, 246
Canadian School Trustees' Association, 576
Canadian Suffrage Association, 197
Canadian Teachers' Federation, 576
Canadian Television (CTV), 544
Canadian University Foundation, 353
Canadian University Service Overseas, 566
Canadien, Le, 526
CANDU, 439, 566
Caouette, Réal, 352-3
Capital investment
  increase (1890s), 129
  railways (1916), 507
Cappon, James, 657
Cardin, P. J. A., 294
Cardwell, Edward, 27
Careless, J. M. S., 657

Carlo, Yvonne De, 691
Carmack, (Lying) George, 130
Carman, Bliss, 225, 640, 644, 645, 648
Carnarvon, Lord, and B.C. Railway, 59
Caron, Sir Joseph, 123
Carr, Emily, 705-6
Carson, Jack, 691
Carter, Frederick, 41, 42
Cartier, George Etienne, 9, 56, 90, 164
    at Charlottetown Conference, 19, 20
    Coalition (1864), 17
    as Minister of Militia, 765
    mission to London, 28
    negotiations for H.B.Co. land, 33-4
    resignation (1862), 12
Cartier, Jacques, cure for scurvy, 553
Cartier, Michel, 690, 696
Cartwright, Sir Richard, 92, 109, 118,
    126, 128
Casgrain, Abbé Henri Raymond, 660,
    665, 671, 673
Catherwood, Ethel, 607, 615
Catholic Church Extension Society, 592
Cauchon, Noulan, 635
Central Mortgage and Housing Cor-
    poration, 316
Chalk River, 561, 566
Chamber of Commerce, congress of Brit-
    ish Empire chambers, 137-8
Chamberlain, Joseph, 132, 133, 769
Chamberlain, Neville, 271
Chamberland, Paul, 671, 672
Chant, S. N. F., 552
Chapais, Thomas, 665
Chapleau, J. A., 122, 124
Chapman, William, 661
Chaput, Marcel, 370, 375
Charbonneau, Jean, 662
Charlesworth, Hector, 541
Charlesworth, Marigold, 690
Charlottetown Conference, 17-19
Charlton, John, 121
Chauveau, Pierre, on racial division,
    120
Chesapeake affair, 26
Children's Aid Societies, 755, 758
China (Mainland)
    Canadian attitudes to, 359
    Canadian relations with, 329
    Canadian trade with, 333, 361
    civil war, 326-7
    release of U.N. war prisoners, 328
Chiriaeff, Ludmilla, 684, 690, 696
Chopin, René, 663, 671
Choquette, Robert, 663, 671

Christian Guardian, on social classes,
    116
Christian Social Service Council of
    Canada, 593
Chronicle (Halifax), on Confederation,
    77-8
Church
    relinquishing universities, 313
    and State, separation of, 587, 713
Churches
    accommodating affluence, respectabil-
        ity, 594
    adapting to urban, industrial society,
        592
    attitude to First World War, 597
    Church Union, 228, 594-7
    denominational unions and Canadian
        ministry, 588-9
    and the depression, 597-8
    effects of religious modernism, 593
    foreign missions, 603-5
    gains from immigration, 598
    held back by rural conservatism,
        226-9
    ignore working class, 115-16
    influence of speculative idealism, 224
    and international issues, 598
    lose ground in 1920s, 206
    missionary enterprises, 601-5
    problems of the Orthodox commun-
        ion, 599-600
    problems related to national growth,
        592
    and prohibition, 199-200, 228-9
    puritanical approach to moral and
        social issues, 587
    religious communities or social agen-
        cies, 605
    spared slavery issue, 588
    and trade-unionism, 592, 597
    urban missions, 603
    and Winnipeg General Strike, 597
Churchill, Sir Winston, 279, 285, 289,
    291, 310
Churchill Falls, 319
Cité Libre, 370
Citizen (Ottawa), 526
Civil Service, 310, 341
Claxton, Brooke, 680, 783
Clegue, Francis H., 630
Climo, J. S., 66
Clouser, James, 696
Coalition of 1864
    delegates to Maritime union confer-
        ence, 17-19

fcdcration schemes, 17
and York County by-election (New Brunswick), 30
Coburn, Kathleen, 657
Cochrane, Charles, 657
Cohen, Leonard, 654
Cohen, Nathan, 311
Coldwell, M. J., 253
Coldwell, William, 527
Collin, W. E., 657
Collip, J. B., 556, 557, 564
Colombo Plan, 567
Colonial Conference (1902), 168
Colonial Economic Conference, 119
Columbia River treaty, 319, 332-3
Colville, Alex, 709
Commercial Cable Company, 535
Commercial Graduates Basketball Club, 616
Commonwealth
aid plan, 329-30
Air Training Plan, 282, 286, 776
Canada's new concept of, 329-30
Canada's role as middleman, 360
decline, 801
evolution from Empire, 232, 794
inclusion of Afro-Asian nations, 329-30
permanent secretariat, 360
racial division, 360
South Africa, departure of, 330
trade agreements (1932), 243
Communications, 525-45
corporation profits, 452
effect on visual arts, 698-9
effects on cities, 632-3
moving pictures, 536-9
newspapers, 526-9, 531-2
O'Leary Commission, 529-31
periodicals, 529-31
radio, 539-43, 544, 545
telegraph systems, 532-5
telephone systems, 534, 535
television, benefited from rearmament program, 466
threat to French Canada, 372
Communism
dissenters labelled 'red', 249, 250
Duplessis's Padlock Law, 258
espionage activities, 303
McCarthy's reign of terror, 333
Company of Young Canadians, 357
Comtois, Ulysse, 707, 712
Conan, Laure, 660, 661
Conant, James B., on secondary education in U.S., 580
Confederation
alternatives to, 29
B.N.A. contrasted with U.S., 21-2
and the churches, 590, 594
contribution of *Trent* affair, 10-11
debates on, 3-24
and defeat of Tilley government, 24
defiance of geography, 789, 804
Diamond Jubilee, 233
disintegrative forces (1880s), 89-93 *passim*, 98-107
English-Canadian objections to Quebec domination, 78
extension westward, 788-9
federalism adapted to British traditions, 20-1
first interest in, 7
further work needed to complete (1867), 32-6
a government, not a popular, project, 61, 69
helped by Fenian raids, 31
helped by threat of invasion, 764-5
importance of including Red River settlement, 35
importance of railways, 503
Maritime discontent with, 77-8
necessary for western expansion, eastern communications, 14
Newfoundland's entry, 305-6, 786
passed, 32-3
prerequisites, 14-15
v. provincial loyalties, 69, 80
Quebec's place in, 78-9, 371-81
reached its limits (1890), 107, 108
reasons for federal union, 20
residuary powers question, 22
set up against U.S., 45, 786, 803
undermining of, 98-102, 103-5, 107
work completed (1886), 87
York County by-election (New Brunswick), 30
Confederation of National Trade Unions, 488, 495, 496, 501
Congo, Canada's role, 331
Congregational Church
Church Union, 228, 595
in 1867, 586, 589
foreign missions, 604, 605
numbers (1871-1961), 596
Congress of Industrial Organizations
v. A.F.L., 496
and the C.C.F., 252, 257
and General Motors strike (1937), 257

unions expelled from T.L.C., 494,
  495-6
Connaught Laboratories, 562-3, 566
Connor, Ralph, 225, 646
Conroy, Mgr., 127
Conscription, 187-90, 202-3, 777
  controversy in French Canada, 373
  crisis of 1917, effects in 1939, 277
  crisis of Second World War, 794
  racial split over, 799
  in two wars, 300
Conseil Canadien de la Coopération,
  488
Conservation, 410-48 passim
Conservatives
  accomplishments by 1896, 789
  alliance with Nationalists, 176, 792
  anti-agricultural bias, 191
  Beauharnois scandal, 252
  Bennett's New Deal, 260-1
  break between French and English,
    162, 166-7
  Cabinet revolt (1963), 347
  cash contribution to British navy, 177
  coalition with Reform Grits, 16-17
  no conscription for overseas service,
    277, 293
  conservatism and social welfare, 763
  corruption in Department of Public
    Works, 106
  criticism of Pearson in Suez crisis, 330
  dearth of talent (1880s), 90-1, 105-6
  débâcle in international relations, 359
  dependence on Macdonald, 105-6
  under Diefenbaker, 338-9, 346
  'double majority' scheme, 12-13
  early natural-resources policy, 411
  ecclesiastical support in Quebec, 79,
    124
  efforts to increase prosperity (1890s),
    119
  elections: (1900) 135-6, (1926) 218,
    (1945) 297, (1949) 307, (1963) 348;
    defeats: (1896) 125-6, (1935) 260;
    lose majority (1921), 211; survive
    (1896), 119; victories: New Bruns-
    wick, Nova Scotia, 342, (1891) 111-
    12, (1911) 176, (1930) 237, 238, (1957)
    335, 338; win plurality (1925), 216
  eschewed opportunism, 215
  failure to shift trade to Britain, 330
  good times (1880s), 70-1
  Herridge presses for economic inter-
    vention, 260
  increase Ontario seats (1891-3), 113

  lose in Quebec to Parti National, 100
  losing popular support, 340
  loyalty campaign (1891), 110-11
  and Mackenzie's railway problem, 59
  mainly in Ontario, 212, 335-6
  and mandement of Quebec bishops,
    124
  and Manitoba separate-schools issue,
    122-6, 591-2
  National Policy, 111, 117, 150
  nationalism v. imperialism, 206
  Naval Service Act, 169
  oppose trade agreement (1911), 176
  outmoded approach to depression,
    242
  Pacific Scandal, 56-7
  plan for federation of B.N.A. (1858),
    9, 17
  political bargaining for support of
    C.P.R. measures, 88, 92
  pressure for atomic-test-ban treaty,
    330
  problems with weak Quebec lieuten-
    ants, 721-2
  protectionism (late 1870s), 52-3
  protective tariff and western farmers,
    155, 215
  provincial right to choose education-
    al system, 161
  and railways, 220
  and Riel's execution, 98-9
  see need for reform, 251
  semi-police state in depression, 249-50
  social legislation, 356
  split over Bennett's 'radicalism', 254
  split over conscription issue, 188-9
  Stevens crisis, 260
  success of policies (1880s), 75
  Taché-Macdonald government (1864),
    16
  tariffs (1879-96), 456
  and threat of absorption by U.S., 334
  Tilley tariff (1879), 53
  Union Government, 188-9
  and U.S. investment, 361
  unpopularity of foreign policy in
    U.S., 330
  weak war-time opposition, 281
Construction industry, 315, 636-7
Continental Union movement, 117-18
Cooke, Jay, 56
Co-operative Commonwealth Federation (C.C.F.); see also New Democratic Party
  absorbed by N.D.P., 500

on Bennett New Deal, 261, 262
blocked by Duplessis, 258, 259
in British Columbia, 342
on Canadian contribution to war, 73-4
and the C.I.O., 257
conscription vote, 799
effects of Diefenbaker victory (1957), 340-1
elections, 253, (1935) 260, (1945) 297
founding and rise of, 241, 251-4, 500
influence on Liberal government, 253, 255
and labour movement, 251, 341
machinery for changing leader, 721
movement and party, 252
in Ontario, 257
as a political experiment, 718
Regina Manifesto, 597
and Social Gospel movement, 593, 597
supported by League for Social Reconstruction, 253
and United Farmers of Ontario, 257
wavering on neutrality question, 273
Coopérative Fédérée, 498
Co-operative Union of Canada, 488, 497
Co-operatives, 487-501
beginnings of movement, 490
caisses populaires, 497
development of, 496-8
Prairie 'pools', 498
rise of Wheat Pools, 230
Corbett, E. A., on Dr. Tory's dismissal from N.R.C., 559
Corporations and Labour Unions Returns Act, 474, 478
Cosmos, Amor de, 40, 86, 526n.
Costain, Thomas B., 657
Côté, Gérard, 611
Coughtry, Graham, 710
Coulter, John, 695
Courrier de St-Hyacinthe, Le, 526
Cox, George, 118, 129
Coyne, James, 361
Craigie, J. H., 550
Craigie, James, 562
Crawley, Budge, 687
Crawley Films, 538
Creighton, Donald, 657
Crémazie, Octave, 660, 663, 671
Crerar, H. D. G., 290, 777, 778
Crerar, Thomas A., 192, 237, 291
Criminal Code, 249-50, 254
Croft, Henry Holmes, 547, 548
Croll, David, 257

Crothers, Bill, 607
Crown, the, 719-20, 733
Crown corporations, 727-8
Crow's Nest Pass freight rates, 215, 216
Cuba, Canadian trade with, 333, 361
Cullen, Maurice, 703
Curling, first bonspiel, 67
Curnoe, Greg, 710
Currie, Sir Arthur, 288, 772
Czechoslovakia, 303, 328

Dafoe, John, on Munich, 271
Daily News (New York), on Canada's foreign minister, 333
Daily Star (Toronto), 528
Dandurand, Leo, 612
Daniells, Roy, 657
Dantin, Louis, 662, 665
Davey, Frank, 653
David, L. O., 127
Davies, Meredith, 690
Davies, Robertson, 654, 655
on plight of Canadian theatre, 324
Davin, Nicholas Flood, 74-5
Davis, Dorothy, 198
Davis, Murray, 690
Dawson, R. MacGregor, on King's tactics, 798
Dawson, Sir William, 547, 548-9
Dawson City, in gold rush, 130
Defence, 764-84
Avro Arrow, 332
BOMARC missiles, 334, 346-7, 782-3
Britain attempts to shift burden to colonies, 27
British responsibility (1860s), 12
Canada as a buffer state, 331-2
Canadian-British agreement (1864), 28
Canadian navy question, 168-9, 174-5, 770, 791
Conservative non-policy (1860s), 13
continuance after war, 298
criticism by Sir John French, 771
Diefenbaker and nuclear war-heads, 346-7
first regular Canadian units, 766
First World War, 178-90, 771-4
integration, 783-4
Jervois sent to revamp system, 27
Korea, 465-6, 781
militia, vote of, 765, 779-80
Militia Council (1904), 769
NATO, 304, 780-1
Naval Bill (1910), 770

peace-keeping role, 781
Permanent Joint Board Canada–U.S., 302-3
post-First World War, 774-5
post-Second World War, 778-84
Schemes 1, 2, 3: 774-6
Second World War, 279-93, 776-8
U.S. joint arrangements with, 331-2, 781-3, 804
withdrawal of British troops proposed (1870), 46
Defence Production Act, 337
Defence Research Board, 331, 582, 779
Defence Research Medical Laboratories, 562
Defries, R. D., 563
De la Roche, Mazo, 231, 645, 647, 658
Democracy, weakness of cultural minority in crisis, 133
Denison, Flora, 198
Denison, George, 110, 131
Depression, Great, 238-74
    blamed on capitalism by Bennett, 261
    Conservative measures, 242-8
    development of semi-police state, 249-50
    eclipsed other considerations, 797
    economic paralysis, 794
    effects, on cities, 632-3; on government and politics, 241, 250-1
    expectation of return, 316
    impact on the churches, 597-8
    need for federal action, 241, 250-1
Desjardins, Alphonse, 497
Desrochers, Alfred, 663, 671
Desrosiers, Léo-Paul, 665
Development Road Program (Yukon and N.W.T.), 519
Devoir, Le, on Ontario Regulation 17, 187
Dewey, John, 311
Dickens, Charles, 683
Diefenbaker, John G.
    and anti-Quebec feeling in west, 381
    character, 338-9
    Commonwealth affairs, 360
    on foreign capital investment, 475-6
    loss of majority, 346
    and nuclear war-heads, 346-7
    and process of decentralization, 353
    Quebec support, 338
    reasons for defeat, 348-9
    reformation of Conservative party, 338

and South Africa's departure from Commonwealth, 330
    victory (1957), 335
    victory (1958), 310, 335, 346
Dieppe, 289, 777
Director of Employment Services, 571
Disabled Persons' Allowances, 750, 758
Disraeli, Benjamin, 71, 72
DEW Line, 782
Dobell, R. R., in Laurier cabinet, 126
Dominion Bridge, protests Standard Oil monopoly, 130
Dominion Drama Festival, 325, 684
Dominion Government Telegraph Services, 533-4
Dominion-Provincial Conference (1927), 232-3
Dominion Telegraph Company, 533
Dominions, and abdication crisis, 267-8
Donald, William, 699
Dorion, Antoine Aimé, 12
Dorion, Chief Justice Frédéric, 350
Douglas, C. H., 231
Douglas, T. C., 253
Douglas, Wm. Moir, 549
Dow, Herbert H., 564
Dow Chemical Company, 564
Dreux, Albert, 662
Drew, George, 307, 310, 335, 338
Drocourt-Quéant Line, 183
Drummond, Sir George Alexander, 123
Drummond, William Henry, 642, 647, 648-9
Dubé, Marcel, 668-9, 695
Duck Lake massacre, 95
Dufferin, Lord, 57, 59-60
Dugas, Fr. Georges, 35
Dugas, Marcel, 671
Dulles, John Foster, 310, 335
Dumont, Gabriel, 94, 97
Dumouchel, Albert, 707
Duncan, Sara Jeanette, 225
Dundonald, Earl of, 769
Dunning, Charles, 237
Duplessis, Maurice, 241, 271, 312, 336, 341
    anti-trade-union measures, 258-9
    assertion of provincial rights, 257-8
    conservatism, 365
    consolidates power, 257-8
    defeat (1939), 280-1
    Padlock Law, 258-9
    quasi-police state, 258-9
    regime, 392
    returned to power, 301

and Roman Catholic Church, 258, 259
Dupuis, Yvon, 352
Durbin, Deanna, 691
Duvernay, Ludger, 526

Eastern Provincial Airlines, 515
Eaton, Charles, on English Tory bigotry, 136
Eaton's of Canada, 318
Economic Council of Canada, on problems of manufacturing industry, 470-1
Economist, on U.S. capital investment in Canada, 129
Economy
  and architecture, 622-4
  based on natural resources, 446
  boom (1910-13), 173-4
  capital expenditures, by sectors, 451
  changes in 1860s, 6-7
  control exerted by banks, 208
  conversion to peace-time, 465
  corporation profits, by sectors, 452
  crash (1893), 113
  crash (1929), 234-5, 236
  deflation, 208, 209-10
  depression, (1873-95) 455-6, (1930s) 236-74 *passim*, 461; pre-First World War, 458
  down-swing (1957-61), 466-7
  drawbacks of rigid price structure, 242
  1867-1967 compared, 453-4
  in 1870s, 63-5
  in 1890s, 112-14
  expansion (1960s), 467
  expansion, unplanned, 317
  First World War, stimulus, 178
  and free trade, 6-7
  growth, creating divided society, 109; (through 1920s) 221-2; (1950s) 311, 314-18
  high transport overhead, 523
  importance of foreign capital, 474
  importance of manufacturing, 452
  increased dependence on U.S., 299
  increased U.S. investment, 793-4, 796
  industrial expansion, 460-1
  Manitoba land market breaks (1883), 89
  need for balance between sectors, 480, 485-6
  peril of 1887 election to national economy, 105

post-Confederation conditions, 455
post-war adjustment, 193-4, 203, 345, 465
post-war boom and inflation, 207
post-war growth, 297-9
pre-Confederation commercialism, 6-7
pre-war recession, 178
prosperity, first decade of century, 138-9
prosperity (late 1920s), 234
recession (mid 1880s), 89
recession (mid 1890s), 128
recession (1957), 340
recovery from deflation, 216
recovery from depression, slow, 273-4, 461-2
recovery (late 1890s), 129-30
regions becoming interdependent, 150-1
Second World War, 274, 283-4, 450-1
self-regulating theory, 207
shift to peace-time goals, 345
slump (1880s), 109
standard of living, 744-5
up-swing (1890), 109-10
Edgar, James, 57-8
Edgar, Pelham, 657
Edinburgh International Festival of Documentary Films, 538
Edmonton, and the Far North, 223
Edmonton Grads, 616
Education, 568-85; *see also* Universities
  based on science (1920s), 223
  deficiencies, 404-7
  denominational schools, 368, 577-8
  1867 and 1967 contrasted, 569
  emphasis on quality, 572-3
  expenditure, 581-3
  federal involvement, 575
  French language in school not allowed, 213
  fundamental questions, 570
  government activity increased, 341
  humanities lagging, 224
  for individual needs, 570-3
  and industrialization, 403-8
  junior colleges, 572
  levels, by ethnic group, 405-6
  levels, by provinces, 405
  local boards, 574
  local units, reorganization of, 579-81
  modified system of separate schools in west, 159-62
  moving pictures, use of, 536-7
  need for democratization, 404, 408

need for improvement in forestry,
    429, 430
need for interprovincial co-ordina-
    tion, 575-6
Ontario controversies (1880s), 80
organization and control, 574-81
post-secondary formal, 572
provinces' largest budget item, 314
a provincial matter, 345, 573-5
Quebec, 78-9, 367-8, 371
and religion, 406-7
royal commissions, 569-70
schools as agents of social policy,
    224-5
self-instructional devices, 584-5
separate-schools issues, 373, 589; New
    Brunswick, 60; Manitoba, 102, 110,
    121-8, 159, 160, 213, 373, 591-2
teachers, 583-4
Toronto bishop v. Minister of Educa-
    tion, 80
veterans' benefits, 297-8
vocational and technical, 571-2
Edward VIII, abdication, 267-8
Egalitarianism (in 1880s), 73-5 passim
Eisenhower, Dwight, 310
Elections
    (1896) issues, 125-6
    (1911) 170, 176
    (1926) 218
    1930 upset, 237-8
    (1935) 259-63; protest vote, 253-5
    (1940) King victory, 281
    (1945) 296-7
    (1949) Liberal victory, 307
    (1957) 335, 338
    (1958) 310, 335, 338, 346
    (1963) issues, 347-8
    change in suffrage (1917), 189
    Drummond-Arthabaska, and Naval
        Service Act, 170
    importance of party leader, 336, 338
    need for majority, 345
    plethora of (in 1960s), 345
    province testing-ground for changes
        in system, 718
    secret ballot introduced, 61, 68
Elizabeth II, visit to Quebec City, 375-6
Emigration
    almost equal to immigration, 390
    exceeds immigration around 1890, 112
    keeps step with population increase
        (1880), 90
    Quebec farm families, to New Eng-
        land, 164

to U.S. (1870s), 62
Energy
    atomic, 439, 561, 566
    coal, 436
    electrical, export of, 440
    hydro-electric power, 437-9, 458
    oil, 436-7
    sources, 436
    thermal-electric power, 438-9
Equal Franchise League, 197
Equal Rights Association, 102, 111, 121,
    591
    anti-Catholicism, 120
    and imperialism, 132
Equal Suffrage Society, 197
Erickson, Arthur, 326
Eskimos, 398-400
    effects of opening of north, 637
    lack of influence on government, 715
    missions to, 601
Esson, James, 66
Etcheverry, Sam, 617
Ethnic groups, 394-400, 408-9
Europe
    effect of family ties with, 390
    industrial recovery, 317
    recovery accomplished, 331
Examiner (Charlottetown), 526
'Expo 67', 382, 712
External affairs, 302-5, 312-13, 785-805;
        see also Commonwealth; Great
        Britain; NATO; United Nations;
        United States
    aid, increase in (1950s, 1960s), 329-30
    Canada as emerging nation, 790-2
    Canadian High Commissioner in
        London, 790
    Chanak affair, 215, 269, 795
    the Cold War, 303-5
    Commonwealth relations, 360
    and the constitution, 266-7
    Cuban crisis, 363
    department established, 792
    diplomatic mission in Washington,
        785
    and domestic crises, 794-5
    economic background, 791
    emergence of a Canadian policy, 362-3
    evolution of Canada's middle-power
        role, 794
    extension of sphere of interests, 328-
        30
    foreign policy of 1930s, 796-8
    Imperial Conference (1926), 796
    internationalism v. isolationism, 795

isolationism, 303-4, 794
issue-dodging (1930s), 266, 268-71, 273-4
during King's administration, 259, 268-74, 797-8
Legation opened in Washington, 796
and Liberal tradition, 266-7
ministers of, 304
in 1960s, 359-63
peace-keeping missions, 359, 363
policy since Confederation, 786
post-Second World War, 800-5
provincial power to make treaties?, 264
pursuit of national rights, 213, 215
role of disinterested middleman, 359
and Second World War, 798-800
Suez crisis, 363
U.S., relations with, 360-2, 790, 793, 803-4
U.S.S.R., recognition of, 795
External Affairs, Department of, 792

Fairfield, Robert, 326
Fairley, Barker, 657
Family Allowance Act, 300
Family Allowances, 748, 753
Faraday, Michael, 547
Favreau, Guy, 350
Federal District Commission, 632, 635
Federal government
agricultural legislation now emergency only, 414
aid to provinces (1930s), 244, 247, 250-1
and church missions to natives, 602-3
constitutionally hampered in dealing with depression, 236, 250-1
control of Crown lands in west, 160
control of natural resources in west, 142
and defence industries, 298
disallows Social Credit legislation, 255
empowered to protect minority rights, 122-3
evolving labour policy, 157-8
fisheries, 433
formal links with provincial government structure, 719
funds for education, 582
geological survey work, 419-20
ignores constitutional conference, 104-5
increased power, during and after war, 341

intervention in Winnipeg Strike, 196
involvement in education, 575
lack of leadership, 345
leadership required in resource management, 447-8
over-extension of powers by Bennett, 261-4
policies on industrial growth, 479-84; Howe's guidelines, 482
powers, 302, 310, 729
and Quebec, 370-4, 379
and Queen Elizabeth's visit, 376
and railways, 504, 505
recreational resources policy, 441, 442-3
revenues (1938), 276
role in forestry, 428-9, 430
St. Lawrence Seaway project, 520
social legislation, 356-8
social welfare programs, 748-51
structure of, 719-25
subsidizes construction of branch railway lines, 145-6, 148
support of universities, 314, 353-4
veterans' rehabilitation, 194
weakening of powers (1880s), 81, 103
weaknesses, 353
wheat-buying, 244
Federalism, 376-80, 715-16, 729-32
Federal-provincial relations
attempts to resolve crisis, 377-80
conferences, 377, 728, 733; (1887) 104-5; (1927) 232-3, 264; (1941) 266; (1964) 355
constitutional framework, 728-9
consultation, 380
'co-operative federalism', 354-5, 377
decentralization, 353-4
federal structure turned upside down, 729-31
legislation by conference?, 355-6
medical care insurance, 762
need for reassessment in depression, 236, 241, 250-1, 255, 263-5
no federal department, 728
problems (1940s), 305
provinces, 81, 104-5, 109, 266; financial problems, 731-2; increasing power, 341, 363-4; Ontario's fight for provincial rights (1880s), 80-1, 103; Quebec encroaching on federal powers, 377-8
reassessment, 354
resource management, 412

shared-cost welfare programs, 747-8,
  750-1
significance of Property and Civil
  Rights clause, 80-1, 103
social services, 736-7, 747-52
social welfare controversy, 357, 358
special status for Quebec?, 378-80
strong provincial figures in Laurier
  cabinet, 126
tax-sharing agreements – opting-out
  formula, 354
Federal Resources Conference (1954),
  412
Fédérations des Collèges Classiques, 368
Feldbrill, Victor, 690
Female Suffrage movement, 196-9
Fenian raids, 31, 45, 46, 93, 764
Fenians, in Saskatchewan rebellion, 96
Ferguson, J. K. W., 563
Ferron, Jacques, 670
Fielding, Wm. Stevens
  at constitutional conference, 104
  heads Nova Scotia government, 103
  Minister of Finance, 126
  secession plan, 103
  tariff hearings, 128
  and western separate schools, 161
First World War, 172-90, 771-4
  as argument for prohibition, 200
  attitude of churches, 597
  Canada's involvement automatic, 792
  Canadian action, 179-83
  Canadian voice in policy-making,
    792-3
  casualties on Western Front, 290-1
  cure for recession, 458-9
  disintegrative effects, 202, 205-6
  Dominions represented at peace con-
    ference, 793
  effect on national unity, 793
  effect on railways, 505-6
  effects on Canada's role, 201-2, 203-4
  end, 183, 190
  general approval of Canadian parti-
    cipation, 178-9
  outbreak, 173, 177
  profiteering, 180
  shortage of reinforcements, 187-8
  the Somme, 773
  Vimy Ridge, 773
  voluntary enlistment mostly British-
    born, 184
  Ypres, 179, 182, 772-3
Fish, Hamilton, 34, 46, 47, 49-50

Fisheries, 430-6
  Americans in Canadian waters, 46-7,
    48
  Atlantic coast, 430, 431, 434
  changes needed, 434-6
  early importance, 410
  and early settlement, 431
  exports, 432
  future outlook, 435-6
  Great Lakes, 432
  importance of international treaties,
    430-1
  Joint High Commission (1898-9), 131
  management, 433
  modern methods, 432
  Pacific coast, 430, 431-2, 434
  production, 432-3
  proposed twelve-mile limit, 432
  research, 435
  sports fishery, 435
  Treaty of Washington, 48
Fitzpatrick, Charles, 127
Flag, the, 350, 382
Fleming, Sandford, 54, 55
Flemming, Hugh John, 342
Ford Motor Company of Canada, 333
Foreign affairs, see External affairs
Forest resources
  changes needed, 429-30
  and early settlement, 410
  in 1870s, 65
  exploitation, 630
  exports, 424, 428
  growth, early twentieth century, 457
  importance besides timber, 425
  importance of reforestation, 428
  legislation, 427-8
  logging methods, 425-6
  main regions, 425
  management, 426-7, 428-30
  need for research, 429, 430
  processing, 425-6
  a provincial responsibility, 426-8
  pulp and paper, 222, 425-6, 428
  research, 563
  species of commercial value, 424-5
  tenure, 426-7
  U.S. capital investment in Canada
    (1890s), 129
Forrester, Maureen, 325, 691, 692
Fort Norman, discovery of oil, 223
Foster, George, 91, 106, 119
Foster, William, 69
Fowler, R. M., 545
Franca, Celia, 684, 690

France
  attitudes of Canada and U.S., 360
  Canadian diplomatic mission, 277
  fall (1940), 283, 293
  in NATO and U.N., 360
Franck, Albert, 708
Fréchette, Louis, 75, 661, 663
Free Methodists, 594
Free Press Publications, 528
Free trade; *see also* Reciprocity Treaty
  auto parts agreement, 362
  effects of British adoption of, 6-7
  Liberal efforts to restore Reciprocity
    Treaty, 49-50
  Liberal plank (1887), 105
  in natural products, negotiations with
    U.S., 150, 175-6
  opinion swings in favour of protec-
    tion, 52-3
Freedman, Harry, 696
French, Sir John, 771
French Canada; *see also* Quebec
  beyond Quebec, 381-2
  Blishen's occupational scale, 396-7
  and Boer War, 133-4
  cohesion of society, 391
  Conservatives consider breaking with
    English, 162
  difficulties outside Quebec, 381
  disturbed by increasing English in-
    fluences, 139
  and English-Canadian ties with Brit-
    ain, 169-70
  increasing traditionalism, 159, 163-4
  industrialization, 392-3, 397
  influence on structure of government,
    715
  lack of enthusiasm for nation-build-
    ing, 159-60, 162
  limited to Quebec by English Cana-
    dians, 373, 381
  literature, 659-74
  little migration west, 159-60, 161-2
  and Naval Service Act, 169-70
  new chapter with Liberal victory, 343
  population, 391, 394
  pro-Spanish sympathies, 133
  problems of federal politics, 372-4
  radio network, 542
  relations with English Canada, effects
    of Second World War, 300-1
  and religious guarantee for western
    separate schools, 161-2
  and St. Laurent, 336
  threat of assimilation, 372

  and Union Government, 188
French language, 121-2, 186-7
Front de Libération Québécois, 375
Frye, Northrop, 656, 657
Fulton-Favreau Formula, 355
Fund for Rural Economic Development,
  416
Fur trade, 410, 444
Furie, Sidney J., 691

Gagnon, Ernest, 668
Galt, Alexander T.
  as Canadian High Commissioner, 74
  at Charlottetown Conference, 19, 20
  and Imperial Federation League, 106
  mission to London, 28
  proposal to move surplus Irish to
    Canada, 90
Gardiner, Robert, 252
Gardner, John W., 569
Garneau, Alfred, 661
Garneau, François-Xavier, 660, 674
Garneau, Saint-Denys, 666, 673
Gas, natural, 437, 440, 465, 468
Gascon, Jean, 690
Gaspé, Philippe Aubert de, 660
Gaucher, Yves, 710
Gaulle, Charles de, 360
Gazette (Montreal), 526
Geiger-Torel, Herman, 690, 691
Gélinas, Gratien, 668, 690, 695
General Finance Corporation, 369
General Motors, Oshawa strike (1937),
  257
Genereux, George, 607
Geological Survey of Canada, 420
George, Lloyd, 201, 773
George VI, 268, 273
Gérin-Lajoie, Paul, 368
Germany
  air offensive against, 287
  in League of Nations, 234
  repossession of the Rhineland, 269
  threat to British naval supremacy,
    167-8, 172-3, 175
Giguère, Roland, 667
Gil, Charles, 662
Gilbert, Edward, 690
Giroux, André, 670
Gladstone, Gerald, 712
Gladstone, William Ewart, 27, 33
Globe (Toronto), 526
  annexationist organ? 117
  on religious conflict, 120
  on Royal Society of Canada, 75

support of Hepburn, 257
Globe and Mail, 526, 532
  correspondent in Peking, 329
  on Liberal Conference at Kingston,
    340
Gnarowski, Michael, 653
Godbout, Jacques, 670-1
Godin, Gérald, 672
Goldenberg, H. Carl, on two-tier school
    government, 581
Goldsmith, Oliver, 642, 644
Gompers, Samuel, 195
Good, W. C., cyclical theory of budget-
    ing, 231
Gooderham, Albert E., 562
Gordon, Arthur Hamilton, 14-15, 24, 30
Gordon, Rev. Charles W., 225
Gordon, Margaret, 198
Gordon, Walter, 349, 361, 476
Gordon Report, 310
Gorman, Richard, 710
Gould, Glenn, 325, 691
Gouzenko, Igor, 328, 333
Government, structure of, 713-33
  American influence, 714
  assessment, 732-3
  British influence, 713, 724
  the Cabinet, 721
  complexity, 715-16
  the Crown, 719-20
  the Crown corporation, 727-8
  the federal position, 719-25
  federal system turned upside down,
    729-31
  federal-provincial conference, 728,
    733
  federal-provincial links, 719
  House of Commons, 723-5
  increased power of those in power,
    722
  judiciary separate from legislative,
    executive branches, 713
  local government, 715-17
  philosophy, 482
  pragmatic, 713-14
  pre-Confederation basis, 713
  prime minister, 720-1; and his cab-
    inet, 721-2
  provinces, 717-19
  public service, 726-7
  Senate, changing role of, 722-3
  war-time Crown corporations, 464
Governor General, role of, 720, 721, 722
Graham, Hugh, 134
Grain Act (1900), 153

Grain Exchange, farmers fight to sell
    wheat on, 154
Grain Growers' Association, 210-11
Grain Growers' Grain Company, 154,
    497
Grain Growers' Guide, on politics, 155
Grand Trunk Pacific, 141, 220, 505, 507;
    telegraph, 533
Grand Trunk Railway, 6, 60
  all-Canadian route proposed, 149
  connected with Intercolonial, 503
  expansion into west, 147-8
  extended into U.S. mid-west, 78
  financial troubles, 503
  line-building (1850s, 1860s), 53-4
  and National Transcontinental, 149-
    50
  nationalization, 506
  opposition to C.P.R., 88
  preferential rates on oil, 130
  public investment (1916), 507
Grandbois, Alain, 666
Grandpré, A. De, 526
Grands Ballets Canadiens, Les, 684
Grant, George Monro, 131, 594
Grant, Ulysses S., 34, 47
Gray, Jack, 695
Gray, William, 526
Great Britain; *see also* British Isles
  abdication crisis, 267-8
  accused of pro-Southern sympathies,
    26
  Admiralty pressure for Dominion
    naval contributions, 168-9
  and amendment of Canadian Con-
    stitution, 232
  anti-colonial sentiment, 27, 29
  attitude to colonies (1860s), 10-12
  British North America shouldering
    some obligations, 12
  Canada's best customer (1930s), 318
  Canadian commitments to, 305
  and Canadian Commonwealth role,
    360
  and Canadian expansion, 788-9
  Canadian independence of, increas-
    ing, 233
  and Canadian navy, 168-9, 174-5
  and Canadian preferential tariffs, 128,
    243-4
  Canadian relations with, late 19th
    century, 790
  and Canadian resolutions re Irish
    Home Rule, 93

and Canadian servicemen, 288-9
capital investment in Canada (1900-14), 458
colonies as a burden, 788
Commonwealth air-training program proposed, 271
conciliatory attitude to U.S. on joint high commission, 47-8
Conservative attempt to shift trade to, 330
control of Canadian foreign policy, 788
and defence of Canada, 765-7
depression (1870s), 455
educational expenditure, 583
in the European Common Market, 360
expanding agricultural market, 113
exports to, increased, 243-4
foreign aid, 330
and Germany's naval power, 769
government control of universities, 577
guarantees loan for British Columbia railway, 49
guarantees loan for Intercolonial (1863), 13
High Commissioner in Ottawa, 233
Imperial Army Reserve idea, 769-70
importance of relations with, 791
industries in world market, 471-2
investment in Canada declines, 318
naval construction program (1909), 167-8
new appreciation of colonies (1880s), 71-2
and new concept of Commonwealth, 329
and Newfoundland, 305-6
parties in municipal politics, 716
preferential tariffs – and American branch plants in Canada, 460, 462
Privy Council Judicial Committee, 263-4, 265, 302
Privy Council Railway Committee, 510
promise to influence Maritimes re Confederation, 28
promise to pay Fenian claims, 48
proposal to withdraw troops from Canada, 46
reasons for approving of Confederation, 27-8
reception of Nova Scotia Anti-Confederate delegation, 33

suggests joint high commission with U.S., 47
and U.S. claims for reparation after Civil War, 34
university costs, 408
West Berlin airlift, 303
world status, 327
Great Lakes Fisheries Convention, 432
Great North Western telegraph company, 533
Great Slave Railway Commission, 519
Greber, Jacques, 634
Green, Howard, 330
Greenburg, Clement, 709
Greene, Lorne, 691
Greenway, Thomas, 102, 127
Gregg, Alan, 558
Griffith, H. R., 563
Grignon, Claude-Henri, 671-2
Gross National Product
   (1867) 453
   (1933-63) 737, 742-3
   (1945-8) 297
   (1950-60) 314
   (1967) 453
Groulx, Abbé Lionel, 213, 234, 664, 665
Group of Canadian Painters, 705
Group of Seven, 226, 326
Grove, Frederick Philip, 225, 231, 640, 642, 650
Guest, Jack, 611
Guèvremont, Germaine, 670
Guité, J. P., 526
Guthrie, Hugh, 249-50
Guthrie, Tyrone, 685, 689
Guttman, Irving, 690

Hahn, Otto, 551
Haig, Sir Douglas, 180, 181
Haliburton, Thomas Chandler, 643, 650
Halifax
   and *Chesapeake* affair, 26
   effects of St. Lawrence Ship Canal, 522
   growth as first entrepôt (1870s), 64
   and Royal Canadian Navy, 286
   to be terminus of Intercolonial, 53-4
Halifax Gazette, 526
Hamilton, Lord George, on female suffrage, 198
Handy, Arthur, 712
Hanlan, Ned, 607, 610-11, 613
Hansen, Fritzie, 615
Harkness, Douglas, 347
Harris, Lawren, 704

Harris, Robert, 99, 702
Harris, William, 526
Harris company, 65
Hart, Harvey, 691
Harvey, Jean-Charles, 664
Havana Convention, 540
Hayden, Melissa, 691
Hays, Charles, 147-8
Haythorne, Robert, 44
Haywood, Bob, 607
Head, Sir Edmund Walker, 548
Heagerty, J. J., 553-4
Hearst, William Randolph, 311
Heavysege, Charles, 640, 644
Hebb, D. O., 552
Hébert, Anne, 667
Hébert, Louis-Philippe, 702
Hedrick, Robert, 710
Heenan, Peter, 237
Hees, George, 347, 361
Hellyer, Paul, 783
Hémon, Louis, 165-6, 366, 640, 663-4
Hénault, Gilles, 667
Henderson, G. H., 561
Henderson, Velyien E., 563
Hepburn, Mitchell F., 256-7, 258
    anti-labour campaign, 259
    criticism of federal war policies, 281
    opposition to Rowell-Sirois Report,
        266
Herald (Battleford), 527
Herald (Montreal), 526
Herbert, Ivan, 767
Herridge, W. D., 260
Highways
    development of systems, 508
    economic effects, 508-9
    expenditure, 509
    extending (1920s), 234
    government activity, increased, 341
    inadequacy (1920s), 219
    into north, 518-19
    social effects, 508-9
Hill, Arthur, 691
Hill, J. J., 112
Hiller, Arthur, 691
Hindenburg Line, 183
Hirsch, John, 690
Hofmann, Hans, 708
Holiness Movement, 594
Holland, Anthony, 526
Holmes, John W., on Canada as Inter-
        preter, 802-3
Holton, Luther, 12
Homburger, Walter, 689, 690

Homestead Act (1872), 413
Hoover, Herbert, 237, 238
Hopkins, Castell, 208
Horner, Harry, 687
Hospital Insurance Act, 750-1
House of Commons, 722, 723-5; see also
    Parliament
Howe, C. D., 278, 310, 336, 340
    contribution to industrial develop-
        ment, 481-3
    and the pipeline, 337
    role in Liberal defeat, 337
Howe, Joseph, 529
    agitation for repeal of Confederation,
        33
    colonial representation scheme, 29
    criticism of Quebec Resolutions, 24
Howith, Harry, 653
Howland, W. P., 12
Hubbard, Robert, 703, 704
Hudson Bay Mining Company, 517
Hudson Bay Railway, 215, 223, 517
Hudson's Bay Company, 86
    blocking westward expansion, 7, 13,
        27
    hold on North-west, 32
    Minnesotan interest in lands, 46
    transfer of North-west to Canada,
        33-4, 37, 39, 140
Hughes, E. C., 397
Hughes, Sir Samuel, 178, 186, 771
Humanities, lagging behind science in
        1920s, 224
Huntington, Seth, 56-7
Huskins, Leonard, 550
Hutchison, Bruce, 657
Hutton, E. T. H., 768
Hyde Park agreement, 800
Hydro-electric power, 222, 437-9

Ilsley, J. L., 278
Immigrants, 5, 142, 395-8, 636
Immigration, 413
    and Canadian Northern Railway, 505
    and the churches, 598
    declining (1891), 112
    in 1870s, 62
    in 1880s, 70-1, 90
    flood to west, 140-4, 150, 790
    increased, 173
    little greater than emigration, 389-90
    in 1950s, 316
    skilled and professional workers,
        407-8
Immigration Act, 249

Imperial conferences, 232-3, 267, 269
(1923) 216
(1926) 232-3, 795, 796
(1930) 243
Imperial Economic Conference, 242-3
Imperial Federation League, 100, 110
antagonizes French Canadians, 106
antidote to annexation, 131
in 1891 election, 111
non-involvement in Dominion matters, 793
Imperial War Cabinet, 292, 792
Imperialism
as basis of national unity, 71-3, 233
Boer War, 133-4
Canada First, 243
and Canadian autonomy, 168-9
Conservative jingoism, 169
and 1897 tariff, 131
enthusiasm over Canadian participation in First World War, 178
finished off by King, 327
King's brand of, 268-9
Laurier at Diamond Jubilee, 131-2
naval issue (1909-10), 168-9, 177
role of Imperial Federation League, 106
stimulated by anti-Americanism, 131
threat to national unity, 132
v. nationalism, 206
India, 327, 330, 566
Indians, 398-400
on Blishen's occupational scale, 399
federal policies concerning, 83-4
lack of influence on government, 715
lacrosse, 609-10
located on reserves, 142
missions to, 601-3
poverty, 315
support of Riel, 96
treaties (1870s), 61
vestige of influence, 625
Indo-China Control Commission, 329
Indonesia, 327
Industrial Development Bank, 483
Industrial Disputes Investigation Act, 158
Industrial Research Council (Quebec), 369
Industrial Revolution, 6-7
Industrial Workers of the World, 195
Industrialization, 400-4, 487
and the churches, 592-3, 597-8, 601, 603

and democratization, 386-7
effect of war, 634
effects on farm families, 416
effects on occupational structure, 397, 400-4
effects in Quebec (1930s), 257
implications for education, 403-8
social effects, 403-4
socio-economic consequences, 129-30
Industry, 449-86
assessment of development, 485-6
automotive, 298-9
Canada's rank in world, 449
capital expenditure, 451
catching up with agriculture, 210
causes northern expansion, 222
corporation profits, 452
the depression, 461
effect of highway transport, 508
expansion, 151; (after 1896) 456-7;
First World War, 459; (1940s) 297-9;
(after 1950) 465-6
foreign investment, capital, and control, 458, 473-8
government policies to encourage, 479, 480-5
growth after 1900, 457-8
growth (1950s), 314-15
impetus of Second World War, 463-5, 468
importance of available energy, 437
iron and steel in Maritimes, and railway construction, 150-1
Korean war, 465-6
labour force (1920s), 460
manufacturing, advance into, from resource industries, 446; auto parts agreement, 362, 484; concentration in major cities, 636; at Confederation, 454-5; cut-back (1957-61), 466-7; 1867-1967 compared, 453-4; decline in Maritimes, 150; employment, 450; exports, 451-2; farm machinery, 65, 315; implications for farmers, 142; importance to economy, 450-1, 452; investment, (1960s) 472, (1918) 459-60, (1920s) 460-1, (1945) 464-5; predominance of Montreal and Toronto, 77; problem of foreign control, 475-8; range of, 450; recovery, 461-2; recovery (1960s), 467; and tariffs, 128, 150, 154-5, 456; U.S. capital investment in Canada, 129, 318; value, 150, 450; in world markets, 467-73

need for balance of primary, secondary, tertiary, 480, 485-6

opportunities for Canadian participation, 478

primary, mainstay to 1939, 450

problem of mass unemployment, 235

role of provincial governments, 484-5

spread, 221

steel, growth of, First World War, 459

steel mills and mineral development, 424

stimulus of western boom, 129

U.S. control, 361

U.S. investment, (1890s) 129, (1920s) 460

U.S. subsidiaries, Canadian guidelines for, 477-8

Industry, Department of, and Area Development Agency, 483-4

Influenza epidemic, 200

Innis, Harold A., 657

Institut Canadien, 52

Institut Canadien des Affaires Publiques, 370

Intelligencer (Belleville), 526

Intercolonial Railway, 7, 9, 58

amalgamation with other lines, 506

Canada rejects scheme (1863), 13, 14

as condition of Confederation, 54

connected with Grand Trunk, 503

construction of, 503

as defence link, 765

effects of completion, 64

financial drag on government, 55-6

Halifax, rather than St. Andrews, to be terminus, 53-4

importance to Confederation, 14

opened (1876), 55

P.E.I. linked with, 44

P.E.I. opposition, 43

public investment (1916), 507

route settled on, 54

traffic mainly eastward, 77

International Brotherhood of Teamsters, 334

International Halibut Treaty, 216

International Labor Organization, 263

International Nickel Company, 315

International Pacific Halibut Convention, 431

International Pacific Salmon Fisheries Convention, 431

International Telecommunications Union, 540

International Whaling Convention, 432

Interoceanic railway company, 56

Interprovincial pipeline, 522

Irish Home Rule, influence on Canadian Irish, 92-3

Irving, K. C., 311, 343

Isaacs Gallery, 326

Iskowitz, Gershon, 699

Isolationism, 271, 276-7

Italians, construction labour, 296, 407

Jackson, A. Y., 704

Jacobs, Indian Jack, 617

Japan, 269, 272

Canadian diplomatic mission, 277

industrial recovery, 317

in Second World War, 284, 289, 292, 293

Jarvis, Donald, 699, 706

Jasmin, Claude, 672

Jehovah's Witnesses, 312

Jenner, Senator, 333

Jervois, Lt.-Col., 27

Jesuit Estates Act, 101-2, 591

Jewison, Norman, 691

Jews, 397, 600-1

Jodoin, Claude, 341

Johnson, Lyndon B., 359, 360

Johnstone, J. H. L., 561

Joint High Commission (1898-9), 128, 131

'Joual', 650

Judiciary, 713, 718

Justice, Department of, and delegation of unemployed, 249

Kahane, Anne, 701

Kaiser Wilhelm II, 172-3

Kane, Paul, 701, 702

Keen, George, 497

Keenleyside, H. L., 562, 797

Kellogg-Briand Pact, 234

Kenner, Hugh, 657

Keyfitz, Nathan, on net population increase, 390

Keynes, John Maynard, 231

Khorana, Gobind, 564

Kierans, Eric, 352

King, William Lyon Mackenzie, 134, 233, 289, 304, 336, 340

and abdication crisis, 268

agreement with Progressives, 216, 218

avoided defining policy regarding war, 271-3, 274

becomes party leader, 202

on Bennett, 237, 262

campaign of moderation, 259-60
Canadian–U.S. relations, 302-3
character, 214, 307-8
Commonwealth Air Training Plan, 282
conception of war effort defeated, 281-2
conscription crisis, 276-7, 281-2, 293-4, 300-1
and 'constitutional crisis', 216-19
contrasted with St. Laurent, 307
contribution, summary, 307-8
death, 307
defeat (1925), 216
defeated by service vote (1945), 296
dependence on Quebec, 300
faith in plebiscites, 267
fear of Duplessis, 259
fear of war in Korea, 328
feud with Hepburn, 257
foreign policy, 267-74 *passim*; vagueness of, 797-8
hostility of Canadian forces to, 278-9
interest in industrial relations, 157-8
and isolationism, 271, 327
and Meighen, 203, 237
and nationalism, 254-5
and Newfoundland, 306-7
nervousness about French Canada, 269-70
1939 Quebec election crisis, 280-1
1945 election, 296-7
opposed to Imperial War Cabinet, 292
political goals, 214-15
retains power after defeat, 216-17
and social reform, 254, 263, 299-300
on war conference at Quebec, 293
war-time administration, 277-8, 280
work in labour-management relations, 202
Kirby, William, 640, 647
Kirkconnell, Watson, 657
Kirschmann, August, 552
Kiyooka, Roy, 710
Klein, A. M., 642, 651, 652, 655
Klinck, Carl F., 657
Klondike gold rush, 130-1
Klondike Nugget (Dawson City), 527
Knights of Labor, 115, 493, 494, 497, 499
opposed by Roman Catholicism, 592
Knowles, Stanley, 341
Knudson, George, 617
Korean war, 317, 328, 781
Korner, John, 706

Kricghoff, Cornelius, 701, 702
Kurelek, William, 708

Labelle, François-Xavier Antoine, 164
Laberge, Albert, 664
LaBine, Gilbert, 560-1
Labour force
    adolescents, 742
    effects of industrialization, 400-4
    income, 742-3
    manufacturing industries, 450
    second jobs, 743
    total, 741
    women, 741-2, 743
    working conditions (1867-1967), compared, 453-4
    working hours, 261, 743
Labour party, 218, 234
Labour unions, 487-501
    A.F.L. *v.* C.I.O., 496
    at Confederation, 488
    considered threat by Hepburn, 256-7
    consolidating gains, 309
    and the C.C.F., 251-2, 341
    craft *v.* industrial unions, 495
    crippled by Duplessis, 258
    decline in membership, 249
    election of first Labour M.L.A., 498
    employers not required to negotiate with, 157
    federal intervention to delay strikes, 157-8
    federal policy in industrial disputes, 156-8
    growth in late 1890s, 130
    Hepburn's anti-labour policy, 256-7
    influence of U.S., 195
    legislation against, 489-90
    membership increase (1900-10), 156
    opposed by churches, 592, 597
    organizations, 488, 492-5
    and politics, 498-500
    post-war radicalism, 192-6
    predominance of international unions, 156
    railway strikes and national economy, 157-8
    railway unions, 496
    rash of strikes (1918-19), 195-6
    reasons for, 489-90
    right to join guaranteed, 254
    rights guaranteed, Ontario, 256
    rights unprotected, 250
    Roman Catholic organizations in Quebec, 157, 598

R.C.M.P. invigilation, 249
schisms, 495
small and ineffectual (1890s), 115
Toronto printers' strike (1872), 592
T.L.C., united with C.C.L., 496
Labrador, 314, 419, 422
Lacombe, Albert, 124
Lacroix, Richard, 710
Laflèche, Bishop, 79, 127
  denunciation of Laurier, 125
Laissez-faire, social and economic, ex-
    tinction of, 230-1
Lajeunesse, Emma (Mme Albani), 691
Lake, Percy, 769
Lalonde, Newsy, 610
Lampman, Archibald, 115, 642, 647, 648,
    649
Landy, John, 607
Langevin, André, 670
Langevin, Sir Hector, 98, 106, 122
Langham, Michael, 690
Languirand, Jacques, 669, 695
Lansdowne, Lord, 93
Lapointe, Ernest, 213, 237, 278, 336
  agreement with King on external
    policies, 272
  and Alberta Social Credit legislation,
    259
  and 'constitutional crisis', 218
  and French-Canadian attitudes to
    Second World War, 798-9
  and Hepburn's anti-labour campaign,
    259
  1939 Quebec election crisis, 281
  opposes police-state measures, 249
  on the Padlock Law, 259
Lapointe, Gatien, 667
Lasnier, Rina, 666-7
Laurence, George C., 561
Laurendeau, André, 280, 294
'Laurentian republic', 213
Laurentide Company (mining), 514
Laurie, P. G., 527
Laurier, Sir Wilfrid, 117, 123, 311, 338,
    789
  on British connection, 118
  cabinet (1896), 126
  Commission of Conservation, 412
  confidence in 1896 election, 113-14
  death, 202
  defeat (1911), 174-6, 791
  deserted on conscription issue, 188
  at Diamond Jubilee, 131-2
  election campaign (1900), 135, 136
  emerges as Liberal leader (1887), 105

expected dissolution of Confedera-
    tion, 108
  on future of Canada, 454
  and imperialism, 791-2
  liberal trade policies, 480
  on Liberal unity, 123
  loses hold on Quebec, 176
  and Manitoba schools question, 123-4,
    126-8, 591
  naval crisis (1909), 167-70, 174-5
  new Liberalism in Quebec, 52, 79
  on Ottawa, 631-2
  'parliament will decide', 134, 272
  on participation in First World War,
    184
  and Quebec bishops, 126-8
  Quebec colonization policy, 165
  refusal to join Union Government,
    188
  on Riel, 99
  and South African War, 134-5, 768
  suspicion of, in Ontario, 125
  victory (1896), 125
  view on Canadian autonomy, 168
  and the west, 148, 155, 160-2, 173, 505
Laval University, 79
Layton, Irving, 651, 653
Leach, Archdeacon W. T., 657
Leacock, Stephen, 645, 646, 650, 658
League for Social Reconstruction, 253
League of Nations, 778
  Article X, 795
  Canada's contribution to failure of,
    269, 303, 327
  Canadian belief in, 775
  and Canadian national assertion, 216
  dominions represented, 201-2, 793
  Germany included, 234
  and national self-determination, 233
  oil sanction against Italy proposed,
    269
  weakening of, 269
Lee, Pinky, 691
Léger, Paul-Emile, 311
Leja, Walter, 375
Lemay, Pamphile, 661
Lemieux, Jean-Paul, 708
Lemieux, Rodolphe, 795-6
Le Moyne, Jean, 668, 673
Lesage, Jean
  communiqué from federal-provincial
    conference (1964), 355
  defeat (1966), 345n.
  and Fulton-Favreau Formula, 355

and off-shore mineral rights quarrel, 379-80
program of social reconstruction, 365
Lescarbot, Marc, 683
Lestanc, Fr., 35
LeSueur, Ernest A., 564
Lévesque, René, 311, 369
Leyrac, Monique, 691
Liberals
accept principles of National Policy, 118, 150
assertion of Ontario provincial rights, 103
attempt to win back west, 215
Beauharnois scandal, 252
and Bennett's New Deal, 262
in British Columbia (1930s), 256
and British Columbia railway, 57-60, 86
change in conscription policy, 293
Clear Grit plan for federal union of Canada, 9, 17
in Coalition of 1864, 16-17
conscription issue (1944), 799-800
crisis over western separate schools, 161
defeat (1911), 174-6
defeat (1930), 237, 238
disrupted by conscription issue, 188
divisions in Quebec wing, 373-4
economic problems (1896-7), 128-9
elections, (1900) 135-6, (1925) 216, (1926) 218; victory (1935), 259-60; victory (1945), 296-7; (1949) 307
encouragement of Canadian control of industries, 476
fear of Duplessis, 259
and the flag, 350
free-trade efforts (1870s), 49-50
health service programs, 762
and imperialism, 131
incapable of coping with depression, 236-8
influence on Bennett New Deal, 261
influence of C.C.F., 253-4
Kingston Conference, 340
liberalism in Quebec, 79
and Manitoba Schools Question, 123-4, 126-8, 591-2
minority government (1921), 211
national convention (1893), 118
nationalism *v.* internationalism, 206
New Brunswick, victory (1960), 343
no conscription for overseas service, 277, 280, 293

nuclear policy, 348
Ontario, 124, 256-7
opposition to C.P.R., 86, 88
and Pacific scandal, 56-7
pipeline debate, 337, 346
problems of foreign policy, early 1900s, 791-2
and Quebec bishops, 124-5, 126-8
Quebec defeat (1944), 301; reforms brought in, 366-70; victory, 343
reasons for defeat (1957), 335, 337-8
and Riel's execution, 99
scandals, 350
'Sixty days of Decision', 349
social legislation, 356-8
social welfare, 299-300
split over trade agreement (1911), 176
support Continental Union movement, 117
and threat of absorption by U.S., 334
troubles in Quebec (1870s), 52
unemployment insurance made national, 266
in Union Government, 188-9
and U.S. investment, 361
victory (1896), 125-6
war on poverty, 357
Lieutenant-Governor, appointment, 718, 719, 729
Ligue pour la défense du Canada, 294
Lillie, Adam, 589
Limitation of Hours of Work Act, 261
Line, William, 552
Lipset, S. M., on Canadian values, 386
Lismer, Arthur, 704
Literary Garland, 529
Literature (English), 639-58
breaks with past traditions, 645-50, 652-3
development, 656, 658
European influence, 640, 641-3
fiction, 642-3, 645-7, 650, 652, 654-6
poetry, 75, 642, 643-4, 646, 647-9, 650-2
problems, 640-1
reflection of social change, 658
scholarship, 656-7
who is Canadian? 640-2
Literature (French), 75, 659-74
assessment, 673-4
drama, 668-9
language problem, 671-2
Montreal School, 662-3
North American and French ties, 667-8

the novel, 663-5, 669-71
poetry, 661, 662-3, 665-7
pre-Confederation, 659-61
Lloyd, Gwyneth, 684
Locarno treaty, 795
Lochhead, Kenneth, 709
Lodge, R. C., 224
Logan, Sir William, 420, 549
London Conference, 32
London Free Press, 526
Longboat, Tom, 611
Loranger, Françoise, 669
Loring, Frances, 711
Lorne, Lord, 71-2, 83, 84
Louise, Princess, 71-2
Lower, A. R. M., 657, 699, 786-7
Lowry, Malcolm, 640, 655
Lozeau, Albert, 662
Lucas, G. H. W., 563
Ludwig, Jack, 654
Lutheran Church
    in 1867, 586, 589
    gains from immigration, 598
    and German culture, 589-90
    numbers (1871-1961), 596
Lyell, Sir Charles, 548
Lynch, Charles, 334
Lyon, Peyton V., on Pearson in world
    affairs, 359

MacCallum, John Bruce, 555, 556
MacCallum, William G., 555-6
McCarran, Senator, 333
McCarthy, D'Alton, 90, 125, 591
    advocates imperial preferential tar-
    iffs, 109
    anti-French-language bill, 102
    anti-French tour of west, 102
    on English-French problem, 120-1
    and Imperial Federation League, 106,
    131
McCarthy, Joseph, 333
McClung, Nellie, 198, 199
McCrae, John, 555, 567
McCrae, Thomas, 555
Macdonald, Angus L., 278
Macdonald, Brian, 696
MacDonald, J. E. H., 704
Macdonald, J. W. G., 708
Macdonald, Sir John A., 68, 69, 70, 764-
    5, 789
    action on railway to British Colum-
    bia, 86-7
    acts to quell Saskatchewan rebellion,
    96

on British-Canadian reciprocal aid,
    767
and British Columbia railway, 57, 86
British Columbia won over to Con-
    federation, 40-1
and British proposal to withdraw
    troops, 46
on British–U.S. joint high commis-
    sion, 47-8
and Canada Firsters, 74
and Canadian Pacific Railway Com-
    pany, 60, 88
at Charlottetown Conference, 19, 20
Coalition of 1864, 17
on Confederation, 44
death, 111-12
defeat over Pacific Scandal, 57
defence of National Policy, 110
dismissal of Métis claims on Saskat-
    chewan, 94, 95
holds to goal of building nation, 106,
    108
and Joseph Howe, 33
Irish vote (1882), 93
joint leader of Conservatives, 9
losing hold, 105-6, 108, 122
and Manitoban railway demands, 92
and Mowat's ideas of provincial
    rights, 80-1
on national independence, 784
National Policy, 52-3, 411, 480
and the need for a western railway,
    84-5
and Newfoundland in Confederation,
    42
and Ontario-Manitoba dispute, 82
and Pacific railway, 55-6
persuades Parliament to ratify Treaty
    of Washington, 48-9
pressure from Irish Home Rule sup-
    porters, 93
problem of land speculation in
    North-west, 83
and proposed repeal of Confedera-
    tion, 33
and Red River uprising, 36
resignation (1862), 12
response to resolutions of constitu-
    tional conference, 104
retains power (1887), 105
return to power (1878), 53, 60
and Riel, 97-8, 591
search for successor, 90
speech to Quebec Conference, 20-1

troubles with Quebec supporters, 78
victory (1887), 105
Macdonald, John Sandfield, 12, 13, 16
MacDonald, Ramsay, 243
Macdonald, Sir William, 550
Macdonnell, Allan, 55
McDougall, Colin, 654
MacDougall, William, 33-4, 36, 37
McEwen, Jean, 707
McGee, Thomas D'Arcy, 18-19, 764
McGill University, 546-66 *passim*
  Forest Products Laboratory, 563
  Space Research Institute, 565
MacInnes, Tom, 648
McKay, Arthur, 709
Mackenzie, Alexander, 49, 81
  administration, summed up, 60-1
  and British Columbia Railway, 57-60, 86
  and Canada First movement, 50
  defeated over British Columbia railway, 60
  and failure of Brown's Washington mission, 50
  takes office after Pacific Scandal, 57
  weakness through 1880s, 91-2
Mackenzie, C. J., 560
Mackenzie, Ian, 272, 776
Mackenzie, William, and Canadian Northern Railway, 146-7
Mackenzie Highway, 518
McLaren, Norman, 325
McLarnin, Jimmy, 613, 615
Maclean's Magazine, 1950 predictions, 312
MacLennan, Hugh, 652, 654
McLennan, John Cunningham, 550, 551
Macleod, J. J. R., 557
McLuhan, Marshall, 311, 657, 698
Macmillan, Harold, 310
McMullen, G. W., 56, 57
McNaughton, A. G. L., 778
  and Canadian Expeditionary Force, 288
  Chairman of National Research Council, 559
  commander of Army, 777
  defeat at polls, 296
  favoured integration of forces, 774
  forced out of command, 289
  Minister of National Defence, 295
  necessity of conscription, 295
  opposed to needless fighting, 289
  reorganization of forces, 775

war and politics, 778
Macpherson, David, 56
Mafia, 334
Mail (Toronto), 101, 111, 257
Mail and Empire, on Spanish-American war, 133
Maintenant, 370
Mair, Charles, 642, 647
Major, André, 672
Major, Leon, 690
Malmros, Oscar, 35
Mandel, Eli, 656
'Manifest Destiny', doctrine of, 45
Manion, R. J., formula for Canadian participation in war, 277, 280
Manitoba
  becomes province, 39, 788
  and Canadian Northern Railway, 146-7, 505
  and C.P.R. monopoly, 104
  colonization (1880s), 82
  C.C.F. progress, 253
  dissatisfaction with C.P.R., 92
  economic problems (mid-1880s), 89
  election, 166, 345n.
  federal control of natural resources, 142
  French language loses constitutional guarantee, 102, 159
  government takes over some grain elevators, 154
  McCarthy's anti-French tour, 102
  mineral resources, 421, 424
  natural-resources issue (1870s), 60
  natural selection of most efficient farmers, 112
  originally officially bilingual, 102, 718
  Patrons of Industry, 117
  population (1900), 140
  Schools Question, 102, 110, 121-8, 159, 160-1, 212-13, 373, 591-2
  settlement of Interlake, 221
  territorial dispute with Ontario, 81-2
  United Farmers, 211, 219, 499-500
Manitoba Act, 55
Manitoba Grain Growers Association, 491
Manitoba Theatre Centre, 325
Mann, Donald, and Canadian Northern Railway, 146-7
Mann, Stanley, 691
Manufacturing, *see under* Industry
Maple Leaf Hockey organization, 607
Marconi, Guglielmo Marchese, 539

Marconi Wireless Telegraph Company, 540

Marcotte, Gilles, 673

Maritime Marshland Rehabilitation Act, 415

Maritime Provinces
adverse effect of high tariffs (1880s), 77
architecture, 622, 625-6, 638
attitude to Confederation (1880s), 77-8
Canadian Northern Railway, 505
Co-operative Commonwealth Federation, 253
development of government, 724
drop police budget, 249
economic decline, late nineteenth century, 77, 112, 626
economy (1870s), 64
effects of railways, 626-7
hard hit by depression, 239-40
iron and steel, and railway construction, 150-1
jealous of central Canada, 139
and Jesuit Estates Act, 102
manufacturing declines under National Policy, 150
Maritime union movement, 14-16
'New Light', revival, 589
percentage of Europeans, 398
politics in depression, 241
population, 387, 388
post-Confederation disillusionment, 50
pre-Confederation railways, 503; railway line through Maine, 92
shipping (1880s), 74

Maritime Union
Canadians invite themselves to Conference, 17-18
lukewarm reception, 15-16
as preliminary step in Confederation, 14-15
reasons for, 14-15
waived in favour of Confederation, 18-19

Marshall, Lois, 325, 691

Martin, Chester, 224

Martin, Claire, 670

Martin, Paul, 360

Massey, Raymond, 691

Massey, Vincent, 233

Massey company, 65

Massey Report, 323, 326

Massey-Harris Company, 130

Matton, Roger, 696

Medical Research Council, 566

Medicare, 354, 358, 364

Medicine, 546, 553-8, 562-3, 566-7
anaesthesia, 563
findings shared with other nations, 566-7
general esteem for, 223

Medico, 566

Mehta, Zuban, 689

Meighen, Arthur
above opportunism, 215
becomes Conservative party leader, 202-3
becomes Prime Minister, 218
calls election (1921), 211
closure rule, 177, 202
and 'constitutional crisis', 217-18
defeat (1942), 295
and King, 203
no concessions, 1926 election, 218

Mental health services, 752, 759

Mercier, Honoré, 102, 164
advocates formation of Parti National, 99, 100
calls constitutional conference, 104
cause of Liberal division, 110
dream of a North American French state, 100
English reaction to his ascendancy, 100
and Imperial Federation League, 100, 106
leads Quebec government, 100
and press reaction to his ascendancy, 100
problem of Jesuit Estates, 101
and Riel's execution, 99, 591

Mergers, 151
Canada Cement Company, 151
early twentieth century, 458
Steel Company of Canada, 151

Mesplet, Fleury, 526

Methodist Church
Church Union, 228, 595
concern with 'Social Gospel', 227
in 1867, 586, 588
foreign missions, 603, 605
inroads by Holiness Movement, 594
national union, 588, 589, 590, 594, 595
native missions, 602
numbers (1871-1961), 596
persecution of Workman, 593
and working class, 116

Métis
  execution of Scott, 38
  and Fenians in Manitoba (1871), 39
  grievances on the Saskatchewan, 94
  invite Riel back, 94
  National Committee, 37
  problems today, 399
  in Red River uprising, 35-6
Middleton, Frederick B., 96, 767, 768
Midnight Sun (Dawson City), 527
Military Service Act, 189-90
Militia Act (1868), 765
Militia Act (1883), 766
Militia Bill (Province of Canada, 1862), 12
Miller, F. R., 784
Miller, W. Lash, on Croft, 547
Milne, David, 705, 706
Mine, Mill and Smelter Workers, 496
Mineral resources
  air transport, 514
  asbestos, 65
  coal production, 436
  corporation profits, 452
  discoveries, major, 421-2, 424; post-war, 465, 468; recent, 420
  exploitation, 630
  geological survey work, 419-20
  growth (1920s), 222, (1950s), 314-15
  importance of aero-magnetic surveys, 420
  iron ore, 65
  problem of foreign capital, 475-8
  production, 418-19, 421-2, 423
  and railways, 517, 628, 630
  regions, 419
  role of provinces, 420
  silver, 65
  and steel mills, 424
  undiscovered, 422-4
  U.S. capital investment in Canada (1890s), 129
Minerve, La, 526
Minifie, James, 334
Minimum Wages Act, 261
Minnesota, interest in Hudson's Bay Company lands, 46
Minority rights
  religious guarantee for western separate schools, 160-2
  weakness pointed up by Boer War, 133
Minto, Lord, 134, 135-6
Miron, Gastron, 667
Mitchell, John, 232

Mitchell, Peter, 47
Mitchell, W. O., 650
Mittelman, Norman, 691
Monck, Lord, 13
Monde, Le, on Laurier cabinet, 126
Monetary policy, rigidity under Bennett, 242, 244, 247-8
Monk, F. D., 162
  and Bourassa, on schools question, 166-7
  on Naval Services Act, 170, 175
  resigns from Cabinet, 177
Monopolies
  encouraged by outmoded policies, 250
  flourished (1890), 129-30
  Stevens Commission, 260
Monroe Doctrine, and Confederation, 45
Montgomery, Lucy Maud, 646
Montreal
  boasts about, 137-8
  growing importance, 162-3
  growth (1870s), 65
  improvement of port, 522
  population (1861), 4, 5
  predominance of English influence, 163-4
Montreal Neurological Institute, 558
Montreal Society of Artists, 702
Montreal Telegraph Company, 533
Moody, Dwight L., 604
Moore, Brian, 654, 655-6
Moore, Mavor, 690, 695
Morel, François, 696
Morin, Paul, 663, 671
Morrice, James Wilson, 703
Morse, Barry, 691
Morse, Samuel, 532
Mosher, C. B., 251
Mothers' Allowance, 752, 754, 758, 759
Motor Vehicle Transport Act, 510
Mousseau, Jean-Paul, 707
Mouvement Laïque de Langue Française, 370
Moving pictures
  as Canadian cultural medium, 537-8
  Canadian film-making, 325, 537-8, 687
  censorship, 536
  effects of television, 537, 538-9, 681
Mowat, Oliver
  on British connection, 118
  champion of provincial rights, 81
  at constitutional conference, 104
  and Continental Union, 117-18

doubts about unrestricted reciprocity,
110
gains Keewatin for Ontario, 82
in Laurier cabinet, 126
legal victories over Ottawa, 103
silence in 1891 campaign, 110
statutes re working conditions, 115
Mulock, William, 118, 126, 135
Munich agreement, 277
Murchie, Lt.-Gen. J. C., 295
Murray, Robert, 700, 709, 712
Muscular Dystrophy Association, 566
Musgrave, Anthony, 40-1
Music, 325
Myers, C. R., 552

Nakamura, Kazuo, 708, 710
Narrache, Jean, 650
National Ballet of Canada, 325, 684
National Capital Commission, 634-5
National Conference of Canadian Uni-
versities, 353
National Defence, Department of, 324,
783
camps for transient unemployed, 248
National Defence College, 779
National Energy Board, 523
National Film Board, 325, 537, 687
National Film Society, 536-7
National Gallery, 326
National Health and Welfare, Depart-
ment of, 552
National Hockey Association, 612
National Hockey League, 612, 616-17
National Party (Quebec), 99-100
National Progressive Party, 192, 499
National Research Council, 550, 558, 566
Chairmen, 559-60
psychological research, 552
in Second World War, 560
work in 1920s, 223
National Resources Mobilization Act,
283, 293, 777
amendment (overseas conscription),
294, 777
National Revenue, Department of
censorship of 'seditious books', 249
National Review, 529
National Trades and Labour Congress,
495
National Transcontinental railway
and colonization of French Canada,
165
and Grand Trunk, 149-50

public investment (1916), 507
telegraph, 533
Nationalism
achievement of national status, 232-3,
234
and annexation, 74
apparent unity (1939-40), 280
based on imperialism, 233
British High Commissioner in Ottawa, 233
'Canadian citizen' status, 302
concept in 1870s, 70-1
and conscription crisis of Second
World War, 794
consequences in Empire, 233
and 'continental resources', 362
contribution of air transport, 516-17
contribution of CBC, 246
contribution of National Film Board,
537-8
disrupted by sectional parties, 212
economic control by U.S., 475-6
economic interdependence, 170
effect of depression, 238, 251
effect of First World War, 793
effects of Second World War, 277,
300-1, 798-800
English-Canadian concept, 132
gaining ground in 1880s, 74-5
and the Group of Seven, 704-5
hampered by unclear constitution,
266
v. imperialism, 206
importance of transport system, 523-4
independence of Commonwealth, 302
and industrial development, 479-86
passim
influence of newspapers, 531-2
v. internationalism, 206
and issue-dodging, 273-4
King's achievement, 308
lack due to incomplete use of communications, 545
more than economy, 138-9
national identity still being sought,
139
and need for reforms, 251
and opting-out formula, 354
and the performing arts, 695-6
post-war difficulties, 203
problem of bilingualism, 372
problems of 1960s, 344-5
Quebec brand, exploited by Duplessis, 241, 257-9; forerunner of increased provincial power; 341;

lulled (late 1920s), 234; terrorism, 375

and Queen Elizabeth's visit to Quebec City, 375-6

and radio, 539-45 *passim*

and railways, 148, 149, 502-7 *passim*

reconciling autonomy and colonial subordination, 168-9

Rowell-Sirois Report as expression of, 265

stimulated by anti-Americanism, 131, 333-4, 804

superficiality of, in 1920s, 231-2

Nationalist Party

alliance with Tories, 176, 792

and Naval Service Act, 175, 176

Natural Products Marketing Act, 261

Natural resources, 410-48

beginnings of conservation, 411

'continental resources' approach, 469

control of, 142, 718

distribution, 411

energy, 436-40

exploitation of prairies, 413-14

extensive, not intensive, use, 446

farmlands, 413-18

federal control of, 142

fisheries, 430-6

forestry, 424-30

importance to economy, 446-8

increasing exploitation (1920s), 222-3

mainly under provincial jurisdiction, 447

management of, 361-2

minerals, 418-24

the myth of abundance, 411

national and provincial parks, 411

need for federal leadership, 447-8

need for sound management policies, 447-8

prosperity in Alberta and British Columbia, 341

recreational, 440-5

Naval Service Act (1910), 168, 169, 175, 770

Nelligan, Emile, 642, 662-3, 666, 673

Nelsova, Zara, 691

New Brunswick

Anti-Confederates divided, 29

collapse of Anti-Confederates, 30-1

Confederate victory (1866), 30-1

Confederates win York County by-election, 30

Conservative victory, 343

criticism of Quebec Resolutions, 23-5

defeat of Tilley government, 24

economic recovery, 343

and the Grand Trunk, 505

Intercolonial financial problems, 14

Liberal victory (1960), 343

Maritime union movement, 14-16

mineral resources, 420

population (1861), 4

railways (1860s), 6

refusal to provide French-language schools, 381

revolt against Liberals, 342

separate-school issue, 60, 373

shipbuilding, 6

war on poverty, 363-4

'Western Extension' plan, 29

Youth Assistance Act, 363

New Democratic Party

absorbed C.C.F., 500

and C.L.C., 500-1

founding, 252, 341, 350-2

machinery for changing leader, 721

near victory in B.C., 342

1963 election, 348

program, 351-2

and Quebec's quiet revolution, 352

role in Parliament, 341

New York State, St. Lawrence power development, 520

Newfoundland

anti-Confederate vote (1869), 41-2

becomes province, 305-6, 786, 789

denominational schools, 578

election (1966), 345n.

free university education, 363

obdurate against Confederation, 31, 32, 35

only provincial Liberal government left (1960), 343

opposition to Quebec Resolutions, 23, 25

population (1861), 4

resource development, 343

Newfoundland Escort Force, 285

Newfoundland Regiment, 180

Newlove, John, 653

Newman, Barnett, 709

Newman, Peter, on Diefenbaker's defeat, 349

News (Toronto), on question of participation in Boer War, 134

Newspapers, 526-9, 531-2

chains, 528-9

changes since 1900, 527-8

contribution to national unity, 531-2

facsimile, 532
libertarian climate, 529
mechanical improvements, 526, 527-8
wire services, 531-2
Newton, Margaret, 550
Nichols, Jack, 708
Nicol, Eric, 695
Nisbet, James, 602
Noland, Kenneth, 709
Norman, Herbert, 333
Norquay, John, 104
North, the
    Arctic islands given to Canada, 789
    church missions, 602-3
    development contrasted with west,
        519
    DEW Line, 304, 332
    highways into, 518-19
    importance of aeroplane, 634
    inaccessibility, 222-3
    natural resources, 411
    new communities, 637
    opening of, by bush planes, 223
    railways into, 219, 223
    U.S. activities in, 302, 303
North American Defence Command,
    332, 346, 782-3
    Canada's commitment to, 327
    N.D.P. opposition, 352
North Atlantic Treaty Organization,
    359, 363
    Canadian contribution to, 305, 313,
        780, 803
    Canadian hopes of, 801
    formation, 304
    N.D.P. opposition, 352
    new role, 346
    U.S. proposal for nuclear force, 360,
        780-1
North Pacific Fur Seal Convention, 432
North Pacific High Seas Fisheries Con-
    vention, 432
Northern Alberta Railway, 517
Northern Pacific railway company
    (U.S.), 56-7, 84-5
North-west
    administration during 1870s, 39
    ceded to Canada by Hudson's Bay
        Company, 33-4, 39
    importance of a railway, 84-5, 96
    McCarthy's anti-French-language
        bill, 102
    natural selection of most efficient
        farmers, 112
    Patrons of Industry, 117

predominance of cattle (1880s), 83-4
problems of disposal of land, 94
publicity of Lord Lorne's tour, 84
Saskatchewan rebellion, 89, 94-6
transfer from Hudson's Bay Company
    delayed by Red River uprising, 37
Northwest Atlantic Fisheries Conven-
    tion, 432
North West Mounted Police, 61
    effective guardianship of west, 68, 84
    in Klondike, 130
    second Riel uprising, 95-6, 767-8
Northwest Territories
    French denied equal language rights,
        121
    growth (1880s), 82-4
    mineral resources, 422
    originally officially bilingual, 718
    radio network, 542
    roads, 518-19
North West Transportation, Naviga-
    tion and Railway Company, 55
Nor'Wester (Fort Garry), 527
Norwood, Gilbert, 657
Notman, James, 66
Notman, William, 66
Nouveau Journal, Le, 528
Nova Scotia
    Anti-Confederates, final capitulation,
        33
    coal mining, 419
    Conservative victory (1956), 342
    criticism of Quebec Resolutions, 23-5
    effect of Confederate victory in New
        Brunswick, 30-1
    effects of Intercolonial railway, 64
    favours secession of Maritimes, 103
    Intercolonial problems (1863), 14
    Maritime union movement, 14-16
    new industries, 343
    population (1861), 4
    post-Confederate unrest, 33, 35
    Presbyterian mission to New Heb-
        rides, 603
    railways (1860s), 6
    repression of Cape Breton coal
        miners, 249
    research council, 564
    sends delegates to London, 31
    shipbuilding, 6
Nova Scotian, 103, 526
Nuclear power, 439

O'Brien, W. E., 102
Ogdensburg Agreement, 292, 302, 781,
    800

Oil
 exports and imports, 437, 440
 found at Fort Norman, 223
 growth, 314
 major post-war discoveries, 465, 468
 production, 437
 U.S. capital investment in Canada
  (1890s), 129
O'Keefe Centre, 323
Old Age Assistance, 750, 752-3, 759
Old Age Pension Act, 230
Old Age Security, 749, 753, 759
Old Age Security Act, 300, 749
O'Leary Commission, 529-31
Olitski, Jules, 709
Oliver, Frank, 527
Oliver, Michael, 365
Olympic Games, hockey, 606-8
Onderdonk, Andrew, 87
One Big Union, 195, 495, 496
O'Neill, W. V., 375
Ontario
 architecture, 623-4, 628-9, 631, 638
 attitude to Riel, 97-8
 and Canadian Northern Railway, 505
 cities at Confederation, 623-4
 claims for provincial rights, 264
 Conservative sweep, 176
 controversy over Canada Pension
  Plan, 357, 358
 Co-operative Commonwealth Federation, 241, 253, 257, 340
 cultural exchange program with Quebec, 381
 decline of agricultural labour force,
  401
 Department of University Affairs, 577
 early statutes re working conditions,
  115
 economy (1870s), 65
 effects of railways, 628-9
 Equal Rights Association, 102
 expansion northward, 624
 export of Crown land logs prohibited,
  128
 French in low-status jobs, 398
 French language restricted in schools,
  102, 186-7, 213
 growing ascendancy (1880s), 79-82
 Hepburn's anti-labour campaign, 259
 identification with national interests,
  92
 junior colleges, 572
 King-Hepburn feud, 257
 Liberals, 124, 125, 256-7

 local school unit reorganization, 580
 market lures Grand Trunk, 505
 mineral resources, 420, 421, 422, 424
 1940 federal election, 281
 out of federal-provincial agreements,
  305
 population, 150, 387, 388
 proportion of Europeans, 398
 and Quebec dominance of Commons,
  725
 reaction to Jesuit Estates Act, 101-2
 reaction to Riel's execution of Scott,
  591
 research council, 564
 and Rowell-Sirois Report, 265-6, 305
 and St. Lawrence power development,
  520
 separate schools, 373, 578
 spread of Patrons of Industry, 117
 territorial dispute with Manitoba,
  81-2
 U.F.O. electoral victory, 192, 211, 499
 water conservation projects, 415
Ontario Northland railway, 518
Ontario Society of Artists, 702, 705
Orangeism, 38-9, 120, 136
Organization of American States, 801
Orion, 75
Osler, William, 553, 554, 556
Ostenso, Martha, 650
Ottawa Improvement Commission, 632
Otter, Sir William, 768, 769, 774
Ouellette, Fernand, 667
Ouimet, Joseph A., 123
Ozawa, Seiji, 689

Pacaud, Ernest, 127
Pacey, Desmond, 639, 657
Pacific Cable Board, 535
Pacific Great Eastern, 518
Pacific Scandal, 49, 56-7
Packet (Bytown), 526
Padlock Law, 258-9
Painting, 699-700, 701-10
 French-Canadian, 706-7
 Group of Seven, 703-5
 Painters Eleven, 708
Pakistan, 327, 566
Palmerston, Lord, 27
Palomino, Mercedes, 690
Pan-American Union, 801
Papineau, Louis Joseph, 162
Papineau-Couture, Jean, 696
Parent, Etienne, 526
Parker, Sir Gilbert, 225, 640

Parkin, George, 132
Parkin, John C., 326
Parks, 440, 441-3
  national, 441-2, 619-20, 631
  problem in cities, 631-2, 634-6
  provincial, 442-3, 619-20
Parliament
  attacks on French language in eastern
    Ontario schools, 102
  compromise on participation in Boer
    War, 134-5
  and Crown corporation, 727
  declares Canadian entry into war,
    272-3
  differences between Senate and Com-
    mons, 722-3
  establishes C.B.C., 246
  Female Suffrage, 198-9
  first, 32
  first division by race, 102
  flag debate, 350
  ill-suited to Canadian situation, 335
  and Irish Home Rule, 92-3
  King's ambivalence toward, 267
  largest majority, 346
  minorities the rule (1960s), 341
  Newfoundland members added, 306
  not called for abdication crisis, 267-8
  opposes trade agreement (1911), 176
  passes feeble anti-combines bill, 114
  passes Military Service Act, 189
  problem if Quebec associate state, 378
  ratifies transfer of Hudson's Bay Com-
    pany land, 34
  refusal to disallow Jesuit Estates Act,
    102
  rejects Borden's Naval Air Bill, 177
  replaced by conferences, 355-6
  resolution re British Columbia be-
    coming province, 41
  role of Speaker, 733
  St. Lawrence Deep Waterway agree-
    ment (1932), 246
  saves C.P.R. from creditors, 88, 89
  sets up Northwest Territories, 34
  too-large majorities, 335
  weak tradition, 732
Parliament Building, 69
Parti National, 99-100
Parti-Pris, 370
Parti Rouge, 588
Partridge, E. A., 153-4
Passchendaele, 182
Patrick, Principal, 595

Patrons of Industry, 118, 125
  growth and decline, 490-1
  in Ontario, 117
  political action, 499
Patterson, J. C., 111
Patterson, William, 126, 128
Pattullo, T. D., 256
Peace River country, settlement of, 140
Pearce, Bob, 611
Pearson, Lester B., 330, 355
  'American New Frontier', 346
  and anti-French feeling, 381
  attitude to U.S. involvement in Viet
    Nam, 359
  Commonwealth affairs, 360
  communiqué from federal-provincial
    conference (1964), 355
  and Gordon's budget, 349
  in international scene, 327-8, 359
  and Lyndon B. Johnson, 360
  and King's position on U.N. Korean
    election commission, 328
  Minister of External Affairs, 304
  1963 election, 348
  as prime minister, 349-50
  realistic foreign policy, 363
  rebuilds Liberal party, 340
  Suez crisis, 804
Peden, Torchy, 615
Pellan, Alfred, 705, 706, 707
Penfield, Wilder, 558-9
Penticton Vs, 606
Peppiatt, Frank, 691
Periodicals, 529-31
Permanent Joint Defence Board, 781-2
Peterson, Len, 692-3, 695
Phillips, C. E., 573
Pilon, Jean-Guy, 667
Pine Point railway line, 517
Pipelines, 522-3
Pius XII, 310
Plaskett, Joe, 708
Plummer, Christopher, 691
Political Equality League, 198
Politics
  changes wrought by Diefenbaker, 338
  churches as pressure groups, 587, 593
  conscription issue, 189, 190
  departure of Laurier and Borden, 202
  dominance of farmers in west, 154
  emergence of French-Canadian party,
    166-7, 170
  emergence of left-wing programs, 115
  English v. French Canada, 214

entry of Patrons of Industry, 117
farmers form third party, 170, 211
and Farmers organizations, 498-500
five parties, 353
formation of farmers provincial parties, 190-2
French-Canadian problems, 372-4
inability of most parties to change leader, 720-1
increasing corruption (1890s), 109
influence of King, 310
and labour unions, 498-501
Liberal opportunism, 215
new parties in depression, 240-1, 251-9
new party needed for western farmers 155
opportunism of 1920s, 233-4
post-war radicalism, 190-3
racial conflict, 120
return to two-party system (1926), 218
returned to politicians, 216
routes to the Cabinet, 336
sectional character of parties, 212
and social welfare, 763
Polymer Corporation, 483
Pope, J. C., 44
Population, 385-409
  (1861) 4-5
  (1870s) 61-3
  levelling off (1880s), 90
  decrease (1891), 112
  (1914) 276
  (1921) 210
  (1939) 275
  (1941, 1951) 298
  (1960) 317
  (1961) 445
  distribution, by age, 738-9; by ethnic origin, 394-5; geographical, 411; (1900-1910) 150; by provinces, 387-8
  increase, and construction industry, 636-7; (1867-1967) 389-90; postwar, 737-8; on prairies (1900-1910) 140; and social services, 737-8, 739
  Indians and Eskimos, 398-9
  major cities, 62
  by major religions, 596
  regionalism and ethnic origins, 398
  rural rather than urban, 5
  shift to cities, 221
Power, C. G., 296
  'Canadianization' of air force units, 282-3, 286
Prairie Farm Rehabilitation Act, 414

Prairie Provinces
  architecture, 628-30, 638
  collective action of wheat farmers, 152-5
  concentration on wheat, 414
  control of natural resources, 718
  development of wheat economy, 129
  dropped police budgets, 249
  drought and resource management, 412
  effects of mechanization and one-crop cultivation, 632
  effects of railways, 628-9
  new parties in depression, 240-1, 251-9
  to be English-speaking region, 161
  farmers' parties, 170, 190-1, 211
  farmers propose devaluation of dollar, 247
  farmers turn from political to economic action, 216
  federal control of land policy, 160
  few French Canadians migrate to, 159-60, 161-2
  flood of immigration, 140-4, 150, 173, 790
  French language abolished in schools, 373
  grain-growers' organization, 489, 491
  and the Grand Trunk, 505
  hard hit by depression and drought, 239
  importance of railway, 413, 503, 504-5
  jealous of central Canada, 139
  life of settlers (early 1900s), 143-4
  necessity of being productive, 140
  new parties in depression, 240-1, 251-6
  northern settlement, 221
  organized in readiness for settlers, 142
  politically inexperienced, 214
  pooling of wheat sales, 216
  population, 387, 388
  proportion of Europeans, 398
  record wheat crop (1928), 234, 235
  religious diversity, 594
  settlement as part of National Policy, 150
  stopgap measures in depression, 244
  structure of governments, 715
  unrest of workers, 193-6
  the 'wheat blockade', 145, 146
  and the Wheat Board, 208-9
Pratt, E. J., 225, 231, 650-1, 658
Presbyterian Church
  anti-unionists, 595

Church Union, 228, 594-5
  in 1867, 586, 588
  foreign missions, 603, 604-5
  national union, 588, 589, 590, 594,
    594-5
  native missions, 602
  numbers (1871-1961), 596
  and religious modernism, 593
Presse, La, 134, 527
Pressey, Sidney, 585
Prime Minister, role of, 720-1
Prince Edward Island
  attitude to Confederation, 42-5
  becomes province, 44, 789
  Butler's offer of Reciprocity, 35, 36,
    43
  election (1966), 345n.
  Maritime union movement, 15
  obdurate against Confederation, 31,
    32, 35
  opposition to Quebec Resolutions, 23,
    25
  over-ambitious railway program, 43-4
  population (1861), 4
  Prohibition Act, 199, 200
  tunnel promised, 111
Progressive party
  disintegration of, 215
  Douglas and Banking Act review, 231
  elections, (1921) 211, 500, (1925) 216,
    (1926) 218
  goals, 215
  influence on Bennett New Deal, 261
  mainly western party, 212
  new National Policy, 211
  support Liberal party (1926), 218
Prohibition
  and the churches, 228-9
  effects on small communities, 633
  majority too slight, 135
  the movement, 199-201
  reaction against, 200-1
  replaced by government control, 235
  weakness, 229
Prophetic Bible Institute, 254
Protestant Committee of Public In-
    struction, 101
Protestant Protective Association, 120,
    132, 136
Protestantism
  and Catholic minority in Manitoba,
    121ff.
  against Catholic schools, 125
  Church Union, 228

  doctrine of separation of Church and
    State, 101
  extreme hatred of Catholicism, 120
  lack of social philosophy, 601
  and prohibition, 228-9
  pursuits (1950s), 309-10
  reaction to Jesuit Estates Act, 101-2
  social preoccupation, 227-9
Proulx, Abbé, mission to Rome, 127
Provancher, Abbé Léon, 550
Provinces
  best vehicles for economic and social
    development, 353
  chauvinism (1870s), 69
  cross-currents (1880s), 92
  education, 573-4
  expansion of role, 341, 345-6, 363-4,
    729-30, 737, 747-8
  federal aid (1930), 244, 247, 250-1
  fisheries, 433
  forest resources, 426-8
  form of government, 718-19
  formal links with federal government
    structure, 719
  and highway transport, 509-10
  increasing independence (1920s), 795
  industrial policies, 484-5
  influences on federal parties, 259
  influence on universities, 577
  judiciary, 718
  mainly governed by executive branch,
    718-19
  and mineral resources, 420
  parks, 442-3, 619-20
  political opposition to federal gov-
    ernment, 341-3
  position within government struc-
    ture, 717-19
  relationship with municipalities, 717
  revenues below obligations, 731-2
  rights, 236, 241, 250-1; amendments
    concerning, still go to British Par-
    liament, 302; assertion of, in 1930s,
    257-8; demands for, intensified un-
    der Liberals, 264; generally played
    down (1950s), 310
  rivalry with federal government, 727-
    30
  social welfare program, 750-3
  taking over agricultural legislation,
    414
  telephone systems, 534
  testing-ground for changes in elec-
    tion system, 718
Publishing, growth (1950s), 322

Quebec; *see also* French Canada; Nationalism: Quebec brand
agricultural market lures Grand Trunk, 505
architecture, 623, 627-8, 638
associate state, 378
attitude to Riel, 97, 98
bicameral form of government, 718
bishops and Laurier, 126-7
bishops' *mandement* on separate schools, 124
Canada Pension Plan controversy, 357-8
on Canadian contribution to war, 274
and Canadian entry into war, 272
challenges federal authority in radio, 541
claims control over external relations, 264
claims for provincial rights, 264
colonization policy, limitations, 164-6
concept of liberalism, 79
and conscription, 269-70, 273, 293-6, 300-1
Conseil d'Education Supérieur, 577
Conservative-Nationalist alliance, 176, 177, 792
continuation in national politics essential to Liberals, 215
C.C.F. opposed by Roman Catholic hierarchy, 253
and 'co-operative federalism', 355
corruption in politics, 213, 217-18
cultural *entente* with France, 369-70
cultural exchange program with Ontario, 381
cultural expression and identity, 695
decline of agricultural labour force, 401
defence against racial conflict, 121
differences from other provinces, 379, 713
divisions in federal Liberal party, 373-4
dream of North American French state, 100
Drummond-Arthabaska by-election, and Naval Services Act, 170
early sculpture, 700
Eastern Townships becoming French, 78-9
ecclesiastical support for Conservatives, 124
economic development, 368-9
economy (1870s), 64-5

effect of Riel's execution, 591
effects of King's wariness of, 269-70
effects of prosperity, 162-4
effects of railways, 627-8
election (1966), 345n.
emergence of French-Canadian party, 166-7, 170
emigration of farmers' families, 164
factors hindering development, 371
out of federal-provincial agreements, 305
and federal-provincial financial relations, 731
and First World War, 183-6, 189-90
form of the revolt, 212-13
formation of Le Parti National, 99-100
French-Canadian nationalism, 212-13
as French-Canadian stronghold, 373-5
French Canadians in industry, 369
goals of quiet revolution, 366-7
government activities in industry, 369
and Sam Hughes, 186
importance of Prime Minister's lieutenant, 721-2
increased separateness under Duplessis, 259
increasing feeling of apartness, 162
internal reform, 381
iron-ore deposits, 314
and Jehovah's Witnesses, 312
Jesuit Estates issue, 101-2, 591
junior colleges, 572
and King's brand of nationalism, 216
Liberal victory, (1896) 125, (1960) 343
local school unit reorganization, 580
M.P.s' interpretation of roles, 725
Mercier alienates English Canadians, 110
mineral resources, 421, 424
Ministry of Education, 367-8
Montreal an English enclave, 163
nationalism, 219, 344-5, 375-6
nationalization of power companies, 369
new French communities (1880s), 78-9
1939 election crisis, 280-1
1940 federal election, 281
no prohibition, 200
obliged to be officially bilingual, 718
off-shore mineral rights, 379
and Ontario dominance of Commons, 725
and opting-out formula, 354, 737

over-extension of railway lines, 92
Padlock Law, 258-9, 529
Parent Commission, 367-8
parish-school system, 78-9
Parti National forms government, 100
particular status, 378-80
percentage of Europeans, 398
political unrest (1930s), 257-9
politics in depression, 241, 257-9
population, 150, 387, 388
predominantly Roman Catholic (1867), 586
pro-Diefenbaker vote, 338
pro-Franco sympathies, 274
problem of *collèges classiques*, 368
prosperity of 1880s, 78
protest against inferior status, 392, 397
provincial *v.* Canadian nationalism, 259
quasi-police state under Duplessis, 258-9
quiet revolution, 345, 364-71, 392, 397; effects, 376; and the N.D.P., 352
railways to northern mining area, 518
reaction to Riel execution, 98-9
re-evaluation of traditional institutions, 370
v. rest of Canada after 1917 election, 189
Roman Catholic attacks on liberalism, 590-1
Roman Catholic Church and industrialization, 598
Roman Catholic schools, 578
Rouges and ultramontanes, 52
and Rowell-Sirois Report, 265-6
and royal commission on bilingualism, 376-7
and Second World War, 274, 280-1
separatism, 370, 377
Social Credit upsurge, 352
social services, 755
social welfare, changing approach to, 369
spearheaded provincial-power trend, 341
spurns federal aid to universities, 353-4
status in Confederation, 78-9
a sub-culture, 391-2
support of King, 300-1
support of Liberal party (1921), 212
la survivance, 163-4
trade unions, 495

and Trans-Canada Highway, 301
terrorism, 375-6
a unified nation in itself, 370-1
Union Nationale, returned, 301
Quebec City, and the Far North, 223, 293
Quebec Conference, 3, 19-22
Quebec Council of Economic Reorientation, 369
Quebec Provincial Police, and Queen Elizabeth's visit, 376
Quebec Resolutions, 22-5
Queen's Plate, 607

Racial conflict
  conscription issue, 189-90, 293-6
  'dialogue' of the sixties, 380
  dissatisfaction of Quebeckers, 370-82
  eruptions, 373
  fanned by imperialism, 131
  greatest strain on federalism, 131
  growing estrangement of French Canadians, 166-7
  intensified (1960s), 391-3
  less in Second World War than in First World War, 300-1
  and New Brunswick's war on poverty, 381
  outlet in politics, 120
  public service, merit system and bilingualism, 726
Racial origin
  and the churches, 589-90, 598-601
  of immigrants to prairies, 143
  pre-Confederation, 5
Raddall, Thomas, 657
Radio, 539-43, 544, 545
  drama, 685-6
  northern network, 542
  private broadcasting, 540-1
  Signal Corps, 542
Radio Telegraph Act, 539
Railway Labour Dispute Act, 157-8
Railways, 53-60, 502-7; *see also* Canadian National Railways; Canadian Northern Railway; Canadian Pacific Railway; Grand Trunk Pacific; Grand Trunk Railway; Pacific Great Eastern
  automation, 320
  before Confederation, 502-3
  beginning of competition, 505
  beginning of recovery, 320
  branch line construction subsidized, 145-6, 148

to British Columbia, 41, 49, 55-60, 86, 504

competition from highway transport, 298-9, 507, 508-10, 513-14

competitive check on rates, 511

construction stimulates Maritime iron and steel industry, 150, 151

drawbacks to Maritimes, 103

effects, 64, 625-30

in 1860s, 6

(1875-85) 504

factors in proliferation, 505

fall behind settlement and traffic, 145

to Far North, 219

financial troubles, 502-7 *passim*

Grand Trunk, 6

Halifax and Montreal linked, 55

impetus to industry, 456-7

importance to Confederation, 7-8, 9, 503

importance to development of west, 84-5, 144-5, 413, 626

importance to nation, 53-5, 219-21, 455

Intercolonial, 7, 9, 13, 14

lines built, 1850s and 1860s, 53-4

MacPherson Commission, 511-13

and mineral finds, 422, 628, 630

and National Policy, 148, 150

and national unity, 170

nationalization, 203, 220-1, 506

need for government action in west, 145

need for system, streamlining, 523-4

to the north, 517-18

over-extension, 220-1

Pacific Scandal, 49

piggy-back, 320

P.E.I. overreaches, is rescued, 43-4

problems in depression, 245-6

proposed western extension in N.B., 29

Quebec over-extends herself, 92

rates, 510-12

royal commission recommends branch-line rationalization, 507

Saint John–Montreal line through Maine, 92

spate of building, 626

strikes, and national economy, 157-8

subsidies recommended, 511-12

success of Conservative policies (1880s), 75

supremacy challenged by automobile, 221

threat of Northern Pacific, 84-5

threat of U.S. railways, 112, 504

two more transcontinental systems proposed, 148

two transcontinental lines, 174

U.S. capital investment in Canada (1890s), 129

Winnipeg to Portage la Prairie, 83

Yukon, 130-1

Ralliement des Créditistes, 352, 353

Ralston, J. L., 278, 289, 293
and conscription policy, 293, 296
resignation, 294

Ramsay, Alexander, 35

Rand Corporation, 332

Rat Portage, Ontario-Manitoba jurisdictional dispute, 82

Rawhide, 312

Rayner, Gordon, 699, 710

Reaney, James, 644, 652, 653, 656

Reciprocity (with U.S.)
arguments against, 176
defeat of agreement, 191
Joint High Commission (1898-9), 131
and Laurier's defeat, 791
Treaty of 1854, 7; abrogation of, 29-30, 35, 46-7, 175

Reconstruction Conference (1945), 412

Reconstruction Party, 254, 260

Recorder (Brockville), 526

Red River, 5, 34, 35-6, 38, 39, 788-9

Reeve, Ted, 610

Régie des Ondes, 545

Regina Manifesto, 251, 253

Regionalism, 151, 170-1

Reid, Kate, 691

Religion, 586-605
absence of anti-clericalism, 588
conflict and outlet in politics, 120
as a divisive element, 406-7
heritage from Europe, 587, 588
Jewish, 600-1
Manitoba Schools Question, 121-8, 159, 160-1, 373, 591-2
pluralism, 586, 605
population, by major denominations, 596
re-interpretation of role of, 598
sectarian reaction to 'respectable' churches, 594
sectarian social philosophy, 601
university courses, 313

Renaud, Jacques, 672

Rep. by Pop., 8

Research Enterprises Ltd., 560
Réseau de Résistance, 375
Resources for Tomorrow Conference
    (1961), 412, 448
  fisheries, 433
  forestry, 429
Restrictive trade practices, 114, 153
Rhodes, Edgar, on tax increases (1932),
    247
Rhodesia, and the Commonwealth, 360
Richler, Mordecai, 642, 650, 654
Ricker, W. E., 433
Riddell, W. A., 269
Riel, Louis, 127
  ambitions, 94-5
  character, 95
  delegation to Ottawa, 55
  establishes provincial government on
    Saskatchewan, 95
  execution, 97-9, 373, 591
  execution of Scott, 38, 591
  Indian supporters, 96
  invited to take leadership of Battle-
    ford, 94
  Red River uprising, 35-6, 37, 39, 765,
    788-9
  second uprising, 94-6, 767-8
  surrender, 96
  trial, 97-8
Ringuet, 665
Riopelle, Jean-Paul, 707
Ritchot, Fr., 35
Rivard, Lucien, 350
'Roads to Resources' program, 519
Roberts, Charles G. D., 75, 640-1, 644,
    645, 646, 648, 649
Roberts, Goodridge, 708
Roberts, J. H., 199
Roberts, Jean, 690
Robichaud, Louis, 343
Roblin, Sir Rodmond, 198
Rockingham, J. M., 781
Roebuck, Arthur, 257
Rogers, Major, 87
Roman Catholic Church
  Antigonish co-operative venture, 598
  anti-socialist pronouncements in Que-
    bec, 253
  attack on Liberalism, 79, 590-1
  declarations against annexation
    (1891), 110
  and Duplessis, 258, 259
  and educational rights, 406
  foreign missions, 604
  gains from immigration, 598

  integral part of Quebec nation, 589
  maintenance of French culture, 212-
    13
  Manitoba Schools question, 121-8,
    159, 160-1, 373, 591-2
  modified system of separate schools
    in west, 159-62
  native missions, 601-2
  numbers (1871-1961), 596
  outnumber Protestants in Toronto,
    322
  post-Confederation expansion, 590
  preoccupations (1920s), 227
  Quebec (1867), 586
  and religious modernism, 593
  slow to become national, 589
  social welfare in Quebec, 755
  and trade unions in Quebec, 157
Ronald, William, 708, 710
Roosevelt, Franklin D., 238, 279, 285
  death, 302-3
  meeting with King (1940), 292
  New Deal, 260, 261
Ross, James Sinclair, 650
Ross, Malcolm, 657
Ross, Ronald, 556
Rouges, 52, 79
  merge with Ultramontanes in Parti
    National, 99
  and Quebec Resolutions, 23
Routhier, Judge, 126
Roux, Jean-Louis, 690
Rowell, N. W., 264
Rowell-Sirois Report, 265-6
  on industrial development, 460
  and resource management, 412
  social services, 736
Roy, Camille, 665
Roy, Gabrielle, 669-70, 673
Royal Air Force, and Royal Canadian
    Air Force personnel, 282
Royal Canadian Academy, 75, 702, 705
Royal Canadian Air Force, 781, 782
  problems, 282-3
  in Second World War, 286-8, 776
Royal Canadian Dragoons, 766
Royal Canadian Mounted Police, 259
  antagonism to, in Quebec, 375
  'labour spies', 249
  in prairies and Maritimes, 249
  and unemployed (1930s), 248-9
Royal Canadian Navy
  North-west Atlantic command, 285
  in Second World War, 285-6, 287, 776
Royal Canadian Regiment, 766, 768

Royal Commission on Bilingualism and Biculturalism, 376-7
Royal Commission on Broadcasting (Fowler), 543-4
Royal Commission on Dominion-Provincial Relations (Rowell-Sirois), 265-6, 305
Royal Commission on Government Organization (Glassco), 783
Royal Commission on Health Services (Hall), 762
Royal Commission on National Developments in the Arts, Letters and Sciences (Massey), 353, 679-80
Royal Commission on Price Spreads (Stevens), 250, 260
Royal Commission on Radio Communications (Aird), 541
Royal Commission on Restrictive Trade Practices (1889), 130
Royal Commission on Transportation (MacPherson), 511-13
Royal Military College, 61, 766, 771, 779
Royal Navy bases at Halifax, Esquimalt, 766
Royal North West Mounted Police, *see* North West Mounted Police
Royal Society of Canada, 75
Royal Winnipeg Ballet, 325, 684
Royalist sentiment, extent in 1880s, 72-3
Rupert's Land Act, 788
Rush-Bagot agreement, 26, 796
Russia, 182, 195, 196
Russian Orthodox Church, 599
Rutherford, Ernest, 546, 550-1

Sager, Peter, 700
St. Albans raid, 26
Saint John, effects of St. Lawrence Ship Channel, 522
St. John's, anti-confederation vote, 306
St. Laurent, Louis S., 278, 310, 336-7
  auspicious start as Prime Minister, 307
  becomes Prime Minister, 301, 304
  contrasted with King, 307
  declares need for collective defence, 304
  extension of Canada's commitments, 327
  first Canadian Governor General appointed, 337
  and King's position on U.N. Korean-election commission, 328

Minister of External Affairs, 304
NATO, 804
St. Lawrence Deep Waterway agreement (1932), 246, 520
St. Lawrence–Great Lakes navigational system, 521, 523
St. Lawrence River, Americans obtain free navigation on, 48
St. Lawrence Seaway, 319, 520-2
St. Lawrence Seaway Authority, 520
St. Lawrence Ship Channel, 521
Salisbury Plain, 178-9
Salvation Army, 116, 133, 594
Samedi de la matraque, 376
Sangster, Charles, 643-4
San Jacinto, 10
Sarrazin, Michel, 553
Saskatchewan
  becomes province, 39, 159, 789
  C.C.F. official opposition, 253
  decline of agricultural labour force, 400-1
  federal control of natural resources, 142
  Land Utilization Act, 414
  Medical Care Act, 364
  royal commission re government operating elevators, 154
  Second World War recruiting, 280
  separate schools, 159-62, 373, 578, 591-2
  total economic collapse, 239
Saskatchewan Grain Growers, 500
Saskatoon, beginnings, 140-1
Saunders, Charles Edward, 414, 549
Saunders, Percy, 414
Saunders, William, 414, 549
Sauvé, Maurice, 374
Sauvé, Paul, 365
Savard, Félix-Antoine, 664
Scholes, Lou, 611
Science, 546-53, 559-67
  agriculture, 549-50
  Alouette, 565
  biology, 562-3
  industrial research, 563-4
  National Research Council, 559ff.
  physics, 550-1
  psychology, 552-3
  sharing with other nations, 566-7
  solidly established by 1920s, 223
  space, 565
  war-time research, 560-2, 563
Scott, Barbara Ann, 618

Scott, Duncan Campbell, 115, 225, 644, 647
Scott, Frank R., 651, 652
Scott, Thomas, 38, 97, 591
Sculpture, 700-1, 711-12
Sealing
  Canadian vessels seized by U.S., 106
  Joint High Commission (1898-9), 131
Second World War, 275-97, 776-8
  Air Force, 286-7
  Army, 287-91
  Canada as 'linchpin' in Anglo-American relations, 291-2
  Canada declares war separately, 272-3, 277, 798
  Canadian-American co-operation, 462, 794
  Canadian entry ambiguous, 274
  Canadian leadership uninspiring, 278
  Canadian servicemen and British people, 288-9
  and the churches, 598
  Combined Chiefs of Staff, 292
  conferences at Quebec City, 293
  conscription crisis, 293-6
  direction of war, 291-3
  effects on cities, 634
  fall of France, 283, 293
  French and English in the services, 301
  home front, 284
  industrial expansion, 463-5, 468
  'limited liability' policy to 1940, 279, 280-2, 283
  military program, 282-3
  Navy, 285-6
  as problem-solver, 274
  production effort, 283-4
  recruiting, 279-80
  RCAF casualties, 287
  scientific research, 560, 563
  war effort, 279-84
Sedgewick, G. G., 657
Selby-Smyth, Edward, 767
Selye, Hans, 657
Senate, 559, 722-3
Senate Committee on Investigations (U.S.), and Herbert Norman, 333
Service, Robert, 640, 644, 647-8
Sévigny, Pierre, 347
Seward, William, 45
Seymour, Frederick, 40
Shadbolt, Jack, 699, 706, 711
Shaughnessy, Lord, 506
Shaw, George Bernard, 311

Shaw, Norman, on Lord Rutherford, 551
Sheridan Research Park, 564-5
Sherring, Bill, 611
Shields, T. T., 312
Shortt, Adam, 224
Shutt, Frank B., 549
Sicotte, L. V., 12
'Siege of Ottawa', 155
Siegfried, André, on Canada's foreign policy, 786
Sifton, Clifford, 126-7, 529
  chairman of Conservation Commission, 412
  on free trade, 128
  and immigration to prairies, 143-4
  in Laurier cabinet, 126
  on railway monopoly, 507
  on railway policies, 145
  and western separate schools, 161
Simard, Jean, 668
Sinclair, James, 329
Sirois, Joseph, 264
Sitting Bull, 84
Skelton, O. D., 224, 302, 452-3
Skookum Jim, 130
Slater, Patrick, 232
Slemon, R., 782
Smallwood, J. R., 306, 343
Smiley, Robert, 526
Smith, A. J. M., 640, 651, 652, 657
Smith, Albert J., 29, 30
Smith, Arnold, 360
Smith, Sir Donald, 87, 123
Smith, Donald A., 38
Smith, Goldwin, 70
  advocates annexation to U.S., 50-1
  and Continental Union movement, 117
  on French peasant, 120
  on future of Canada, 137
  on Irish Home Rule resolutions, 93
  on Mackenzie, 61
Smith, Gordon, 699, 706, 712
Smith, Ralph, 499
Smith, William (Amor de Cosmos), 40
Smythe, Conn, 612, 613
Snow, Michael, 710
Social Credit, 235, 254-6, 500
  and Aberhart's sect, 601
  and Banking Act review, 231
  in British Columbia, 342
  conscription vote, 799
  early legislation in Alberta, 255-6, 259
  1962 election, 352

1963 election, 347-8, 352-3
as a political experiment, 718
spread from England, 230-1
Social Gospel movement, 593
Social reform, jurisdictional problem of, 260-4
Social Security Act (U.S.), 736
Social welfare, 734-63
   abortive old age pensions act, 300
   advent of (1920s), 230
   assessment of Canadian families, 745, 761-2
   burden on municipalities, provinces, 241, 250-1
   complications of mobility, 740-1
   constitutional problems, 747-8
   C.C.F. pressure, 254
   effects on consumer purchasing power, 316
   effects of depression, 736
   and expansion of civil service, 310
   extent, 736-7
   federal programs, 748-51
   federal-provincial programs, 750-1
   federal-provincial-municipal programs, 751-2
   fields of service, 756-7
   groups of 'dependent poor', 757-9
   housing, 763
   implications of increased population, 738
   importance of health services, 762
   increased government activity, 341
   increased power of provinces, 729-30
   legislation, 254, 356-8, 747-8
   methods of payment, 753-4
   municipal responsibilities, 753
   a new era, 358
   in Newfoundland, 306-7
   percentage of net national income, 734
   post-war measures, 299-300
   poverty in industrial society, 745-7
   pre-depression, 735-6
   prerequisites, 761-3
   private voluntary agencies, 754-7
   professional social work, 756-7
   a provincial matter, 345
   provincial programs, 750-3
   rising expenditures, 761-2
   'self-supporting poor', 760
   6 per cent of families – 50 per cent of services, 740
   'socially responsible state', 734-5, 761
   supported by all parties, 763

   unemployment, 742, 743-4, 757-8, 762
   and urbanization, 358
   and working mothers, 741-2
Socialism, 230, 251
Society, 385-409
   basic conservatism (1870s), 68-9
   becoming divided by economic growth, 109
   British pattern alien, 73-4
   Canadian and American compared, 385-6, 395-6
   Canadian values, 386
   changes in structure, 230
   common outlook (1920s), 229-30
   dissatisfaction with inequalities, 203-4
   economic élite from broader spectrum, 311
   (1870s) 66-9
   emigration and social structure, 390-1
   ethnic differentiation and class structure, 395-8
   ethnic fragmentation, 394-6
   inequities of structure, 193-4
   maintenance of status quo, 309-10
   'mosaic' rather than melting-pot, 386
   and the motor car, 298-9
   not determined as 'Canadian' (1900), 139
   predominantly rural outlook, 588
   sources of status, 744
   typical Canadian way of life, 389
   typical citizen, 745
   underlying changes (1950s), 310-11
   unity through diversity? 393
   upward mobility, 404
   urban working class, 115-16
   weakness of community ties, 390-1
Soddy, Frederick, 550
Somers, Harry, 696
Somerville, C. Ross 'Sandy', 613, 614-15, 617
Somme, 180, 773
Sons of England, 136
Souster, Raymond, 651-2, 653
South Africa, and the Commonwealth, 330, 360
South East Asia Treaty Organization, 330
Southam newspaper chain, 528
Spanish-American War, pro-American feeling prevalent in Canada, 133
Spanish Civil War, Quebec sympathies, 274
Spectator (Hamilton), 526
Spence, Ben, 199

Spohr, Arnold, 684, 690
Sport
  camping, 619-20
  at Confederation, 608-10
  Edmonton Grads, 616
  (1870s) 67
  hockey, 606-8, 611-13, 620
  lacrosse, 608, 609-10
  marathon running, 611
  national impact, 617-18
  participators, 618-20
  polo, 609
  post-war boom, 616-20
  sculling, 610-11
Stalin, Joseph, 310, 313
Standard Oil, monopoly, central Canada, 130
Stanfield, Robert, 311, 342
Stanley, Frederick Arthur, Lord, 612
Stanley Cup, 612
Star (Montreal), on participation in Boer War, 134
Statute of Westminster, 232, 267, 277, 794, 796
Stead, Robert J. C., 650
Steel Company of Canada, 151
Steele, W. A., 559
Steinhouse, Herbert, 654
Stephen, George, 60, 86, 87, 88
Stern, Karl, 657
Stevens, G. R., on Canadian Northern Railway, 505
Stevens, H. H., 260
Stevens Report, 250
Stewart, Marlene, 618
Storey, Red, 615
Strachan, John, 547
Strange, Thomas, 96
Stratas, Teresa, 691
Strate, Grant, 696
Stratford Festival, 325, 676-7, 680
Stuart, Kenneth, 289
Student Volunteer Movement, 604
Subsidies
  indirect, to airlines, 516-17
  inequitable effects, 250
  railway, 511-12
Suez Canal crisis, 330, 335, 363
Sumner, Charles, 45, 47
Supreme Court of Canada
  as champion of Parliament power, 730
  disqualified to settle constitutional questions? 379
  established, 61

highest court of appeal, 302, 730
  ruling on Bennett New Deal, 263
Sutherland, R. A., 331
Sutherland, William, 526
Suttie, E. R., 780
Suzor-Coté, Aurèle, 703
Swinehart, G. B., 527
Sylvestre, Guy, 674
Symphony orchestras, 684, 685

Taché, Bishop, 38
Taché, Etienne, 16
Tagish Charley, 130
Tanzania, 331
Tardivel, Jules-Paul, 121
Tariffs
  agitation for increases in, 456
  anti-dumping provisions, 242
  Dingley tariff, 128
  disadvantageous to farmers, 154-5
  disadvantageous to Maritimes, 77, 103
  effect of high U.S. tariffs (1890), 109
  1897 tariff and imperialism, 131
  end of retaliation with U.S., 273
  farm machinery, 89, 116
  farmers agitate for lowering of, 211, 215
  favourable to Ontario (1880s), 80
  further raises (1932), 243
  gradual removal, 469-70, 472, 481
  growing dissatisfaction with policy (1880s), 109, 110
  hearings held in industrial centres, 128
  high inequitable effects of, 250
  imperial preference, 150, 243-4
  importance to national economy, 105, 108
  Liberals change policy, 118
  manufacturing at a disadvantage, 469-70
  McCarthy's advocacy of imperial preferences, 109
  as part of National Policy, 140, 150
  Patrons of Industry agitate for reform, 117
  preferential system (1897), 128
  protection removable if monopolies encouraged (1890s), 129-30
  raised (1930), 242
  reductions (1894), 119
  success of Conservative policies (1880s), 75
  survive peril of 1887 election, 105
  U.S., 106-7, 113, 238

and U.S. branch plants in Canada, 460, 462

Tarte, Israel, 349
on Canadian participation in Boer War, 134
on Laurier, 124
in Laurier cabinet, 126
resignation in balance, 134-5
target of Conservative attacks, 135

Taschereau, L. A., 213, 257
Taylor, Ron, 617
Technical and Vocational Assistance Act, 356
Teitelbaum, Mashel, 699
Telegram (Toronto), Canadians a nation of toadies, 73
Television, 543-5, 681
drama, 685-6
need for improvement, 687-8
'Temperance' movement, 199-201
Temps, Le, on Laurier cabinet, 126
Theatre, 325, 683-4, 687
Théâtre du Nouveau Monde, 325
Thériault, Yves, 670
Thermal-electric power, 438-9
Thompson, Bill, 614
Thompson, Frank, 614
Thompson, Sir John S. D., 90-1, 122
Thompson, Robert, 352, 353
Thomson, Tom, 704
Thomson Company, 529
Thornton, Henry, 220
Thorson, J. T., 272
Thorton, Edward, 46
Tilley, Samuel Leonard, 41, 90
defeat (1864), 24
and diminishing revenues (1880s), 89
and Maritime union, 15
and Quebec Resolutions, 24
returned to office (1866), 31
Times, The
on Canadian resolutions re Irish Home Rule, 93
on Canadian west, 84
Todd, F. G., 635
Topley, W. J., 66
Toronto
changes (1950s), 321-2
effect of immigration, 636
growing local pride, 80
metropolitan government, 636
population (1861), 5
Toronto Stock Exchange, 316-17
Tory, Henry Marshall, 550, 559, 560, 564

Toupin, Paul, 668
Town, Harold, 311, 699, 708, 709-10
Trade; *see also* Free Trade; Reciprocity; Tariffs
agreements with Commonwealth members, 243
agreement with U.S. (1937), 273
balance-of-payments problem, 362, 466
Britain top customer (1930s), 318
Canada's rank in world, 449
Canadian ambivalence toward, 361
Conservative attempt to shift to Britain, 330
decline (1870s), 455
decline in European imports, Second World War, 459
disadvantage of high Canadian dollar, 317
exports, 239-40, 453; agricultural, 417-18; electrical energy, 440; fish, 432; forest products, 424, 428; hydroelectric power question, 319; manufactured goods, 451-2; oil etc. to U.S. restricted, 332; wheat, 329, 332, 362, 469
increasing transatlantic commerce, 162
Joint U.S.–Canadian Committee on Trade and Economic Affairs, 477
Kennedy Round, 472-3
manufacturing industries in world markets, 467-73
(1939) 276
oil and natural gas, 437, 440
pros and cons of surplus, 242
reciprocity *v.* protection, 456
sales to China and Cuba, 361
shift in pattern (1930s), 243-4
with U.S., increase in 1950s, 318
Trade and Commerce, Department of, 119
Trade unions, *see* Labour unions
Trades and Labour Congress of Canada
allegiance to international unions, 495
and A.F. of L., 156, 493-5
endorses co-operatives, 497
endorses political action, 498
expels C.I.O. unions, 494, 495-6
favours farmer-labour co-operation, 499
formation, 156
history, 492-3
merged with C.C.L., 341, 493, 500

politically ineffectual, 115
Trans-Canada Air Lines, see Air Canada
Trans-Canada Highway, 301, 508, 634
Trans-Canada pipeline, 319, 522
Trans-Mountain pipeline, 522
Transport, 502-4; see also Highways;
  Railways
  advent of steam, 6
  air, 319-20, 514-17, 634
  automobile, 221, 320
  changes (1950s), 319-20
  and cities, 633-4
  corporation profits, 452
  and development of country, 446
  highway, 507-10, 524
  investment in, by underdeveloped
    countries, 504
  motor vehicles, rising numbers, 298-9,
    507-8
  and national unity, 523-4
  need for planning, 524
  into north, 222-3, 517-19
  oil and gas pipelines, 337, 522-3
  on Saskatchewan River, 83
  streetcar, effects on cities, 630-1
  urban problems, 320
Transport, Department of
  enlightened policy of design, 323
  establishment, 515
  northern radio network, 542
Treaty of Versailles, 201, 793
Treaty of Washington, 48-9, 766
Trent affair, 10-12, 26
Tribune (Chicago), on Canada's foreign
  minister, 333
Trimble, James, 40
Trotter, R. G., 224
Trottier, Pierre, 667
Trudeau, Yves, 712
Truman, Harry S., 328
Tupper, Sir Charles, 41, 111, 123, 125,
  135
  becomes Prime Minister, 124
  and British Columbia railway, 59
  C.P.R. contract, 60, 86
  and Fenian raid, 31
  High Commissioner in London, 90
  and Maritime union, 15
Tupper, Charles Hibbert, 123
Turner, R. E. W., 768-9
Tyler, Henry, 88

Ukrainian Greek Orthodox Church,
  596, 600
Ukrainians, opening up the west, 396

Ultramontanism
  in the ascendant, 52
  end of, 592
  and liberalism, 79, 590-1
  and nationalism, 212-13
  and the Parti National, 99
  supported by Jesuit Order, 101
Underhill, Frank, 657
Unemployment
  adolescents, 742
  burden in municipalities, provinces,
    241, 250-1
  as cause of poverty, 745-6, 757-8
  ceased to be tolerated, 209
  in depression, 238, 240
  federal aid, 244, 250-1
  Hepburn's approach, 257-8
  1929 et seq., 235
  in 1939, 273, 276
  1957-61 high, 466-7
  1960 level with 1939, 316
  persisting in industry, 216
  post-war, 297
  protest delegations (1930s), 248
  and Second World War, 273
  and social service, 743-4, 757-8
  and social welfare, 762
  transient camps established, 248
Unemployment Assistance Act, 751-2
Unemployment Insurance, 749-50, 754
  fund exhausted (1959-61), 762
  made a federal responsibility, 254,
    300
Unemployment Insurance Act, 300
Unemployment and Social Insurance
  Act, 261
Union Carbide Company, 564
Union Government
  conscription, 189-90
  facilitated formation of farmers'
    party, 192
  formation of, 188
  ignores farmers' appeals for lower
    tariffs, 211
  and railways, 220
  Wartime Election Act, 189
  a war-time necessity, 192
  and Winnipeg General Strike, 196
Union Nationale
  defeat (1960), 343
  and denominational school system,
    368n.
  regime in the late 1930s, 257-9
  returned, 301
  victory (1966), 345n.

Union of Soviet Socialist Republics, 331
Berlin Blockade, 303
educational expenditure, 583
espionage activities, 328
pressured for atomic-test-ban treaty, 330
and Quemoy and Matsu, 329
world status, 327
United Automobile Workers, 257
United Church of Canada
creation, 594
in ecumenical movements, 599
General Conference, 252
intended as a national church, 595-7
numbers (1871-1961), 596
union discussions with Anglicans, 598-9
United Co-operatives of Ontario, 498
United Electrical, Radio and Machine Workers, 496
United Empire Loyalists, 717
United Farmers' Co-operative Company Limited, 497-8
United Farmers of Alberta, 252, 255, 500
formation, 491
form government, 211, 500
1926 election, 218
quiet in Commons, 234
United Farmers of Canada, 500
United Farmers of Manitoba, 211, 500
United Farmers of New Brunswick, 499
United Farmers of Ontario
affiliated with C.C.F., 257
formation of, 491
form government, 192, 211, 499
United Grain Growers Limited, 210-11, 497, 498
United Mine Workers, 496
United Nations, 312-13, 801
Canada's activities in, 303, 327-8, 359, 363
Canadian role, 802, 803
commission on Korean elections, 328
Cyprus, 331
Suez crisis, 330-1
UNESCO, 567
United Nations Emergency Force, 330
United Nations Military Observer Group, 781
United Press International, 531-2
United States; *see also* American Civil War
Alaska purchase, 45-6, 74

American Alien Contract Labor Law, 494
attitude to France, 360
attitudes to Communism (1950s), 333-4
auto parts agreement, 362, 484
balance of payments, problem with, 362
branch plants in Canada, 333, 460, 462, 477
in British Columbia mineral lands and timberlands, 112
and Canada, conflict of economic interests, 332-3
and Canada, mutual best customers, 318
Canadian commitments to, 305
Canadian diplomatic mission, 277
Canadian economy linked with, 317-19
and Canadian film industry, 537
Canadian industrial dependence on, 299
and Canadian magazine market, 334, 529-30
and Canadian 'neutrality', 273
in Canadian north, 130-1, 303
and Canadian radio broadcasting, 540
Canadian relations with, 791, 803; late nineteenth century, 45-7, 790; (1940s) changes, 302-3; Second World War, 292-3
and Canadian trade unions, 493-6
and Canadian trade with China and Cuba, 333, 361
Columbia River treaty, 332-3, 362
command of Newfoundland Escort Force, 285
commercial control in northern British Columbia contested, 129
and Communist China, 329
Confederation set up against, 786
Congress approves trade ageement (1911), 176
Congress's attitude to Confederation, 45
Conservative attempt to shift trade from, 330
continental natural resources, 469
continentalist movement, 45
control over Canadian industry, 361
Co-operative Extension Service, 418
defence, collaboration with Canada, 331-2, 781-3
depression (1870s), 455

DEW Line, 304
differences from Canada, 333-4
economic link increased by Seaway, pipelines, 319
educational expenditure, 583
effect of family ties with, 390
emigration to, 61-2, 90, 112, 317, 390
emigration to Canadian west, 142, 143
enters First World War, 182
exports to, 437, 469, 470
failure of trade negotiations (1930s), 243, 244
fishing privileges under Reciprocity Treaty, 46-7
football imports from, 617
foreign aid, 330
and Gordon's 1963 budget, 349
Great Lakes Fisheries Convention, 432
grievances after Civil War, 34-5, 46
growth of capital investment in Canada, 129
guidelines to reduce capital outflow, 477
Halibut treaty, 795
implied acknowledgment of Canada as nation, 48
increasing Canadian dependence on, 233, 331-5
increasing Canadian independence of, in world affairs, 359
influence of agrarian movements, 191
influence on Canadian external policy, 360-1
influence on Canadian trade-union movement, 195
influence on extension of Confederation, 788
influence in visual arts, 698-9
International Joint Commission, 796
investment in Canadian industry, 361, 473-8, 793-4, 796; (1900-14) 458; (1950s) 318
involvement in Viet Nam, Canadian attitudes toward, 359
isolationism, 271
Joint High Commission with Great Britain, 47-8
Kennedy Round, 472
land-grant colleges, 418
Manifest Destiny, 45
Monroe Doctrine, 45
in Newfoundland, 306
parties in municipal politics, 716
plans for Panama protectorate, 74

pressured for atomic-test-ban treaty, 330
and Quemoy and Matsu, 329
radio and TV programs, 684-5
railways, threat to Canadian nationalism, 148
reciprocity, 46-7, 49-50, 150, 155
Rush-Bagot Agreement, 796
St. Lawrence Deep Waterway Treaty stopped by Senate, 246, 520
St. Lawrence Seaway project, 520
in Second World War, 462
seizure of Canadian sealing vessels in Bering Sea, 106
separation of Church and State in education, 577
social security, 734, 736
threat of absorption of Canada, 334
threat to Canadian west, 85
threat to disunite B.N.A., 45
threat to west coast by railway, 504
trade (1890s), 128-9
university costs, 408
water as 'continental resource', 447
West Berlin airlift, 303
westward expansion threatening B.N.A., 7
world status, 327
Universities, 546-66
and Canada Council Funds, 324
costs, in Canada, U.S., U.K., 408
decline of church influence, 579
federal support, 314, 353-4
free, in Newfoundland, 363
'hotbeds of quietism', 309
1950s and 1960s contrasted, 313-14
organization and control, 576-7
University of Toronto, 546-66 passim
Aerospace Institute, 565
Urbanization, 487, 621-38
adding to subversion of constitution, 730
approaches 50 per cent mark, 210
and the churches, 592, 597-8, 601, 603
as complication in Quebec (1930), 257
effects on rural life, 230-1, 234, 235 (1871-1961), 388
extent, 387
first decade of century, 150
increased rate of, 358, 445-6; (1880-1900) 116; (1940s) 298; and social services, 739-40
increasing problems (1950s), 320-1
lack of planning, 631, 632-3
problems of expanding suburbs, 635-6

a provincial problem, 364
public transportation and the suburbs, 508-9
in Quebec, 241, 365
relative decline of agriculture, 415-16
result of National Policy (1880-1900), 112
slowed in 1930s, 239
socio-economic consequences (1890s), 129
suburban increase, 739

Vaillancourt, Armand, 712
Val, Mgr. Merry del, 127
Valcartier Camp, 178
Vallé, Louis, 66
Van Horne, Sir William Cornelius, 87, 111
Vancouver, founding, 625
Vancouver Island, 5, 32
Vandenburg Resolution, 304
VE day, Halifax riot, 286
Vernon, C. W., 593
Verville, Alphonse, 499
Veterans
First World War, rehabilitation, 194
Second World War, benefits, 297-8
social welfare program, 750
Viau, M. Guy, on *la tradition mourante*, 700
Vickers, Jon, 325, 691, 692
Victoria, Queen, as symbol of imperial unity, 72
Victoria Gazette and Anglo-American, 526-7
Viet Nam, Canadian attitudes, 359
Vigneault, Gilles, 691
Vimy Ridge, 181, 773

Walkem, George, 58, 59, 86
Walker, Edmund, 145
Wall Street crash (1929), 234
Wallace, Clarke, 122, 123, 125
War Cry, 132-3
Ward, Pete, 617
Wartime Elections Act, 189, 193, 198
Wartime Prices and Trade Board, 284
Water Conservation Assistance Act, 415
Watkin, Edward, 55
Watson, Homer, 701
Watson, John, 224
Watson, Sheila, 654
Watters, R. E., 657
Weekly Rest in Industrial Undertakings Act, 261

Welland Canal, need for expansion, 521
Westcoast Transmission pipeline, 522
Western Associated Press, 531
Whalley, George, 657
Whelan, Edward, 526
Wilkes, Charles, 10
Willan, Healey, 696
Williams, Percy, 613-14, 615
Willison, John, 121
Williston, H. C., 526
Wilmot, R. D., 29, 30
Wilson, Ethel, 654
Wilson, Thomas L., 564
Wilson, Woodrow, 793
Winnipeg, 82-3, 221, 223
Winnipeg Ballet Company, 684
Winnipeg *Free Press*, on Munich, 271
Winnipeg General Strike, 196, 203
opposed by churches, 597
resulted in labour representation in Commons, 230
Winnipeg Trades and Labour Council, 196
Winters, Robert H., 477
Wiseman, Adele, 654
Wolseley, Garnet, 765, 767
Women's Christian Temperance Union, 198, 199
Woodcock, George, 657
Woodhouse, A. S. P., 657
Woodsworth, J. S., 253
on Bennett and delegations, 248
on Canadian entry into Second World War, 273
on devaluation of dollar, 247
on King and constitutional difficulties, 237
leader of C.C.F., 252
on need for reinvigorating League of Nations, 271
Old Age Pensions Act, 230
opposes police-state measures, 249
on the Padlock Law, 258
on Parliament and Act of Succession, 268
shocked by slums, 152
'Social Gospel', 227, 593
on the unemployed, 240
and Winnipeg General Strike, 597
Wooten-Boten Commission, 520
Workers' Unity League, 495
Working class
bore brunt of depression, 239
city tenements, 152

discontent with share of prosperity, 139
ignored by churches, 115-16
poor conditions (1890s), 115
post-war disillusionment, 193-6
social structure altered to include, 230
in west, hard hit by war effort, 193
working conditions, legislation concerning, 115, 256
Workman, George, 593
Workmen's Compensation, 752, 754
World (Toronto), on 1900 election, 136
World Council of Churches, 599
World Health Organization, 567

Wright, G. F., 560
Wright, Joe, 611
Wyle, Florence, 711

Yale Convention, 40
Young, G. M., 91n.
Young, George (the *Nova-scotian*), 526
Young, George, 615
Young, Henry Esson, 554
Youth Allowances, 748, 753
Ypres Salient, 179, 182, 772-3
Yukon, 130-1, 421, 518-19

Zambia, 360